Essential Public Affairs for Journalists

THIRD EDITION

James Morrison

OXFORD
UNIVERSITY PRESS

OXFORD
UNIVERSITY PRESS

Great Clarendon Street, Oxford OX2 6DP,
United Kingdom

Oxford University Press is a department of the University of Oxford.
It furthers the University's objective of excellence in research, scholarship,
and education by publishing worldwide. Oxford is a registered trade mark of
Oxford University Press in the UK and in certain other countries

First edition published 2009

Second edition published 2011

Impression: 3

British Library Cataloguing in Publication Data
Data available

ISBN 978-0-19-966385-9

Printed in Great Britain by
Clays Ltd, St Ives plc

Essential Public Affairs for Journalists

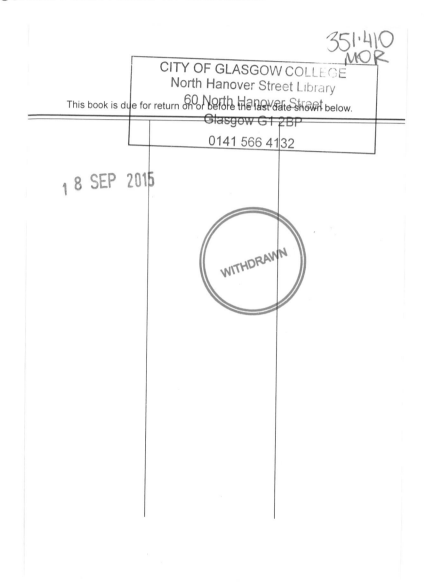

For my beloved Annalise, Scarlet, Rosella, and Ivor Munro

New to this edition

- Full explanations of the huge programmes of reform introduced by the coalition government.
- Concise and engaging explanations of major recent and ongoing political events including the Libor-fixing scandal, the eurozone sovereign debt crisis, the 2012 budget, and the background to the Leveson Inquiry.
- New sections focusing on key topical issues and debates including changes to the pension system, the current debate about the future of contributory and universal welfare benefits, and access to social housing.

Preface—the changing face of public affairs

Two years ago, when I last sat down to pen this missive, I wrote that there was never an ideal time to update a textbook on contemporary public affairs. Without wishing to lay claim to the gift of prescience, twenty-six months into the first British coalition government since the Second World War it seems fair to say that those words have been vindicated.

While the seismic event that was the May 2010 election cast a long shadow over the process of updating the first edition, the blizzard of radical legislation passed since the second went to press late that year has necessitated even heftier revisions to some chapters this time round. The past two years have seen Work and Pensions Secretary Iain Duncan Smith embark on the biggest shake-up (and cuts programme) in the history of the welfare state, with the Coalition doggedly pursuing an equally unprecedented restructure of the National Health Service. In education, as is often observed of late, Michael Gove has been beavering away to consolidate a quiet revolution in state schooling. And in all manner of other spending areas—from the Home Office to the Ministry of Defence—the most far-reaching fiscal squeeze in generations has really started to bite.

As if all this didn't offer enough political red meat for early-career journalists to sink their teeth into, recent months have also witnessed further turmoil in the British economy (by October struggling to emerge from the dreaded 'double-dip' recession) and the near-collapse of the euro. The latter is one subject about which everything included here risks being a hostage to fortune by time of publication, so fragile does the 'eurozone' presently look. And while the 2008–9 financial crisis provided a last-minute headache just as the finishing touches were being put to edition one, the spectre of 'casino banking' has returned to haunt this one, too, in the form of the ongoing rows about reform and regulation and, as the July 2012 copy deadline loomed, explosive new revelations about Libor-rigging. And this is to say nothing of the Leveson Inquiry, the various party lobbying scandals, the failed alternative vote referendum (Britain's first for thirty-six years), or the numerous reports and reviews ordered by ministers into everything from the future of state pensions and social care for the elderly to since mothballed plans to reform the House of Lords.

How, then, have these multifarious developments affected the content and format of this book? Well, aside from some significant changes to the text itself, remarkably little. When edition two was being written the NCTJ was in the midst of compiling its rationalized 'Essential Public Affairs (EPA)' programme of study—necessitating that more thought be given to the pedagogic material included as end matter in each chapter. The resulting additions—principally the 'topical feature ideas' and 'current issues'—were largely well received, so these have been retained for edition three, but refreshed with more up-to-date questions and examples. Having taken soundings from my fellow EPA board members, I also resolved to keep the glossary (albeit now shorn of the label 'key terms', following the NCTJ's decision to remove its annually revised list of 'official' terminology from the EPA syllabus). In fact, the strong support colleagues expressed for the principle of continuing to drill important terms and phrases into trainee journalists encouraged me to expand it. Again, heavy revisions were needed to remove some now-defunct terms ('Audit Commission' anyone?) and add in new ones (the names of several new financial regulators introduced by the Coalition). In other respects, no longer having to define only those terms on a prescribed list proved to be a boon—enabling me to add some previously absent entries that seemed worthy of inclusion, such as 'Budget', 'growth', and 'quantitative easing'.

So what aspects of the book's layout *have* changed? Perhaps the most noteworthy tweaks are those intended to 'tidy up' the look of certain pages and make them look less 'busy' and easier on the eye. The microphone icon used in the margin to signpost readers to examples of reporting in practice has been replaced by a shorthand notebook (arguably more suitable and self-explanatory), while the first appearances of glossary terms in the chapter text alongside explanations of their meanings are highlighted in bold, rather than bold italics.

Other than that, it's back to business as usual—though what 'usual' means in these politically tempestuous, economically insecure, scandal-ridden times is anybody's guess.

JM

More praise for *Essential Public Affairs for Journalists*

'Journalists need to know what they need to know. Government, at every level, and public bodies are where they will find the stories that really affect their readers, listeners, and the viewers. This is a practical guide to help cut through the bureaucracy, jargon, smoke-screens, and secrecy.'

Bob Satchwell, Executive Director, Society of Editors

'Accurate reporting of the ever-changing political landscape is at the heart of thorough and trustworthy journalism. James Morrison delivers a definitive account of how national and local government works, packed with all the detail every journalist needs. This book is vital for anyone serious about responsible news reporting.'

Janet Jones, NCTJ Chief Examiner in Public Affairs

'This is a wonderfully thorough, clear, and up-to-date guide to the political mechanics of the country. James Morrison takes readers by the hand and leads them expertly through the twisty byways of British public life and its multifarious institutions.'

Roger Alton, Editor, *The Times*

Acknowledgements

I would like to thank my colleagues on the NCTJ's public affairs board. Thanks, too, are due to the various other lecturers and journalists who reviewed the chapters as I wrote them, for their invariably salient advice. Special mention must go to Ron Fenney, and to David Kett—the nearest Britain has, surely, to a PA guru—for the huge amount of legwork they both did before me to make sense of the tangle of legislation and 'officialese' that bedevils local and central government today. I would also like to thank the Department for Communities and Local Government (DCLG), the National Archive, and the Economic and Social Research Council (ESRC) for their prompt responses to requests for data, and their willingness for us to reproduce tables and charts (which we have credited where this is the case). Finally, thanks to the various other government departments, executive agencies, and quangos that have helped with enquiries in one way or other both in relation to this and the previous editions: HM Treasury; the Department for Work and Pensions (DWP); the Foreign and Commonwealth Office's Europe Delivery Group; the School Improvement Division of the erstwhile Department for Children, Schools, and Families; the Commission for Social Care Inspection; the Department of Health; the United Nations Department of Public Information; the Directorate General for Budget of the European Commission; and the Institute of Fiscal Studies.

For permission to reproduce articles and documents in the topical feature ideas we are grateful to the *Manchester Evening News* (MEN Media), Guardian News and Media Ltd 2010, *Birmingham Mail*, *Oxford Mail*, Tamworth Borough Council, City of Bradford Metropolitan District Council, *Exeter Express and Echo*, *The Independent*, and Cambridgeshire County Council. Finally, I'd like to thank the 'class of 95' on my first paper, the *North Devon Journal*—James Cornish, Mark Devane, Tahira Yaqoob, Kent Upshon, and Matt Radley—for keeping my spirits up.

Brief contents

Detailed contents

Guide to the book's features

Each chapter in *Essential Public Affairs for Journalist* contains a selection of features to help you to navigate your way through the book, and to direct you to sources of further information.

> Magna Carta (the Great Charter), signed by Kin
> the foundation stone of Britain's constitution, in
> of **rule of law**. This embodied the inalienable ri
> criminal offence to a free and fair trial before his
> the principle that no one—not even the reigning
> Of course, even today, the idea that not even the

Glossary terms

Key terms are emboldened in the text and are defined in a glossary at the end of the book.

☰ Topical feature idea

The article in Figure 6.4 is taken from the *Manchester Evening News*. It cond
leaked document revealing plans by Central Manchester University Hospita
Foundation Trust—one of a new generation of 'super trusts' granted permi
over struggling neighbouring trusts—to reduce accident and emergency pr
Trafford General Hospital to cut its debt. The move, which followed a local d
save Trafford's A&E unit, reflected several recent trends in management of
England: an emphasis on balancing the books of individual trusts as if the

Topical feature ideas

Topical feature ideas at the end of chapters suggest possible sources of a story on each subject.

✳ Current issues

- **Votes for prisoners:** the European Court of Human Rights has issued se
  turns to British governments since 2005, ordering first Labour then the
  grant serving prisoners the vote, in defiance of long-standing electoral p
  the UK. Though the Court gave ministers just six months to change their
  in November 2010, warning it would permit at least 2,500 inmates to su
  for breaching their human rights if the deadline was missed, MPs voted
  overwhelmingly to uphold the country's current position in February 20

Current issues

Current issues highlight contemporary topics that are particularly relevant to journalists, and provide a starting point for further exploration.

? Review questions

1. Which is the oldest UK political party—Conservative, Labour, or Liberal
2. To what extent has Labour stayed true to its democratic socialist roots,
   ditional labels such as 'left-wing', 'right-wing', and 'centrist' still relevan
3. Outline the similarities and differences between the roles of the 1922 C
   the Conservative Party and the Parliamentary Labour Party.
4. What is the difference between a political donation and loan in UK law?

Review questions

A set of questions allows you to test your knowledge of what has been covered in each chapter.

Further reading

Take your learning further by using the reading lists at the end of each chapter to find more detailed information on a specific topic.

> **→ Further reading**
>
> Budge, I., Crewe, I., McKay, D., and Newton, K. (2007) *The New British Politics* London: Longman. **Fourth edition of acclaimed critical introduction to B politics at the dawn of the twenty-first century, updated to cover Brown administration**.
>
> Burnham, J. and Pyper, R. (2008) *Britain's Modernised Civil Service*, London: Macmillan. **Thorough examination of recent Civil Service developments**.

In the margin you will also find a number of icons with the following meanings:

This icon indicates discussion of an issue concerned with **devolution** in the United Kingdom. It allows you to see at a glance where devolved subjects are explored.

This icon occurs where there is discussion of public affairs **reporting in practice**.

Certain subjects are matters for both central and local government. In those cases the **central/local cross-references** direct you to the appropriate coverage elsewhere in the book.

The **Online Resource Centre** icon appears to remind you when additional or updated material can be found on the book's accompanying website. www.oxfordtextbooks.co.uk/orc/morrison_3e/

Guide to the Online Resource Centre

Essential Public Affairs for Journalists is accompanied by an Online Resource Centre with a range of helpful additional materials to augment the printed text. These resources are free of charge and can be found at:

http://www.oxfordtextbooks.co.uk/orc/morrison3e/

Regular updates

Key new developments in public affairs are succinctly summarised so that you can always keep up to date.

News feeds

Links to real articles from various news sites are provided via RSS.

Additional and updated tables

Tables with information that changes regularly can be found in an updated form online, alongside additional tables that do not appear in the book.

Table 4.2 Distribution of seats in the House of Commons following the May 2010 election							
Party	Seats	Gains	Losses	Net gain/loss	Votes (%)	Votes	Swing
Conservative	307	101	3	+97	36.1	10,706,647	+3.8%
Labour	258	3	94	-91	29.0	8,604,358	-6.2%
Liberal Democrat	57	8	13	-5	23.0	6,827,938	+1.0%

Topical feature ideas

Further topical feature ideas are provided to help you consider where to find a story or to prepare for the NCTJ portfolio assessment.

Web links

Useful websites relating to the topics in each chapter are listed to allow you to find further information.

> **Chapter 6**
>
> www.dh.gov.uk
> Official website of Department of Health in England and Wales. A hugely comprehensive website with links other resources, plus detailed breakdowns on individual areas of responsibility, including National Service Frameworks, NHS trusts, and foundation hospitals.
>
> www.nice.org.uk/aboutnice/
> Website of the National Institute for Health and Clinical Excellent (NICE). Includes an overview of its remit and powers and details of recent rulings on medication and treatment.
>
> www.ombudsman.org.uk/about_us/our_history/index.html
> Official website of the Health Service Ombudsman, including details of the types of complaints investigated and the procedure for complaining.
>
> www.healthcarecommission.org.uk
> Website of the Healthcare Commission, which monitors NHS and private healthcare standards in England.

Introduction

▶ Confessions of a local council reporter

I'll always remember the name Mervyn Lane. From the moment I arrived as a naive raw recruit on the *North Devon Journal* in Barnstaple—bristling with high ideas, most of them hugely unrealistic and some more than a little 'conspiracy theorist'—Mervyn and I were destined to clash. I'd been taken on as a junior reporter without a car (or, for that matter, driving licence) and was only hired on condition I passed my test within six months of starting. Logically enough, I was immediately posted to Bideford—the area's 'second town', some ten miles west of the paper's Barnstaple headquarters—but still expected to soldier into head office each day, and cover a sprawling patch of rustic terrain into the bargain.

To top it all, I was required to generate a district edition single-handedly each week, filling three pages of news and finding at least one front-page lead without fail. Bideford being Bideford, there were few obvious sources of scoops: the edgiest events tended to be an annual Easter fair, known dubiously (but all too descriptively) as 'Cow Pat Fun Day', and the occasional drugs raid on a pint-sized sink estate at East-the-Water, the town's ungrammatically named answer to Moss Side.

Unsurprisingly, it wasn't long before I was turning to the local authority for inspiration (or, more accurately, out of desperation). Little did I know how fruitful this would be. Those wintry evenings spent pinching myself awake through meetings of Torridge District Council's planning committee invariably threw up a last-minute gem that, with a bit of creative editing (and barring news of an international sheep-rustling scam), would generate enough ire to merit a splash.

From the humdrum ('Supermarket Threat to Town Centre') to the absurd ('Ships in Our Back Garden'), Torridge seldom failed to deliver the goods. Inevitably, it was only a matter of time before I crossed swords with the venerable Mr Lane—at that time leader of the district council's ruling Liberal Democrat group, chairman of its powerful policy and resources committee, and both a Bideford town councillor and Devon county councillor to boot.

The first of our many run-ins was sparked by a front-page story I wrote about a decision to award free parking permits to all Torridge councillors and ninety-two senior officers (dubbed 'essential users' by the council) for use in council car parks in central Bideford whenever they were on local authority business. As controversies go, this may sound small beer—there was nothing illegal or improper about the policy—but boy did it upset the locals. To understand the scale of the furore among residents and businesses, a little context is needed. Parking and the wider subject of transport were perhaps the most toxic issues facing Bidefordians. For various reasons driving was pretty much the only way most people had of gaining access to the town for shopping or tourism, thanks to a train line that was (literally) a museum piece (take a bow Dr Beeching) and an antediluvian bus service. The notoriously perilous North Devon Link Road and a winding, hazardous 'coastal route' were all that connected it to civilization (or Barnstaple, at any rate)—providing lifelines for those living in outlying villages. Yet, in central Bideford—in the words of one councillor, 'a medieval town with a twentieth-century traffic problem'—any street wide enough to admit vehicles seemed to have been daubed with double-yellow lines, putting the limited parking spaces available at a premium. Hence the incendiary reaction.

My parking story was one of many to irritate Mr Lane during my eighteen-month tenure as Bideford district reporter. But he wasn't the only local dignitary to be the focus of embarrassing headlines on the *Journal* during this time . . .

Let's not forget George Moss, the Bideford mayor who arrived in full regalia to turn on the town's Christmas lights one November only to find that a timer switch had done so automatically several hours earlier—the moment dusk had descended. He didn't fare any better a year later, when the precautions that council engineers took to avoid a similar fiasco proved so watertight that the lights couldn't be switched on at all.

Of course, council stories don't need to emanate from committee meetings—or, for that matter, councillors. Take the example of Les Garland, a community activist from Northam—a strip of suburban housing, pockmarked with scrappy golf courses, which runs along the Torridge Estuary to the east of Bideford. Armed with little more than a tape measure, he led a one-man campaign to rid the whole of Devon of the peril of 'hazardously placed' A-boards. (To the uninitiated, A-boards are the signs one finds outside newsagents bearing misspelt headlines from papers like the *Journal*.)

Insisting they posed a hazard to pedestrians, by blocking pavements and tripping people up, Les set about scouring the small print of Devon County Council's highways regulations—not to mention various Acts of Parliament—in search of a clause that would back his assertion that they contravened health and safety legislation. I clearly remember a conversation with an apoplectic county councillor, who stormed into the *Journal's* Bideford office to inform me that the county could be faced with rewriting its entire highways policy, at a cost of tens of thousands of pounds, if Les were to force the issue.

Perhaps inevitably, Les had the last laugh. When I last visited North Devon, in 2003, I picked up a copy of that hallowed Bideford edition of the *Journal*. Turning to the district pages, I was greeted by a familiar visage, grinning at me over a caption about a good citizenship award he'd received for serving the local community. As I wandered down Bideford high street later that day, I couldn't help noticing several shops still had A-boards placed perilously distant from their doorways. But the memory of Les's beaming face reminded me that, in one way or other, his dogged devotion to civic duty had paid off.

My purpose in highlighting these anecdotal examples is to illustrate a simple point: that knowledge of public affairs (and, for the rookie journalist, local government especially) *matters*. Whether it be protests by angry parents over changes to school catchment areas, demands from worried residents for 'speed bumps' to prevent accidents on dangerous roads, or controversies about New Age traveller camps, waste disposal sites, or parasitical out-of-town superstores, local newspapers are chock-full of council-related stories on a daily and weekly basis. And to identify, research, and write up these stories in a way that is comprehensible and meaningful to their readers, journalists first need to grasp the basics of how government works and the parameters within which it operates.

This book aims to make that process easier.

1

The British constitution and monarchy

▌ What is a 'constitution'?

For any state to achieve a sense of order and identity it requires a shared set of values to be recognized and accepted by its subjects. Such values tend to be instilled by a system of fundamental laws and principles, and upheld by parliaments, courts, and other institutions established to maintain and reinforce them.

This notion of shared membership, of collective rights and responsibilities—as common to commercial companies and supranational organizations like the European Union (EU) as to organs of individual governments—is known as a 'constitution'.

Constitutions come in all shapes and sizes. They can be formal or informal, long or short, absolute or merely advisory. Most significant, though, is the difference between the two broad types of constitution adopted by individual states: *written* and *unwritten*. Naturally, for any set of ideas related to one's citizenship of a state to be communicated and sustained effectively some kind of written record will need to exist. Yet there is an important distinction between constitutions described as 'written' and ones that are not. All constitutions of any worth comprise elements that have been written in a literal sense—for example, laws or decrees set down in documentary form. But this does not make them 'written constitutions' per se. Written constitutions are, rather, *codified* frameworks: single manuscripts summarizing the rights, values, and responsibilities attached to membership of the states to which they relate.

For historical reasons, some states have adopted written constitutions while others have not. In general, written constitutions have tended to emerge in countries where there has been a sudden change in the entire system of government caused by a political upheaval like a war, invasion, or revolution. This was certainly the case for two nations with which the term is perhaps most closely associated: France and the USA.

France's constitution derives from the *Declaration of the Rights of Man and of the Citizen*, adopted on 26 August 1789 by the National Constituent Assembly convened in the aftermath of the French Revolution, and later amended to enshrine the three abiding principles of 'liberty, equality, and fraternity'. The USA adopted its equivalent a decade after declaring independence from Britain, on 17 September 1787, at a landmark constitutional convention in Philadelphia, Pennsylvania, addressed by Enlightenment philosopher Benjamin Franklin.

The origins and sources of the British constitution

Britain—or more accurately the 'United Kingdom of Great Britain and Northern Ireland'—is a different case entirely. The story of the UK's constitutional evolution is of, first, the gradual unification of disparate kingdoms under one national sovereign (monarch), then, in due course, the struggle for supremacy between the sovereign and the Christian Church, and ultimately between the sovereign and Parliament.

As these various power struggles have been played out, at several points in its history Britain has come close to adopting a formal framework specifying the rights and responsibilities of its citizenry. Up to now, however, it has stopped short of producing a definitive statement. Despite the fact that documents of one kind or another form a huge part of the constitutional framework governing the lives of its citizens, there exists no single statement of principles. Therefore, in defiance of campaigns by pressure groups ranging from the Chartists of 1848 to the coalition of liberal thinkers who put their names to Charter 88 a century and a half later, to all intents and purposes Britain still has an unwritten constitution.

As such, the British constitution has clear advantages: it is *flexible* enough to be amended, added to, or subtracted from according to the will of the elected Parliament of the day, without any of the tortuous procedures required in the USA and elsewhere whenever the slightest break with tradition is sought in the interests of political progress. Conversely, it has the disadvantage of provoking as much wrangling among lawyers, politicians, and historians as it can ever claim to circumvent, by leaving layers of ambiguity around sometimes crucial issues relating to its subjects' liberties and entitlements. The controversy surrounding Gordon Brown's decision to sign the EU's 2007 Lisbon Treaty—seen by some as a 'European constitution' in all but name—is one example of how easily the UK can adopt potentially significant changes to its constitutional fabric without any of the debate rendered necessary by the *rigid* rule systems of other countries. Meanwhile, the perceived 'Big Brother' assault on individuals' civil liberties represented by the rash of anti-terror legislation since the attacks on the Twin Towers on 11 September 2001, not to mention the launch of a national DNA database and the recently abandoned identity card scheme, was viewed by human rights campaigners as an example of the dangers of failing to enshrine core principles in a solid constitutional statement.

So what are the primary sources of Britain's constitution? The main constituent components fall into the following five broad categories:

- *statute*—individual laws or 'Acts of Parliament';
- *common law*—sometimes known as 'judge-made', 'case law', or 'precedent';
- *conventions*—customs, traditions, and long-standing practices;
- *treatises*—historical works of legal and/or constitutional authority;
- *treaties*—EU and other international agreements.

Statute

Magna Carta (the Great Charter), signed by King John in 1215, is often cited as the foundation stone of Britain's constitution, invoking as it does the principle of **rule of law**. This embodied the inalienable right of any citizen accused of a criminal offence to a free and fair trial before his peers and, crucially, enshrined the principle that no one—not even the reigning sovereign—is 'above the law'. Of course, even today, the idea that not even the sovereign is immune to prosecution is (like many constitutional concepts) a little problematic. In practice, because criminal prosecutions are instigated in the name of the Crown, if the king or queen were accused of a crime and brought before a court of law this would provoke a constitutional crisis.

Perhaps more significant even than Magna Carta was the 1689 Bill of Rights, passed in the wake of the turbulent period stemming from the execution forty years earlier of the Anglican King Charles I, and the eleven-year interregnum that followed under his vanquisher, the self-styled Puritan 'Lord Protector' Oliver Cromwell. Although the titular head of the Church of England, Charles was felt by many to be too sympathetic to Roman Catholicism, having married the Catholic princess Henrietta Maria of France. There was also deep unease about his invocation of the loose constitutional principle (popular among medieval monarchs) known as the *Divine Right of Kings*—a notion that the authority of the sovereign derived from his/her relationship to God and was thus immutable. In the event, the Parliamentarians secured victory over Charles's Royalist supporters in the ensuing English Civil War (1642–51), ending centuries of rule under this premise.

The Bill of Rights itself arose out of the alliance between the Protestant-dominated Parliament and William of Orange, the Dutch king whom it helped to depose Charles's younger son, James II, during the 'Glorious Revolution' of 1688. Having worked in an uneasy stalemate with James's elder brother, Charles II, following his return from exile in France after Cromwell's death in

1660, Parliament used the ascension of his uncompromising sibling (a devout Catholic) as a pretext for cementing its authority as Britain's supreme seat of power.

To this end it identified James's Protestant daughter, Mary, as the rightful heir to the throne. Together with her husband, William, Mary effectively deposed James as monarch. In exchange for Parliament's loyalty to the couple, they permitted the passage of the Bill, which formalized for the first time the transfer of constitutional supremacy from Crown to elected Parliament. Its central tenet was to ratify the principle that in future the sovereign could only rule *through* Parliament—rather than tell it what to do, as in the past. In other words, monarchs would henceforth have to seek the official consent of members of Parliament (MPs)—and, more particularly, government ministers—before passing legislation (Acts), declaring war, or invoking any of the other sovereign powers they had traditionally wielded. In this way the Bill effectively ended centuries of 'royal sovereignty' and ushered in the concept (even today a fundamental cornerstone of Britain's democracy) of **parliamentary sovereignty**.

This core constitutional principle is the one that most symbolizes the oft-cited flexibility of an unwritten constitution. The term 'sovereignty'—or **political sovereignty**—refers to the notion of an individual or institution exercising supreme control over a geographical realm, a people, or themselves. The concept of parliamentary sovereignty flows from this: as well as asserting the hegemony of the *institution* of Parliament over British subjects, it confers on *each individual* UK Parliament—the body of MPs elected at a given general election—the authority to make its own laws and repeal any of those passed by previous Parliaments. To this extent it prevents any one Parliament being 'bound by the actions of a predecessor'.

Many constitutional experts argue that this idea is incompatible with that of a conventional written constitution because, if we were to have such a document, one Parliament could theoretically use its sovereignty to repeal the Act that introduced it. Advocates of a codified document dismiss this as a bogus argument, contending that many countries with written constitutions manage to maintain them alongside their own versions of parliamentary sovereignty without encountering such conflicts. One way of embedding a written constitution into the political fabric of a state is to compose it out of a web of interlocking legislation, rather than single Acts—making them harder to repeal. Another might be to set up an independent superior court with the power to adjudicate in constitutional disputes. Britain's new US-style Supreme Court (see p. 66) could conceivably fulfil this role.

In addition to formalizing the notion of parliamentary sovereignty, the Bill of Rights granted several privileges to all 'Englishmen'—with the exception, in certain cases, of Roman Catholics. Its main tenets are listed in the table entitled 'Main entitlements listed in Bill of Rights 1689', to be found on the Online Resource Centre that accompanies this book.

The Bill also specified conditions governing the future succession of the monarchy, in light of the coronation of William and Mary over the dethroned James II:

- James's flight from England following Mary's accession was defined as an 'abdication';
- William and Mary were officially declared James's successors;
- the throne should subsequently pass to Mary's heirs, then her sister, Princess Anne of Denmark, and her heirs, then to heirs of William by later marriage.

Finally, the Bill also introduced a further constitutional principle that remains fundamental to the workings of Parliament. Often incorrectly described as a 'convention' (rather than a product of statute, which it is), this is **parliamentary privilege**. In brief, the primary role of parliamentary privilege is to enable any elected MP sitting in the House of Commons or peer in the House of Lords to make accusations about individuals or companies in open debate in the chambers without fear of prosecution for defamation.

Recent years have seen several high-profile examples of parliamentary privilege being used by members to 'name and shame' private individuals in ways that would be considered defamatory (and which might invite legal action) if repeated outside Parliament. In 2000, Peter Hain (then Foreign Office Minister for Africa) invoked privilege to identify brothers Maurice and David Zollman as the owners of an Antwerp diamond trading business that he said was breaking United Nations (UN) sanctions by helping to bankroll the civil war in Angola. A year later Peter Robinson (then deputy leader of the Democratic Unionist Party (DUP)) used it to 'out' Brian Keenan and Brian Gillen as members of the Provisional Irish Republican Army (IRA) ruling army council.

A flip side of the legal protection afforded by parliamentary privilege is the fact that certain words and phrases are construed as 'unparliamentary language' and therefore unacceptable if directed at fellow members in either the Commons or Lords chambers. Most notorious is the word 'liar', which is seen to conflict constitutionally with the freedom given to members under parliamentary privilege to speak their minds. In November 1993 the Reverend Ian Paisley (then leader of the Democratic Unionists) was famously suspended from the Commons for five days for accusing then Prime Minister John Major of lying after it emerged that, despite previously insisting that the idea of negotiating with Northern Irish republicans (whom he dubbed 'terrorists') would 'turn his stomach', he'd actually been holding secret talks for more than a year with Sinn Féin, the main republican party.

More recently, Commons Speaker John Bercow has frequently hauled MPs into line for hurling insults in the chamber—in May 2012 he even ordered David Cameron to apologize for dismissing Shadow Chancellor Ed Balls as a 'muttering idiot' while answering Prime Minister's Questions (see p. 46). Controversially, the following month he failed to reprimand Shadow Immigration Minister Chris

Bryant for accusing Culture Secretary Jeremy Hunt of having 'lied' to the Commons over the extent of his contacts with senior figures at News Corporation during the run-up to a decision by Ofcom about whether it should be allowed to buy up BSkyB (see p. 93). On this occasion Mr Bercow cited an obscure ruling to justify his leniency: namely that Mr Bryant's language was acceptable in light of the fact that the Opposition motion being debated by MPs concerned the question of 'whether he [Hunt] breached paragraph 1.2c (giving accurate and truthful information to Parliament) . . . of the Ministerial Code'. In other words, the motion implicitly revolved around Mr Hunt's honesty.

Just as parliamentary privilege protects MPs and peers from being sued in court for defamatory statements made in Parliament, it also safeguards the media and public from action arising out of repeating those claims. By way of further complicating explanations of this privilege, however, according to a literal interpretation of the Bill of Rights it also protects the press from proceedings arising from 'a report alleging wrongdoing in Parliament by an MP'. This legal argument was used to enable *The Guardian* to defend a libel action brought in 1996 by former Conservative minister, Neil Hamilton, over its allegations two years earlier that he had accepted cash from Harrods owner Mohamed Al Fayed for asking parliamentary questions designed to further the latter's business interests. To muddy the constitutional waters further, as a sitting MP Mr Hamilton had to obtain formal permission to sue the newspaper in the first place. In the event, a new clause was inserted into the 1996 Defamation Act (s. 13) enabling him to waive his right to parliamentary privilege by suing the newspaper as a private citizen (an action that, in any case, failed).

In November 2008 a major political row erupted about a more obscure aspect of parliamentary privilege, when it emerged that the Conservatives' immigration spokesman, Damian Green, had been arrested and questioned by police over allegations that he unlawfully solicited leaks about government policy from a sympathetic civil servant in the Home Office. Both Opposition and government MPs united in criticizing the police action. Many saw it as an abuse of the long-established constitutional right of members to conduct free and open conversations with officials in the Palace of Westminster—and a throwback to Charles I's challenge to the freedoms of Parliament in the seventeenth century. MPs on all sides of the House turned their fire on the then Commons Speaker, Michael Martin, who, as its overall custodian, was accused of having given his permission to officers to search Mr Green's office—potentially jeopardizing the confidentiality of sensitive information relating to his constituents. It later transpired that Mr Martin had in fact delegated the decision to a more obscure Commons officer, the Sergeant-at-Arms (see p. 72).

Perhaps the most contentious attempt to use parliamentary privilege as a protection was the interpretation cited by Labour MPs Elliot Morley, Jim Devine, and David Chaytor and Tory peer Lord Hanningfield after they were each charged with false accounting over their Commons expenses claims. They invoked Article 9 of the 1689 Bill of Rights to argue that, as any alleged wrong-doing had been committed by them while carrying out official duties, it was for Parliament alone to try (if necessary) to punish them. In the event, their argument was overruled by the courts and all four were convicted (see p. 58).

Of Britain's other key constitutional statutes, the most historically significant are the 1701 Act of Settlement and 1706–7 Acts of Union. The former built on the newly introduced rules relating to monarchical succession in the Bill of Rights by setting out the conditions for future sovereigns, as outlined in Table 1.1.

The Acts of Union, meanwhile, were twin laws passed first in England then Scotland, in 1706 and 1707 respectively, formalizing the Treaty of Union—the agreement that unified the countries as one United Kingdom under a single sovereign and Parliament. Key Acts absorbed into UK law more recently include those listed in Table 1.2.

The penultimate Act listed in Table 1.2—the Human Rights Act (HRA) 1998—justifies some discussion here, given the growing contention by many lawyers, human rights campaigners, and constitutional experts that it conflicts with the British constitution as it previously stood. For this and other

Table 1.1 The rules governing monarchical succession in the Act of Settlement 1701

	Details
Protestants only	The Crown should pass to Protestant descendants of Electress Sophie of Hanover (first cousin once removed of Queen Anne, who inherited throne after deaths of Mary and William)
No marriages to Catholics	Monarchs '*shall join in communion*' with Church of England and not marry Roman Catholics
England for the English	If anyone not native to England inherits throne, the country will not wage war for '*any dominions or territories which do not belong to the Crown of England without the consent of Parliament*'
Loyalty from the Crown	No monarch may leave 'British Isles' without Parliament's consent (repealed by George I in 1716)
Openness before Parliament	All government matters within Privy Council's jurisdiction (see p. 20) should be transacted there and all such resolutions must be signed, so Parliament knows who has agreed them
Constitutional privileges for the English only	No foreigner, even if naturalized (unless born of English parents), shall be allowed to be a privy councillor or member of either House of Parliament, or hold '*any office or place of trust, either civil or military, or to have any grant of lands, tenements or hereditaments from the Crown, to himself or to any other or others in trust for him*' (repealed by later citizenship laws)
Ban on election for Crown servants	No person working for the monarch or receiving a Crown pension may be an MP—to avoid 'unwelcome' royal interference in Parliament's work
Judiciary answerable to Parliament	Judges' commissions valid *quamdiu se bene gesserint* (during good behaviour) and can be removed only by both Houses
Parliament has ultimate sanction	No royal pardon (see p. 21) can save a person from impeachment by the Commons

Table 1.2 Key statutes absorbed into the UK constitution in the twentieth century

Statute	Effect
Race Relations Acts 1965, 1968, and 1976	Outlawed discrimination on racial grounds
Government of Scotland and Government of Wales Acts 1998	Paved way for national referendums to establish devolved power in Scotland and Wales
Human Rights Act (HRA) 1998	Incorporated into British law the *Convention on the Protection of Human Rights and Fundamental Freedoms* (European Convention on Human Rights), signed by Council of Europe in 1950
House of Lords Act 1999	Removed all but ninety-two hereditary peers then remaining and created 'transitional' Lords to remain until decisive reform was agreed by both Houses (see p. 62)

reasons, the Conservatives entered the 2010 general election with a manifesto commitment to repeal the Act, in favour of a new Bill of Rights tailored specifically to UK citizens. But with its coalition partners, the Liberal Democrats, committed to the HRA, in the short term the Conservative Party settled for a wide-ranging inquiry by an independent commission. At time of writing the Act remained in place—but tensions were mounting over the repeated insistence by the European Court of Human Rights (ECtHR) in Strasbourg that the British government abandon its long-standing opposition to allowing convicted prisoners the vote (see p. 120).

Although it received royal assent in November 1998, the HRA only came into force in October 2000. Among its stipulations was that every future Bill put before Parliament must now include a preface confirming that the relevant secretary of state is happy that it conforms with the Convention. The principal rights safeguarded by the Convention are as outlined in Table 1.3.

In addition, the UK has accepted the First and Sixth (now Thirteenth) Protocols to the *European Convention on Human Rights* (ECHR), of which there are fourteen altogether. The First Protocol includes additional rights for property (Art. 1), education (Art. 2), and free and fair elections (Art. 3).

The Thirteenth Protocol formally abolishes the death penalty (previously, the Sixth Protocol prohibited it in peacetime only).

The Act has, in theory, strengthened the ability of ordinary people to challenge the actions of governments, public bodies, and private companies in the UK and EU courts, by if necessary taking legal action through the **ECtHR**—the primary judicial body of the Council of Europe (see pp. 314–15). There are, however, notable limitations to its pre-eminence, and it remains a moot point as to how far it takes absolute precedence over national laws and conventions. By general consensus, for example, the principle of parliamentary privilege remains unaffected by the Act. In addition, British judges—although required by it to take account of ECtHR judgments when making rulings in British courts—are

Table 1.3 The Articles of the European Convention on Human Rights (ECHR)

Article	Right enshrined
1	Obligation to respect human rights
2	Life
3	Protection from torture and inhuman or degrading treatment
4	Protection from slavery and forced or compulsory labour
5	Right to liberty and security of person
6	Right to a fair trial
7	Protection from retrospective criminalization of acts or omissions
8	Protection of private and family life
9	Freedom of thought, conscience, and religion
10	Freedom of expression
11	Freedom of association and assembly
12	Right to marry and found a family
13	Freedom from discrimination
14	Prohibition of discrimination
15	Derogations
16	Exemption for political activities of aliens
17	Prohibition of abuse of rights
18	Limitations on permitted restrictions of rights

not permitted simply to override extant parliamentary legislation that appears to contravene the Convention.

In addition, the following formal qualifications exist in relation to the Act's implementation and enforcement:

- claims must be brought against the offending state or public body 'within one year of the action about which the complaint is being made';
- some rights can theoretically be breached if not 'in accordance with the laws of the country' that is a signatory;
- breaches are tolerated 'in the interests of national security, public safety, or the country's economic well-being; for the prevention of crime and disorder, the protection of health or morals, or to protect the freedom and rights of others . . .'.

In Britain the HRA has arguably been repeatedly breached by successive home secretaries. The Anti-terrorism, Crime, and Security Act 2001 allowed the detention and deportation without trial of people suspected of terrorist links, and Tony Blair repeatedly threatened to amend the Act to prevent judges blocking further proposed crackdowns—particularly on the activities of extremist Islamist preachers—following the 2005 London bombings.

In Scotland the Act came into force in 1998—two years ahead of England. By November 1999 the High Court had already declared unlawful the appointment of 129 temporary sheriffs (judges in the Scottish criminal courts) because they had been hired by the Lord Advocate, the member of the Scottish Executive responsible for prosecutions—a clear conflict with one of the constitution's fundamental guiding principles, the separation of powers (see p. 16).

One potential outcome of the Act's adoption in the longer term could be the abolition of the Act of Settlement, which has long arguably infringed human rights by preventing non-Protestants acceding to the British throne and maintaining a system whereby the succession passes through the male line—two principles finally set to be abandoned by the Conservative–Liberal Democrat Coalition (see p. 26). For some time *The Guardian* has argued that the very *existence* of a monarchy is incompatible with the HRA and that the 1701 Act should therefore be repealed. Because it is still technically illegal (under the Treason Felony Act 1848) to advocate the monarchy's abolition, the paper once even applied for a High Court declaration that the 1848 Act was incompatible with Art. 10 of the HRA. Its attempt failed, due to a loophole, because the Court ruled that the Attorney General's refusal to grant immunity to its editor was not an 'act of the state'—meaning it fell outside the HRA's remit.

Besides the showpiece constitutional Acts listed in Table 1.2, several others have contained key clauses with serious implications for the workings of the British constitution. Among these are the myriad Parliament Acts passed before the Second World War (see pp. 60–1). Perhaps the single most significant constitutional reform introduced by any of these Acts was the stipulation, in the Parliament Act 1911, that a general election must be held *a maximum of five years after the previous Parliament was convened* (in other words, a little over five years after the previous polling day). Until then parliaments could theoretically last up to seven years, under the terms of the Septennial Act 1715. It would be another century, however, before fixed-term parliaments in the more widely understood sense were introduced, by the Coalition (see p. 118).

Common law

For several centuries before the emergence of parliamentary democracy many laws passed in England were decided by judges, on a case-by-case basis. When this system began emerging in the eleventh and twelfth centuries, judicial decisions were often taken in an ad hoc way, at local level, leading to significant disparities between one area of the kingdom and another—both in terms of what was (and wasn't) perceived as a criminal offence and the range and severity of punishments meted out when laws were broken.

In 1166 the first Plantagenet king, Henry II, began the process of institutionalizing a unified national framework of common law derived from 'case law' or 'precedent'—in other words, what he regarded as the more reasoned judgments made in individual local hearings over previous decades. This new framework—which came to apply throughout England and Wales, though not Scotland—elevated some local laws to national status, sought to eliminate arbitrary or eccentric rulings, and established a great enduring constitutional right of citizens charged with criminal offences: a jury system, which would enshrine defendants' entitlement to be tried by 'twelve good men and true' from among their fellow citizens. To ensure that these new practices were implemented consistently and fairly nationwide, Henry appointed judges at his own central court and sent them around the country to adjudicate on local disputes.

Many statutes passed—and constitutional conventions that evolved—subsequently had their roots in common law. Even now, common law is still occasionally 'created': judges often have to make rulings based on their interpretations of ambiguously worded Acts or apparent conflicts between domestic and international laws. Such 'test cases' are, in their way, common law hearings.

Conventions

Other than from formal statutes and court judgments, perhaps the single most characteristic feature of Britain's unwritten constitution is its incorporation of all manner of idiosyncratic, quaint, and occasionally absurd traditions and customs. These well-worn practices have become accepted as part of Britain's constitutional framework through little more than endless repetition.

Many of the principal conventions operating in Parliament and government today are discussed in detail elsewhere in this book. These include the doctrines of collective responsibility and individual ministerial responsibility, and the tradition that the sovereign accepts Parliament's will by rubber-stamping legislation with the royal assent. More amusing conventions include the fact that the Speaker in the House of Lords (until recently the *Lord Chancellor*, but now an elected Lord Speaker) sits on a woolsack and wears a wig. The annual State Opening of Parliament by the reigning monarch is heralded by a procession led by a ceremonial officer known as 'The Gentleman Usher of the Black Rod'. It is the task of Black Rod—as he is commonly known—to lead MPs (or 'strangers') from the Commons to the Lords to hear the Queen's Speech (see p. 16). On arriving at the Commons to summon MPs, he has the door slammed in his face, and is forced to gain entry by rapping on it three times with (naturally) a black rod. This ritual is derived from a confrontation between Parliament and the sovereign in 1642, when King Charles I tried to arrest five MPs in what the Commons regarded as a breach of parliamentary privilege. Within Parliament today a form of light 'class warfare' between the chambers remains: MPs only refer to the Lords as 'another place'.

Treatises

Just as judges often have to disentangle apparently contradictory elements of Britain's unwritten constitution when making court rulings, so, too, constitutional historians, philosophers, and political scientists have long struggled to make sense of it.

Of the myriad books and theses written about the UK constitution over the centuries, a handful have become so revered that they are now seen to qualify as constitutional documents themselves. Some are considered so indispensable that they are effectively used as 'handbooks' (albeit unwieldy ones) by everyone from the Speaker of the House of Commons to High Court barristers and judges. Many of today's new laws and court judgments are framed in reference to the wisdom imparted in such tomes, the most celebrated of which are listed in Table 1.4.

Treaties

Over recent decades Britain has signed many international treaties. Of these, only a handful are arguably 'constitutional' (legally binding). Most—such as the 1945 Charter of the United Nations and the North Atlantic Treaty, which established the North Atlantic Treaty Organization (NATO) in 1949—are really little more than membership agreements and, as such, could theoretically be 'opted out of' at any time.

Table 1.4 Seminal British constitutional treatises

Treatise	Author	Significance
A Practical Treatise on the Law, Privileges, Proceedings and Usage of Parliament (Parliamentary Practice)	Erskine May (1844)	Sir Thomas Erskine May (1815–86), first Baron Farnborough and distinguished parliamentary officer, became Chief Librarian of House of Commons Library and Clerk to the Commons. His most famous work remains his seminal examination of Parliament's role, rights, and responsibilities.
The English Constitution	Walter Bagehot (1867)	A maths graduate from University College London, Bagehot (1826–77) was called to the Bar, but rejected it for a career in banking and shipping. He later edited *The Economist* (last column of which still bears his name in tribute), before writing his most esteemed work: a rumination on relationship between Parliament and monarchy and the contrast between the UK and US constitutions.
An Introduction to the Study of the Law of the Constitution	A. V. Dicey (1885)	Albert Venn Dicey (1835–1922) was an accomplished scholar, appointed to Vinerian Chair of English Law at University of Oxford in 1882, later becoming professor of law at London School of Economics. Of all great constitutional treatises, Dicey's is considered the most authoritative and far-reaching. Its central thesis was that 'freedom' of British subjects was under attack by increasingly aggressive rule of law. He saw impartiality of courts (which he believed essential to preserving this freedom) as even then under attack from governments intent on limiting fundamental civil liberties.

However, some—such as the ECHR, ratified by Labour in 1998—have effectively been incorporated into Britain's constitution and would therefore require legislation to 'remove' the obligations they impose on the state. There has also been considerable debate about the growing powers of the EU, which the UK joined (amid some controversy) in 1973, when it was still known as the European Economic Community (EEC). Recent treaties—notably the 2007 Lisbon Treaty—have solidified the relationship between member states and the EU's governing institutions, leading 'Eurosceptics' to claim that Britain has signed up to an 'EU constitution' by the back door and is now part of a 'European superstate' governed from Brussels, rather than an independent sovereign nation. This is discussed further in Chapter 9.

The separation of powers in the UK

Perhaps the most fundamental guiding principle underlying the British constitution is the **separation of powers**. Based on the theories of French political thinker Baron de Montesquieu (1689–1755), the *Trias Politica* is a notional model that splits the state into three branches:

- 'executive' (the government);
- 'legislature' (Parliament);
- 'judiciary' (the courts).

The idea is that, to avoid arbitrary or dictatorial government, a constitutional framework is needed that does not confer too much power on a single individual (or small group of individuals). In theory, if the executive is wholly 'separated' from the legislature, and in turn the judiciary, each acts as a 'check and balance' on the other.

Montesquieu purportedly formulated his theory based on the workings of the UK system, although Britain's democracy arguably adheres far less strictly to this model than many that have emerged since. In practice, numerous overlaps have emerged down the centuries between the roles, powers, and even membership of the key institutions charged with preserving the separation of powers. These include that:

- constitutionally, the reigning monarch (as 'head of state') is titular head of all three branches of the constitution;
- until 2007, when the post was reformed (see pp. 73–5), the Lord Chancellor was a member of all three institutions, as Speaker of the House of Lords (legislature), 'manager' of the legal profession (judiciary), and a minister in Cabinet (executive);
- the prime minister and most other ministers are members of both government (executive) and Parliament (legislature);

- before the establishment of an independent Supreme Court in October 2009, the Law Lords collectively constituted Britain's highest court of appeal (judiciary), as well as being voting peers (legislature).

Such constitutional overlaps are not confined to Britain. Many other parliamentary democracies—particularly those directly modelled on the UK's, as in many Commonwealth countries—display a similar fusion of powers, rather than the 'separation' to which they aspire. Constitutional historians increasingly draw distinctions in this regard between countries that practise 'presidential government' and those characterized by 'parliamentary government'. In the former (which include the USA, France, South Africa, and Australia), separation is felt to be both more practised and practicable than in countries like Britain, where the most senior politician (the prime minister) is today drawn from among the ranks of ordinary MPs and, as such, represents a constituency in the same way as his/her peers.

In the UK, executive decisions are taken primarily by prime ministers and their ministers, before being presented for approval to Parliament (where most of them are also present, this time as voting MPs and peers). In the USA and other states, in contrast, the most senior elected politician is the president—who, in the absence of a reigning monarch, is also head of state. Crucially, unlike in Britain and other parliamentary states, presidents are usually elected on different timetables to their national parliaments. The separation of powers in the USA is more pronounced than in Britain because Congress (comprising the Senate and House of Representatives—the US equivalent of Britain's Parliament) is elected in large part on a different date, and in a different manner, from the president. More crucially, the president (unlike the British prime minister) is not a member of either House; so while he/she may present policies to Congress for approval, he/she does not preside over the ensuing debates within the chambers in the way prime ministers do in the Commons.

Another feature of the separation of powers enjoyed by presidential states is the fact that, historically, they tend to have developed a more provably independent judicial system than in many prime ministerial ones. The USA has long had a Supreme Court that (in theory at least) is entirely separate from the political process. Notwithstanding controversies over the president's ability to nominate judges to replace those who retire (President Bush was castigated in 2005 for choosing Harriet Miers, his former adviser and a long-time conservative ally, who later withdrew her own candidacy), this system is felt to be more appropriate than one in which judges straddle the divide between legislature and judiciary by serving in both a legal and law-making capacity. To this end, in 2007 Jack Straw, as inaugural Secretary of State for Justice (and de facto Lord Chancellor), announced that the Law Lords would be effectively removed from Parliament in 2009, to sit in the new Supreme Court.

Further reforms, including a written constitution and a Bill to give Parliament the final say over any future decision to take Britain to war, were floated by Gordon Brown at various points in his tenure, but never acted on. At the time of writing, the Coalition was still reviewing the question of whether a new Bill of Rights was needed—though the minister chairing the review, Deputy Prime Minister Nick Clegg, was lukewarm about the idea, given that for many Conservatives it is seen as paving the way for a withdrawal from the ECHR (see p. 12).

▌ The monarchy

Britain's reigning sovereign is the head of a 'constitutional monarchy'. This means that, while he/she remains UK head of state, with the notional prerogative to govern and take major constitutional decisions, in practice he/she does not do so. Unlike in presidential countries, Britain's head of state is a figurehead with little real power. Instead, day-to-day decisions regarding domestic and foreign policy are left to Her Majesty's government, led by the 'First Lord of the Treasury'—or prime minister.

The authority invested in successive prime ministers to choose their own ministers, devise and draft legislation, and decide whether to take Britain to war is derived from another key constitutional principle: the **royal prerogative**. In essence, this is the body of customary privileges and powers historically acquired by reigning monarchs (predominantly in the Middle Ages). Today, the majority of so-called 'prerogative powers' derived from this principle are exercised not by the Crown itself but by Parliament.

Origins of the modern British monarchy

Although the present monarchy is also descended from several powerful families with roots outside the UK, Queen Elizabeth II can reputedly trace her line on one side directly to King Egbert, the ruler who united England under one throne in AD 829. The position she occupies is that of Britain's longest standing secular institution (its only interruption being the previously mentioned interregnum from 1649 to 1660).

Although short-lived, this period—sometimes referred to as the 'English Revolution'—marked a break with the past that was to change the monarchy's role forever. Beforehand, the prevailing 'rationale' for the existence of the sovereign derived from the 'Divine Right of Kings'. By propagating the idea that they should not be answerable to 'man-made' institutions, European medieval monarchs sought to reign with the minimum of outside interference—with the possible exception of that of the Church, which, in some notable instances (including Henry VIII's inability to obtain permission from the Pope to divorce his first wife, Catherine of Aragon), directly challenged their pre-eminence. Parliaments were generally regarded as tools to enable kings and queens to raise taxes, pass edicts, and declare wars with impunity.

In England all of this changed after the execution of Charles I. While his eldest son, Charles II, ultimately succeeded him following Cromwell's death, the concept that any monarch had a divine right to rule unchallenged had by then been all but rescinded. Through a succession of landmark constitutional statutes—principally the Bill of Rights and Act of Settlement (see pp. 7–10)—a newly liberated Parliament stamped its authority on the nation, and (in all but name) the monarch.

The role of the monarchy today

In *The English Constitution*, Bagehot (1826–77) argued that it was incumbent on monarchs to embody the following qualities:

❝ The right to be consulted, the right to encourage, the right to warn. ❞

Specifically, the role and powers of the monarch are best explained by splitting them into two broad categories: *actual* and *notional*.

Actual prerogative powers—those exercised by the monarch

Despite the huge upheavals of recent centuries, the sovereign still holds the following key constitutional offices:

- head of state;
- head of the executive, legislature, and judiciary;
- commander-in-chief of the Armed Forces;
- supreme governor of the established Church of England;
- head of the Commonwealth (and head of state of fifteen of its fifty-three members);
- the authority from which the Royal Mint derives its licence to coin and print money (at present, in his/her image).

But so much for their official titles: what do monarchs actually *do*? And, more specifically, which prerogative powers do monarchs personally still exercise in an age when governments hold sway over most key political decisions?

The core roles and duties of the monarch—many largely ceremonial—include:

- reading Her Majesty's Most Gracious Speech, or the 'Gracious Address'—better known as the Queen's Speech—at the State Opening of Parliament each October or November, or shortly after a general election;

- governing the Church of England;
- the formal act of 'creating' peers and conferring knighthoods and honours;
- meeting the prime minister once a week (usually on Tuesdays) to discuss Cabinet business and offer advice on affairs of state;
- entertaining visiting heads of state at Buckingham Palace;
- touring other nations on official state visits—including those of the Commonwealth—as Britain's premier overseas ambassador;
- chairing meetings of the **Privy Council** (a body of advisers made up of members of the current and previous Cabinets, plus other distinguished individuals, which issues Royal Charters and Orders in Council—see p. 69);
- attending 'Trooping the Colour' (the monarch's annual birthday parade, led by regiments of HM Armed Forces).

Although this list of 'powers' may appear feeble in the scheme of things, there is considerable anecdotal evidence to suggest that recent monarchs have discharged their duties with rigour. In her first audience with then newly elected Labour Prime Minister Harold Wilson in 1964, Queen Elizabeth II famously wrong-footed him by expressing interest in proposals for a 'new town' near Bletchley. Having not yet read his Cabinet papers, he knew nothing of them. In his 1976 resignation speech, Wilson made a joke of the episode, saying he would advise his successors to 'do their homework' before meeting the Queen.

In addition to the above prerogative powers retained by the monarch and his/her immediate family, the sovereign has traditionally been called on to fulfil a unifying role as a national figurehead at times of crisis. The late HM Queen Elizabeth the Queen Mother famously toured bomb sites in London's East End to provide comfort to dispossessed families during the Blitz, while the Queen's annual televised Christmas Day address is designed as much to 'sum up' the past year and look to the one ahead on behalf of the whole nation as to update her subjects on her own regal affairs. Such is the onus placed on the sovereign to 'speak for the nation' at times of tragedy or disaster that the Queen's initial silence following the death of Diana, Princess of Wales and her lover Dodi Fayed in a Paris car crash in 1997 became a cause célèbre among her critics—allegedly prompting newly elected premier Tony Blair to appeal to her to make a statement in tribute to her daughter-in-law.

Notional prerogative powers—those deferred to government

Most sovereign powers are exercised 'on the advice of ministers', which means it is ministers—and the prime minister mostly—who actually take the decisions. In practice, then, it is the monarch who offers 'advice' to prime ministers, rather than the other way round, and prime ministers who discharge the following functions:

- dissolving and summoning Parliament—calling elections and forming new parliaments after the results are in;
- giving the **royal assent** (the final 'rubber-stamp' of approval) to Bills passed by Parliament;
- appointing ministers and other senior public officials, including judges, diplomats, governors, officers in the Armed Forces, police chief constables, and Church of England bishops and archbishops;
- devising the legislative agenda for each parliamentary session (year of Parliament) and *writing* the **Queen's Speech**, which outlines that agenda and is read out by the sovereign at the State Opening of Parliament—the ceremony heralding the start of a session;
- declaring war and peace;
- the **prorogation** of Parliament—that is, suspending its activities over holiday periods, such as the summer recess and annual Christmas and Easter breaks;
- drawing up lists of nominations—in consultation with the leaders of opposition parties—for peerages, knighthoods, and other honours to be confirmed by the sovereign in the New Year Honours List and Queen's Birthday Honours List.

In addition, the monarch may occasionally issue a 'royal pardon'—known formally as the 'royal prerogative of mercy'—to convicted criminals. This tends to happen either when an individual convicted of a crime is subsequently pardoned in light of new evidence, or (very rarely) when the actions and/or behaviour of a prisoner are deemed to warrant their early release from a sentence. Unlike all other sovereign powers exercised by the government on the monarch's behalf, pardons are issued on the advice not of the prime minister but the Justice Secretary (in England and Wales), Scottish First Minister (Scotland), or Northern Ireland Secretary (Northern Ireland), following the introduction of devolution. A recent example of a royal pardon was the posthumous forgiveness offered to families of all British soldiers executed for cowardice during the Second World War.

How the monarchy is funded

For forty years before the 2012–13 tax year, the income of the reigning monarch and his/her immediate family—the 'Royal Household'—derived from four principal sources:

- the Civil List;
- grants-in-aid;

- the Privy Purse;
- personal income.

Following the passage of the Sovereign Grant Act 2011, however, a rationalized funding regime was introduced, which has seen the first two sources of sovereign income (both funded by the taxpayer) supplanted by a single annual payment: the sovereign grant.

From the old to the new system—finances in transition

Often used by those who favour abolishing the monarchy as shorthand for the Royal Family as a whole, the Civil List originated in the Bill of Rights. With the accession of William and Mary, Parliament voted to give the Royal Household £600,000 to aid it in 'civil government'. The Civil List in its more recent form was established in 1760, during George III's reign. In return for the king surrendering to Parliament his 'hereditary revenues'—the income generated by the Crown Lands (estates owned previously by the monarch)—MPs agreed to pledge a fixed annual income to the Royal Household. In practice, this exchange would reap huge dividends for Parliament: in 2008–9, the income generated for the Treasury by the Crown Lands (as administered by the Crown Estate Commissioners) was £226.5m, compared to £40m paid to the monarch.

In 2001 the Civil List itself was fixed at £7.9m a year for the Queen until at least 2011, with her husband, the Duke of Edinburgh (Prince Philip), receiving a separate annuity of £359,000. In a deal struck with Mr Brown while Chancellor, the Queen agreed to finance any increases in her outgoings from a 'reserve fund' worth up to £30m, accumulated over the previous decade. In return, her own and her husband's 'fixed' incomes would rise by 7.5 per cent a year to keep them abreast of inflation (which, at 3 per cent in 2001, was less than half as high). As a result, by the end of 2009–10, the Civil List had actually swelled to £14.2m. In common with many households, though, the royals emerged from the recession rather less solvent than beforehand: when the 2009–10 Buckingham Palace accounts were published in July 2010, they revealed that the Queen had been forced to supplement the official Civil List pot by a record £6.5m during that year, reducing her reserve fund to £15.2m. With an expected drawdown of £7.2m in 2010–11, she faced the prospect of running out of reserves by 2012—her Diamond Jubilee year. Chancellor George Osborne also announced in his June 2010 Budget that future Civil List settlements would be subject to the same scrutiny as government departments, amending the Civil List Audit Act 1816 to hand auditing powers to the National Audit Office and the influential Public Accounts Committee of MPs. And in his subsequent Comprehensive Spending Review (CSR) (see p. 195), he revealed that the Queen had agreed to shoulder her share of the burden of his swingeing £81bn package of spending cuts by consenting to a two-year freeze in her grant funding, in 2011–12 and 2012–13, which would necessitate a 14 per cent reduction in the Royal Household's spending.

In the last few years before it was abolished, the Civil List funded the following expenses for both the Queen and Duke of Edinburgh:

- salaries of the retinue of 645 servants, butlers, and other Royal Household employees (70 per cent);
- costs of royal garden parties (attended by some 48,000 people each year) and hospitality during state visits (30 per cent).

In addition, a number of parliamentary allowances have been issued annually to individual members of the Royal Family, including the Duke of York (Prince Andrew) and the Princess Royal (Princess Anne), under the Civil List Acts. These have generally amounted to £2.5m extra, though since April 1993 the Queen has in practice refunded £1.5m to Parliament, using her personal pot of money, the Privy Purse (see p. 25). The remaining £1m has been retained each year as income for the Duke of Edinburgh and, until her death in 2002, the Queen Mother (who received £643,000 a year). All other senior royals performing official duties have received annuities from the Privy Purse rather than the Civil List.

Perhaps surprisingly, one of the few key Royal Household members who has not benefited from such an annuity is the present heir, the Prince of Wales (Prince Charles), who as Duke of Cornwall earns substantial income from his sprawling 130,000-acre Duchy of Cornwall estate. Originally bestowed on the Black Prince in 1337, despite its name the Duchy extends over twenty-three counties. According to the Prince's official website, in 2011–12 it generated income worth £20.48m—a year-on-year increase of £700,000, or 3.6 per cent (though it appeared that this boost was needed, in light of a £721,000 rise in the Prince's spending, in part due to the cost of the royal wedding of his son and daughter-in-law, the Duke and Duchess of Cambridge, in April 2011).

While the Civil List was used to cover the day-to-day living costs of the Royal Household, the other customary pot of taxpayers' money, *grants-in-aid*, was set aside for maintaining the 'occupied royal palaces'—those in which members of the Royal Family still live—and the family's personal transport. Awarded to the Crown by the Department of Culture, Media, and Sport (DCMS), grants totalling around £15m a year were bestowed on the palaces, chief among which were the following:

- Buckingham Palace (home of the Queen and Prince Philip);
- St James's Palace (home of Prince Charles);
- Kensington Palace;
- Windsor Castle (the Queen's second home).

In addition to grants-in-aid, Buckingham Palace and Windsor Castle also helped to maintain themselves by means of their summer public openings. Grants were not available for the upkeep of two royal estates—Sandringham in Norfolk and Balmoral in Scotland—which are the Queen's private property and not her legacy as head of state.

A further set of grants was awarded by the Department for Transport (DfT), amounting to some £6m a year. These covered the cost of transporting family members to and from their 3,000 annual engagements in Britain and overseas. Until she was decommissioned in 1997, the biggest grant was used to maintain the Royal Yacht Britannia, the Queen's official ship, which was launched in 1953. The other principal transport expenses were the Royal Air Force (RAF) aircraft of the No. 32 (The Royal) Squadron, the Royal Train, and numerous chartered and scheduled flights used by senior royals for official visits.

In recent years, disclosures of the Royal Family's travels in the preceding twelve months have attracted heavy media attention. In 2011–12 the Duke and Duchess of Cambridge (Prince William and Princess Catherine) spent £52,000 on one-way flights from Los Angeles to London for them and their seven-strong entourage. The heavily publicized globe-trotting 'Jubilee Tour' undertaken by the Duke's younger brother, Prince Harry, to mark the Queen's sixtieth year on the throne set taxpayers back £107,098, while his uncle, the Duke of York—long ago nicknamed 'Airmiles Andy' on account of his extravagant exploits—spent £378,000 on flights during the last months of his much-criticized stint as Britain's global ambassador for trade and industry.

A growing public backlash against extravagant royal transport costs, combined with the new mood of frugality arising from recent recessions, has encouraged the Royal Household to rein back significantly on travel spending, particularly its use of commercial flights. Total travel expenditure dropped from £6.5m in 2008–9 to £3.9m in 2009–10—though by 2011–12 (the last year of a separate grants-in-aid budget) it had bounced back to £6.1m.

The remaining portion of the grants-in-aid budget (typically amounting to around 10 per cent of the total) was spent on royal 'communications': letters, telephone bills, and other correspondences, including invitations to garden parties.

As explained earlier, the Civil List and grants-in-aid were due to be consolidated from 2012–13 into a single **sovereign grant**. The grant has been set initially at 15 per cent of the net revenue generated each year by the Crown Estates—early estimates suggest this could actually increase the Royal Household's taxpayer-funded income to as much as £36m a year (up from £32.2m in 2011–12). It is envisaged that the new, more generous, grant will enable the Queen to finance long overdue repairs to several of her palaces. The practice of the Queen 'subsidizing' the state by reimbursing it for the cost of annuities for family members other than her husband has also been formalized under the new regime, with these parliamentary annuities officially ceasing. If there is money left from the sovereign grant in a given year, this will be paid into a reserve fund overseen by the Royal Trustees (up to a maximum value of half of the grant awarded). Conversely, if the Queen requires more money one year she can dip into this fund to meet any unforeseen expenses.

The Privy Purse

Dating back to 1399, the Privy Purse is derived largely from the income generated by the Duchy of Lancaster—a huge expanse of land covering 19,268 acres and the sole surviving Crown estate to remain in the monarch's possession. It is kept under lock and key by her personal accountant and administered by the Chancellor of the Duchy of Lancaster—today almost always a senior Cabinet minister—and the Keeper of the Privy Purse (currently Sir Alan Reid).

Personal income

Like anyone else, senior members of the Royal Family, despite deriving significant income from the state, are free to generate their own earnings—provided they pay Income Tax on them (see p. 192). Personal incomes earned by individual members of the Royal Household include the military salaries drawn by Prince Charles, who served for a time in the Royal Navy, Prince Andrew, who saw action during the Falklands War, and Prince Harry, currently in the Household Cavalry (Blues and Royals). Other examples include the income earned by Prince Charles's Duchy of Cornwall estate from land rent and sales of its produce—for example, his 'Duchy Originals' biscuits. His youngest brother, Prince Edward, Duke of Wessex, owned a film and television company, Ardent Productions, until its liquidation in 2009.

More sporadic sources of income might include everything from share dividends to windfalls from betting on the races (the Queen Mother famously liked a flutter).

Taxation and the monarchy

Like everyone else, the Queen has always paid indirect taxes—value added tax (VAT) and other tariffs levied on consumer goods and services. She has also long paid, on a voluntary basis, local taxes—Council Tax and, before that, the Community Charge (or 'Poll Tax') and rates. It was not until 1993, however, that she agreed to pay direct taxes—principally Income Tax. This decision was taken following a public backlash over the revelation that much of the £60m cost of repairing Windsor Castle after a devastating fire in 1992 was funded by taxpayers, despite the fact that they already hugely subsidized the Royal Household.

The monarch and certain members of her immediate family do, however, continue to enjoy substantial tax breaks not granted to her subjects. In particular, while the Privy Purse pays tax and the Queen's personal estate is subject to Inheritance Tax, the sovereign grant is not regarded as taxable, and neither is any transfer of property 'from sovereign to sovereign'—that is, between the Queen and her successor.

The succession

For many centuries, as is commonly the case in other European nation states, the monarchy has tended to pass from father to son in Britain, through a process known as 'eldest male primogeniture'. Only when a male line (going through the eldest son) has been exhausted does the crown pass to the eldest male sibling of the originator of that line, and only after that will it ever go to a female sibling. Under this system, Prince Charles would inherit the throne from his mother on her death and, after he died, it would pass to his eldest son, William, and from him to the eldest of his own sons. If William were to die without leaving a male heir but he did have a daughter, it would eventually pass to her, but if he were to have no children and die before his brother, Harry, the crown would finally pass to him.

However, in a radical constitutional departure, the Coalition has dispensed with centuries of tradition by confirming in its 2012 Queen's Speech that legislation will be brought forward to end the principle of eldest male primogeniture, with effect from the succession of Prince William. This will mean that if the first child of the Duke and Duchess of Cambridge is a girl she will automatically succeed to the throne following his death, rather than it passing over her head to a younger son (and thence, potentially, down his male line). Before confirming the change, ministers first had to formally seek approval from the fifteen other Commonwealth countries reigned over by the Queen (see pp. 320–3), but all approved the move at a summit in 2011. In a further significant change, the Bill of Rights, Act of Settlement, and Royal Marriages Act 1772 are all to be amended to allow future sovereigns to marry Roman Catholics without forfeiting their titles. The legal obligation of every descendant of George II to seek the monarch's permission before getting married will also end. In future, only the six Royal Family members closest to the Crown will require this prior consent.

The other key 'rules' governing the succession—between them derived from the Bill of Rights and Act of Settlement—are listed in Table 1.1.

Monarchy versus presidency—which way forward?

Although Britain has had a monarchy for the best part of 1,500 years, today it is one of the few 'developed' nations to retain one—let alone to boast an extended Royal Family, funded largely by taxpayers. Perhaps unsurprisingly, recent years have witnessed growing calls for the monarchy to be replaced by an elected head of state. These have been fuelled by a succession of controversies surrounding the Royal Household and, in particular, that relating to Prince Charles's divorce from the late Diana, Princess of Wales, and revelations about his long-standing relationship with Camilla Parker-Bowles (now his second wife and Duchess of Cornwall). Further succour was given to those arguing for Britain's hereditary figurehead to be replaced by an elected one by the

Australian electorate's narrow decision to retain the Queen as Australia's head of state in November 1999. In 2007 the country's newly elected Labour Prime Minister, Kevin Rudd, pledged to hold a further referendum, but had not achieved this by the time he left office in 2010 (after being deposed by his deputy, Julia Gillard).

The argument for an elected head of state is self-explanatory: in a modern democracy, so the republican case goes, it is surely only right that the state's ultimate ambassador—the individual who publicly represents its interests on the global stage—should gain a 'mandate' to do so from his/her subjects. But what are the arguments for retaining a monarch? Opinions differ among constitutional historians about the merits of the institution, but an oft-cited argument in favour of the hereditary principle is that it produces heads of state who have the luxury of being able to maintain an objective, independent-minded *distance* from the day-to-day workings of the political process—rather than being hidebound by the narrow, short-term thinking that constrains politicians reliant on the votes of a fickle electorate. In addition, the presence of Queen Elizabeth II through sixty years of changing governments and shifting political priorities has provided, some argue, a degree of continuity absent from presidential states.

▌ Devolution—from union to government in the nations

Most of this chapter has focused on outlining the process by which the modern British state came into being, and the rules, customs, and laws that have evolved to determine the balance of powers between Parliament, the monarchy, and citizens.

The UK is a 'representative democracy'—a state whose power is exercised through democratically elected representatives (in Britain's case, MPs in the House of Commons). Broadly speaking, there are two main types of democracy: *federal* and *unitary*. In federal democracies, countries are divided into separate political units, each with considerable autonomy over its own affairs. The USA is an example of a federal democracy: major foreign and domestic policy decisions are taken by the national government (president and Congress), but many day-to-day matters are decided on a state-by-state basis. The most oft-cited example of federalism in action relates to the way that different states punish felons convicted of serious crimes like murder and rape: while fourteen of the states making up the USA favour custodial sentences, the remaining thirty-six still practise capital punishment.

Britain, in contrast to the USA, is a *unitary* democracy. This means the bulk of power remains in the hands of central government and the Westminster

Parliament. But, while the constitutional story of Britain since the late medieval period has mostly been one of the gradual consolidation of a single UK run from the centre, in recent years this has been compromised by moves towards a more decentralized form of government, taking power closer to the people from whom it derives.

The story of the emergence of local government—elected councils, funded by local taxpayers, which run local services—is told in detail in the second half of this book. But, at a higher level than the strictly 'local', there now exists in Scotland, Wales, and Northern Ireland a further tier of government to which significant powers have been devolved by Westminster. This statutory transfer of power from central government to the separate nations that make up the UK alongside England is known as **devolution**.

Before proceeding further, it is worth explaining the distinction between 'devolution' and 'independence'. Although the parties most enthusiastically embracing devolution in Scotland, Wales, and Northern Ireland tend to be 'nationalist' ones—those that would ultimately like to break away from the UK to become independent states—devolved power does not amount to independence in itself. Neither does it inevitably follow that, having gained devolution, a country will one day become independent. Indeed, one of the principal arguments used by Labour to justify devolution was that, in granting it, the party was safeguarding the union of Britain, by permitting a limited degree of autonomy that made practical sense and would answer many of the frustrations expressed by dissatisfied, but otherwise loyal, British subjects in those countries. Conversely, advocates of independence have argued that in the long term it makes little sense for national assemblies in Scotland or Wales, that take most of their own day-to-day decisions without needing formal permission from Westminster, to remain its vassals, and that full self-government is the logical next step. Although technically Parliament's approval would be required before independence could be granted, demands for a breakaway government became a clamour when Alex Salmond, leader of the Scottish Nationalist Party, was elected his country's First Minister in May 2007, eradicating Labour's majority share of the vote in Scotland for the first time in fifty years. They became even more acute when, four years later, his party was returned to power, this time with an outright majority.

Mr Salmond's repeated pledges to hold an independence referendum were addressed in part by a draft Bill published in February 2010, in which he outlined proposals for two separate ballots of Scottish voters. The first would ask them if they supported the Scottish Parliament being granted more devolved autonomy, with two alternative models proposed: one, dubbed 'devolution max', involved the handover of all remaining powers from Westminster to Holyrood apart from defence policy, foreign affairs, and financial regulation, and the other envisaged a more limited extension of devolution, along the lines of changes suggested in June 2009 by Sir Kenneth Calman. Mr Salmond also proposed asking voters, in a second ballot, if they wanted Holyrood's powers extended to enable full-blooded independence to be achieved. But even under these plans, the Queen would remain Scotland's head of state. The country would also seek to retain membership of the European Union (though it's ability to do so without formally 'reapplying' as an independent state has since been questioned by the European Commission). Mr Salmond's speech had a mixed reception with critics stressing that the near-collapse of both Halifax Bank of Scotland (HBOS) and the Royal Bank of Scotland (RBS) during the 2008–9 financial crisis, and their subsequent bailouts by HM Treasury (see pp. 213–16), had emphasized the economic security provided by the union.

Mr Salmond renewed his calls for independence in January 2012 when, in the face of a challenge by Mr Cameron to put up or shut up, he called the Coalition's bluff by publishing a consultation paper setting out a detailed timetable for achieving his goal—including the desired wording of his referendum 'question'. Stating that he intended to hold the crucial vote some time in autumn 2014, he revived the notion of putting more than one scenario to the Scottish people, including a 'devolution max' option. The main item on the ballot paper, however, would be an 'in or out' question worded as follows:

❝ Do you agree that Scotland should be an independent country? ❞

Buoyed by opinion polls suggesting that seven out of ten Scots wanted to preserve the union, the Coalition argued that the referendum should concern itself solely with gauging support for full-blown independence. After weeks of intense further negotiations, Mr Salmond and Mr Cameron finally shook hands on a deal in October 2012 which will put a single 'yes/no' question to the Scottish people. In return for dropping his demand for a second, 'devo-max', question Scotland's First Minister secured the Coalition's promise that the outcome of the referendum would be binding under the terms of an obscure constitutional instrument known a 'Section 30': in other words, if the Scots vote to withdraw from the UK then formal independence will now be granted in accordance with their wishes. Unlike in any previous election, 16- and 17-year olds will also be allowed to vote.

Prior to the dispute erupting over the putative referendum, the Coalition had used its inaugural Queen's Speech on 25 May 2010 to confirm plans for a Scotland Bill that would implement many of the Calman Commission's recommendations. Convened in 2007 to review the progress of Scottish devolution ten years on, the Commission had made several suggestions, including that 10p should be top-sliced from the basic and higher rates of Income Tax in Scotland, with the Scottish Parliament left to decide whether to make up the difference by levying its own top-up tax. Sir Kenneth had also recommended devolution of all manner of minor policing matters—from airgun control to drink driving and speeding policies.

The unification of Great Britain

Wales

Like much of the UK's constitutional heritage, the concept of devolution originated in the Middle Ages, when Wales and Scotland first began demanding the right to rule themselves independently of the English sovereign. Of the two countries, Wales has the longest formal association with England. The main stages in its moves towards incorporation into the UK are outlined in the table entitled 'Timeline for the incorporation of Wales into the UK', to be found on the Online Resource Centre that accompanies this book.

Scotland

Scotland's progress towards integration in the UK was more complex—due, in part, to the fact that it had never been formally absorbed into the Roman Empire. It took centuries of conflict during the medieval period for it finally to succumb to the authority of the English Crown—a timeline showing this is outlined in the table entitled 'Timeline for the incorporation of Scotland into the UK', to be found on the Online Resource Centre.

Northern Ireland

Northern Ireland's incorporation into the UK was more problematic, encompassing as it did its split from Southern Ireland (Eire). The early stages of the process are outlined in the table entitled 'Timeline for the incorporation of Northern Ireland into the UK', to be found on the Online Resource Centre.

The path to Scottish devolution

The workings of the governing institutions established under devolution in Scotland, Wales, and Northern Ireland are explored in more detail in Chapter 2. What follows here is an outline of the process by which these institutions were created following the 1997 referendums and the levels of devolution granted in each case.

Of the three countries, Scotland has the most extensive degree of devolved government, following the enabling legislation passed to formalize devolution in 1998. In part this is a reflection of the fact that, for complex historical reasons, the country has long had certain devolved functions—most notably its distinctive legal system. More significantly, however, it is a legacy of the growing calls north of the border, after eighteen years of Conservative rule at Westminster, for greater autonomy from a national Parliament that seemed increasingly remote (both politically and geographically) from Scottish interests.

Table 1.5 Timeline for the introduction of devolution in Scotland

Date	Event
1973	Royal Commission on the Constitution, set up by Wilson's Labour government in late 1960s, recommends devolution to Edward Heath's Conservatives
1978	Re-elected Labour government passes Scotland Act, paving way for referendum on Scottish self-government: 40 per cent of Scottish electorate must vote for devolution for it to be granted
March 1979	Devolution put on hold indefinitely because, although 52 per cent of those who voted supported it, this was equivalent to only 32 per cent of total electorate
July 1997	Newly re-elected Labour government publishes *Scotland's Parliament*, a White Paper advocating devolution
11 September 1997	This time, referendum attracts 60 per cent turnout, with 74 per cent of voters backing devolution and 64 per cent voting 'yes' in answer to second question, backing Scottish Parliament's having *tax-varying* powers
1998	Government of Scotland Act passed, conferring devolution
12 May 1999	The Queen opens new Scottish Parliament after its precise powers confirmed by consultative steering group
7 September 2004	Grand opening of £420m purpose-built Scottish Parliament at Holyrood, by foot of Edinburgh's Royal Mile

The path to Scottish devolution began in the 1960s, when the then Labour government established a Royal Commission to examine the arguments for some form of home rule. The sequence of events leading to eventual devolution is outlined in Table 1.5.

Unlike Wales and Northern Ireland, where (at present) devolved powers have so far been more limited, the Scottish Parliament has considerable authority—only foreign affairs, defence policy, the welfare system, and the introduction of new taxes are outside its remit. Its powers include determining education, health, environment, and transport policy in Scotland, and being able to 'vary'—that is, raise or lower—Income Tax by up to 3p in the pound (the so-called 'Tartan Tax' option). In July 2010, a commission set up by the Welsh Assembly Government recommended that Wales be given similar authority to vary Income Tax levels, but this change has yet to be approved by the Coalition government.

The 'West Lothian Question'

The growing assertiveness of the Scottish Parliament in light of its powers—for example, it voted to reject foundation hospitals and undergraduate top-up fees, two deeply unpopular Blair policies adopted south of the border—has raised significant constitutional issues. None is more explosive than the 'West Lothian Question': the argument that it is unfair for Scottish MPs to be allowed to continue voting on matters that have no bearing on their own country, but directly affect England and Wales, while English and Welsh members have no say over issues particular to Scotland. Although devolution was only introduced relatively recently, this quandary was first raised in debate in the Commons by Labour backbencher Tam Dalyell in the 1970s. It was dubbed the 'West Lothian Question' by then Tory MP Enoch Powell after the name of Dalyell's constituency.

Today the West Lothian Question rages more than ever—not least because, on more than one occasion, Mr Blair managed to bolster shaky Commons majorities in votes on controversial legislation with the help of Scottish MPs who had let it be known that they did not support the same policies being applied in their own country (see p. 177). The fact that his successor, Mr Brown, was a Scot (and one representing a Scottish constituency) did little to dampen the issue on his departure.

The path to Welsh devolution

Welsh devolution was introduced as outlined in Table 1.6.

The rocky road to Northern Irish devolution

Due to the fallout from 'The Troubles', the devolution process in Northern Ireland was more drawn out, with the various parties unable to agree a workable framework for devolved government until very recently. A landmark agreement signed in 2007 appeared finally, however, to have buried the hatchet between the main republican and unionist parties, with the ruling Democratic Unionists accepting that the IRA had decommissioned its weapons, as it had long claimed. The Northern Ireland Assembly has since been restored.

The saga that led to the granting of meaningful devolution to Northern Ireland lasted decades, so it would be impractical to list every twist and turn here, but the most significant events are outlined in Table 1.7.

Table 1.6 Timeline for the introduction of devolution in Wales

Date	Event
July 1997	White Paper entitled *A Voice for Wales* introduced, outlining proposals for Welsh devolution
18 September 1997	Referendum attracts low turnout of around 50 per cent, but 50.3 per cent approve devolution
1998	Government of Wales Act passed to lay out framework
1999	National Assembly for Wales (Transfer of Functions) Order introduced, providing a legal and constitutional framework
6 May 1999	First election for National Assembly for Wales
12 May 1999	National Assembly for Wales meets for first time
1 March 2006	The Queen officially opens new purpose-built £67m Welsh Assembly building in Cardiff

Table 1.7 Timeline for the introduction of devolution in Northern Ireland

Date	Event
1968	Civil Rights Movement starts in Ulster; street violence erupts between Protestants and Catholics (dawn of 'The Troubles')
1972	Most notorious explosion of violence in history of 'The Troubles'— 'Bloody Sunday'—occurs in Londonderry, culminating at the Bogside, a Catholic ghetto
1972	Northern Ireland constitution, prime minister, and Parliament suspended for a year due to escalating violence
November 1985	Anglo-Irish Agreement (officially 'The Hillsborough Agreement'), signed by Britain and Ireland, recognizes that any constitutional change in Northern Ireland can only come about with agreement of population through a referendum
November 1992	Inconclusive end to talks flowing from Anglo-Irish Agreement
December 1993	UK Prime Minister John Major and Irish Taoiseach Albert Reynolds issue Joint Declaration from 10 Downing Street ('The Downing Street Declaration'), stipulating that future participation in discussions about government of Northern Ireland should be restricted to parties committed to 'exclusively peaceful means'
August 1994	IRA announces ceasefire, described as 'complete cessation of military operations'; Combined Loyalist Military Command swiftly does likewise
February 1995	British and Irish governments launch *A New Framework for Accountable Government in Northern Ireland*, outlining proposals for new democratic institutions
February 1996	Docklands bomb brings IRA ceasefire to an end
June 1996	Former US Senator George Mitchell convenes Northern Ireland Forum, outlining six 'Mitchell Principles' for moves towards peace; Sinn Féin excluded until IRA formally readopts its ceasefire; two further IRA bomb blasts follow, in Manchester and County Antrim
July 1997	Sinn Féin president Gerry Adams and vice-president Martin McGuinness elected as Westminster MPs, and IRA resumes its ceasefire; International Commission on Decommissioning set up under Canadian general John de Chastelain to oversee process
September 1997	Sinn Féin signs up to the Mitchell Principles and multiparty talks start at Stormont; after being switched to Lancaster House in London, deadline of 9 April 1998 set for agreement
10 April 1998	'Good Friday Agreement' (Belfast Agreement) published as basis for dual referendums on devolution in Northern and Southern Ireland; constitutionally, the way is paved by Northern Ireland (Elections) Act 1998 and nineteenth Amendment to Irish Constitution (renouncing Eire's claim on the north)
22 May 1998	Referendum of whole of Ireland produces 94 per cent backing for devolution among residents of Eire and 71 per cent 'yes' vote in Northern Ireland
25 June 1998	First elections for Northern Ireland Assembly see Ulster Unionist Party gaining most seats (28), with Social Democratic and Labour Party second (24)

(*continued*)

Table 1.7 (*continued*)

Date	Event
1 July 1998	New assembly meets for first time, with Lord Alderdice as first Presiding Officer and David Trimble, Ulster Unionist Party leader, as First Minister Designate; at least three nationalists and three designated unionists meant to be included in government under devolution deal (known as the 'd'Hondt procedure'—formula named after Belgian Victor d'Hondt, whereby each party is allocated seats on a 'largest average' basis relating to number of votes it receives)
15 August 1998	Twenty-nine people die in Omagh bomb planted by 'Real IRA' splinter group
1 December 1999	Direct rule of Northern Ireland from Westminster ends with the Queen's signing of Northern Ireland Act 1998
2 December 1999	Anglo-Irish Agreement replaced by British-Irish Agreement, formally creating the North–South Ministerial Council and British–Irish Ministerial Council envisaged in Good Friday Agreement; on same day, Irish Parliament replaces Arts 2 and 3 of Irish Constitution—formally abandoning Eire's historic claim to hegemony over Northern Ireland
11 February 2000	Assembly suspended due to continuing disagreement about the pace of terrorists' decommissioning of weapons; prolonged period of intermittent direct rule resumes while General de Chasterlain continues trying to confirm IRA claims it has put its arms beyond use
December 2003	Assembly elections give largest number of seats (30) to Reverend Ian Paisley's Democratic Unionist Party, followed by Ulster Unionist Party (27), Sinn Féin (24), and moderate nationalist SDLP (18)
March 2007	After further elections in Northern Ireland and power-sharing talks, agreement finally struck to restore devolution
April 2007	Loyalist Volunteer Force follows IRA's declaration of 'final cessation of hostilities' in August 2005 by announcing it is winding up
May 2007	Power-sharing resumes in the Assembly

Ironically, the *level* of power devolved to the province is much more limited than that of Scotland. As in Wales, Northern Ireland was until recently restricted to:

- determining some budgetary priorities in education, health, etc.;
- funding, directing, and appointing managers of its National Health Service (NHS) bodies;
- administering any EU structural funds;
- determining the content of its version of the National Curriculum in schools.

However, in a highly significant and symbolic development recognizing the unique historical and geographical factors distinguishing Northern Ireland from Scotland and Wales, April 2010 saw the devolution of policing and justice powers to Stormont (see p. 80). Defying trenchant opposition from the Ulster Unionists (who voted against the proposal despite last-minute entreaties from then UK Opposition leader Mr Cameron, US Secretary of State Hillary Clinton, and former President George W. Bush), the ruling DUP–Sinn Féin coalition won sufficient cross-community approval to drive the process to its next, decisive stage: the appointment of a Justice Minister. The vote was won by eighty-eight to seventeen, receiving the backing of all forty-four nationalist members and thirty-five out of the fifty-two unionists. David Ford, leader of the Alliance Party, was duly elected to the post of Justice Minister on 13 May.

A month later another watershed was reached, with the long-awaited publication of the final report of an official inquiry set up by Mr Blair into the events of 'Bloody Sunday'—after twelve years of hearings, costing £200m. The 5,000-page report concluded that when, on 30 January 1972, British paratroopers fired on a civil rights march in Londonderry, killing thirteen civilians, none of the dead had been armed, the paras had shot first and without warning, and some had subsequently lied about their actions. In a Commons statement Mr Cameron apologized to the bereaved families on behalf of the UK government, describing the shootings as 'unjustified and unjustifiable'.

Devolution in England—the end of the road?

The increasing autonomy given to Scotland, Wales, and Northern Ireland has led to growing demands from some quarters for major English regions outside London to be given similar powers to determine their own affairs.

Tentative moves towards an embryonic English regional devolution actually emerged under the Tories, when John Major set up regional offices manned by civil servants seconded from the main spending departments at Whitehall. As befitted these nine 'Government Offices of the Regions', however, their role was largely administrative and there were no moves to extend the remit of this 'devolved' power to embrace any form of elected government.

When Labour returned to power in 1997, however, steps were taken to introduce the idea of some form of elected regional authorities by then Deputy Prime Minister John Prescott's short-lived 'super-ministry': the Department for the Environment, Transport, and the Regions (DETR). The first development was the creation of *regional development agencies* (RDAs) to drive sustainable development/regeneration and job creation in the eight English regions: East Midlands, East of England, North East, North West, South East, South West, West Midlands, and Yorkshire and Humber (see p. 474). Each region was also given a *regional chamber*, intended to pave the way, in time, for elected assemblies à la Scotland, Wales, and Northern Ireland's. Despite their title, membership of these 'shadow' bodies was initially composed of a combination of seconded civil servants (70 per cent) and members of other interested parties like the Confederation of British Industry (CBI), Trades Union Congress (TUC), and various statutory agencies (30 per cent).

After a lengthy but (many argued) poorly publicized consultation process, DETR went on to pass a series of Bills designed to enable referendums to be held simultaneously in each of the eight regions in November 2004. But, in the event, the North East Regional Assembly was the only one actually to hold its vote on the designated date—a postal-only ballot that proved hugely controversial, in the wake of allegations of corruption in similar-style votes for Birmingham City Council a few months earlier. The region decisively rejected the idea of an elected assembly—by 78 to 22 per cent—kicking regional devolution into touch for the foreseeable future. Local people appeared not to want yet another tier of government, and to be unclear about the tangible benefits that would have derived from such a body. Although chastened at the time, Mr Prescott vowed to resurrect the regional plan at a later date, but it was not to be. So far, the one decisive gesture made by the Conservative–Liberal Democrat Coalition on regional devolution has been to abolish RDAs.

☰ Topical feature idea

According to a poll published by the think tank Policy Exchange and YouGov in April 2012, three-quarters of British people consider the Human Rights Act 1998 as a 'charter for criminals' because of the protection it gives people accused of offences to challenge court cases brought against them under the ECHR. The survey findings came a year after a February 2011 report by legal publisher Sweet & Maxwell revealed that 5,000 individuals had used the Convention to defend themselves against criminal proceedings—equivalent to ten cases a day. With the British government having used its recent six-month chairmanship of the Council of Europe to table a paper calling for radical reform of the Convention, your editor is keen for you to write a background feature on the subject. How widely, if at all, has the HRA been used in court cases in your area? What do local people know about the HRA and the protections it contains? What might they stand to gain or lose by the UK's withdrawal from the ECHR?

✳ Current issues

■ **Future of the union:** Scotland's First Minister, Alex Salmond, has set a provisional 'date' of autumn 2014 for a referendum on Scottish independence—sparking disagreement with the Westminster administration about the wording of the question to be put to voters and the authority of any ensuing decision if it turns out to favour the break-up of the UK.

- **Fixed-term parliaments:** the Coalition has introduced fixed-term parliaments to prevent future prime ministers 'cutting and running' to call elections at times when it suits their own political fortunes, rather than the interests of the country. Five-year fixed-term parliaments are due to be introduced from the next election, which means that poll should be held on Thursday 7 May 2015.

- **Introduction of the sovereign grant:** the Coalition has embarked on radical reform of royal funding, bundling the Civil List and grants-in-aid together into a single sovereign grant, to be drawn from a percentage of new annual revenues from the Crown Estates. The new regime rationalizes the existing set-up, but could well generate even more taxpayer-funded income for the Queen than the previous arrangements.

? Review questions

1. Outline the main sources and principles of the British constitution. What are the advantages and disadvantages of an unwritten constitution?

2. What is meant by the principle of 'separation of powers' and to what extent does it work in practice in the UK?

3. What are the main roles and powers of the British monarch—notional and actual—and how is the Royal Family funded?

4. Given that royal sovereignty has been superseded by parliamentary sovereignty, what are the arguments for retaining the British monarchy?

5. Is there an 'answer' to the West Lothian Question?

→ Further reading

Cannon, J. and Griffiths, R. (1998) *The Oxford Illustrated History of the British Monarchy*, Oxford: Oxford Paperbacks. **Full-colour history of the British monarchy, from King Egbert to Elizabeth Windsor, including evaluation of its role in modern Britain.**

Hardman, R. (2007) *Monarchy: The Royal Family at Work*, London: Ebury Press. **Populist but informative companion book to the BBC series of the same name, giving insights into the day-to-day reality of how the monarchy works.**

Harrison, K. and Boyd, T. (2006) *The Changing Constitution*, Edinburgh: Edinburgh University Press. **A comprehensive examination of the origins and history of the British constitution, with an emphasis on recent reforms, including devolution and the introduction of the Supreme Court.**

Hazell, R. and Rawlings, R. (2007) *Devolution, Law Making and the Constitution*, Exeter: Imprint Academic. **A detailed look at the mechanics of law-making through the devolved administrations in Scotland, Wales, and Northern Ireland.**

Leach, R., Coxall, B., and Robins, L. (2006) *British Politics*, London: Palgrave Macmillan.
Excellent guide to the nuts and bolts of contemporary British political institutions and processes at local, regional, national, and international levels.

Moran, M. (2006) *Politics and Governance in the UK*, London: Palgrave Macmillan.
Forward-looking textbook focusing on new and evolving forces at work in local, regional, national, and international governance in an increasingly globalized world.

Online Resource Centre

www.oxfordtextbooks.co.uk/orc/Morrison3e/
Visit the Online Resource Centre that accompanies this book for web links and regular updates.

2

Parliamentary democracy in the UK

▶ The origins of the British Parliament

As Chapter 1 explained, the reins of power in Britain no longer lie with the sovereign. Rather, they are vested primarily in the Houses of Parliament, and specifically in the **members of Parliament (MPs)** elected to the primary legislative chamber: the House of Commons.

But what are the origins of today's 'bicameral legislature'—a Parliament comprising twin chambers, each with its own distinct constitutional role? How does it discharge its functions and exercise the prerogative powers vested in it by the Crown? And what are the implications of recent moves towards devolution in the provinces?

Britain's Parliament (famously dubbed the 'mother of parliaments' by nineteenth-century social reformer John Bright) has its roots in successive institutions that emerged in the medieval period—initially to bolster, but ultimately to counteract, the power of the monarch. The most significant of these originated in Norman times, in the era of root-and-branch constitutional upheaval that also witnessed the publication of the Domesday Book—England's first great population census—for William I in 1086. To provide mechanisms through which the sovereign could tax and rule his subjects on a practical basis, a succession of bodies was established—one or two of which survive, notionally, to this day. These included the Privy Council, a group of personal confidantes of the sovereign—at whose meetings they continue to officiate (see p. 20)—comprising all past and present Cabinet ministers and responsible for agreeing Orders in Council (see p. 69) and supervising the use of the Privy Purse (see p. 25). For a more detailed explanation of the role of the Privy Council and the two other proto-parliamentary bodies, the *Magnum Concilium* and *Curia Regis*, see the table entitled 'The role and composition of forerunners of the Houses of Parliament', to be found on the Online Resource Centre.

Parliament today

Parliament long ago took precedence over the sovereign in the day-to-day exercise of constitutional power. As early as the fourteenth century, monarchs were increasingly forced to recognize that the earls and barons on whom they depended to maintain their authority must, for that reason, be consulted (and heeded) on major affairs of state. It was during this tumultuous century that kings reluctantly came to accept the need to gain consent from their landed supporters to levy taxes, and in ensuing decades that a newly assertive Parliament of 'Commoners' secured the right to play an active part in converting royal petitions (or Bills) into statutes (Acts).

Then, in the seventeenth century, came the English Civil War and with it the sequence of decisive breaks with tradition outlined in Chapter 1. While these began the process of ushering in a new order, it would be another 200 years or more (despite the lofty ambitions of the more revolutionary Parliamentarians) before most people were granted a vote—and with it a true stake in parliamentary democracy.

These developments are discussed in detail in Chapter 4, which explores the British electoral system. But what exactly is this Parliament—this great organ of government and citizenship—in which UK citizens are expected to invest such faith? This chapter explores two key aspects of Britain's parliamentary democracy: the nature and composition of the various institutions of Parliament, and the roles, duties, and responsibilities that its members discharge on the country's behalf.

Hansard

Before examining the workings of Parliament it is worth pausing to mention how its practices are recorded. Since 1909 all debates, votes, and other proceedings have been transcribed for a sprawling record known as **Hansard**. Excepting the words of serving prime ministers, it is not verbatim—'repetitions, redundancies, and obvious errors' are deliberately omitted—but it is the nearest we have to a definitive account of Parliament's business.

Although Hansard has only been published by Parliament itself for about a hundred years, it has existed for longer. As early as 1771 a printer named Miller was hauled before the Lord Mayor of London for producing illicit reports of parliamentary debates, while radical free speech campaigners John Wilkes and William Cobbett fought for the right to publish their own versions. The first detailed parliamentary reports appeared from 1803 in Cobbett's *Political Register*, courtesy of one Thomas Curson 'TC' Hansard—the printer after whom the 'official' record was formally named in 1943. Today, Hansard is one of the most reliable sources of news stories for political journalists at both local and national level, providing full details not only of contemporaneously reported debates but also written parliamentary questions and answers, early day motions (see p. 43), and petitions. Like live debates it carries qualified privilege, and can be accessed electronically (via http://www.publications.parliament.uk/pa/cm/cmhansrd.htm). A more critical overview of how individual MPs and peers vote in Parliament can be found at http://www.theyworkforyou.com.

▌ The House of Commons

The linchpin of modern constitutional government in the UK is the 'lower house': the House of Commons. It currently comprises 650 MPs, but as of 2015—the date scheduled for the next general election—this number may or may not be cut to 600. Though a pledge to equalize the size of constituencies was included in the Coalition agreement, in August 2012 the Lib Dems withdrew their support for the proposal (expected to disproportionately benefit the Conservatives) in protest at Tory backbenchers' refusal to support their plans for House of Lords reform (see p. 65). As things stand, each MP represents a **constituency** or 'seat' (electoral district) averaging 65,000 inhabitants, though wide disparities exist between some relatively underpopulated rural seats and others covering more built-up areas. To this end, the Tories' intended reduction in the size of the Commons was designed to coincide with a comprehensive redrawing of constituency boundaries to 'equalize' the sizes of the populations covered by each one.

Unlike many other parliaments, including the European Parliament (Chapter 9), the Commons chamber is ranged along two sets of opposing benches, presided over by its chairperson, the **Speaker** (referred to by members as 'Mr Speaker' or 'Madam Speaker'). To the right of the Speaker's chair are the government benches, while to the left are the benches occupied by 'Her Majesty's Loyal Opposition' (the Opposition)—generally the second biggest party after a general election. All other MPs not allied to the governing party (or parties) of the day sit along this side.

The Commons' adversarial layout mirrors the 'two-party politics' that (barring occasional interludes of coalition government) has characterized the British parliamentary scene for centuries. Since the later medieval period debate has been divided broadly along conservative versus radical/reformist lines with, at various times, Royalists ranged against Parliamentarians; landowning Whigs battling to preserve the status quo against an upwardly mobile, entrepreneurial breed of Tories during the Industrial Revolution; and latterly Liberal, then Labour, MPs championing the rights of the 'common man' against the forces of a more establishment 'big C' Conservatism.

In modern times two-party politics has continued to prevail, largely due to the inequities of the UK's electoral system. As we will see in Chapter 4, the so-called 'first-past-the-post' (FPTP) process sees only candidates who win a *relative majority* of votes cast in their constituencies—that is, more than any of their rivals—elected to the Commons. This means all votes cast in favour of anyone else are effectively 'wasted'. As a result, the electoral process favours parties that can muster sufficient concentrations of support in enough constituencies to win the number of seats needed to form a government—so discriminating against minority interests and independent candidates.

While Commons debates are chaired by the Speaker, its business timetable is set by a Cabinet minister: the **Leader of the House**. The typical Commons year is outlined in Table 2.1, while its usual weekly sittings are set out in Table 2.2.

The role of an MP in relation to constituents

Since April 2010 the salaries of ordinary MPs have been frozen at £65,738 a year by the body which now determines them: the Independent Parliamentary Standards Authority (IPSA) (see p. 59). It has maintained this freeze both as a mark of respect for the millions of British workers enduring pay cuts as a result of recent recessions and the Coalition's austerity drive and a legacy of the parliamentary expenses scandal that first led to its formation (see pp. 55–8). Not

Table 2.1 Annual House of Commons timetable

Date	Event
May (first week)	State Opening of Parliament
May (one week over Spring Bank Holiday)	Whit recess
July–September (two months)	Summer recess
September/October (three weeks)	Party conference season
October/November	Prorogation
December–January (for four weeks)	Christmas recess
February (one week)	Half-term recess
March/April (two weeks)	Easter recess

Table 2.2 Weekly House of Commons timetable

Day	Time of sitting
Monday	2.30–10.30 p.m.
Tuesday	2.30–10.30 p.m.
Wednesday	11.30 a.m.–7.30 p.m.
Thursday	10.30 a.m.–6.30 p.m.
Friday (13 days a year for private members' business, including private members' Bills)	9.30 a.m.–3.00 p.m.

that MPs have been short-changed: in addition to their salaries, they retain generous personal allowances enabling them to employ their own secretaries and/or researchers. In return, they are expected to represent the concerns and interests of *all* their constituents—regardless of individual voters' political affiliations.

At any time the serving government numbers between eighty and 100-odd MPs. All other MPs—save Opposition 'shadow ministers'—are known as 'back-bench MPs' or **backbenchers**.

The principal ways in which MPs discharge their constituency responsibilities include:

- holding weekly 'surgeries' in their constituencies;
- writing to ministers responsible for relevant government departments to try to resolve grievances voiced by constituents;
- asking written or oral questions in the Commons at Question Time—both 'Prime Minister's Questions' on a Wednesday and other regular slots, during which senior departmental ministers answer for their ministries;
- canvassing support among fellow MPs for *early day motions* (EDMs)—formal parliamentary records expressing strong views on an issue dear to them;
- requesting leave from the Speaker for adjournment debates, urgent debates, or debates on *e-petitions*;
- introducing private members' Bills (PMBs)—a form of primary legislation that, if passed, would change the law of the land (see pp. 67–8);
- coordinating e-petitions on behalf of constituents and/or the wider public interest.

The four main forms of debate that may be tabled or promoted by backbenchers are explained in Table 2.3, but certain of their roles justify more detailed explanation.

Surgeries

Also known as 'clinics', these weekly drop-in sessions may be attended by constituents wishing to voice concerns. They are normally held on Fridays (when little parliamentary business is timetabled), or Saturdays in the case of MPs whose constituencies are distant from London. Although many MPs hold surgeries in their constituency offices, today they frequently take place in more informal surroundings—church halls, community centres, and even pubs.

Question Time

An opportunity to quiz senior departmental ministers directly about their policy decisions and the day-to-day workings of their ministries, **Question Time** is

Table 2.3 Types of Commons debate that may be tabled or promoted by backbenchers

Name	How it works	Example
Early day motions (EDMs)	'Paper' record of strong view expressed by number of MPs. Rarely result in actual 'motions' (votes) and seldom win sufficient signatures to warrant full debate—only usually happens when at least half the sitting MPs support the motion. But as part of official Commons record they have official status greater than minor procedures. EDMs often provide journalists with stories—and in age of media-driven policy initiatives they can, over time, influence governments. Most important function is enabling backbenchers to highlight issues of personal concern, gauging support among colleagues for more definite attempts to initiate change through PMBs (see pp. 67–8) etc.	Most significant EDM of recent times was that tabled by then Opposition leader Margaret Thatcher in 1979, censuring Jim Callaghan's ailing Labour government. Callaghan's administration had been unstable since collapse of 'Lib-Lab Pact' negotiated with David Steel's Liberal Party the previous August and, in time, Mrs Thatcher's motion precipitated the vote of no confidence that brought it down. What followed for Labour, on 4 May 1979, was election defeat to Tories. Others have included influential EDM signed by 412 of 646 MPs, days after 2005 election, calling for Climate Change Bill, which followed in 2006. Only three other EDMs ever received more than 400 signatures.
Adjournment debates	Half-hour debates on motion that 'this House do now adjourn', held either in Commons or neighbouring Westminster Hall at end of day's business. Present opportunity for backbencher to raise issue of concern to his/her constituents—and 'summon' minister to respond. As with EDMs, adjournment debates rarely result in votes, but occasionally happens when debate raises nationally significant issue over which there is strong disagreement.	Conservative Prime Minister Neville Chamberlain, signatory to ill-fated Munich Agreement with Nazi Germany, was brought down by motion flowing from adjournment debate: while government won vote—effectively motion of confidence in his leadership following Hitler's breach of agreement by invading Poland—the narrow margin fatally weakened his position. He was swiftly replaced by Winston Churchill.

Urgent debates	A backbencher may apply to Speaker for urgent debate—formerly 'emergency debate'—'on a specific and important matter that should have urgent consideration' under Standing Order No. 24. In practice, far more MPs apply than are granted debates and Speaker only allows one or two per session. If granted, debate takes place within twenty-four hours.	Recent urgent debates have included a three-hour session on future of British troop deployments in Afghanistan, forced by then Shadow Defence Minister Bernard Jenkin on 20 March 2002.
e-petition debates	The Coalition introduced e-petitions to boost public engagement in Westminster politics. Anyone can start an e-petition by setting it up on <http://epetitions.direct.gov.uk>. If it receives backing of 100,000 or more signatories it is referred to Backbench Business Committee for consideration for full Commons debate on one of thirty-five days set aside for this purpose each session. Campaigning backbenchers increasingly help to coordinate petitions in effort to win parliamentary time for debates on issues they consider important.	A number of debates have been held in Parliament as result of e-petitions, with grass-roots campaign groups like 38 Degrees and Avaaz leading calls for MPs to debate issues ranging from 'Robin Hood Tax' on the big banks (see p. 215) to electoral reform. Labour used justification of e-petition attracting 170,000 backers in support of urgent debate on Coalition's NHS reforms to table last-minute attempt to block them in March 2012—weeks after ministers had blocked an e-petition debate on same issue, arguing it had already been heavily debated in Commons. Backers of a petition demanding reinstatement of death penalty (coordinated by political blogger Guido Fawkes via his *order-order.com* website) failed to secure debate after attracting just 26,000 signatures in support.

held for at least one hour a day whenever the Commons is sitting. On Mondays and Tuesdays it takes place between 2.30 p.m. and 3.30 p.m.; on Wednesdays, from 11.30 a.m. to 12.30 p.m.; on Thursdays, from 10.30 a.m. to 12.30 p.m. (the two-hour slot on this day is intended to make up for the fact that Parliament rarely sits on a Friday).

Each department takes turns to answer questions from the Commons floor on a fortnightly rota. In addition to these departmental question times, questions can be put to the prime minister on Wednesday lunchtimes, between 12 noon and 12.30 p.m. Between its introduction in 1961 and Mr Blair's election in 1997, 'Prime Minister's Questions' (or PMQs) occupied a twice-weekly fifteen-minute slot: on Tuesdays and Thursdays, between 3.00 p.m. and 3.15 p.m. Mr Blair's decision to combine the two into a single session was widely criticized as a high-handed presidential-style gesture calculated to limit opportunities for Parliament and his own party to scrutinize him publicly. Nonetheless, the bumper Wednesday PMQ slot—which, since 1989, has been televised live on BBC2—has become a knockabout media highlight of the weekly Commons timetable.

Questions posed at departmental Question Time sessions tend to be for a verbal (oral) response. They are answered by ministers according to a rota called the 'Order of Oral Questions'. Prime Minister's Questions, in contrast, takes one of two forms: oral or written (officially 'questions for a written answer').

Posed, as they are, in front of television cameras, oral questions attract the most media attention—often for their 'Punch and Judy' nature rather than substance. Because PMQs can be heavily oversubscribed, MPs keen to ask questions are advised to give the Speaker three days' advance notice of their intentions, to ensure their names appear sufficiently early on the order paper for them to be called in the allotted time. Giving such notice does *not* mean MPs must specify the *exact wording* of their questions at that stage—merely that they let it be known they wish to ask one.

PMQs follow several curious conventions. The first question is always one asking the prime minister about the other engagements he/she has scheduled for that day. This will usually be immediately tailed by a 'follow-up' question tabled by whichever MP posed the initial procedural one. This is the *real* question and, while the prime minister may have prior notice of the subject to which it relates, he/she rarely knows exactly how it will be phrased. The prime minister's hope is that he/she will have been adequately briefed by civil servants on the issue concerned to be able to ad-lib a convincing answer (or sidestep it effectively). When, later in the session, premiers refer before taking a question to 'the reply I gave some moments ago', they are alluding to the fact that the MP about to ask them a question has used the same procedural nicety about their engagements to get his/her name on the order paper.

Despite being the most talked about parliamentary activity, PMQs is often criticized by serious-minded observers for being superficial and insincere, and playing to the cameras. And it is not only the prime minister and his/her would-be replacement on the Opposition frontbenches who are accused of this: the most derided questions are often those asked by jobbing backbenchers using the session as an opportunity either to curry favour with the media in their own constituencies (and by extension their electorates) by focusing on extraordinarily specific local issues, or to massage ministers' egos in the hope of gaining promotion.

In general, MPs genuinely seeking to hold ministers to account for their actions and influence decision-making on behalf of their constituents will pose *written questions* (which, as well as being 'put on paper' themselves, are intended for written answers). This enables them to be forensic—seeking more detailed replies than are likely to be delivered during the theatrical point-scoring exercise that PMQs often resembles. Although ministers invariably try to put a positive gloss on their policies—and the luxury of being able to map out a considered written answer gives them ample scope to do so—they are under a constitutional obligation to reply to these questions thoroughly and accurately. From a journalistic viewpoint, while snappy sound bites offered up in the heat of battle between harassed ministers and their Opposition counterparts may generate easy headlines, stories that emerge from skilfully worded written questions can be more newsworthy in the long run.

An alternative is to table what until recently were known as 'private notice questions' (now *urgent questions*). These are questions on issues that have suddenly come to light, and do not require MPs to give the usual three days' notice. In recent times this device has increasingly been used by shadow ministers, as well as backbenchers, to hold ministers to account: Labour tabled a series of urgent questions in 2011 and 2012, as the Coalition sailed into choppy waters with its controversial reforms of welfare and the NHS (see p. 63); the UK economy's return to recession (see pp. 203–5); and what many viewed to be the simmering scandal over Conservative ministers' close links to Rupert Murdoch's News International (see pp. 92–3).

None of this is meant to downplay the importance of straightforward oral questions—PMQs in particular. As a weekly barometer of how the political wind is swaying, there is nothing to rival it. While ordinary backbenchers may ask only one question, the Leader of the Opposition is allowed to pose six supplementaries and that of the second largest opposing party (normally the Liberal Democrats) two. In May 2010 Lib Dem leader Nick Clegg forfeited his right to ask questions for the duration of the coalition government he formed with Conservative leader David Cameron. Indeed, as Deputy Prime Minister, Mr Clegg has since stood in at the despatch box for Mr Cameron at times when he is away.

PMQs have long generated lively, even heated, exchanges between serving prime ministers and the pretenders who would dethrone them—and have been said to make or break party leaders. Despite a shaky start, Mr Blair became an adept Question Time operator in his decade in power. Nonetheless, on stepping down in summer 2007, he confessed he had always privately dreaded the weekly ordeal. While there was criticism of Mr Brown's testy, stilted perfor-mances at PMQs (despite his experience of ten years as Chancellor of the Exchequer), Mr Cameron represented something of a return, at least initially, to the breezier style of Mr Blair.

Role of an MP in relation to Parliament and party

MPs' primary duty of care lies, constitutionally, with their constituents. In ad-dition, they have a responsibility to Parliament and, through it, the British peo-ple in general to participate in debate and scrutinize and hold accountable the executive (government and Cabinet). One of the chief ways they discharge this responsibility is through the committee system—one of several 'checks and balances' built into the workings of the legislature to ensure the transparency and accountability of government.

In practice, however, the nature of Britain's party system means these con-stitutional responsibilities can conflict with the pressure most MPs are under to act in accordance with the official policies of their parties. This sense of instilled discipline—increasingly enforced by a strict whip system—is known as 'toeing the party line'. The idiomatic expression refers to the clearly delin-eated lines drawn along the length of the Commons in front of each set of benches, behind which members sitting on either side are required to stand while debating. It relates to the somewhat arcane principle that opposing MPs should be made to stand sufficiently far apart to ensure that, if they were to draw their swords in the heat of debate, they would be able to hold their arms fully outstretched without their weapons clashing.

Parliamentary scrutiny and the committee system

Most backbenchers—and peers, who have an equivalent system in the Lords—are members of at least one committee. Each comprises between eleven and fourteen members and is chaired by a fellow member. The proportion of commit-tees chaired by MPs/peers drawn from one party or other has customarily reflected the distribution of Commons seats. Between May 1997 and May 2010, therefore, Labour had proportionately more chairpersons than all other parties put together, reflecting its majority, while the same is currently true of the Tories.

Although committees have become more 'fluid' in the forms they have taken recently—a Committee against Anti-Semitism was formed in 2005—they can generally be divided into three broad types:

- select committees;
- general committees (including public and private Bill committees and grand committees);
- joint committees.

Select committees

The most frequently publicized type, **select committees** scrutinize the workings of individual government departments and Parliament itself, and as such are permanent (at least until the department they relate to is renamed or disbanded). At present, there are eighteen select committees covering departmental matters, and seventeen others focusing on internal parliamentary and wider constitutional issues—everything from the Backbench Business Committee that decides how the (limited) time allotted to backbenchers is divided up, to a European Scrutiny Committee charged with assessing the legal and/or political importance of each new document produced by the European Union (EU). Departmental committees include the Education Committee—which scrutinizes the Department for Education—and the Culture, Media, and Sport Select Committee. There is also a Commons Liaison Committee (established by Mr Blair), comprising the chairpersons of all other select committees, to which the prime minister submits him/herself for questioning on government policy twice a year.

Select committees have the power to call MPs, senior civil servants, and other public officials as witnesses, and to publish reports on their findings. One of the most explosive hearings of recent times occurred on 15 July 2003, when late weapons inspector David Kelly was grilled by the Foreign Affairs Select Committee amid the controversy over a dossier compiled by the Blair government to justify its case for war against Saddam Hussein's Iraq. Members subjected Dr Kelly to intense questioning about whether he was the source of a report by BBC defence correspondent Andrew Gilligan for Radio 4's *Today* programme, which claimed senior intelligence sources were concerned that ministers had 'sexed up' the dossier by exaggerating the likelihood that Saddam's forces could unleash weapons of mass destruction (WMDs) within forty-five minutes of being ordered to do so. Dr Kelly was found dead in a wood near his Gloucestershire home two days later.

Because they are permanent, the composition of select committees has become increasingly contentious, in light of their customary inbuilt bias towards governing parties. During the Thatcher and early Blair years, Parliament was often criticized for failing to do enough to hold serving ministers to account, and committees in particular often seemed neutered—not least because premiers had a habit of using their party whips to parachute favoured placemen and women into chairmanships. It was against this backdrop (as well as the general loss of public trust in MPs sparked by the expenses controversy) that the Commons Parliamentary Reform Select Committee recommended in 2010 that all future chairpersons should be formally elected by their fellow MPs. The Coalition implemented this recommendation, introducing elections by alternative vote (see p. 133) for most chairs, and extending the scope of elections further, to cover all members of such committees. Henceforth, committee seats allotted to each party proportionally would be filled by MPs elected by their fellow party members.

General (including public and private Bill) committees

The other most influential type of committee is the **general committee**—an overarching category embracing **public Bill committees**, **private Bill committees**, and grand committees. Most numerous are public Bill committees (formerly known as 'standing' committees—an archaic reference to the fact that their members were not around long enough to warrant permanent seats). The new name better reflects the function of this type of committee: to scrutinize, comment on, amend, and/or refer back to the Commons for further consideration Bills in the process of becoming Acts. Unlike the standing committees of old, public Bill committees have enhanced powers, including the ability to summon expert witnesses and officials from outside Parliament to give evidence.

As the work of public and private Bill committees can take weeks or months, governments sometimes try to bypass them when rushing to pass legislation they deem urgent. When ministers are trying to rush through 'emergency' legislation, if agreed by the Speaker, the Commons itself takes on their role, as a 'Committee of the Whole House'. (During its own committee stages, the Lords normally does the same.) The committee stage of Bills is explored in more detail below.

Most **grand committees** are concerned with debating the impact of legislation on specific geographical nations and regions. There is, for example, a grand committee for the East Midlands and another for Scotland. Grand committees also exist for delegated legislation, European documents, and the House of Lords—which uses them for committee stages not taken on the floor of the House.

Joint committees

So-called because they are composed jointly of MPs and peers, joint committees include the Joint Committee on House of Lords Reform, formed in 2002 to consider a range of alternative options for the composition of the 'Upper House' in the wake of the, as yet incomplete, Lords reforms (see p. 65). Since 1894 there has been a joint committee devoted to assisting the swift passage of laws designed to rationalize the number of Acts on the statute book (the record of all parliamentary legislation in place at any one time). These 'consolidation Bills', normally introduced in the Lords rather than the Commons, seek to combine disparate Acts on the same or similar subjects into single all-encompassing statutes.

Into the twenty-first century—juggling parliamentary and constituency work

A significant, if somewhat surprising, development approved in October 2011 was the use of Twitter in the Commons. After the House Procedure Committee recommended that portable electronic devices be permitted in the main chamber, MPs voted by 206 to 63 against a motion to block use of the social media web service, defying warnings by opponents, including Lib Dem Deputy Leader Simon Hughes, that this could lead to tweeting members appearing 'disconnected' from the debates in which they were meant to be participating.

In theory, the use of Twitter (and indeed SMS text messaging and email) via mobile smartphones could prove revolutionary, enabling MPs to juggle parliamentary duties with answering constituents' queries and receiving their feedback. In practice, though, questions remain about whether most members are up to such multitasking. Even as the Commons voted in favour of tweeting (provided it was done silently), the *Huffington Post* ran a news feature revealing that the MPs who tweeted most frequently, and/or had the greatest number of followers, tended to be those with the poorest parliamentary attendance. Meanwhile, in July 2012 members of the Commons Treasury Committee were widely criticized in the media for tweeting while they were supposed to be concentrating on questioning former Barclays chief executive Bob Diamond over the Libor-rigging scandal (see p. 217)—prompting some members of the public to tweet back urging them to get on with the job in hand, and suggesting alternative (in some cases, sharper) questions.

Party loyalty and the whip system

As discussed earlier, British MPs tend to be affiliated to political parties. There have been notable exceptions, like Martin Bell, the one-time BBC foreign correspondent who overturned disgraced former Conservative minister Neil Hamilton's huge majority in Tatton in 1997, standing as an independent candidate on an 'anti-sleaze' ticket. But, mostly, the nature of Britain's electoral system tends to guarantee candidates backed by party machines—particularly those representing the three main ones—the best chances of election. More recently, the 2010 election saw Caroline Lucas elected as Britain's first Green Party MP in Brighton Pavilion, while in March 2012 former Labour backbencher George Galloway trounced his old party in a dramatic by-election win for Respect in Bradford West. As the sole members for their parties, Ms Lucas and Mr Galloway are arguably independent MPs in all but name.

Party membership is a double-edged sword. Being selected as an official candidate for a major party gives you access to a huge support network, including significant financial backing running up to elections. Independents, in contrast, must largely use their own money to finance campaigns or canvass for donations. But being a partisan MP also comes at a price. Parties in Britain have traditionally painted themselves as 'broad churches' representing people united by common ideals, but who may hold a variety of shades of opinion on specific issues. In recent times, however, party leaders (particularly serving prime ministers) have been criticized for stifling dissent in their ranks by using the whip system to force their MPs to back the official line when voting.

There are three broad definitions of the term 'whip':

- whips;
- party whip;
- three-line whips.

Whips are individuals (MPs or peers) charged with 'whipping into line' back-benchers when a debate or vote regarded as important by their leadership is pending. It is the job of whips, led by a chief whip, to persuade MPs whose views are known to differ from those of their leadership to attend debates and vote with their party at the appropriate time.

Whips have frequently been accused of cajoling or bullying MPs into doing their leaders' bidding. When John Major was struggling to pass the Maastricht Treaty into British law in May 1992 in the face of a backbench rebellion by Eurosceptic Tories (see pp. 295–6), ailing loyalists—including one who had just had brain surgery—were taxied to the Commons to act as 'lobby fodder' for the government. The media dubbed this the 'stretcher vote'. Under Labour, whips would notoriously bombard MPs with pager alerts urging them to turn up and vote along party lines and stay 'on message' when making speeches and giving interviews.

Mr Blair's prolonged honeymoon with both voters and his own MPs after his 1997 election victory ended with a bump in his second term, when he faced a succession of knife-edge votes, despite retaining a large Commons majority. He squeezed through some of his more controversial reforms, such as foundation hospitals and university top-up fees, by wafer-thin margins. In his third term he actually lost the vote to extend the length of time terrorist suspects may be questioned by police without charge from fourteen to ninety days, in spite of rigorous arm-twisting by Labour Chief Whip and future Home Secretary Jacqui Smith.

In addition to being fixers, the whips also play a more 'constructive' role. Crucially, they act as unofficial personnel officers for the party leadership, talent-spotting potential future ministers and frontbench spokespeople, and providing important lines of communication between leader and party.

The term 'party whip' effectively refers to an MP or peer's 'membership' of his/her parliamentary party. Like any such affiliation, this can be withdrawn if the member is felt to have broken the 'rules' attached to membership. Mr Major temporarily withdrew the whip from the twenty-two Maastricht rebels—including future party leader Iain Duncan Smith—as a punishment for their disloyalty. Mr Galloway, as Labour MP for Glasgow Kelvin, had the whip removed in October 2003 following his repeated public attacks on Mr Blair over the invasion of Iraq. The same fate befell several Labour backbenchers prosecuted for bogus allowance claims in the wake of the 2009 expenses scandal, while in 2012 another Labour backbencher, Eric Joyce, was expelled from the party after assaulting four fellow MPs in the Commons Strangers' Bar—an incident leading to his subsequent conviction.

Votes judged by party leaders to be of the highest importance are highlighted—and underlined three times—in a weekly circular, *The Whip*, sent to their MPs and peers. These votes are known as 'three-line whips', and attendance and voting along party lines is regarded by party leaders as mandatory. There are two lower levels of voting:

- 'one-line whips' (or 'free votes') tend to be called on 'matters of conscience'—non-party political issues, like fox hunting or euthanasia;
- with 'two-line whips' MPs are told they 'must attend' unless they have made legitimate arrangements to be absent under the *pairing* system.

Pairing is a traditional parliamentary convention allowing an MP sitting on one side of the House to miss a vote on which they would have voted one way, at the same time as an MP with opposing views on the opposite side of the chamber—thereby 'cancelling each other out'. Although regarded as acceptable, leaders would obviously prefer all of their MPs to attend and vote with their party, regardless of whether members on the other side are absent, to increase their chances of winning votes. In turn, certain 'tribal' members, notably former Labour MP Tony Benn, have refused on principle to participate in pairing.

Although technically still possible, pairing was last used in 1996. At that time the Labour and Lib Dem Chief Whips (Donald Dewar and Archy Kirkwood respectively) suspended the arrangement indefinitely in protest at an incident in which three Conservative MPs cheated by each pairing up with members from both major Opposition parties—thereby cancelling out six, rather than three, votes.

Three-line whips have long been used as the ultimate call to arms (and disciplinary device) by party leaders—so much so that the term has passed into the popular vernacular to denote events and activities at which attendance is compulsory. But, as with collective responsibility (see pp. 101–2), the Coalition agreed early on to compromise established practice in areas of principled disagreement between the parties, in the interests of preserving their overall alliance. For example, the official coalition agreement included provision for a three-line whip to be used to force through the Referendum Bill, paving the way for a public vote on electoral reform, though Tories were permitted to campaign *against* changing the voting system when the referendum came (as Mr Cameron and fellow ministers duly did).

MPs, conflicts of interest, abuses of privilege—and how to avoid them

In addition to being responsible to their constituents, Parliament, and their parties, recent years have seen MPs accused of compromising their integrity by affiliating themselves to 'outside interests' over and above those to which they have constitutional obligations. To promote greater openness about such outside interests—and avoid charges of corruption or deceit about their motives—since 1974 they have been expected to declare any gifts or income received over and above their parliamentary salaries on a **register of members' interests** (now known as the **register of members' financial interests**).

The idea that an MP might have a financial or non-pecuniary interest in an organization other than the Commons is hardly new. MPs of the eighteenth and early nineteenth centuries were invariably industrialists, agriculturalists, and/or landlords first and foremost, and elected representatives second—their decision to stand in the first place normally motivated as much by commercial self-interest as concern to improve the lot of their fellow man. Conversely, when the Labour Party was formed, one of its aims was to get working-class candidates elected to the Commons, to counter the long-standing dominance of the middle and upper classes. To enable people from poorer backgrounds to fight elections, the trade union movement (one of several bodies that united to form the party) offered to 'sponsor' them—a traditional source of funding that continued for more than a century, but was recently switched from MPs themselves to their constituencies. Mr Blair was himself sponsored by the now defunct Transport and General Workers' Union (TGWU, later T&G) for much of his time as an MP, while the constituencies of some 102 of Ed Miliband's MPs receive funding from its successor, the Unite union.

While Labour has long been accused of being in the unions' pocket, similar charges have been levelled at the Conservatives in relation to big business. When Kenneth Clarke, a former Tory Health Secretary and Chancellor, retired (temporarily) to the backbenches in 1997, after losing a leadership bid to William Hague, he took on several company directorships as well as the chairmanship of British American Tobacco. But the outside interests of some of his erstwhile frontbench colleagues were more controversial still. Jonathan Aitken, Minister for Defence Procurement in Mr Major's government, notoriously signed a 'gagging order' during the 'Iraqi Supergun' affair, preventing it being disclosed that a British arms company of which he was a non-executive director, BMARC, had sold weapons to Saddam's regime. Another major lobbying saga under Mr Major erupted over 'cash for questions'. In October 1994 Trade Minister Neil Hamilton and a colleague, Tim Smith, were accused in *The Guardian* of receiving money in brown paper envelopes from Harrods owner Mohamed Al Fayed in exchange for asking parliamentary questions on his behalf—a clear breach of Commons rules. Both were forced to resign and, although Hamilton was granted immunity from parliamentary privilege to sue both the paper and Al Fayed (see p. 9), he was unsuccessful.

Following the Hamilton debacle and a series of personal scandals involving other ministers, Mr Major established a new Committee on Standards in Public Life under distinguished judge Lord Nolan. After six months' deliberation, the Nolan Committee published *Seven Principles of Public Life* (see Table 2.4), to which it stated MPs and other senior public officials should in future adhere.

Table 2.4 'Seven Principles of Public Life'

Principle	Meaning
Selflessness	Duty to act solely in terms of public interest (i.e. not for financial gain for him/herself, his/her family, or friends)
Integrity	Duty not to sustain any financial obligation to outside individuals or organizations that might seek to influence him/her in performance of his/her duties
Objectivity	Principle that appointment to his/her position be based purely on merit
Accountability	Duty to be accountable for his/her actions to public and submit him/herself to 'whatever scrutiny is appropriate' to his/her office
Openness	Duty to be open about his/her actions and decisions in office
Honesty	Duty to declare any private interests relating to his/her public duties and take steps to resolve any conflicts of interest
Leadership	Duty to promote all principles by leadership and example

If 'cash for questions' marked a low point for Mr Major's government, the scale of its fallout was as nothing compared to that from the MPs' expenses scandal that erupted under Gordon Brown. What began as a trickle of minor revelations about the questionable claims of a handful of MPs—exposed by Freedom of Information Act 2000 (FoI) requests from journalists Ben Leapman, Jon Ungoed-Thomas, and Heather Brooke—had, by May 2009, become a flood, with the release of unexpurgated details of the accounts of hundreds of MPs in a flurry of front-page scoops by *The Daily Telegraph*.

An early casualty of the furore was Conservative backbencher Derek Conway, who had the whip withdrawn by Mr Cameron after it emerged he had used his parliamentary allowance to pay his younger son, Freddie, £40,000 and his eldest, Henry, a further £32,000 for purportedly working as his researchers. The scandal centred less on their being employed by their father—it soon emerged that such nepotism was commonplace at Westminster—but over whether they actually carried out the duties, of which no records were kept. The three main parties swiftly ordered their MPs to make full declarations about any relatives whom they were employing, the nature of their engagement, and details of their remuneration.

The ensuing controversy led to further disclosures about the arcane allowances regime governing MPs. It transpired that many MPs—including then Speaker Michael Martin—were claiming up to £22,000 a year to help with mortgage repayments on second homes (those in their constituencies), despite the fact that some had long since repaid the loans. Embarrassingly, Mr Martin was chairing a committee tasked with reviewing the expenses system at the time.

Scenting blood, the media was soon chasing every shred of information about the obscure rule system governing MPs' expenses. An early twist in the saga came when it emerged that MPs claiming £250 or less on expenses were not even required to submit receipts to the authority then in charge, the Commons Fees Office (formally titled the 'Operations Directorate of the House of Commons Department of Resources'). Although Mr Brown immediately slashed the minimum receipted claim to £25, this change only came into effect in June 2009—by which time the saga had moved on. That March, details were released under FoI requests of a so-called 'John Lewis list' of perks for which MPs were eligible in relation to their second homes. Members were able to claim (at taxpayers' expense) for furnishing the properties—including around £10,000 for a new kitchen, £300 for air-conditioning units, £35 per square metre for new carpets or wooden flooring, and £750 apiece for television sets.

Two months later, the High Court ruled that a request for full disclosure of MPs' expenses, made some two years earlier under FoI, should be granted. Under intense media pressure, the custodian of this information, Mr Martin, reluctantly agreed to publish a receipt-by-receipt breakdown—in so doing, revealing that Mr Brown had claimed £4,471 to modernize his kitchen in 2005, with Mr Blair reimbursed £10,600 for a new one at his former constituency home in Sedgefield. Only weeks after these disclosures, husband and wife Tory MPs Nicholas and Ann Winterton were found guilty by the Parliamentary Commissioner, John Lyon, of breaching rules introduced two years earlier to stop MPs reclaiming rent on properties owned by family members. Having paid off the mortgage on their £700,000 London flat in the early 1990s, the couple had placed it in a family trust to avoid Inheritance Tax. But since 2002 they had occupied it again as tenants, paying the trust £21,600 a year out of a Commons entitlement known as the 'additional costs allowance' (ACA)—a subsidy of up to £24,000 a year to help MPs who needed second homes because of the distance between their constituencies and Parliament. In the ensuing weeks and months it emerged that 'abuse' of the ACA by MPs was widespread—with many members going so far as to 'flip' the houses and flats they designated as their second homes to claim help with the cost of furnishing and/or refurbishing more than one residence. Among the serving and shadow ministers exposed for misusing the ACA were Communities Secretary Hazel Blears, Transport Secretary Geoff Hoon, and future Education Secretary Michael Gove. Some members had even added value to a property at taxpayers' expense before selling it—avoiding Capital Gains Tax (see p. 192) to boot if they had designated it their first home.

But 'home-flipping' was only part of the picture. In January 2009 Leader of the House Harriet Harman made a final vain attempt to prevent full disclosure of all MPs' expense accounts, after nearly two years of stonewalling by members since the journalists' initial FoI requests. When the trio had passed their original enquiries to Information Commissioner Richard Thomas (see p. 262) in June 2007 an immediate tussle began between him and the Commons. While he had ordered the disclosure of some of the requested information, Commons authorities formally objected and MPs voted to exempt their correspondences from his jurisdiction by approving the Freedom of Information (Amendment) Bill (see p. 602)—with the excuse that wholesale disclosure of MPs' personal information might compromise that of constituents with whom they had corresponded. In the event, the Bill was swiftly withdrawn when it became clear no peer could be found to 'sponsor' it (introduce it formally) in the Lords. So when, under intense media scrutiny, Ms Harman tried to revive the block to the wholesale release of expenses, it was only a matter of time before the authorities buckled. Following the government's climbdown, it announced that full disclosure of all MPs' expense receipts going back to April 2004 would be published on 1 July that year.

But those impatient to know more did not have to wait that long. In May 2009 *The Daily Telegraph* published the first of many sensational instalments revealing just what MPs had been using their parliamentary allowances for—after a disc containing data on all 646 serving MPs was leaked to it by an ex-SAS officer, John Wick. For weeks, newspapers and radio and television bulletins were dominated by unravelling details of a variety of sometimes lavish, more usually trivial, and occasionally downright bizarre claims. But for the *Telegraph* investigation much of this detail might never have emerged: when the Commons finally got round to publishing MPs' receipts two months later, chunks of information had been 'redacted' (blacked out), supposedly to protect individuals' personal details.

Among the outlandish claims exposed by the *Telegraph* were the purchase of a £1,645 'duck island' by Conservative MP Peter Viggers, the £2,115 reimbursement to former minister Douglas Hogg for the cost of cleaning his moat, and a rejected claim made by then Home Secretary Jacqui Smith (apparently unwittingly) for a £67 Virgin Media bill that included two pornographic pay-per-view films ordered by her husband. She eventually resigned (officially for family reasons) just ahead of the 2009 European elections, but after losing her seat in the 2010 Westminster poll conceded that one of her reasons for quitting had actually been her elevation to the status of 'poster girl' of the expenses scandal.

Inevitably, ministers had to act—and decisively. A handful of hurried tweaks to existing Commons rules would never be enough to satisfy a baying media. Wholesale reform was needed. In the end Mr Brown's response was threefold:

- commissioning Sir Christopher Kelly, chairman of the Committee on Standards in Public Life, to examine the existing expenses regime and recommend reform;
- establishing IPSA to assume responsibility for policing the expenses system from the existing in-house Commons authorities, Members' Estimate Committee, and Fees Office;

- ensuring questionable second home expenses claimed since 2004 were repaid by MPs in full, by authorizing retired permanent secretary Sir Thomas Legg to conduct a backdated audit—invoicing anyone he judged in breach of existing rules.

Sir Christopher's report, published in October 2009, contained several recommendations, all of which Mr Brown accepted. The most significant were:

- Scrapping the ACA following an 'appropriate' transitional period.
- Banning MPs from employing members of their families within five years.
- Ending the generous 'resettlement grants' to which retiring MPs had been entitled. These were worth up to a year's salary (around £65,000) depending on members' age and length of service—the first £30,000 being tax-free. Now all they are entitled to is eight weeks' pay.
- Transferring responsibility to IPSA for determining both MPs' expenses and their salaries and pensions.

Not all MPs 'outed' for excessive or inappropriate claims took their punishments meekly. When, in February 2010, Sir Thomas began issuing individual letters demanding repayment from 390 MPs (who had collectively 'over-claimed' £1.3m), some said they did not have enough money available, while others criticized the 'injustice' of applying a putative new set of rules to claims made in good faith under an old one. By the time his final report was published—exposing a 'culture of deference' at the Fees Office—seventy MPs had lodged appeals against his demands (at least nine winning them). In the end the most substantial repayments Sir Thomas requested included one for £42,458 from then Communities Minister Barbara Follett, and one for £24,878 from Liam Fox, later to serve for a time as Mr Cameron's Defence Secretary.

More unedifying still was the prosecution for false accounting of five Labour MPs—former Fisheries Minister Elliot Morley, David Chaytor, Jim Devine, Eric Illsley, and Margaret Moran—and Conservative peers Lord Hanningfield and Lord Taylor. All but one of these parliamentarians were subsequently convicted (Ms Moran was judged unfit to stand trial due to depression)—but not before Messrs Morley, Chaytor, and Devine had tried to invoke the constitutional protection of parliamentary privilege (see p. 10), arguing that allowing a court of law to try them would breach the principle of the separation of powers between judiciary and legislature. They cited the wording of Article Nine of the 1689 Bill of Rights, which reads:

" The freedom of speech and debates or proceedings in Parliament ought not to be impeached or questioned in any court or place out of Parliament. "

Their efforts to avoid a high-profile trial were short-lived, however: in June 2010 Mr Justice Saunders ruled there was no 'logical, practical, or moral justification' for their immunity.

The Parliamentary Commissioner for Standards

To reinforce his determination to stamp out the perceived culture of 'sleaze' among certain members of his party, Mr Major had a formal code of conduct for MPs drawn up and appointed Sir Gordon Downey the first **Parliamentary Commissioner for Standards** in 1995. The Commissioner's job is to oversee the register of interests, summoning and holding to account any member felt to have breached the code. He was later replaced by Elizabeth Filkin, but in late 2001 her job was controversially advertised while she was still in office. Many argued this was because she had taken her job too seriously. Her successor, Sir Philip Mawer, was replaced by Mr Lyon in summer 2008. To ensure the Commissioner is correctly discharging his/her duties, a further layer of oversight exists, in the guise of the Committee on Standards and Privileges. Not to be confused with the Committee on Standards in Public Life, this is composed of sitting MPs, and has the same membership as the House of Commons Commission (see p. 72). A separate Lords Commissioner for Standards oversees probity in the Upper House. Among his recent investigations was a probe into the accommodation expenses of Conservative co-chairman Baroness Warsi, after she referred herself to him in June 2012 amid allegations she had claimed her allowance while staying with a friend rent-free in 2008.

Independent Parliamentary Standards Authority (IPSA)

Established in Mr Brown's last year of power, **IPSA** was charged not only with drawing up a new allowances system but also with setting and reviewing MPs' salaries and pensions. Although it began developing a firm 'scheme' of changes to the old expenses system in 2009, it took until after the May 2010 election to implement it. While it was substantially the same as the recommendations made by Sir Christopher, finer details included:

- Replacing MPs' ability to claim second home expenses with an entitlement to help with rented accommodation costs. From summer 2010 a two-year transitional period was introduced for MPs claiming mortgage interest expenses, enabling them to adapt to the changes.

- Widening the definition of the term 'London area', hitherto used by MPs claiming accommodation expenses on the grounds that their constituencies were too far from Westminster for them to commute. Members would no longer be eligible for help with overnight stays if any part of their constituency was within twenty miles of Parliament, or when a commute from any part of their constituency to Westminster was possible within sixty minutes by public transport at peak times.

- Limiting expenditure for any train journey to the cost of a standard-class open ticket, as opposed to a first-class one.

▎ The House of Lords

Before describing the means by which Parliament passes legislation, it is necessary to look at the nature and composition of the second chamber: the House of Lords. Since the passage of the House of Lords Act 1999, which Labour introduced to start the process of reforming or replacing this institution, it has been in a state of effective limbo—and currently remains a 'transitional' House. At the behest of Lib Dem MPs (and to the chagrin of many Tories), Mr Clegg unveiled his long-awaited House of Lords Reform Bill in June 2012, but even this attempt to finish the job Labour had failed to was to prove short-lived (see next section).

What is the point of the Lords?

Even among parliamentarians who dispute the current make-up of the Lords there is widespread support for the principle that the main law-making chamber in a bicameral legislature should be held to account by a second. The arguments that have raged in recent decades over whether the Lords should be reformed or abolished have been less about any real desire to scrap the Upper House altogether than a growing recognition that, in a modern democratic state, a second chamber composed primarily of political appointees and people entitled to sit there by birthright is fundamentally undemocratic.

As long ago as the early twentieth century the Lords had begun to seem outmoded to many—its staunchly establishment outlook increasingly colliding with the reformist Liberal governments of Herbert Asquith and David Lloyd George. It was as Asquith's Chancellor that Lloyd George brought the matter of Lords reform to a head by introducing his seminal 'People's Budget' in 1909, which sought to raise taxes to fund social reform. The Budget was rejected by the disproportionately Conservative Lords, so after Asquith narrowly won a further election the following year he made it his mission to prevent the Lords ever again being able to reject legislation outright. Backed by a threat from the then monarch, George V, to force through reform of the Upper House by creating sufficient Liberal peers to overcome the Lords' inbuilt Conservative majority in the crucial vote, Asquith succeeded in passing the Parliament Act 1911. This replaced the Lords' power of veto with a right merely to *delay* Bills— and for a maximum of two calendar years (or three parliamentary sessions). Subsequently, the Lords voluntarily ceded further powers in recognition of the unequivocal mandate for change achieved by Labour following its landslide 1945 election victory, but opposed on political grounds by the Conservative-dominated chamber. In a constitutional tweak which became known as the 'Salisbury convention'—or 'Salisbury doctrine'—then Tory leader in the Lords Viscount Cranborne (later Lord Salisbury) agreed to establish the principle that the Upper House should not oppose the second or third readings of legislation promised in a governing party's election manifesto.

The Lords' delaying period, meanwhile, was further truncated by the Parliament Act 1949, to two sessions over thirteen months. Any attempt to delay further, in defiance of the Commons' will, has since seen governments 'invoke the Parliament Act(s)'. The Lords' repeated attempts to thwart Labour's hunting ban during Mr Blair's second term were defeated in this way.

Since Asquith's run-in with the Lords, and despite repeated promises by Labour to further curtail its powers, little decisive action has been taken. Little, that is, apart from the House of Lords Act 1999, which finally sounded the starter pistol for reform of the chamber by abolishing all but a handful of the remaining hereditary peers at the time still sitting in the House. Its long-term aim was to replace the hereditary principle with some form of membership entitlement based on individuals' contribution to society through public service or other major achievement.

The composition of the Lords prior to 1999 was as follows.

1. **Lords Spiritual**—26 peers comprising:
   (a) Archbishops of Canterbury and York;
   (b) Bishops of London, Durham, and Winchester;
   (c) twenty-one next most senior Church of England diocesan bishops.

2. Lords Temporal—1,263 peers comprising:
   (a) all 759 *hereditary peers* of England, Scotland, Great Britain, and the United Kingdom (not including Northern Ireland);
   (b) *Lords of Appeal in Ordinary (the Law Lords)*—twenty-seven peers 'created' by successive governments under the Appellate Jurisdiction Act 1876 to help the Lords fulfil its role as the UK's final court of appeal;
   (c) 477 others with **life peerages** created in **honours lists** under the terms of the Life Peerages Act 1958.

Hereditary peers have long been permitted to disclaim their peerages so they may stand as MPs, and this happened on several occasions in the second half of the twentieth century. Mr Benn inherited the title Viscount Stansgate while sitting in the Commons—thereby finding himself banned by law from retaining his seat. After several years of campaigning for the right to renounce his peerage and resume his Commons seat, he persuaded Harold Macmillan's Conservative government to set up a joint committee to examine the issue and, ultimately, change the law through the Peerage Act 1963.

Others followed his lead. Quintin Hogg (Lord Hailsham) disclaimed his family seat to fight a by-election—ironically, in his father's old constituency of St Marylebone. He ultimately changed his mind, however, reverting to his inherited title to become a Tory Lord Chancellor. Most peculiarly, in 1963 Lord Home performed a double-flip by giving up an inherited title that had earlier forced him to resign a Commons seat to return to the Lower House as prime minister. His action—prompted by his election to replace Macmillan as Conservative leader—had the unique consequence of creating a two-week interval between his 'resignation' as a peer and re-election as an MP, during which Britain's prime minister was a member of neither the Commons nor the Lords.

The House of Lords Act 1999

The 1999 Act contained five key clauses designed to pave the way for an, at least partially, elected second chamber. After a series of run-ins between Mr Blair, his own backbenchers, the Tories, and the Lords itself, however, it was decided to move towards reform gradually by setting up a 'transitional' chamber which would initially do little more than remove the automatic membership rights of all but ninety-two hereditary peers. In the meantime, the thorny question of what the final composition of a new Upper House should be was handed to a Royal Commission headed by former Tory minister Lord Wakeham.

Of the ninety-two hereditary peers allowed to remain in the House during the transition period, ninety were elected—but by their fellow peers, not the public. The aim from the outset was to retain individuals with a history of making valuable contributions to debates, rather than the many who seldom attended proceedings. Since 2002, whenever elected hereditary peers have died their places have been taken not by the heirs to their own titles but by other hereditaries drawn from the pool of those initially debarred from the Lords in 1999. By-elections, conducted using the alternative vote (AV) system (see p. 133), have to be held within three months of the peers' deaths. The only peers eligible to vote at such times are other serving hereditary members drawn from the same party grouping—or, in the case of cross-bench peers, fellow cross-benchers. Recent 'new arrivals' include Lord Ashton of Hyde, who inherited the Conservative whip from the late Earl of Onslow in May 2011, and cross-bench peer Viscount Colville of Ross, who succeeded Lord Ampthill the previous month.

As well as the ninety lords with **elected hereditary peerages**, however, a further two hereditary peers have been permitted to remain as *ex officio* members, on the basis of their ceremonial significance to the chamber. These were the Earl Marshal, the Duke of Norfolk, and the Lord Great Chamberlain, the Marquess of Cholmondeley. In addition, ten new life peerages were controversially created to enable several hereditary peers *not* elected to remain. These included former Tory Leader of the House Lord Cranborne, ex-Foreign Secretary Lord Carrington, and the Earl of Longford. The process by which the transitional House was set up was brokered as a compromise amendment to the Bill by Lord Weatherill, a former Commons Speaker.

After the internal election following passage of the 'Weatherill Amendment', the composition of the Lords was as follows:

- twenty-six Lords Spiritual;
- 598 Lords Temporal, comprising twenty-seven Law Lords, two non-elected hereditary peers, ninety elected hereditary peers, and 477 life peers.

Since then life peers have continued to be appointed at a prodigious rate and the balance of power between parties has fluctuated, with Labour finally reaching the symbolic tipping-point at which it had as many peers as the Tories and Lib Dems put together in 2009—twelve years after regaining power. Shortly after signing their coalition agreement, Mr Cameron and Mr Clegg unveiled plans to create up to 172 new party-affiliated peers between them to ensure their Bills' uninterrupted passage through the Lords—a move condemned by Labour MP Chris Bryant, a former Deputy Leader of the Commons, as 'the single largest simultaneous act of political patronage probably since Charles II came to the throne in 1660'. As of May 2012, the Tories and Lib Dems boasted 304 peers between them, to Labour's 235.

In practice, though the Lords' political composition tends to broadly mirror that of the Commons, members drawn from the governing party (or parties) often behave in a more independent-minded way than their ministerial 'masters' would like. In early 2012 the Coalition weathered a string of embarrassing defeats at the hands of peers over its controversial Health and Social Care and Welfare Reform Bills—some spearheaded by prominent Tory and Lib Dem MPs. Following months of horse-trading with rebel Lib Dem peers led by veteran former minister Baroness Williams, then Health Secretary Andrew Lansley finally dragged his Bill onto the statute book, but only after several attempts by those still wary of the legislation to frustrate its passage with eleventh-hour amendments (see p. 180). And former Tory ministers Lords Mackay, Mawhinney, and Newton were among government peers who tried to thwart aspects of the welfare Bill, which suffered more than half a dozen defeats in the Lords over measures ranging from a new rule requiring disabled people to undergo means-testing for entitlement to Employment and Support Allowance after a year to the introduction of a household 'benefit cap' (see pp. 512–13).

In the end, the Bill only reached the statute book with the help of an obscure procedural rule designed to limit the amount of 'parliamentary ping-pong' between Commons and Lords. So-called 'financial privilege' rules allow governments to overturn amendments tabled in the Lords to public Bills that are intended to 'make significant changes to public expenditure' and/or 'affect national or local taxation or National Insurance' (see p. 236). Given that the Bill in question introduced the biggest shake-up of the welfare state since its inception—and related directly to National Insurance-funded benefits—it was judged to pass this test.

Lords who have no declared party affiliation are known as *cross-benchers*. Appropriately, they sit on benches ranged in short rows across the width of the House, with the government benches to their left and the Opposition to their right. Though independent of party ties, cross-benchers are not afraid to flex their political muscles. During the choppy passage of the NHS reforms some of the most persistent opposition to the detail of the Bill came from Lord Owen, non-affiliated former leader of the Social Democratic Party (SDP).

From Wakeham to the Coalition reforms and beyond

Lord Wakeham's influential 2000 report, *A House for the Future*, made several recommendations, subsequently crystallized in a 2001 House of Lords White Paper. This advocated a neutered version of the Wakeham proposals, including the removal of all remaining hereditary peers, the retention of existing life peers 'transitionally', and the eventual capping of Lords membership at about 600. The one concrete development that happened almost immediately was the establishment of an independent **House of Lords Appointments Commission** to ensure that, while transitional arrangements remained, life peerages would be awarded principally on merit, rather than by political patronage. The Commission's main role was to vet individuals nominated by the party leaders for any sign of rewards for favours—a power it memorably used to block three of Mr Blair's nominees in 2005 (see pp. 160–1). But it is also allowed to propose its own peers, focusing on non-partisan individuals with 'a record of significant achievement' in their 'chosen way of life'. To date, some fifty 'people's peers' have been appointed.

During his remaining years in office, Mr Blair slowly edged away from advocating a partially elected chamber to a fully appointed one—in defiance of an all-party motion in March 1999 demanding it be entirely elected. Although he would cite in his defence well-rehearsed Conservative arguments—including the potential challenge an elected Lords might pose to the status of the Commons as Britain's primary legislature—the Tories branded his alternative idea an attempt to shore up his power base by appointing 'Tony's Cronies'. Memories were evoked of the 'Lavender List', a notorious string of honours for trusted allies and confidantes that another Labour Prime Minister, Harold Wilson, had patronized on his retirement in 1976.

The 'settled' view of MPs now appears to favour a largely or fully elected second chamber. Between 2006 and 2008 Jack Straw (first as Leader of the Commons, then Lord Chancellor) introduced two further White Papers: one proposing a fifty-fifty split between elected and appointed peers, with new £50,000 salaries to encourage attendance, and the other an elected component of between 80 and 100 per cent (earning £55,000–60,000). This legislation would also have reduced the size of the Lords to 400–50 members, with anyone found guilty of being 'lazy' or 'corrupt' expelled (a rule that would surely have removed Lord Archer, the Tory peer jailed for perjury in 2000).

By the time Labour entered the 2010 election it had finally committed itself to full elections as part of a wider package of constitutional reforms, including a referendum on replacing Britain's first-past-the-post (FPTP) electoral system with AV. With the Lib Dems advocating similar reforms, Mr Clegg persuaded Mr Cameron to include a commitment in their coalition agreement to push for a new 'Senate', to be wholly or largely elected using proportional representation (see p. 63). A further White Paper, accompanied by a draft Bill, followed in

2011, reviving Mr Straw's idea of an eighty–twenty split between elected and appointed members, but proposing to cap membership at no more than 300, with initial elections to be held around the time of the next Commons poll in 2015. After a period of scrutiny by a new joint committee of both Houses, Mr Clegg's long-awaited House of Lords Reform Bill finally made it to a first reading in June 2012. However, despite defying a ninety-one-strong rebellion by Tory backbenchers to nominally reach second reading stage the following month, it was formally abandoned for the duration of the parliament that August after Mr Cameron informed Mr Clegg he would be unable to secure sufficient support from his MPs to take the reforms any further. The Bill's key proposals had been to:

- halve membership of the chamber from 826 to 450, with all but ninety peers to be elected, including representatives from every region, and the remainder to be chosen (on a non-partisan basis) by an independent appointments commission;
- introduce non-renewable terms for future peers of fifteen years, beginning with a first election in 2015 and subsequent ones at five-year intervals, with a third of the membership retiring on each occasion, and all existing members to be 'phased out';
- preserve the right of Church of England bishops to sit in the Lords, while more than halving their number from twenty-six to twelve;
- retain the title 'House of Lords'.

The Bill's fate was ultimately decided by an unholy alliance of Conservatives stolidly opposed to Lords elections and what Mr Clegg branded an 'opportunistic' Labour Opposition intent on exploiting the situation to promote cracks in the Coalition. Labour's leadership had indicated support for the legislation in principle (though it would prefer a public referendum first), but before voting 'yes' to the second reading it forced ministers into dropping a proposed 'programme motion' to limit scrutiny at that stage to ten days—a vote the government would certainly have lost. In the end, weeks into the summer recess, Mr Clegg was forced to call a press conference to confirm he was reluctantly mothballing the Bill. However, in doing so he raised the prospect of heightened infighting within the Coalition, by announcing he would instruct his fellow Lib Dem MPs to oppose Tory-led proposals for changes to Commons constituency boundaries when they came to a vote (see p. 41). Though Mr Clegg made it clear he felt the Conservatives had collectively reneged on their half of the coalition agreement by withholding support for Lords reform, his official reason for opposing the boundary proposals was that, in the *absence* of changes to the composition of the second chamber, reducing the number of elected MPs risked undermining the Commons' authority.

The decidedly tepid reception towards the prospect of fully fledged reform—London mayor Boris Johnson spoke for many Tories when he condemned the putative election of 'has-beens and never-wozzers'—belied the widespread support among MPs for compromise moves proposed in the House of Lords (Amendment) Bill, a private member's Bill (see p. 67) introduced by Lib Dem peer Lord Steel in 2011. The main proposals in the PMB, which completed its passage through the Lords in March 2012, included new rules removing the patronage of party leaders in the creation of future life peers, in favour of purely merit-based decisions by a statutory appointments commission; the removal of any members sentenced to more than a year in prison for serious criminal offences; and the scrapping of future by-elections to replace deceased hereditary peers (a move which would, over time, effectively 'abolish' the remaining elected hereditary members as the ninety present incumbents died).

The one significant further reform between 1999 and 2012 to affect the Lords has been the creation in the Constitutional Reform Act 2005 of a new US-style Supreme Court—formally known as the **Supreme Court of the United Kingdom**. To reinforce the principle of separation of powers in practice, then Lord Chancellor Mr Straw divested the House of Lords of its judicial function, transferred its status as highest court of justice and appeal in the UK to the Supreme Court, and installed twelve of the then twenty-seven Law Lords as inaugural Justices of the Supreme Court. The Court began work on 1 October 2009. For the duration of their service as Justices, its members' ability to sit in the Lords was curtailed, although they would be entitled to return to the chamber on retirement (assuming it still existed). Future appointees would not have seats in the Lords. Although the new Court is the ultimate bastion of English, Northern Irish, and Scottish law, and has taken over adjudicating devolutionary matters from the Judicial Committee of the Privy Council, Scotland retains its own supreme court in criminal matters: the High Court of Justiciary.

▌ Types of legislation

As Britain's legislature, the primary purpose of Parliament is to legislate. So how does it do this and what forms can legislation take?

British legislation is divided into two broad types: primary and secondary. Primary legislation is the umbrella term for all Bills passed by both Houses of Parliament and given the royal assent to become Acts. It is also known as 'enabling legislation', in that Acts must be passed to 'enable' the government and Parliament to issue the various rules, regulations, and instructions needed to implement changes in law on the ground.

Primary legislation

The four main categories of primary Bill are as follows:

- public Bills;
- private Bills;
- hybrid Bills;
- private members' Bills.

Public, private, and hybrid Bills

Public, private, and hybrid Bills all have one thing in common: they are all initiated at the government's behest. But that is where their similarities end. Whereas **public Bills** change 'the law of the land', **private Bills** seek only to affect specific individuals or organizations—for example, companies or local authorities.

Briefly, the majority of new laws that gain media attention—and about which journalists normally find themselves reporting—are public Bills. The Academies Bill 2010, which controversially paved the way for free schools, the Health and Social Care Bill, and the numerous 'anti-terror' Bills of recent years all are (or were) public Bills affecting the entire population of England, if not Britain. Private Bills, in contrast, are usually introduced at the request of specific individuals or bodies, either to exempt them from a law otherwise affecting the whole country, or to grant them other discrete privileges. The Highways Agency—the executive agency of the Department for Transport responsible for building and maintaining major trunk roads, 'A' roads, and motorways—has often been granted private Bills to enable it to extend, or introduce, roads in new areas. Hybrid Bills are a mix of the other two. Like public Bills, they affect the whole population, but resemble private Bills in that they impinge on some people more than others. Examples of hybrid Bills include the one enabling work to begin on the long-delayed Crossrail project in London, which affects some residents of the country (those living along the link) more than others.

Private members' Bills (PMBs)

Private members' Bills (PMBs) warrant a separate category because, unlike all of the above types of legislation, they are introduced not by governments but backbench MPs. PMBs may be introduced in one of three ways, listed in Table 2.5.

The primary purpose of ten-minute rule Bills is to enable MPs to raise issues they deem important—rather than actually get their measures onto the statute book. In practice, it is unlikely an MP will persuade his/her party, or the government, to allocate sufficient parliamentary time to take his/her Bill further (although there have been some celebrated cases in which this has occurred—see p. 68).

Table 2.5 The three ways of introducing private member's Bills (PMBs)

Method	Procedure
PMB Fridays	Early in each parliamentary session, MPs can enter 'ballot' for opportunity to introduce their own Bill on one of thirteen 'PMB Fridays'. On these days PMBs take precedence over government and Opposition business. First twenty names drawn in ballot—effectively out of a 'hat'—may introduce their Bills. The six or seven at top of list are likely to have their proposals discussed in detail in Commons.
The **ten-minute rule**	MPs may instead use 'ten-minute rule' (officially, Standing Order No. 23), which applies on most Tuesdays and Wednesdays at start of public business in Commons. They may make ten-minute speech outlining their proposals, provided they have support of ten other members. An opponent may make ten-minute speech in reply.
Presentation Bills	MPs may introduce presentation Bill (under Standing Order No. 57). This is a means of drawing limited attention to issue of concern to MP, because—unlike other two methods—it does not allow him/her to make speech outlining Bill's details in House.

To qualify to introduce a ten-minute rule Bill, an MP must be 'the first member through the door' to the Public Bill Office on the Tuesday or Wednesday fifteen working days before the date on which they wish to present it. They must also have the Bill proposed and seconded and receive written backing from ten colleagues.

Many significant issues have been raised through PMBs. In 1997, after initial indications he would receive government backing, Labour backbencher Michael Foster introduced a PMB proposing a ban on hunting with dogs (a measure proposed in his party's manifesto). He later withdrew it when it became clear ministers were not going to accord it sufficient parliamentary time to see it through all the necessary stages in the face of mounting opposition from Conservatives and the Lords.

The most famous PMB was former Liberal leader Mr Steel's Abortion Bill 1967, which legalized terminations of unwanted pregnancies for the first time in Britain, albeit only up to twenty-four weeks after conception. Touching on an issue of huge public concern at the time, it was allotted ample time for full debate and scrutiny, and duly passed.

Secondary legislation

It has increasingly been the convention for primary legislation to cover only the fundamental *principles* underpinning a change in the law. In contrast, **secondary**—or subordinate or **delegated**—**legislation** refers to powers 'flowing from' Acts themselves, and rules, regulations, and guidelines drawn up to implement them. For primary legislation to be put into practice, ministers need the authority to introduce the measures it contains on the ground. This authority is exercised through 'delegated' legislative powers, the main types of which are listed in Table 2.6.

Table 2.6 Main types of secondary legislation

Name	Definition	Example
Statutory instrument	Rules, regulations, and guidelines issued by ministers to flesh out newly passed Acts and implement on ground. Although no further Act is required to implement measures, they still require formal agreement of Parliament. 'Parent' Act usually specifies whether affirmative or negative agreement is required (former means statutory instrument will not come into play unless Parliament formally approves a resolution, while latter means it will automatically do so if, after forty days, no motion passed objecting to it).	Complex instructions issued by Department for Culture, Media, and Sport to give local authorities and police responsibility for issuing liquor and public entertainment licences under Licensing Act 2003. These took so long to come into force that 'twenty-four-hour drinking' was only introduced in pubs in November 2005—two years after royal assent.
By-law	Localized laws passed on approval of relevant minister, scope of which is enshrined in existing Act.	City centre street drinking bans introduced by councils in problem areas.
Order in Council	Submitted by ministers for approval by sovereign at meeting of Privy Council. Draft normally agreed by Parliament before being submitted by ministers.	Orders in Council were used to introduce much delegated anti-terror legislation relating to Northern Ireland in 1960s and 1970s.

▌ The passage of a Bill

Before it can be introduced into Parliament as a fully fledged Bill, the detail of prospective government legislation is publicly aired in two early draft forms: a **Green Paper** and a **White Paper**. The former is a sketchy consultation document outlining the *broad spirit* of a proposed Bill. It is open to significant redefinition depending on the response it elicits from the public and other interested parties. The latter is a more crystallized outline of a proposed law—again issued for consultation purposes—that normally prefigures a Bill to be introduced in the next session.

Bills can be introduced in either the Commons or the Lords, although they are normally instigated in the former. The process is outlined in Table 2.7.

Speeding up the legislative process

The legislative process can be very involved, and over the decades MPs of all parties have become increasingly adept at delaying Bills to which they object. Traditionally they have conspired to do so by making excessively long speeches to frustrate the government's attempts to get through the various stages through which a Bill must pass to become law. Such 'filibustering' has at times

Table 2.7 The passage of a Bill

Stage	Process
First reading	Reading out of new Bill's title in Commons. In practice this can take several minutes, because full titles of Bills tend to sum up substance of proposals and can be lengthy.
Second reading	General principles of Bill read out, debated, and voted on for first time. This normally happens in 'an afternoon' between 4 p.m. and 10 p.m. (barring brief experiment, when late Leader of the House Robin Cook introduced 'family-friendly' parliamentary timetable). Second reading can run over several days if Bill has major implications.
Committee stage	Public or private Bill committee undertakes detailed consideration of main clauses in Bill. Sometimes this stage takes place in Commons itself, sitting as Committee of the Whole House (this normally happens when treaty is being ratified, or when Bill needs to be passed urgently—e.g. recent anti-terror legislation). This also happens automatically following annual Budget Speech, when aspects of Finance Act flowing from it are fast-tracked.
Report stage	Committee's recommendations referred to Commons in written report and further amendments can follow before Bill proceeds to third reading. This stage often involves late sittings.
Third reading	Bill reviewed and debated in final intended form. At this stage all opportunities for Commons to make amendments have passed (although Lords can still do so).
Bill now referred to Lords (or 'another place' in parliamentary parlance). Here it follows similar sequence of stages as those of Commons, but this time committee stage usually taken on floor of House.	
The House of Lords and the Lords' report to the Commons	Amendments made by Lords must be agreed by Commons before it can proceed to statute book. Should there be significant differences of opinion between them (e.g. over fox hunting legislation during Mr Blair's tenure), joint committee usually set up to resolve them. Under successive Parliament Acts, Lords cannot delay money Bill and can only delay other Bills by up to thirteen months.
Royal assent	Final seal of approval for Bill, turning it into an Act, is notionally still given by monarch, but last time this formally happened was in 1854. It is conferred in Norman French, *La Reine le Veult*, and has not been refused since 1707, when Queen Anne declined to grant it for Bill to settle militia in Scotland. Sentence preceding every Act reads: 'Be it enacted by the Queen's Most Excellent Majesty, by and with the advice and consent of the Lords Spiritual and Temporal, and Commons, in this Parliament assembled, and by authority of the same, as follows . . .'

been used sufficiently obstructively to delay indefinitely, or even 'kill off', prospective Acts. If a Bill were delayed by time-wasters long enough for a government to be voted out of office in an election this might well spell its end, because the Opposition waiting to take over would be unlikely to resurrect it. Similarly, so-called 'wrecking amendments' have often been made by the Lords towards the end of a parliament in an effort to 'time out' a Bill, in the hope the next government will abandon it.

Table 2.8 Devices used to speed up debate in the Commons

Device	Definition
Allocation of time motion (the 'guillotine')	Used by Leader of House to restrict time that can be taken by specific stages of Bill (i.e. to set deadline). First used in 1887 to push through Criminal Law Amendment (Ireland) Bill following debate lasting thirty-five days (including all-night sittings), largely because of obstruction by Irish MPs. Six years earlier, Commons had sustained its single longest ever sitting: debate over Protection of Person and Property (Ireland) Bill 1881, lasting forty-one hours and thirty-one minutes. Guillotine used in June 1997 to force through Referendums (Scotland and Wales) Bill, when opponents had tabled 250 amendments.
A motion of closure	Requires petition of 100-plus MPs to be submitted to Speaker calling for vote to be taken swiftly.
The 'kangaroo'	Speaker chooses to combine, in one vote, number of virtually identical motions or amendments tabled by different MPs.
Programme orders	Relatively new device, replacing guillotine in many cases, that allows Leader of House to set fixed number of sittings for Bill's passage or fixed date for its completion. Programme orders may be moved after second reading stage.

The term 'filibustering' was first coined in reference to pro-independence Irish MPs in the nineteenth century, who, in an effort to force the Westminster government to hand over 'home rule' for Ireland, would deliberately hold up Bills on other issues. Today, filibustering and other forms of time-wasting, repetition, and drawn-out debate can be countered in one of the four ways outlined in Table 2.8.

▌ Role of the Commons Speaker

The most important officer of the Commons, the Speaker is official chair of its business. As such he/she must preside over votes and debates; intervene to restore 'order' when members become rowdy; and choose which member should be next to speak when confronted by MPs waving their order papers in a bid to 'catch the Speaker's eye'. The Speaker is always drawn from the ranks of elected MPs, but on taking office he/she discards his/her previous party allegiance for the duration of his/her time in post.

The Speaker's main roles today are:

- Controlling debates, including deciding when those on specific subjects should end and be voted on, and suspending or adjourning sittings if they get out of hand. Debate over the Hutton Report into the death of Dr Kelly (see p. 49) was suspended after protesters invaded the Commons public gallery. Similar action was taken during two other protests in the House: in May 2004, when activists from Fathers4Justice, a pressure group campaigning for equal access rights to children for separated fathers, threw a missile containing purple powder from the guests' gallery at Mr Blair, and again that September, when pro-hunt protestors led by Otis Ferry, son of singer Bryan Ferry, invaded the floor of the chamber.

- Ordering MPs who have broken Commons rules to leave the chamber. Mr Galloway was barred from the Commons for eighteen days in July 2007 for failing to declare his links to the United Nations (UN) 'Oil for Food' programme—a charitable appeal allegedly partly funded by a supporter involved in the sale of oil under Saddam Hussein.

- Certifying some Bills as 'money Bills' to give them swift approval.

- Signing warrants to send members to jail for contempt of the House.

- Chairing the House of Commons Commission—the main body that administers the procedures of the Commons.

- Chairing the Speaker's Committee on the Electoral Commission, which recommends appointments to the board of the Commission (see p. 129).

Traditionally, the Speaker (the first of whom, Peter de Montfort, was appointed as Parlour of the Commons in 1258) is chosen by an election of MPs called by the 'Father of the House'—the backbench MP with the longest unbroken membership of the Commons. For nearly forty years it has also been customary for the two main political parties to alternate in providing Speakers. But when the post became vacant in October 2000 with the retirement of Betty (now Baroness) Boothroyd, backbenchers became so annoyed by the government's insistence that this tradition be upheld that they defied it by voting in another Labour MP, Mr Martin, instead of Mr Blair's preferred candidate, former Tory minister Sir George Young. After the 2005 election, however, then Father of the House Tam Dalyell faced the prospect of Mr Martin's re-election as Speaker being contested amid criticisms from the Tories about his alleged government bias.

Although Mr Martin survived several whispering campaigns in the ensuing parliament, his tenacity would ultimately deprive him of any opportunity to retire gracefully. A series of perceived errors of judgement began in November 2008, with his mishandling of the Damian Green affair (see p. 9). More damaging still were revelations that he had claimed £20,000 of taxpayers' money to pay City law firm Carter Ruck to defend him against negative press stories and subsequent disclosures that his wife had been reimbursed by taxpayers for £4,000 in taxi fares while on a series of shopping trips to buy food and refreshment for receptions, and that refurbishments to the couple's official residence, the Speaker's House, had cost £1.7m.

The final straw, though, was Mr Martin's faltering response to the wave of revelations about MPs' expenses claims (see pp. 55–8). After appearing to do too little too late—by proposing only a prolonged sequence of meetings between party leaders and other internal Commons bodies to decide how best to reform the system, rather than any larger-scale changes—on 12 May 2009 he became the first Speaker in memory to face a no confidence vote (tabled by Conservative backbencher Douglas Carswell). Within days, Mr Clegg became the first party leader to demand his resignation and Mr Martin had to defend his refusal to allow a debate on the confidence motion in the House—hesitantly citing obscure rules that, he said, prevented it unless either the government or Opposition formally made room in their timetables. Finally, on 19 May, a week after his initial motion, Mr Carswell tabled another—this time backed by twenty-two further MPs. Before matters proceeded to a formal vote, Mr Martin announced his resignation in the chamber, becoming the first Speaker since Sir John Trevor in 1695 to be forced out of office.

With Mr Martin's successor, the Commons reverted to its customary pendulum swing from Labour to Conservatives: in a hotly contested election that marked a break from the 'coronations' of past Speakers, John Bercow beat a host of other hopefuls, including fellow Tories Ann Widdecombe and Sir George Young, and former Labour Foreign Secretary Margaret Beckett. He was reconfirmed in office after the May 2010 election.

Though it is the Speaker who officially presides in the Commons, recent events have acted as a timely reminder of the presence of a further, more shadowy, figure whose constitutional role is also to oversee debate in the chamber—though on behalf of a very particular vested interest. The *City Remembrancer*—who has a chair reserved for him/her behind the Speaker's 'throne'—occupies an obscure office of state dating back to 1571. His/her task is to act as a channel of information between, on the one hand, the City of London Corporation and its chief dignitary, the Lord Mayor of London (see p. 339), and, on the other, Parliament and the Sovereign. Critics view this arcane post as a somewhat sinister manifestation of the grip Britain's financial sector has long been seen to exercise over the seat of British democracy—a concern sharpened in the wake of the 2007–8 banking collapse and, in February 2012, the eviction by Corporation authorities of a camp set up by supporters of anti-capitalist protest movement Occupy from the area surrounding St Paul's Cathedral.

▶ The changing role of the Lord Chancellor

Officially the 'Lord High Chancellor of Great Britain', this ancient post—dating back at least as far as the 1066 Norman Conquest—has undergone significant (if not always smooth) changes over recent years. The office of Lord Chancellor is the second most senior of the so-called 'Great Officers of State of the UK'—the highest ranking being the Lord High Steward (a post generally kept vacant, except during coronations, when it is filled temporarily). As explained in Chapter 1, the Lord Chancellor was, for centuries, a bastion of all three branches of the British constitution, being head of the judiciary, Speaker of the Lords (legislature), and, as Cabinet minister responsible for what until recently was known as the 'Lord Chancellor's Department', a member of the executive.

The Lord Chancellor still retains many ancient ceremonial roles. As 'Custodian of The Great Seal of the Realm', or 'The Great Seal of the United Kingdom', he/she has the ability to authorize the reigning sovereign's documents (most notably the royal assent) on his/her behalf—saving the monarch from having to sign each one personally. The Lord Chancellor also remains a minister.

Since 2003, however, post-holders have ceased to retain quite the authority enjoyed by their predecessors—to the annoyance of the Lords, which sought initially to prevent Mr Blair denuding these powers. In a notoriously botched Cabinet reshuffle, Mr Blair replaced outgoing Lord Chancellor Derry Irvine with Lord Falconer of Thoroton. In doing so, he sought to rename the post 'Secretary of State for Constitutional Affairs'—effectively *abolishing* a constitutional role that had existed since the Middle Ages.

Mr Blair was forced to step back from scrapping the post outright and, though he did abolish the Lord Chancellor's Department, Lord Falconer retained the dual titles of Constitutional Affairs Secretary and Lord Chancellor throughout his four years in office. Further changes, however, came about after the 2005 election, when the Constitutional Affairs Act 2005 handed responsibility for running the judiciary to the Lord Chief Justice and created a new post of **Lord Speaker**—elected by his/her fellow peers using the alternative vote (AV) (see p. 133)—to assume the Lord Chancellor's role as chair of the Lords. The inaugural Lord Speaker, Baroness Hayman, was confirmed in office on 4 July 2006, and succeeded by former Convenor of the Crossbench Peers Baroness D'Souza in 2011.

During Mr Brown's first reshuffle the Department for Constitutional Reform was renamed the Ministry of Justice (MoJ). More significantly, Lord Falconer's successor, Mr Straw, became the first Lord Chancellor, since Henry VIII's Cardinal Wolsey gave way to several laymen in the sixteenth century, to be an MP—*not* a lord. Early signs under Mr Cameron's government were that this 'new tradition' would continue: Mr Straw's successor was to be another MP, Mr Clarke.

▌ The Opposition

The largest party other than the governing one (in terms of the number of seats it has in the Commons) is known as 'Her Majesty's Loyal Opposition'. In recognition of its official status, the Leader of the Opposition, the Opposition Chief

Whip, and the Opposition Deputy Chief Whip each receive allowances on top of their normal parliamentary ones to help with their responsibilities.

The Opposition is charged with:

- holding the government to account by appointing a 'Shadow Cabinet' covering the main departmental briefs;
- contributing to the legislative process by proposing amendments;
- setting out its policies as an alternative government using designated 'Opposition Days', which are scheduled into the parliamentary timetable to allow it, rather than the government, to dictate the flow of Commons business. In each session there are twenty Opposition Days (seventeen usually go to the largest Opposition party and three to the second largest).

▮ Devolution in practice—parliaments in the provinces

The first chapter laid out the overall constitutional framework governing the UK, while introducing the concept of devolution and how it was applied in the constituent countries of Britain outside England. This section explains how devolution has come to work in practice through the aegis of the new chambers created to implement it.

The Scottish Parliament

Comprising 129 **members of the Scottish Parliament (MSPs)**, the **Scottish Parliament** is, unlike Westminster's, a 'unicameral' legislature—meaning it only has one House.

During the initial transition stage flowing from its establishment in 1998, some of the inaugural MSPs were permitted to remain members of the House of Commons as well (a similar arrangement currently exists in the Northern Ireland Assembly, following restoration of devolved government in that province). This swiftly changed, however, when they assumed their place as MSPs full time, and by-elections were held to find replacements for them in their previous Commons constituencies.

Long before Scottish devolution was established, concerns were raised about the 'West Lothian Question' (see p. 31): the perceived inequity of allowing MSPs to sit and vote on English issues in the London Parliament while their Westminster equivalents would be barred from doing so in Scotland. Since devolution was introduced, the arrangement has proved incendiary: in November 2003, the votes of Scottish Labour backbenchers secured a knife-edge victory for the most controversial clauses of the government's Bill to introduce foundation hospitals in England (legislation with no bearing on their own constituencies). The Scottish Parliament—buoyed by the votes of Labour MSPs—had previously rejected the imposition of foundation hospitals in Scotland.

MSPs are elected using the additional member system (AMS) form of PR (see p. 136), with seventy-three voted in via the UK's traditional first-past-the-post (FPTP) system and the remaining fifty-six from a regional list designed to give a fairer allocation of seats to each party at national level. Each elector is allotted two votes: one for his/her constituency, and the other for a political party, the names of which appear on the list.

MSPs originally met in a temporary chamber at Edinburgh's Church of Scotland Assembly Hall on The Mound. This was belatedly replaced by a purpose-built Parliament in Holyrood, at the foot of the Royal Mile, in 2004. One MSP is elected to be 'Presiding Officer' (equivalent to the Commons Speaker), supported by two deputies. Parliament is elected for fixed terms lasting four years from the date of an election, and each year is divided into a parliamentary session, which is further split into 'sitting days' and 'recess periods'. On sitting days, Parliament tries to finish its business at 5.30 p.m., except on Fridays, which tend to wrap up at 12.30 p.m.

MSPs can raise issues by:

- asking oral questions during parliamentary sittings;
- submitting written questions;
- giving notice of, or moving, a motion.

Scottish parliamentary committees

Unlike at Westminster, much of the Scottish Parliament's work is performed by its eighteen committees—a system intended to make it easier for individual members to hold the devolved administration to account. Committees comprise five to fifteen MSPs and are chaired by 'conveners'. Meetings take place in public and can be held anywhere in Scotland. This is meant to provide more direct access to the democratic process for ordinary people. One committee member is appointed as a 'reporter', and MSPs are allowed to participate in meetings of committees of which they are not members (although they cannot vote).

Committees are charged with examining:

- policy, administration, and financial arrangements of the Scottish Government or Scottish Executive (see p. 113);
- proposed legislation in the Scottish and Westminster Parliaments;
- application of EU and international laws or conventions in Scotland.

Role and responsibilities of the Scottish Parliament

The Scottish Parliament is responsible for *domestic* issues specifically relevant to Scotland, but not foreign policy. Roles retained by the Commons include:

- foreign and defence policy;
- most economic policy;
- social security;
- medical ethics.

The legislative process in Scotland

The four main types of Bill that can be introduced into the Scottish Parliament are:

- *executive*—introduced by a minister;
- *committee*—introduced by the convener (chair) of a committee;
- *member's*—introduced by individual MSPs, like private member's Bills at Westminster, with the support of eleven fellow members;
- *private*—introduced by private individuals or promoters.

When introduced in the Scottish Parliament, Bills must be accompanied by the documents listed in the table entitled 'The documents required to accompany different types of Scottish Bill' on the Online Resource Centre. To become law, they must pass through the four stages outlined in Table 2.9, in a streamlined version of the Westminster process.

The National Assembly for Wales

Elected every four years, the Cardiff-based **National Assembly for Wales** has sixty members—forty elected for constituencies, and twenty on the basis of four for each of five larger regions. As in Scotland and Northern Ireland, these

Table 2.9 The passage of a Bill through the Scottish Parliament

Stage	Process
Stage one	Examination of Bill's general principles, normally handled by *lead committee* (i.e. committee specializing in relevant subject).
Stage two	Detailed line-by-line examination of Bill, either by lead committee, another committee, or whole Parliament. Amendments made and debated.
Stage three	Final consideration of Bill by full Parliament. Amendments made and debated, and Parliament decides whether to pass. More than quarter of all MSPs must vote on issue either way for it to pass.
Final stage	Parliament decides whether to approve Bill when referred back to meeting of full House. It is then automatically submitted by presiding officer for royal assent (there is no Lords stage).

assembly members (AMs) are no longer permitted to simultaneously sit as Westminster MPs.

Each Welsh elector has two votes: one for a constituency member and the other for one from the relevant regional list. The Secretary of State for Wales retains a degree of responsibility for the province and, unlike in Scotland, the Assembly does not yet have tax-varying powers. He/she is charged with ensuring devolution works effectively, by chairing a joint ministerial committee between Westminster and Cardiff.

The Assembly's responsibilities originally covered only the following:

- determining budgetary priorities;
- funding, directing, and appointing managers of NHS bodies in Wales;
- administering EU structural funds aimed at Wales;
- determining the content of the National Curriculum in Wales.

Although it remains a poor relation of the Scottish Parliament in terms of remit, the Assembly gained notable new legislative powers with the passage of the Government of Wales Act 2006. This introduced the 'Measure of the National Assembly for Wales' (or 'Assembly Measure')—a form of second-tier primary legislation that allows ministers in the Welsh Assembly Government to enact statutory instruments in relation to twenty 'fields' and 'matters' over which it had devolved authority. Assembly Measures could be proposed by any member of the Assembly, including backbenchers, and had to be scrutinized by committees, debated in plenary session, and approved in votes before being adopted. Importantly, the 2006 Act also broadened the ambit of the Assembly's powers to cover a wider range of areas (devolution of which had to first be approved through the passage of a form of Order in Council (see p. 69) known as a Legislative Competence Order (LCO)):

- agriculture, fisheries, forestry, and rural development;
- ancient monuments and historic buildings;
- culture;
- economic development;
- education and training;
- environment;
- fire and rescue services and promotion of fire safety;
- food;
- health and health services;
- highways and transport;
- housing;
- local government;

- public administration;
- social welfare;
- sport and recreation;
- tourism;
- town and country planning;
- water and flood defence;
- Welsh language;
- the Assembly itself.

More recently, in a referendum held on 3 March 2011, Welsh people voted by a 63.5 to 36.5 per cent majority to grant the Assembly powers to pass its own laws—known as Acts of the Assembly—on all matters in the twenty 'subject areas' over which it has authority.

The law-making process in Wales

The Welsh legislative procedure resembles that of Scotland, in that it is overseen by a presiding officer and his/her deputy, elected by other AMs. Again, executive functions are wielded by a First Minister at the head of a devolved government. This was initially called the **Welsh Executive** (now referred to as the **Welsh Assembly Government**).

The Assembly meets in public plenary session in Cardiff, and business is directed by the presiding officer through a business secretary and business committee. Every session allows at least fifteen minutes for oral questions of the First Minister and, every four weeks, similar sessions for each departmental minister. In addition, any AM can propose a specific motion once a week, before the conclusion of plenary business, and there are two forms of committee to consider matters in plenary session: 'subject committees', and 'regional committees' covering specific areas of the country.

The Northern Ireland Assembly

It was only in 2007 that devolved government at the **Northern Ireland Assembly** in Stormont finally came about, with the signing of a landmark power-sharing agreement between the two biggest parties—Ian Paisley's Democratic Unionist Party (DUP) and Gerry Adams's Sinn Féin—following fresh elections in the province. In April 2008 Dr Paisley (a stalwart of Northern Irish politics for more than four decades) retired as First Minister and DUP leader, to be replaced by East Belfast MP Peter Robinson (who subsequently lost his Westminster seat at the 2010 election, but continued as head of the Assembly). At time of writing, former Sinn Féin chief negotiator Martin McGuinness remained Deputy First Minister.

Areas of responsibility retained over Northern Ireland by Westminster

The Secretary of State for Northern Ireland remains responsible for:

- international relations;
- defence;
- taxation.

Several Whitehall agencies remain responsible for overseeing specific areas, including the Northern Ireland Prison Service, Compensation Agency, and Forensic Agency of Northern Ireland. Policing and justice powers were devolved in April 2010 (see p. 35). The former is overseen by a recently reconstituted Northern Ireland Policing Board, with members drawn from all the main political parties.

The legislative process in Northern Ireland

The Northern Ireland Assembly is home to 108 elected representatives, known as **members of the Legislative Assembly (MLAs)**. The nature and titles of its senior politicians and officers and the nature of its legislative process are virtually identical to those in Wales.

☰ Topical feature idea

Since 2010 it has been possible for ordinary citizens—and local MPs representing them—to engage in a more 'direct' form of democracy than was previously possible, through the Coalition's introduction of e-petitions. Anyone who can mobilize at least 100,000 signatories to back an online petition supporting their cause can press the Commons Backbench Business Committee to timetable a full debate on that issue in the chamber. The advent of online activist movements like Avaaz and 38 Degrees has made it easier for individuals and small community groups to mobilize support for e-petitions. But, in practice, petitions are usually 'presented' to the committee by backbench MPs representing particular constituencies or with personal interests in a campaign. Have there been any successful e-petitions mounted in your area? Are any current or pending? Why not set up your own e-petition as an experiment to see how much support can be rallied for a campaign on a local issue?

✳ Current issues

- **House of Lords reform:** the Lords' slow transformation from an unelected to an elected chamber began with the 1999 House of Lords Act. Labour failed to finish the job, but Mr Clegg introduced a new reform Bill in July 2012—but was forced to drop it in August 2012 after Mr Cameron confirmed he would be unable to muster sufficient Tory backbench support. The best hope for Lords reform now rests with a PMB introduced by former Liberal leader Lord Steel.

■ **Deadlock over proposed boundary changes:** the quid pro quo for Mr Cameron's support for Lords reform was the Lib Dems' for a cut in the number of constituencies from 650 to 600, with constituency population sizes equalized to ensure a fairer allocation of votes at elections (and, in all likelihood, up to twenty more Tory seats). But, in announcing he was placing his plans for Lords reform on hold indefinitely, Mr Clegg confirmed his MPs would be voting against the boundary proposals in the Commons.

■ **Reassertion of Parliament's scrutiny function:** since the introduction of elected select committees in 2010, backbench MPs have had a new lease of life—revelling in their increased legitimacy as scrutinizers of government policy. Among the more combative committee chairpersons have been Keith Vaz, Chairman of the Home Affairs Committee, and Margaret Hodge, who chairs the Public Accounts Committee. Even the Lords has been more assertive, inflicting notable defeats on ministers during the turbulent passage of health and welfare legislation.

? Review questions

1. Outline the role of backbench MPs. To whom do MPs owe primary responsibility—Parliament, party, or public?

2. What is meant by the terms 'party whip', the 'whip', and 'three-line whip'?

3. What are the arguments for and against an elected second chamber?

4. What is the role of private member's Bills and what do they actually achieve?

5. Has the creation of the Lord Speaker and the removal of the condition that the Lord Chancellor must be a peer rendered the position redundant?

→ Further reading

Jones, B. (2004) *Dictionary of British Politics*, Manchester: Manchester University Press. **Thorough, accessible A–Z of terms and recent developments in British politics**.

Jones, B., Kavanagh, D., Moran, M., and Norton, P. (2006) *Politics UK*, 6th edn, London: Longman. **Full-colour edition of established core text giving comprehensive overview of structure and workings of British political system up to 2005**.

Norton, P. (2005) *Parliament in British Politics*, London: Palgrave Macmillan. **Thoughtful evaluation of changing significance of British Parliament in light of recent constitutional developments, such as devolution and partial reform of the Lords**.

Rogers, R. and Walters, R. (2006) *How Parliament Works*, 6th edn, London: Longman.
   Sixth edition of indispensable layman's guide to often complex, sometimes archaic workings of British Parliament.

ⓐ **Online Resource Centre**

www.oxfordtextbooks.co.uk/orc/Morrison3e/
   Visit the Online Resource Centre that accompanies this book for web links and regular updates.

3

Prime minister, Cabinet, and government

Having examined the competing seats of constitutional power in Britain—the sovereign and Parliament—it is necessary to look in detail at the means by which most of that power is exercised in practice. This chapter focuses on the make-up and workings of the executive branch of the UK constitution—the government—and in particular the role of the inner circle of ministers known as the Cabinet, and the most senior of these: the prime minister.

▌ Origins of the role of prime minister

Compared to ancient posts like that of Lord Chancellor, the role of prime minister (or PM) emerged surprisingly recently, and owes its origins to historical accident. When German-born George I succeeded to the British throne in 1714 he could speak little English. Traditionally the Cabinet had always been chaired by the monarch, but with the newly crowned king literally incapable of understanding the language of UK government a practical need arose for a senior minister to perform this duty in his stead. Thus was born the idea of a post that became that of de facto head of government in Britain—or 'prime' minister.

But which government minister should assume this privileged position? After some debate the honour fell to Sir Robert Walpole, holder of the extant post 'First Lord of the Treasury' (in effect, the Lord High Treasurer or official head of HM Treasury—the department responsible for raising taxes to finance government policy). His previous duties were generally assumed from this date by the Lord High Commissioners of the Treasury.

Despite assuming the day-to-day role of prime minister, however, Walpole retained his official Cabinet title, as did his successors for the best part of a century. In fact, although the term 'prime minister' was used informally within government from 1714 onwards and started appearing on government documents in the 1860s, under Benjamin Disraeli, it was only coined publicly during the term of Liberal Sir Henry Campbell-Bannerman (1905–8).

Given the disproportionate degree of power wielded by the PM, since the position arose it has been constitutionally contentious. Before its introduction, all ministers of the Crown were regarded as equals, with shared responsibility for governing the nation. The emergence of a Cabinet chairperson from within its own ranks made an immediate mockery of this idea, by implicitly elevating him/her to a level *more equal* than that of the others. This curious, somewhat contradictory, position spawned a Latin phrase associated with PMs ever since: *primus inter pares*—or 'first among equals'. The notion is that PMs are 'equal' to their peers in Cabinet—and, indeed, the House of Commons (the legislature)— in that, as elected members of Parliament (the last peer to be PM was Lord Salisbury, who left office in 1902), they must be voted in to represent constituencies and can be removed by local people if they become unpopular. To this extent they are ordinary MPs like any other. In contrast, they are 'first among' those notional 'equals' by dint of not only being senior ministers in the government, but also presiding over Cabinet meetings.

The role of prime minister today

Today there are many established conventions surrounding the office of **prime minister**, almost all of which have grown up since the time of Walpole. The PM— or 'premier'—tends to be the leader of the party that wins the most seats in the Commons at a general election. To this extent, although British voters are theoretically turning out to elect their local MP on polling day (not to mention the small matter of a national government for their country), the emphasis of elections is inherently 'presidential'. Everyone knows that if X party gets in, Y leader will become PM. Historically, premiers have always hailed from one of the two biggest parliamentary parties at any one time. In the twentieth century only five PMs were Labour, compared to twelve Conservatives. The Tories' dominance of the office until recently saw them regarded as the 'natural party of government'.

Although many prerogative powers exercised on the sovereign's behalf are discharged collectively by Cabinet (at least notionally), the PM is customarily the only minister ever granted a private audience with the monarch. Incoming premiers first meet the Queen in this capacity when they visit her at Buckingham Palace to be offered the post formally after their election. This behind-the-scenes ritual is known as the 'kissing of the hands'. Reportedly, Tony Blair actually did kiss the Queen's hands, although this has not generally been the practice for generations.

The PM's official London residence is at 10 Downing Street, and he/she also has the use of a sprawling country estate at Chequers in the Chilterns. Like many conventions, of course, such rules are there to be bent when circumstances dictate: when Mr Blair came to power he struck a deal to swap domestic quarters with his Chancellor, Gordon Brown, whose official residence was next door at Number 11, where there is more living space. Mr Blair had a growing family of three children, while at the time Mr Brown was living alone.

By far the most important convention relating to the PM, however, is the fact that whoever holds the office has the authority to exercise, on behalf of the sovereign, the majority of the powers entrusted to him/her by the royal prerogative.

The principal prerogative powers discharged by the premier are to:

- appoint fellow ministers of the Crown;
- chair meetings of the Cabinet at least once a week;
- appoint members of Cabinet committees;
- keep the sovereign informed of government business on a weekly basis;
- declare war and peace;
- recommend passage of government Bills to royal assent;
- recommend **dissolution** of Parliament for general elections;
- recommend prorogation of Parliament for summer recess and other holidays;
- draw up his/her party's manifesto at elections and write the Queen's Speech—the annual announcement of proposed government legislation;
- recommend for sovereign's approval appointees to senior clergy positions, including the Church of England bishops and deans;
- recommend the appointment of senior judges;
- recommend appointees for senior positions in public corporations, including the British Broadcasting Corporation (BBC);
- recommend prospective recipients of honours and peerages in the Queen's Birthday Honours List and New Year Honours List;
- answer for his/her government's policies and actions at Prime Minister's Questions (PMQs).

The PM also has an additional job title: Minister for the Civil Service. The 'department' he/she oversees in this capacity is the Cabinet Office (effectively the 'Ministry for the Civil Service'), and until recently his/her permanent secretary (the most senior civil servant) was the Cabinet Secretary. On the retirement of then incumbent Sir Gus O'Donnell, at the end of 2011, a decision was taken to split his previous role three ways—with Sir Jeremy Heywood succeeding him as Cabinet Secretary, Ian Watmore as permanent secretary to the Cabinet Office, and Sir Bob Kerslake in the (now part-time) post of Head of the Home Civil Service.

Towards 'elective dictatorship'—are prime ministers now too presidential?

Britain's premier may not be its head of state, but to many outside observers he/she often appears to be. No monarch has had the temerity to challenge the passage of a government Bill since Queen Anne did so more than 300 years ago. And the notion that he/she would defy the will of the electorate to block the appointment of a PM whose policies he/she opposed is the stuff of establishment conspiracy theories.

Perhaps unsurprisingly, power has been known to go to some PMs' heads. As long ago as 1976, Quintin Hogg—who, as Lord Hailsham, twice served as Conservative Lord Chancellor—used his Richard Dimbleby Lecture to criticize the 'elective dictatorship' of British governments. The thrust of his argument was that successive PMs had accrued substantial additional power over and above that vested in them constitutionally, and were increasingly using their parliamentary colleagues to steamroller policies through Parliament. Moreover, he argued, those same policies were often thought up (and effectively decided upon) behind closed doors—long before being debated in Parliament. At best this backstage policymaking would take place around the Cabinet table, among premiers and their ministerial colleagues; at worst it might be dreamed up informally between the PM and a close-knit inner circle of trusted confidantes, not all of whom were even ministers. This mode of governing is often referred to as 'prime ministerial government'—or, more recently, 'sofa government'—as opposed to the collective decision-making embodied by traditional 'Cabinet government'.

Indeed, it was often said that the governments of the late 1960s and 1970s were prone to striking deals in 'smoke-filled rooms', with business leaders, trade union bosses, and other interest groups having a direct and unofficial input into policymaking. In the case of Labour governments, the phrase 'beer and sandwiches' was coined to refer to the cosy chats the likes of Harold Wilson and James Callaghan reportedly had with the union leaders who helped bankroll the party prior to announcing new wage and industrial policies.

But these tactics—increasingly common to governments of both main parties—are far from the only examples of perceived presidential behaviour by modern PMs. Occasional slips of the tongue by pressurized premiers have spoken volumes about their apparent sense of superiority or infallibility. In 1989, Margaret Thatcher notoriously greeted news that her son Mark's wife had given birth with the 'royal we', telling the waiting media: 'We are a grandmother.'

Mr Blair—of all other recent PMs, the one most frequently described as presidential—was also prone to such lapses during his later years in office. In an interview on ITV1 chat show *Parkinson* in March 2006 it was put to him by host Michael Parkinson that his job brought with it a huge amount of responsibility, in light of his status as commander-in-chief of the British Armed Forces.

Mr Blair failed to challenge this assertion, despite the fact that, constitution-ally, this office still resides with the Queen. In the same interview he intimated that God had guided his actions over Iraq (an echo of words used by President George W. Bush several years earlier).

So much for the sound bites, though: in what ways do PMs *act* high-handedly? Broadly, the examples of such presidential actions can be broken down into four major categories:

- bypassing/downgrading the Cabinet's role in devising policy;
- announcing policies to the media before informing Parliament/Cabinet;
- ignoring popular opinion and protest;
- grandstanding on the international stage.

Bypassing/downgrading the Cabinet's role in devising policy

PMs chair meetings of Cabinet. It is here that policies are traditionally thrashed out and fine-tuned, before being announced to the press and public. In recent decades, however, there has been a tendency for premiers to downgrade the Cabinet's role in policymaking—and, in some cases, bypass it entirely, in favour of relying for advice on small posses of trusted friends and colleagues known as 'kitchen Cabinets'.

'Kitchen Cabinets' have taken various forms, often closely reflecting the par-ticular politics and personalities of individual PMs. One of the first manifesta-tions of a UK kitchen Cabinet was Conservative PM Ted Heath's Central Policy Review Staff (CPRS), a group of advisers within the Cabinet Office (see p. 85) entrusted with streamlining the formulation of government policy across de-partments. The formation of the CPRS had been recommended by the Fulton Committee, set up by his predecessor, Labour PM Wilson, in 1966 to review the workings of the Civil Service. The Committee had also suggested a separate 'policy unit' be formed to coordinate long-term planning in each ministry, and when Wilson returned to power in 1974 he acted on this suggestion by forming the Downing Street Policy Unit (effectively his own kitchen Cabinet), chaired by Sir Bernard Donoughue.

Indeed, Mr Wilson (more than any earlier PM) had a reputation for valuing the views of personal friends over those of Cabinet colleagues. Among his closest confidantes were his private secretary, Marcia Williams, and press secretary, Joe Haines. This fashion for consulting close allies—elected or otherwise—before presenting ideas to Cabinet (let alone Parliament) was also favoured by his successor-but-one, Mrs Thatcher, whose closest aides included her press secretary, Sir Bernard Ingham, and private secretary, former businessman Charles Powell.

More recently, the plotting and ruminations of the kitchen Cabinet have become increasingly associated with the work of 'special advisers' and, in particular, the spin doctors employed by ministers to put a positive gloss on government policy. This development will be discussed more fully later in this chapter, but it is worth reflecting on here in relation to one particular casualty of the 'sofa government' favoured by Mr Blair: Cabinet decision-making. As with his weekly meetings with the Queen, when the Iraq War was in full swing Mr Blair downgraded formal Cabinet meetings to such an extent that deliberations that traditionally took two or three hours were often reduced to thirty minutes or less. In addition, he is said to have left many detailed policy debates, customarily held in full Cabinet, to be discussed by Cabinet committees—appointing his most loyal colleagues to chair those hearings to reduce the likelihood of his own ideas being disputed. It was for this and other tendencies that she saw as fundamentally undemocratic that former Cabinet minister Clare Short later publicly dubbed Mr Blair a 'control freak'.

Recent PMs—notably Mrs Thatcher and Mr Blair—have also been accused of bypassing or downgrading Parliament's role in the legislative process. They commonly do this by using the party whip system to coerce MPs and peers to back the party line. Mr Blair was frequently accused of abusing his large Commons majority to 'steamroller' through policies unpopular with the public (not to mention his own backbenchers). Examples include the various anti-terror measures introduced following the attacks on the Twin Towers in New York and the 7 July 2005 bombings in London—many of which were rushed through in a matter of days, with committee stages taking place on the floor of the Commons. In October 2011, Mr Cameron used a three-line whip to stifle a backbench revolt by Tory MPs demanding a referendum on Britain's membership of the European Union (EU). Despite this the resulting rebellion remained the single biggest over Europe since the Second World War, with eighty-one backbenchers defying the whip to support it. Nine months later, ninety-one Tory MPs defied the whips over Lords reform (see p. 65), while almost exactly a year after the present EU showdown with his backbenchers Mr Cameron suffered a defeat over his proposal to argue for a freeze, rather than real-terms cut, in the Union's budget.

Announcing policies to the media before Parliament/Cabinet

Briefing the media (or targeted sections of it sympathetic to government) on policy proposals ahead of formal announcements to Parliament and public has become a much criticized trend under recent administrations. Indeed, in some instances under Mr Blair this secondary form of bypassing the normal machinery of government saw ministers close to the PM spoon-feeding policy details to favoured journalists before even the Cabinet (let alone the Commons) had deliberated over them. Arrangements for the briefings invariably involved the spin doctors and/or special advisers with which Mr Blair surrounded himself—principally his official spokesman and long-time Director of Communications, Alastair Campbell, and/or Downing Street Chief of Staff Jonathan Powell.

So what forms do these 'off the record' briefings actually take, and how often have they involved policy announcements yet to be debated in Cabinet? The most widely used tactics are explained in the table entitled, 'Types of media briefing used by ministers and special advisers' to be found on the Online Resource Centre.

From a policy viewpoint, one of the most infamous examples of serious proposals being released to the press in advance of even full Cabinet discussion occurred in 2002, when then Health Secretary and close Blair ally Alan Milburn gave *The Times* a detailed explanation of his so-called 'Ten-Year Plan for the National Health Service' (see p. 176).

Ignoring popular opinion/protest

During his first term, Mr Blair was notorious for consulting opinion pollsters and focus groups before taking radical policy decisions. His critics (including many within his own party) argued this was, at best, a waste of the mandate he had achieved by winning such a large majority in the 1997 election and, at worst, a betrayal of promises made in Labour's manifesto.

In his second term, Mr Blair developed a tendency to do precisely the opposite—becoming increasingly bold in his political judgements. The most notorious example of this headstrong approach was his pursuit of the case for war with Iraq, citing supposed evidence (which turned out to be deeply flawed) that Saddam Hussein was stockpiling weapons of mass destruction (WMDs). Defying huge opposition in the country—articulated by the biggest peacetime demonstration in Britain's history, when up to 500,000 protestors converged on Trafalgar Square just days before the war—he persuaded a reluctant Commons to vote for the invasion.

Mr Blair's appetite for defying public opposition echoed Mrs Thatcher's. The policy that most clearly demonstrated her stubbornness in the teeth of huge public opposition would ultimately—like the Iraq War for Mr Blair—hasten her downfall. Introducing the deeply unpopular Community Charge (see p. 366), to replace the age-old rates system, provoked some of the largest-scale public protests in British history. Mrs Thatcher remained resolute, however, and it was only when her successor, John Major, came to power a year or so later that the tax was abandoned.

Grandstanding on the international stage

As Britain's de facto head of state, the PM has the biggest global profile of any UK politician. Nonetheless, some premiers take to the role of international statesperson more than others. In the nineteenth century, Liberal William Gladstone and Tory Benjamin Disraeli were two most accomplished and successful British premiers, but it was arguably the latter—famous, like Mrs Thatcher and Mr Blair, for his interventionist foreign policy—who impressed most on the international stage. Of twentieth-century PMs, Winston Churchill was widely regarded as the greatest statesman, principally because of the leadership he gave to Europe during the Second World War.

Examples of 'presidential-style' grandstanding on the global stage in recent times have included Mrs Thatcher's decisive handling of the Falklands War and high-profile White House 'love-ins' with US president Ronald Reagan. Her implacable opposition to communism and her determined negotiation of various British opt-outs from EU legislation also helped to maintain her high international profile.

Mr Blair, meanwhile, waged four wars during his decade in Downing Street—pursuing a proactive defence policy known as liberal interventionism. During his first term he helped launch two military campaigns: the North Atlantic Treaty Organization (NATO) intervention over alleged 'ethnic cleansing' of Albanians by Slobodan Milošović's Serbs in Kosovo, and a decisive move to halt the civil war in the former British colony of Sierra Leone. In his second he became forever wedded in the public eye to George Bush's US administration by pledging to 'stand shoulder to shoulder' with him following the 11 September terrorist attacks, and actively supporting the invasions of Afghanistan and Iraq.

Mr Blair's exhausting schedule of shuttle diplomacy in the run-up to the Iraq War—criss-crossing Africa to persuade smaller United Nations (UN) member states to support Britain and the USA's calls for a 'second' resolution to justify military action—buoyed his profile still further. So, too, did his earlier missions to tackle poverty in Africa, forge peace in Northern Ireland, and promote a decisive 'two-state solution' to the long-running stand-off between Israel and Palestine in the Middle East. His involvement in brokering the latter saw him rewarded after stepping down as PM with a new diplomatic role as Middle East peace envoy for 'the Quartet'—a loose international consortium representing the EU, UN, USA, and Russia.

Finally, although the Queen is still responsible constitutionally for entertaining visiting heads of state on official visits (which she did for President Bush in 2004 and France's President Sarkozy in 2008), PMs also tend to get in on the action, often inviting world leaders to stay at Chequers after they have left her.

Holding the PM to account

Given the degree of power accrued by PMs, what mechanisms exist to hold them to account? As we know, monarchs have long since lost their inclination (if not ability) to challenge premiers—Queen Anne's notable stand against a government Bill in 1707 being the last to date. Notwithstanding Queen Elizabeth II's predilection for wrong-footing Wilson and her reputedly frosty relationship with Mrs Thatcher, there has been little evidence in modern times of reigning monarchs displaying any appetite for confrontation. Nonetheless, there remain significant means by which the actions of PMs can be influenced, if not directly controlled. These can be divided into four areas:

- public;
- press;
- Parliament;
- party.

Public

The primary means of holding premiers to account goes back to that first principle—that they are ultimately MPs like any other, and must stand for re-election in their constituencies come polling day. Their parties are similarly dependent on mandates for their Commons majorities: if enough of their MPs lose their constituencies' support at an election, other parties will emerge with more seats to supplant them in government.

The resounding defeat of Mr Major's Conservative government in 1997 by 'New Labour' was perhaps the clearest example in recent times of an ailing administration being unceremoniously ejected by an electorate intent on change. Not only did the Tories suffer a landslide defeat, but many senior MPs—including Defence Secretary Michael Portillo—lost their seats. Although Mr Major escaped this ignominy, it has been known for PMs in some countries to lose their own constituency seats, as well as their parliamentary majorities. Australian premier John Howard lost his parliamentary seat in that country's 2007 election, after more than a decade in power, while Northern Ireland First Minister Peter Robinson suffered a similar fate in the 2010 UK general election, despite retaining his MLA constituency at Stormont (see p. 79).

PMs are also accountable in other ways. It has long been the practice, for example, for by-elections, local authority, and European elections to be treated as anti-government 'protest votes', giving PM's a 'bloody nose'. Other voters prefer to withhold their support from governing parties they might still back at general elections by abstaining altogether. There was significant anecdotal evidence that protest votes rose under New Labour, especially among traditional party voters disillusioned by the invasion of Iraq. The combined effect of protest votes and abstentions on one side, and renewed determination to harness support on the other, can lead to situations like that witnessed in the 2007 and 2008 local elections, both of which were 'won' by David Cameron's then resurgent Conservatives.

Other forms of public pressure that can be put on PMs include demonstrations (such as the Stop the War Coalition marches over Iraq and the Countryside Alliance's over the hunting ban), industrial action by public sector employees—for example, the recent wave of strikes in protest at the Coalition's austerity measures and pension reforms—and rejections of key policies in national

referendums. Although British governments rarely put individual questions to the public vote in this way—preferring to invoke the constitutional principle of parliamentary sovereignty, which leaves decisions to Parliament between elections—both Mr Blair and Mr Brown were accused of purposely avoiding referendums on the EU's 2007 Lisbon Treaty for fear of losing (see p. 273).

Press

If there is one thing guaranteed to send a PM scurrying in pursuit of populist policy ideas to regain public support, it is a run of negative headlines in Britain's tabloids.

In recent years the national press—particularly the biggest-selling daily papers, *The Sun* and the *Daily Mail*—has been seen to wield disproportionately more influence than other media on the actions of successive governments. Mrs Thatcher's hat-trick of election wins in the late 1970s and 1980s were put down, in part, to the support of 'white van' or 'Essex man'—terms used to denote a new breed of aspirational working-class voter weary of the 'class warfare' espoused by old-school Labour politicians, and attracted by the doctrines of self-help and share and home ownership ushered in by Thatcherite ideology. Although formerly a red-blooded Labour paper (the *Daily Herald*), *The Sun* under Rupert Murdoch came to epitomize this new spirit of entrepreneurship, just as the high moral tone of the *Daily Mail* appealed to 'traditional' Conservatives.

Throughout the 1980s *The Sun*, under bullish editor Kelvin Mackenzie, remained one of the staunchest advocates of Thatcherism, using many memorable front-page headlines to bolster support for her resolute, patriotic brand of politics. Among its most controversial splashes was its celebration of the sinking of the Argentine warship *General Belgrano* with the headline 'Gotcha!' and the one with which it urged voters to support Mr Major rather than Labour leader Neil Kinnock in the 1992 election: 'If Neil Kinnock wins today would the last person to leave Britain please turn out the lights.' After years of supporting the Conservatives, though, Britain's biggest-selling paper switched horses in the run-up to the 1997 election, backing Mr Blair (although it eventually returned to the Tories, declaring 'Labour's lost it' on the morning after Mr Brown's speech to the 2009 Labour Party Conference).

Although this was strenuously denied by both Mr Blair and Mr Brown, the liberalization of UK media ownership laws that enabled Mr Murdoch (despite his significant share of the national newspaper market) to buy a stake in ITV was rumoured to have come as a result of his behind-the-scenes lobbying. Mr Cameron also faced serious questions over his perceived closeness to the Murdoch empire following his decision, while still in Opposition, to hire former *News of the World* editor Andy Coulson as his personal spokesman shortly after the latter's 2007 resignation over a then incipient scandal about the practice of reporters at the Sunday paper hacking into their contacts' mobile phone voicemail messages. Though Mr Coulson quit his Downing Street post in February 2011, amid growing allegations about his collusion in a cover-up at the *News of the World*, the perhaps uncomfortably close relations between the Murdoch press and Mr Cameron's Tories was laid bare in more detail during a series of hearings at the public inquiry convened in 2011 by Lord Justice Leveson to examine the culture and practices of the British media in light of further revelations about the prevalence of phone-hacking. Among the nuggets to emerge were anecdotes about Mr Cameron's cosy chat with then News International chairman James Murdoch in a Mayfair club, during which he learned of the decision by the paper's sister title, *The Sun*, to revert to supporting the Conservatives in the coming election, and the furious phone exchanges between the company's chief executive, Rebekah Brooks, Labour's serving premier, Mr Brown, and his First Secretary, Lord Mandelson, that followed the paper's formal switch of loyalties later in 2009.

More controversial still were questions that emerged during the inquiry about the extent of unofficial Coalition endorsement of the attempt by News International's parent company, News Corporation, to purchase the 61 per cent of shares it did not already own in UK-based satellite television broadcaster BSkyB. At time of writing it remained unclear how closely Mr Cameron was involved in any behind-the-scenes discussions designed to smooth the way for the takeover, but in his evidence to the inquiry Mr Murdoch junior dropped a bombshell by disclosing a slew of email exchanges between Adam Smith, a special adviser to then Culture Secretary Jeremy Hunt, and News Corp lobbyist Frederic Michel, which appeared to reflect the minister's implied support for the bid. At a later hearing, Mr Smith revealed the existence of a memo sent to Mr Cameron by Mr Hunt himself, in which he apparently urged the PM to back the takeover. The note was sent on 19 November 2010—a month before Mr Cameron appointed Mr Hunt to succeed Business Secretary Vince Cable in determining the outcome of the BSkyB bid, following the latter's indiscreet confession to two undercover reporters from *The Daily Telegraph* that he had 'declared war' on Mr Murdoch.

Set alongside Mr Murdoch's recollection of chatting to Mr Cameron about the takeover plans over Christmas dinner at Mrs Brooks's Cotswolds home, and the regular text messages sent to the latter by the PM (signed off with a familiar 'DC'), an impression emerged of unprecedented levels of intimacy between Britain's most powerful media company and the holder of its highest office.

While it has long been commonplace for newspapers to take a partisan stand, in Britain broadcasters are bound by a strict code of impartiality upheld by the Office of Communications (Ofcom) (see p. 226) and, in the case of the licence fee-funded BBC, the BBC Trust. There have been recent calls, so far unheeded, from Mr Mackenzie and others for commercial broadcasters to be allowed to adopt a more political voice akin to that of the pro-Republican, Murdoch-owned Fox News Network in the USA.

Parliament

PMs are held to account by Parliament in various ways, the most demonstrable being Prime Minister's Questions (PMQs)—the Wednesday lunchtime half-hour session in which he/she is quizzed about his/her actions (see p. 46).

Most MPs also sit on committees. On select committees they examine the workings of individual government departments—and, indirectly, the Cabinet over which the PM presides. General committees, meanwhile, scrutinize prospective legislation, the bulk of which will have originated in the in-trays of the PM and his/her most senior ministerial colleagues. PMs also now subject themselves to twice-yearly scrutiny by the Commons Liaison Committee (see p. 49).

MPs can also use a variety of other parliamentary procedures outlined in the last chapter—including early day motions (EDMs), urgent debates, adjournment debates, and e-petition debates—to influence/criticize PMs. But perhaps the single most powerful way in which MPs—and, to a lesser extent, peers—conspire to embarrass serving PMs is by voting down their policies in Parliament. Because most governments tend to have working Commons majorities and can usually marshal sufficient support from loyalists, historically government legislation is rarely comprehensively defeated. Occasionally, however, PMs have found themselves so out of step with their parliamentary parties that (whatever their nominal majorities) they have struggled to get their proposals passed.

Party

When Parliament conspires to censure PMs, derail their legislative programmes, or otherwise undermine their authority, it usually succeeds only with the complicity of government backbenchers so dismayed at their leader's direction that they are prepared to vote against it en masse. During Mr Blair's second and third terms, backbench rebellions became so frequent at times that Labour MPs were increasingly described as the 'unofficial Opposition' (particularly when the *real* Opposition, the Tories, were still under the stuttering leaderships of William Hague, Iain Duncan Smith, and Michael Howard).

The most serious form backbench rebellions can take is a 'motion of no confidence' (also known as a 'vote of no confidence' or 'censure motion'). This is when a device such as an EDM is put before the Commons—customarily by the Leader of the Opposition—inviting MPs to pass a motion (vote) expressing a loss of 'confidence' in the serving PM. If he/she loses the motion this normally means that even his/her own MPs have withdrawn their support, and an election must therefore be called.

The election that saw the end of Callaghan's Labour government in May 1979 was ultimately precipitated by a confidence vote tabled by Opposition leader Mrs Thatcher. Because Callaghan had been leading a minority government following the collapse of a fragile deal with the Liberal Party that stopped short of formal coalition—the 'Lib-Lab Pact'—he was increasingly reliant on support from the Ulster Unionists and Scottish Nationalists. When his government refused to implement a proposed Scotland Act to introduce devolution (a referendum had backed it, but only on a relatively low voter turnout), the nationalists tabled a confidence motion, which Mrs Thatcher swiftly emulated.

PMs in desperate straits have even been known to call their own confidence votes to instil discipline in their party ranks and force through unpopular legislation. In 1993 Mr Major tabled a high-risk 'back-me-or-sack-me' motion to force the hand of the 'Maastricht rebels' (Eurosceptic Conservative backbenchers who had repeatedly voted against the Treaty on the European Union—or 'Maastricht Treaty'—that he was struggling to ratify). In the event, he won—not least because most of the rebels represented marginal seats, and could easily have lost them to other candidates or parties in the event of an election.

Traditionally, confidence motions have only ever required *simple majorities* of MPs' votes—50 per cent of those cast, plus one—to bring down a government. So it was with alarm that some constitutional experts and politicians on both sides of the Commons initially greeted the Coalition's proposals in May 2010 to introduce not only five-year fixed-term parliaments (see p. 118), but a new rule preventing elections being called mid-term unless 55 per cent of MPs voted in favour of dissolution. Critics argued that the proposed '55 per cent rule' could be used to insure Mr Cameron against the possibility of his coalition partners pulling the plug on it prematurely (between them the Lib Dems, Labour, and all of the minority parties would only have been able to muster 53 per cent of Commons votes if the former were to switch loyalties).

They also complained it would render redundant the confidence procedure. Although a government could theoretically still be defeated by a simple no confidence vote, the backing of a further 5 per cent of MPs would be needed to force an election—potentially leaving a 'defeated' administration limping on indefinitely like a 'zombie'. In the Coalition's defence, Leader of the House Sir George Young argued that its opponents were missing the point: rather than enabling PMs to prolong their tenures against Parliament's wishes, the new rule would instead liberate the Commons by equipping it with a mechanism to demand dissolution without the need for a formal confidence vote. Nevertheless, when Mr Clegg confirmed the final shape of the proposals in a Commons statement two months later, he announced the 55 per cent rule was being dropped, and elections would instead continue to be triggered by a no confidence vote alone. However, in performing his U-turn, he introduced a new lifeline for struggling minority governments—granting them a two-week breathing space after losing a confidence vote to try to form an alternative administration and avert an election. At the same time, he said the Commons would still have the ability to prompt dissolution by a straight vote, although only if two-thirds of MPs (as opposed to the mooted 55 per cent) were to approve it. The proposed new power echoed one previously adopted by the Scottish Parliament.

There are, of course, various other ways in which governing parties can hold their leaders to account—and even depose them. Once a week when Labour is in government leaders subject themselves to a lengthy meeting of the Parliamentary Labour Party (PLP)—essentially the body representing all elected Labour MPs. Although Mr Blair was given a famously easy ride for his first few years in power, in the aftermath of the Iraq debacle PLP meetings reportedly became increasingly strained, with the PM fielding harder questions and occasionally being heckled.

Conservatives have an even more ferocious means of grilling—and occasionally removing—their leaders. The 1922 Committee is a body made up of all Tory MPs. Actually formed in 1923 (but taking its name from the 1922 election), this influential committee has an eighteen-strong executive committee charged with overseeing the election of new leaders, and has, at times, acted to replace existing ones. As the 'voice' of Tory MPs, the 1922 Committee is seen to represent the collective 'mood' of the parliamentary party. If it passes a vote of no confidence, therefore, it is normally only a matter of time before the leader jumps (assuming that he/she is not pushed).

The 1922 Committee is examined in more detail in Chapter 5, but it is relevant here in relation to its involvement in the removal of a recent Tory premier: Mrs Thatcher. Her downfall was effectively instigated by her former Cabinet colleague, Michael Heseltine, when he challenged her for the party leadership in November 1990. Although she won the first round of voting, she did so by too small a margin to seal the contest outright. To do so she had to secure the backing of an *absolute majority*—that is, more than half—of all Tory MPs and achieve 15 per cent more votes than her nearest rival. She narrowly missed the target. Despite initially announcing her intention to continue fighting through the second round, in the interim Mrs Thatcher was visited by a deputation of backbenchers who made it clear she had lost the backing of many MPs. After taking counsel from fellow ministers she withdrew her candidacy—paving the way for Mr Major's election.

Cabinet versus government—what's the difference?

Despite the clear moves towards more presidential—or 'prime ministerial'—forms of government, constitutionally the role of Cabinet remains of paramount importance in the exercise of elected power in Britain. So what exactly is the 'Cabinet', and how does it differ from and relate to the 'government'?

The **Cabinet** is a 'subset' of the government. While the latter comprises *all* ministers appointed by the PM, the former is composed of only the most senior.

Governments and Cabinets have been known to vary wildly in size from one administration to another, with some favouring a more compact, rationalized approach and others a more all-embracing one.

As explained in Chapter 2, governments can number anything between eighty and 100-plus ministers. Indeed, in October 2011 the Coalition was criticized by the Commons Public Administration Committee for hitting record highs—with some 119 ministers and forty-six ministerial aides on the government's payroll. Historically, the average Cabinet size has been twenty—though at times it has been significantly larger or smaller. For much of the Second World War, Winston Churchill ran a Cabinet numbering sixty-eight ministers, while in 1922 Andrew Bonar Law formed a peacetime Cabinet of only sixteen. In contrast, Labour PMs have tended to appoint larger Cabinets—at least in part as a bulwark against what the party for many years saw as the intransigence of senior civil servants when presented with its policies in government. Wilson had one Cabinet comprising twenty-four members and Mr Blair raised the bar to twenty-six. Mr Brown, meanwhile, appointed an enlarged 'hybrid' first Cabinet, effectively numbering twenty-nine—before expanding it still further, to thirty-four (including 'occasional' members like Olympics Minister Tessa Jowell), in his October 2008 reshuffle. Its numbers were boosted, in part, by Mr Brown's decision to create a new Department of Energy and Climate Change (DECC), and reinstate two distinct offices for Defence and Scotland, in response to criticisms from military chiefs and the devolved Scottish Government respectively of his earlier decision to combine the two under one minister. Despite the overall size of the government of which it is part, the Coalition Cabinet has generally numbered around twenty-three ministers.

Cabinet ministers have, until recently, always been either MPs or peers. Though some critics and constitutional historians regard the idea of peers—lords or ladies who have no democratic mandate—being entrusted with ministerial briefs as contentious, there have been many high-profile examples of such appointments, including Lord Young of Graffham (Trade and Industry Secretary under Mrs Thatcher and appointed by Mr Cameron to lead a review of health and safety laws) and Lord Adonis (first Education Minister then Transport Secretary in Blair's and Brown's administrations). Today the appointment of peers to senior positions (if not that of PM) scarcely raises an eyebrow.

Mr Brown took the PM's discretion to choose ministers from outside the Commons to a new level, with his declaration on entering office that he wanted a pluralistic 'government of all the talents'. This assertion—an extension of the 'big tent' politics for which Mr Blair was often criticized by Labour traditionalists—saw several individuals from outside his party appointed to senior advisory positions in government. Baron Jones of Birmingham, former director-general of the Confederation of British Industry (CBI), was appointed a minister at the then Department of Business, Enterprise, and Regulatory

Reform (BERR)—despite making it clear he had no intention of joining the Labour Party. Sir Mark Malloch Brown, former UN deputy secretary-general and neither a peer nor an MP, was appointed Minister for Africa, Asia, and the UN. Mr Brown also dispensed with another Cabinet tradition: since 1963 its meetings had generally been held on Thursdays, but he switched them to Tuesdays.

Most Cabinet ministers have the title **secretary of state**, rather than **minister of state**, denoting their seniority. This normally means they head up a major spending department, such as health, and often have several junior ministers—in government but not Cabinet—answerable to them. The choice of ministerial posts included in the Cabinet can vary greatly, depending on the political priorities of the day. Until Mr Blair's election win in 1997, overseas aid/development was treated as a relatively minor ministerial area and was the responsibility of a non-Cabinet minister in the Foreign Office. When Labour was re-elected the post was promoted to become 'International Development Secretary', with his/her own dedicated ministry.

In addition to obvious senior departmental posts, traditionally the Cabinet also contains one or two honorary ones awarded to loyal lieutenants of the prime minister whom he/she wants to keep close at hand, but for more general duties than overseeing specific portfolios. One such post is that of 'Chancellor of the Duchy of Lancaster'—a sinecure deriving from an office once involved in the daily management of the sovereign's one significant surviving estate following the handover of the Crown Lands to the state (see p. 22). When veteran Labour MP Jack Cunningham was appointed to this post in 1998 the media dubbed him variously 'Cabinet enforcer' and 'Cabinet fixer' because his brief was taking charge of coordinating the government's message in its dealings with press and public. Another such post is the recent addition of 'Minister without Portfolio', an office briefly assumed after the 1997 election by Mr Blair's close ally, Peter Mandelson (who made two subsequent returns to the Cabinet). In forming his coalition, meanwhile, Mr Cameron dispensed with convention by appointing the Lib Dem leader, Nick Clegg, Deputy Prime Minister without allocating him a departmental brief. On day one of their collaborative administration, the two leaders jointly took the stand at a press conference in the Downing Street garden, as if intending to share the top job. As of November 2012, following Mr Cameron's reshuffle that September, the Coalition Cabinet was as listed in Table 3.1.

So much for the Cabinet: what of the government as a whole? Its size can also vary, but in modern times it has become customary for it to number anything up to a hundred ministers. The most junior ministerial post is that of **parliamentary under-secretary**, ranking beneath both ministers and secretaries of state. Also included in the overall tally are government whips and any MP appointed a **parliamentary private secretary (PPS)**. These are junior posts ascribed to ambitious MPs who aspire to become ministers. They serve as

Table 3.1 Composition of the UK Cabinet (November 2012)

Title	Name
Prime Minister/First Lord of the Treasury/Minister for the Civil Service	David Cameron
Deputy Prime Minister, Lord President of the Council	Nick Clegg
Chancellor of the Exchequer	George Osborne
Secretary of State for Foreign and Commonwealth Affairs (Foreign Secretary) and First Secretary of State	William Hague
Secretary of State for Justice/Lord Chancellor	Chris Grayling
Secretary of State for the Home Department (Home Secretary) and Minister for Women and Equality	Theresa May
Secretary of State for Defence	Phillip Hammond
Secretary of State for Health	Jeremy Hunt
Secretary of State for Energy and Climate Change	Edward Davey
Secretary of State for the Environment, Food, and Rural Affairs	Owen Paterson
Secretary of State for International Development	Justine Greening
Secretary of State for Business, Innovation, and Skills	Vince Cable
Secretary of State for Work and Pensions	Iain Duncan Smith
Secretary of State for Transport	Patrick McLoughlin
Secretary of State for Communities and Local Government	Eric Pickles
Chief Whip	Sir George Young
Secretary of State for Education	Michael Gove
Secretary of State for Culture, Olympics, Media, and Sport	Maria Miller
Secretary of State for Northern Ireland	Theresa Villiers
Secretary of State for Wales	David Jones
Secretary of State for Scotland	Michael Moore
Leader of the House of Lords, Chancellor of the Duchy of Lancaster	Lord Strathclyde
Chief Secretary to the Treasury	Danny Alexander
The following senior ministers are also allowed to attend Cabinet:	
Minister for Universities, Science, and Skills	David Willetts
Attorney General	Dominic Grieve
Solicitor General	Oliver Heald
Minister for the Cabinet Office, Paymaster General	Francis Maude
Minister without Portfolio, with responsibility for economic policy	Kenneth Clarke
Minister without Portfolio	Grant Shapps
Minister of State for the Cabinet Office, with responsibility to the PM for policy	Oliver Letwin
Leader of the House of Commons	Andrew Lansley

NOTE: A regularly updated version of this table can be found on the Online Resource Centre.

points of contact/liaison in Parliament (or, as some would have it, 'spies') for serving ministers and are informally connected to their departments. The PM tends to have two PPSs.

Ministerial salaries

In recognition of their higher levels of responsibility, ministers who are MPs receive substantially higher salaries than backbenchers. The precise levels of ministerial salaries can vary significantly, depending on the degree of their additional responsibilities and the complexity of their jobs. As of the 2008/9 tax year then PM Mr Brown and his ministers declined their automatic annual 1.5 per cent salary increases in a gesture of solidarity with public sector workers, whose pay rises were being limited because of (in his words) the 'economic uncertainty' of the times. This initially meant Mr Brown was paid £132,923 on top of his basic MP salary of £64,766 (a total income of £198,661—several thousand less than his entitlement), but soon after he left office in May 2010 it emerged that for the previous year he had quietly taken a further cut—bringing his salary nearer the level of ordinary senior ministers (£150,000). For the two years prior to Labour's electoral defeat, Cabinet ministers and the government Chief Whip had each earned £145,492 in total. During his first week in power, Mr Cameron went further, in an apparent goodwill gesture ahead of public spending cuts. By cutting salaries of those around the top table by 5 per cent in absolute terms, and freezing them at those levels for the rest of the parliament, he brought his own political earnings down to £142,500, those of Cabinet ministers to £134,565, and pay for ministers of state outside Cabinet from £100,568 under Labour to £98,740.

Although peers are not yet paid, those occupying government positions do receive parliamentary remuneration. Cabinet ministers drawn from the Lords receive £101,038, while ministers of state get £78,891. Until 2007 the highest-paid minister of all was not the PM but the Lord Chancellor, who was entitled to the princely sum of £232,900. But both Coalition incumbents thus far, Kenneth Clarke and Chris Grayling, and their immediate predecessor, Jack Straw, are MPs, and have therefore drawn £145,492 and £134,565 respectively.

Substantial salaries are also paid to senior Opposition frontbenchers, although at a lower level than those of their government counterparts. The Leader of the Opposition currently earns £139,355 a year.

Collective responsibility, ministerial responsibility, and the ministerial code

The actions of ministers, especially those in Cabinet, are governed by two constitutional conventions—collective responsibility and individual ministerial responsibility—and an increasingly strict statutory 'rule book' known as the ministerial code.

Collective responsibility

Cabinet ministers are expected to endorse publicly the actions of governments of which they are members, even if they do not agree with them privately. This doctrine—known as **collective responsibility**—rests on the assumption that individual ministers are broadly in favour of the policy programme adopted by their government but may occasionally disagree with specific proposals. It has therefore long been the custom for ministers to bite their tongues. On many notable occasions, however, individuals have found themselves increasingly out of step with the views of their Cabinet colleagues over time and have ultimately resigned—freeing themselves to speak out.

In 1986 then Defence Secretary Mr Heseltine quit the Cabinet over the proposed merger of Westland, Britain's last surviving helicopter manufacturer, with US company Sikorsky. He stormed out of a Cabinet meeting in full view of waiting television cameras, making it clear he was exasperated with what he saw as Mrs Thatcher's dictatorial decision-making style. In 2003 the late Robin Cook, then Leader of the House, resigned from government in protest at Mr Blair's decision to invade Iraq. He was followed, some time after the invasion, by International Development Secretary Ms Short, who blamed the country's chaotic reconstruction following Saddam's defeat for her decision. John Denham, reappointed to the Cabinet under Mr Brown, resigned from a junior post over Iraq. More recently, in July 2012 ministerial aide Conor Burns quit his Coalition government post, and fellow Tory Angie Bray was sacked, over their opposition to Lords reform.

Very occasionally collective responsibility has been waived by PMs to encourage frank and open debate about serious constitutional matters. In a risky, but ultimately shrewd, tactical manoeuvre, in 1975 Labour PM Wilson temporarily suspended it in relation to a debate over an issue he feared would otherwise create potentially fatal Cabinet divisions. Having called a national referendum on Britain's continued membership of the European Community (which he subsequently won), he allowed Cabinet members strongly opposed to the policy to campaign for a 'no' vote. Among the Eurosceptics was left-winger Tony Benn, who argued the 'Common Market' (as it was widely known) would destroy British jobs by preventing Britain using protectionism—or customs duties—to inflate the price of imports of manufactured goods, in the interests of persuading people to 'buy British'. Asked about his similarly inclusive policy towards troublesome colleagues, US President Lyndon B. Johnson once remarked of FBI director J. Edgar Hoover:

❝ It's probably better to have him inside the tent pissing out than outside the tent pissing in. ❞

In the early days of the Coalition there were signs that Messrs Cameron and Clegg were looking to mimic Mr Wilson's tactic in relation to policies over which there remained clear divisions between their parties. In a major dilution of the binding nature of collective responsibility, to win the latter's support the Conservatives agreed to let Lib Dem frontbenchers 'continue to make the case for' alternative policies in areas like the proposed renewal of Britain's Trident nuclear programme, while Tory ministers were allowed to campaign against the introduction of the alternative vote (see p. 133) in the run-up to the May 2011 referendum on electoral reform. But, while the coalition agreement allowed for limited open Cabinet 'dissent' in specified areas, Lib Dem MPs (both front and backbench) were generally bound by an undertaking not to vote *against* policy proposals—only abstain.

Individual ministerial responsibility

The other major convention relating to ministers' work is that of **individual ministerial responsibility**. This is the doctrine that, should a serious error or scandal occur 'on the watch' of a departmental minister, he/she should do the honourable thing and resign. Lord Carrington, for example, stepped down as Foreign Secretary over the Argentine invasion of the Falkland Islands in 1982.

In contrast, recent history is littered with examples of significant departmental errors for which ministers have been reluctant to take the blame. The fiasco over Britain's sudden withdrawal from the European exchange rate mechanism (ERM) in 1992 would, on many other occasions, have seen the immediate departure of the Chancellor of the Exchequer—the minister in charge of the economy. In fact, then Chancellor Norman Lamont stayed on for several months before belatedly being sacked by PM Mr Major.

Geoff Hoon, Defence Secretary at the time of the Iraq invasion, survived numerous controversies surrounding everything from the non-discovery of Saddam's alleged WMDs to a scandal over the inadequate military equipment with which British soldiers were revealed to be fighting in both Iraq and Afghanistan. And, nearly a decade later, Culture Secretary Mr Hunt doggedly defied calls for his scalp following the Leveson Inquiry's revelations about email exchanges between his special adviser and a senior News Corp lobbyist focusing on the company's bid to take over BSkyB—an example of ministerial responsibility which some critics, including outspoken Culture, Media, and Sport Select Committee member Tom Watson, argued was also a breach of the ministerial code (see pp. 103–4).

Those who have 'fallen on their swords' recently include Liam Fox, who was forced to resign as Defence Secretary in October 2011 following revelations he had allowed his former best man, Adam Werritty, to accompany him on official overseas visits and attend sensitive meetings that might have aided the latter's business interests. Mr Werritty, a freelance corporate lobbyist who had not received Ministry of Defence security clearance, had exacerbated the situation by handing out business cards falsely claiming to be an adviser to Dr Fox. Questions were also raised about Dr Fox's ongoing, taxpayer-funded trips to Sri Lanka, where he had previously been involved in facilitating a peace process between government and Tamil forces, but for which he held no formal ministerial brief.

In practice, ministers are often sacked before they have a chance to quit. The premier's ability to remove colleagues unceremoniously dates back to a convention initiated by William Pitt in the early nineteenth century and perfected by his Tory successor, Harold Macmillan, when on Friday 13 July 1962 he sacked seven ministers in one go in a notorious 'Night of the Long Knives'. Sackings almost always precipitate 'Cabinet reshuffles', during which other ministers are moved from one job to another to fill gaps created by the removal of their colleagues.

The ministerial code

The most recent redraft of the **ministerial code** was agreed by the then newly formed Coalition government in May 2010. Its opening line sets the tone of the document, stating:

❝ Ministers of the Crown are expected to behave in a way that upholds the highest standards of propriety. ❞

The implication is clear: while Lord Nolan's Seven Principles of Public Life (see Table 2.4) are intended to encourage responsible behaviour by MPs and peers generally, the bar is raised higher for members of Her Majesty's government. To this end, it lays out the following ten additional principles governing ministerial conduct:

(a) The principle of collective responsibility, save where it is explicitly set aside, applies to all ministers.

(b) Ministers have a duty to Parliament to account, and be held to account, for the policies, decisions, and actions of their departments and agencies.

(c) It is of paramount importance that ministers give accurate and truthful information to Parliament, correcting any inadvertent error at the earliest opportunity. Ministers who knowingly mislead Parliament will be expected to offer their resignations.

(d) Ministers should be as open as possible with Parliament and public, refusing to provide information only when disclosure would not be in the public interest, which should be decided in accordance with the relevant statutes and the Freedom of Information Act 2000.

(e) Ministers should similarly require civil servants who give evidence before Parliamentary Committees on their behalf and under their direction to be as helpful as possible in providing accurate, truthful, and full information in accordance with the duties and responsibilities of civil servants as set out in the Civil Service Code.

(f) Ministers must ensure that no conflict arises, or appears to arise, between their public duties and private interests.

(g) Ministers should not accept any gift or hospitality which might, or might reasonably appear to, compromise their judgement or place them under an improper obligation.

(h) Ministers in the Commons must keep separate their roles as minister and constituency member.

(i) Ministers must not use government resources for party political purposes.

(j) Ministers must uphold the political impartiality of the civil service and not ask civil servants to act in any way which would conflict with the Civil Service Code as set out in the Constitutional Reform and Governance Act 2010.

The code stipulates that it is the PM's personal responsibility to refer alleged breaches to an Independent Adviser on Ministerial Interests (at time of writing Sir Alex Allan), which Mr Cameron did in June 2012 in relation to the expenses claims of the Conservative Party's then Co-chairman Baroness Warsi (see p. 59). It goes on to lay out at some length the array of duties that accompany ministerial office—ranging from their obligation to chair departmental board meetings to their responsibility for the conduct of those they themselves appoint, including special advisers (see p. 112). It was in relation to this latter point that Mr Hunt faced calls for his resignation over the Murdoch emails affair. Even more important, perhaps, than their responsibility for their staff's conduct is ministers' obligation to ensure no conflicts of interest arise—or 'could reasonably be perceived to arise'—between their ministerial positions and private interests, 'financial or otherwise'. To this end, a formal List of Ministers' Interests is now published online, and regularly updated, as an additional level of transparency beyond the Register of Members' Interests to which all MPs are subject. Among the interests declared by Mr Cameron on the list as of December 2011 were his vice-presidency of the National Society for Epilepsy, presidency of the Oxfordshire Beekeepers' Association, and honorary membership of Ellesborough Golf Club. Both Mr Cameron and Mr Clegg also declared relevant roles held by their wives, including Samantha Cameron's post as creative consultant of upmarket Bond Street stationers Smythson, and Miriam Clegg's as both a partner at international law firm Dechert and independent adviser to Spanish construction company Acciona.

The Cabinet Office and Cabinet committees

The Cabinet Office is effectively the 'Civil Service of the Cabinet'—the administrative staff and machinery that organizes its meetings and business on a day-to-day basis. It comprises a Cabinet Secretariat, responsible for recording the minutes of Cabinet meetings, and the Office of Public Service, which over-sees overall government business. It is headed by the Cabinet Secretary (see p. 85).

In turn, the Secretariat is made up of six separate departmental secretariats:

- Economic and Domestic Affairs Secretariat;
- Defence and Overseas Affairs Secretariat;
- European Secretariat;
- Constitution Secretariat;
- Central Secretariat;
- Intelligence Support Secretariat.

In addition, **Cabinet committees** are increasingly formed to deal with the finer points of policymaking. They tend to be chaired by ministers whose personal views are close to those of the PM. Under the Coalition, most of the nine full cabinet committees and their sixteen subcommittees have been chaired by the so-called 'quartet' of most senior ministers: Mr Cameron, Mr Clegg, Mr Osborne, and Chief Secretary to the Treasury Danny Alexander. There are sev-eral types of Cabinet committee, as outlined in the table entitled 'Types of cab-inet committee' to be found on the Online Resource Centre.

The Civil Service

If ministers are the architects of government—brainstorming and formulating policies in Cabinet—civil servants are the stolid engineers on the factory floor, responsible for oiling the machinery of state that puts these ideas into practice. The 'Civil Service' is the collective term for the administrative structure that carries out the work of government departments and the numerous agencies that implement policies on their behalf.

Dating back to the secretariats that first emerged, piecemeal, in the eigh-teenth century, the Civil Service has become the one constant in the UK system of government. The fact that government continues to operate uninterrupted even after a governing party has changed at an election (and, indeed, while the country is without any MPs—although not without ministers—during election campaigns) is largely down to the continuity guaranteed by the professionals responsible for 'keeping things running'. Its continuity role has rarely been more starkly apparent than during the five days between the May 2010 election and the formation of the Coalition, when caretaker PM Mr Brown agreed to give both other main parties access to then Cabinet Secretary Sir Gus and other high-level mandarins as they worked on the terms of their prospective deal. He also revealed the existence of a working document he had asked Sir Gus (jokingly nicknamed 'GOD' by colleagues) to produce in the run-up to the election clarifying the constitutional position of sitting premiers and Opposition leaders in a hung Parliament.

The foundations of today's Civil Service were laid in the Northcote–Trevelyan Report 1854, which stipulated that:

- all appointments should be made on *merit*;
- there should be *fair and open competition* for advertised posts.

Efforts were quickly made to establish a professional structure for the Civil Service, and successive governments have made this progressively more rigorous. Senior civil servants—known as 'mandarins'—are recruited by independent Civil Service Commissioners through the Civil Service Board. Some recruits rise to senior ranks very quickly, via the Fast Stream development programme, which admits around 300 graduates a year.

Altogether, Her Majesty's Civil Service comprises around 500,000 officials working across anything up to sixty departments and a hundred associated bodies—primarily executive agencies (see pp. 107–10)—based principally at Whitehall and Millbank, a stone's throw from Parliament. Each department is headed by a **permanent secretary**. As with lower-ranking civil servants, they are employed because of their expertise in the particular areas overseen by their departments. They are not to be confused with secretaries of state, and indeed often have far longer records of service to their departments than such individuals, given that they are permanent Crown employees and, as such, will remain in post irrespective of whether the government changes at an election. Although they come into close daily contact with ministers and often advise them on policy, as paid officials permanent secretaries are expected to be politically neutral at all times.

Political neutrality in practice

Although the doctrine of 'political neutrality' is held sacrosanct in the Civil Service, controversies have sometimes arisen over civil servants who have acted in an apparently politically motivated way. The machinations of Sir Humphrey Appleby—the odious permanent secretary for the Ministry for Administrative Affairs in the classic 1980s BBC1 sitcoms *Yes, Minister* and *Yes, Prime Minister*—are said to have been inspired by real-life shenanigans in Whitehall circles. But perhaps the most significant Civil Service scandal of modern times occurred in 1985, when Clive Ponting, a civil servant in the Ministry of Defence, was tried under the Official Secrets Act 1911 for passing classified details to an unauthorized person about the sinking during the Falklands War of the Argentine ship the *General Belgrano*—allegedly while it was both retreating and outside the 'exclusion zone' declared by the British government around the islands. Although Ponting, who went on to be a successful writer, was acquitted of breaching s. 2 of the Act, the case prompted then

Cabinet Secretary Sir Robin Butler to issue the following 'Note'—by way of an addendum to the code of conduct earlier drafted for the Civil Service:

> ❝ The determination of policy is the responsibility of the minister . . . When, having been given all the relevant information and advice, the minister has taken the decision, it is the duty of civil servants loyally to carry out that decision . . . Civil servants are under an obligation to keep the confidences to which they become privy in the course of their official duties. ❞

Following the Ponting affair and a series of smaller-scale 'leaks' by similarly ethically motivated 'whistle-blowers', new stipulations were drawn up to clarify the *levels* of political neutrality expected of civil servants on different rungs of the professional ladder. While civil servants of all ranks were expected to remain politically impartial in their day-to-day behaviour in the workplace, it was decided the extent to which they had to be entirely neutral *outside* work would depend on their seniority (see table entitled 'Levels of political impartiality in the Civil Service', on the Online Resource Centre). Yet leaks have continued. The Home Office was embroiled in controversy after a series of leaks to then Opposition MP Damian Green led to the police searching his office (see p. 9) in November 2008, and months later a disc containing details of MPs' expenses claims was leaked to *The Daily Telegraph* (see p. 55).

In running their departments on a day-to-day basis, civil servants are expected to abide by the 'three Es'—'economy, efficiency, and effectiveness'. This maxim has been underlined by two key milestones: the Efficiency Strategy published in 1979 by Sir Derek (now Lord) Rayner and the 1982 Financial Management Initiative, which sought to provide departmental managers with 'a clear view' of the responsibilities of their individual ministries.

Civil Service accountability

Several recent government initiatives have attempted to give the Civil Service a better name by making it appear leaner and meaner. In 1991 Mr Major launched a 'Citizen's Charter' calling for a 'revolution in public services'. In theory, this gave the public recourse to complain about everything from lack of information to discourtesy in their dealings with government departments. In January 2002 Charter Mark services were extended to cover the conduct of purely *internal* departmental divisions that did not come into direct contact with the public. New Labour coined the buzz-phrase 'joined-up government' to refer to its attempts to encourage separate departments to collaborate.

Executive agencies

The work of the Civil Service is so all-consuming and involved that governments have often tried to rationalize departments, breaking them down into smaller, more manageable units. These units—effectively *subsets* of their parent departments—focus exclusively on the *delivery*, rather than *formulation*, of policy. Today most are known as '**executive agencies**'.

Initially established in 1988 by Mrs Thatcher—who sought to move away from what she saw as an overcentralized, monolithic structure—these smaller-scale, breakaway departmental bodies were designed to resemble commercial companies rather than traditional organs of government. As such, they were each given their own chief executive, who presided over a board of directors—at the time a radical departure from the bureaucratic way the Civil Service had previously been run. Unlike commercial companies, agencies had no shareholders (and therefore no profit motive) and were staffed by civil servants seconded from their parent departments. But as time went on, their managers were increasingly drafted in from industry, rather than graduating from the ranks of the Service itself (the theory being that importing talent from the private sector would increase efficiency). This approach was ultimately to have a sweeping impact across the public sector that continues to be felt today, with everything from local NHS trusts to further education colleges adopting a chief executive and board model at their helm.

Initially there were only a handful of executive agencies, the first of which, the Vehicle Inspectorate—now the Vehicle and Operator Services Agency (VOSA)—was established in August 1988. Their number went on to mushroom, particularly under Labour, which ended up with 130 in total—ninety-plus reporting to government departments at Whitehall, with the remaining number answering to the three devolved administrations in Scotland, Wales, and Northern Ireland. While some smaller spending departments have only one or two agencies working under them, bigger ones like the Home Office and Department for Work and Pensions (DWP) allocate much of their day-to-day work to agencies. The single biggest agency, in terms of staffing and budget, is Jobcentre Plus, which employs 100,000 people and spends £4bn a year of taxpayers' money. With thirty-six, the Ministry of Defence (MoD) has the most.

One of the major criticisms of executive agencies is that they are used by ministers to absolve themselves from individual ministerial responsibility. By devolving power to 'breakaway' sections of their departments, ministers might disclaim personal liability for their mistakes. This arguably happened in November 2007 when Chancellor Alistair Darling refused to accept culpability for the loss of two unencrypted computer discs containing the names, addresses, birthdates, National Insurance (NI) numbers, and bank details of 25 million families by HM Revenue and Customs (HMRC), an executive agency of the Treasury (see p. 244). The Child Benefit-related data had been on its way to the National Audit Office (NAO) when it was mislaid. In the ensuing furore it was HMRC's chief executive, Paul Gray, who resigned—not Mr Darling.

Quangos

Long before executive agencies existed there were already a large number of taxpayer-funded organizations carrying out work delegated by government departments. But, historically, these non-departmental public bodies (NDPBs) tended to be staffed not by seconded civil servants from specific departments of state, but their own employees, which they recruited as discrete entities, notionally independent of government. Over time an umbrella term has evolved for these bodies: 'quasi-autonomous non-governmental organizations'—or '**quangos**'.

Quangos are often confused with executive agencies, and it is easy to see why. Like agencies they have their own management boards—although these are headed by honorary chairpersons, rather than salaried chief executives. They also control significant, largely taxpayer-funded, budgets.

Perhaps unsurprisingly, quangos frequently come under fire from the media for lacking accountability. Whereas agencies are at least answerable to ministers who can be ejected at elections, quangos have traditionally had levels of autonomy putting them beyond such direct 'control'. Yet, like agencies, they receive most of their funding from taxpayers—through the aegis of related departments. Much of the budget for Arts Council England (ACE), for example, comes from the Department for Culture, Media, and Sport (DCMS).

Lack of accountability is one criticism levelled at quangos; another is nepotism. How can we be certain that boards appointed by ministers are genuinely chosen on merit, rather than because they are friends and/or political allies? The recently disbanded BBC Board of Governors—charged with holding the Corporation to account for its public service broadcasting responsibilities—was a quango in all but name. Little surprise, then, that Mr Blair was criticized for choosing former Labour donor Gavyn Davies as its chairman in 2000.

Sustained criticism of the 'quangocracy' has led to several recent moves to address the nepotism question. In 2000 the government introduced an Appointments Commission to propose chairpersons and non-executive directors of NHS bodies, including hospitals, primary care trusts, and strategic health authorities (see Chapter 6). It also has powers to vet appointees to other local, regional, and national quangos. These appointments are themselves regulated by an Office of the Commissioner for Public Appointments (OCPA).

In July 1996 a democratic audit identified 6,224 executive and advisory quangos, run by 66,000–73,500 people and responsible for spending £60.4bn. On entering power, Mr Blair vowed to scrap 'unaccountable quangos' and Mr Brown spoke of a 'bonfire of the quangos'. But in August 2007 Cabinet Office figures revealed quangos had spent £167.5bn the previous year. The Coalition was quick to revive the 'bonfire' concept on entering office, with Cabinet Office Minister Francis Maude publishing a list of 192 destined to be culled and a further 118 intended for merger in October 2010. While few can have lamented the passing of obscure bodies like the Zoos Forum or the Government Hospitality Advisory Committee on the Purchase of Wines, there was widespread criticism of the decision to scrap the UK Film Council, which had co-funded a string of globally successful British-made movies, including that year's big Oscar winner, the *King's Speech*, while the government's pledge to replace the Audit Commission—the national quango responsible for auditing council accounts—with a patchwork of private contractors was seen by some as an example of free market ideology trumping transparency. As time passed, the Coalition was also accused of 'smoke and mirrors'—liberally chopping quangos in some areas, while introducing swathes of new ones elsewhere. According to a widely reported exchange between Mr Cameron and Labour leader Ed Miliband during PMQs on 29 June 2011, the Coalition's health reforms are likely to see the number of quangos in the NHS alone more than triple, from 163 to 521.

Taskforces and tsars

A new form of non-elected body created by New Labour, particularly during its first term, the number of taskforces in place by 2000 was already forty-four. They were generally set up to deal with short-term issues of public concern, and were headed by senior public figures dubbed 'tsars' (effectively, hired troubleshooters). Examples include the Rough Sleepers' Unit, led by 'Homelessness Tsar' Louise Casey, which set out to tackle street homelessness, and a short-lived drugs taskforce run by 'Drugs Tsar' Keith Hellawell. Though the term 'taskforce' is seldom heard today, Mr Cameron has continued the trend for 'tsars', allowing the term to be used to denote advisory roles he gave to former Labour MPs Alan Milburn and Lord Hutton (as 'Social Mobility Tsar' and 'Pensions Tsar' respectively), current Labour MP Frank Field ('Poverty Tsar'), and Will Hutton, ex-editor of the *Observer* ('Fair Pay Tsar').

Think tanks, the private sector, and the future of public policymaking

At time of writing it appeared that even policymaking—long the preserve of Whitehall mandarins and their underlings—was on the verge of being outsourced to the private sector. In a controversial address to independent think tank the Institute for Government, May 2012 saw then recently installed Cabinet Secretary Sir Jeremy moot the 'perfectly legitimate' idea of contracting private companies to come up with future ministerial initiatives. In so doing, he appeared to be advocating a move which, critics argued, could open up the highly sensitive area of policy formulation to commercial conflicts of interest; dilute the institutional memory of the Civil Service itself; and relegate highly knowledgeable and experienced officials to the status of mere implementers and administrators. Within weeks Mr Maude had published even more radical proposals, including allowing ministers to appoint future permanent secretaries, rather than relying on the Civil Service's own promotional structure—an idea which immediately revived concerns about the 'politicization' of policy delivery. The proposals—which followed the departure from Downing Street of Steve Hilton, Mr Cameron's policy guru and an originator of his 'Big Society' concept for franchising out public services—appeared to have been prompted by a desire by ministers to retain an appearance of radical zeal for public sector reform. It remains to be seen if it will be acted on.

Spin doctors and special advisers

Under the ministerial code, each Cabinet minister is entitled to employ up to two special advisers—colloquially known as 'SPADs'—while other government ministers permitted to attend Cabinet meetings may each appoint one. The total number of special advisers and, in particular, **spin doctors**—those largely concerned with presenting policy effectively through the media—has hugely multiplied in recent years. By the end of Mr Major's reign they had increased to thirty-eight, but under Mr Blair there were consistently as many as seventy-four at the highest level. At its peak the advisers' salary bill topped £3.6m, but their number has since declined.

Unlike civil servants, special advisers and spin doctors are normally *party*, rather than government, appointees. This was the case with most Downing Street big-hitters of the Blair years, including Mr Campbell and Mr Powell. Sometimes the edges are more blurred, however: Sir Bernard Ingham started out as a civil servant, before switching to the Conservative Party's payroll while Mrs Thatcher was PM. When a party is in opposition it pays for its advisers, but once in government they (like civil servants) are usually paid from public funds.

Under Mr Blair some special advisers became bywords for cold-hearted calculation. Jo Moore, an adviser at the Department of Transport, Local Government, and the Regions (DTLR), was forced to resign in February 2002 following a series of controversies about her management style, and in particular the publication of an explosive email she sent on 11 September the previous year—the date of the terrorist attacks on the Twin Towers—describing it as a 'very good day' to 'bury' bad news.

Mr Blair's reliance on advice from spin doctors and party appointees over senior civil servants frequently saw him accused of 'politicizing' the Civil Service by the back door. One of his first actions on taking office was to pass an executive order allowing senior advisers like Mr Campbell and Mr Powell to issue orders to civil servants. Mr Brown revoked this, symbolically, within hours of replacing Mr Blair at Number 10, but cynics dismissed even this gesture as spin, in light of recent statistics indicating that the number of government special advisers, spin doctors, and press and marketing staff continued to climb during his time in power. A Whitehall audit found that sixty-eight additional special advisers were employed by ministers during 2007, and all were still in post at the end of the year—six months after Mr Brown took office. The overall number of press office staff (many civil servants, but nonetheless employed to put a positive gloss on government policy) had risen to 3,250. Between 1997 and 2007 Labour increased the annual cost of 'government PR' (public relations) to £338m—with a £15m rise in 2007 alone.

In July 2001, following years of controversy about Labour's reliance on political advisers, a Code of Conduct for Special Advisers was published. It defined them as 'temporary civil servants', who did not necessarily have to be appointed 'on merit' but were nonetheless expected to comply with the Civil Service Code, and could not use 'official resources', such as stationery, for party political purposes. If they wished to campaign on behalf of their ministers during the lead-up to an election, they must first resign from their posts in recognition of their political affiliation. Mr Campbell did this in 2005.

The Parliamentary Ombudsman

Despite its title, the **Parliamentary Commissioner for Administration** (part of a wider regulatory body known as the **Parliamentary and Health Service Ombudsman**) is charged with investigating public complaints not about Parliament itself, but government departments and other public bodies, including quangos. The basis of an individual's complaint has to be that he/she has suffered an injustice due to maladministration arising from delay, faulty procedures, errors, unfairness, and/or bias. Complaints against judges, police officers, and councils are investigated by separate bodies and procedures.

The Ombudsman is sometimes derided as 'a watchdog without teeth' because, even though it can recommend that a department or body should 'remedy' mistakes, its findings of maladministration cannot be *enforced*.

Since devolution there have been separate ombudsmen for Scotland and Wales.

▌Devolved government—executive decision-making in the regions

Chapters 1 and 2 laid out, first, the manner in which devolution unfolded in Britain and the forms of government subsequently settled on in each of the three countries outside England. There follows a brief overview of the manner in which government is constituted in those countries.

The Scottish Government/Executive

Just as the legislative process prevailing in Scotland is distinct from that which applies in Wales and Northern Ireland, so too is its executive framework. Scotland now boasts its own **Scottish Government**. Until recently this was known as the **Scottish Executive**, but when the Scottish Nationalist Party (SNP) became the largest party in the Holyrood Parliament in May 2007 and its leader, Alex Salmond, replaced Labour's Jack McConnell as First Minister, he renamed it. The Scottish Government is much more fully formed than its cousins in Cardiff and Stormont. Like the British government it has its own Cabinet, which meets on Tuesday mornings at Bute House in Edinburgh's Charlotte Square, the First Minister's official residence. The administration itself is based at St Andrew's House, along with its own secretariat, and has two subcommittees: a Cabinet subcommittee on legislation and an emergency room Cabinet subcommittee.

The Welsh Assembly Government/Welsh Executive

Like the Scottish Executive the Welsh Executive recently changed its name to the Welsh Assembly Government to reflect the increasing autonomy granted to it. It, too, is led by a First Minister—Labour leader Carwyn Jones, who replaced his long-time predecessor, Rhodri Morgan, in December 2009. After the 2007 Welsh Assembly election Labour entered a coalition with the Welsh nationalist party, Plaid Cymru, under the banner 'One Wales', but since May 2011, when it scored its biggest victory since the introduction of devolution, it has governed alone.

The Northern Ireland Executive

The 'power-sharing executive' in Northern Ireland has been a coalition since its rocky inception more than seven years ago—and only began to function properly following the conclusion of a substantive peace agreement in spring 2007. As of May 2011 the executive remained a coalition of the two biggest parties, the Democratic Unionist Party (DUP) and Sinn Féin.

☰ Topical feature idea

The Civil Service is Britain's single biggest employer, with departmental head offices at Whitehall but staff based the length and breadth of the country—working everywhere from local tax offices to branches of Jobcentre Plus. But the past two years have witnessed wage freezes and thousands of redundancies across the UK. The Coalition is now planning to abandon the decades-old practice of negotiating Civil Service pay on a national basis, meaning that wide regional disparities in salary levels could soon emerge. How big an employer is the Civil Service in your area and how many job losses, if any, have there been? What does a typical day in the life of a civil servant working in your local Jobcentre Plus branch or tax office entail, how much are they paid, and what would happen if they were not there to do their job? How are staff coping with a recruitment freeze, pay cuts, and a high workload due to recent rises in unemployment?

✳ Current issues

- **The difficulties of coalition government:** both Tory and Lib Dem backbenchers are becoming increasingly restive over the policy compromises agreed by their leaders in government, and their parties' falling opinion poll ratings, meaning the second half of the Coalition's term looks set to be a rockier ride.

- **The future of collective responsibility, the whip system, and party discipline:** despite being in coalition, the Conservatives and Lib Dems continue to fight council and European elections on different manifestos, and Mr Cameron and his fellow Tories actively campaigned against electoral reform in the run-up to the May 2011 AV referendum. Similarly, the Lib Dems are still allowed to speak out against certain Tory policies, such as the renewal of Trident. At time of writing there were tensions within the Coalition over the future of wind farms—with Lib Dem Energy Secretary Ed Davey supporting them but Tory Energy Minister John Hayes saying of them 'enough is enough'.

- **Contraction of the Civil Service:** the Coalition has frozen Civil Service recruitment indefinitely. Although portrayed as stasis rather than a reduction in civil servants, Opposition MPs and independent commentators argue it means job losses, as individuals who retire or move on will not be replaced. In June 2010 John Philpott, chief economic adviser for the Chartered Institute of Personnel and Development, warned up to 725,000 public sector jobs were likely to be lost as a result.

? Review questions

1. Outline the role and powers of the PM. To what extent, in practice, does his/her position differ from a head of state's?

2. To what extent can recent PMs be accused of being 'presidential'—and can they still claim to adhere to the maxim of 'first among equals'?

3. What is the distinction between 'collective' and 'individual ministerial' responsibility, and do Cabinet ministers always abide by either/both?

4. What is the difference between Cabinet and government? Is there an optimum size and composition for either/both?

5. To what extent can the use of 'kitchen Cabinets', special advisers, and spin doctors be said to have 'politicized' the Civil Service?

→ **Further reading**

Budge, I., Crewe, I., McKay, D., and Newton, K. (2007) *The New British Politics*, 4th edn, London: Longman. **Fourth edition of acclaimed critical introduction to British politics at the dawn of the twenty-first century, updated to cover Brown's administration**.

Burnham, J. and Pyper, R. (2008) *Britain's Modernised Civil Service*, London: Palgrave Macmillan. **Thorough examination of recent Civil Service developments, incorporating analysis of the impact of changes introduced by the Thatcher, Major, Blair, and Brown governments**.

Campbell, A. (2012) *The Burden of Power: Countdown to Iraq*, London: Hutchinson. **Candid, if 'on message', fourth volume of personal diaries by Tony Blair's chief spin doctor, charting the turbulent period between the terrorist attacks of 11 September 2001 and Britain and America's 2003 invasion of Iraq**.

Crossman, R. (1979) *The Crossman Diaries: Selections from the Diaries of a Cabinet Minister, 1964–1970*, London: Book Club Associates. **Widely regarded as among the most incisive and revealing political diaries written by a British minister, these highlights are edited by one of Britain's foremost contemporary political biographers**.

Mullin, C. (2010) *View from the Foothills*, London: Profile Books. **Witty, warts-and-all account of the follies and foibles of the Blair government by a former junior minister. Best read as a counterpoint or companion piece to the more positive spin in Campbell's diaries**.

Online Resource Centre

www.oxfordtextbooks.co.uk/orc/Morrison3e/
Visit the Online Resource Centre that accompanies this book for web links and regular updates.

4

The electoral system

Chapters 1–3 examined the constitutional framework governing the UK and the gradual shift from royal to parliamentary sovereignty that has taken place over the past four centuries. But the legitimacy of the UK legislature—and the executive, the members of which are drawn from it—today derives from more than mere historical precedent: it stems from the system of democratic elections that is the bedrock of modern British government.

▌ The origins of the British franchise

British social reformers were demanding the vote for their fellow citizens for centuries before it was granted. For the rank and file comprising the New Model Army, the Levellers, and the Diggers, propelling Oliver Cromwell to power, the English Civil War was about far more than a tussle for constitutional supremacy between Parliament and Crown. To John Lilburne, radical leader of the Levellers, parliamentary sovereignty meant nothing if it was not exercised by ordinary people. For this to happen, he argued, all 'free-born Englishmen' must be given a direct say in how Parliament was run: in other words, a vote.

Lilburne's arguments would echo down the decades for some 200 years before being answered, even in part—through the writings of Thomas Paine, the marches of the nineteenth-century Chartists, the speeches of the Labour Party's firebrand first MP, James Keir Hardie, and the campaigns of the suffragettes. But it was to be a further century or more before every adult (regardless of class or gender) was granted a say in the running of his/her country's affairs. The slow extension of voting rights in parliamentary elections is charted in the table entitled 'Acts of Parliament that extended the UK franchise' on the Online Resource Centre.

While the primary significance of these Acts was to extend the voting entitlement to more people, the most radical went further. To ensure that parliamentary democracy operates in as fair and equitable a way as possible, it has been necessary for governments periodically to introduce additional structural and procedural reforms.

The 'Great Reform Act 1832' owes its place in history less to a wholesale extension of the franchise and more to its abolition of so-called 'rotten boroughs'—by that point an anachronistic and shameful hangover from medieval times. The term 'rotten borough' was used to refer to areas in which constituency boundaries ought to have been altered to reflect dwindling population numbers, but had not. In other words, there existed (prior to the Act) boroughs in which MPs were dependent for their election on a fraction of the number of adults whose votes had to be sought by their parliamentary colleagues.

In some cases the number of local electors was so minimal that it was possible for a parliamentary candidate to win a seat by bribing voters. In 1831, the year before the Act was passed, the constituency of Old Sarum in Wiltshire had just three houses and eleven registered voters. Gatton, in Surrey, had twenty-three houses, but only seven voters. As a result, rotten boroughs had become a byword for corruption, with some constituencies effectively being bought and sold, and others passed from father to son like inheritances. Before being awarded a peerage (and eventually becoming prime minister) Arthur Wellesley, the Duke of Wellington, once served as MP for the rotten borough of Trim, County Meath. Rotten boroughs were memorably satirized in the BBC1 sitcom *Blackadder the Third*, in which a dog won the fictitious seat of 'Dunny-on-the-Wold'.

Another significant reform was the abolition of 'plural voting'. This was the tradition allowing individuals who owned properties in two or more areas—or those attending university in one area when their family home was in another—to have a multiple say in the outcome of an election, by voting in each constituency. This practice (not to be confused with that, still common today, which allows individuals in these positions to choose in which constituency they would like to vote) was ended by the Representation of the People Act 1948.

The British franchise today—who can vote?

Elections to the House of Commons are known as **general elections**. They have traditionally taken place up to five years to the day after the previous Parliament was assembled following a poll (between the Septennial Act 1715 and the Parliament Act 1911, the gap between elections had been as long as seven years). For convoluted historical reasons, polling day tends to be on a Thursday.

However, the ability of sitting UK prime ministers (unlike governments in practically any other developed democracy) to call elections at times that suit them—often quitting while they are ahead in the polls, rather than seeing through policies that might be for the good of the country, if not their own approval ratings—has long been contentious. So, in its maiden Queen's Speech in May 2010, the Coalition confirmed legislative plans to introduce fixed-term parliaments—commencing with an election on Thursday 7 May 2015—as part of a wider-ranging package of constitutional reform. The decision to plump straight for five-year (rather than the more usual four-year) terms provoked some early criticism. Similarly contentious was the Coalition's (arguably unconstitutional) decision in September 2010 to drop the customary autumn Queen's Speech that year and in 2011, thereby extending the length of its first full parliamentary session until spring 2012—two years after it had entered power. The result was the longest interval between state openings for 150 years. The excuse given for this by then Leader of the House Sir George Young was that a generous time slot was needed to allow MPs and peers to fully scrutinize the fledgling government's packed legislative agenda.

As its name implies, at a general election all sitting MPs formally resign to contest their seats. This means elections are held simultaneously in all 650 Commons constituencies and a new Parliament is normally summoned by the sovereign as soon as all votes are counted and seats allocated. After the 2010 election the distribution of seats in the Commons was as outlined in the table entitled 'The distribution of seats in the House of Commons following the May 2010 election' on the Online Resource Centre.

This result left Britain facing its first hung Parliament since February 1974. Under these circumstances it typically takes several days for a new government to be finalized, and, true to form, the Lib-Con 'coalition agreement' was only signed, after days of febrile media speculation about its every nuance, on Tuesday 11 May—five days after the polls had closed.

Whereas in local and European elections the franchise has gradually been extended to include European Union (EU) citizens resident in Britain on polling day, voting is more restricted in general elections. Currently it is open to citizens of Britain, the Irish Republic, and Commonwealth normally resident in the UK, subject to their:

- names being on the **electoral register** for the constituencies in which they live;
- being over 18 at the time of the election—although they may enter their names on the electoral register when aged 17.

Despite these broad qualification criteria, the following individuals are barred from voting:

- peers entitled to sit in the Lords;
- foreign nationals (including citizens of other EU states);
- patients detained under mental health legislation for crimes;

- people detained in prison (but not those awaiting trial on remand);
- people convicted during the preceding five years of 'corrupt' or 'illegal election practices'.

The rules governing eligibility to vote in general elections also have the following quirks:

- Members of the Armed Forces and Crown servants of British embassies, the Diplomatic Service, and British Council employed overseas (and their partners and other family members) may vote in the constituencies 'where they would normally live'.

- UK citizens living abroad ('ex-pats'), but resident in Britain and registered as electors within the previous fifteen years, can make annual declarations allowing their names to be included in the register for constituencies 'where they were living before they went abroad'. They can vote by proxy—appointing friends or relatives to vote on their behalf—at any Westminster, Scottish Parliament, Welsh Assembly, and European Parliament (but not local) election.

- Holidaymakers are allowed 'absent votes' in national elections under the Representation of the People Act 1985—provided that the electoral registration officer is 'satisfied that the applicant's circumstances on the date of the poll will be or are likely to be such that he cannot reasonably be expected to vote in person'.

- Although there is nothing stopping reigning monarchs and their immediate heirs from voting in theory, were they to do so in practice, this would be seen as unconstitutional.

Registers of electors are compiled by local electoral registration officers, and completion of electoral registration forms is compulsory—although, unlike in countries such as Australia, voting is *not*. Many people technically broke the law when local taxpayers were charged the Community Charge ('Poll Tax')—a head tax payable by each individual, rather than household (see p. 366)—by deliberately not filling in forms to avoid being billed.

The Representation of the People Act 2000 has changed the way registration takes place in the following respects.

- Before the Act, electors were registered to vote wherever they were living on 10 October each year. Although an annual canvass is still conducted—on 15 October—a rolling registration system now exists, enabling electors to register themselves at a new address at the beginning of any month.

- Draft registers used to be open for inspection until 16 December. This date has now been brought forward to 1 December. The register cannot be altered (except as the result of a formal appeal) once the final date for registration has passed.

The Labour government also liberalized some pre-existing voting disqualifications, while remaining strict about others. Until recently, many people detained under mental health legislation in hospitals or other institutions (as opposed to being there voluntarily) were barred from voting, on the ground that they were not of 'sound mind'. This is no longer the case (unless they have been convicted of a crime). Homeless people were also enfranchised formally for the first time with the passage of the 2000 Act. People with no permanent address may now vote subject to a 'declaration of local connection'. Following repeated appeals by convicted prisoners against their prohibition from voting under the European Convention on Human Rights (see p. 11), Coalition ministers have been considering amending the law to allow some categories of inmate to vote—despite angry tirades from Tory backbenchers and Mr Cameron's protestation that the thought of doing so made him feel 'physically sick'. At time of writing, however, this matter remained unresolved.

Although its stance was more liberal than those of previous governments in some respects, Labour tightened up certain qualifications. The Representation of the People Act 1989 made it easier for ex-pats to vote in general elections, by allowing them to do so up to twenty years after emigrating. At the time this was viewed by critics of the then Conservative government as a manoeuvre designed to boost its vote (the assumption being that many people who had retired abroad were likely to be wealthy and inclined to vote Tory). After the 2001 election Labour reduced this entitlement period to fifteen years.

▌ General elections and candidacy—who can stand?

Since June 2007 any citizen of Britain, the Irish Republic, or a Commonwealth country resident in Britain and over 18 on the day he/she is nominated (the age qualification was previously 21) has been able to stand for election—provided that he/she is not disqualified from sitting in the Commons. Such disqualification might arise because he/she is:

- a peer retained in the House of Lords;
- an undischarged bankrupt subject to a bankruptcy restriction order under the Enterprise Act 2002 in England and Wales (these are made by the Insolvency Service—an executive agency of the Department of Business, Enterprise, and Regulatory Reform (BERR)—if a bankrupt individual is found to have acted dishonestly or in an otherwise 'blameworthy' way); in Northern Ireland anyone adjudged bankrupt is barred from standing, while in Scotland anyone whose estate has been sequestered is banned;

- a patient detained for criminal activities under mental health legislation;
- someone sentenced to, and currently serving, more than one year's imprisonment;
- someone found personally guilty of *corrupt* election practices during the preceding ten years (if in the same constituency) or in the last five years (if in a different one);
- someone found personally guilty of *illegal* election practices in the last seven years (if in his/her constituency) or five years (if elsewhere);
- a holder of the offices listed in the House of Commons Disqualification Act 1975:
  - **politically restricted posts** in the Civil Service—that is, senior civil servants in close day-to-day contact with government ministers or elected councillors;
  - members of the regular Armed Forces or the Ulster Defence Regiment;
  - serving police officers;
  - holders of judicial office;
  - members of specified commissions—for example, the Equality and Human Rights Commission (EHRC), the Independent Police Complaints Commission (IPCC), and the Lands Tribunal.

Some disqualifications are more liberal than others. While convicted prisoners have long been denied the vote in general elections, they may stand as candidates—provided they are serving twelve months or less. This 'loophole' was once even more open-minded: Provisional Irish Republican Army (IRA) member Bobby Sands was imprisoned for fourteen years for possessing firearms in 1977, yet managed to get himself elected as MP for Fermanagh and South Tyrone in April 1981, after standing on a so-called 'Anti-H Block/Armagh Political Prisoner' ticket. He was on hunger strike at the time, however, and died a few weeks later. After his death Margaret Thatcher's government hastily passed the Representation of the People Act 1981, which introduced the current 'maximum twelve-month sentence' qualification for serving prisoners with parliamentary ambitions. The swiftness with which it did so stopped any of Sands's fellow hunger strikers standing for election in his stead.

How the British electoral system works

The system used to elect MPs in British general elections is colloquially known as 'first-past-the-post' (FPTP) (its technical name is *plurality voting*). Essentially, this means that in each constituency the candidate receiving the most votes—a relative majority—is automatically elected its MP. Similarly, the political party that has gained the most seats in the Commons once all constituency votes are counted nationwide normally forms the government. Historically, one party has tended to win an *overall majority* at national level—more seats than all other parties and independent MPs put together (or a majority 'over all'). In rarer circumstances one party emerges with only a handful more seats than its nearest rival—allowing it to form only a *minority* administration (as Labour did temporarily in February 1974) or forge a coalition with another party or parties. This type of result is known as a **hung Parliament**.

Britain's most recent hung Parliament followed the 2010 election, when no single party won an overall majority, but the Conservatives secured 307 Commons seats, Labour 258, and the Lib Dems 57. With Lib Dem leader Nick Clegg holding the balance of power—despite a disappointing election-night result, which saw his party make a net loss of five seats—he was invited into swift negotiations with David Cameron's Tories. After five days of furtive deal-making, which at one point saw Mr Clegg holding parallel talks with Labour, the Lib Dems formally agreed to join a Conservative-led government—marking the start of the UK's first formal coalition since the end of the Second World War. Unlike the fragile 'Lib-Lab Pact', which saw David Steel's then Liberal Party keep James Callaghan's Labour government in power for fifteen months between 1977 and 1978, the 2010 arrangement—dubbed 'a new politics' by Mr Clegg—saw Lib Dem frontbenchers enter the Cabinet in senior positions, with their leader anointed deputy prime minister.

The British electoral system has long been controversial, because of the frequent imbalance between the number of votes cast for a particular party and the share of seats into which they translate. As only the first-placed candidate in a given constituency is elected, all other votes cast (often numbering tens of thousands) are effectively 'wasted'. For many years it has been only the Conservatives and Labour who have stood a realistic chance of forming governments in their own right, because in order to win sufficient seats to do so parties have had to rely on *concentrations* of support. Traditional heartlands—for the Tories, the affluent south-east; for Labour, the north and Scotland—tend to swing the pendulum from one to the other.

General elections have also produced governments with numbers of seats vastly outstripping their shares of the vote. Recent examples include the 1997 election, which saw not one Conservative MP elected in Scotland—despite the fact that more than one in six Scots still voted for the party. The 2005 poll saw Labour win well over half the available seats, despite only gaining 35 per cent of the vote (equivalent to 21 per cent of registered voters, given the low turnout on the day). And the inbuilt Labour bias under FPTP was underlined still further when in 2010 the Tories won 36 per cent of the votes, compared to Labour's 29 per cent and the Lib Dems' 23 per cent, but were nineteen seats short of the winning post. Detailed analysis of the 2005 election results had found that the average Labour MP needed only 26,858 votes to be re-elected at that time, whereas Tories required 44,241 and Lib Dems 98,484.

Hardly surprising that, in a move presented as an attempt to rectify this imbalance (as well as cutting the cost of Parliament to taxpayers), Mr Cameron hopes to reduce the number of MPs to 600 and make constituency populations more equal as of the 2015 election. However, while one might have expected this move to go down well with Coalition backbenchers, as details emerged about the arbitrary new constituency boundaries being proposed by the **Boundary Commission for England** in September 2011, both Tory and Lib Dem MPs became restive. As the commissions for Scotland, Wales, and Northern Ireland continued their ruminations, it emerged that the process of making English constituency sizes more equal was likely to lead to some politically sensitive situations. Assuming the current proposals remained in place (which looked doubtful at the time of writing, given the Lib Dems' decision to withdraw support for them following Conservative MPs' rebellion against Lords reform—see p. 65), Coalition Business Secretary Vince Cable would face a close-fought duel with Tory golden boy Zac Goldsmith in a proposed new seat of Richmond and Twickenham—a carved-up amalgam of both their existing fiefdoms—while fellow ministers George Osborne, Iain Duncan Smith, and Kenneth Clarke would all be battling to retain their seats. More alarming still for the Lib Dems was an analysis of how the party's dwindling opinion poll ratings were likely to translate into Commons seats in 2015, conducted by polling organization YouGov and published in *The Sun* on 16 April 2012. The survey, carried out among 1,524 voters in seventy-six prospective new constituency areas, suggested all but seven of the fifty-seven Lib Dem members returned in 2010 were likely to lose their seats—including Deputy Prime Minister Nick Clegg and every other frontbencher drawn from his party, barring Energy and Climate Change Secretary Ed Davey.

Few dispute, however, that some reform is needed. An example of the wild disparities in the sizes of UK electorates at the 2010 election was the fact that the Isle of Wight (a Tory stronghold) boasted 110,000 voters, while a populace of 22,000 was sufficient to return a Scottish Nationalist Party (SNP) MP in the Western Isles. If the planned changes go ahead, the Isle of Wight is expected to be split into two constituencies, each covering some 50,000 electors. While still embracing twice as many people as the Western Isles, each seat will nonetheless be well below the customary 65,000-voter average.

Some election results have been notoriously unfair. In February 1974 incumbent Prime Minister Ted Heath's Tories won 200,000 more votes than Labour, but secured four fewer seats. Heath's attempts to secure a deal to keep himself in power with then Liberal leader Jeremy Thorpe failed within days—due largely to the Conservatives' unwillingness to give ground on electoral reform. Within days Wilson took office, consolidating his victory in October that year by securing a small working majority of three, and a million more votes than the Tories, but this did little to defuse the initial sense of injustice. It has not always been this way around: in 1951 Labour Prime Minister Clement Attlee was beaten by Winston Churchill's Tories, who won seven more seats despite polling more than a million fewer votes.

Tactical voting

In recent elections it has become increasingly common for people in certain constituencies to vote *strategically*—backing candidates other than those they would most like to see elected, in the hope of preventing the election of those they like least. This method of casting votes—rejecting one's 'sincere prefer-ence' in favour of a compromise candidate who is more likely to win—is known as **tactical voting**.

An oft-cited example of this is when a voter who strongly identifies with Labour, but lives in a constituency in which the sitting MP is Conservative, votes Lib Dem instead. If, at the previous election, the Labour candidate had come third, behind not only the Tories but also the Lib Dems, on this basis a vote for Labour would be 'wasted'. So, as the Lib Dems are better placed to beat the Tories, it is worth the Labour supporter voting tactically, backing his/her 'least worst option' over the one he/she most favours.

Examples of MPs elected by tactical voting abound in recent years. Lib Dem Mark Oaten's decisive 1997 victory in the Winchester by-election prompted by an electoral petition from Tory Gerry Malone, described later in this chap-ter, is believed to have been due largely to a wholesale tactical switch by Labour supporters to the Lib Dems. Indeed, by 1997 the Conservatives had become so unpopular, after eighteen years in power, that widespread tactical voting was used to boot them out—whatever the cost—across the UK. In 2001, protest singer Billy Bragg organized a national campaign designed to prevent the Tories winning seats by getting fellow opponents of the party to 'trade' their tactical votes with electors living elsewhere in Britain. A Lib Dem voter living in a Labour/Tory marginal constituency, for example, might 'vote by remote' for his/her preferred party in a distant Lib Dem/Tory marginal—trading his/her own constituency vote with a Labour supporter whose home was in that area.

▌ The election process

The sequence of events leading to a general election is outlined in Table 4.1.

Each candidate must put down a £500 **election deposit**, which is returned provided that he/she receives at least 5 per cent of votes cast in the relevant constituency. The deposit was introduced in 1918 to discourage 'frivolous'

Table 4.1 The general election process

Event	Condition
Election date announced	Elections must be called *at least seventeen working days* before polling day.
Nominations for candidates—until recently, prospective parliamentary candidates (PPCs)—entered	Nomination process closes at 12 p.m. on nineteenth day before election (excluding Sundays and Bank Holidays).
Application for postal ballots closes	All applications for **postal votes** must be made by 5 p.m. on eleventh working day before poll.
Checking that nomination meets basic conditions for eligibility and registration	Each candidate must have his/her nomination proposed and seconded by two 'subscribing' electors, and signed by eight other 'assenting' electors—all registered in constituency. Nominations include brief description of candidate (up to six words including name and political affiliation) identifying them on ballot paper. Candidates do not have to be backed by parties (i.e. can be 'independent'). Each allowed to post one 'election communication' to registered voters.
Disqualification of invalid nominations	Returning officers may reject nomination papers deemed 'out of order' on day of voting.

candidates—and, cynics suggest, boost the Treasury's coffers (it made £800,000 from forfeited deposits in 2001).

Voting procedure on the day—role of the returning officer

Local administration of voting in general elections follows a tightly regulated procedure. After polling closes it culminates in an election-night 'count' at a chosen venue—normally a large local authority building somewhere near the constituency's geographical centre—overseen by a **returning officer**. In practice, the role of returning officer has tended to be discharged by a senior officer in the local authority containing, coterminous with, or neighbouring the constituency—often its chief executive. But in theory it is the responsibility of the council's chairperson or mayor, except in 'county constituencies' (rural ones), in which the role now falls to 'acting returning officers' (electoral registration officers employed by specified nearby district councils). Electoral procedure on the day is outlined in Table 4.2.

Should results be especially close and it is felt that disallowed ballot papers might have produced a different result if included, dissatisfied candidates can apply to the High Court for an 'election petition' against the returning officer. This happened in 1997, when Mr Malone lost his Winchester seat by just two votes to Mr Oaten (see p. 124)—the closest result since 1945. Mr Malone's petition succeeded, but when the election was rerun that November he lost by a 21,566-vote landslide (suggesting there is more than a little truth to the adage that

Table 4.2 The electoral process on polling day

Event	Conditions
Polling stations open at 7 a.m. and close at 10 p.m.	Registered electors who have not chosen to vote by post, email, or proxy may cast votes at stations based at schools, community centres, and, increasingly, pubs and supermarkets. Ballot papers are issued to voters at polling stations by election staff (with official marks impressed on papers at this stage).
Absent votes may be cast in advance	Those who cannot reasonably be expected to vote in person (e.g. are on holiday) can apply for 'absent votes', while people physically incapacitated or unable to vote because of nature of their work or fact they have moved to new constituency since electoral roll last updated can apply for 'indefinite absent votes'. Anyone entitled to absent vote can either vote by post or have someone else do so in person at polling station on his/her behalf ('proxy vote'); postal ballot papers *cannot*, however, be sent to addresses outside UK.
Secrecy of ballot preserved—no interference with ballot boxes	Ballot boxes sealed at close of poll, before being taken to counting place to be counted.
Official count starts after close of poll—only valid papers counted	Count supervised by returning officer—observed by candidates, agents, media, and small number of 'scrutineers'. Any 'spoilt' ballot papers—e.g. those defaced or with crosses beside names of more than one candidate—disallowed.
Deadline for voting—including receipt of postal votes	All votes must have been cast and postal ballot papers received, by 10 p.m. on polling day.
Recount if result too close to call	If winner's victory is marginal, candidates can demand recount (on occasion, more than one—until returning officer decides result is clear). In event of dead heat, returning officer is required by law to settle victory by intervening more directly. He/she will normally do so either by tossing coin or asking neck-and-neck candidates to write their names on slips of paper and drawing winner from hat.

nobody likes a bad loser!). The by-election result is almost certain to have been nearer the electorate's original wishes than the knife-edge outcome of the general election poll, given that on the earlier occasion many voters had been confused by the candidacy of Richard Huggett, who listed himself on the official ballot paper as 'Liberal Democrat Top Choice for Parliament' (forcing Mr Oaten to have the words 'Liberal Democrat Leader Paddy Ashdown' written beside his name). Mr Huggett stood again in the ensuing by-election—under the label 'Literal Democrat'—but the adverse publicity generated by his first campaign blunted his vote. The use of such deliberately confusing labels was subsequently banned by the Registration of Political Parties Act 1998, which established the Electoral Commission (see p. 129).

On the exceptionally rare occasions when an election results in a dead heat—with multiple recounts confirming that two candidates have received exactly the same number of votes—it falls on the returning officer to supervise the most primitive possible way of deciding the contest: asking the joint winners to draw lots. Most recently, 'sortition' (as it is technically known, after the name coined for the process in ancient Athens) was used in the 2011 local elections (see Chapter 14) to determine political control of Bury. On this occasion, Joanne Columbine drew the longest straw to clinch the borough council for Labour from the Tories.

Disputes over close-run contests are far from the only thing that can cause headaches on election night. Occasionally, more serious administrative problems occur. Besides being the first election for thirty-six years to produce a hung Parliament, the 2010 poll was notable for widespread controversy over the number of electors unable to cast their votes because of localized organizational hiccups. As early results were announced on the evening of 6 May, live reports about registered voters being denied the right to vote began flooding in from areas as disparate as Hackney, Liverpool, and Newcastle-upon-Tyne. Some voters had spent hours queuing, only to be locked out of polling stations when the clocks struck 10 p.m. In Sheffield Hallam (Mr Clegg's constituency), the returning officer blamed a last-minute influx of students without polling cards for delays that resulted in a number of people being denied votes. A swift investigation by the Electoral Commission (see p. 129) found that 1,200 voters were barred from voting. The Commission's initial recommendation was for a wholesale modernization of the voting process—which to date has relied largely on paper records, rather than computerized ones—to avert similar problems in future. The 2010 election also saw a significant increase in postal voting—one of the main devices used by recent governments to boost otherwise dwindling turnouts on polling day (see p. 137). In some areas of the UK the number of people voting by post soared by as much as 60 per cent, but with this increase in apparent electoral engagement came a wave of allegations that supporters of one party or other were using it as a way of fraudulently bolstering the positions of their favoured candidates. In Oxfordshire, 667 postal ballot packs went missing a week before the election, by error or design, while some fifty separate investigations into alleged fraud were under way on the eve of polling. Notoriously, however, it can take years for police to bring successful prosecutions. It wasn't until September 2010—four months after the election—that two former councillors and three other men were jailed for an unsuccessful attempt at the 2005 poll to use fraudulent postal votes to swing the marginal seat of Bradford West behind then Tory candidate Haroon Rashid.

Limits on election spending

Election spending is closely controlled by the Electoral Commission to stop any candidate or party having a significant advantage over his/her/its competitors. Each candidate must appoint an election agent with an office in the constituency.

The maximum sum candidates may spend campaigning in their seats is fixed by law. At time of writing, it was just under £7,150, plus 5p per voter in urban constituencies and 7p in rural ones. At a national level, however, parties may also spend £30,000 fielding each candidate.

In addition, so-called 'recognized third parties' may separately spend money campaigning in support of (or against) a candidate—up to £500 apiece. They are, however, permitted to spend considerably more in support of a party as a whole. UNISON is registered as a 'recognized third party' supporter of Labour. It is allowed to spend up to £793,000 on the party's behalf at a general election, or £30,000 in elections to devolved assemblies. Other organizations or individuals wishing to campaign on behalf of a political party (rather than an individual candidate)—but 'unregistered'—are legally limited to spending £10,000 in England, or £5,000 in the other UK countries.

In referendums, meanwhile, 'permitted participants'—those registered to campaign for 'yes' or 'no' votes—may spend up to £500,000 on a UK-wide poll, but only £10,000 may be spent by anyone *not* so permitted. The Commission may 'designate' specific permitted participants to campaign for a 'yes' or 'no' vote to ensure order. Such bodies may claim up to £600,000 to finance their campaigns and spend up to £5m.

▌ Before the event—how constituency boundaries are decided

As explained earlier, there are currently 650 Commons constituencies in England, Wales, Scotland, and Northern Ireland, but until recently there were 659. Historically, the number has fluctuated 'naturally' in line with population changes—aside from periods, like the present, when governments have consciously tried to shake up the system to distribute electors more fairly (see p. 123). Variations in population not only have an impact on the number of constituencies, however; they also influence the size and shape of seats. In some cases, constituencies with falling populations cease to exist or are merged with neighbouring ones, while large localized increases in population can lead to the introduction of additional seats or existing ones being split.

Regular reviews of parliamentary electoral boundaries occur on a cycle of eight to twelve years, to ensure they keep pace with demographic fluctuations. The task of conducting these reviews falls to four independent 'boundary commissions'—covering England, Scotland, Wales, and Northern Ireland. Under the Political Parties, Elections, and Referendums Act 2000 Labour had planned to transfer the commissions' duties to the Electoral Commission (see p. 129). However, the Local Democracy, Economic Development, and Construction Act

2009 repealed this prospective change, and there are now no plans for the boundary commissions to cede their boundary-drawing functions.

Boundary changes have always been controversial. The act of abolishing constituencies, creating new ones, subdividing them, and/or merging two or more can often have a significant impact on the ability of particular political parties to win seats at subsequent elections. Although the commissions are meant to be non-partisan, successive governments have been accused of trying to influence their decisions, to ensure that proposed changes are favourable to their own parties at election time. That said, New Labour's last boundary review was widely interpreted as a boost to the Tories, particularly given the eventual outcome of the May 2010 election. Confirmed by the English and Welsh Commissions in April 2007, with new boundaries for assembly member (AM) constituencies in place for the National Assembly of Wales elections in May that year, it proved controversial in some parts of the north and other Labour heartlands, because all four new constituencies were in the south. The Coalition has since undertaken an even more extensive boundary review, designed officially to equalize the size of constituencies (see p. 123), though at time of writing the future of this policy looked uncertain following Mr Clegg's announcement that Lib Dem MPs would not be voting for it in Parliament in light of Tory backbenchers' refusal to back reform of the Lords (see p. 65).

Role of the Electoral Commission

Having been divested of its status as boundary-setting authority—a responsibility it also lost in relation to local elections under the 2009 Act—the **Electoral Commission** nonetheless retains a suite of responsibilities. These include:

- registering political parties (and preventing their names being used by others);
- ensuring people understand and follow the rules on party and election finance;
- setting standards for running elections and reporting on how well this is done;
- ensuring people understand they should register to vote, and know how to do so;
- making sure candidates fund their election campaigns in a legal and transparent way.

In addition to overseeing election-related funding, the Commission is also responsible for policing party finance as a whole, by vetting how parties raise money and declare their donations (see pp. 158–9).

How parties select candidates

Just as different political parties have their own membership policies, they also have their own preferences about how to select the candidates they wish to field at general elections. The workings of Britain's main political parties, and the internal structures and procedures distinguishing one from the other, are the subject of Chapter 5, but it is worth looking here at significant trends and developments in candidate selection procedures.

The Conservative Party

Historically, the Conservatives have favoured a centrally controlled selection procedure, with a list of 'approved candidates' compiled by Conservative Campaign Headquarters. This initially involves staff from the party's Candidates' Department sifting through CVs and letters from applicants, and inviting a selection to attend a 'candidates' weekend', at which they face aptitude tests to ascertain their suitability. A central list is then drawn up and distributed to local Conservative constituency associations, who advertise vacancies for prospective candidates in their areas as and when they arise (sitting MPs wishing to run again are normally automatically reselected, as in the other main parties). After several public meetings, at which three to five competing applicants have the chance to prove their mettle in debates with rivals, a vote is held among local party members on which individual should be adopted to fight the seat.

Mr Cameron's tenure as party leader has seen contradictory moves towards greater centralization on the one hand and localization on the other. A controversial early move was his drawing up of an 'A-list' of aspiring Tory MPs prior to the 2010 election, including the likes of 'chick-lit' author Louise Bagshawe (now Louise Mensch) and Mr Goldsmith, editor of the *Ecologist* magazine and son of late Tory defector Sir James Goldsmith (whose Referendum Party had stood against Europhile Tory MPs in the 1997 election). Both were subsequently elected. But Mr Cameron has also pioneered 'open primaries' modelled on the US voting system. These give everyone on the electoral register in a constituency a chance to vote on which prospective candidate should stand for the Conservatives at an election—irrespective of whether they are Tory members (or even supporters).

The Labour Party

Labour's selection process has traditionally been more democratic than the Conservatives'. Under Mr Blair, however, it became increasingly centralized and, given moves by the Tories to encourage greater public involvement in their internal party procedures, Labour can no longer so easily claim to be more transparent.

Up to 31 January 2001, constituency Labour parties (equivalent to the Tories' constituency associations) and affiliated organizations, including unions, could each nominate up to two candidates from lists approved by local party leaderships. The general councils of Constituency Labour Party (CLP) branches then drew up shortlists, which were circulated to local party members to vote, either by postal ballot or at 'hustings'—public meetings involving debates between the rival candidates (as described above).

On the pretext of speeding up this time-consuming process, Mr Blair introduced a streamlined version of it after 31 January 2001. To reduce the time taken up with initial vetting procedures, future candidate lists would be centrally approved by the party's 'ruling' National Executive Committee (NEC). CLPs needing new candidates would be presented with these lists and asked to vote for one of the approved names. Mr Blair's critics saw this as a clear attempt to weed out left-wing candidates and impose a more Blairite agenda on the party's grass roots.

An earlier example of the centralizing tendency among recent Labour leaders was the party's adoption of all-women shortlists for parliamentary candidates in 1993. The positive discrimination policy was brought in to increase the number of women MPs, to reflect better the gender balance in the British population (which is 51 per cent female). In 1996 Labour's stand was judged unlawful, in a case brought under the Sex Discrimination Act 1975, but once in power Labour introduced the Sex Discrimination (Election Candidates) Act 2002, which guaranteed the legality of all-women shortlists until 2015. More recently, in the run-up to the May 2010 election, Mr Cameron became a convert to all-women shortlists. Nonetheless, the policy still has its critics—most notably some groups representing ethnic minorities, who argue that white women may get selected in some areas known for their racial diversity at the expense of strong potential candidates from minority communities.

The Liberal Democrat Party

Although they often claim to be more democratic than their bigger Westminster rivals, the Lib Dems use a similarly centralized selection system. A list of approved names is drawn up centrally. Constituencies looking for new candidates must first advertise this fact in *Liberal Democrat News*, the party's main publication, and individuals whose names are on that list may apply for vacancies. A selection committee then interviews them and a shortlist is put before the local party membership.

Quirks of the electoral system

Parliamentary candidates may stand, and even be elected, in more than one constituency. If returned in both, however, they must immediately decide which constituency they would like to represent and 'stand down' from the other. The seat forgone will pass to the second-choice candidate in that constituency. This follows rules set out in Erskine May (see p. 15) and laid down in House of Commons procedures.

Candidates may withdraw their nominations for election, provided they do so in writing (with one witness attesting) by noon on the sixteenth day before polling day. This throws up the intriguing possibility that an individual might one day be elected to serve as an MP, despite having decided against standing at the last minute.

Since 1935, elections have generally been held on Thursdays. The precise historical reasons for this are obscure, but the day is thought to have been arrived at through a process of elimination. As the traditional Christian day of worship, Sundays are out, and weekends, as a whole, are seen to present too many leisure options to ensure voters will discipline themselves to vote. Mondays have the highest employee absence record of any working day—making it difficult to be sure of a solid turnout—while Tuesdays and Wednesdays are the main working days (providing few opportunities for people to escape the workplace to vote). As the traditional market day in many towns and cities, Thursday has traditionally been favoured. In addition, holding elections before a weekend is seen to have advantages if there is a change of government, as it allows new administrations to use Saturday and Sunday to prepare themselves to start work in earnest the following week.

The British electoral system produces a clear divide between 'marginal constituencies' (or 'marginals') and 'safe seats'. In marginals—the key battlegrounds on election day—incumbent MPs have small majorities (in some cases, having won only a handful more votes than their nearest rivals at the previous election), so their seat is considered vulnerable and a key target for competing candidates. Candidates concentrate their energies on attracting the support of 'swing voters': individuals with no firm historical loyalty to any one party. Safe seats, in contrast, are those in which sitting MPs have large majorities that (barring a huge upset) they are unlikely to lose. These tend to be located in party political heartlands—for example, the north for Labour and Home Counties for the Tories. Such seats would require huge 'swings' (switches of support from one candidate or party to another) if they were to change hands.

Other than local and European elections, one of the biggest litmus tests of British public opinion has traditionally been the by-election—a vote in a single constituency to replace a sitting MP who has either retired, been deselected, or died between general elections. Towards the end of Mrs Thatcher's time in the late 1980s and under Mr Major in the early 1990s, by-elections frequently produced bruising results for the Tories, reflecting their growing unpopularity across the country. By 2008 it was Labour's turn to suffer. Over a three-month period before the summer recess, the party sustained a series of humiliating defeats, including two in previously safe seats: the Crewe and Nantwich constituency of veteran backbencher Gwyneth Dunwoody, whose 7,000–strong majority was overturned by the Conservatives in their first by-election victory over Labour for thirty years, and Glasgow East, a dyed-in-the-wool Labour seat on Mr Brown's doorstep, where the Scottish Nationalists achieved a 22.5 per cent swing to snatch the seat (although Labour regained it at the 2010 election).

❙ Proportional representation (PR) and other voting systems

Such are the inequities of the British electoral system that pro-democracy campaigners have long argued for its replacement by one the outcome of which more accurately reflects the distribution of votes between rival candidates or parties. Pressure groups like the Electoral Reform Society and Charter 88 (recently incorporated into Unlock Democracy) advocate **proportional representation (PR)**—an umbrella term referring to a variety of alternative models they judge to be fairer (see Table 4.3). Such a switch has, for many years, been official policy for the Lib Dems, who have long suffered more than any other party under FPTP, due to the wide dispersal of their vote across the country.

It has often been observed that, given Labour and the Tories' vested interest in keeping the old system in place, the Lib Dems would need to get into power to be able to introduce it—but that without it this is unlikely to ever happen. However, the eventual outcome of the 2010 election—which saw Mr Clegg and several Lib Dem colleagues take their seats at Mr Cameron's Cabinet table— forced the Tory leader to agree to hold a referendum on whether to adopt PR. As a result, on 5 May 2011 (a year after the Coalition's formation), the public was given its say on whether FPTP should be abandoned—but not in favour of the **single transferable vote (STV)**, the complex if more proportional system favoured by the Lib Dems, but the so-called **alternative vote (AV)**. This system, used in Australia (and, interestingly, in most elections for the chairpersons of Commons select committees—see p. 49), requires electors in each constituency to mark candidates in order of preference. Depending on how the system is implemented in a given territory, a candidate will be elected if he/she wins either a simple majority (50 per cent plus one of all votes cast) or absolute majority (the support of 50 per cent plus one of all eligible voters). If (as commonly happens) no one reaches this level on the basis of first preferences alone, the name of the lowest-placed candidate is struck off the ballot paper and his/ her second preferences redistributed among the remaining contenders as if they were first choices. This process continues until one candidate finally has a simple or absolute majority. In the event, after a lacklustre 'yes' campaign, and amid fearsome opposition from a much better funded and organized 'no' lobby, the Lib Dems and their supporters (including Labour leader Ed Miliband) lost the AV referendum—and with it, perhaps, a once-in-a-generation chance to improve Britain's increasingly outmoded-looking electoral system. On a nationwide turnout of just 42.2 per cent—a striking symbol of the disengagement with parliamentary politics that reformers had hoped to rectify—the 'no' vote triumphed by 68 to 32 per cent.

Nonetheless, the referendum had been significant in two respects: it was the first such public vote to be held across the whole UK since Britons were asked

Table 4.3 Different types of proportional representation (PR) and how they work

Name	How it works	Where used
Single transferable vote (STV)	System favoured by Liberal Democrats. STV states have multi-member constituencies—making it more likely voters will end up with representation by party they support. Electors mark candidates in order of preference and, once one achieves predetermined quota (e.g. one-fifth of votes cast if five seats available) he/she is elected. Second choices listed on all 'surplus' papers naming that candidate as 'first choice' treated as first choices and distributed accordingly among remaining candidates. Means by which some ballot papers designated 'surplus' varies: in some countries 'surplus' papers are selected randomly from all those with initial winning candidate as first choice, while elsewhere papers are accorded primacy on 'first come, first served' basis (those submitted later become 'surplus'). Process of reallocating second choices, third choices, etc. as 'first choices' continues until required number of candidates are elected.	The Irish Dáil Scottish local authorities The Northern Ireland Assembly Local and European elections in Northern Ireland
Party list systems	Seats allocated to parties in direct proportion to their vote share. Candidates chosen by voters from lists supplied by their parties—meaning they can theoretically opt for someone with local connection to area, even if 'constituency link' preserved by UK elections is more remote. In 'open' list system, they can vote for both party and individual: parties supply lists of candidates; electors choose ones they want; party then allocates seats it wins to named candidates, according to those expressed preferences. In 'closed' list systems parties have already decided which candidates they wish to take seats in parliament, if they win enough votes. Britain, like all other EU member states, already uses party list system as its means of electing members of European Parliament (MEPs). In 2004 European Parliament elections UK Independence Party used closed list system to cherry-pick candidates it wanted to represent it as MEPs—ensuring former BBC talk show presenter and ex-Labour MP Robert Kilroy-Silk was elected.	European elections in most member states Regional and national parliamentary elections in European states, including Sweden and Netherlands Israel's Knesset

Table 4.3 (*continued*)

Name	How it works	Where used
Alternative vote (AV) or preferential voting	Similar to STV, except only one MP elected per constituency—meaning extent to which election's outcome pleases most voters is more limited. AV is, however, widely seen as producing more accurate reflections of voters' preferences than FPTP. If, after votes counted, one candidate has simple majority—more than half votes cast—he/she is immediately elected. Otherwise, candidate with least 'first choice' votes is struck out and 'second choices' on all papers putting them top redistributed among others as if first choices. Process continues until one candidate has more than half the votes cast.	Australia's House of Representatives
Supplementary vote (SV)	Modified version of AV. If no candidate initially obtains absolute majority—support of more than half eligible voters—all but top two eliminated and their 'second choices' reallocated to produce winner.	English mayoral elections, including that for London mayor
Additional member system (AMS)	Hybrid of different systems: some candidates elected in single-member constituencies (normally using FPTP) and second—'additional'—votes used to top up from regional lists, introducing measure of 'proportionality' between votes and parties. As with party list system, lists can be either open or closed.	Elections for Scottish Parliament, Welsh Assembly, and London Assembly Parliaments in Germany, Italy, Mexico, New Zealand, and Venezuela

if they wanted to remain in the then European Community (now the EU) by Harold Wilson's government in 1975, and it marked the belated revival of a review of the electoral system that had originally commenced under Tony Blair, in December 1997. Unsure that it would win a working majority in the May 1997 election, Labour committed itself to re-examining FPTP, and duly did so with the appointment of an Independent Commission on the Voting System under the chairmanship of the late Lord Jenkins, a Lib Dem peer and former Labour Chancellor. He reported in 1998, advocating either a hybrid system modelled on that to be used in Scotland and Wales (see below and p. 76) or a new system called 'alternative vote plus' (AV+).

AV+ would have involved a reduction in the number of constituencies, but with the total number of MPs remaining the same as at present. Between 80 and 85 per cent of MPs would have continued to be elected on a constituency basis, with the rest voted in via a 'top-up process'. This would work 'correctively'—on the basis of electors' second votes—to better reflect their overall preferences.

Table 4.4 Pros and cons of PR

For	Against
Governments elected under FPTP are often parties that win majority of seats despite only securing minority of votes.	PR produces more **coalition governments**. These can be less decisive and coordinated in policymaking. Extremist parties (e.g. France's Front National) can sometimes hold balance of power because their support is vital to enable mainstream ones to form governments.
Many votes wasted because numerous electors denied representation by MPs of same or similar persuasion. PR produces overall results that are fairer reflections of distribution of votes cast.	PR means voters less able to hold particular government responsible for its actions by decisively voting it out.
Changes in government between Left and Right can bring abrupt changes of policy and direction—leading to lack of long-term continuity.	Some PR systems break constituency link between individual voters and MPs—a cornerstone of Britain's democracy.
FPTP denies voice in Parliament to minority parties with significant support in country but no elected MPs.	PR can lead to frequent elections and big policy compromises, because many coalitions are unstable. Sometimes leadership and firmer action are needed.

Although Lord Jenkins never lived to see his advice acted upon, in the aftermath of the May 2010 election several senior Labour politicians, including outgoing Home Secretary Alan Johnson and Welsh Secretary Peter Hain, indicated their enthusiasm for a form of PR modelled on AV+.

Key arguments used by advocates and opponents of the introduction of PR in the UK are outlined in Table 4.4.

▌ Elections under devolution

The devolved parliaments in Scotland, Wales, and Northern Ireland are elected on a set timetable every four years—an electoral cycle bearing more resemblance to those of local authorities than the Commons. But this is not the only difference from Westminster: more significantly, the voting systems used to elect members of the Scottish Parliament (MSPs), assembly members (AMs), and members of the Legislative Assembly in Northern Ireland (MLAs) use elements of PR.

In Northern Ireland the single transferable vote (STV) is now used, in line with the system used in Southern Ireland since 1919. Both Scotland and Wales have adopted the 'additional member' system (see p. 76).

▌ The future of voting

Since 2001, electoral turnout has been consistently lower than at any time since the Second World War, although it rose by nearly 4 per cent in 2010—from 61.3 to 65.1 per cent—in the midst of a period of political and economic upheaval following the recession and the MPs' expenses scandal. This has prompted an ongoing debate about the perceived disengagement of voters—whether due to the increasingly indistinguishable nature of many Labour and Conservative policies, or the perception that politicians say one thing in their manifestos and do another once elected.

Although there remains a wide spectrum of different views on the merits and pitfalls of FPTP, there is a growing cross-party consensus that more needs to be done to encourage people to vote. One approach to this quandary—in recognition of the increasingly hectic lifestyles led by many British adults—is to make voting *easier*. The Representation of the People Act 2000 authorized various pilot schemes to see which worked best, including:

- electronic voting—via email, text messaging, the Internet;
- global postal voting;
- voting spread over a number of days;
- voting on Saturdays;
- taking polling stations to the voter—to supermarkets, GP surgeries, etc.

Although Labour was a big advocate of postal voting, presiding over a 60 per cent rise in its take-up in some areas in 2010, there have been huge controversies over its vulnerability to fraud. In multi-occupancy households one resident could theoretically vote multiple times by filling in his/her housemates' forms. Indeed, elections for Birmingham City Council in 2004 exposed systematic corruption after a number of Labour Party workers were implicated in fraudulently submitting forms in support of it.

☷ Topical feature idea

As of 2015 parliamentary electoral boundaries are set for their most radical realignment in living memory, with hundreds of seats due to be merged, split, or even abolished. What are the current plans for the constituency, or constituencies, covered by your organization? Which parties and/or MPs are expected to be the biggest winners and losers? What do they and their constituents/supporters have to say about the Coalition's proposals?

✳ Current issues

- **Votes for prisoners:** the European Court of Human Rights has issued several ultima-tums to British governments since 2005, ordering first Labour then the Coalition to grant serving prisoners the vote, in defiance of long-standing electoral practice in the UK. Though the Court gave ministers just six months to change their position in November 2010, warning it would permit at least 2,500 inmates to sue Britain for breaching their human rights if the deadline was missed, MPs voted overwhelmingly to uphold the country's current position in February 2011. A further six-month deadline expired in May 2012.

- **Fixed-term parliaments:** the Coalition is introducing fixed-term parliaments—ending the age-old constitutional convention allowing prime ministers to 'quit while they're ahead' by dissolving Parliament mid-term. Elections will be held every five years, rather than four (as in the USA), and to bring down a sitting gov-ernment in between would require either a no confidence vote or a motion with the backing of two-thirds of MPs.

- **Open primaries:** the Conservatives have become the first UK party to experiment with the idea of a US-style *open primary* selection process for their parliamentary hopefuls (that is, allowing electors living in a given constituency, regardless of their past political affiliations, to vote on which prospective Tory candidates they would like to stand for election to the Commons). Will others follow?

? Review questions

1. What are the arguments for lowering the voting age in the UK to 16?

2. Given the imbalance between votes cast and seats won under the first-past-the-post (FPTP) system, what are the arguments for and against proportional representation (PR)? Give an explanation of two or more different types of PR.

3. What are the qualifications for electors and candidates in UK parliamentary elections, and how can people be barred from standing for the Commons?

4. How are constituency boundaries determined, how many constituencies are there at present, and what are the plans for after the 2015 general election?

5. How have recent governments tried to increase turnout at general elections, and can you think of any additional or alternative ways of improving voter engagement?

→ Further reading

Blais, A. (ed.) (2008) *To Keep or to Change First Past the Post? The Politics of Electoral Reform*, New York: Oxford University Press, USA. **Expert analysis of the relative merits of 'first-past-the-post' and other electoral systems, and critique of failures of UK, US, and other countries using FPTP to achieve reform.**

Braune, J. (2011) *Comparing Electoral Systems: First-Past-the-Post versus Proportional Representation*, Kindle edition: Amazon Digital Services. **Handy 'bluffers' guide' to main differences between Britain's parliamentary voting system and PR systems, examining advantages and disadvantages of each**.

Denver, D. (2006) *Elections and Voters in Britain*, 2nd edn, London: Palgrave Macmillan. **Second edition of authoritative text focusing on UK voting patterns. Includes data from British Electoral Study (BES) surveys**.

Gallagher, M. and Mitchell, P. (2008) *The Politics of Electoral Systems*, Oxford: Oxford University Press. **Comprehensive examination of different electoral systems used in twenty-two countries, including Britain, incorporating comparative data and examples**.

Online Resource Centre

www.oxfordtextbooks.co.uk/orc/Morrison3e/
Visit the Online Resource Centre that accompanies this book for web links and regular updates.

5

Political parties, party funding, and lobbying

The 'party system' has long been a cornerstone of Britain's brand of representative democracy. It derives from a series of nineteenth- and early twentieth-century works of political science, most notably *American Commonwealth* (1885) by English scholar James Bryce and later writings by Charles Merriam and William Nisbet Chambers—all focusing on the emergence of what was seen as a model democratic system in the USA. The notion of groups of like-minded individuals banding together to form 'parties' and campaigning collectively to win power might have been relatively new across the Atlantic, but in Britain the party was already a long-established institution, as was the country's own peculiar version of party politics—the 'two-party system'.

The 'first-past-the-post' (FPTP) electoral system has always favoured candidates representing the two or three main parties. Given that British general elections produce a 'winner-takes-all' outcome at constituency level—with a single representative returned in each—it has tended to be those candidates most closely identified with the (frequently polarized) concerns of each area who have been elected (historically, social reformers in the industrial north and conservatives in the wealthier south). The formation of a coherent nationwide government is only possible if a number of elected representatives agree to share power and ascribe particular responsibilities to individuals from among their number. For both these reasons, the emergence of a party system in Britain was logical, pragmatic, and arguably inevitable.

From the point at which Parliament wrested sovereignty from the monarch in 1689 up to the emergence of the Liberal Party some 170 years later, the two-party system revolved around two political groupings: Whigs and Tories. While the former are often crudely identified with the progressive tendencies later embodied by the nineteenth-century Liberals of William Gladstone, and the latter with the modern-day Conservative Party (the term 'Tory' is still used as shorthand for 'Conservative'), in truth the distinction between the two was more nebulous. Both were associated, to a greater or lesser degree, with the moneyed classes and aristocracy. What differences there were initially rested largely on Christian denominational grounds, with the Whigs identifying more with non-Anglican believers ('dissenters' such as the evolving Presbyterian Church in Scotland) and the Tories the Church of England establishment.

By the late eighteenth century, however, clearer party lines had emerged, with the ascendancy of Charles James Fox and William Pitt the Younger as Whig leader and Tory prime minister respectively. Within a few short decades the Whigs would be advocating the abolition of slavery, the introduction of overseas free trade, and wider voting rights.

Although the purpose of this book is to give journalists a clear understanding of the present-day political framework governing the UK, no explanation of the British party system would be complete without a brief summary of how today's main parties came about.

▌ The Conservative Party—a potted history

For much of the period from the 1950s to the 1990s the Conservative and Unionist Party, to use its full title, was viewed as the 'natural party of government'. Of the twenty-one prime ministers in the twentieth century, thirteen were Conservative, compared to three Liberals and five from Labour. The Tories were in power for fifty-five years, the Liberals for seventeen, and Labour twenty-eight.

Although William Pitt the Younger is widely regarded as the first true 'Conservative' prime minister, he was really the last of a long line of political leaders whose affiliation was rooted in that looser, more general Tory persuasion spawned in the seventeenth century. It was only after his death, in 1812, that a cohesive Tory Party organization began to emerge, initially under Lord Liverpool (who, as prime minister for fifteen years, remains the longest-serving premier to date). Not until a decade later, however, was the term 'Conservative' tentatively coined by his short-lived successor, George Canning.

The title 'Conservative Party' was officially adopted in 1834 by Sir Robert Peel, widely credited as its true founder, who formalized it in a paper viewed as the blueprint for its later constitution: *The Tamworth Manifesto*. Ironically, he later all but destroyed the party, splitting it down the middle over his decision to repeal the 'corn laws'—tariffs protecting the profits of British agriculturalists by artificially inflating the prices of imported foreign crops—to allay the suffering caused by the Irish potato famine of 1845–6. After being deposed, Peel formed his own faction in Parliament—the 'Peelites'—and was briefly courted by a coalition of Whigs and Radicals (later to form the Liberal Party) in 1849.

The late nineteenth century was notable for the emergence of two progressive political giants in the Conservative Party: Benjamin Disraeli, who served twice as prime minister between 1868 and 1880, and his successor, Lord Salisbury. Despite his imperialistic approach to foreign policy, Disraeli marked a break with tradition in the Tory ranks, extending the right to vote and embodying a more paternalistic attitude towards the poor. He even introduced a right to peaceful picketing in industrial disputes.

Disraeli's brand of moderate conservatism foreshadowed the 'One Nation Toryism' that would characterize post-war twentieth-century premiers such as Harold Macmillan and Sir Alec Douglas-Home. Only with the emergence of Thatcherism—and its adherents' derogatory labelling of their ilk as 'Wets'—did the party's pendulum swing decisively back to the right, adopting a more solidly free market approach to its handling of the economy and social welfare than ever before.

The last Conservative prime minister of the twentieth century was John Major, who served from 1990 to 1997. Today the party is still associated with certain core Tory values—privatization, low taxes, tough anti-crime measures, and a free market approach to the economy—but its latest premier, David Cameron, initially also modernized its approach to issues traditionally associated with Labour, the Lib Dems, and even the Greens. While in opposition, he launched several policy reviews focusing on everything from renewable energy to the widening gap between rich and poor. The author of the latter report, former leader Iain Duncan Smith, coined the term 'broken society' to describe Labour's legacy after a decade in power, and Mr Cameron's 2010 election campaign centred around his pledge to promote a 'Big Society'. Yet, if this was intended as a rhetorical rebuff to Margaret Thatcher's oft-cited (if slightly misquoted) remark that there was 'no such thing as society', it was also founded, in part, on a repackaging of Thatcherite values like self-help, individual responsibility, and small government.

The Labour Party—a potted history

Despite having long since supplanted the Liberal Party (today the Liberal Democrats) as the second of Britain's two main political parties, Labour is little more than a hundred years old. For much of the nineteenth century the Liberals were the 'progressive' party—advocating what would later become core Labour values, such as social reform, wider democracy, and a foreign policy founded on internationalism rather than imperialism. Only when the vote was finally extended to men on more modest incomes—ironically, a policy ushered in by both Disraeli's Tories and Gladstone's Liberals—did rumbling calls for a voice in Parliament for the working classes, to counter that of the middle and upper echelons who had so far dominated, become a clamour.

Unlike the Conservative Party, which emerged 'organically' from the ranks of the propertied classes over a period of decades, Labour was formed through the coordinated amalgamation of several organizations founded to safeguard the interests of ordinary working people, and united by a shared belief in democratic socialism. The first of these were the trades unions, which had evolved out of the aftermath of the Industrial Revolution to provide protection and representation for employees in the workplace. Having failed to persuade the Liberals to sponsor sufficient numbers of working-class candidates to stand in general elections in the later nineteenth century, the unions turned their attentions towards establishing their own party.

Around the turn of the century, several like-minded organizations began talking seriously about forming a new party: notably two early think tanks, the Fabian Society and the Social Democratic Federation, and a body of aspiring parliamentary candidates and their supporters calling itself the Independent Labour Party (ILP). In 1900, at a special conference convened by the Trades Union Congress (TUC) in Farringdon, London, they formed between them the Labour Representation Committee (LRC). With future Labour Prime Minister James Ramsay Macdonald as secretary, the LRC began sponsoring candidates to fight the coming election. In the event, the so-called 'khaki election', which returned the Tories under Arthur Balfour that October following his perceived success in the Boer War, delivered the first two Labour MPs: Richard Bell for Derby and James Keir Hardie for Merthyr Tydfil, who was to become its first leader.

Although hardly meteoric, the party's progress in Parliament was steady from here on in. The 1906 election ushered in seventeen years of reforming Liberal government, but a combination of infighting and growing Labour momentum during its later years ensured that this marked the party's last term as a majority administration. Labour had gained twenty-seven additional seats in 1906—thanks in part to a secret pact between Macdonald and Liberal Chief Whip Herbert Gladstone, designed to stop Labour and Liberal candidates cancelling out each other's votes by contesting the same seats—but by 1910 it was up to forty-two. In 1924, aided by the Liberals' divisions, it won 191—enough to form its first government under Macdonald.

By now Labour was the second party. It secured its first decisive election victory in the wake of the Second World War, in 1945—a landslide win for Clement Attlee and a radical team of ministers, who introduced the National Health Service (NHS) and free state education, and consolidated earlier moves towards establishing a welfare state to provide benefits for the unemployed, the low paid, and the elderly. Three further periods of government followed:

under Harold Wilson (1964–70); Wilson and James Callaghan (1974–9); and Tony Blair and Gordon Brown (1997–2010).

▌ The Liberal Democrat Party—a potted history

Although technically the youngest of the three main parties, the Liberal Democrats—or 'Lib Dems'—are essentially the successors to the Liberal Party. The Liberals were a dominant force in British politics until a combination of the erosion of their grass-roots support by Labour and internal divisions caused by the bitter rivalry between the last Liberal Prime Minister, David Lloyd George, and his predecessor, Herbert Asquith, led to their sharp decline in the late 1920s.

Between the 1920s and 1980s the Liberals cemented their status as Britain's 'third party', with modest parliamentary gains that were never again sufficient to propel them to power in their own right, but at times gave them a toehold in government. In 1977, buffeted by rising inflation and wildcat union strikes, Callaghan kept himself in Number 10 by negotiating a Lib-Lab Pact with Liberal leader David Steel. The Liberals held the balance of power for a year, but the alliance soon broke up, and Labour were brought down on a Tory-instigated confidence vote in March 1979 (see p. 94).

In 1981, as Labour swung to the left following its election defeat, four senior moderates—former Chancellor Roy Jenkins, Foreign Secretary David Owen, Science Minister Shirley Williams, and Transport Secretary Bill Rodgers—quit to form the Social Democratic Party (SDP). By 1983 the so-called 'Gang of Four' had recruited enough supporters to form a credible new party, joining Steel's Liberals to form the SDP–Liberal Alliance. Such was the state of the UK economy in the early 1980s that the Tories began flat-lining in opinion polls—with the Alliance initially reaping the benefit, due to infighting within Labour. At one point in 1982 it reached a poll rating of 50 per cent, with the Tories and Labour virtually neck and neck on around half that. But for the Falklands War, it is possible the next election would have produced a hung Parliament, with the Alliance the biggest 'party'. In the event, buoyed by victory in the South Atlantic, Mrs Thatcher increased her majority and the Alliance went on to perform modestly in both the 1983 and 1987 polls, before disbanding.

In 1988 more than two-thirds of the existing Liberal and SDP members—and all their serving MPs—regrouped to form a new party: the Liberal Democrats. Initially led jointly, like the Alliance, by Steel and Robert Maclennan (Mr Owen's successor as SDP leader), it soon elected Paddy Ashdown to replace them. He was succeeded by Charles Kennedy, Sir Menzies 'Ming' Campbell, and Nick Clegg.

▌ Structure and constitution of the modern Conservative Party

Many aspects of the internal organization of the Conservative Party remain the same today as a hundred years ago. It has, however, introduced significant changes since the 1990s, most notably democratizing its leadership elections.

As with any organization, the lifeblood of the party is its grass-roots membership. It is ordinary members who swell the party's coffers by paying annual subscriptions and raising funds, who troop out, unpaid, on cold winter evenings to canvass in the run-up to elections—and who can usually be relied on to vote loyally come polling day. In return, it is incumbent on the party's leadership to give something back to members—policies they can support, and a sense of involvement. This can come through everything from participating in fund-raising events to attending the annual party conference. Like those of Labour and the Lib Dems, this is held at the end of the summer recess, traditionally in a large coastal town such as Brighton, Bournemouth, or Blackpool.

Notwithstanding Labour's close ties with the unions, traditionally the Conservatives have had the largest individual subscribing membership of any British party. Although recent years have witnessed a decline in party membership across the board, the Tories remain the biggest at grass-roots level, with around 250,000 members in September 2010. Members are connected to the national party through local constituency associations, which began springing up around the UK in the wake of the Reform Act 1832. Unlike in the Labour Party, in which membership activities have always been centrally directed, these associations initially sprouted independently. They could, however, wield considerable clout: in affluent areas, associations would recruit candidates and finance their campaigns.

Despite being gradually incorporated into the overall party structure, associations had considerable independence until 1998, when then newly elected leader William Hague formalized their party status in an effort to discipline what he perceived as errant elements (which he controversially labelled 'out of touch' and 'racist'), and kick-start a grass-roots Tory revival. To this end he introduced the party's first codified constitutional document, *Fresh Future*. This imposed new conditions on associations, but gave them significant new rights. Their position in the modern Tory Party's internal hierarchy—beneath its constitutional college and Conservative Campaign Headquarters (formerly 'Conservative Central Office')—is explained in Table 5.1, while the way the various components of the party's central organization fit together is shown in Table 5.2.

Although the Tories traditionally perform poorly in elections in Scotland and Wales—they secured only one Scottish MP in May 2010—unlike Labour they still contest some seats in Northern Ireland. This is a hangover from the party's strong historical ties to the province, as evidenced by its official 'Conservative

Table 5.1 Internal structure of the modern Conservative Party

Level	Party in the country	Party in Parliament
Top table	**Chairman of the Conservative Party** (head of Conservative Campaign Headquarters) and Conservative Party Board	Leader
Middle tier	Constitutional college, incorporating National Conservative Convention (comprising MPs, members of the European Parliament (MEPs), and other senior activists)	1922 Committee
Grass roots	Constituency associations	Individual backbenchers

Table 5.2 Main components of central Conservative Party organization

Body	Role and composition
Conservative Party Board	Ultimate decision-making body, comprising eighteen members, including chairman of Conservative Party and deputy chairman. Tories' equivalent of National Executive Committee (NEC) of Labour Party.
Conservative Campaign Headquarters	Main fund-raising, campaigning, and recruitment body, which coordinates its electioneering and marketing. Headed by Party Chairman.
Constitutional college	Body comprising representatives from all levels of party, including constituency associations and rank-and-file members, with say in questions of reform and long-term policy strategy. Incorporates National Conservative Convention—made up of MPs, MEPs, and senior activists.
Constituency associations	Grass-roots member organizations, originally only loosely affiliated to the party, but now formally incorporated. Now permitted to play significant role in selecting prospective candidates for Parliament, European Parliament, and elections for devolved assemblies.

and Unionist Party' title. In July 2008 Mr Cameron and the leader of the Ulster Unionists, Sir Reg Empey, published a joint letter in *The Daily Telegraph* pledging to revive their parties' historic electoral alliance, dating back to the 1880s, which had been severed some thirty years earlier due to infighting.

How the Conservatives choose their leader

From the mid-1960s until 1998 Conservative leaders were always elected by their parliamentary colleagues—with no formal input from rank-and-file members. Today, only the first stage of this process is handled exclusively by MPs and peers. Once two frontrunners have emerged this way, their names are put forward to ordinary members nationwide—on a 'one member, one vote' basis—and the final say rests with them.

While the introduction of this huge extension of party democracy signalled that then new and youthful Tory leader Hague (he was just 36 at the time) was serious about modernizing his party, it was not long before his fellow MPs were rueing the day they voted for it. When Hague was defeated at the 2001 election he swiftly resigned, to be replaced by little-known Mr Duncan Smith. Although widely perceived by both colleagues in Parliament and political commentators as uncharismatic, he beat his more dynamic challengers, Kenneth Clarke and Michael Portillo, because of his solid grass-roots support. An ex-Army officer, devoted family man, practising Christian and Eurosceptic, he chimed far more than his rivals with typical Tory members—the average age of whom (despite Hague's reforms) was 64. In contrast, Clarke's Europhile views and Portillo's admission of a youthful homosexual relationship did little to endear them.

Duncan Smith's later removal in a confidence vote instigated by disgruntled Tory MPs paved the way for another new leader, former Home Secretary, Michael Howard. Recognizing the need to ensure the party elected leaders more in touch with the wider public in future, after losing the May 2005 election he tried to reverse Hague's reforms in his remaining months in office. His proposals were defeated, however, after failing to win the required two-thirds majority among Tory MPs and activists in the party's 1,141-strong constitutional college.

The 1922 Committee

Also known as the '1922 Backbench Committee', this comprises all Conservative MPs apart from the leader, and can therefore number in the hundreds. It has often been referred to as 'influential'—an understatement, given that it represents all elected Tory members and is therefore able to articulate the 'mood' of the parliamentary party like no other organization. Traditionally, leaders have ignored its views at their peril.

Far from being a talking shop, the **1922 Committee** retains huge constitutional clout. It is headed by an eighteen-member executive committee, the chairperson of which is often referred to as the party's 'shop steward', charged as he/she is with organizing elections for its leadership (even under the new rules). He/she also oversees votes of confidence. Such a vote can be triggered by a letter to the chairperson signed by 15 per cent of Tory MPs. The last time this happened was in 2003, when Mr Duncan Smith was deposed. The Committee also instigated the final twist of the knife that unseated Mrs Thatcher following Michael Heseltine's 1990 leadership challenge (see p. 96).

The Committee meets every week when Parliament is in session, and is governed by curious conventions. For the first eighty-eight years of its existence, frontbenchers were only permitted to attend its meetings when the party was in opposition. Even then, the leader was barred—so his/her Shadow Cabinet colleagues would act as his/her intermediaries. When in government, neither leader nor Cabinet colleagues used to be able to attend, but barely a week after forming his May 2010 Coalition government Mr Cameron surprised the committee by demanding an immediate vote on whether frontbenchers should be both admitted and granted full voting rights. Arguing that the Conservatives needed to be 'one party' in Parliament, he successfully orchestrated a secret ballot, and his rule change was passed by 168 votes to 118. He was later forced into a partial U-turn, agreeing to drop his call for frontbenchers to be allowed a vote in the committee. His initial move had provoked fierce reactions from stalwart backbenchers. Eurosceptic, Bill Cash, described it in the media as 'a great tragedy' and warned that, when seen in conjunction with other constitutional changes Mr Cameron was proposing at the time (including the '55 per cent rule'—see p. 95), it smacked less of the 'new politics' about which he and Mr Clegg had evangelized than an 'old politics' of empire-building.

Although the 1922 Committee is by far the most powerful subgroup of the party, MPs and peers may choose to join several smaller such 'clubs', depending on where their views fall on the wide Conservative political spectrum. These associations of like-minded left- or right-wingers—or members united over particular issues, like Europe—have traditionally been known as 'ginger groups', although many have recently morphed into semi-professional think tanks. Among the most active today are the Bow Group, which describes itself as Britain's 'oldest centre-right think tank', and the Thatcherite group Conservative Way Forward. As befits the online age, however, the most influential of all is arguably a collaborative website—ConservativeHome—whose editor, Tim Montgomerie, has cultivated a good relationship with both the party rank and file and more outspoken internal critics of its leadership. An excellent source of news and gossip for political reporters (and occasional headaches for Mr Cameron), its web address is http://conservativehome.blogs.com.

Intriguingly, in May 2012 a newly formed ginger group was to liven up the first elections for the 1922 Committee executive since the Coalition's formation. Loyalist MPs, Nicholas Soames and Tracey Crouch, quit the top table voluntarily in protest at the 'factional' tactics of the '301 Group'—a pro-Cameron faction named after the number of Commons seats the Tories need to win an overall majority at the 2015 election—when it published a list of candidates it hoped would be elected to counteract the views of 'bloody rude' critics of his leadership, including Eurosceptic Bernard Jenkin.

In addition to its various ginger groups, the Conservative Party has a long tradition of support from upmarket gentlemen's associations including the Carlton Club.

▌ Structure and constitution of the modern Labour Party

Unlike the Conservative Party, which emerged in 'top-down' fashion from one of the two principal parliamentary factions that evolved in the late seventeenth and early eighteenth centuries, Labour was created in a 'bottom-up' way—as a membership-led movement formed through a coalition of establishment outsiders campaigning for greater parliamentary representation for the working classes. Its formation was altogether more 'deliberate', with several distinct groupings coalescing to establish it formally in 1900. As such, it has had a codified constitution since its inception.

In addition to its de facto union members, the Labour Party today is made up of some 177,000 subscribing individuals. For a brief period under Tony Blair its membership reached an all-time peak of 400,000—overtaking the Conservative Party's—but this later fell due to growing disenchantment with his leadership. Although it has had traditional strongholds in Scotland, Wales, and northern England, Labour does not organize in Northern Ireland. In that province its closest equivalent is the centre-left Social Democratic and Labour Party (SDLP).

The main constituent elements of the Labour Party today are outlined in Table 5.3. Of its principal leadership bodies, the most significant is the National Executive Committee of the Labour Party (NEC). Its role in relation to two other organizations, the National Policy Forum (NPF) and the Labour Party Conference, is explained in Table 5.4.

Clause 4 and the birth of 'New Labour'

The most significant internal victory for Mr Blair's leadership came not in his frequent run-ins with his own backbenchers after being elected premier, but in his first year as leader, with the party still in opposition. At its 1995 Easter conference, bolstered by his rabble-rousing deputy, John Prescott (whose similarly tub-thumping speech had helped John Smith, Mr Blair's predecessor, win the 'one member, one vote' debate—see Table 5.3), Mr Blair successfully passed a motion rewording one of the most sensitive and symbolic sentences in Labour's constitution.

'Clause 4' had been written in the context of a pre-war British society in which ownership of the country's assets and wealth was concentrated in the hands of very few individuals, and the absence of any state provision meant 'public services' like free health care and education were largely reliant on charity. As a result, its wording bore the imprint of the Marxist ideology on which the party's original values were based—focusing on the need to take into public ownership the 'means of production' (industry and agriculture) and give workers a greater share in their fruits. The clause, penned by Marxist intellectual Sidney Webb in 1917 and formally adopted by the party a year later, vowed:

❝ To secure for the workers by hand or by brain the full fruits of their industry and the most equitable distribution thereof that may be possible upon the basis of the common ownership of the means of production, distribution and exchange, and the best obtainable system of popular administration and control of each industry or service. ❞

Basing his version on a pamphlet he had written for the Fabian Society, Mr Blair reworded it:

Table 5.3 Member organizations of the Labour Party

Organization	Role and functions
Constituency Labour Parties (CLPs)	Equivalent to Conservatives' constituency associations, and 'voice' of ordinary party members and activists. Their influence has diminished in recent years, as leadership exerts greater control over selection of parliamentary candidates and other activities. CLPs still technically have final say over who represents their constituencies, but must choose from centrally vetted list of applicants. NEC may overrule decisions of selection panels, parachuting in favoured candidates over the heads of those chosen locally.
	CLPs normally run by two committees: general management committee (GC) and executive committee (EC). Former comprises delegates from branch Labour parties (smaller-scale ones in individual towns), local socialist societies, Co-operative Party branches, and unions. Each CLP has several elected officers, including a chair, two vice-chairs, secretary, treasurer, women's officer, youth and student officer, and, increasingly, black and ethnic minority officer. CLPs elect representatives to national policymaking bodies, including Labour Party Conference, and nominates candidates for election to the other two ruling bodies: National Policy Forum and NEC.
Affiliated trades unions	Certain unions formally affiliated to party—many 'sponsoring' individual constituencies. These include UNISON and Unite. Among those that disaffiliated, in protest at Labour's policies in government, are Rail and Maritime Union (RMT) and Fire Brigades Union. If employee is member of affiliated union, he/she automatically becomes de facto Labour member, although he/she may opt out of party.
	Affiliated unions select twelve of the thirty-two members of NEC and elect half the party conference delegates. However, until early 1990s unions still wielded 'block vote' at conferences—allowing them to pass or kill off policy proposals en masse on behalf of their memberships, regardless of individual members' views. This led to numerous run-ins between 'moderate' leaderships and union leaders pursuing more socialist agendas. In 1993 Kinnock's successor, John Smith, replaced block vote with 'one member, one vote'.
Socialist societies	Umbrella term referring to various smaller associations instrumental in party's foundation. Like unions they pay affiliation fee and may elect one delegate between them to sit on NEC. Most famous socialist society is the Fabian Society, with early members including George Bernard Shaw, H. G. Wells, and Emmeline Pankhurst, founder of British suffragette movement.
The Co-operative Party	Small socialist party formed in 1881 through establishment of joint parliamentary committee to act as watchdog on activities at Westminster from viewpoint of under-represented working people. This has long-standing arrangement with Labour not to contest same seats separately at elections—instead, often fields joint candidates with Labour under 'Labour and Co-operative Party' banner.

Table 5.4 Main constitutional bodies of the Labour Party

Body	Role and composition	Notes
National Executive Committee of the Labour Party (NEC)	Often described as Labour's 'ruling' body, National Executive Committee (NEC) is meant to represent all wings at national policymaking level, taking delegates from all affiliated groupings (see Table 5.3). Has traditionally acted as counterweight to leadership, although its influence declined under Mr Blair, who formed the National Policy Forum. As of September 2012 NEC had thirty-one members—not counting its two *ex officio* ones: party leader and deputy leader. These included former *EastEnders* actor and MEP Michael Cashman, stalwart backbencher Dennis Skinner, and former London Mayor Ken Livingstone. NEC also enforces party discipline. In 2003 its 'constitutional committee' expelled George Galloway, former Labour MP for Glasgow Kelvin, for bringing party into disrepute in series of speeches criticizing Mr Blair's actions in Iraq.	Mr Blair's neutering of NEC followed frequent run-ins his predecessors had in the 1980s and early 1990s over proposed policy changes, like the party's abandonment of commitment to scrap Britain's nuclear weapons, and repeated election to its membership of vocal critics of the leadership, such as veteran left-winger Tony Benn.
National Policy Forum (NPF)	Formed by Mr Blair in 1997, under 'Partnership in Power' initiative, this draws 184 members from all levels of the party. It meets two or three weekends a year to analyse proposal documents generated by six policy commissions, members of which include representatives of leadership, NEC, and NPF. Recommendations pass to conference for ratification.	Introduced officially as means of widening party democracy in Labour's ranks, but often perceived as leadership's instrument for quelling dissent.
Labour Party Conference	Unlike Conservative and Lib Dem conferences, Labour's is traditionally viewed less as event than decision-making body. Presiding over Conference is general-secretary: one of Labour Party's most senior officers.	Theoretically, Conference still has final say on major policy/constitutional changes. Since 1997 leadership has made clear its willingness to overrule Conference decisions. Mr Blair also reduced weight of Conference vote by affiliated organizations from 80 to 50 per cent (four-fifths still wielded by union members).

> 66 The Labour Party is a democratic socialist party. It believes that by the strength of our common endeavour we achieve more than we achieve alone, so as to create for each of us the means to realise our true potential and for all of us a community in which power, wealth and opportunity are in the hands of the many, not the few, where the rights we enjoy reflect the duties we owe, and where we live together, freely, in a spirit of solidarity, tolerance and respect. 99

The rewriting of Clause 4 was a defining moment in the creation of the 'New Labour' brand—a project initiated years earlier under Neil Kinnock, who had softened the party's image by replacing its Soviet-style, Red Flag-inspired logo (and conference anthem) with the now familiar red rose motif. Under Mr Blair this process was accelerated, as the party embraced more mainstream policies, the language and aspirations of business, and an affinity for media management— or 'spin'—designed to improve its public image after years in the political wilderness. Soon terms such as 'third way', 'big tent politics', and 'triangulation' had entered the political vernacular to explain the tactics used by Mr Blair and his apparatchiks to neutralize their opponents, by bringing together people from different shades of 'liberal' opinion in a new coalition against what he would describe in a later conference speech as 'the forces of conservatism'.

How Labour chooses its leader

Labour's leadership election procedure has trodden a long, slow road towards democratization over recent decades—though it began this process well in advance of more recent Tory moves to involve ordinary party members. From 1922 to 1981 leaders were elected solely by the party's MPs. Annual contests were held at the party Conference, but in practice leaders were normally re-elected unopposed, so these were mere formalities.

In 1981, although it was to be some years before wholesale reform of the party's constitution, Labour established an electoral college: in future, only three out of ten votes in leadership elections would be cast by Labour MPs, with 30 per cent going to Constituency Labour Parties (CLPs) and 40 per cent to the unions. Further reform followed in 1993, when the union block vote was scrapped and the weighting equalized to give each grouping a one-third share of the vote. There remain some inequities, however: individuals who are members of two or more affiliated organizations—for example, a union and a CLP—may vote more than once. Other anomalies abound: although Labour balked at electoral reform while in office (see p. 135), it uses the alternative vote (AV) system for its leadership elections.

While the process by which Labour elects its leader may now be more democratic, the power wielded by that individual, once chosen, has also been enhanced. In July 2011 Ed Miliband persuaded his backbenchers to abandon a decades-old tradition forcing frontbenchers to stand for re-election by the rest of the party's MPs every two years whenever Labour was in opposition. His victory enabled him to embark on an early Shadow Cabinet reshuffle which, in the eyes of many, shifted the balance of power away from the Blairite wing and began the process of stamping a more left-leaning agenda on the parliamentary party. On appointing his initial frontbench team nine months earlier, Mr Miliband had been forced to choose from a selection of MPs arrived at in the traditional way.

The Parliamentary Labour Party (PLP)

Like the Conservative Party, Labour has a body that represents the views of rank-and-file MPs: the **Parliamentary Labour Party (PLP)**. It, too, meets weekly in a room in Parliament and has a chairperson elected annually, normally at the start of the parliamentary session.

Between 1921 and 1970 the chair of the PLP was the party leader. But since 1970 the two posts have been permanently split, and the PLP has become (like the 1922 Committee) largely a means for backbenchers to hold their leaders to account. Unlike the 1922 Committee, however, leaders have always been able to attend the PLP, even when in government. Towards the end of his premiership, Mr Blair endured several hostile receptions from the PLP (although he received a standing ovation at the meeting following his resignation). Like the 1922 Committee, the PLP can instigate a vote of no confidence in its leadership, but in practice Labour has refrained from dumping unpopular leaders, who have generally jumped before being pushed despite murmurings of rebellion.

As well as the PLP, Labour has within it several ginger groups and is associated with various think tanks. These include three left-leaning factions: the Campaign Group, Compass, and Tribune, which was revived in 2005 by backbencher Clive Efford as a direct challenge to the leadership's perceived move to the right. More Blairite examples have included Progress, Demos, and the Institute of Public Policy Research (IPPR), although the latter recently distanced itself from Labour. A big influence on Mr Miliband's policy ideas (at least for a time) was 'Blue Labour'—brainchild of Westminster University sociologist and Labour peer Lord Glasman. This movement rejected the neo-liberal free market economics embraced by first Thatcher then Blair, while advocating a return to socially conservative policies on immigration and crime and the promotion of social justice through community-level, rather than 'big state', action.

▌ Structure and constitution of the Liberal Democrat Party

As the 'youngest' of Britain's major political parties, the Liberal Democrat Party also has the newest constitution. Unlike either Labour or Conservatives, the party has a *federal* organization, comprising separate but conjoined parties for England, Scotland, and Wales. It had 64,000 paying members in 2010, and, like Labour, encompasses several affiliated groupings, known as 'specified associated organizations' (SAOs). Each represents a particular section of its membership, such as women, ethnic minorities, lesbian, gay, bisexual, and transgender (LGBT) members, trade unionists, and youths and students.

Like Labour and the Tories, the Lib Dems have a parliamentary party to act as a voice for ordinary MPs: in fact they have three, in recognition of their federal structure. The party also organizes in Northern Ireland, but, rather than contesting elections under its own banner, has a semi-official arrangement to support the Alliance Party of Northern Ireland.

How Liberal Democrats choose their leader

Of the three main Westminster political parties, the Lib Dems have the most democratic process for electing their leaders. Once an election is called, every paid-up member of the party—from Commons frontbenchers down to local activists—has an equal say in its outcome. The various means by which elections may be triggered, however, range from grass-roots-led (receipt by the party's president of a requisition from at least 75 per cent of local parties) to decidedly 'top-down' (a no confidence vote passed by a majority of Lib Dem MPs).

In recent years the Lib Dems have been willing to depose leaders with whom they become dissatisfied. Despite leading his troops to their biggest tally of Commons seats to date under the Lib Dem banner in 2005 (sixty-two), Mr Kennedy was persuaded to resign in January 2007 following his public admission of a drink problem. The weeks beforehand had seen several of his parliamentary colleagues call for his resignation, and a poll of his MPs for BBC2's *Newsnight* suggested only seventeen were willing to give him their unqualified backing. Less than two years later, his successor, Mr Campbell, also quit, after senior colleagues (including his deputy, Vince Cable) disclosed to journalists their concerns about his lacklustre performance in the media and during Prime Minister's Questions.

The Lib Dem ideology—left, right, or somewhere in-between?

The question of where the Lib Dems fall on the left–right political spectrum has long been debatable. Traditionally, like the Liberals before them, they have been seen as centrists—pro-welfare state on the one hand, but in favour of the free market (subject to effective regulation) on the other. It is this that has arguably been their great electoral asset—enabling them to appeal to Labour voters in Tory-held marginals and Conservatives in Labour ones. In recent years, however, the Lib Dems have often appeared more conventionally left-wing in their policy ideas than Labour—thanks in part to Labour's rhetorical embrace of many Thatcherite economic reforms, the encroachment of market forces into public services, and its increasingly interventionist foreign policy. For many years, the Lib Dems advocated a 50 per cent higher rate of Income

Tax (something Labour abandoned for some time until its introduction in April 2010 of a new 'top rate' pegged at that level for people earning £150,000 a year or more). The Lib Dems still support a local income tax to replace the Council Tax, arguing it would take more account of individuals' ability to pay.

Under Nick Clegg's immediate predecessors the party reasserted many centre-left tendencies, particularly in relation to civil liberties and constitutional reform, but more recently there have been signs of the return of a more 'classical Liberal' free market approach. In 2004 Mr Clegg, along with several fellow leading lights, including Mr Cable, co-authored the *Orange Book*, a collection of essays advocating a return to a Gladstonian, nineteenth-century vision of Liberalism. The resurgence of this 'laissez-faire' philosophy appeared to be confirmed when, after the 2010 election returned no majority government for a single party, Mr Clegg allied himself with Mr Cameron's Conservatives rather than join a 'coalition of the defeated' with Mr Brown. It was not long before many left-leaning Lib Dem supporters and activists began openly voicing concern about the long-term implications for the party's independence.

The 'rightward shift' at the top has arguably continued in government, with Lib Dem ministers publicly endorsing, and at times initiating, market reforms in public services and other 'business-friendly' policies the party might have opposed under leaders like Mr Kennedy or Mr Campbell. As Business Secretary, Mr Cable found himself in the invidious position of having to introduce a tripling of undergraduate tuition fees from the 2012/13 academic year (like most other Lib Dem MPs, he had signed a pledge before the 2010 election stating his opposition to fees in principle). At the same time he was arguing for cuts in the so-called 'red tape' encumbering small businesses in an effort to stimulate economic growth, which amounted to diluting many people's employment rights by, for instance, preventing them from taking their employers to tribunals for unfair dismissal until they had worked for them continuously for two years (rather than one, as in the past). Chief Secretary to the Treasury Danny Alexander was made personally responsible for delivering the Coalition's swingeing public spending cuts, while the entire parliamentary party was whipped into supporting controversial reforms of the NHS and welfare system. However, Mr Clegg and colleagues have repeatedly retorted that, despite being the 'junior coalition partner', the party has succeeded in getting around three-quarters of its manifesto commitments onto the statute book—citing Chancellor George Osborne's repeated rises in the personal Income Tax allowance, designed to lift Britain's poorest workers out of tax altogether (see p. 192).

As a testament to the unease felt by some party leading lights about their leadership's drift away from what they considered to be its founding principles, barely a week after the formal 'coalition agreement' was signed, ex-leader Mr Kennedy—one of a long line of Liberal leaders who had nurtured the idea of an eventual 'realignment of the centre-left'—became the first 'big shot' to out himself as opposing it. (He had abstained when the parliamentary party voted to endorse it.) In an article for *The Guardian* on 15 May 2010, he expressed alarm at Mr Cameron's use of the term 'Liberal Conservative' to describe the new government in his first Downing Street press conference, and warned that the Tories might try to absorb the Lib Dems in time. This had happened to sections of the party on two previous occasions—first, when Joseph Chamberlain split it over home rule for Ireland in 1886 (ending up a Liberal Unionist), and second, when a decision by Lloyd George to continue in coalition with the Conservatives after the end of the First World War sparked a prolonged period of factional infighting, resulting in the formation of various splinter groups and the Liberals' ultimate relegation to 'third party' status.

More recently, in April 2011 a poll of grass-roots members lifted the lid on the extent of disillusionment among the party faithful—with some 64 per cent of respondents describing themselves as 'social liberals' (a term used to denote a centre-left ideology, and associated more with members of the party previously in the SDP), and just 35 per cent as 'economic liberals' (the term linked to more right-leaning 'Orange Bookers' like Mr Clegg). However, nearly a year later, a survey by influential online ginger group http://www.libdemvoice.org appeared to offer a contradictory picture—suggesting eight out of ten members still backed the Coalition.

Perhaps the rank and file are consoled by knowledge of how much leverage they can ultimately wield over their leaders. As well as possessing the tools to remove him/her, members have access to an unusual constitutional mechanism enabling them to prevent their leadership steering them in political directions with which they are uncomfortable. The 'triple-lock' was originally agreed by the party's conference in 1998 amid growing concern among some members about increasingly close relations between then Lib Dem leader Ashdown and the Labour government. It is designed to come into effect whenever the leadership makes a 'substantial proposal that could affect the party's independence of political action'—for example, announcing its intention to join a coalition. To secure such a deal, leaders are required to first win support from at least three-quarters of members of both the parliamentary party and the Lib Dems' Federal Executive (an elected committee of thirty-five senior activists, MPs, and party officials). If no such backing can be obtained, a special conference must be convened to decide the matter, mirroring the composition and voting rights of a standard annual gathering of the party. The triple-lock was invoked for the first time on 12 May 2010, to approve the Lib Dems' entry into government.

▌ The deselection process

Once a parliamentary candidate has been selected by his/her constituency party or association and elected to Parliament, he/she usually serves until voted out at another election or until he/she retires. Under certain circumstances, however, it is possible for a candidate to be 'deselected'—or sacked—by either his/her local party or leadership. The process by which this can happen varies from party to party, but in general terms follows much the same pattern.

The most recent formal deselection was that of Jane Moffat, Labour MP for East Lothian, who was removed by her local party in March 2010 for allegedly failing to work hard enough for her constituents. In exceptional circumstances MPs can be 'sacked' in other ways: former Immigration Minister Phil Woolas was barred from standing again for Labour after a specially convened election court stripped him of his Oldham East and Saddleworth seat for lying about his Lib Dem rival during the 2010 election campaign.

Notable examples of MPs who have avoided deselection include several Conservatives who defected to other parties in the last years of Mr Major's government. Emma Nicholson, MP for Torridge and West Devon, switched to the Lib Dems in 1995, but continued serving her constituency (despite quitting her local Tory Party) until 1997. Fellow Tories Alan Howarth and Shaun Woodward both jumped ship to Labour, but retained their seats after the election and went on to serve as ministers.

Between general elections, the deselection of an MP normally leads to a by-election—an election in his/her constituency alone, giving his/her local party a chance to field a replacement candidate and retain the seat, and its opponents an opportunity to win.

The Coalition plans to go one step further than previous governments in making serving MPs accountable to their electorates, by introducing new rules enabling voters to sack their MPs between parliaments if they are found guilty of serious wrongdoing, such as fiddling their expenses (see pp. 55–8).

▌ Party funding now and in future

One endlessly debated issue surrounding the party system is that of funding. Because parties are intrinsic to British parliamentary democracy there has long been a vocal lobby calling for them to be financed, at least partly, by the state. At present, only Opposition parties receive state subsidies in Britain—a privilege designed to counteract the advantage governing parties have because of the resources that can be marshalled by their sitting MPs. Introducing wholesale state funding of parties would signal a major change. Given the scale of Britain's current Budget deficit, without significantly increasing the tax burden where would 'the state' find the extra cash needed to fund parties? And, if state funding were to become an entitlement for registered political parties, would it only be the larger and/or more mainstream ones that benefited—or could taxpayers expect some of their money to go to minority extremist organizations like the British National Party (BNP)?

For these and other reasons, successive governments have sidestepped the issue. But in the absence of such grants, how should parties fund their campaigns? Because membership subscriptions provide only modest, if regular, revenue, parties have come to rely increasingly on bequests, loans, and donations from wealthy supporters. Naturally, this has given rise to charges of inequity—if one party attracts higher donations than another it can mount bigger campaigns—and suspicions that rich donors are using their money to buy levels of influence denied ordinary supporters.

The 1990s witnessed various controversies over party finance. During the Major years there was growing unease about the Conservatives' use of anonymous multimillionaire donors and money originating in offshore tax havens—particularly the 'Ashcroft millions' funnelled away by the party's ex-patriot treasurer, Lord Ashcroft. Labour promised to deal with these issues by limiting the ability of 'non-domiciles'—individuals living and/or working in Britain but registered for tax purposes in another country—to finance parties, and making the source of their donations transparent. But within months of his election Mr Blair was embroiled in his own controversy when Formula One boss, Sir Bernie Ecclestone, was identified as the source of a £1m donation to his campaign. The fact that the racing mogul had just been granted a temporary exemption from an impending ban on tobacco sponsorship fuelled suspicions he had bought influence.

To wrest back the moral high ground, the party returned the donation and began reforming the rules governing party funding in two ways: introducing a statutory register of all significant donations and creating new criminal offences relating to false and late declarations. But eleven years afterwards newly released papers suggested that, contrary to Mr Blair's protestations that he was a 'pretty straight kind of guy', within hours of holding a meeting with Ecclestone he had begun frantically looking for ways of exempting Formula One from the sponsorship ban.

Under the Political Parties, Elections, and Referendums Act 2000, registration of donations now rests with the Electoral Commission, which, in addition to overseeing election procedures, has the responsibilities laid out in Table 5.5.

Thirteen years after the 1997 election the Ashcroft saga resurfaced in the run-up to the 2010 poll. This time Mr Brown's former spin doctor, Charlie Whelan (by now political director of the Unite union), mounted an aggressive counter-attack in marginal constituencies the peer was said to be targeting. Lord Ashcroft, who it emerged was still a 'non-dom' despite having given undertakings to then Tory leader Mr Hague a decade earlier that he intended to take up UK residency (and tax liability), was accused of pumping millions into target seats before the official launch of the campaign (thereby avoiding breaking election rules) to 'buy' votes. Two months after the election, with a Conservative once more in Downing Street, Lord Ashcroft finally relinquished his non-dom status—agreeing to pay UK tax in return for keeping his seat in the Lords.

Table 5.5 Role of Electoral Commission in relation to donations and loans

Role	Process
Registers donations and loans	Established statutory register of donations, requiring all political parties and affiliated organizations to declare donations, loans, or benefits in kind of more than £1,000 made to constituencies or local party offices in single year, and donations or loans of £5,000-plus paid to central offices. Parties must detail them in quarterly reports.
Defines 'permissible donors'	Clamps down on anonymous donors. Anyone donating more than £200 to party is named on register and such donations only accepted from 'permissible donors'—individuals on UK electoral register or organizations registered in European Union (EU) and carrying out business in UK. 'Donations in kind' (e.g. office space, printing of campaign literature) treated as donations.
Limits spending	Monitors compliance with spending controls during election campaigns (see Chapter 4).
Refers abuses to Crown Prosecution Service (CPS)	Three levels of offence relate to false/late declarations: 1. failure to submit return in time—a civil offence by party and criminal offence by treasurer; 2. submitting return that fails to comply with Act—criminal offence by treasurer; 3. making false declarations on return—criminal offence by treasurer.

By way of a postscript, figures published by the Commission in August 2010 found overall donations made to Britain's political parties in the run-up to that year's election had been £6m higher than before the 2005 poll—reaching a record level of £26.3m. For the first time since 1997, the Conservatives trumped Labour, raising £12m to its £11m, although the two biggest single donations went to the latter (including £1m from a long-time supporter, steel magnate Lakshmi Mittal).

▌'Lobbygate', 'cash for honours', and other recent funding scandals

Mr Blair's government was frequently embroiled in controversies concerning alleged lack of financial transparency on the one hand and underhand links with business on the other. By the time Mr Brown succeeded him in Downing Street the tension between ministers' pledge to be 'whiter than white' financially while still raising enough money to keep the Labour Party machine afloat had reached breaking point. Successive scandals about undeclared (or, at best, under-declared) donations and loans had forced ministers into embarrassing admissions. The political initiative was consequently handed to Mr Cameron, who demanded a £50,000 cap on all individual payments, including its main lifeline: union donations. Whatever his political instincts, Mr Brown was hardly in a position to comply, arguing instead that union contributions should be viewed as comprising a number of smaller individual donations. With 'Middle England' deserting the party in favour of the resurgent Conservatives, disclosure of Labour's annual accounts in July 2008 revealed the full extent of the party's mounting debt—£24m was owed to various creditors, including several individual donors.

'Lobbygate'

Political lobbying is nothing new. The Conservatives have never been coy about their links to business, while Labour MPs in certain constituencies have been sponsored by unions for decades. But the emergence of specialist lobbying companies purposely set up to help individuals and interest groups gain access to ministers, in the hope of influencing government policy, was a phenomenon not widely witnessed until the 1990s.

The involvement of one such company, Ian Greer Associates, as an alleged intermediary in the 'cash for questions' affair (see p. 54) was for many the first they had heard of such practices. Labour promised to eradicate such activities, but within a year of regaining power senior ministers—including Mr Blair's right-hand man, Peter Mandelson—were being linked to lobbying firms boasting of their ability to buy access to ministers. One such firm was Lawson Lucas Mendelsohn, run by former Labour campaign strategy adviser Neal Lawson, business intermediary Jon Mendelsohn, and Ben Lucas, one of Mr Blair's political briefers. Another, GPC Market Access, employed one of Mandelson's ex-special advisers, Derek Draper, who is alleged to have bragged to clients he could buy them tea with Geoffrey Robinson, Labour's then Paymaster General, or dinner with Mr Blair.

'Cash for honours'

If 'Lobbygate' and the Ecclestone affair were early shots across the bows for Labour, then the various 'cash for honours' rows that followed provided the smoking gun that proved for many the party was as guilty of succumbing to the advances of big business as the Conservatives.

Of these, by far the most damaging was the so-called 'loans for peerages' scandal exposed by *The Independent on Sunday* in October 2005. The controversy erupted in earnest the following March, when the then recently formed House of Lords Appointments Commission rejected several nominees Mr Blair had put forward for life peerages. It quickly emerged that each of the men concerned had anonymously loaned the Labour Party substantial sums of money. A loophole in the 2000 Act meant that, although all *donations* of £200-plus had to be properly declared, the same rule did not apply to loans—provided they were taken out on normal commercial terms.

With the party in huge debt in the run-up to the 2005 election, Mr Blair and his advisers appeared to have deliberately sidestepped a law they themselves had introduced under the premise of wanting to make party funding more transparent, by courting loans rather than actual donations. Although the revelation that the party had gone 'cap in hand' to anonymous lenders was embarrassing enough for the government, there was no suggestion the letter of election law had been breached (even if its spirit might have been). What led to the subsequent criminal investigation—and the spectacle of Mr Blair becoming the first serving prime minister to be questioned by police, albeit as a witness—was the allegation, levelled by Scottish Nationalist MP Angus McNeil, that attempts had been made by some of his aides to 'sell' honours (an offence under the Sale of Peerages Act 1925).

In the ensuing months the spotlight came to focus on Lord Levy, Labour's chief fundraiser (who was alleged to have asked one of the lenders, Dr Chai Patel, director of the Priory healthcare group, to change a gift he planned to offer the party into an unsecured loan for £1.5m, to sidestep the new donation rules). As the controversy escalated, Lord Levy—known as 'Lord Cashpoint' in some Labour circles—briefly faced the prospect of being charged with conspiracy to pervert the course of justice, while Downing Street adviser Ruth Turner was subjected to a dawn raid by the Metropolitan Police amid rumours she faced similar charges.

No charges were ultimately brought, but the year-long investigation, which ended weeks before Mr Blair left Downing Street, cast a shadow over his final year in office. To regain the political initiative at the height of the controversy, he launched a cross-party review of political funding, chaired by Sir Hayden Phillips, chairman of the National Theatre and a senior partner with corporate financiers Hanson Westhouse. But in October 2007 the talks were suspended amid scenes of dissent between Labour and the Tories. This did not stop Sir Hayden making his own recommendations public. They included a proposal to cap individual donations after a transitional period at £50,000.

The murky world of lobbying reared its head yet again within a short time of Mr Cameron entering Downing Street. When the Coalition was formed, the Tory leader had described politicians' cosy relationship with lobbyists as the 'next great political scandal' awaiting the British Parliament—after then recent furores over MPs' expenses and the near-collapse of the banking system. His words came back to haunt him, with the explosion of the *News of the World* phone-hacking saga; the prosecution of his close friend and fellow Old Etonian Charlie Brooks and wife Rebekah (the paper's former editor); and the suggestion of collusion between senior ministers and News International executives over the bid by the latter's parent company, News Corp, to take over BSkyB (see p. 93). A few weeks earlier, in a separate scandal, Mr Cameron had been forced to sack his party's treasurer, Peter Cruddas, after he was filmed in a 'sting' operation by *Sunday Times* journalists boasting that Tory donors could buy 'Premier League access' to the prime minister, and even influence his policymaking decisions, by giving the party £250,000.

The Coalition has mooted the introduction of a new statutory register of third parties involved in lobbying on others' behalf. But in July 2012 these proposals prompted a highly critical report from the Commons Political and Constitutional Reform Committee, which argued that a register will be meaningless unless it also covers organizations that lobby ministers directly, as in the USA.

☷ Topical feature idea

The 2010 general election delivered no overall majority for any individual party, and produced nineteen MPs representing interests other than those of Labour, the Conservatives, or Liberal Democrats. The Green Party secured its first MP, Caroline Lucas for Brighton Pavilion, after fielding candidates across Britain, and while neither the United Kingdom Independence Party (UKIP) nor the British National Party (BNP) won any seats, they put up 560 and 326 candidates respectively and secured thousands of votes in some constituencies. What level of support do minority parties have in your area? How are they likely to fare in light of the public's recent rejection of electoral reform?

✷ Current issues

- **The future of traditional party politics:** the advent of the Coalition broke the eighty-year hegemony of the 'two-party' system. Despite rejecting electoral reform in the 2011 referendum, British voters have demonstrated a growing disconnect with all three main Westminster parties. The first Green MP was elected in 2010, while maverick George Galloway was returned to the Commons as Respect Party MP for Bradford West in a by-election in March 2012. If voting patterns in recent council, devolved assembly, and European elections are repeated at national level in coming years there could be a sizeable increase in the number of Scottish Nationalist MPs, while UKIP could supplant the Lib Dems as Britain's 'third party'.
- **Party funding:** controversies over political loans and donations have led to renewed calls for the introduction of state funding for parties, as practised in other countries.

- **'Deselection' by public:** the Coalition has pledged to introduce new rules to enable constituents to sack their own MPs between Parliaments if they are found guilty of serious wrongdoing.

? Review questions

1. Which is the oldest UK political party—Conservative, Labour, or Liberal Democrat?

2. To what extent has Labour stayed true to its democratic socialist roots, and are traditional labels such as 'left-wing', 'right-wing', and 'centrist' still relevant today?

3. Outline the similarities and differences between the roles of the 1922 Committee in the Conservative Party and the Parliamentary Labour Party.

4. What is the difference between a political donation and loan in UK law?

5. What are the arguments for and against state funding of political parties in Britain?

→ Further reading

Marr, A. (2008) *A History of Modern Britain*, London: Pan Books. **Critically acclaimed tie-in to 2007 BBC2 documentary series of same name, chronicling British socio-political history from post-war period to present day**.

Roy, D. (2005) Liberals: A History of the Liberal and Liberal Democratic Parties, London: Hambledon Continuum. **Overview of complex history of Liberal Party and its successors, tracing origins of liberalism, party's twentieth-century decline, and its 1970s and 1980s resurgence**.

Seldon, A. and Snowdon, P. (2004) *The Conservative Party*, Stroud: The History Press. **Colourful history of Conservative Party from late eighteenth century to present, including analysis of its recent troubles over Europe**.

Thorpe, A. (2001) *A History of the British Labour Party*, 2nd edn, London: Palgrave Macmillan. **Second edition of comprehensive overview, chronicling evolution of its policies and institutions from late nineteenth-century origins up to 2001 election**.

⊚ Online Resource Centre

www.oxfordtextbooks.co.uk/orc/Morrison3e/
Visit the Online Resource Centre that accompanies this book for web links and regular updates.

6

The National Health Service (NHS)

If there is one British institution beside Parliament capable of dictating the country's news agenda it is the National Health Service (NHS). For many journalists, however, the newsworthiness of the NHS is matched only by its complexity.

Founded in 1948, three years into Clement Attlee's reforming post-war Labour government, the NHS was designed to be exactly what it said on the tin: a *national* health service providing high-quality medical treatment, 'free at the point of need', on a uniform basis wherever one lived in the UK. But the story of subsequent decades—in particular the past thirty years—has been of the gradual fragmentation of this idealized model of socialized health care. What was once a single, monolithic health service, run directly by central government, was transformed in the 1980s and 1990s into an umbrella organization encompassing a series of connected, but increasingly autonomous, units. Much like individual companies in the commercial marketplace, most were given their own boards of directors and delegated budgets, and allowed to 'purchase' or 'commission' services from and 'sell' services to one another. And with the introduction of the concept of 'patient choice'—allowing those in need of operations and other treatments to shop around between hospitals like customers—they even began to compete for business.

With the advent of the Conservative-led Coalition government, market reforms initiated by Margaret Thatcher and consolidated by first John Major then Tony Blair are being taken to a new level in England, through the wholesale dismantling of parts of the NHS—with general practitioners (GPs) and other health professionals given direct charge of purchasing care for their patients, and many hospitals allowed to opt out of the health service altogether to become fully fledged not-for-profit companies. This chapter charts how the NHS in its current (and likely future) form came about, and tries to explain how its many strands link together.

▶ The origins of the NHS

Although not formally established until the National Health Service Act 1946, the NHS emerged from mounting concern over several decades about the ever-starker inequalities in personal well-being between the richest and poorest Britons. It had its roots in two key developments. These were the 'Beveridge Report' (of which more in a moment) and the introduction by Liberal Chancellor David Lloyd George, as far back as 1911, of a National Insurance (NI) scheme, which, in exchange for docking 4d a week from their wages, insured low-paid workers against sickness and unemployment.

When this modest measure was introduced, the concept of an NHS offering a comprehensive range of treatments was still some way off. It was not until Labour ministers were invited into Winston Churchill's wartime 'national government' in 1940 that the idea of a universal, needs-based health service was born. Arthur Greenwood, then Minister without Portfolio, commissioned Liberal economist William Beveridge to head up an interdepartmental committee on social insurance and allied services in 1941. Its report, published a year later, was to form the blueprint for not only the NHS but also the all-encompassing 'welfare state' of which it became part—leading to Attlee's famous pledge, on entering Downing Street, to harness the spirit of collectivism born out of the war effort to look after the poor, sick, and vulnerable 'from the cradle to the grave' during peacetime.

The Health Minister entrusted with launching the embryonic NHS was Aneurin 'Nye' Bevan, whose vision was inspired by his memories of witnessing the suffering of steelworkers and miners in his native Tredegar, south-east Wales, as a younger man, and the work voluntary societies and charity-funded cottage hospitals had done, in the absence of government funding, to care for such people. He reputedly modelled the NHS on the Tredegar Medical Aid Society, a community-run health care collective set up in 1874.

With no pre-existing national template for the NHS, Bevan initially had a fight on his hands persuading family doctors and consultants—most of whom had previously been able to dictate their own working conditions and pay—to sign up to his project. In the end he did so by offering them generous contracts that, by his own admission, 'stuffed their mouths with gold'. When he triumphantly unveiled the new NHS at its inaugural outlet, Park Hospital in Manchester, on 5 July 1948, Bevan declared:

❝ We now have the moral leadership of the world. ❞

Although Bevan's vision of a health service for all was largely fulfilled, it was not long before the economics of providing universal health care on such a massive scale began to chip away at some of its guiding principles—notably that of universal free access to treatment, regardless of ability to pay. In May 1951, buffeted by global economic turbulence and its dependence on US loans to continue financing its social welfare programme, the Labour government reluctantly introduced the first NHS charges: £1 for spectacles prescribed by an optician, and a half-cost price for dentures. A year later a flat rate £1 fee for visiting the dentist was introduced, along with a one-shilling generic prescription charge. In what was ultimately to be a mortal blow for Attlee, Bevan—the architect of his greatest achievement—resigned from the government even before the first of these charges had taken effect. Among those who joined him was a young Harold Wilson, a future prime minister.

How the NHS is funded

Although the proportion of Britain's gross domestic product (GDP) ploughed into the NHS each year has varied wildly between governments—with Labour traditionally investing more, even if not always wisely—the general breakdown of sources from which this investment derives has remained broadly the same as in the early 1950s. Around 80 per cent comes from general taxation (Income Tax, VAT, duties on tobacco and alcohol), with the remaining 20 per cent deriving from:

- NHS element of National Insurance contributions;
- charges to patients for drugs (prescriptions) and treatment;
- income from land sales and income-generation schemes;
- funds raised from voluntary sources—for example, local hospital appeals.

Given the direction in which the Coalition is currently pushing health policy, this balance is likely to shift in future years, with substantially more coming from income-generation.

▌ End of the post-war consensus and the birth of NHS markets

For forty years or more the NHS retained largely the same structure: it was funded centrally through taxation, with ministers and civil servants filtering the money down to hospitals, surgeries, and ambulance services. Of the tens of thousands of nurses, doctors, and paramedics (not to mention catering and cleaning staff) working in the health service at any one time, most were effectively on the government's payroll.

This is no longer the case. A series of institutional reforms since the late 1980s have transformed the NHS into a different organization entirely. Nowadays, the bulk of family doctors, or 'general practitioners' (GPs), are self-employed; many specialists work as freelance locums, moving from hospital to hospital (and public to private sector) as demand arises; and junior doctors, nurses, and care workers are increasingly hired through agencies, rather than as full-time members of staff. Catering, cleaning, and security workers are routinely supplied by outside contractors, rather than being employed in-house, and even treatment itself is increasingly contracted out to external and/or commercial providers.

So how and why did this apparent sea change in the day-to-day running of the NHS come about, and who is responsible for running the modern-day health service?

It is impossible to understand the shape of the NHS today without first examining the emergence of the 'internal market'. As long ago as 1973, the National Health Service Reorganization Act, spearheaded by then Conservative Health and Social Security Secretary Keith Joseph (one of the architects of 'Thatcherism'), aimed to shake up the NHS by introducing a more efficient management structure, with 'generalist' managers joining existing clinical experts on hospital boards, and incentives to generate revenue by letting out unused wards for the use of private patients. These themes were revisited a decade later when, alarmed at the escalating cost of NHS treatment and wage bills, another Tory Health Secretary, Norman Fowler, commissioned then deputy chairman and managing director of Sainsbury's, Sir Roy Griffiths, to chair an inquiry into making the health service more efficient. His remit was to recommend an alternative management structure, and find ways of cutting running costs by using resources more economically.

The resulting Griffiths Report proposed a major restructuring of the NHS, putting the onus on two key recommendations:

- Introduction of *general managers* to run existing district health authorities (DHAs)—essentially the administrative presence on the ground in each area of then Department of Health and Social Security (DHSS), and responsible for directing funding to local hospitals and surgeries. These would oversee the efficient use of local NHS budgets, replacing the previous 'management by consensus' philosophy (under which medical practitioners had effectively been their own managers). Griffiths felt this approach had provided little more than crisis management.

- Greater focus on *community-based* health care—with GPs, dentists, and other primary care providers given control of their own budgets, along with the freedom to commission services on behalf of their patients without needing to go through the government, or even their local health authorities. The aim was to make the allocation of finite NHS funds more efficient by replacing the 'one-size-fits-all' approach to funding GP surgeries with more targeted allocations tailored to their own patients' needs.

Amid criticisms from Labour that they were primarily motivated by saving money (and accusations that they were privatizing the health service by stealth), the Tories initially took only tentative steps towards implementing the report's findings. But a series of White Papers flowing from the inquiry in ensuing years eventually paved the way for an internal market that was, if anything, more far-reaching.

The Act that finally established this internal market (in so doing, defining this term for the first time) flowed from a further review of the NHS announced by Prime Minister Margaret Thatcher in 1988. At about the same time, she decided to split the mammoth DHSS in two, in recognition of its burgeoning workload: creating the Department of Social Security (DSS) to run the benefits system and a separate Department of Health (DH).

The National Health Service and Community Care Act 1990 implemented two White Papers: *Caring for People* and *Working for Patients*. It ushered in a phased reorganization with the following key features:

- Hospitals, mental health units, ambulance services, and other NHS bodies directly involved in patient care became **NHS trusts**—with their own management boards, incorporating both practitioners (consultants and other senior clinical staff) and general managers charged with improving efficiency.

- GPs were offered the opportunity to become 'fund-holders'—'opting out' of district health authority control to take charge of their own budgets.

- GP fund-holding practices, DHAs, and family health service authorities (FHSAs) were redefined as 'purchasers' of NHS care on behalf of their patients. While GPs would now focus on *primary care*—providing 'first-port-of-call' treatments such as diagnoses, vaccinations, and purchasing X-rays, tests, and small operations on behalf of their surgery patients—FHSAs would buy in other community-based services, with DHAs 'purchasing' acute hospital services such as accident and emergency (A&E) facilities.

- NHS trusts were defined as service 'providers'.

In theory, the new internal market would operate as illustrated in Figure 6.1.

In practice, its implementation was far from smooth. For a start, as independent contractors GPs had to *want* to be integrated into it in the first place. While some relished the opportunity to control their own budgets and direct spending towards areas they felt needed cash, others were alarmed at the increased workload and the prospect of making the wrong decisions about how to spend their money—only to face tricky dilemmas should unforeseen needs arise during a financial year. Only family practices with more than 5,000 patients in England and Northern Ireland (4,000 in Wales and Scotland) were allowed to apply for fund-holder status. By the time Labour came to power in 1997, some 3,500 practices and 15,000 GPs—fewer than half the estimated 40,000

Figure 6.1 How the Conservatives' NHS internal market was structured

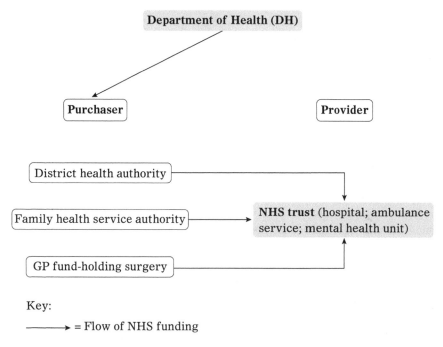

Key:

——————▶ = Flow of NHS funding

practising across the UK—had signed up. By mid-1996 there were more than 520 trusts in place, but mergers had reduced this tally to 450 by 1999.

The internal market was also criticized for placing too much emphasis on management and recruiting high-salaried senior staff, armed with clipboards and flow charts, at the expense of frontline workers like nurses. Managers were increasingly headhunted from the private sector—a reflection of the Conservatives' belief that those with business expertise were likely to be better at running the organization than medical practitioners, whose skills lay primarily in patient care. This trend has continued to this day, with chief executives of most NHS trust boards earning six-figure salaries. In May 2012 a survey by Incomes Data Services identified Jan Filochowski, of West Hertfordshire Hospitals Trust, as the highest-paid CEO—having earned £282,500 in 2010/11, including a bonus for the previous year. It also found that three-quarters of hospital trust chief executives were paid more than prime minister David Cameron in the same period, with average earnings of £163,500.

The (initially short-lived) introduction of fund-holding GP surgeries—the key plank of the Tories' internal market ideal—remains an important innovation, as it was to ultimately shape the party's approach to further reforming the NHS after its return to power in 2010 (see p. 178).

Emergence of the 'postcode lottery' and treatment rationing

There was widespread agreement before the introduction of the internal market that the original 'top-down' NHS model needed adapting to the changing needs of a society on the cusp of a new century—not least because of the widening disparities between different areas in terms of average income, age, health care needs, and other demographic factors. Nonetheless, the decision to grant increased autonomy to DHAs and individual GPs was to have one unintended consequence: the steady emergence of significant variations in the level and nature of treatment available to people with the same conditions living in different areas. This increasing trend—dubbed the 'postcode lottery' or 'postcode prescribing'—led many to question whether the NHS could any longer be described as a 'national' health service.

A famous cause célèbre for those arguing against the delegation of funding decisions to local level was the case of beta interferon—an expensive drug that, according to some experts, dramatically decreases the number of relapses suffered by people with multiple sclerosis. In the early 1990s it emerged that a number of DHAs were refusing to fund beta interferon on the NHS—arguing that the £10,000 a year cost per patient would be better spent on other treatments, such as physiotherapy. Its supporters claimed prescribing the medicine early could save the NHS money in the long run, by delaying the need for residential and/or palliative care. Another commonly cited example of the postcode lottery is the differential availability of fertility treatment for childless couples and, in particular, *in vitro* fertilization (IVF)—the process by which egg cells are fertilized by a man's sperm outside a woman's womb before being transferred back to stimulate pregnancy.

Despite Labour's early attempt to end the postcode lottery by establishing national service frameworks (NSFs) to harmonize provision of essential health services across the country (see p. 174), wide disparities remain. In November 2005 it emerged that Ipswich Hospital NHS Trust and a number of Suffolk primary care trusts (PCTs) were rationing hip and knee replacement operations by refusing to offer them to patients judged obese, other than in exceptional circumstances. Dr Brian Keeble, director of public health for Ipswich PCT, justified the decision by telling the press it was for patients' own good, because overweight people 'do worse after operations' and hip replacements might fail. But critics of the move—since emulated by several other trusts—condemned it as discrimination against patients whose conditions were judged to be self-inflicted. Their concerns were compounded when, just days later, a leaked paper from the **National Institute for Health and Clinical Excellence (NICE)**—the agency that vets potential new treatments and recommends to the government whether they should be funded on the NHS—indicated plans were afoot to ration treatment for heavy smokers and drinkers.

The postcode lottery is now such a political issue that ministers have increasingly found themselves drawn into disputes over individual cases of patients denied treatment by their local PCTs. So potentially damaging had the issue become by June 2008 that then Health Secretary Alan Johnson pledged to end it once and for all—by banning PCTs from denying patients costly treatments approved by NICE for NHS use. Despite this, inequities remain, and there are fears that a combination of real-terms budget cuts and the introduction of wholesale GP commissioning heralded by then Coalition Health Secretary Andrew Lansley (see p. 178) could see widening disparities emerge in primary health provision from area to area. In June 2012, a Freedom of Information Act request by *GP Magazine* revealed that nine out of ten NHS trusts were restricting the availability of certain operations—with tonsillectomies most heavily rationed, and cataract surgery similarly heavily restricted (by 89 and 66 per cent of trusts respectively). While ministers maintained that rationing on grounds of cost (as opposed to clinical judgement) was unacceptable, David Stout, deputy chief executive of the NHS Confederation, which represents PCTs, argued that restrictions were justified in some cases, in light of the 'considerable financial pressures and scarce resources' engendered by the Coalition's deficit-reduction programme (see p. 184).

NHS waiting lists and the origins of Blair's health reforms

Perhaps more controversial still, in light of escalating criticisms of the Thatcher and Major governments' emphasis on spending NHS money more efficiently rather than pouring more in, was the waiting list crisis that emerged in the early 1990s. By the time Labour was elected in May 1997, 1.3 million people were listed as awaiting operations or other inpatient treatments, with 'guaranteed maximum waits' from initial GP referral to actual treatment of eighteen months. In the final months of Mr Major's government the tabloids were filled with stories about elderly and vulnerable patients falling seriously ill or even dying while waiting for surgery. Equally alarming were the numerous stories printed about the lengthy queues people were enduring in A&E units—and the often overcrowded and undignified conditions they were forced to accept.

Such was the public outcry that one of Tony Blair's central election pledges in the campaign leading to his 1997 landslide was to cut waiting lists by 100,000 by releasing £100m from so-called 'NHS red tape'. Despite a sluggish start, by November 2004 official figures indicated waiting lists had hit a seventeen-year low: although 857,000 people were still listed, this was down 300,000 on 1997. Perhaps more importantly for the individuals concerned, waiting *times* had fallen, with only nineteen patients waiting longer than a year for treatment, and 122 more than nine months. Health Minister John Hutton declared at the time that, by the end of 2008, no patient should be waiting longer than eighteen weeks—and this target remained official government policy until Labour left office in 2010. However, within weeks of becoming Health Secretary, Mr Lansley signalled an end to 'target culture' (a long-standing bête noire of the Conservatives) by scrapping the eighteen-week appointment 'guarantee' in England, together with the stipulation that all NHS patients should be seen by a GP within forty-eight hours of requesting an appointment.

New Labour's restructuring of the NHS

The success of Mr Blair's blizzard of NHS reforms was mixed. Significant achievements in some areas—bolstered by unprecedented public investment—were marred by inconsistent, even contradictory, policymaking in others.

When Labour returned to power after eighteen years in opposition, it inherited a health service widely seen as in crisis. After an initial period of caution, during which the new government stuck to spending limits imposed by the Tories, then Chancellor of the Exchequer Gordon Brown announced a huge increase in NHS funding—taking it above and beyond the average annual investment of other European countries in public health care. In 1997 the proportion of Britain's GDP spent annually on the NHS was 6.7 per cent, but in his 2002 Budget Mr Brown used his first tax rise (a 1 per cent National Insurance increase) to raise it to 7.4 per cent a year. By 2010, health spending was equivalent to 9.7 per cent of GDP, but even before the Coalition took power and announced its multibillion-pound savings programme the influential King's Fund charity was predicting that by 2016/17 it would fall back to 7.9 per cent as a result of public spending cuts—wiping out all real terms increases since 2000.

Mr Blair quickly decided that pouring more money into the NHS was not enough. To ensure this investment was spent wisely, like Mrs Thatcher before him, he set about restructuring the health service. Having promised to dismantle the 'wasteful' internal market while in opposition (and initially doing so under his first Health Secretary, Frank Dobson), he began to introduce a new form of localized management and budgetary control seen by many as his own version of the Tory model.

New Labour's version of the internal market originated in the Health Act 1999 and the White Paper preceding it, *The New NHS: Modern and Dependable*. Its main emphasis was on the primacy of community-based health care—steering patients wherever possible away from hospital, and giving GPs and other primary care providers the money and autonomy needed to offer a wider range of treatments through their practices.

On the face of it, the resulting reforms were initially modest. In place of fundholding, which had effectively fostered an element of 'competition' between GP surgeries, Mr Blair introduced greater cooperation between practices, by establishing *primary care groups* (PCGs). These collaborative bodies brought together GPs, community nurses, and other related practitioners in a given geographical area to promote closer liaison and, ultimately, a more coordinated use of NHS resources. The idea was that, as PCGs grew in confidence and evolved, increasing levels of responsibility would be delegated to them. In the end, like fund-holding GP practices, they also assumed control of their own budgets, establishing NHS trust-style boards to take their financial decisions for them.

By 2002 the bones of the following new NHS structure were established:

- PCGs were replaced by *primary care trusts* (PCTs)—local administrative organizations covering populations of 100,000 or more. Like fund-holding GP practices, these bought in clinical services from NHS trusts on behalf of patients—except that, rather than calling this 'purchasing', Labour used the term 'commissioning'. PCTs took control of 80 per cent of the overall NHS budget, and with it virtually all local commissioning. But it was only a matter of time before health policy would return full circle, with the Coalition's pledge to abolish PCTs and hand commissioning powers direct to GPs (see p. 178).

- After initially being replaced by ninety-six health authorities (HAs), DHAs later gave way to much more arm's-length administrative bodies, *strategic health authorities* (SHAs), of which there were initially twenty-eight—a number reduced to ten in July 2006. As the population covered by each authority increased, its level of direct involvement in patient care dwindled. In October 2011 they were merged to form four regional 'clusters' tasked with managing the NHS at local level pending the introduction of a new long-term health service structure in April 2013 (see p. 180). In the meantime, they remained responsible for monitoring local health care to ensure fair access to services like GP surgeries and dentists, and for publishing three-yearly 'health improvement plans' (HIPs) identifying local health concerns (such as rates of heart disease or diabetes) and promoting healthier lifestyles and disease prevention.

- NHS trusts continued to be classed as service 'providers', but with the prospect of gaining greater financial autonomy if they performed well in 'league tables'. Ultimately, many were granted the 'self-governing' status of **foundation trusts**—a form of autonomy now granted to all NHS trusts by the Coalition (see p. 181).

- County councils and unitary authorities established *local involvement networks* (LINks) to act as the voice of service users. Run directly by local taxpayers, LINks could demand specific changes to health and social care in their areas. They replaced a prior Labour invention, patients' forums, which had been staffed by volunteers from local communities, and earlier 'community health councils' (CHCs), run by paid officers. LINks had to be formally consulted on major structural changes in their areas and allowed to view related documentation.

Labour's revamped internal market therefore works as outlined in Figure 6.2.

Figure 6.2 Labour's version of the internal market

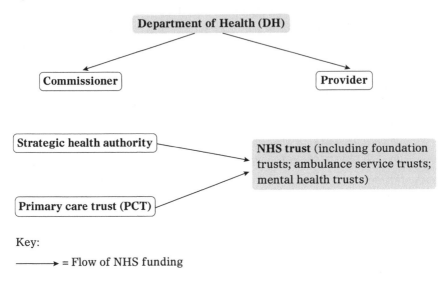

Key:

⟶ = Flow of NHS funding

After Labour's initial restructure, the NHS was rationalized more than once. On 1 October 2006 the number of PCTs was halved, from 303 to 151. The mergers enabling this to happen were intended to produce efficiency savings by preventing duplication between trusts in neighbouring areas with broadly similar needs. By the time the Coalition announced it was scrapping PCTs many covered populations of up to 600,000. The number of hospital trusts had also been reduced (partly due to closures and mergers). Prior to the Coalition's reorganization there were 168 acute trusts and seventy-three mental health trusts covering 1,600 hospitals and specialist care centres.

In addition to its structural reforms, Labour strengthened the hand of the DH and the Secretary of State, giving them the power to set nationwide targets and standards of care in priority areas, to which all SHAs, PCTs, and NHS trusts must adhere. These 'national service frameworks' (NSFs), established in 1998, were 'long-term strategies' designed to provide consistency of care across the UK. In effect, they amounted to a prospectus, similar to the National Curriculum used to enforce uniformity of teaching in core subjects in schools. By the time Labour left office there were NSFs and strategies covering ten high-priority conditions—ranging from cancer to coronary heart disease and diabetes. These are outlined in the table entitled 'NHS national service frameworks and strategies (to 2 February 2014)', to be found on the Online Resource Centre. The number of NSFs and strategies was reduced to nine by the Coalition in early 2012, with another review due on 1 February 2014.

Though the Coalition has nominally retained NSFs, a closer look at the 'small print' of the newly revised frameworks and strategies bears witness to greater emphasis on patient choice—with individuals encouraged to take informed decisions from a range of options presented to them by professionals about how best to manage their own care. This more individualized approach—an extension of ideas road-tested by both the Major and Blair governments—arguably undermines one of the original purposes of NSFs, namely to reintroduce a degree of 'uniformity' to health provision across England. Supporters of the new approach would counter that it has never been the purpose of NSFs to dictate a one-size-fits-all approach to treating patients with the same conditions, irrespective of their individual circumstances. Rather, they would argue that it is the job of NSFs to establish a consistent 'menu' of treatment options across the country—an idea not incompatible with allowing each patient to choose the option they feel is best suited to them.

Nonetheless, the pursuit of greater standardization of health care was a central thread of some other Labour initiatives, including the early introduction of 'health action zones' (HAZs) in deprived areas. These were used to address 'health inequalities' between rich and poor districts by targeting additional resources at communities with high rates of unemployment, poverty, and poor housing, to ensure that public health—and quality of health care—in those areas kept pace with that in more affluent ones.

A further attempt to tackle postcode lotteries came with the formation of NICE in 1999. This executive agency of the DH is charged with approving drugs and treatments for NHS use, promoting improved public health, and ensuring that consistent, high-quality health care is available across the country, by:

- offering guidance on the prevention of illness to NHS workers, local authorities, and the wider public and voluntary sectors;

- advising government on whether new and existing clinical treatments, medicines, and procedures should be made (or remain) available on the NHS;

- giving advice to ministers and the public on the most appropriate treatment for individuals with specific ailments and diseases.

NICE's decisions are frequently controversial. Campaigners representing sufferers from specific conditions have accused it of penny-pinching by failing to endorse new drugs or recommending the abandonment of others (in a preliminary ruling in 2001 it ruled beta interferon should no longer be available on the NHS—see p. 170). On occasion, however, its interventions have been more 'positive': in June 2006 NICE issued draft guidance to PCTs recommending the use of the then recently licensed drug Herceptin® for early-stage breast cancer. Its decision followed the case of Barbara Clark, a 49-year-old nurse who persuaded Somerset Coast PCT to pay for the £20,000-a-year drug by threatening it with litigation in the European Court of Human Rights (ECtHR).

The DH's other key roles in recent years have included:

- setting the *direction* of health policy—by outlining overall NHS strategies, formulating policies, passing legislation, setting regulations, allocating resources, and fostering local partnerships to implement DH policy on the ground;

- supporting NHS service delivery—by monitoring and evaluating the performance of health service bodies and professionals, increasing capacity, improving the skills base, and ensuring value for money for service users;

- promoting health and well-being among citizens—by working with public, private, and voluntary sectors to encourage healthier lifestyles, and liaising with international bodies like the European Union (EU), World Health Organization (WHO), and Organisation for Economic Co-operation and Development (OECD);

- accounting to Parliament and the public for the NHS' performance—by answering parliamentary questions, responding to correspondences from the public, and communicating through speeches and public events.

From patients to consumers—the 'marketization' of the NHS

The blueprint for taking Thatcher and Major's NHS reforms to their logical conclusion, and much that has followed under the Coalition, came with the publication of New Labour's 'Ten-Year NHS Plan' in 2000. Pledging to 'give the people of Britain a health service fit for the twenty-first century', modernizing Health Secretary Alan Milburn launched NHS 'taskforces' to 'drive' the promotion of market concepts like 'choice' and 'competition'. At carefully choreographed intervals between early 2001 and 2003, Mr Milburn risked the ire of many medical practitioners—and Labour traditionalists—by outlining the radical plans listed in the table entitled 'Key reforms flowing from Ten-Year NHS Plan', to be found on the Online Resource Centre.

Mr Milburn's introduction of a 'Concordat' allowing patients to be treated in private hospitals and clinics to speed up reductions in waiting times was just one of the measures that proved deeply unpopular with some long-serving party loyalists, for whom the idea of *any* private sector involvement in the NHS (direct or indirect) was heresy.

It wasn't long before ministers were being accused of privatizing the NHS by the back door. But Mr Blair was unapologetic, arguing that it was ends not means that mattered, and if using a spare BUPA ward meant frail pensioners would have to wait eighteen months less for hip replacements, neither they nor their families were likely to be fussed about outdated ideological objections. Yet the media was quick to highlight the incongruous spectacle of NHS patients being flown overseas for surgery that ought to be available to them locally.

Vocal critics of this shake-up included Mr Dobson, who accused his party's leadership of being 'elitist' and 'following a Tory consensus'. He argued that, by naming and shaming 'failing' hospitals in league tables and allowing 'success-ful' ones (foundation trusts) to offer inflated salaries for the most qualified and experienced staff, Labour risked creating a 'two-tier health service'. High-performing trusts would inevitably become yet more successful, gaining even greater freedoms in the process, while those stuck at the bottom would con-tinue spiralling downhill, devoid of the reputation, resources, and autonomy needed to improve their performance. Others argued 'patient choice' was a sham. Given the option of having an operation at a local poor-performing hospi-tal or a better one elsewhere, few patients would surely choose the former, making 'choice' illusory. And like the most popular schools, the best-perform-ing hospitals ultimately had finite capacity—meaning they might quickly become oversubscribed and unable to cope with demand.

As if taunting his critics, Mr Milburn went further in an interview with *The Times* in January 2002, by describing the NHS as 'Britain's last great national-ized industry'—and suggesting it represented a model unsuitable for the twen-ty-first century (see p. 89).

But for Labour opponents of the changes, the final insult came at the hands of their fellow backbenchers, on a glacial November evening in 2003. With the help of a handful of Scottish MPs—many personally opposed to having founda-tion hospitals in their own country, where MSPs had rejected them—Mr Blair scored his lowest Commons victory to date, squeezing the Health and Social Care Bill through by seventeen votes.

As for the devolved nations, the overall structure of the NHS in Scotland today bears a strong resemblance to the way it looked nationwide before Mrs Thatcher. Meanwhile, in Wales the internal market was abandoned in time for the sixtieth birthday of the health service in 2008—returning to an old-style model that saw funding channelled directly from the health department down to trusts and *health boards*, the Welsh equivalent of SHAs.

Nonetheless, by the time of the 2010 election a broad consensus existed between the three main parties supporting moves to grant all English-based NHS trusts foundation status—giving staff and local residents increasingly hands-on involvement in their running. Today's foundation trusts, overseen by **Monitor, an Independent Regulator of NHS Foundation Trusts**, have been lik-ened by advocates to mutuals or cooperatives. Staff and members of the public can become 'members', earning the right to elect members to their boards or even stand themselves. Once on a board they have a direct say in the appoint-ment (and dismissal) of the trust's chairpersons and non-executive directors, and a veto over their choices of chief executive.

The Health and Social Care Act 2012 and the reinvention of the NHS

If Mr Blair's repeated restructuring of the NHS was controversial, the biggest earthquake was to come. Despite earlier declaring a 'moratorium' on any further 'top-down' reform of the health service—and Mr Cameron's personal assurances in the run-up to the 2010 election that the letters 'N-H-S' were his top policy priority (in an echo of Mr Blair's 'education, education, education' mantra prior to 1997)—two months after entering office, Mr Lansley unveiled a root-and-branch reform package unlike anything seen before. In a throwback to the abortive fund-holding policies of the Major years, he announced the abolition of PCTs and handover of their commissioning role to GPs. Unlike fund-holding practices (which managed their finances individually), the new breed of GP commissioners would form local 'consortia'—later dubbed **clinical commissioning groups (CCGs)**—to purchase services collaboratively. But this time GPs would be *forced* to participate, rather than deciding for themselves whether to 'opt in' (as was the case with fund-holders)—a curious element of compulsion amid a raft of other proposals predicated on the freedom of choice principle. More controversial still, potentially, was Mr Lansley's pledge to create 'the largest social enterprise sector in the world' by encouraging foundation trusts to effectively break out of the NHS superstructure—becoming not-for-profit, mutual-style companies with the ability to generate their own revenue by charging paying customers for private treatment as well as providing traditional health care free at the point of delivery. The flip side of these freedoms is that, like commercial firms, hospitals that mismanage their finances could go bust. Moreover, the complex and costly transformation was to begin at the same time as the NHS was ordered to find £20 billion in administrative savings—a demand introduced by Mr Lansley as a quid pro quo for Chancellor George Osborne's guarantee in his June 2010 'emergency Budget' (see p. 196) that real-terms increases in health spending would continue until 2014. Fears about the danger of NHS trusts being left to fend for themselves financially appeared to be borne out when in June 2012 South London Healthcare, formed through the merger of three smaller trusts in 2009, was formally put into administration by Mr Lansley and warned it faced being dissolved or losing several key services after racking up a £69m debt. Though Labour warned this was merely a taste of things to come under a new look, deconstructed NHS, ironically the root of this trust's problems appeared to lie in the cost of servicing crippling private finance initiative (PFI) contracts for facilities built under the previous government (see pp. 230–1). Tellingly, the government warned that twenty-two other trusts were facing similar problems.

One of the biggest charges directed at Mr Lansley is the accusation that his reforms effectively hand £60bn of NHS funds over to private contractors—with no PCTs or SHAs left to police them. He has countered that GPs' decisions will be scrutinized by a new regulator, **Healthwatch**, with local offshoots based on the extant LINks bodies, and a beefed-up version of the **health service scrutiny committees** established by Labour (see p. 185). To oversee commissioning of specialist services—and primary care itself—there is a new quango, the **NHS Commissioning Board**, which (along with the DH) will act as a hub of the new look health care market.

As for that market, the Bill's most contentious inclusion initially was a clause which smacked to many of paving the way for the NHS' transformation into a US-style insurance-based system. Under the new model of marketized health care, NHS hospitals and foundation trusts would be forced to compete for business with 'any willing provider' from the private and/or voluntary sectors—raising the prospect of multinational companies reaping huge profits off the backs of British taxpayers by 'cherry-picking' simple procedures conducive to economies of scale, and leaving the NHS to deal with more complex cases.

So seismic was the proposed overhaul that in August 2010 health care union **UNISON** (concerned about its members' job security) launched legal action in protest at the speed and scale of DH reform. It argued that the public consultation ministers had instigated was a 'sham', as within twenty-four hours of Mr Lansley's unveiling his White Paper, NHS chief executive Sir David Nicholson had written to all English trusts urging them to start implementing the changes 'immediately'. But respected health charity the King's Fund warned that, while GPs were best placed to judge the needs of patients, many had little inclination (or ability) to become accountants. Sure enough, fears that the new consortia might end up paying for the costly expertise of commercial consultancy firms appeared to be borne out when, as early as January 2011—two years before the reforms were introduced countrywide—GP magazine *Pulse* conducted an analysis of ten of the first fifty-two 'pathfinder' CCGs set up by the government to road-test the new commissioning structure. It found that six of them had already signed contracts with private firms, including KPMG, or were about to do so. The alternative, critics argued, would be for CCGs to effectively reinvent PCTs by hiring in-house managers, administrators, and finance directors. In a further criticism of the direction of government policy, the British Medical Association (BMA), the professional body representing doctors, warned that giving GPs direct control of their own budgets (and the associated tough spending decisions) risked fostering distrust between them and patients with strong ideas about their own medical needs.

So unprecedented was the scale of opposition to the reforms among medical professionals—with, for example, the Royal College of Nursing passing a no confidence vote in the Health Secretary and the loyalist Liberal Democrat peer Baroness Williams leading a revolt at her party's 2011 spring conference—that ministers were forced to introduce a six-week 'pause' in the Bill's passage while a specially convened panel of independent experts, the NHS Future Forum, investigated ways of introducing additional regulatory safeguards to allay critics' fears. Among the recommendations Mr Lansley accepted to mollify his opponents was to water down a clause in the original Bill requiring Monitor to 'promote competition' within the NHS—which some suggested would (by accident or design) open the health service up to EU competition law. Instead, the Bill was amended to emphasize the need to 'promote integration' between different health care bodies and the treatments they offered, in the interests of increasing 'citizens' rights' and 'improving quality'. The Health Secretary's 'duty to provide' a comprehensive NHS to the public was also reinstated—or, as ministers would have it, re-emphasized—to reassure all concerned that the fragmentation of old structures did not amount to wholesale privatization and deregulation.

In the end, after withstanding several defeats in the Lords, knife-edge Commons debates (see p. 63), and more than a hundred amendments from ministers alone, the Health and Social Care Bill finally received royal assent in March 2012—a full fourteen months after it was first presented to Parliament, and nineteen months after publication of the White Paper that spawned it. The structural reforms that survived its turbulent passage were as follows:

- Clinical commissioning groups (CCGs) to take over commissioning from PCTs in April 2013. Unlike in the original Bill, the groups—numbering 257 at time of writing—will not be solely GP-led, but collaborations between doctors and other medical professionals, including nurses.

- NHS Commissioning Board (NHS CB) to take responsibility for commissioning primary care itself and ensuring specialist services are maintained at national and regional levels. The Board will convene *clinical senates* to provide medical advice on commissioning plans and *clinical networks* to advise on local service integration.

- Local authorities to replace SHAs as the main bodies promoting health improvement and shaping overall health care provision in their areas. Their role in scrutinizing the quality of local NHS services will be extended to cover all health providers in their areas—including those from the private and voluntary sectors—and councils will also assume devolved powers to scrutinize public health services. Scrutiny powers will either be exercised by councils' existing health service scrutiny committees or a 'suitable' alternative arrangement approved by ministers.

- **Health and well-being boards** to be formed by all 152 English local authorities to bring together all commissioners of health and social care in each area, along with local representatives of Healthwatch, to promote integrated approaches to improving health. Boards to include elected local councillors.

- Secondary care to be offered by 'any qualified provider' (as opposed to any 'willing' one), embracing competition between public, private, and third sectors.

- The Care Quality Commission (see p. 545) to assume responsibility for regulating standards of health and social care across *all* providers, while Monitor will issue (and withdraw) licences to registered health care providers, including private companies and charities. It will also be responsible for promoting 'efficiency', setting prices for NHS treatment, and ensuring competition works in 'patients' interests'. To ensure NHS providers are not undercut by commercial rivals, competition is to be on the basis of 'quality'—not price.

- **Public Health England (PHE)**, a new executive agency of the DH, to promote healthier lifestyles and fund £4bn worth of public health initiatives across the country. Public health services to be commissioned by local authorities from ring-fenced budgets (see p. 360) or the NHS at local level, using PHE finance.

The DH has also announced the creation of several other quangos, in addition to the raft of new bodies listed above—many of which were themselves only introduced at the various amendment stages. While Monitor's role overseeing foundation trusts will be retained for the time being, this will only be 'temporarily', while an *NHS Trust Development Authority* completes the process of converting all remaining trusts to foundation status. Another body, *Health Education England*, will oversee the training of future NHS professionals. Figure 6.3 gives a visual description of the new internal commissioning structure.

Though the new structure is all but in place, there is no sign of resistance to the reforms abating. Even as the Bill battled its way through its final stages, the *Guardian* and *Independent* newspapers reported that struggling NHS hospitals were already being quietly 'taken over' by private companies. In September 2011 the former used requests under the Freedom of Information Act (see Chapter 20) to reveal how top-level talks were already under way between the DH, McKinsey, and private German health care chain Helios about 'potential opportunities in London'. The first 'public–private partnership' contract to actually be signed in relation to the day-to-day management of an NHS hospital was the deal completed by Circle Partnership and Hinchingbrooke Hospital, Huntington—coincidentally, Mr Major's former constituency—in February 2012. Under this arrangement, Circle was tasked with introducing savings to turn around the trust's £40m debt, in return for which it would keep the first £2m of any 'profit' generated by the hospital and a quarter of all subsequent earnings. Precisely what form these 'savings' will take has sparked fresh opposition from unions, concerned about the contractual implications of having their employment effectively transferred from public to private sector.

Meanwhile, the Coalition's decision to raise the cap on how much of their incomes foundation trusts may raise through treating private patients to as

Figure 6.3 How the Coalition's new 'internal–external' NHS market is structured

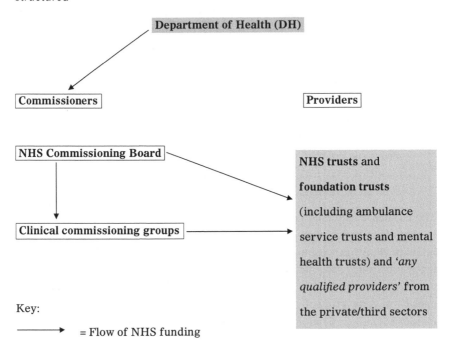

Key:

———————▶ = Flow of NHS funding

high as 49 per cent has also met stiff opposition. Shadow ministers and union leaders have accused the government of subsidizing the private sector with taxpayers' money and running the risk of increasing NHS waiting lists by prioritizing more lucrative fee-paying customers. For its part, Labour has pledged to repeal key sections of the Act when it returns to power.

The Faculty of Public Health, the professional body which monitors standards of care provided by public health specialists, has also issued warnings about the dangers of marketizing the NHS—arguing that tying hospital funding to the number of procedures they carry out will incentivize them (and rival private and charitable providers) to treat patients needlessly to raise profits. The organization's vice-president, John Middleton, added it would become increasingly difficult for patients with long-term conditions to receive 'joined-up care' as this would require separate organizations to collaborate—and Monitor and/or EU competition authorities might see this as 'anti-competitive' behaviour. A market-based health service will also, he argued, disadvantage less educated and/or pushy patients—and increase the likelihood of further child abuse cases like those of Victoria Climbié and Peter Connelly (see p. 519) going unnoticed until too late, by ending the tradition of designated professionals having ongoing supervisory roles over individual caseloads.

Other recent controversies in the NHS

Mr Lansley and his Coalition successor, Jeremy Hunt, are far from the first ministers to have to deal with NHS trusts in financial trouble. In 2006, then Health Secretary Patricia Hewitt responded to an escalating deficit crisis in some areas by giving debt-ridden trusts permission to borrow money from 'better performing' ones with financial surpluses. The Coalition might also reflect on the difficulties Labour encountered when negotiating with GPs. In 2004 it emerged Mr Blair's government had 'botched' a new contract for family doctors by offering them bonuses for providing certain services—for example, flu vaccinations for asthmatics and the elderly—over and above their general practice, inflating their salaries to £100,000 or more. Rumbling controversy over this perceived injustice at a time when many practices offered little or no out-of-hours service led eventually to a new agreement between ministers and the BMA, in which GPs reluctantly agreed to renegotiate their collective contract, and offer limited weekend and evening appointments. Mr Lansley was tougher in his negotiations with doctors—most controversially, changing the rules governing their pensions, forcing them to work longer and pay bigger monthly contributions for less reward in retirement. In the case of GPs and hospital doctors this will mean working until 68 rather than 65, and paying as much as 14.5 per cent of their salaries each year into personal pension pots if they are to retire on the £68,000 a year colleagues previously enjoyed. In a show of defiance, the normally moderate BMA mounted its first strike in forty years in June 2012, leading to widespread cancellation of non-urgent operations, surgeries, and hospital appointments.

Mr Lansley's run-ins with the medical profession did not stop here: he also forced local GPs to reclaim formal control of all out-of-hours provision from the private companies that delivered it under Labour, and pledged to ensure all foreign doctors providing out-of-hours care can speak good English. This change followed several scandals relating to allegedly poor levels of care administered by some overseas practitioners under the previous system. In the most high-profile case, retired engineer David Gray died after being given ten times the correct dose of diamorphine by German locum Daniel Urbani.

Other recent controversies have revolved around a familiar bugbear of reform critics: the fines and bonuses culture. In 2008 then Health Minister Lord Darzi published the recommendations of a year-long review into NHS funding, unveiling plans to award hospitals multimillion-pound bonuses for demonstrating top-quality clinical performance. Assessments of their success would be based both on hard data—covering everything from waiting times to individual surgeons' 'death rates'—and patients' own views about the quality of their treatment. Also proposed was a new 'NHS constitution' outlining what patients had a right to expect from the health service, including dignity, privacy, and confidentiality (an echo of the Major and Blair 'Patients' Charter'). In addition,

→
see also
local
government,
pp. 541–2

15 million people with long-term health conditions, including asthma and diabetes, would receive personalized care plans, with 5,000 participating in a pilot giving them greater control over their treatment through 'personal health budgets'—a reform already in place in relation to domiciliary care provided by council social services departments for elderly and mentally ill people.

The Coalition has adopted a tactic broadly the reverse of Lord Darzi's—forcing hospitals that readmit patients within thirty days of discharging them for related complaints to carry out any additional treatment at their own expense. Defending the penalties when he introduced them in 2010, Mr Lansley cited statistics showing hospitals had become overzealous in discharging patients to alleviate 'bed-blocking' (see p. 544). As a result, between 1998/9 and 2007/8 emergency readmissions in England had risen from 359,719 to 546,354.

Deficit reduction was also the motivation for Lib Dem and Tory manifesto promises to cut wasteful spending on consultants, managers, and IT projects. Once in office, however, the Coalition quickly reneged on a related pledge: its undertaking to scrap the Summary Care Record (SCR) database, commissioned by Labour to store all electronic patient records centrally so they can be accessed by NHS professionals working anywhere in England. The database—which patients must 'opt out' of if they want their details kept private—began rolling out in April 2010.

▌ Complaining about NHS treatment

Anyone dissatisfied with his/her NHS care may make a formal complaint, initially at local level, and his/her case may be referred to one of four ombudsmen—one each for England, Scotland, Wales, and Northern Ireland. In England complaints about the NHS are handled by the *Parliamentary and Health Service Ombudsman*, in Wales the *Public Services Ombudsman for Wales*, in Scotland the *Scottish Public Services Ombudsman*, and in Northern Ireland the *Northern Ireland Ombudsman*.

Each ombudsman produces an annual report for consideration by its national assembly or parliament, and handles complaints in relation to:

- failure in NHS service standards;
- failure to provide a service 'to which a person is entitled';
- maladministration by an NHS body;
- failure in the exercise of clinical judgement by hospitals or GPs.

Complaints are handled according to the sequence outlined in the table entitled 'The complaints process to the Health Service Commissioner (Health Service Ombudsman)', to be found on the Online Resource Centre.

In addition, there is an independent watchdog charged with promoting ongoing improvements in the health service and reviewing complaints by service users unhappy with the local resolution of their cases. Individuals must, however, have gone through the full NHS complaints procedure before their cases can be referred to this quango. Since April 2008, health and social care providers in England have been monitored by the CQC. Formed from the merger of the Healthcare Commission and Commission for Social Care Inspection (CSCI), it is authorized to issue trusts with fines, fixed penalties, and enforcement notices for breaking the terms of their registrations. It can even withdraw NHS licences from acute hospitals that persistently fail cleanliness inspections. In Scotland the CQC's role is assumed by the *Scottish Commission for the Regulation of Care* (SCRC) (Care Commission for short), in Wales by *Healthcare Inspectorate Wales* (HIW), and in Northern Ireland by the *Regulation and Quality Improvement Authority* (RQIA).

→
see also local government— chapter 18

In recent years the performance of local NHS services has also been monitored by health service scrutiny committees set up by county councils and unitary authorities (see p. 180). These comprise around fifteen members, including a chairperson and vice-chairperson. Membership is drawn not only from these authorities, but also local district/borough councils and relevant voluntary organizations, including Age Concern, National Society for the Prevention of Cruelty to Children (NSPCC), and National Association for Mental Health (Mind).

▌ NHS changes under devolution

Handing day-to-day NHS management to the devolved executives in Scotland, Wales, and Northern Ireland was always likely to create disparities in the way the health service was administered in different areas. Aside from major structural contrasts—for example, the continued absence of foundation trusts in Scotland—the past few years have seen clear 'inequalities' emerge between the nations, arising from political decisions taken by individual legislatures. In April 2007 the National Assembly for Wales became the first devolved chamber to scrap prescription charges, having previously halved them from the £6 an item levied elsewhere in Britain at that time to £3. The Northern Ireland Assembly followed suit in April 2010 and the Scottish Parliament a year later. There have been (as yet unheeded) demands for the same to happen in England.

Marginally less controversial have been the decisions by all three devolved administrations to abandon parking charges at NHS hospitals—a move former Labour Health Minister Ben Bradshaw refused to adopt in England, arguing that many trusts needed the revenue generated to subsidize patient care.

⬛ Topical feature idea

The article in Figure 6.4 is taken from the *Manchester Evening News*. It concerns a leaked document revealing plans by Central Manchester University Hospitals NHS Foundation Trust—one of a new generation of 'super trusts' granted permission to take over struggling neighbouring trusts—to reduce accident and emergency provision at Trafford General Hospital to cut its debt. The move, which followed a local campaign to save Trafford's A&E unit, reflected several recent trends in management of the NHS in England: an emphasis on balancing the books of individual trusts as if they were independent businesses; the emergence of different 'tiers' of trusts, with 'successful' ones allowed to absorb 'failing' ones; and rationalization of health provision at local level. How would you develop this story into a background feature? Who would you approach for interviews, and what questions would you ask them?

Figure 6.4 Article from the *Manchester Evening News*, 9 May 2012

Anger at plans to downgrade Trafford General Hospital's A&E

Katherine Vine and Alice McKeegan

Manchester Evening News

9 May 2012

Web link: http://menmedia.co.uk/trafford/news/s/1493317_anger-at-plans-to-downgrade-trafford-general-hospitals-ae

The accident and emergency department at Trafford General is set to be downgraded under plans leaked this week.

Documents show four possible options for the emergency unit at the hospital—with the most likely being the downgrading of A&E.

The papers are understood to be drafts and were drawn up by NHS Trafford ahead of an anticipated public consultation this summer.

The first proposal involves keeping A&E as it is—but it is thought health bosses do not consider this as a viable option.

The second would see A&E downgraded to an urgent care centre, which would still take some emergency patients and would be open from 8am until 8pm, or until midnight. Emergency surgical admissions would be axed and there would be no inpatient surgery.

The third would be for an urgent care centre with a nurse-led minor illnesses and injuries unit, which would not take ambulance transfers.

The final option would be the same as the third but with no dedicated treatment room for patients before they are taken to a ward.

Changes are being proposed after a takeover by neighbouring Central Manchester University Hospitals NHS Foundation Trust.

The merger took place because Trafford was struggling with an historic debt and was too small to operate independently.

Health campaigners, who are fighting to save A&E, slammed the plans and described them as a 'full scale attack on the hospital services currently provided'.

Matthew Finnegan, chairman of the Save Trafford General campaign, said: 'They are trying to persuade the public to accept a watered down version of a 24/7 A&E unit.

'This is the most serious ever threat to the future of Trafford General.'

Campaign co-ordinator Jo Harding demanded that the first option—to keep A&E as it is—is included in the final consultation.

A spokesman from NHS North West said: 'Any plans to change services of this nature would have to be consulted upon with patients and staff.'

'NHS Trafford must gain approval from the board of NHS North West prior to embarking upon any consultation.'

✳ Current issues

- **Return of GP commissioning and creation of independent hospitals:** the Conservative-led Coalition has introduced the most radical reorganization of the NHS since its inception. Clinical commissioning groups (CCGs) of GPs and other health professionals will now commission services direct from 'any qualified provider'—a category which embraces NHS trusts, foundation trusts, charities, and multinational corporations.

- **Future of NHS prescription charges:** prior to the May 2010 election, Labour pledged to abolish prescription charges for those with long-term conditions in England, but this was put on hold by the Coalition. Since 2011 no one living in Scotland, Wales, or Northern Ireland has had to pay for prescribed medicines.

- **Scaling back of NHS targets, or just changing their emphasis?** The Coalition has vowed to reduce the use of top-down NHS targets, placing greater emphasis on assessing 'quality' of care, rather than simply the quantity and speed of procedures performed. However, as then Health Secretary, Mr Lansley launched several new datasets to be published regularly to inform patients. The first, introduced in June 2010, were weekly updates on rates of infection at individual hospitals by meticillin-resistant *Staphylococcus aureus* (MRSA) and *Clostridium difficile* (C. diff.). These are now published on a single national website: http://data.gov.uk.

? Review questions

1. What were the founding NHS principles? To what extent were they ever achieved—and how far can they be said to be still upheld by government policy?

2. The Coalition denies Opposition claims that it is privatizing the NHS—despite allowing 'any qualified provider' to compete to treat health service patients, and encouraging foundation trusts to become self-supporting independent businesses, with the ability to raise up to 49 per cent of their income from private patients. Who is right, and why?

3. Can the NHS still be described as a 'national' health service? If not, why not?

4. Given the variable needs and demands of different areas of the UK, what are the arguments for and against pursuing the NHS ideal?

5. Outline what is meant by the concept of 'patient choice'. What measures have been introduced so far to put this idea into practice—and how successful have they been?

→ Further reading

Ham, C. (2004) *Health Policy in Britain: The Politics and Organisation of The National Health Service*, 5th edn, London: Palgrave Macmillan. **Fifth edition of leading text on history of NHS, including updates on Labour's reforms and developments in Scotland, Wales, and Northern Ireland.**

Klein, R. (2010) *The New Politics of the NHS: From Creation to Reinvention*, 6th edn, Abingdon: Radcliffe Publishing. **Comprehensive overview of evolution of the health service, encompassing recent market reforms.**

Leys, C. and Player, S. (2011) *The Plot Against the NHS*, Perth: Merlin Press. **Provocative interrogation of political agenda underlying Coalition's reform plans for the NHS, envisaging emergence of US-style insurance-based health system.**

Pollock, A. M. (2006) *NHS plc: The Privatisation of Our Health Care*, London: Verso Books. **Thoughtful critique of growing involvement of private sector in running NHS by professor of health policy and health services research at University College London.**

ⓦ Online Resource Centre

www.oxfordtextbooks.co.uk/orc/Morrison3e/
   Visit the Online Resource Centre that accompanies this book for web links and regular updates.

7

The Treasury, industry, and the utilities

During the 1992 US presidential election race, James Carville, campaign strategist for then aspiring Democratic nominee Bill Clinton, coined a phrase that would go down in political (and journalistic) folklore. Identifying the issue he judged most crucial to persuading the US electorate to back a candidate, he said simply, 'the economy, stupid'. So it is, arguably, in Britain. Although political historians have observed that UK voters do not always switch horses at times of economic crisis (the deep recession of the early 1990s saw John Major return the Conservatives to power, albeit with a drastically reduced majority), perceived economic competence has proved the making of certain prime ministers (Margaret Thatcher, Tony Blair) and incompetence the downfall of others (Ted Heath, James Callaghan).

This chapter explores the work of the two principal government departments charged with overseeing the British economy: HM Treasury and the Department for Business, Innovation, and Skills (BIS). It also examines the remit and composition of the main non-departmental bodies charged with managing specific areas of economic performance, such as the Bank of England's Monetary Policy Committee (MPC), the Office of Fair Trading (OFT), the Financial Services Authority (FSA), and the recently established Office for Budget Responsibility (OBR).

▌ The role of the Treasury and Chancellor of the Exchequer

In recent years it has become customary for prime ministers to appoint deputy prime ministers to stand in for them when they are absent on foreign business or on holiday. If the premier can be said to have a true 'number two', however, it is the Chancellor of the Exchequer. Charged with controlling the government's purse strings, the Chancellor is indisputably the most powerful minister in the Cabinet beside the prime minister. The workings of government would grind to a halt if it were not for taxes and loans, and it is the Chancellor's job to raise this money. Even the name of the department he/she heads—the Treasury—testifies to his/her authority. Not for nothing is the prime minister's own official title 'First Lord of the Treasury'.

The Chancellor has the following key responsibilities:

- overseeing the government's public spending commitments by managing fiscal policy—raising or lowering taxes/duties, and investing them in public services (schools, hospitals, roads);
- managing national debt—the level of borrowing needed to top up taxation revenues to finance the government's spending programme;
- promoting economic growth in Britain's economy and encouraging exports;
- controlling domestic inflation (rises in the cost of living) and unemployment.

In recognition of the huge degree of responsibility that comes with the post, he/she is assisted by one of the largest ministerial teams of any Whitehall department. Unlike most other ministries, the Treasury boasts at least three secretaries of state in addition to the Chancellor: the Chief Secretary to the Treasury, the Financial Secretary to the Treasury, and the Economic Secretary to the Treasury.

Fiscal policy and taxation

One of the principal means by which British governments have traditionally attempted to control the economy is through 'tax and spend' tactics—more formally known as 'fiscal policy'. Based on the writings of Liberal economist John Maynard Keynes, fiscal policy involves raising or lowering taxation to influence consumer behaviour—and to improve the health of the government's finances. A 'Keynesian' approach might see the Chancellor raise Income Tax rates, for example, in so doing cutting individuals' take-home pay and, by extension, spending power. In theory this should have the knock-on effect of reducing demand for goods and services, thereby curbing inflation. Increasing taxes also boosts government revenue for public spending on schools, hospitals, etc., reducing the need for the Chancellor to *borrow* money (increasing the UK's Budget deficit and, over time, 'national debt').

Until the 1980s there was a broad post-war consensus in favour of managing the economy through fiscal policy—although, on balance, this approach tended to be favoured more by Labour than Conservative governments. Labour's enthusiasm arose largely out of its traditional emphasis on taxation as an instrument for redistributing income from higher to lower earners through benefits (see Chapter 8). From the advent of the National Health Service (NHS) onwards, Labour also gained a reputation as the 'high tax party' because of its ideological commitment to strong investment in state health care and education (which required substantial revenues). Before the Thatcher years, the party also favoured the public ownership of many industries and these, too, required huge injections of money to maintain them. The Conservatives, in contrast, have traditionally been the party of tax cuts and breaks (particularly for business)—favouring a 'supply-side' approach to running the economy that leaves more money in individuals' pockets in the hope of boosting growth through private, rather than public, expenditure. The theory is that keeping taxes as low as possible for everyone, including the rich, ultimately has a beneficial 'trickle-down' effect on the wider economy and, by extension, lower-income households.

There are two broad forms of taxation: **direct taxes** and **indirect taxes**. Direct taxes are 'upfront'—explicitly taken from individuals or businesses as deductions from their basic earnings. The main types are outlined in Table 7.1.

The fact direct taxation is charged at different rates, according to an individual's or company's income, means it is often referred to as 'progressive taxation'. By taking into account people's ability to pay, it is seen as fairer than a flat-rate charge—like a water bill or television licence—which costs the same to everyone, regardless of their earnings. This has not stopped some campaigners arguing for a more once-size-fits-all approach, however. And in light of recent debates about the perceived need to simplify Britain's hideously complex 'tax code' (the rulebook governing how much each individual is charged, based on their precise financial circumstances) the notion of an across-the-board rate of, say, 30 per cent has been revived, not only by conservatives, but also some pragmatists who see this as a way of making it harder for the rich to use creative accounting to avoid paying taxes.

In contrast to direct taxes, indirect ones are often described as 'regressive'. Unlike Income or Corporation Taxes, they are built into the prices of goods and services consumers buy (including basic utilities like gas and electricity). Because these 'pay-as-you-spend' charges—often described as 'hidden' or 'stealth' taxes—are levied at universal rates, they take no account of individuals' ability to pay. The most familiar—VAT, tobacco/alcohol duties, and fuel duty—are set out in Table 7.2.

The British tax system has long been characterized by its complexity. For this reason Mr Osborne established a new *Office for Tax Simplification* in July 2010 to rationalize the 11,000-page Exchequer code he had inherited, and end what he described as the 'spaghetti bowl' of UK tax law. Meanwhile, in an effort to crack down on tax evasion and avoidance—together estimated to cost Britain's economy some £14bn a year—Mr Osborne's Lib Dem deputy, Chief

Table 7.1 Types of direct taxation in the UK—and how they work

Tax	How administered	Rates (2013/14)	Notes
Income Tax	Paid by working people through either Pay-As-You-Earn (PAYE) contributions deducted from their gross salaries by employers, or retrospective payments to HM Revenue and Customs (HMRC) by self-employed	Personal allowance for under 65-year-olds—£8,105 in 2012/13 and £9,205 in 2013/14 Personal allowance for 65 to 74-year-olds—£10,500 Personal allowance for those aged 75 and over—£10,660 Standard rate—20% (20p in £) Higher rate—40% (40p in £) Additional rate for those earning £150,000 or more—45% (45p in £)	The Income Tax 'personal allowance' (the amount a person can earn before paying tax) has risen incrementally each year since Coalition entered office, with aim of eventually taking all those earning less than £10,000 a year out of tax altogether (a Lib Dem manifesto pledge). Level at which 40% higher rate kicks in was lowered in 2011/12 to £35,001, and £34,371 in 2012/13. Additional rate is being lowered from 50% (50p in £) from April 2013.
Corporation Tax	Paid by companies on their profits—an 'income tax for companies'	Small profits rate—20% (20p in £) from April 2011—down from 21% (21p in £) Main rate—24% (24p in £) from April 2012—down from 26% (26p in £), and due to fall to 23% (23p in £) in 2013/14	Standard rate (known as 'main rate') was due to fall by 1% every year for four years beginning April 2011. Main rate applies to any company whose profits in given tax year are £1.5m or more. Small profits rate has fallen back incrementally from high of 22% in 2009 (when 100% relief for small businesses on any capital investment up to £50,000 and 175% tax credit to encourage research and development also introduced). Small profits rate applies to companies generating profits up to £300,000.
Capital Gains Tax (CGT)	Paid by owners of financial assets, property, and other items, like expensive jewellery or sports cars, sold for personal gain	Entrepreneurs' rate—10% (10p in £) on first £5m made during lifetime General rate—18% (18p in £) Higher rate taxpayers' rate—28% (28p in £)	There has been prolonged controversy about capital gains in UK media, in light of mammoth profits made by 'private equity firms'—groups of wealthy speculators who club together to buy underperforming

Table 7.1 (*continued*)

Tax	How administered	Rates (2013/14)	Notes
			companies, improve their fortunes, and sell them for profit. Amid mounting criticism of this sector (some directors were reputed to be paying less tax than their cleaners), Labour introduced 18% flat rate for CGT for anyone whose gains exceeded £1m (albeit with 10% 'entrepreneurs' rate' for gains of less than £1m). Before George Osborne's first Budget there was speculation CGT might rise to 40 or 50%, but it was finally raised to just 28%—and only for higher rate Income Tax payers. At same time entrepreneurs' rate was extended to apply to first £5m of individual's lifetime gains.
Inheritance Tax (IHT)	A 'death duty' paid on value of estates (including financial assets, property, and other valuable items) handed down from deceased to friends or family members by executors of their wills	Legacies of over £325,000—40% (40p in £), or 36% (36p in £) for those who leave 10% or more of their net estate to charity, since April 2012	Until recently, IHT was charged at 40% on all estates worth £300,000-plus, but mounting controversy over this low threshold (average house prices were near that level by 2007) prompted Labour Chancellor Alistair Darling to introduce 'exempt transfers' for individuals who leave estates to a spouse, civil partner, or charity. In effect this means recipients may use both their own allowances and those of the deceased parties—doubling their thresholds to £650,000. Mr Darling was widely criticized for 'stealing' Conservative policy, and Tories entered May 2010 election pledging to raise threshold to £1m (although Lib Dems have blocked this policy).

NOTE: A regularly updated version of this table can be found on the Online Resource Centre.

Essential public affairs for journalists

Table 7.2 Types of indirect taxation in the UK—and how they work

Name	How administered	Rates (2011/12)	Notes
Value added tax (VAT)	'Hidden tax' embedded in retail prices of items consumers buy in supermarkets, high-street stores, and online	20% (20p in £)	For essential items like domestic fuel and power there is reduced rate of 5%, while certain items are exempt—including food, children's clothes, books, newspapers and magazines, and some disability equipment. During 2008–10 recession Labour cut rate for 13 months from 17.5% (17.5p in £) to 15% (15p in £). Coalition raised it in January 2011 to 20% (20p in £).
Tobacco products duty and alcohol excise duties	Embedded in retail prices of items subject to excise duty	16.5% of the retail price of a packet of 20 cigarettes, plus £167.41 per 1,000 cigarettes as of 21 March 2012

26.81% (26.8p in £) per litre of spirits and wine exceeding 22% ABV

253.39% (253.39p in £) per hectolitre of made-wine and sparkling wine of 5.5–15% alcohol by volume (ABV)

19.51% (19.51p in £) per hectolitre of general beer, with 4.88p in £ extra for high-strength beer, and lower rate of 9.76p in £ for lower-strength beer | Always controversial among smokers and drinkers, these are higher in Britain than elsewhere in EU. Duties on alcohol products range widely from one to another. Petrol duties have also been a source of unrest recently, in light of the increasing underlying price of car fuel caused by ongoing global peak oil crisis. Mr Osborne froze tobacco and most alcohol duties in June 2010 Budget, and announced no further rise in fuel duty, but motorists still hit by ensuing increase in VAT. |
| Fuel duty | Additional tax added to VAT on motor fuel | 58p in £ per litre for unleaded petrol, diesel, biodiesel, and bioethanol from 23 March 2011, due to rise to 61p in £ from 1 January 2013 | In 2000 Mr Brown angered farmers and long-distance hauliers by raising fuel duty—and introducing automatic annual rise known as 'fuel tax escalator'—at time of already rising petrol prices. His action led to first large-scale protest of Blair era, as convoys of fuel protestors clogged M1 and M6. In his last Budget Mr Darling announced he was phasing in proposed 'all-in-one-go' rise of nearly 3p a litre in three stages—in April 2010, October 2010, and December 2011, but Mr Osborne cut duty by 1p in £ in his March 2011 Budget and scrapped escalator. He has since repeatedly delayed planned rises because of soaring pump prices, but was due to introduce further increase in January 2013 |

NOTE: A regularly updated version of this table can be found on the Online Resource Centre.

Secretary to the Treasury Danny Alexander, announced at his party's 2010 conference that he would be scrutinizing the accounts of everyone earning £150,000 or more, aiming to recoup at least half of these lost fiscal receipts. Since then the issue of 'tax-dodging' has moved up the political agenda—particularly in light of campaigns by groups such as UK Uncut and 38 Degrees highlighting the fact that the annual cost to the Exchequer of those at the top of the pile who abuse the tax system is anything up to thirty-eight times as much as that of 'benefit fraud' (see p. 241).

Major public spending announcements have historically been reserved for the Budget (see pp. 205–6), but in 1997 Mr Brown introduced an innovation designed to set out publicly his spending plans for three years at a time. The idea was partly motivated by a desire to create the appearance of greater financial transparency. It was also intended to encourage individual spending departments dependent on Treasury handouts to plan in a more long-term way, rather than from year to year as previously. Spending reviews have generally been held on a three-yearly basis since then, with less frequent (but more far-reaching) **Comprehensive Spending Reviews (CSRs)** occurring so far on just three occasions (in 1998, 2007, and 2010). Labour delayed its final CSR until after the May 2010 election, and it eventually fell to the Coalition to deliver it that October (see p. 246).

Managing national debt

National debt—sometimes referred to as 'public', 'government', or increasingly 'sovereign debt' (see p. 292)—is the term describing the total of all credit owed at any one time by every level of government (or government-owned institution) in a given state. Other than raising taxes, the principal way in which governments finance public spending is through borrowing. On a month-by-month basis, Chancellors run a **public sector net cash requirement (PSNCR)**. Formerly the 'public sector borrowing requirement' (PSBR), this is effectively the difference between the total ministers intend to spend on public services in a given year and the amount available through taxation. To avoid unpopular tax rises or spending cuts, governments have historically favoured loans as a means of financing costly public expenditure. Usually these are raised by selling bonds (known as 'gilt-edged securities' or 'gilts') to the public. By borrowing from investors to maintain or increase spending, governments often run up short-term 'debts'—much like individuals using their bank overdrafts or credit cards. Overspends of this kind within a given financial year are known as *annual deficits*.

Since a more 'monetarist' approach to running the economy was adopted in the 1980s (see pp. 201–2), successive governments have made a virtue of trying to 'balance the books' within overall *economic cycles* (periods, usually of a few years, during which economies 'naturally' fluctuate between bouts of expansion and contraction) by reining in taxation and controlling spending. But the impact of the 2008 global financial collapse and ensuing recessions and 'eurozone' sovereign debt crisis (see pp. 292–5) changed this. In 2009/10, the last tax year before the May 2010 election, government borrowing reached a peacetime record of £163.4bn—*excluding* the cost of aid to the banking sector.

The principal debate in Britain since the Coalition came to power has centred on the state of the country's 'structural', rather than 'cyclical', deficit. The latter phenomenon—a familiar concept in most market economies—is the periodic budgetary overspend most governments incur during periods of short-term economic turbulence (such as recessions). The former is deeper-rooted. It results from what the *Financial Times* newspaper describes as a 'fundamental imbalance in a government's receipts and expenditure, as opposed to one-off or short-term factors'. In other words, a structural deficit tends to emerge after a prolonged period during which a government has consistently spent more money than it was able to raise through taxes or selling off state assets—forcing it to borrow more (often at high commercial interest rates) as a consequence.

When the Coalition took office and examined the previous government's balance sheets in detail, its ministers claimed the 'black hole' in Britain's public finances—and the true extent of its structural deficit—was even worse than previously feared. In his last Budget, Labour Chancellor Alistair Darling said this overspend (estimated at around £77bn of Britain's overall £167bn deficit) had peaked at 8.4 per cent of GDP during 2009/10, and would fall to 2.5 per cent by 2014/15 on the back of a phased programme of £73bn in spending cuts and tax rises. He repeated an earlier Labour pledge to halve the country's overall deficit within four years.

But neither Mr Darling's figures nor the speed of his response to Britain's debt crisis impressed the Conservatives. Delivering his own 'emergency' Budget barely two months later, Mr Osborne unveiled a swingeing package of austerity measures—principally a squeeze on welfare benefits (see pp. 246–8) and annual spending cuts of £40bn by 2015, *in addition to* the billions earmarked by Labour. In so doing, he put government spending departments other than those with previously ring-fenced frontline budgets on notice that their funding would fall by up to a quarter (later asking ministers to 'model' cuts of up to 40 per cent to identify any further slack). By 2015/16, Mr Osborne predicted, the structural *current* deficit—the part of the structural deficit used to fund public sector running costs like wages and maintenance, rather than capital investment—would become a modest surplus, allowing him to start addressing Britain's overall national debt. Based on his Budget, the OBR predicted this debt would peak at £70.3bn in 2013/14—compared to the £74.9bn anticipated for 2014/15 under Labour's plans. He was later forced to revise his timetable for eradicating the deficit, principally blaming the sovereign debt crisis in the 'eurozone' (see pp. 292–5) for delaying it until at least 2017—two years after the next election. At time of writing, further revisions were widely anticipated, after statistics published in June 2012 revealed that public sector net borrowing had soared by £3bn since the previous year—from £15.2bn to £17.9bn—due to a 7.3 per cent fall in tax receipts combined with an 11.7 per cent rise in welfare benefits caused by rising unemployment and stalling growth.

The fallout from Mr Osborne's rhetoric was significant. Given his repeated public pronouncement that 'we are all in this together', his contention (and that of his Lib Dem allies) that his Budget had been 'fair'—by, for example, raising the personal Income Tax allowance to £7,475, thus taking 900,000 low-paid workers out of tax altogether—was questioned in August 2010, when the independent Institute of Fiscal Studies (IFS) think tank published an in-depth analysis of its likely impact on different income groups up to and including 2014. Branding the Budget 'clearly regressive', it claimed the poorest 10 per cent of households stood to lose 5 per cent of their income as a result of its measures, while non-pensioner households without children in the richest tenth would sacrifice less than 1 per cent. The IFS analysis—reflected in a similar assessment four months later when Mr Osborne slashed welfare further in his October CSR—prompted an unusual intervention by the director general of the Equality and Human Rights Commission, Neil Kingham, who publicly reminded ministers of their obligation under the Equality Act 2010 (passed months before Labour left office) to 'have due regard', before announcing Budget measures, to their likely impact on the disabled and other 'vulnerable groups'. He warned that the Commission might need to take 'enforcement action' if the Treasury could not prove it had properly assessed the likely long-term fallout of the Budget against 'equality impact assessments'.

The CSR itself went on to slash some £81bn from public expenditure—the biggest cut by a British government since at least the 1970s—and the Treasury's own predictions estimated nearly 500,000 public sector jobs would be lost as a result.

During acute economic crises, it has sometimes been necessary for governments to approach global financial institutions. In the mid-1970s then Labour Prime Minister James Callaghan borrowed money from the International Monetary Fund (IMF)—a crisis bank Britain had co-founded in the wake of the Second World War (see pp. 317–18)—to stabilize Britain's economy as it was buffeted by stagflation (simultaneous rises in inflation and unemployment). The IMF only agreed on condition that the government made substantial public spending cuts to save money. Documents released by the National Archive in December 2006 under the 'Thirty-Year Rule' (see pp. 603–4)—a convention stipulating all but the most sensitive government papers should be made public thirty years after being written (a gift for journalists!)—revealed Britain had nearly had to scrap its nuclear deterrent simply to balance the books.

More recently, it emerged that the huge injections of extra funding into health and education under New Labour were financed largely by borrowing—meaning that, even before it was forced into considering a multibillion-pound bailout for the banks, the government was accumulating a mounting structural deficit (see p. 196). According to figures released in 2008, having initially dropped sharply after the party returned to power in 1997, national debt more than doubled between 2001/2 and 2007/8, leaping from £315.5bn to £650bn. It rose by £100bn in one stroke when the government bailed out the Northern Rock bank to save its customers' deposits and restore confidence in the financial sector following its near-collapse in 2007. Northern Rock—which had overstretched itself by making high-risk home loans to customers without the guaranteed means of repaying them—initially made an emergency plea for support to the Bank of England (reflecting trends in the US 'sub-prime market'—see pp. 213–14). It was eventually nationalized by the government as a 'temporary measure', after months of talks to find a private buyer failed, but in November 2011 Mr Osborne confirmed plans to sell it to Virgin Money, albeit for 'only' £747 million—barely half the £1.4 billion Labour had spent taking it into public ownership.

By the time of Northern Rock's nationalization, the bill for propping it up had topped £100bn (equivalent to the total annual spend on the NHS), and repaying Britain's national debt was costing taxpayers £31bn a year in interest alone—marginally less than the country's defence budget. In July 2008 Mr Darling was forced to admit he was reviewing Mr Brown's fiscal 'Golden Rule': the principle, adhered to for a decade or more, that government should only borrow for *investment*, rather than *current spending*. In a swift move designed to signify ministers had learned lessons from the Northern Rock debacle, in September 2008 Mr Darling wasted little time nationalizing the assets of another bank, the Bradford and Bingley, to avert its collapse. While some critics immediately accused him and Mr Brown of again using taxpayers' money to secure irresponsible loans made by a reckless bank at the height of the credit boom, they were widely praised for some innovations, including the creation of a new Financial Services Compensation Scheme (FSCS). Triggered by the FSA, this effectively forced the banking sector as a whole to absorb Bradford and Bingley's losses, while still guaranteeing protection to those with savings of up to £35,000.

Towards the end of its thirteen-year rule, Labour reverted even more overtly to a Keynesian approach to buoying up the economy. As the recession bit, Mr Brown and Mr Darling committed themselves to a 'fiscal stimulus' designed to limit job losses by boosting growth through strategic tax cuts (including a short-term cut in VAT—see Table 7.2) and increased public investment. The idea was that, by bringing forward capital projects originally earmarked for future years, the sharp decline in activity in the by then free-falling housing and small business sectors could be offset by the state keeping people in employment directly. Figures published by the Office for National Statistics (ONS) in July 2010 suggested it might indeed have been the fiscal stimulus that hauled the British economy out of recession (growth reached 1.2 per cent in the second quarter).

At the height of the downturn, Labour also launched a number of discrete aid initiatives to help those hit hardest. These included a Homeowner Mortgage

Support Scheme, to give short-term financial aid to those with mortgages of up to £400,000 and savings of £16,000 or less who had lost their jobs but expected to find work soon. Its aim was to avoid a repeat of the 1980s and 1990s recessions, during which home repossessions had soared. By 2010 there were indications that its impact had been positive: according to the Council of Mortgage Lenders, while 46,000 homes were repossessed in 2009, this was only 61 per cent of the 75,500 seized by banks and building societies in 1991.

To stimulate a recovery in property and small business, meanwhile, the government began using its stake in the part-nationalized banks to nudge them into lending more money (at affordable rates) to consumers and struggling companies. An Asset Protection Scheme was also introduced to insure the major British banks against potential losses caused by previous 'toxic debts' (see pp. 213–14). At the same time, in a move unseen for decades, the Bank of England opted to use its own device to encourage more lending, pumping liquidity into the system by increasing the supply of sterling through boosting its own bank balance electronically: a process known as **quantitative easing (QE)**.

Briefly, QE involves central banks purchasing bonds or equities from retail banks, in so doing increasing the prices of those assets and reducing the interest rates payable on them. The effect of this (at least theoretically) is to help 'recapitalize' banks, lower overall interest rates in the economy, and pass on these cheaper borrowing costs to ordinary customers, including individuals and businesses seeking loans for investment (and, by extension, taking on more staff). In light of Britain's stalling recovery, and subsequent slip back into recession, QE has continued to be used periodically under the Coalition, but at time of writing it remained unclear how effective it had been—with some economists arguing it had achieved little more than enabling banks to shore up their own finances without passing on the benefits. Others predicted QE could have the long-term effect of increasing inflation by leading to another boom in consumer spending like those of the late 1980s and Noughties.

Another recent tactic used by the Coalition to help small businesses secure finance they need to expand is so-called 'credit-easing'—the practice of the Treasury lending money, via banks, to companies with turnovers of up to £50m at a cut-price interest rate, designed to lessen the repayment costs. Mr Osborne released £5bn of taxpayers' money over an initial six-month period at a rate 1 per cent below that commonly available commercially, with a further £15bn expected to follow over the ensuing eighteen months. Participating banks included RBS, Lloyds, Barclays, Santander, and a new specialist lender, Aldermore.

Bond markets, borrowing costs, and the tyranny of 'credit ratings'

Just as individuals and companies have to be deemed 'credit-worthy' to qualify for loans from financial institutions, so too do governments. An enduring principle underpinning the Coalition's fiscal squeeze has been its conviction that

Britain must be seen to stand firm in its resolve to rebalance the nation's books—and that only by doing so will it reassure the all-important bond markets (pension funds, venture capitalists, and other institutional and individual investors) that 'UK plc' remains a safe haven for their investment.

In addition, today's Chancellors are all too mindful of the ominous influence on the markets of *credit rating agencies*—the pronouncements of which can have the power of life and death over a state's long-term financial health. To date, the three main agencies, Standard and Poor's, Fitch Ratings, and Moody's, have continued to award Britain the maximum gold-starred 'triple-A' rating—ensuring the interest rates the country is charged for its borrowing remain low. However, in February 2012 Moody's contributed to a wobble in UK markets by putting it on notice that its status might be cut in future because of the potential impact on its growth prospects of the eurozone crisis, which had already seen several EU economies lose their top ratings and the so-called 'PIGS' states (Portugal, Ireland, Greece, and Spain) reduced to 'junk bond' level. For a fuller explanation of the eurozone crisis, see Chapter 9.

Office for Budget Responsibility

In a symbolic move intended to take responsibility for making medium- to longer-term economic forecasts out of the hands of politically motivated Chancellors, Mr Osborne introduced the **Office for Budget Responsibility (OBR)** shortly after entering Number 11 Downing Street. While the OBR gave a broad thumbs-up to the cutbacks and tax changes he introduced to tackle Britain's deficit in his maiden Budget, one of its earliest pronouncements was remarkably positive about the economic competence of his predecessor. Although it revised down Mr Darling's predicted growth rates of 3 per cent or more from 2011 onwards (instead predicting fluctuations between 2.6 and 2.8 per cent), it revealed that surprisingly buoyant tax receipts in the early part of 2010—boosted by the introduction of a (since abandoned) 50p top Income Tax rate—meant government borrowing over the following five years was likely to be £22bn less than he had warned. More directly embarrassing for the Coalition was the OBR's prediction in June 2010 that by 2015 around 1.2 million fewer people would be employed across the public and private sectors (although ministers emphasized other figures suggesting this could be offset by the creation of new jobs).

Controlling inflation and unemployment

When inflation is rising unemployment tends to be low, and vice versa. Only usually at a major crisis point—such as the 1930s Depression or late 1970s oil crash—do both rise noticeably at the same time. This is known as *stagflation*.

The reasons for this trade-off relate to basic 'supply and demand' economics. When the prices of goods and services rise, this tends to mean one of two things:

either demand for them is high ('demand-pull inflation') or the cost of producing them is rising ('cost-push inflation'). Demand-pull inflation comes about when shops and manufacturers find they can get away with charging more for goods and services, because high average disposable incomes mean people are willing and able to pay. Cost-push inflation is a result of rising production costs, often (but not always) down to mounting wage bills: in other words, more workers have been taken on to produce and deliver those goods and services and/or their salaries have risen.

At times when demand for goods is falling, the first casualties tend to be at least some of the workers employed to produce them. Employers lay off staff to reduce their running costs and enable them to continue in business on a more manageable scale, cutting prices to attract more custom if necessary. If such redundancies become more widespread in the economy, overall unemployment will rise. And, of course, at times of high unemployment, people have less money to spend on goods and services—so prices will have to fall further if consumer demand is to be sustained.

Therefore, rising unemployment tends to lead to falling inflation. A knock-on effect of this is a reduction in economic growth—the expansion of the economy through rising demand for goods and services, and increased private sector investment, job creation, and exports. Theoretically, growth can be a virtuous circle: more jobs should mean more people with money to buy things, more companies manufacturing goods, and higher employment. In practice, the promotion of free trade has meant that many of the products British people buy today are cheap imports from the Far East and elsewhere—which means they no longer necessarily lead to industrial expansion and job creation in Britain.

Given the tensile nature of this relationship between inflation and unemployment—referred to by economists as the 'inflation–unemployment see-saw'—governments find it difficult to keep a grip on both for very long. When Labour was elected in 1997 Mr Brown pledged to end 'boom and bust' by doing just this—words that returned to haunt him years later. Despite the fact that Britain proceeded to enjoy a decade of sustained growth, at time of writing the country's economy had recently slipped into its second recession in four years.

The Bank of England's role in monetary policy

If fiscal policy was the favoured approach to keeping the British economy afloat in the 1950s and 1960s, 'monetary policy' has been the vogue since the 1980s. Widely credited as the 'invention' of free market US economist Milton Friedman (a hero of Mrs Thatcher's), the contrasting approach to economic management favoured by monetarism involves **interest rates**—the cost of borrowing money— being used to direct consumer behaviour and control inflation. The theory is that if rates rise, people will be more likely to *save* (banks and building societies should theoretically be offering them a profitable return for their investment) and less likely to borrow and spend (credit cards and loans cost more).

In Britain **inflation** is calculated monthly. The government uses two tools to measure it: the **retail price index (RPI)** and the **consumer price index (CPI)**. Both track movements in the prices of notional 'baskets' of 650-odd items bought regularly by 'typical' households—including food, clothing, and tobacco. The difference between the two is that the CPI—the measure preferred by governments and the European Central Bank (see p. 291)—*excludes* housing costs such as Council Tax and mortgage rates, while 'core CPI' (also often quoted) omits day-to-day expenses, including food and energy bills. Both place more emphasis on goods people buy only occasionally—for example, DVD players and other electronic products. Given that routine purchases like food and utilities are the costs that most burden households, critics view the CPI as highly misleading. Nonetheless, the use of these statistics enabled Labour to maintain low rates of both 'headline' (CPI) and 'underlying' inflation (CPI adjusted to exclude volatile items, like tax rises) on the whole, even when the RPI figures cited by the Opposition and some economists began to rise.

Until 1997, responsibility for reviewing interest rates monthly rested with the Chancellor. Within days of taking on that job, however, Mr Brown made the **Bank of England** independent—and handed it the task of controlling inflation on his behalf. Decisions about interest rates have since rested with the **Monetary Policy Committee (MPC)**, composed of nine members, including the bank's chief economist, and chaired by its governor. The government sets an inflation target—currently 2 per cent—and if this is missed by more than one percentage point (according to CPI figures) the governor is expected to write to the Chancellor explaining, and setting out the action the MPC intends to take to lower it. In April 2007 Mervyn King became the first incumbent to have to do this, when headline inflation hit 3.1 per cent. Until May 2012, when inflation finally fell back to 3 per cent for the first time in nine quarters, for several years this was to become a monthly ritual.

The quest for full employment

Successive Chancellors, particularly Labour ones, have dreamed of the holy grail of 'full employment'—an ideal state in which everyone capable of work can find a job suited to their abilities and aspirations. In practice this goal has remained elusive.

At certain times, unemployment in Britain has reached levels that have been politically damaging for the government of the day. In the early 1980s Mrs Thatcher's mass closure of coalpits, steelworks, and shipyards in northern England, Wales, and Scotland, combined with her crackdown on trades union power (see pp. 220–1), saw the national jobless total rise to between 3 million and 4 million. While Labour largely maintained a much lower official unemployment rate than this—using a combination of 'carrot' and 'stick' policies, such as tax credits and its 'New Deal' to entice people off benefits and back to work—nationwide unemployment still hovered around 1.5 million-plus, even before the recession pushed it nearer to 2.5 million. Moreover, there has been huge criticism of the increasing 'casualization' now widespread in the British working environment—with many new jobs created since the early 1990s taking the form of part-time and/or short-term contracts devoid of the entitlements (for example, pensions, holiday pay) available to full-time, permanent staff.

Unemployment has been an ongoing issue for the Coalition—not least because of the rising number of public sector job losses caused by the deep austerity cuts introduced by Mr Osborne. Since shortly after the government's election, the jobless total has hovered around 2.5 million—a level that marked a sixteen-year high when it was breached in November 2010—with record numbers of women and young people since having to sign on for want of work. By twelve months later, overall unemployment had reached 2.62 million, with the number of 16 to 24-year-olds out of work breaking through the symbolic one million barrier for the first time. Labour market analysis published by independent think tank IPPR North in February 2012 found that in some employment 'cold spots', such as Clackmannanshire near Perth in Scotland, as many as thirty-five people were chasing every available vacancy.

Though headline unemployment was falling slightly at time of writing, the fact that economic growth (see next section) was still proving stubbornly elusive provoked considerable head-scratching about what this could mean. Two other worrying long-term trends have also emerged in recent statistics: by June 2012, 1.41 million people were working part time purely because they could not find full-time posts, while the number of long-term unemployed (those out of work for at least six months) had risen to 886,000.

Promoting growth and UK exports

If one word strikes terror into the hearts of prime ministers and Chancellors it is **recession**—the term denoting two successive economic quarters in which the economy 'shrinks'. Such periods of negative growth generally lead to less money being borrowed and spent by consumers, lower sales and profits for businesses, the scaling back of production, and redundancies. Britain has lived through four recent recessions: in the early 1980s, early 1990s, from April 2008 to December 2009, and again between the first and third quarters of 2012, when the country's economy slipped into a so-called 'double dip' barely two years after breaking into a recovery.

Little wonder governments have become so obsessed with achieving **growth**. Two engines are traditionally used to achieve this: rising employment and prosperity among a country's citizens, leading to increasing domestic demand, and development of overseas export markets for products manufactured at home. In theory, each should lead to wealth creation.

This chapter has already examined the inflation–unemployment conundrum, and how British governments have tried to boost the economy by juggling these 'twin evils'. But how do they go about promoting the UK's exports abroad—and measuring their success or failure in doing so? Taking the latter question first, there are two measures:

- **Balance of trade**—the difference in value between the total of all goods and services bought by British residents from overseas (imports) and all UK-made products sold abroad (exports) each year. This includes both 'visible' items (physical goods, like food, clothes, and television sets) and 'invisible' ones (virtual goods, including information technology and financial services).

- **Balance of payments**—the difference in value between the total of *all* payments of every kind flowing between the UK and other countries, including financial transfers and debt payments to foreigners. The balance of trade is therefore a 'subset' of the balance of payments.

If, in a given financial year, Britain purchases more foreign imports than it sells exports overseas, its current account will be in *deficit*. In contrast, if it sells more abroad than it buys in it is in *surplus*.

Recent decades—particularly since Britain joined the European Union (EU) (see Chapter 9)—have seen the country importing disproportionate quantities of cheap foreign clothing, toys, electrical items, and motor vehicles. The slow decline of indigenous industries like shipbuilding and coalmining, meanwhile, has seen the emphasis of the country's economic output switch to services like telecommunications, information technology (IT), and finance. As a result, while the UK has historically had a significant balance of trade deficit in terms of visible items, its service sector has often generated a surplus.

In addition to the balance of trade and balance of payments there are two other 'litmus tests' of growth in the economy:

- **gross domestic product (GDP)**—the market value of all goods and services produced within Britain's borders each year, irrespective of which country derives income from them (sometimes referred to as 'national output');

- **gross national product (GNP)**—the market value of all goods and services produced by British-owned companies, labour, and property each year, irrespective of where those assets are based (sometimes referred to as 'national income').

It has become customary for governments to cite favourable GDP as evidence of strong economic performance. In reality, however, while a high GDP should reduce unemployment (a foreign-owned company on UK soil is as likely to generate jobs and consumer spending as a British one), this is only part of the picture. Most income generated by foreign-owned companies flows back to the countries in which they are based, limiting the longer-term benefits to the

British economy brought by businesses that choose to locate here. GNP may often give a truer indication of levels of wealth generation for 'UK plc': the numerous British-based telecoms firms that have recently outsourced their call centres to the Far East, where labour costs are cheaper, may do little to help Britain's employment figures, but much of their income returns to the Treasury.

Given the UK's recent slide into a 'double-dip recession'—defined as a return to recession after only a brief period in which the economy has expanded—the pursuit of growth has become a topic of huge political significance. While several authoritative voices have leant their support to the Coalition's drive for 'fiscal consolidation' (in plain-speaking terms, 'cuts')—among them IMF managing director Christine Lagarde—several prominent economists are backing the more Keynesian approach to tackling lack of demand in Britain's economy favoured by Shadow Chancellor Ed Balls. These include former MPC member David Blanchflower, cross-bench peer (and Keynes biographer) Lord Skidelsky, and Nobel prize-winners Joseph E. Stiglitz and Paul Krugman. Though stolidly sticking to their priority of cutting Britain's record deficit, rising youth unemployment (more than a million 18- to 24-year-olds were out of work at time of writing), stalling consumer demand, and an ever-worsening 'eurozone' crisis have motivated ministers to come up with a raft of initiatives to stimulate expansion—including an 'infrastructure plan' involving major private investors, such as pension funds, and a 'sovereign guarantee' scheme (based on those used in other states) which would see the Treasury underwrite loans to businesses investing in capital projects deemed to be in the public interest.

▌ The Budget process

The highlight of the Treasury's calendar is the annual **Budget**. This used to take place in autumn, but is now held each spring. However, Mr Brown introduced an annual *Pre-Budget Report* (PBR—also known as the 'Pre-Budget' or 'Autumn Statement'), which has since been delivered each October or November. This was initially intended simply to set the scene for prospective tax and spending plans to be announced in the Budget, acting as a 'health check' on the performance of Britain's economy over the preceding twelve months. More recently, it has become almost as much of a media event as the Budget itself—with Chancellors making increasingly firm policy announcements, and using these as opportunities to test public opinion on changes they are considering.

The Budget itself, generally held in early March, has two elements: the Budget Speech and the Finance Act.

The Budget Speech

The Budget Speech is designed to:

- forecast short- to medium-term movements in the economy (one to three years) and review how it has performed in the preceding twelve months;

- announce rises and/or cuts in direct and indirect taxation and public spending—and prioritize particular areas over others (for example health, education, defence);

- announce new taxes, tax breaks, and/or benefits to finance investment and/or help low-income groups (for example tax credits, cold weather payments for the elderly);

- give the Chancellor a platform for political grandstanding—allowing him/her to boast about the country's economic performance.

The Speech—which regularly runs for around an hour—is immediately followed by a similarly lengthy retort from the Leader of the Opposition (the Shadow Chancellor has his/her chance the same evening on national television), and a debate in the Commons. More than 150 years after the event, William Gladstone holds the dubious honour of having delivered the longest ever continuous Budget Speech. His 1853 address lasted four hours and forty-five minutes.

The Finance Act

For measures announced in the Budget to be implemented, the Commons must legislate. Unlike most laws, however, the Bill needed to deliver the proposals is given swift passage and substantially passed on the same day as the Speech. Dubbed the Finance Bill, it is automatically designated a 'money Bill' by the Speaker—enabling it to bypass the usual stages Bills must negotiate before receiving royal assent (see p. 70). The initial 'stages' are effectively gone through in one go, with the Speech itself treated as the first reading. The Commons must pass individual resolutions to approve each specific tax or duty change within ten sitting days, but, under the Collection of Taxes Act 1968, minor changes can be agreed immediately—enabling government business to continue in the interim. A second reading must be heard within thirty days, but the committee stage may be split, with more important resolutions heard by a committee of the whole house and remaining ones considered by a standing committee of thirty to forty MPs. Following this, the third reading will be steamrollered through, usually on the second day of the report stage.

Since the confrontation between the Commons and House of Lords over Lloyd George's 1909 'People's Budget', there has been no Lords stage to the Finance Bill. Nonetheless, even today there is scope for Budgets to fall at a late hurdle. The row over Labour's abolition of the 10p starting rate of Income Tax so raised the hackles of backbench rebels led by former Welfare Minister Mr Field that, before announcing a compensation package for low earners penalized by the change, it looked as if Mr Darling's first Budget (in 2008) might be defeated, forcing his resignation. In the event he staved off this prospect by issuing an 'emergency Budget' designed to compensate the losers—some of whom stood to be left £230 a year worse off. If Mr Darling's 2008 Budget proved a political minefield, so too did Mr Osborne's third. Over a period of three months or more after his March 2012 Commons speech, several provisions in the accompanying Finance Bill unravelled—with ministers performing a succession of U-turns over controversial measures ranging from a tabloid-christened 'granny tax' (proposed cuts to the personal tax allowance for over 65-year-olds) to a 'pasty tax' on hot takeaway snacks. The slew of policy reversals led to the Budget memorably being dubbed an 'omnishambles' by Labour leader Ed Miliband—a reference to a term coined by fictional spin doctor Malcolm Tucker in BBC sitcom *The Thick of It.*

Public spending outside England—the Barnett Formula

To ensure that Scotland, Wales, and Northern Ireland benefit fairly from central government tax revenues, public spending is allocated on a per capita basis across Britain, using a system called the 'Barnett Formula'. In theory, the formula—devised in the late 1970s by then Labour Chief Secretary to the Treasury Joel (now Lord) Barnett—ensures the amount given to each country corresponds to its population size (and, by definition, the extent to which its inhabitants contribute to taxes).

In practice, the formula remains highly controversial—successive recalculations have disproportionately benefited Scotland, and the distribution of funding has moved increasingly out of step with levels of economic need in different parts of Britain. Resentment between Scotland and England, in particular, has escalated since devolution was introduced in 1998, because not only has Holyrood continued to do disproportionately well out of taxes, but the Scottish Parliament has used its freedom to spend its share of the money as it chooses, to subsidize its public sector in ways unseen elsewhere. Barnett has, among other things, enabled Scotland to reject university tuition fees (for the time being) and phase out NHS prescription charges—two highly controversial levies that remain in England (if not Wales and Northern Ireland).

Mr Osborne has so far resisted calls from Tory backbenchers for the formula to be reviewed. But with Treasury figures released in 2011 showing the gap in annual government spending on England and Scotland had risen to £1,600 per person, and Lord Barnett himself urging reform to make the formula more responsive to need rather than simple population size, it remains a source of heated debate.

▶ The government's role in promoting industry and commerce

For the past thirty years British governments have taken an increasingly lais-sez-faire approach to running the economy as a whole. The mass privatization pro-gramme of the 1980s saw a swathe of industries sold into private ownership, from motor manufacturer British Leyland to British Airways, British Steel, all major utilities (gas, electricity, water), and ultimately the railways (see pp. 229–30). In the decades since, the mantra has been one of 'consumer choice', with successive governments promoting competition between rival private sector providers over any state monopoly. In theory, this allows people to shop around for the best deals on virtually any product—with market forces (supply and demand) ensuring they are high quality and competitively priced.

In practice, however, the government continues to play an interventionist role in promoting British industry and protecting it from the worst ravages of globalization—the process by which national economies are becoming increas-ingly interdependent. Recent decisions by ministers to shore up failing banks and broker rescue packages for car manufacturers, including Nissan (which received £6.2 million from the Coalition's Regional Growth Fund for its Sunderland plant in November 2011) and Rover—the last surviving British-owned motor company until its collapse in 2005—have demonstrated this. Moreover, the free market ideal of a private sector that, left alone, will 'regulate itself' efficiently and fairly has proved elusive—forcing the state to introduce greater regulation.

The Department for Business, Innovation, and Skills (BIS)

The department responsible for promoting British industry and commerce and overseeing regulation of the free market in the UK, BIS was known as the Department for Business, Enterprise, and Regulatory Reform (BERR) under Mr Brown, and before that as, variously, the Department of Trade and Industry (DTI), Department of Trade, and Board of Trade.

The Department's website describes it as 'the voice for business across government'. It is responsible for:

- creating conditions for business success and raising productivity in the UK economy;
- championing the interests of employees and employers;
- promoting consumer interests;
- encouraging sustainable business development.

Although formal regulation of the business environment is delegated to a series of non-departmental bodies, when BERR replaced the DTI under Labour, its

Secretary of State began to play a more hands-on role than previously. In January 2009, then Business Secretary Lord Mandelson tried to jump-start Britain's ailing car industry by pledging £2.3bn in loan guarantees—including £1.3bn from the European Investment Bank—for motor manufacturers prepared to invest in 'high technology' and green alternatives to conventional engines. BERR was proactive in enforcing regulatory judgments, too. In 2008 Lord Mandelson's predecessor, John Hutton, publicly ordered BSkyB, the satellite broadcaster part-owned by Rupert Murdoch's multinational media company News Corp, to sell more than half its shares in rival company ITV. He was endorsing a ruling by the Competition Commission (see pp. 211–12) that the shareholding represented 'a substantial lessening of competition' in the television market.

As well as overseeing the regulatory framework, it is the Business Secretary's job to liaise regularly with the main bodies representing employees and employers: the Trades Union Congress (TUC) (see p. 220) and the CBI respectively.

Regulatory authorities

While BIS is required to draft the laws governing fair competition, consumer protection, and sustainable business, these have for some time been administered on the ground by two principal regulatory authorities: the Office of Fair Trading (OFT) and Competition Commission. In April 2014 the two bodies are set to be merged to form one overarching new regulator: the **Competition and Markets Authority (CMA)**.

The Office of Fair Trading (OFT)

Established in 1973, this has been charged with ensuring the 'rules' of fair play—genuine choice and competition—are applied in practice. Its founding remit was to protect both consumers and companies, shielding small businesses from anti-competitive practices by larger, more established rivals. Until 2003 it was headed by a Director General of Fair Trading, but it has since been run by a board and chairperson.

The OFT's duties are to:

- encourage businesses to comply with competition and consumer law, and improve their trading practices through self-regulation;
- act decisively to stop hardcore or flagrant offenders;
- study markets and recommend action where required;
- empower consumers to make informed choices and get the best value from markets, and help them resolve problems with suppliers through Consumer Direct—a regionally based, government-funded advice service established in 2000.

It has been for the OFT to launch investigations into allegations of 'restrictive practices'. Most commonly a small or medium-sized business has complained that its attempt to break into an established market (such as telecoms) was being frustrated by larger-scale companies offering product discounts it could not hope to match as it struggled with initial overheads. To some extent, being initially 'out-competed' by the big boys is inevitable as one tries to set oneself up in a new marketplace, but history is littered with examples of competition being deliberately stifled by established players using underhand means—for example, pegging their prices at the same level and/or undercutting potential new competitors by offering 'loss leaders' (cheap deals at below-cost price) to lure customers. These unofficial alliances—'cartels'—can effectively stop new competitors getting established, by using economies of scale achieved through years of trading in the sector to sell certain items at unrealistically low prices.

Companies have also been accused of unfair trading in relation to the prices they pay their suppliers. In recent years there has been concern about the below-cost prices allegedly offered by supermarket chains like Tesco and Asda to producers in developing countries for everything from bananas to coffee, while British farmers have complained of being offered unsustainably low prices for meat and dairy products. The appalling press generated by such controversies has prompted retailers to embrace 'fair trade' goods and invest millions in corporate social responsibility programmes.

Of course it is not only other businesses that are hurt by restrictive practices: price-fixing can work upwards, as well as downwards, and at times consumers get the worst deal. In December 2007 Asda and Sainsbury's admitted having conspired to fix the price of milk, following an OFT investigation. The supermarkets charged inflated prices for the product—despite offering farmers minimal payment—and British consumers were left £270m out of pocket.

In 1997 a separate regulator was set up to oversee the financial services sector—banks, building societies, and insurance companies—assuming responsibilities previously held by the Bank of England. But the effectiveness of this body, the **Financial Services Authority (FSA)**, was called into question following its failure to act on the banking sector's increasingly cavalier mortgage lending policies prior to the collapse of Northern Rock and wider subsequent banking crisis (see pp. 213–16). Following the Labour government's multibillion-pound bailout of the banks—and the soaring structural deficit that resulted—the party was roundly condemned for adopting such 'light-touch' regulation in the financial sector. Another criticism concerned the 'tripartite' nature of the regulatory regime it presided over—effectively splitting responsibilities for policing banking between the FSA, Bank of England, and Treasury, and creating confusion over which should intervene and when. In truth, introducing the FSA had slightly tightened the regulatory framework, compared to the laissez-faire regime ushered in by Margaret Thatcher's overnight 'Big Bang' deregulation of the City on 27 October 1986. Nonetheless, it has fallen to the Coalition to toughen up banking regulation for the future, by dividing the responsibilities of the soon-to-be-abolished FSA between three authorities, as follows:

- **Financial Conduct Authority (FCA)** (originally to be called the Consumer Protection and Markets Authority) to police the overall conduct of every financial company authorized to provide services to the public and maintain the overall integrity of the UK's money markets from 2013;

- **Prudential Regulatory Authority (PRA)**, created as a subsidiary of the Bank of England to prevent financial companies—from banks and building societies to insurers and brokers—taking imprudent risks with their investors' money, also from 2013;

- **Financial Policy Committee (FPC)**, again within the Bank of England and modelled in composition on the MPC. Charged with identifying potential financial and macroeconomic risks to the stability of the UK economy and, where possible, taking pre-emptive action to avert them, it took over this role from the FSA in March 2012.

The Competition Commission

Formerly the Monopolies and Mergers Commission, the Commission has been less concerned with the day-to-day market practices preoccupying the OFT than movements in company ownership that may affect future competition. Although most markets are now 'deregulated'—open to full free market competition—in practice there has been huge consolidation in many of them over recent decades, with more profitable companies taking over or merging with smaller ones. As a result, markets that once offered dozens of alternatives from which consumers could choose are increasingly dominated by a handful of providers—and sometimes only one or two.

Nowhere is this lack of genuine competition more obvious than on supermarket shelves. While most stores offer myriad varieties of essentially the same products, superficially different brands are often made by the same company. Other than supermarkets' own-brand options, household cleaning products tend to be manufactured by Unilever or Procter and Gamble; many chocolate bars lining confectionery counters will somewhere bear the small print 'Nestlé' or 'Cadbury'.

It has been the Commission's job to ensure that, wherever possible, choice has been genuine. One way of doing this has been to prevent mergers and takeovers that would otherwise restrict it—avoiding 'monopolies', which occur when one company has more than a 25 per cent market share in a particular product. Recent high-profile rulings by the Commission have included its decision to approve supermarket chain Morrisons' takeover of rival Safeway in 2003—provided it first agreed to sell fifty-three stores in areas where local competition might suffer due to the acquisition. In February 2008 the Commission issued a report focusing on whether the proliferation of out-of-town supermarkets was contributing to the decline of town centres and local grocery stores. It angered critics by finding no conclusive evidence to support this assertion—although it did argue a new 'competition test' should be applied by local authorities when deciding whether to grant superstores planning permission. It cited the example of the 'Tesco town' of Bicester in Oxfordshire, which is ringed by five branches of the chain. The report also disappointed campaigners by failing to compel major supermarkets to dispose of 'land banks'—areas of prime development land they had acquired to prevent rivals building there.

→
see also local government, p. 484 and pp. 486–7

Types of company

There are three main types of UK corporate structure:

- limited liability company (ltd);
- private limited company;
- **public limited company (plc).**

The principal differences between the three are explained in Table 7.3.

The role of the Stock Exchange

Shares in plcs are traded on global stock markets, one of the biggest being the London Stock Exchange (LSE). Established in 1760, when 150 brokers expelled from the Royal Exchange for rowdiness formed a spontaneous share-trading

Table 7.3 Types of UK company

Type of company	Definition
Limited liability companies (ltds)	One up from sole trader, a common form of small and medium-sized enterprise (SME) (small business). Introduced to provide security for individuals who would otherwise have to shoulder whole burden of risk associated with running own businesses, it provides statutory guarantees not enjoyed by larger companies. Limited companies—which can include theatres, charities, and voluntary trusts—only allocate 'liability' (risk) to investors to value of nominal sum (usually £1). This is agreed when they initially sign company's 'original memorandum' and 'articles of association'.
Private limited companies	Again usually SMEs, these may not issue shares to public. Liability of individual investors for shortfalls/debts limited to nominal value of shares they are initially issued.
Public limited companies (plcs)	Have at least two shareholders and may offer shares to public. Owners 'float' them and they are listed on London Stock Exchange. Shareholders usually receive annual 'loyalty payments' (dividends) and can vote on certain aspects of company policy/strategic direction. Enterprise and Regulatory Reform Bill 2012 will give shareholders in UK-quoted companies 'binding rights' to reject executive pay deals, following series of grass-roots rebellions against boards of banks and other firms in 2012. Plcs must have issued shares to value of £50,000 before being allowed to trade. Larger plcs often referred to as 'blue-chip' companies, including BP and Marks and Spencer.

club at Jonathan's Coffee House, it registered as a private limited company in 1986, and finally a plc in 2000. Like all plcs, the LSE is susceptible to potential takeover bids. In 2004 it became the first stock market to be targeted by a prospective purchaser when it faced an £822m hostile bid from little-known Swedish company the OM Group, a technology manufacturer that runs the Swedish Stock Exchange. Four years later, its shareholders rejected a £1.35bn offer by its German rival, Deutsche Börse.

Today, the LSE has regional bases in Belfast, Birmingham, Glasgow, Leeds, and Manchester. Some 2,600 UK and overseas companies are listed on it at any one time, and shares are traded electronically via a computerized system called 'CREST'. Minute-by-minute movements in share prices of listed companies are tracked by a series of nine indices, collectively known as the 'Financial Times Stock Exchange' ('FTSE', or 'FOOTSIE'). The most famous of these is the **FT100 Share Index**, which lists the 100 highest-valued companies at any one time in order of value, and monitors the movements in these firms' share prices. The FT All-Share Index, meanwhile, lists all 2,500-plus companies on the stock market, again in order, and monitors daily movements.

All manner of factors can impact on company share prices. Mergers and takeovers—or the mere prospect of them—can send prices soaring or crashing, according to the market's assessment of how favourable such outcomes are for a firm's commercial fortunes. Shares in iconic high-street companies like Marks and Spencer (M&S), meanwhile, are notoriously prone to fluctuations depending on the movements of senior personnel and the state of their sales and profits—particularly at Christmas.

Often companies' share prices suffer because of factors beyond their control. Amid growing suspicions among share traders that the 1980s stock market bubble was about to burst, 'Black Monday' on 1 October 1987 saw the biggest one-day crash in history. By the end of the month the value of LSE shares alone had plummeted by 26.4 per cent.

As well as the LSE, London also now boasts an Alternative Investment Market (AIM), launched in 1995, on which shares in smaller developing companies, ethical traders, and/or those whose value has fallen so low that they have decided to 'delist' from FTSE are traded. Sometimes, the trend goes in reverse: when The Body Shop™ was acquired by French cosmetics giant L'Oréal in 2006, it moved from AIM to FTSE.

The global banking crisis and its fallout

After years of unsustainable growth in the mortgage sector and the credit market as a whole, autumn 2008 witnessed the onset of the biggest global financial meltdown since the 1929 Wall Street Crash and the ensuing Great Depression. Eighteen months after the term 'sub-prime' had first seeped into the mainstream media—in relation to the crisis of insecurity sparked by defaults on 'toxic' mortgage loans made by US banks to people without the means to repay them—major financial institutions from Europe to the Far East were brought to their knees by the knock-on effects of these and similar practices elsewhere. In the end, the position of household-name banks, from Merrill Lynch to Barclays, became so perilous that governments in Britain, the USA, and mainland Europe were forced into doing what the long-standing 'neo-liberal' consensus would previously have deemed unthinkable: pouring vast sums of money into the sector to shore up savings and pensions and keep the institutions afloat. But even this was not enough, and before long Mr Brown's government was leading the way by going a stage further—taking controlling stakes in several major high-street banks. After decades of runaway privatization and deregulation, the term 'nationalization' (see pp. 223–4) re-entered the political lexicon.

The escalating financial crisis came to a head in late September 2008 when, within a week, investment bank Lehman Brothers filed for bankruptcy, Merrill Lynch was taken over by the Bank of America, and the US Federal Reserve Bank (the US equivalent of the Bank of England) announced an $85bn rescue package and effective nationalization of the country's biggest insurance firm, AIG. Within a fortnight an even bigger collapse occurred, when Washington Mutual—the largest US mortgage lender—was shut down by regulators and sold to JPMorgan Chase. To prevent other financial giants facing a similar fate, the White House administration was left battling to force a $700bn rescue package for the country's entire banking sector through a Congress furious at the conduct of reckless bankers.

In Britain even more dramatic state interventions followed. Barely a week after Lloyds TSB stepped in to announce a buyout of Halifax Bank of Scotland (HBOS), one of Britain's biggest mortgage lenders, ministers nationalized the bulk of Bradford and Bingley's assets, while selling off its branches and savings operation to Spanish bank Santander. The Treasury then moved to guarantee all deposits in UK banks of up to £50,000, to prevent a 'run on the banks'—the mass withdrawal of savings by panicked investors worried about losing their money if institutions collapsed.

Then, on 8 October, amid feverish rumours and jittery fluctuations on the stock market, Messrs Brown and Darling announced details of a £500bn bailout for the UK's banking sector, which would see up to eight high-street banks and building societies part-nationalized in a last-ditch attempt to persuade institutions to resume lending to each other, and—more importantly for the 'real economy'—their customers. While only Lloyds TSB, HBOS, and the Royal Bank of Scotland (shares in which had plummeted) initially accepted the government's offer—other major banks like Barclays opting to raise capital on the open market—the price paid by these institutions for their cut of the 'final' £37bn Treasury share offer was significant. First, the FSA ordered the government to acquire not only 'preference shares' (which give shareholders priority in the payment of dividends, but no voting rights), but also 'ordinary' ones—allowing ministers a direct say in running the companies. Second, it emerged that the government would be appointing its own directors to the banks' boards, and no bonuses would be paid to senior staff for at least the first year. This latter measure went some way towards allaying mounting public outrage at the scale of the 'bonus culture' fostered during the boom years, with directors often taking home multimillion-pound perks irrespective of how well their company was performing. The government replaced several leading bankers at the helm of the semi-nationalized institutions, including RBS chief executive Sir Fred 'the Shred' Goodwin (whose knighthood was subsequently rescinded in 2012). RBS was 60 per cent nationalized, while the state took a 41 per cent stake in Lloyds TSB and HBOS.

In the same tumultuous week, Mr Brown entered into a public row with Iceland after several of that country's leading banks collapsed like dominoes, and it emerged dozens of British councils, charities, universities, and other bodies had substantial sums invested in them. When Iceland's prime minister, Geir Haarde, announced he was guaranteeing the safety of all Icelanders' deposits, but not those of Britons, Mr Brown risked international condemnation by using anti-terror legislation to freeze the £7bn in assets held in the UK by Landsbanki, the country's national bank, to recoup some of the costs.

see also local government, pp. 378–9

The aftermath of the banking crisis, and its ongoing impact on Britain's public finances (see pp. 198–200), saw Opposition politicians and media commentators pour scorn on City traders and demand firm action from ministers to ensure there could be no repeat of the reckless practices that led to the near-collapse of so many institutions. Vocal critics included future Lib Dem Business Secretary Vince Cable, who ridiculed what he saw as Mr Darling's ineffectual response—a call for international action to impose strict new trading conditions on the banking sector, and a one-off 50 per cent tax on bonuses of £25,000-plus that was only levied in April 2010 (though it raised £2.3bn). However, once in office, the Coalition wavered in its professed determination to make the sector pay for its past errors: Mr Osborne initially imposed only a modest levy on the banks, based on their overall balance sheets rather than individuals' bonuses. Since then debate has raged over how best to deter future rogue banking practices and ensure the big banks saved by taxpayer-funded bailouts make fair reparations for their wrongdoing. Agreement has been even slower coming over the various proposals for some form of levy on banking transactions, or 'Robin Hood Tax'. The EU came close to adopting a Union-wide financial transaction tax (FTT), modelled on an idea first proposed by Nobel Laureate James Tobin. Its sister plan for a Fiscal Compact (see p. 294)—which was approved by all member states but Britain and the Czech Republic in March 2012—will, if implemented, require signatory countries to commit to maintaining national budget surpluses or balanced accounts from 1 January 2013. However, in

December 2011 Mr Cameron made it clear Britain would opt out of any such deal—arguing it could have a disproportionate impact on the City—and six months later European finance ministers appeared to rein back from a fully fledged pan-European tax on trade in equities, bonds, and derivatives (as proposed by the European Commission), in favour of a stamp duty-style levy on documents and unilateral transaction taxes for countries keen on them. For its part, Labour has repeatedly stated it would make Britain's own bankers' tax an annual levy if returned to power—using the proceeds to reinstate a version of the Future Jobs Fund it set up shortly before leaving office to provide vocational training for unemployed young people.

In government Mr Cable has repeatedly threatened to make good on the Lib Dems' pre-election pledge to 'break up' bigger banks into separate retail and investment arms, to stop ordinary customers ever again being exposed to the perils of high-stakes risk-taking. Following publication of a report by an Independent Commission on Banking (ICB) headed by economist Sir John Vickers, the Treasury finally published a White Paper in June 2012 setting out concrete proposals to restructure the sector. Chief among these was a promise to secure the deposits and overdrafts of individuals and small and medium-sized enterprises (SMEs) in 'ring-fenced banks' banned from conducting 'the vast majority' of wholesale and investment banking or carrying out activities through branches or subsidiaries based outside the European Economic Area (EEA) (see p. 260). The White Paper also set out plans to force retail banks to insulate themselves against sudden shocks by requiring them to hold additional capital reserves/equity of up to 10 per cent.

Short-selling, interest rate 'fixes', and wider questions about banking

Another scandal that emerged at the height of the financial crisis was the widespread practice of 'short-selling'. This shady form of stock market speculation entails gambling on a company's share price falling—it was blamed in some quarters for undermining confidence in the banking system. Short-selling involves seasoned speculators 'borrowing' shares whose value they expect to fall from a third party, selling them on, and then buying them back after their value has plummeted, before returning them to their original owner for a profit. The FSA introduced a short-term ban on this at the height of the banking crisis, and the practice was later unilaterally outlawed in Germany. But in June 2012, under pressure from City-based lobbyists, UK ministers filed a lawsuit to the European Court of Justice (ECJ) challenging EU plans to empower the European Securities and Markets Authority (ESMA) it established in Paris in January 2011 to ban or restrict short-selling across the Union.

Just when the spectre of 'casino banking' finally seemed to have been banished, a major new scandal erupted. This time the initial culprit identified was Barclays, which in June 2012 was fined £291m by the FSA and US Department of Justice for repeatedly lying about the twin interest rates it had to pay to borrow money from other institutions: the so-called London Interbank Offered Rate (Libor) and Euro Interbank Offered Rate (Euribor). The investigation found that from 2005 individual traders in the bank's Barclays Capital division repeatedly lied for personal gain, by claiming rates were higher than they actually were, while at the height of the 2008 crisis their managers ordered them to make out the bank was paying *less* than it was (a tactic known as 'lowballing'), to improve its balance sheets and reduce the rates it was charged elsewhere. It appeared to many that Barclays had deliberately misrepresented its borrowing rates to avert its collapse and/or nationalization by the then Labour government.

At time of writing, the international team probing the scam was investigating links to a wider conspiracy involving up to twenty other institutions; the Serious Fraud Office was looking into potential criminal prosecutions, and Barclays' beleaguered chief executive, Bob Diamond—who just eighteen months earlier had defiantly told MPs he believed it was time for banks to stop apologizing for their misdemeanours—had been pressurized into resigning after being summoned to a special hearing of the Commons Treasury Select Committee. But he did so with a potentially damaging parting shot—releasing details of an internal memo sent to other Barclays executives on 29 October 2008 which appeared to implicate both the Bank of England and, potentially, the government itself in colluding over the rigging of Libor. In the memo, Mr Diamond relayed details of a phone conversation with the Bank's Deputy Governor, Paul Tucker, which he insinuated gave tacit approval to attempts by its staff to find ways of lowering the Libor rates they reported to the British Bankers' Association (the body responsible for logging them). The memo alluded to an implied endorsement of this policy by 'senior Whitehall figures'—raising the prospect that mandarins, special advisers, or even ministers might have been in on the act—though Mr Tucker subsequently denied there had been any such government pressure.

Two separate government inquiries had been launched into rate-fixing—the first into the operation of the Libor system, and the second a parliamentary probe by MPs and peers to be fronted by Andrew Tyrie, Chairman of the Treasury Committee. Yet another dubious banking practice was also exposed in June 2012, with the FSA announcing it had reached settlements with Barclays, HSBC, Lloyds, and RBS over its demands for 'redress' for their 'serious failings' in mis-selling specialist insurance to companies seeking to protect themselves against rising interest rates. News of systemic abuse of the so-called 'interest rate swap' system only added to the renewed sense of distrust towards the culture of bankers and banking.

On a more positive note, the Coalition is proceeding with plans for a **Green Investment Bank** originally announced in Mr Darling's last Budget. Labour envisaged the bank—to be backed by £2bn in combined public and private sector cash—as an engine for investment in green energy projects and high-speed rail links. To be based in Edinburgh, the bank was scheduled to be up and running by autumn 2012. Backed by an initial capitalization fund of £3bn, it has been primarily tasked with funding environmentally sustainable infrastructure projects—addressing private sector market failures and setting out to achieve a so-called 'double bottom line' that will both innovate in green technologies and generate a profit.

▶ The government's role in industrial relations

In the 1960s and 1970s, when many industries were still state-owned, battles between government and trades unions over wages policy, working conditions, and their ability to take industrial action when relations broke down were frequently in the news. After years of struggle between the unions and employers, and growing infighting in the Labour movement, tensions exploded during the 1978–9 'Winter of Discontent'—a prolonged period of wildcat action across the public services during which, at one point, even funerary workers joined the mêlée.

Hand in hand with its mass privatization programme, Mrs Thatcher's government introduced swingeing clampdowns on the rights of workers to take industrial action. Legal barriers were introduced to block strikes, while the new generation of private sector employers with which unions were now confronted no longer even had to 'recognize' their existence—let alone formally negotiate with them over job cuts or changes in working practices. Mrs Thatcher also ended:

- 'the closed shop'—a rule forcing employees in certain trades or industries to join a specific trade union;
- 'secondary picketing'—the ability of workers in trades *related* to others in dispute with their employers to take 'sympathy action'.

Although both the above remain illegal, when Labour returned to power in 1997 certain workers' rights were restored. Many of these—the right to sick pay and paid leave, and a maximum number of weekly working hours—were guaranteed under the European Social Chapter, signed by Mr Blair in 1998 (see p. 295). The new government introduced a **national minimum wage** (NMW). It also extended some rights previously the preserve of full-time permanent employees to those on part-time and temporary contracts. Despite these early moves, it took nearly thirteen years before a more thoroughgoing equalization of the rights of temporary and agency workers and those employed on full-time contracts was introduced, in the Agency Workers Regulations, which were finally adopted by the UK shortly before the May 2010 election. Derived from the EU's Agency Workers Directive, this came into force across the Union on 1 October

2011 and was formally (if grudgingly) introduced by the Coalition on Christmas Eve that year. Its principal achievement was to give temporary and agency employees the same rights as permanent staff after twelve weeks' continuous employment.

The role of unions

As discussed in Chapter 4, the unions initially emerged in the eighteenth and nineteenth centuries. They were formed to provide representation for the large groups of workers recruited by the owners of Britain's emerging manufacturing industries. In time, dismayed by the lack of attention paid to their cause by politicians of their day, they began seeking their own stake in power and, to that end, joined with other bodies to form the Labour Party—to which many of them remain formally affiliated to this day (see pp. 142–4).

Although most workers' rights are today enshrined in British and/or European Union law, unions have historically adhered to a self-help approach to representing their members' interests known as 'voluntarism'—a tradition that shies away from seeking legal intervention in workplace disputes, in favour of a form of group negotiation known as free collective bargaining. In material terms, unions' principal aims are to:

- negotiate and protect a fair wage for given trades and professions;
- negotiate fair working conditions—hours, holiday entitlement, sick pay, and compensation in the event of work-related injuries or illnesses;
- provide their members with training, educational and social opportunities, and a 'fighting fund' for living costs in the event of prolonged industrial disputes.

In addition, unions offer legal and financial support in the event of disputes between employees and employers. Unions have historically achieved many favourable settlements for aggrieved workers unfairly dismissed from their jobs or bullied or harassed by colleagues or bosses. Sometimes this is done on an out-of-court basis, but on other occasions unions represent employees at employment tribunals.

Over the past thirty years the number of unions has declined by a third, with many pooling their resources to strengthen their voice at the negotiating table. The most recent amalgamation was that of the Transport and General Workers' Union (TGWU) and Amicus, Britain's biggest technical union, which merged to form Unite in 2007. As in the Labour Party, the senior officer of a trade union is usually called the 'general secretary'. Again like Labour, it will usually have an elected national executive committee that debates changes of policy and practice, and beneath that regional and district organizations. It will also have branches, often based in individual workplaces, and houses, chapels or shop stewards' committees, which act as focal points for negotiations between employees and employers.

The 'big three' British unions as of 2012 are set out in the table entitled 'Britain's "big three" trade unions', to be found on the Online Resource Centre.

Most unions are affiliated to a single representative body, the Trades Union Congress (TUC), which holds an annual conference like those organized by the main political parties to rally opinion from members and ratify changes in policy. The serving Labour leader is traditionally invited to give its keynote speech.

The TUC dates back to 1868 and its membership currently consists of fifty-eight unions, representing 6.5 million people (equivalent to eight out of ten union members). It has eight regional councils in England and one for Wales. Scotland has its own equivalent body, the Scottish Trades Union Congress (STUC).

Union recognition—and what it is worth

For unions to be able to negotiate with employers about working practices, pay, and conditions, they first need to be formally 'recognized' by employers. After years of having their rights diluted, unions were given a new impetus to recruit in the Employment Relations Act 1999, which introduced a statutory process through which they could demand recognition on meeting specific criteria.

If claims for recognition cannot be satisfied bilaterally between a union and the relevant employers, it may apply for help from a Central Arbitration Committee (CAC), which assigns a three-person panel to each case. There are two main ways a union may achieve recognition through the CAC—regardless of whether this is desired by the employers with which it is in dispute:

- *without* a ballot—a union is entitled in law to *automatic* recognition if *more than 50 per cent* of its 'bargaining unit' (that is, all employees entitled to join it) have done so;
- *with* a ballot—if *at least 40 per cent* of the bargaining unit vote in favour of recognition in a ballot and this number amounts to a majority of those who vote; a worker in a bargaining unit does not need to have joined a union to vote in strike ballots.

Ironically, one of the most notorious industries for union recognition is journalism. There have been many cases in which the managers of larger regional newspapers and some nationals (including Express Newspapers and Independent Newspapers) have fought to prevent it. Prior to the 1999 Act some regional newspaper groups disingenuously argued that, to achieve recognition, the unions representing their journalists would need to obtain the support of 40 per cent of their *overall* workforces—including advertising and sales staff, etc.—rather than simply the writers and subeditors who constituted the bargaining unit.

From the mid-1980s to late 1990s unions were restricted from taking strike action, in the sense that any withdrawal of their labour over a dispute constituted a breach of contract. Theoretically this entitled bosses either to sack striking workers or sue them for damages and loss of business. However, the 1999 Act entitles 'recognized' unions to be consulted formally over changes in working terms and practices for employees they represent—for example, the movement of a British-based call centre to the Far East or a proposed organizational merger. It also gives unions immunity from prosecution for industrial action, provided that:

- the action is 'wholly or mainly in contemplation or furtherance of a trade dispute between workers and their employer' (that is, not secondary picketing);
- the union goes through the correct ballot procedures beforehand—this involves a secret postal ballot, followed by a letter giving the employer seven days' notice of the intended action and details of the ballot result.

Some restrictions remain, however. In addition to being barred from secondary action, unions must keep picket lines to negotiated levels to avoid intimidating colleagues who opt not to take part. This latter clause was inserted to avoid the kinds of harassment to which 'strike-breaking' coalminers and other workers were allegedly subjected in the 1980s by picketers.

Following recent strikes in protest at the Coalition's public spending cuts—by everyone from teachers and lecturers to civil servants and doctors (see p. 251)—some prominent Tories, including London Mayor Boris Johnson, have called for the laws governing industrial action to be tightened, perhaps barring unions from calling stoppages unless at least half of their membership turn out in a ballot to vote in favour. In June 2012, Work and Pensions Secretary Iain Duncan Smith also announced that in future low-paid workers who took part in strikes would lose the working tax credits that would normally top up their pay on the days concerned—in addition to the wages they forego anyway as a result of taking action.

Other proposals have also incurred the unions' wrath. In April 2012 the Coalition announced it was planning to end decades of national wage bargaining by introducing regional pay scales to take account of variations in the cost of living from one part of England to another.

Avoiding strikes—role of ACAS

On occasions when employer–employee negotiations break down, one or other party may seek impartial help in reaching a settlement from the **Advisory, Conciliation, and Arbitration Service (ACAS)**.

This quango's role is to:

- *advise* warring parties on how to avoid industrial action;
- *conciliate* in disputes when invited to do so, and try to encourage the parties to reach agreement peacefully;
- *arbitrate* to restart negotiations in disputes resulting in industrial action;

- *mediate* over grievances between individual employees and their employers—notably in relation to prospective tribunal cases (concerning unfair dismissal, gender, age, or racial discrimination, etc.).

ACAS has been involved in numerous recent disputes. In July 2007 its chair was called in by ministers to report on the issues arising from a strike by Royal Mail workers over the imposition of new modernization plans and a below-inflation 2.5 per cent pay deal. In May 2005 it was approached by the National Union of Journalists (NUJ) to mediate between it and British Broadcasting Corporation (BBC) director general Mark Thompson over his plans to slash 4,000 jobs.

More generally, as part of its drive to cut 'red tape' for business, the Coalition has also moved to speed up employment tribunals, while also cutting the number of cases that are brought before them. The 2012 Enterprise Bill contains proposals to prevent employees bringing cases against their employers until they have worked for them for two years (as opposed to one year, as at present). It also encourages parties to resolve their differences, where possible, using a new 'early conciliation service', to be available through ACAS from April 2014, and/or reach compromises known as 'settlement agreements'. However, a recommendation by Tory donor Adrian Beecroft that Britain adopt a 'no-fault' summary dismissal regime which would, in theory, enable bosses to give staff their marching orders with little or no notice, recompense, or legal redress was roundly rejected by Mr Cable, who dismissed the idea as 'bonkers'. In a heated exchange between the two, played out in the national newspapers in

May 2012, Mr Beecroft retorted that Mr Cable was a 'socialist' who, despite his job title 'appears to do very little to support business'.

Workplace and safety

Health and safety in the workplace is regulated by the Health and Safety at Work Act 1974, which covers the operation of work-based equipment, and various subsequent regulations and statutory instruments, including the Control of Substances Hazardous to Health (COSHH) Regulations 1999, relating to exposure to virtually all potentially dangerous substances.

Since April 2008 the job of both developing policy guidelines on workplace health and safety and enforcing these rules through inspections has fallen to the **Health and Safety Executive (HSE)**.

The HSE's day-to-day work is carried out by its Field Operations Directorate (which incorporates separate factory, agriculture, and quarries inspectorates) and regional officers of the Employment Medical Advisory Service. Its powers are set out in the table entitled 'The responsibilities of the Health and Safety

Executive (HSE)', to be found on the Online Resource Centre.

In addition, some health and safety legislation (covering shops, offices, warehouses, restaurants, etc.) is enforced by local authority environmental health departments. In its drive to reduce red tape—particularly for small businesses—the

Coalition appointed former Tory Trade Secretary Lord Young to review existing legislation in June 2010. That October he published a report, *Common Sense, Common Safety*, which had as its central recommendation a sweeping rationalization of the 'bureaucracy' surrounding health and safety rules. Subsequent legislative proposals have focused on a perceived need to simplify regulations to 'ease the burden on business' and weed out 'rogue health and safety consultants'. A further review, published a year later by Professor Ragnar Lofstedt, proposed scrapping requirements for organizations with 'low-risk' workplaces to maintain qualified first-aid personnel, and stripping the HSE of its role as approver of first-aid trainers. The Coalition has since adopted a 'one in, one out' policy towards introducing new health and safety rules and other regulations, and in true 'Big Society' vein invited members of the public to report irritating and unnecessary regulations they think should be scrapped as part of a so-called 'red tape challenge'.

▌ The utilities

A 'utility' is an organization—whether publicly or privately owned—that is responsible for maintaining and delivering reliable and affordable supplies of a commodity essential to the lives of a country's citizens. The main utilities are those charged with providing 'natural monopolies'—basic services needed to sustain a society, like water and energy (gas and electricity). Traditionally the railways, postal services, and telecommunications have also been grouped under the utilities umbrella.

In recognition of the vital nature of water and power—and the conviction that everyone should have guaranteed, equitable access to them—the post-war Labour government nationalized all utilities in 1948. Until then, like schools and hospitals, they had been owned by an ad hoc medley of local corporations and charities, with the result that service standards varied wildly from place to place.

For forty years the utilities remained in the public sector. While individuals still had to pay their own rail fares and electricity bills (according to how much of any service they individually used), the industries were hugely subsidized through general taxation. Despite the fact there was no outside competition from other suppliers to drive down prices, subsidies generally enabled utilities to keep charges at reasonable levels.

Privatization of the utilities

In the 1980s the ethos governing the way state-owned utilities were perceived began to change, as free market economics infiltrated public services for the first time. Mrs Thatcher's government began a wholesale privatization of the utilities, arguing that the monolithic state-owned industries were inefficient, overbureaucratic, and offered the public too little 'choice'. Arguments for and against privatization are set out in Table 7.4.

The first utility to be privatized was British Telecom—a then state-owned telecommunications provider that was part of the then General Post Office. The British Gas Board followed two years later, with electricity changing hands in 1990, and the railways in 1993. Each privatization is explored in more detail below.

Privatization was to be only the first step in Mrs Thatcher's mission to 'liberalize' Britain's utilities. Unusually for someone revered and reviled in equal measure for her radical handling of the economy, she initially moved tentatively—allowing minimal competition in the privatized utilities to ensure the transition from public to private sectors had time to bed down before being opened to the ravages of the free market. But by the early 1990s gas, electricity, and telecommunications had been totally 'deregulated'—allowing various different companies to compete for business in each sector for the first time. On the railways, travellers were soon being referred to as 'customers' rather than 'passengers'.

Table 7.4 Arguments for and against utility privatization

For	Against
Privatization makes utilities more efficient by introducing competition and enabling providers to woo managers with commercial expertise.	Introducing profits raised suspicions that main priorities of providers were to boost revenue and share dividends, rather than using cost savings to lower prices and improve services.
It enables them to respond to consumers' wishes by reacting to supply and demand with wider choice of services—rather than assuming 'state knows best'.	Periods of intense competition between rival gas and electricity suppliers, and ineffective regulation, led to consolidation under fewer companies. Old-style public monopolies could eventually be replaced by private monopolies—and company boards (unlike governments) not accountable to service users.
Privatization removes 'statist' philosophy imposed on publicly owned utilities, allowing them to cut waste and contract out ancillary services—cleaning, catering, and maintenance—to smaller specialist companies. Doing so cuts overheads, which can be ploughed into improving product.	Some privatized utilities—particularly monopolies like water companies—accused of passing costs on to consumers rather than bearing them internally, to placate shareholders. Major infrastructural investment in water industry required by recent EU directives led to disproportionately high increases in water bills, while dividends kept rising.
Raises revenue for future government spending, while saving taxpayers' money by cutting cost of maintaining huge resources.	Privatization divests country of significant assets built up through prior investment of taxpayers' money and gives commercial companies 'something for nothing'. Former Tory Prime Minister Harold Macmillan called it 'selling off the family silver'.

The onward march of deregulation continues to this day, even in the few sectors still dominated by major public sector providers. In January 2006 the Royal Mail was opened up to free market competition for the first time in 350 years, as then industry regulator the Postal Services Commission (Postcomm) gave the go-ahead for any licensed business to deliver letters.

Although British governments today favour a 'light-touch' approach to regulation—preferring to let market forces determine prices and services—they continue to set certain minimum standards for each sector. For example, BT (successor to British Telecom) is still required by the terms of its licence to maintain public telephone boxes to ensure there is provision for people without mobile phones and in rural areas. In addition, each industry is overseen by at least one regulator with a statutory duty to ensure customers receive value for money and appropriate access to essential services. Overall responsibilities of regulators include:

- setting limits on price increases;
- monitoring service quality;
- ensuring that true competition is maintained.

Over the years, however, there has been considerable criticism of these regulators—often derided as 'watchdogs without teeth' in light of their perceived reluctance to interfere in the ways the utilities are managed. In April 2008, in the absence of regulator action, the chair of an all-party committee on fuel poverty, Labour backbencher John Battle, tabled a Commons motion publicly demanding that ministers force the Office of Gas and Electricity Markets (Ofgem) to stop energy companies charging higher unit rates to poor households reliant on prepayment meters than better off customers paying by direct debit.

Communications

British Telecom was privatized in 1984. Initially, only limited competition was allowed, with a single alternative provider, Mercury Communications Ltd (a digital network then owned by the Cable and Wireless Group), entering the market.

After a well-received trial, this 'duopoly' ended in 1991. Some 150 licensed telecommunications companies soon sprang up, including 125 cable operators and nineteen regional and national public telecoms operators, although the market has since been rationalized through mergers and takeovers. Today consumers can also choose from a range of mobile phone networks, the largest of which include Orange, O2, Vodafone, and T-Mobile, not to mention numerous Internet service providers, including BT Broadband, Virgin, and Tiscali.

Confusingly, most telephone landlines are still provided by engineers from BT, but customers are billed by the suppliers they pay to deliver services to them through those lines. A similar division, between the companies that own the physical infrastructure and those who provide services via it, exists in most utilities.

In recognition of the growing convergence of telecommunications and broadcast media, since 2003 telecoms regulation has been the responsibility of the **Office of Communications (Ofcom)**, a 'super-regulator' that also oversees television, radio, and digital media services providers. As a media regulator, Ofcom is solely concerned with broadcast and digital/online platforms. Oversight of the print media is (pending the outcome of the Leveson Inquiry—see p. 93) the responsibility of the **Press Complaints Commission (PCC)**: unlike Ofcom, a self-regulatory (as opposed to statutory) body with a governing board comprising industry professionals. Its responsibility is to ensure newspapers and magazines comply with an editors' code of practice covering everything from respect for the privacy of the bereaved to protection of confidential sources.

Previously, telecoms were policed by the now defunct Office of Telecommunications (Oftel), while the broadcast industry was overseen by several disparate regulators, including the Independent Television Commission (ITC) and Radiocommunications Agency. The BBC occupied an unusual position, in that it has a discrete overseer to monitor its editorial independence, the BBC Trust, with taste and decency issues falling within Ofcom's remit.

As of 1 October 2011, with the abolition of Postcomm, the postal industry has also come under the ambit of Ofcom. The consumer-run body *Consumer Focus*, which has channelled complaints from the public to government in relation to most of the utilities, is being scrapped, too, with its role franchised to the charity Citizens Advice as part of the government's 'Big Society' roll-out.

Ofcom's role in relation to postal services, acquired from Postcomm, is to:

- protect a universal postal service;
- license postal operators;
- introduce competition into mail services;
- regulate Royal Mail;
- advise the government on the Post Office network.

With nine out of ten letters still delivered by Royal Mail (a former monopoly), it is unsurprising that Postcomm was usually in the news pronouncing on that organization's performance. In May 2008 it issued a report warning that, unless Royal Mail was part-privatized, allowing it to raise investment on the open market, it might have to axe Saturday postal deliveries to save money. Despite already having controversially abandoned twice-daily deliveries on weekdays, in the year to March 2010 the company made a pre-tax loss of £262m, which it blamed on growing competition from private providers and consumer resistance to the rising price of first-class mail during the recession.

Given its continued dominancy of postal services, Royal Mail can also uniquely be fined for failing to meet government targets (a threat used in 2002 to chivvy up Consignia—as it was then known—after it failed to speed up business mail delivery).

In late 2010 Mr Cable confirmed Coalition plans to privatize Royal Mail fully—a step further than Labour had ever dared tread, even under his pro-business predecessor, Lord Mandelson, who shelved proposals for a partial sell-off in the dying months of Mr Brown's government. Under Mr Cable's scheme, at least 10 per cent of Royal Mail shares will be sold to its own employees, with the remainder floated as early as autumn 2013. Ministers were effectively given the go-ahead they required from EU competition authorities in March 2012, when the EC approved their takeover of Royal Mail's £9.5bn pension deficit and proposed write-off of £1bn of its debt—necessary prerequisites for attracting investors. It was also expected that the Post Office—the end of the 'postal chain' responsible for running counter services, rather than delivering mail—would be 'mutualized'. This would entail turning it into a cooperative-style company, run (in 'Big Society' fashion) by its own staff and/or customers.

Energy

In 1986 gas—then the preserve of the British Gas Board—was privatized. Although the newly rechristened 'British Gas' was initially a private monopoly, the industry swiftly became the first utility to be fully deregulated. At first, the emerging new generation of gas companies (like electricity suppliers later) were regionally based—households and businesses in south-east England, for example, were given a choice of only one alternative to British Gas, the headquarters of which was located in their region. Today most people can buy their gas from suppliers based anywhere in Britain, or even abroad, and many companies, including British Gas, supply 'dual fuel' (both gas and electricity).

As with telecoms, there is a division between supply companies that bill customers and the single firm that owns the infrastructure used to 'transport' fuel to them. Both the network of pipes for gas and the cables and pylons used to transmit electricity are owned by National Grid plc, a monopoly. Suppliers pay the company for using the network.

When electricity was privatized in 1990 it was originally split into three generating companies and twelve suppliers. An example of a regional supply company was the South East Electricity Board (Seeboard), subsequently bought by French-owned company Électricité de France (EDF Energy) in 2002. Since then the electricity supply chain has evolved into the three-stage process outlined in the table entitled 'The energy industry supply chain', to be found on the Online Resource Centre.

While England and Wales are governed by this system, Scottish Power plc and Scottish Hydro-Electric generate, transmit, and distribute all electricity in Scotland.

The gas and electricity utilities used to have separate regulators, but are now overseen by **Office of Gas and Electricity Markets (Ofgem)** and the Director General of Gas and Electricity Markets. Following a number of controversies over double-digit rises in energy bills (blamed by companies on the rising price of crude oil—despite the fact most have continued to report substantial profits), a succession of consumer watchdogs have also emerged. The first of these, *Energywatch*, was absorbed by Consumer Focus in 2008.

Water and sewerage

The most controversial utility privatization was that of the water industry, which was sold off in 1989. Given the essential nature of clean, safe water supplies, many critics of privatization (and some supporters) saw the idea of opening it up to market competition as a step too far.

There were also practical objections. Given the peculiar difficulties of 'subdividing' the industry's infrastructure—to take an extreme, splitting stretches of a reservoir between different companies—it quickly became clear that conventional competition would be impossible. To this day, water is supplied to British consumers by companies that are local monopolies—making a mockery, critics argue, of the premise of privatization.

Initially, ten water and sewerage companies were formed. Each was given responsibility for supplying water, storing and recycling it, and treating and disposing of sewerage. Confusingly for consumers (and journalists), the industry today is regulated by not one, but three bodies, the roles of which are outlined in Table 7.5.

Industrial and commercial water users are metered nowadays, and households may be charged on the basis of their Council Tax band or opt to be metered, depending on where they live. Consumers with a record of unpaid bills are often forced to install prepayment meters to avoid them slipping into future arrears. As in the energy industry, there has been periodic controversy about meters, with campaigners arguing they leave poor people vulnerable: if they do not have change available at a given time, their water supply is effectively cut off. Moreover, companies have been criticized for charging higher rates per unit to customers with meters than to those who pay by conventional

Table 7.5 Regulation of the water industry

Regulator	Remit
Water Services Regulatory Authority (Ofwat)—formerly the Office of Water Regulation	Regulates industry's structure and financial transparency (examining annual accounts and vetting proposed mergers/takeovers)
Drinking Water Inspectorate	Regulates quality of water supplied to consumers
Environment Agency	Monitors pollution and regulates water quality in inland, estuary, and coastal waters; also has responsibility for flood protection

bill. These and other concerns prompted the emergence of another watchdog: the **Consumer Council for Water**.

In Scotland, water effectively remains a nationalized utility. Three regional water authorities, covering the north, east, and west of the country, were merged in April 2002 to form a single state-owned company: Scottish Water. Scottish Water is overseen by the Water Industry Commission for Scotland (WICS) and its accounts are audited by Audit Scotland.

Railways

Privatization of the railways took a different route from that of other utilities, and today, albeit by default, the industry remains a public–private partnership (PPP) (see pp. 230–1). In 1993, following years of negotiation with the private sector to sell franchises covering marginal and unprofitable lines, British Rail was finally privatized. It was initially fragmented under 100-plus private operators—companies that bought up engines, carriages, and other rolling stock to manage individual routes on renewable franchises. Meanwhile, as in the energy industry, ownership of the network (tracks, signals, and stations) was transferred from the government to Railtrack: a private monopoly. Following a spate of controversies and rail disasters—including the 1999 Paddington train crash, in which thirty-one people died—ministers wound down Railtrack in 2002, replacing it with a not-for-dividend company: **Network Rail**. The infrastructure was therefore effectively taken back into a form of qualified public ownership.

Network Rail charges the remaining twenty-five operators for using its infrastructure, although in practice many operating companies run their local stations as subcontractors. Franchises are awarded by the government on the basis of a guaranteed 'minimum level of service' specific to each route, and companies are invited to tender for renewable terms of anything between seven and twenty years. The company that wins a franchise will usually be the one willing to run the service with the lowest government subsidy—giving rise to concerns about underinvestment and price rises. Current examples of franchisees include Southern (which runs the main London to Brighton line and manages stations for Network Rail along that route) and South West Trains, which is responsible for a large number of services across southern England and greater London.

In some areas, two or more companies operate services in competition, but elsewhere there are local monopolies. In practice, any competition that does exist is limited because it is physically impossible for two companies to run directly competing services (no two trains can use the same track between the same stations at the same time).

Huge increases in the number of people commuting to work in Britain in recent years have put growing pressure on the rail network, and fare prices have repeatedly risen well above inflation, even at times when service quality has deteriorated. Overcrowded carriages, broken-down engines, late arrivals, and cancellations—at a time when annual government subsidies to the rail network remained significantly higher than those before privatization—have made the railways an enduring ministerial headache. The Coalition's recent reduction in subsidies has only led to further dissatisfaction, as year-on-year price rises for commuters have soared well above inflation (let alone wages), despite the fact the industry continues to receive £4bn a year from the taxpayer.

Regulation of the rail industry is currently split between two authorities. The Office of Rail Regulation is meant to ensure prices are fair and that there is equitable access to tracks for operators. Meanwhile, the Department for Transport (DfT) itself is responsible for awarding and reviewing franchises and fining operators for repeated lateness, cancellations, and other aspects of poor performance. Beforehand, this role fell to the Strategic Rail Authority (SRA).

As with the other utilities, there is also a watchdog to represent consumers: **Passenger Focus**.

▍ Private finance initiative (PFI) and public–private partnerships (PPP)

As with major public sector building projects, the huge infrastructural investments required by utilities are often funded through the **private finance initiative (PFI)**—the system introduced by Mr Major's Conservative government in 1992, initially to finance new prisons at a time of acute overcrowding and repeated breakouts (see pp. 265–6). The classic PFI model sees a private company financing the bulk of the initial capital investment (buildings and equipment), often along with some ancillary staff to man the facility, and effectively 'owning' it for years or decades afterwards. The public sector gradually 'buys it back' in a long-term leaseback arrangement akin to a mortgage.

Although initially sceptical, Labour wholeheartedly embraced the PFI concept as it moved to fund an extensive programme of new schools and hospitals, rechristening such projects **public–private partnerships (PPPs)**. Today virtually all new public capital projects are financed this way—and so, too, are some related to the utilities. The proposed new generation of nuclear power stations approved in 2008 is likely to be largely, if not wholly, financed by private means.

One big advantage to governments of using private finance to fund capital projects is that initial outlays do not appear on the Treasury's balance sheet— meaning they do not technically 'count' as public expenditure. In contrast to the huge start-up costs of some projects, the face value of contracts awarded to

Table 7.6 Criticisms of PFI/PPP

Criticism	Explanation
Can only generally be financed through borrowing	Because governments' borrowing better secured than private sector's, interest rates faced by private companies investing in projects usually higher than those offered to states
Companies put shareholders before public (or 'customers')	Private companies have legal responsibility to earn profits for shareholders—making it likely that, whatever the short-term savings, final costs to taxpayers will, over time, be greater than if state had wholly financed project itself
PFI/PPP agreements like credit card debt or 'hire purchase' agreements of 1960s	PFI/PPP creates confusion over who actually 'owns' project—HP deals mean ministers are using taxpayers' money to mortgage public assets on the 'never never'
Who is responsible if something goes wrong—private investor or taxpayer?	Closure of Railtrack by ministers increased pressure on state to provide guarantees underpinning private sector's investment in prospective PPP projects to avoid deterring them

private businesses as an incentive to carry out building work is relatively low. Critics argue, however, that PPPs have notable disadvantages—as outlined in Table 7.6—and recent difficulties encountered by NHS trusts in servicing their contracts testify to this. At time of writing, there was mounting concern about the looming scale of public debt racked up by PFI/PPP contracts under successive governments, with one NHS trust, South London Healthcare, having recently entered administration, at least partly as a consequence of its capital 'debt', and a number of others said to be facing similar difficulties (see p. 178). Despite this, the success of the Coalition's embryonic 'infrastructure plan' appeared to be resting on hybrid public–private funding arrangements resembling PFI/PPP in all but name.

≣ Topical feature idea

Figure 7.1 contains the first half of a story that appeared in *The Independent* on 14 May 2012. It concerned the announcement by Coalition Chancellor George Osborne of government plans to implement regional pay bargaining for public sector workers, to reflect disparities in living costs from one English region to another. If introduced, the vast majority of public sector workers—from local authority officers to nurses and teachers—would be affected. How would you develop this into a lively backgrounder? To what extent will these changes affect your readers—and which groups of workers stand to suffer the most?

Figure 7.1 Article from *The Independent*, 14 May 2012

Unions attack regional pay plans

Alan Jones and Joe Churcher

The Independent

14 May 2012

Web link: http://www.independent.co.uk/news/
uk/home-news/unions-attack-regional-pay-
plans-7746491.html

Unions today stepped up demands for the
Government to scrap controversial plans for
regional pay in the public sector after the
Deputy Prime Minister said no final decisions
had been taken.

Nick Clegg said during a visit to a school in
London that the idea of 'local' pay was simply
being looked at.

Chancellor George Osborne sparked fury
among public sector unions when he announced in the Budget in March moves
towards introducing different levels of pay in
regions of the UK.

Mr Clegg said: 'There is going to be no
regional pay system. That is not going to
happen. No decisions have been taken.

'All that has been asked is something which
happened under the last government—they
did it in the Crown Court Service—which is "is
there, in specific cases, a justification to allow
local, not regional, local market-based costs to
be reflected in the way people are paid in the
public sector?"

'It is being looked at. Nothing has been
decided. I feel very, very strongly as an MP
from South Yorkshire with a lot of people in
the public services, that we are not going to do
anything which simply willy-nilly exacerbates
a north–south divide.

'There has been some ludicrous scaremongering, particularly from the trade unions,

about what is intended when there is no
proposal on the table at all.

'I really do think it's important that people
should be reassured that we are not just
going to sort of rush headlong in imposing a
system from above which, if it was done in
the way some people describe, would be
totally unjust because it would actually
penalise people working in some of the most
difficult areas.'

Brian Strutton, national officer of the GMB
union, said: 'The Deputy Prime Minister
appears to be softening the line on regional
pay previously put out by the Chancellor. This
is welcome not least because there is no
evidence to support the Chancellor's original
contention that public sector pay somehow
crowds out pay in the private sector. This was
always nonsense and Mr Clegg has successfully refuted the Chancellor's argument.'

Unison called on Mr Clegg to convince Mr
Osborne to ditch the 'divisive' plans to
introduce regional pay in the public sector.

General secretary Dave Prentis said: 'If
Nick Clegg disagrees with regionalised pay he
should convince George Osborne to ditch his
divisive plans. Far from being about making
pay fairer, plans for regionalised pay in the
public are simply a cost-cutting exercise. Not
a single public sector worker will get a pay
rise, but many will see their pay cut.

"Regional pay would hit communities hard,
entrenching low pay in certain areas. This
would cut consumer spending in local economies which they desperately need to recover
from the recession. Stopping the level playing
field in the public sector could also spark a skills
shortage in areas where pay is set lower.'

© The Independent

✳ Current issues

- **Reducing business red tape:** Business Secretary Vince Cable has published
  proposals to lighten red tape faced by SMEs, reducing the health and safety burden,
  while making it harder for employees to bring cases to employment tribunals and
  speeding up decisions when they do.

- **Problems meeting the deficit reduction target:** in Mr Osborne's first Budget he
  pledged spending cuts of up to £31.9bn a year by 2014/15, to eliminate Britain's

Budget deficit. Significant rises in taxes—notably a 2.5 per cent hike in VAT—were also announced in his June 2010 emergency Budget. Two years later, the timetable for clearing the deficit has been put back to at least 2017 and Britain is in a 'double-dip' recession—with falling tax receipts and a rising benefits bill.

- **Regulation of the banking sector:** the Bank of England regained authority for overall bank regulation following the 2010 election, but the FSA is being split up—with beefed-up versions of its previous functions also handed to the Bank. Disagreement remains between the parties about how best to tax bankers as recompense for the 2008/9 bailouts.

? Review questions

1. What role does the Budget play in fiscal and monetary policymaking in Britain?
2. What was the thinking behind Gordon Brown's decision to make the Bank of England independent and to give it responsibility for setting interest rates?
3. Outline the present-day rights of trades unions and the process by which individual unions gain legal recognition. Who has the most power: employers or employees?
4. How effective has regulation of the privatized utilities proved in the UK?
5. What are the arguments for and against the privatization and deregulation of the utilities?

→ Further reading

Edwards, P. (2003) *Industrial Relations: Theory and Practice in Britain*, 2nd edn, London: Wiley-Blackwell. **Second edition of acclaimed text focusing on recent developments in UK worker–employer relations, and growing casualization/ flexibility of labour markets.**

Grimsey, D. and Lewis, M. (2007) *Public Private Partnerships: The Worldwide Revolution in Infrastructure Provision and Project Finance*, London: Edward Elgar. **Illuminating overview of growing role of private capital in public sector infrastructural investment, and costs this brings to public. Includes comparative examples of PPP-style projects from states outside Britain.**

Michie, R. C. (2001) *The London Stock Exchange: A History*, Oxford: Oxford University Press. **Acclaimed history of Britain's biggest money market—one of largest in world—incorporating up-to-date explanations of the Stock Exchange and how FTSE works.**

Monbiot, G. (2001) *Captive State: The Corporate Takeover of Britain*, London: Pan Books. **Critically acclaimed exposé by leading campaigning journalist of the creeping growth in influence of commercial companies in British public affairs.**

Swann, D. (1988) *The Retreat of the State: Deregulation and Privatisation in the UK and US*, London: Prentice-Hall. **Accomplished exploration of privatization revolution on** both sides of Atlantic, and introduction of competition into former state-owned public services.

Wrigley, C. (2002) *British Trade Unions Since 1933*, Cambridge: Cambridge University Press. **Textbook giving comprehensive overview of evolution of industrial relations policy in Britain since 1940s.**

 **Online Resource Centre**

www.oxfordtextbooks.co.uk/orc/Morrison3e/

Visit the Online Resource Centre that accompanies this book for web links and regular updates.

8

Social welfare and home affairs

Alongside the National Health Service (NHS) and education, the twin briefs of 'social affairs' and 'home affairs' occupy more newspaper column inches, broadcast airtime, and web pages than almost any other areas of British life. From government crackdowns on 'welfare scroungers' to controversies about immigration, prison breakouts, or gun crime, barely a week passes without a number of major stories generating screaming headlines.

The story of British citizenship in the modern age is one of 'carrot' and 'stick': carrot, in terms of the rights, entitlements, and benefits to which UK citizens who 'play by the rules' are eligible; stick, in terms of prosecution, punishment, and ultimately imprisonment for those who 'abuse the system' by failing to meet the responsibilities expected of them.

▌ Basis of the 'welfare state'

The primary purpose of the 'welfare state' initiated by the Liberal government of Herbert Asquith and David Lloyd George, and solidified by the post-war reforms of Clement Attlee's Labour administration, was to provide a safety net for members of society who fell on hard times, whether temporarily (through losing a job or falling sick and being unable to work) or more indefinitely (because of a serious injury or long-term illness). Other than in exceptional situations, life 'on the social', 'on the sick', or, in the case of unemployment, 'on the dole' was never envisaged as a permanent state of affairs for anyone. Rather, it was meant to prevent those who, through no fault of their own, found themselves unable to work, earning low wages, or in other economically impoverished circumstances. The concept of 'deserving' and 'undeserving' poor was arguably enshrined in the minds of Britain's governing classes well before the Thatcher revolution.

According to eminent historian Asa Briggs, the term 'welfare state' was first coined by William Temple, Archbishop of Canterbury, during the Second World War. It is widely recognized, however, that the practical foundations of a proto-type welfare state were laid during Lloyd George's time as, first, Chancellor of the Exchequer, then prime minister. His 1909 'People's Budget' (see p. 60) introduced both old-age pensions and **National Insurance (NI)**—the progressive tax that remains the bedrock of the benefits system to this day. From the outset, the welfare state was to be a safety net based on both *need* and *entitlement*: the needy would be looked after, but their eligibility for this support derived from the presumption that when they were able to work and pay their way, they would do so. Even today, a British citizen's ability to claim higher-rate benefits to help them through periods of sickness and/or unemployment is contingent on their having made sufficient NI contributions and paid enough tax during periods of work.

Nonetheless, while a certain amount of 'responsibility' has always been expected of those receiving welfare support, there has been a marked hardening of attitude under recent governments. The early 1980s saw a huge increase in unemployment as entire industries were effectively dismantled through Margaret Thatcher's radical market reforms. Few could argue at the time that the hundreds of thousands of workers made redundant had themselves to blame for their predicament. Yet it was not long before Mrs Thatcher's ministers were invoking the image of the jobless layabout. Shortly after the Handsworth and Brixton Riots of 1981, her Employment Secretary, Norman Tebbit, told a journalist:

❝ I grew up in the 1930s with an unemployed father. He did not riot. He got on his bike and looked for work, and he went on looking until he found it. **❞**

Mr Tebbit's reply has gone down in British political folklore. In many ways it was to set the tone for future policy by not only the Conservatives, but New Labour and the Coalition. When Tony Blair was elected in 1997 his Chancellor, Gordon Brown, initiated an ambitious plan to reduce unemployment under the 'Welfare to Work' banner. His 'New Deal for the Unemployed' (based on a model adopted in some US states) aimed to provide a wider choice of work-related opportunities for the long-term unemployed, rewarding those who undertook specified training programmes and/or voluntary work with initial £10 top-ups to their weekly benefits. In return for these entitlements, however, it would demand ever more stringent demonstrations of their efforts to find work, organizing regular interviews with 'supervisors' in the then Employment Service to monitor their rate of applications and help them with job searches. This built on tough measures introduced under John Major's government, when high-profile crackdowns were introduced to target 'scroungers' and claimants who accepted cash-in-hand work but failed to declare it. Under the Coalition, things have got tougher still. Today the idea of 'contributory welfare' dominates popular discourse about benefits in a way seldom seen since before the welfare state was invented.

▌ Social welfare services today

The social security bill represents the single largest area of government expenditure in Britain. Defined broadly as welfare provision allocated to guarantee 'a basic standard of living for those in financial need', it accounts for more than 30 per cent of Britain's overall public spending budget and 21 per cent of its gross domestic product (GDP) (see p. 204).

Over the years, social welfare services have been administered by a succession of, often overlapping and sometimes conflicting, government departments. Today they are split between the Department for Work and Pensions, Department for Education, Department of Health, and Treasury—as illustrated in the table entitled 'A breakdown of the main government departments involved in social welfare', to be found on the Online Resource Centre.

Because the first half of this chapter is primarily focused on the social security system—specifically the benefits and tax incentives introduced by governments to promote welfare and employment—it concentrates on the work of the two biggest players: the Department for Work and Pensions (DWP) and HM Treasury.

▌ Department for Work and Pensions (DWP)

The DWP has overall responsibility for the 'Welfare to Work' programme. When Labour returned to power in 1997 its immediate concern was to tackle the growing problem of intergenerational unemployment—the increasing numbers of long-term unemployed (those who had been without work for six months or more and, in many cases, some years), as well as the growing number of 18–25-year-olds with little or no employment record (many hailing from the same families as long-term claimants). The 'New Deal' policies that followed were criticized as much for their narrow focus on these two target groups as the stiff conditions they imposed on those they were designed to help. Following the 2001 and 2005 Labour victories, the New Deal was gradually extended to target, in turn, over-25s, over-50s, lone parents, and people with disabilities.

The vast and complex benefits system the DWP presides over is administered in practice by a range of executive agencies. Their roles are outlined in Table 8.1.

Types of benefit and their relationship to NI

The benefits system is currently undergoing its most radical shake-up since its inception, with the phased-in introduction of the Universal Credit (UC), which is due to begin nationwide in October 2013 (see p. 245). However, even under

Table 8.1 Executive agencies involved in social security

Agency	Role
Jobcentre Plus	As 'plus' indicates, this has wider remit than providing employment-related welfare. Replaced Benefits Agency (BA) in administering most state benefits, ranging from Child Benefit, maternity benefits, and widows' pensions to Income Support, Incapacity Benefit, Disability Living Allowance (DLA), and Jobseeker's Allowance (JSA). Council housing departments administer Housing Benefit/Local Housing Allowance (see p. 512) on its behalf.
Child Support Agency (CSA)	Assesses and collects maintenance payments for children from parents under arrangements made in family courts.
Pension Service	Helps people navigate complex web of alternative pension options and related benefits and tax credits.

the new regime—and certainly for the many people who will remain under the current one for the time being—there are two broad 'categories' of UK welfare benefit. Whether a particular payment falls into one or the other depends on the extent to which NI contributions have been made:

- **Contributory benefits** are those available to people if they have paid sufficient NI contributions. These include contributions-based Jobseeker's Allowance (the higher rate of JSA) and Incapacity Benefit.

- **Non-contributory benefits** bear no relationship to an individual's prior NI contributions. Most are 'needs-based' payments for anyone whose income falls below certain levels and/or who meets certain other criteria (e.g. disability in relation to DLA). These include Income Support and the basic level of JSA. Some, however, are 'universal': for example, Winter Fuel Payment, an allowance for everyone over 60, irrespective of their personal financial circumstances.

There are five 'classes' of NI contribution. The one affecting most people is Class 1—paid by both employers and employees in proportion to their levels of earnings. One oft-cited advantage of working for someone else is that for every pound invested into the NI 'pot' entitling a person to future benefit, should they need it, a further pound at least is paid in by his/her employer. By contrast, self-employed people have sole responsibility for making their NI contributions (Class 2, paid weekly, and Class 4, which are profit-based).

There are two further classes of NI: Class 1A, paid by employers operating company car and fuel schemes for their employees for private use, and Class 3, which is paid voluntarily by those with money to do so to safeguard future eligibility to benefits. By way of a long service award, those who continue working after pensionable age no longer have to pay NI. However, their employers continue doing so on their behalf.

Different types of benefit

October 2013 is due to see the start of the roll-out of a new single payment for those receiving welfare support—Universal Credit (UC)—in place of the myriad benefits and tax credits to which individuals have until now been entitled. At present, though—and for some time to come for many existing claimants, who will not be moved over to UC until after new ones—there remain a wide variety of distinct benefits available, depending on whether people are unemployed, disabled, or low-paid.

Jobseeker's Allowance

Jobseeker's allowance (JSA) is paid to adults working fewer than sixteen hours a week and 'available for and actively seeking' full-time work. There are two levels of benefit: contributions-based (related to prior NI contributions) and income-based (for those who satisfy a financial means test, regardless of prior contributions). People with savings of £16,000 or more are unlikely to be eligible for JSA, while those with between £6,000 and £16,000 receive reduced payments.

As with earlier forms of unemployment benefit, JSA has been the subject of periodic criticism from all sides over the nature of the criteria used to award or refuse it, not to mention the level of the benefit itself. For decades, British governments have agonized over the benefits-related 'poverty trap'—put crudely, the fear that giving too much money to the unemployed acts as a disincentive for them to work. In taking up a job, an unemployed person instantly loses any entitlement to unemployment benefit and, even if he/she continues to qualify for certain other payments—for example Housing Benefit/Local Housing Allowance—he/she will instantly be paying Income Tax and NI contributions out of his/her wages. For some, such as single parents, the option of taking up a low-paid, temporary and/or part-time job rather than remaining on JSA often seems impractical: the cost of childcare they would otherwise not need, combined with immediate loss of benefits, can make the prospect of remaining unemployed (however unpalatable) preferable. It has long been acknowledged that at the point at which unemployed people move into work, they are subject to extremely high 'marginal tax rates'—losing up to 95p for every pound earned initially, as benefits cease, tax credits wait to kick in, and emergency tax is deducted from their first pay packets.

Few would dispute that benefit levels need to remain lower than pay rates to encourage people to work when they find a suitable job. But for some campaigners, including social policy think tanks like the Joseph Rowntree Foundation, the poverty trap arises less out of overinflated benefits than the fact that wages for many jobs are too low. In the 2012/13 tax year, maximum weekly rates of JSA stood at £56.25 for 18–25-year-olds and £71 for over-25s—hardly the stuff of which millionaires are made!

Labour tried to address the issue of low wages by introducing Britain's first national minimum wage in 1997 (see p. 218). Yet many workers—particularly those in low-skilled jobs like security and care work—continue to receive poverty wages that take little account of the cost of living in their area. Concern about the poverty trap led Labour to roll out tax credits—a form of welfare payment for people on low incomes, directed to them through their pay packets, rather than the traditional giro cheque-based benefits system. Such measures have, however, been tempered by continuing threats to make life harder for the minority of people that successive governments have insinuated are 'refusing' to work, despite being capable of doing so. In February 2008 Labour launched a major 'rethink' of welfare, contracting out Jobcentre Plus-style jobsearch advice and support services to the private sector—with companies paid for successfully finding work for claimants and keeping them in those jobs for six months or more, and claimants penalized for not attending interviews or appointments with personal supervisors.

The Coalition has taken an even tougher stance. One measure introduced has been a 'three-strikes-and-you're-out' policy for those who repeatedly refuse offers of work. First-time 'offenders' today stand to lose their benefits for three months, second-timers for six months, and third-timers for up to three years—though, when he asked the DWP how many claimants had ever refused three such offers, BBC Home Affairs editor Mark Easton received the answer: 'none'.

The Coalition has also moved further and faster towards requiring unemployed people to work for their benefits, through the aegis of its overarching 'Work Programme'—the umbrella title for the suite of schemes central to its efforts to help the young and long-term jobless find (and remain in) work.

Among its various 'conditionality-based' initiatives—inspired by the 'Workfare' system rolled out across the United States during Bill Clinton's presidency—are a number aimed primarily at 16- to 24-year-olds with little prior workplace experience. The most controversial of these include the self-explanatory 'Mandatory Work Activity', which requires those judged to need extra help to engage (or re-engage) with employment to undertake unpaid four-week stints working on community projects for up to thirty hours a week. Those who fail to turn up, or see placements through to the end, lose their benefits for three months for a 'first offence' and six for a second. In June 2012 Employment Minister Chris Grayling warned that harsher sanctions would be introduced later that year after disclosing that nearly half the first-wave 'jobseekers' referred for placements either failed to turn up or signed off JSA rather than undertake them. Equally unpopular with the unemployed have been new 'work experience' schemes aimed mainly at the young: though notionally voluntary, if participants leave part-way through 'without good reason' they stand to lose up to two weeks' JSA.

Such is the rigid and punitive nature of these twin initiatives that in early 2012 a national media furore erupted around them. The backlash began when it emerged that Cait Reilly, a Birmingham University geology graduate, was suing the Coalition under the Human Rights Act after being forced to give up a sought-after placement in a museum, that might have led to a professional career, to undertake what she described as 'slave labour' in high-street discount chain Poundland. Amid the wave of negative publicity that followed, and a grass-roots protest mobilized by the Right to Work campaign, a succession of major companies withdrew from the scheme—including Sainsbury's, Waterstones, and Superdrug. One of the few prominent surviving participants, Tesco, offered all 1,500 people on placements with the company the choice of either continuing on the government scheme or undertaking a four-week *paid* internship, with the guarantee of a job at the end of it if they performed well.

Similarly incendiary have been the alleged malpractices of some private sector companies contracted to implement the Work Programme on a payment by results basis. In February 2012 it emerged that four employees of A4E—a firm initially hired by Labour, and the biggest recipient of DWP contracts under the Coalition—had been arrested in an investigation into allegations of fraud at its office in Slough. Following a succession of further arrests, and disclosure of an internal audit showing that company bosses were alerted as early as 2009 to potential irregular or criminal activities by employees across Britain, Mr Grayling cancelled its contract to arrange Mandatory Work Activity placements in south-east England. Three months earlier, Emma Harrison, founder of A4E—which stands for 'Action for Employment'—had stepped down as both company chairwoman and the Coalition's 'Family Champion' and 'Back-to-Work Tsar'.

In addition to profiting from the Work Programme directly, the commercial sector also stands to do nicely from an initiative announced by Mr Cameron in August 2010 to crack down on welfare fraud. Defying condemnation from civil liberties groups and some Opposition MPs, and provoking criticism from the Information Commissioner (see Chapter 20), he confirmed that private credit-rating firms—dubbed 'bounty-hunters'—would be used to snoop on the financial affairs of claimants to identify those whose spending habits suggested they were guilty of fraud. Although Mr Cameron highlighted an annual cost to the public purse of £5.2bn from fraud, official DWP and HMRC figures suggested most of this was attributable to overpayment and paperwork errors by officials. Only £1bn was down to wilful fraud.

Income Support

Income Support (IS) is a flexible non-contributory benefit available to 16–60-year-olds on low incomes and not in full-time paid employment, who satisfy various other criteria (for example, being single parents, full-time carers, or registered blind). As of summer 2012/13 there were two rates for single people:

- £56.25 for single 16–24-year-olds;
- £71 for single people aged 25 or over.

As with other benefits, payments to couples take account of their ability to cut costs by shopping and cooking together, and paying joint utility bills. These combined payments are relatively lower as a consequence. The standard rate for all couples in which both partners were 18 or over was £111.45. Eligible single parents were entitled to £56.25 if aged 16 or 17, and £71 if 18 or over, but since 2008 incremental changes have been introduced to encourage parents to take up jobs once their children reach a certain age by withdrawing IS at that point. Lone parents with children over first 12, then 10, had their entitlements stopped in November 2008 and October 2009 respectively, while from October 2010 eligibility was withdrawn from everyone with children due to turn 7 in the following year.

As with JSA, there are restrictions on individuals' ability to claim IS if they have savings of £6,000 or more.

Employment and Support Allowance (ESA) and Disability Living Allowance (DLA)

Just as there are different levels and types of JSA, so, too, there is more than one form of benefit for the sick or disabled. Although soon to be replaced by UC, **Employment and Support Allowance (ESA)** recently supplanted the long-standing Incapacity Benefit (IB) as the main contributions-based payment for people judged incapable of working while under state pension age, who meet one or more of the following criteria:

- they have received Statutory Sick Pay through their employer, that has ended although they remain incapable of working;
- they are self-employed or unemployed;
- they have been receiving Statutory Maternity Pay (SMP), but have not gone back to work because they are sick.

Since 31 January 2011 no new applications for IB have been accepted, and new applicants have instead been assessed for ESA. People who were claiming IB before that date are currently having their eligibility reviewed incrementally—a process due to be completed by 2014. The rate at which ESA is paid initially depends on what stage someone's application is at. During the 'assessment phase'—the first thirteen weeks of a claim, when a decision should be made about the applicant's ability to return to work in the short, medium, or long term, following a Work Capability Assessment (see p. 243)—the rates for 2012/13 were:

- single person under 25—£56.25;
- single person 25 and over—£71.

Then, if the assessment confirms he/she has limited ability to work due to illness or disability, he/she will be placed in one of the following two groups, and paid a corresponding level of benefit:

- Work-Related Activity Group (claimants judged capable of undertaking structured activities designed to prepare them for returning to the work-place)—up to £99.15;
- Support Group (those confirmed as being too sick/disabled to work for the foreseeable future)—up to £105.05.

While income-based ESA is non-taxable, there is also a more generous rate available to those who have made sufficient NI contributions in the past. Claimants receiving these higher payments may be liable for tax, depending on what other income, if any, they receive.

Due to its relative generosity and the sheer number of claimants (2.6 million in 2008, at an annual cost of £12bn), IB became a huge political issue towards the end of its life. First introduced as 'Invalidity Benefit' by Edward Heath's Conservative government, it came into its own during the Thatcher years, when the mass closure of coalpits and factories resulting from privatization and liberalized employment laws saw large numbers of out-of-work men trans-ferred onto it. At the time the Tories—later to lead the charge in bringing down the IB bill—were accused by Labour of deliberately using the benefit as a polit-ical tool to 'massage' the true unemployment figures, while throwing many peo-ple who had previously worked all their lives onto the 'scrapheap'. But since the early 1990s a succession of welfare ministers have made it their mission to weed out those who can work from those who genuinely cannot, through a series of ever-harsher tests.

In 2005 Labour announced a root-and-branch reform of the rules governing IB, vowing to reduce the number of recipients by 1 million. The resulting Welfare Reform Act 2007 introduced these changes, and the concept of the appropriately worded ESA—its title denoting a new emphasis on 'supporting' people, including the large majority with genuine illnesses and disabilities, to re-enter employment as soon as possible.

But introducing the new regime was far from smooth, with particular ques-tions surrounding the conduct of the signature **Work Capability Assessments (WCAs)** used to determine whether new applicants should be granted ESA and existing recipients allowed to continue with it. Subcontracted, controversially, to occupational health company Atos Healthcare (a branch of a French-owned information technology firm), the assessments are carried out by health care professionals—yet last barely thirty minutes, involve no medical examination, and centre on 'tick-box' questions on a computer-based form.

In May 2010, in the very week Mr Duncan Smith first announced plans to roll out the tests to existing IB claimants from 2011, a report by Citizens Advice Scotland (where the assessments were piloted) labelled them 'unfit for purpose' after finding that up to two-thirds of claimants put through the tests under Labour had been declared fit on the basis of their medicals—20 per cent more than anticipated. As a result, 8,000 appeals were being heard each month, with two out of five succeeding. A BBC investigation found that many GPs involved in conducting the medical tests had strong reservations about their efficacy, particularly in relation to people with mental health problems and other less 'visible' illnesses/disabilities. And there were renewed calls for the tests to be scrapped in May 2012, when GPs unanimously backed a motion at the British Medical Association's annual conference condemning them as 'inadequate' and having 'little regard to the nature or complexity of the needs of long-term sick or disabled persons'. By this time, four out of ten appeals reaching tribunals were succeeding—calling into question the basis on which decisions were made.

A more disturbing outcome of the new assessment regime is the circumstantial evidence of its impact on vulnerable claimants. In June 2012 *The Guardian* revealed the existence of an internal email from senior Jobcentre Plus managers urging staff to handle 'customers' with 'utmost care and sensitivity' to acclimatize them to 'difficult changes' they 'may take some time to accept and adjust to'. The Black Triangle Campaign, a grass-roots group representing disabled people, had been established a year earlier, largely in response to the apparent suicide of Paul Reekie, a mentally ill man found dead beside two letters—one notifying him of a decision to cancel his Housing Benefit and the other his IB. These and other horror stories recently led to Labour demanding a review of the way WCAs were being conducted.

Marginally less controversial than ESA is the second principal sickness-related payment: Disability Living Allowance (DLA). Eligibility for this non-contributory benefit is based purely on someone's verified mental or physical needs (regardless of income, savings, or ability to work). Under 65-year-olds have traditionally been able to claim DLA if they are physically or mentally disabled. Because it covers both aspects, DLA comprises both a 'care component' and a 'mobility component', and some individuals have qualified for both. Nonetheless (again ahead of their transfer to UC), ministers have insisted that all new DLA claimants undergo medical assessments from 2013. As of 2012/13, the higher rate of care component was £77.45, middle rate £51.85, and lower rate £20.55. The mobility component has only a higher and a lower rate (£54.05 and £20.55 respectively).

▍ HM Revenue and Customs (HMRC)

HMRC plays an integral role in the welfare system in two respects: it raises taxes to pay for benefits, and makes discrete payments to families, pensioners, and others on limited incomes through tax credits—a system designed to encourage low earners to stay in employment and others to enter it by rewarding them with modest 'rebates' through their pay packets. As the tax credit system has evolved it has expanded to provide 'minimum income guarantees' (MIGs) for other vulnerable groups, including pensioners. The main types are outlined in the table entitled 'A breakdown of the main tax credits available from HMRC', to be found on the Online Resource Centre.

Rationalizing welfare—Universal Credit

The centrepiece of the Coalition's welfare reform programme is **Universal Credit (UC)**—a new 'all-in-one' benefit-cum-tax credit designed to simplify the fiendishly complex array of payment types outlined above (which Mr Duncan Smith himself has confessed even he doesn't understand!). UC is also intended to be more responsive to the specific circumstances of each individual claimant, particularly sudden changes in their financial situations at times when they move into (and out of) employment. A key aim is to remove disincentives to work, by allowing people to retain more of their benefits, at least initially, as they move off the dole queue and into jobs.

Other innovative aspects of the UC regime will include the introduction of online accounts, allowing most claimants to apply for and manage their claims from home, and monthly (rather than fortnightly) payments—to be paid direct into their bank accounts. Support with housing costs will be incorporated into the same payments.

see also local government p. 512

UC was due to be piloted in Greater Manchester and Cheshire from April 2013—in four 'pathfinder' areas: Wigan, Oldham, Tameside, and Warrington. It should be rolled out nationwide from that October. But the mammoth task of moving millions of individuals currently receiving other benefits (and, in some cases, combinations of several different ones) onto a single payment regime meant that, even according to ministers' own estimates, it will take until at least 2017 to shift everyone onto it.

At time of writing, questions were being raised about how realistic even this timetable was. According to a DWP newsletter circulated in May 2012, and highlighted in the Commons by Shadow Work and Pensions Secretary Liam Byrne, the government's original ambition to treat all new applications for out-of-work benefits as UC enquiries from October 2013 was likely to be pushed back to mid-2014. Meanwhile, the projected £2bn cost of introducing UC was expected to rise by at least £100m.

It remains to be seen how smoothly the new system will operate once it is up and running, too. While the idea of streamlining the mind-boggling array of existing benefits and credits into a single payment, tailored to individuals' needs, may make perfect sense in principle, the success of the new system will depend on its ability to make finely tuned, often rapid, calculations that reflect month-to-month (even week-to-week) variations in their circumstances. Whether the final handout a claimant receives has one name (as it now will) or several, the top-ups and/or deductions that will continually need to be made to entitlements by the real-time computer system that will calculate them are likely to make the new regime even more complex than the old. Another concern highlighted by anti-poverty campaigners is that the introduction of new monthly benefit payments may make it difficult for claimants who have up to now received them weekly or fortnightly to budget effectively as the changes come into effect.

The 'universal benefits' versus 'means-testing' debate—the future of welfare for parents and older people

In addition to the needs-based benefits outlined above, several other sources of support have continued to be available on a 'universal' basis. In most, but not all, cases these tend to be payments aimed at children and the elderly.

At time of writing, Child Benefit was still paid to all mothers in respect of every child under 18 (or under 20 and still in full-time education or training). But it has long been controversial, given that high-income families arguably have little need for it, yet receive the same amount per child as low earners and unemployed people. Questioning this rationale (and with an eye to making much-needed savings), Coalition Chancellor George Osborne announced in his 2010 Budget plans to freeze it at its then current rate for three years. Having mooted a more radical approach to cutting the bill, it wasn't long before he plucked up the resolve to challenge the long-standing shibboleth (upheld by both Labour and Tory administrations since the war) that it should remain universal at all costs.

In his Comprehensive Spending Review that October, Mr Osborne unveiled plans to remove the payment as of January 2013 from all families in which at least one adult was a higher-rate taxpayer (earning £43,875-plus at the time). Critics were quick to point out the prima facie injustice of a move that would enable a household of two earners, each taking home up to £43,000, to retain their entitlement while a single parent on just over that amount would lose it. Such was the furore that, in his March 2012 Budget, Mr Osborne backtracked, saying the benefit would be removed only when one earner reached £50,000. Even then, it would be slowly withdrawn from families, at a rate of 1 per cent for every £100 earned over that sum, rather than immediately cut in the 'cliff-edge' way originally envisaged. It will only now be removed entirely once one parent's salary tops £60,000.

That the Child Benefit debate proved such a cause célèbre had its roots in two key issues: the historical context underpinning the payment, and the more over-arching concept of 'universalism'. To deal with the former first, Child Benefit—paid directly to mothers—has been seen as a means of liberating women from dependency on their husbands/partners and giving them direct control over at least part of their household budget (which, in times gone by, might have been their only income). More generally, though, universal benefits like this have long been defended, notably by politicians on the Left, because paying them to everyone, regardless of income, gives those who would not need to claim benefits on financial grounds a 'stake' in the welfare system—thus promoting (in theory) a sense of solidarity about the importance of maintaining it. Labour has also long resisted means-testing—in essence, awarding payments only to those who can prove they are on low incomes and/or have little or no savings—because of a deep-seated aversion to the 'indignity' of requiring people to demonstrate their poverty, and a concern that asking them to do so might discourage many in urgent need of financial help from claiming their entitlements.

A more pragmatic argument against means-testing is that it would be too complex (and, for that reason, costly), given the need to repeatedly reassess households whenever their annual incomes fluctuate for any reason. For example, if the main 'breadwinner' were to lose his/her job, change employer, or become self-employed, this task could be onerous.

The same principle of universality currently applies to certain forms of welfare targeted at the elderly, notably free bus passes for use on local bus services anywhere in England and Wales (for which everyone qualifies from their sixtieth birthdays) and the Winter Fuel Payment (which currently amounts to £200 for individuals living alone who were born on or before 5 July 1951, or £300 for those aged 80 or over on or before 23 September 2012). As with other benefits, couples qualify for reduced sums (£100 and £200 each respectively), but the poorest pensioners (those on Pension Credit, income-based JSA, or income-related ESA) receive £200 or, if over 80, £300 irrespective of whether they live with another adult.

Two further universal benefits for those who meet the criteria on the basis of their family situations, are statutory maternity and paternity pay. These are paid via employers to parents of recently born children. Mothers are now entitled to up to nine months' paid maternity leave, albeit pegged at 90 per cent of their average gross weekly earnings for the first six weeks and whichever is the lower of £135.45 a week or 90 per cent of gross earnings for the remaining thirty-three weeks. Fathers are eligible for two weeks' paid paternity leave, at either 90 per cent of their normal earnings or the £135.45 rate (whichever is lower)—and, since 3 April 2011, have been able to use up to six months of the mother's maternity leave entitlement if she earns more than him and/or decides to return to work sooner.

Other entitlements include Statutory Sick Pay, which is available for up to twenty-eight weeks to full-time employees unable to work through ill health (although the requirement to provide their employers with 'sick notes' was changed to a new emphasis on 'fit notes' in April 2010), and widows' pensions, which are lump sums paid to women whose husbands were below retirement age when they died. Payments begin from the date they would have qualified for pensions had they lived.

Taken together, the sheer scope of their coverage means universal benefits cost the Treasury billions each year. Not surprising, then, that even long-time defenders of universalism are now arguing that the principle has had its day.

Perhaps the most 'regressive' example of the contributory principle in action—and one increasingly highlighted by anti-poverty campaigners—has been the continued entitlement of wealthy ex-patriot Britons who have retired abroad (often to sunnier climes) to the Winter Fuel Allowance. 'Anomalies' like this have led to more independent-minded politicians questioning whether means-testing is now necessary in the interests of fairness to those on the lowest incomes. Other critics of universalism point out that the debate about whether to introduce means-tested benefits more widely is based on a false premise. With fewer and fewer elderly and disabled people entitled to automatic government help with the costs of social care, because their savings and/or other incomes are judged too high, in many areas of life means-testing already exists.

→

see also local
government
pp. 543–4

One type of welfare support that *is* targeted at those on low incomes is the one-off payment. This can take several forms, but the most common are crisis loans (lump sums to help out in the event of emergencies or disasters, like floods or fires), and the Social Fund, which offers either 'regulated' (compulsory) help to those who meet the criteria (for example, one-off payments to help with funeral costs) or 'discretionary' awards, including short-term budgeting loans to help people through rocky patches while waiting for their next pay packets or benefit cheques.

▶ Towards future welfare reform

Despite already being engaged in the most fundamental overhaul of the welfare regime since the Beveridge Report was enacted, there are signs of a growing appetite among the political Right to take things further. This has led some critics of the Coalition's trajectory to suggest the welfare state is slowly being dismantled—including those who view the retention of a strong element of universalism as vital to persuading the majority who seldom claim benefits to 'buy into' the need for a safety net.

In a provocative June 2012 speech on the future of welfare policy under the Tories, Mr Cameron returned to a familiar theme touched on periodically, including in the aftermath of England's 2011 urban riots (see p. 266): the notion of a system that has long 'sent out some incredibly damaging signals', including that it 'pays not to work' and it is possible to get 'something for nothing'. Among the radical future manifesto ideas he floated to combat the 'culture of entitlement' were cuts to benefits for people who failed to obtain work for long periods; forcing claimants with literacy and numeracy problems to learn to read, write, and calculate, to make them more employable; linking benefit levels to wages rather than inflation (abandoning the annual uprating system introduced by Labour in the late 1970s); and paying some benefits 'in kind' rather than cash, to discourage claimants from spending money on the wrong things. In an early draft he even mooted introducing regional benefit levels, to reflect differentials in the cost of living from one part of England to another—an echo of the new policy announced a month earlier by Mr Osbourne in relation to future wage bargaining (see p. 221). Another idea—which came uncomfortably close for some to arguments used by early twentieth-century proponents of eugenics—was the removal of supposed financial incentives to unemployed people to have more children, for example Child Benefit and access to social housing. In October 2012 Mr Duncan Smith suggested benefits might in future be withdrawn from households with as few as three children. Meanwhile, in his December 2012 pre-budget report, Mr Osbourne was widely expected to freeze out-of-work benefits, or peg them to average earnings rather than inflation to avoid the apperance of rewarding the unemployed at a time when many working people were suffering wage cuts.

▶ State pensions and the great retirement debate

Although there has been much debate in recent years about its paltry size, Britons are still automatically entitled to a state retirement pension funded out of general taxation.

Retirement ages for men and women are in the process of being equalized. At time of writing, men born before 6 December 1953 were retiring at 65, and women born after 5 April 1950 but before 6 December 1953 were doing so between the ages of 60 and 65. Following a review of existing retirement ages by an Independent Public Service Pensions Commission chaired by Labour peer Lord Hutton, the Pensions Act 2011 speeded up raising the retirement age for women to 65, and this will now be phased in between April 2016 and November 2018. The Act also stipulated:

- state pension age for all women born on or after 6 April 1953 and all men born on or after 6 December 1953 to start rising to 66 between December 2018 and October 2020;
- pension age to rise further to 67 between 2034 and 2036, and again to 68 between 2044 and 2046.

In November 2011, however, the Coalition announced plans to fast-track the rise to 67 even sooner, bringing it forward to between 2026 and 2028. And in his March 2012 Budget Mr Osborne went further, stating that from that date onwards the retirement age would be linked directly to changes in life expectancy.

The introduction of the basic state retirement pension was one of the founding initiatives of the welfare state in 1948. The basic provision—funded through NI contributions—was supplemented in 1978 with the introduction of the now contentious State Earnings-Related Pension Scheme (SERPS), championed by the late Baroness Castle, who, as then Health and Social Security Secretary, was its main architect. SERPS was seen by many as guaranteeing a civilized degree of comfort to people in retirement because of the principle that under-pinned it: that state pensions should keep pace with average wages.

By the late 1970s, most working people were required by their employers to contribute to second, occupational pensions (normally through their wage packets). Nowadays, however, pension provision in the UK is a patchwork, with many workers having neither the job security nor income levels needed to pay into a scheme over and above their state one.

Mrs Thatcher's government actively encouraged employees to opt out of SERPS and invest instead in potentially more lucrative (if riskier) personal pensions. In recent years the vulnerability of some private pension schemes has been exposed by several major controversies—most notably the mis-sell-ing scandals that hit Royal and Sun Alliance and Standard Life, and fraudulent misuse of the Mirror Group pension fund by late newspaper tycoon Robert Maxwell.

Since the mid-1990s the pensions issue has become increasingly toxic. There is a growing awareness of the fact that, as more people are living longer, radi-cal steps are needed to ensure everyone can retire on a liveable income. As the proportion of the population who are of working age diminishes, the pressure for people to save for retirement increases: no longer is there a guarantee that there will be enough money in the public purse to pay for them when they reach pension age.

The Welfare Reform and Pensions Act 1999 paved the way for potentially radical pension changes. But ministers' attempts to move from this to a defini-tive and coherent framework for state-funded pensions stuttered for years afterwards, and only after several high-profile reviews by independent com-missions and numerous ministerial changes was a conclusion of sorts reached. There are currently three types of government-backed pension, as outlined in Table 8.2.

Following a 2006 report by Lord Turner's Pensions Commission, Labour pro-posed a radical shake-up of state pensions that would have co-opted all workers into a new national pension savings scheme from 2012 and relinked state pen-sions to average earnings—for the first time since SERPS was abolished. This move was brought forward to April 2011 in Mr Osborne's June 2010 Budget.

The Coalition has also pledged to increase pensions annually by the higher of prices, earnings, or 2.5 per cent.

In addition to outlining a timetable for future increases in retirement ages, the Pensions Act 2011 introduced another key reform designed to persuade people to save for their retirements: the principle of 'automatic enrolment' into occupational schemes, beginning on 1 October 2012. The so-called 'earnings trigger' for automatic enrolment—the level of earnings from which employees

Table 8.2 The three types of government-backed pension

Type of pension	How it works
State retirement pension	Contributory benefit, 'real value' of which has plummeted as living costs have risen. Currently linked to inflation, not average earnings (as under SERPS). Those who have not paid enough NI contributions qualify for IS instead.
Stakeholder pension	Introduced to help those without occupational pensions (e.g. self-employed) but earning enough to save for retirement. Distinct from most pension schemes operated by banks and building societies in being cheaper/more flexible (people can move them from job to job). Government pays monthly contributions in place of employers.
State second pension (S2P)	Replaced SERPS in April 2002, providing 'minimum income guarantee (MIG)' for people who cannot afford to save for old age through NI credits. In practice, main beneficiaries are carers and disabled people with sporadic work records.

are automatically signed up—was set at £7,475, but this was later raised to £8,105 (bringing it in line with the PAYE threshold).

And more was to come. The 2012 Queen's Speech included plans for two additional pensions-related laws: a Single-Tier Pension Bill and a Public Sector Pensions Bill. Initially it was the latter that drew media attention, given its aim to enshrine in law a requirement for state workers to retire later than previously and pay in more to their occupational pension pots, but with lower incomes guaranteed in retirement. The Bill's confirmation followed months of acrimonious negotiations between ministers and unions, and several strikes by public servants, including teachers, doctors, and council workers, in protest at ministers' earlier imposition of tougher pension terms (see p. 221). The former Bill is likely to be less contentious, in that it will provide arguably much-needed simplification to the existing state retirement arrangements by combining the basic and state second pensions into one ('single-tier') payment.

▶ Reviews and appeals under the benefits system

If claimants are dissatisfied with a decision on their eligibility for benefit, or moves to withdraw it, they may appeal against the decision. Before appealing, however, they must first go through a lengthy process, requiring them to file formal complaints with 'local decision-makers'. If they are dissatisfied with the outcomes, they may apply for 'reviews' by those decision-makers.

Finally, claimants have recourse to one last stab at 'justice': appeals handled by a branch of the Tribunals Service known as Social Security and Child Support (SSCS) (formerly the Appeals Service). Incorporated into the Tribunals Service in 2006, this agency handles appeals about claims for all kinds of benefit—from DLA to SMP.

Once the SSCS has reached a decision, appeals can only ever be taken further on a 'point of law'. In such circumstances they are dealt with by an independent ombudsman (either a Social Security Commissioner or Child Support Commissioner).

▌ The changing face of home affairs

Officially titled the Home Department, the Home Office was split in two in spring 2007 by Mr Blair's final Home Secretary, John Reid. He had declared it 'not fit for purpose' on succeeding his predecessor, Charles Clarke, in 2006, following a succession of public embarrassments over the unwieldy department's handling of anti-terrorism and asylum policy, and a prison service creaking under the weight of too many inmates.

Mr Reid stepped down when Gordon Brown replaced Mr Blair as prime minister, but not before instigating one of the biggest shake-ups in this sprawling department's 225-year history. For some years there had been an artificial 'Chinese Wall' between the responsibilities of the Home Office (HO) and Lord Chancellor's Department (briefly renamed the 'Department for Constitutional Affairs' in 2005) regarding crime and disorder. With the emergence of major new internal security issues in relation to the growing threat of Islamist terrorism, Mr Reid judged that the department needed to cede some criminal justice powers and focus more effectively on the various other policy areas in its ambit.

When Mr Brown arrived in Downing Street he replaced the Department for Constitutional Affairs with a new 'Ministry of Justice' (MoJ), headed by Lord Falconer's replacement, Jack Straw. Mr Straw became the first Lord Chancellor in 300-plus years to be an MP rather than a peer (a new 'tradition' which has continued under the Coalition, with Kenneth Clarke picking up the baton). Reflecting his status as a 'commoner', Mr Straw was given the additional title 'Secretary of State for Justice'. This better described his powers, in light of the fact that his post had lost several of the Lord Chancellor's traditional trappings—notably his chairmanship of debate in the Lords, which went to a then newly appointed Lord Speaker (see p. 74). The division of responsibilities between the dual departments resulting from these reforms is now as outlined in Table 8.3.

To aid the HO in its new responsibilities for counter-terrorism policy, it was given a new 'subdepartment': the Office for Security and Counter-Terrorism.

Table 8.3 Breakdown of responsibilities of Home Office and Ministry of Justice

Home Office	Ministry of Justice
Policing and crime prevention	Court system and sentencing policy
Security and counter-terrorism	Prisons
Asylum, immigration, and citizenship	Probation and prevention of reoffending

A 'National Security Board' (NSB)—a weekly forum chaired by the Home Secretary—was also formed to discuss security threats when they occurred, as well as a National Criminal Justice Board (NCJB) tasked with promoting 'joined-up government' between the two departments responsible for different aspects of criminal justice policy (chaired jointly by the Home Secretary, Justice Secretary, and Attorney General).

The new-look Home Office

In a break with generations of male dominance in Cabinet, Mr Brown appointed Jacqui Smith as Britain's first female Home Secretary in July 2007. Mr Cameron followed this example, confirming Theresa May in the same post.

Policing and crime prevention

The role of Her Majesty's Constabulary is explored in depth in Chapter 11. In examining the work of the HO, however, it is important to outline the extent to which English and Welsh police forces remain under the department's overall authority.

The HO funds the police and is responsible for recruitment, training, and pay. Responsibility for organizing policing on the ground, like so many areas of public policy, has long since been delegated from central to local government. In theory, it is down to individual local police and crime commissioners (formerly police authorities) to appoint, hold accountable, and occasionally dismiss their local chief constables. In practice, even today the Home Secretary must endorse these appointments and, if there is a perception of declining confidence in either chief constables or commissioners, he/she may intervene to remove them against their wishes. In June 2001 then Home Secretary David Blunkett publicly urged Sussex Police Authority to consider sacking local chief constable Paul Whitehouse over his handling of an inquiry into the fatal shooting by a police marksman of an unarmed alleged drug dealer, James Ashley, in St Leonards-on-sea three-and-a-half years earlier. Mr Whitehouse, who had promoted two of the officers involved in the incident, subsequently resigned.

The Home Secretary's traditional responsibility for overseeing policing in London, through the Metropolitan Police Commissioner, was formally handed to a newly created police authority answerable to the Greater London Authority

see also local government, p. 344

(GLA) in 2000. And the GLA has not been afraid to use these powers. In November 2007 it passed a no confidence vote in Sir Ian Blair, then Met Commissioner, following the Old Bailey's decision to convict his force for breaching health and safety legislation when anti-terror officers mistakenly shot dead Jean Charles De Menezes, an innocent Brazilian man, at Stockwell Tube station in July 2005. An inquest jury subsequently returned an open verdict into his death in December 2008—pointedly disbelieving testimony by police officers who insisted they had shouted a warning to him before opening fire—and it was only a matter of time before Sir Ian was forced out. In October 2008, five months after Conservative Boris Johnson unseated Mr Livingstone as London Mayor, the new mayor publicly demanded a change of leadership at the Met—leaving the Commissioner little option but to resign.

Mr Johnson's immediate criticisms of Sir Ian appeared to be sparked by accusations of unfair treatment for black and Asian officers in the force. Two of his harshest critics, Assistant Commissioner Tarique Ghaffur, Britain's most senior Muslim officer, and Ali Dizaei, had recently been suspended, with the former placed on 'garden leave' in response to his public conduct on filing a £1.2m racial discrimination claim against the Met. Mr Johnson immediately launched a new inquiry into allegations of racism—underlining his insinuation that the former Commissioner had presided over a force that remained 'institutionally racist', despite its protestations to the contrary (a reference to a phrase coined a decade earlier by Sir William Macpherson's report into the botched initial police investigation of the murder of black teenager Stephen Lawrence). The timing of Mr Johnson's intervention coincided with the launch of an advertising campaign by the Met's Black Police Association to deter people from the black and Asian communities from joining the force.

The Met aside, both Labour and the Coalition have had periodic run-ins with the police as a whole—usually over pay, recruitment, and/or pensions. In December 2007 the Metropolitan Police Federation declared itself 'at war' with Mr Brown's government over its decision to stagger a 2.5 per cent pay rise, awarding increases only when it was satisfied productivity targets were being met in relation to crime detection and prevention. But this was nothing compared to the glacial reception Mrs May received when she addressed the 2012 Police Federation conference against the backdrop of 20 per cent budget cuts, a tough new pensions settlement (see pp. 249–51), and mass government-backed outsourcing of policing functions to the private sector.

This last is the most significant reform. Though ministers initially insisted only 'back office' police work would be franchised out under their radical plans to reduce the public sector wage bill—leaving frontline policing to officers employed by the state—by March 2012 it became clear they were minded to go further. That month, West Midlands and Surrey police forces (apparently with ministerial approval, and on behalf of all forces in England and Wales) invited bids from private companies, including the world's biggest security firm, G4S, to take over day-to-day running of a wide range of duties—including criminal investigations and detention of suspects. Earlier in the year, Lincolnshire Police had signed a £200m contract with G4S to 'privatize' its civilian staff by transferring them to the company, which confirmed plans to build and run England's first private police station. By June 2012 David Taylor-Smith, head of G4S for Britain and Africa, was boasting that large parts of the Police Service would be privatized within five years.

Within weeks, the risks of wholesale outsourcing were exposed to the harsh glare of international media attention when, a fortnight before the start of the 2012 London Olympics, G4S was forced to admit to ministers it would not be able to deliver the 10,400 security guards it had been contracted to provide, due to the 'complexity' of training and vetting so many disparate groups—from the unemployed and students looking for summer work experience to individuals who had only recently left other jobs. In the ensuing political fall-out, 3,500 service personnel were drafted in to boost the private security force—raising the unedifying prospect that soldiers recently returned from active overseas service would have to give up long overdue holidays to spend three weeks frisking spectators for unauthorized items and escorting them to their seats.

Like hospitals, schools, and care homes, police forces must submit them-selves to independent inspection. The body responsible, Her Majesty's Inspectorate of Constabulary (HMIC), is actually the oldest organization of its kind—dating back to the County and Borough Police Act 1856. Its remit covers England, Wales, and Northern Ireland (there is a separate inspectorate for Scotland), and it is headed by a Chief Inspector of Constabulary. Like the Chief Inspector for Schools (see p. 458), this official is semi-independent from government—and has been known to speak out critically over aspects of policy. In July 2010 then incumbent Sir Denis O'Connor published a joint report with the Audit Commission and Wales Audit Office warning that the Coalition's projected budget cuts would adversely affect frontline policing. He said that, while 12 per cent could be saved through a 'total redesign' of how forces oper-ated, further cuts would hit beat numbers unless they were 'prioritized over everything else'.

As with Ofsted, the inspectorate can be outspoken. In July 2012 it published a report warning that three regional forces—the Met, Devon and Cornwall, and Lincolnshire—were in danger of being unable 'to provide a sufficiently efficient or effective service' because of the negative impact of budget cuts. Contrary to ministerial assurances, it estimated there would be some 5,800 fewer frontline officers across England and Wales' forty-three forces by 2015, with up to 26,600 other personnel losing their jobs.

At time of writing, the future of policing in the round was the subject of an ongoing inquiry led by former Met Commissioner Lord Stephens, which was due to report in March 2013.

Security and counter-terrorism

When fifty-two commuters were killed in coordinated suicide bombings in central London on 7 July 2005, the British government decided security policy must be at the heart of its future political agenda. Ever since the attacks on New York's World Trade Center on 11 September 2001, and the UK's subsequent support for US-led military action in Afghanistan and Iraq, the country had been periodically threatened with its own atrocity—both covertly, through tip-offs gathered by its intelligence services, and overtly, by the increasingly bellicose online proclamations of the late Osama bin Laden, his chief 'lieutenant' Ayman Al Zawahiri, and Abu Musab al-Zarqawi, then leader of 'Al-Qaeda in Iraq'.

Because of these threats—real and perceived—Mr Blair's government had already passed a succession of 'anti-terror' laws long before the 7 July bombings. In fact, so proactive had it been that critics of his policies (not to mention the Iraq invasion itself) argued that, far from preventing further attacks, they might provoke them.

Of all these anti-terror policies, the most controversial and far-reaching were those relating to the detention of terrorist suspects. At the heart of the controversy was ministers' readiness to dispense with more than 800 years of due legal process by detaining people for prolonged periods without charge. Civil liberties campaigners saw moves like the internment in Belmarsh Prison of individuals suspected of (but not immediately tried for) terror offences as a breach of the sacrosanct constitutional principle of habeas corpus—the right to a fair trial before one's peers—introduced under Magna Carta. Signed by King John in 1215 (see p. 6), this mammoth document stipulated:

> **❝** No free man shall be seized or imprisoned . . . except by the lawful judgement of his equals or by the law of the land. **❞**

The policy of detaining 'terror suspects' summarily (before trial) at Belmarsh began in late 2001, shortly after the 11 September attacks. It was not long before the government—which had opted out of the article of the Human Rights Act 1998 barring it from taking such action—faced significant challenges to its authority. As early as July 2002, the Special Immigration Appeals Commission (SIAC), a Home Office quango, ruled in response to an application by four detainees that the Anti-Terrorism, Crime, and Security Act 2001, under which they had been imprisoned, unjustifiably discriminated against foreign nationals. Although this ruling was later overturned by the Court of Appeal, worse was to come for the Labour government. Most significantly, in December 2004 the Law Lords ruled that continued detention of the twelve individuals still in custody was incompatible with human rights legislation.

Despite an initial show of defiance, Mr Clarke was forced to release the suspects early in 2005, replacing indefinite detention with 'control orders'—sweeping powers to confine suspects in the community by using electronic tagging, curfews, and even house arrest. But these soon ran into trouble too. Because an order could be introduced for between six and twelve months at the Home Secretary's behest, with little opposition, the policy again upset civil liberties campaigners. Neither was it an unqualified success at a practical level: in May 2007 it emerged that three men allegedly plotting to kill British troops abroad, Lamine Adam, 26, his brother Ibrahim, 20, and Cerie Bullivant, 24, had absconded while under control orders. Later, in November 2005, Mr Blair suffered his first Commons defeat in eight years as prime minister by staking his authority on a vote to increase the period of time police are permitted to detain terror suspects for questioning, from an existing limit of fourteen days to ninety days. Mr Blair—who said senior police officers had told him the case for extending their detention powers to nearly three months was 'compelling'— had to accept a compromise of twenty-eight days.

His successor, Mr Brown, later tried to raise this to forty-two days by offering rebellious backbenchers a series of sweeteners and forcing the measure through the Commons on a three-line whip. But he and Ms Smith were forced to shelve the plans after being defeated in the Lords by a 191-vote majority. Among those resisting the measure were Mr Blair's former Attorney General, Lord Goldsmith, and Lord Falconer, ex-Lord Chancellor and one of his closest friends. Erstwhile MI5 heads Dame Eliza Manningham-Buller and Dame Stella Rimington also opposed it.

Having fought the 2010 election on pro-civil liberties platforms, the Tories and Lib Dems launched a wholesale review of anti-terrorism policies on entering government. In January 2011 they confirmed that 'Section 44' police stop-and-search powers (allowing officers to stop people without reasonable grounds for suspicion) would only in future be sanctioned with the permission of very senior officers, and in circumstances when a terrorist attack was believed to be imminent, while the twenty-eight-day detention period for terrorist suspects would be halved to fourteen days. Ministers' recommended replacement for the control order regime was widely mocked, however, when it emerged that they were planning do little more than 'rebrand' them—as **terrorism prevention and investigation measures (TPims)**, lasting up to two years. Meanwhile, the ability of the authorities to impose sixteen-hour curfews on tagged suspects was reduced to a maximum of ten hours—with curfews themselves redefined as **overnight residency requirements**. In July 2012 the first Tpim breach was confirmed when an alleged al-Qaeda sympathizer, identified only as 'CF', was repeatedly intercepted crossing through the Olympic Park in Stratford, east London.

Asylum, immigration, and citizenship

Another of the biggest home affairs issues of recent years has been the dual question of asylum and immigration. The term 'asylum-seeker' entered the media lexicon around the time war broke out in the Balkans in the early 1990s.

The media was quick to focus on this new 'threat' to Britain's borders, and by 2002 the red-tops were filled with scare stories about impending invasions of 'illegal immigrants' lured by the UK's 'soft-touch' benefits system. Their agitated prose was fuelled by the initially laissez-faire attitude of the French government to a burgeoning refugee camp at Sangatte, near Calais, from which 1,600 asylum-seekers were apparently planning to sneak into southern England.

More recently, enlargement of the European Union (EU), first to twenty-five then twenty-seven countries, has led to significant influxes of economic migrants from other countries—particularly those in the former Eastern Bloc—in pursuit of paid work. This, too, has been controversial, with national newspapers like the *Daily Mail* and *Daily Express* pandering to the concerns of local communities in some areas that foreign workers were 'stealing' jobs from long-standing residents and putting pressure on already overstretched public services, such as social housing, schools, and health care. There have also been numerous headlines blaming immigrants for rises in certain types of crime.

In fact, according to two reports published in April 2008, immigrants have had little negative impact on either demand for public services or crime. The first, published by the Association of Chief Police Officers (ACPO), found that offending rates in the Polish, Romanian, and Bulgarian communities (the study's focus, due to the influx of migrants from those countries following their then recent accession to the EU) were proportionate to that in the British population as a whole. The second, a joint study by the Equality and Human Rights Commission (EHRC) and Local Government Association (LGA), found little evidence that migrants were queue-jumping to obtain social housing: in fact 60 per cent of those who had moved to Britain in the previous five years were in private rented accommodation.

But not every survey paints a rosy picture of immigration: in December 2007 analysis of employment data by the Statistics Commission found that eight out of ten new jobs created in Britain since 1997 (1.4 million out of 1.7 million) had gone to foreign-born workers. Around the same time, Ms Smith admitted that as many as 11,000 non-EU nationals licensed to work in the security industry might be illegal immigrants. One had been involved in repairing Mr Blair's car; another was found to be working as a cleaner in the Commons in February 2008. And a report by the Lords Economic Affairs Committee, published in April 2008, concluded that immigrants had had 'little or no impact' on the UK's economic well-being.

Despite widespread perceptions, asylum-seekers, illegal immigrants, and economic migrants often have a far from cushy time when they arrive in Britain. In 1999, newspapers across southern England were filled with reports about the appalling housing conditions some families were enduring while their applications were processed and they awaited 'dispersal' around the country. Meanwhile, an emerging black market in cheap foreign labour at the hands of unscrupulous people-traffickers has led to high-profile tragedies. In

February 2004, twenty-one Chinese refugees were drowned in Morecambe Bay, Lancashire, while illegally working as cockle-pickers.

Sensationalism aside, Britain's population is rising fast: according to the Office for National Statistics (ONS), it soared by 8 per cent between 1971 and 2008, and had reached 62 million by early 2010, while the 2011 census recorded a 3.7 million increase in England and Wales alone in the previous decade (up to 56.1 million), with 55 per cent of the increase attributed to net migration. By 2029 it is expected to top 70 million. In September 2007 the ONS predicted the number of immigrants would continue rising by up to 190,000 a year—three times higher than previous estimates—while three months later it reported the birth rate among foreign-born women living in the UK had overtaken that of British-born mothers.

The decision by aspiring immigrants and economic migrants to relocate to Britain can also have a negative knock-on effect on their countries of origin. The migration of large numbers of skilled Polish workers, such as plumbers and electricians, produced as many negative newspaper headlines in Poland as in Britain. In some media, whole towns were depicted as being 'drained' of their most highly trained artisans by Britain and other western European countries. Meanwhile, the backlash among some sections of the electorate over the perceived impact of inward migration and immigration on the availability of job opportunities for native Britons led to the UK imposing restrictions on migration from the two newest member states, Bulgaria and Romania (both of which joined in January 2007), and Mr Brown's controversial pledge to work towards a guarantee of a 'British job for every British worker'.

But what do terms like 'asylum-seeker' and 'illegal immigrant' actually *mean*—and what is the difference? Put simply, the term 'asylum-seeker' is generally used as a synonym for 'refugee', which the 1951 United Nations (UN) Convention Relating to the Status of Refugees described as a person fleeing their home country because of a 'well-founded fear of being persecuted for reasons of race, religion, nationality, membership of a particular social group, or political opinion'.

The term 'asylum' is also distinct from 'immigration', as it is often used to describe a *temporary* state of affairs—an individual fleeing tyranny in his/her home country is not necessarily seeking to remain permanently in the land to which he/she has fled. 'Immigration', in contrast, is used to describe the process of becoming a 'naturalized' citizen of another country. The term 'illegal immigrant' is frequently used pejoratively by right-wing politicians and newspapers. It refers to individuals who illegally cross borders to enter a country without following the official asylum procedure. Before the Sangatte camp was closed, there were several instances of refugees illicitly entering Britain through the Channel Tunnel.

Asylum policy has, since 2008, been overseen by the UK Border Agency (UKBA)—previously the Border and Immigration Agency—an HO agency.

However, in March 2012 Mrs May formally split the agency in two following a high-profile public row with Brodie Clark, the head of its frontline arm, the UK Border Force, over the suspension of routine checks on overseas visitors with biometric passports the previous year. Briefly, Immigration Minister Damian Green had given the go-ahead for checks to be suspended temporarily over Easter 2011 to cope with lengthy queues at Heathrow and other ports, but according to an inquiry published in February 2012 by John Vince, Chief Inspector of the UKBA, Mr Clark had unilaterally continued to waive them. Following Mr Clark's forced resignation, the Tories effectively revived their pre-election pledge to introduce a new dedicated Border Police Force by announcing the formal separation of its back office and frontline functions.

The question of whether to grant asylum does not arise in the case of Irish Republic or Commonwealth citizens who had the right of abode in Britain before January 1983, nor other EU citizens. It applies only marginally to nationals of the European Economic Area (EEA), a region of *potential* EU countries, which encompasses the Union itself, plus neighbouring states such as Iceland, Liechtenstein, and Norway. Residents of these countries are already allowed to work in Britain (subject to certain limitations) and, if they can support themselves, to live here. But nationals of most countries outside these areas, including many African and Asian nations, require a visa before entering Britain. Some also require 'entry clearance'.

An annual cap on migrants from outside the European Union was promised in the Conservatives' 2010 election manifesto, and on 19 July that year Mrs May introduced a temporary cap on entry into the UK by non-EU citizens (of 24,100 between then and April 2011) to avoid a rush of people trying to migrate before the permanent limit came into force.

The HO has also introduced tough new measures designed to make it harder for foreigners to claim asylum. These are explained in the table entitled 'Recent rule changes covering asylum and immigration policy' on the Online Resource Centre. In addition, successful applicants for British citizenship must now sign up to a number of 'responsibilities' to be able to claim the 'rights' that go with it—a list of conditions recently toughened by Mrs May. These are outlined in Table 8.4.

The great 'Big Brother' debate

If one issue during New Labour's era raised the hackles of civil liberties campaigners more even than detention without trial it was the perceived 'Big Brother' approach ministers took towards crime and terrorism detection and prevention. This tactic was symbolized for many by two signature Blairite policies: national identity cards and the national DNA database.

Between 2009 and 2010 British citizens applying for or renewing adult passports were offered a choice between ID cards containing both their specific personal details (name, age, address, etc.) and biometric data (fingerprints, facial characteristics, irises), or new-style 'biometric passports' containing more

Table 8.4 'Rights and responsibilities' for 'successful' immigration applicants

Device	How it works
Vouchers	Introduced to be exchanged for food and toiletries by refugees applying for asylum. Scheme scrapped by Mr Blunkett in 2002 following riot at Yarl's Wood detention centre, but reintroduced in 2006 amid controversy about cash payments. 'Failed' asylum-seekers not deported to home countries due to human rights concerns also qualify for vouchers, worth £35 a week, in addition to beds—or three meals a day and no financial support.
'Life in the United Kingdom' tests	Labour introduced test for foreign nationals seeking to become UK citizens, focusing on questions about constitution and day-to-day life in Britain. In autumn 2012 Coalition Home Secretary Theresa May introduced more questions about British history, culture, and achievements—including famous battles, monarchs, and inventions—and required applicants to learn first verse of national anthem.
Citizenship ceremonies	Intended to steady community relations between British residents and new foreign immigrants moving into their areas (introduced in 2004). On 26 February that year, in presence of Prince of Wales, nineteen people—including three children—swore allegiance to Queen, sang national anthem, and vowed to respect British rights and freedoms. Citizenship ceremonies since held repeatedly across UK. New immigrants receive 'immigration handbook' and must attend classes in English language, UK institutions, and law, to familiarize themselves with Britain's cultural heritage.
Points system	Introduced for 'economic' migrants in 2008, this five-tier system limits ability of unskilled workers from non-EU countries to work in Britain, while welcoming skilled migrants as 'key contributors' to UK economy. Points for 'highly skilled migrants' awarded on basis of age, qualifications, and previous salary. Around 75 points needed for entry.
Probationary citizenship	Non-EU economic migrants applying to settle in Britain permanently must serve probation period before gaining full citizenship. Under previous system migrants could apply for British passport after five years living and working in UK. New system requires them to serve one- to three-year probationary period of 'earned citizenship' following initial five-year stay. Prospect of someone gaining full citizenship increases if he/she undertakes voluntary work, but reduces if he/she commits a crime. In meantime, benefits and social housing entitlement limited.

limited information. The aim of the 'biographical footprint' held on ID cards was to enable certain accredited organizations to use it—with the cardholders' permission—to confirm their identities. Foreign nationals living and working in the UK began being issued with biometric ID cards in 2008. Although having a card was not initially compulsory, Labour sought to make it so eventually.

Opponents of ID cards broadly fell into two camps: pragmatists and idealists. Pragmatists, like former Conservative Shadow Home Secretary David Davis, argued that questions over the reliability of the technology used to produce the cards, combined with the fact that owning one was not initially intended to be compulsory, threatened to make the scheme ineffective. Idealists, such as campaign group Liberty, saw the cards as a dangerous next step on the road to turning Britain into a paranoid surveillance society. They also highlighted inconsistencies in the arguments ministers used to justify the measure: when first mooted, in the aftermath of 11 September, it appeared they were primarily intended as a weapon in the 'war on terror', but towards the end of Mr Blair's premiership he said the government's main intention was to protect people against the growing threat of identity fraud. ID cards were abandoned by the Coalition.

Concerns about ID cards were compounded by publicity surrounding the expansion of the national DNA database—a sprawling electronic record of genetic samples taken from crime scenes and individuals held in custody. Originally established in 1995, by the end of 2009 it contained 5.9 million samples from 5.1 million people (equivalent to nearly one in ten of the population). Since 2004 anyone penalized for an arrestable offence—even those given a simple police caution—have had their samples added to the database. In December 2006 then Home Secretary Mr Reid admitted that more than a million of those whose details were on the database had not even been cautioned! One reason for the apparent anomaly was the fact that police had failed to remove the details of individuals arrested and charged, but subsequently acquitted.

To ensure the database is not misused, it is regulated by a board comprising members of the HO, ACPO, Association of Police Authorities (APA), and Human Genetics Commission (HGC).

A series of high-profile convictions of serial murderers and sex attackers in early 2008 led to calls from some senior police officers for ministers to extend the scope of the database to include the whole British population. But in its May 2010 Queen's Speech the Coalition announced plans to restrict the future use and growth of the database, and also to regulate closed-circuit television (CCTV) cameras, ease existing limitations on peaceful protest, and reduce the state's ability to monitor individuals' email and Internet records (another crime prevention measure introduced under Mr Brown). As with ID cards, defenders of the database—including those who believe it should be made universal—argued the innocent had nothing to fear from it. But its opponents said such views were counter-intuitive, and that inclusion of non-offenders on a police record contradicted the basic tenet of British justice that individuals were 'innocent until proven guilty'. Not all critics have been Opposition MPs, disgruntled backbenchers, or people with obvious agendas. In August 2004 the Information Commissioner, Richard Thomas, warned in an interview with *The Times* that the country might unwittingly 'sleepwalk into a surveillance society'.

Three years later one of Britain's most senior judges, Lord Justice Sedley, described the database as 'indefensible' and suggested it be extended to cover the whole population—if only to address its intrinsic discrimination against people from ethnic minorities. And yet full-blooded reform has yet to materialize. In July 2011 it emerged that a Coalition commitment to remove the DNA of people subsequently deemed innocent (other than those accused of violent or sexual crimes) was being watered down. Instead, police would be allowed to retain their genetic profiles in anonymized form—leaving open the option of linking these to named individuals in future.

The Coalition parties have also been accused of reneging on their declared opposition to Labour proposals to monitor individuals' Internet use. In June 2012, to the dismay of civil liberties groups and some Lib Dems (not to mention maverick Tory MP Mr Davis), Mrs May published a draft Communications Data Bill—swiftly dubbed a 'snoopers' charter'—which, if passed, would require communications companies to store records of all UK citizens' email conversations, Internet phone calls, games, and other social networking activities for a year, and allow police and intelligence services to access the material in pursuit of terrorists and fraudsters.

Safeguarding human rights for British citizens

Despite Labour's predilection for vigilance, the Human Rights Act 1998 (see p. 10) marked the beginning of a sustained championing of equality of opportunity and other basic freedoms for British citizens, which led to everything from the equalization of the age of consent for gay and heterosexual sex to civil partnerships for homosexual couples.

To spearhead the government's drive to guarantee British citizens equal opportunities—regardless of age, gender, race, or disability—it established three new quangos on entering office in 1997:

- Equal Opportunities Commission (EOC);
- Commission for Racial Equality (CRE);
- Disability Rights Commission (DRC).

Ten years later these bodies were merged into a single Commission for Equality and Human Rights, also known as the **Equality and Human Rights Commission (EHRC)**. The Commission's remit was extended to cover sexual orientation and religious beliefs, in addition to the areas overseen by the three former quangos.

In addition to investigating individual complaints about discrimination, the Commission:

- enforces the law in relation to equal opportunities and rights;
- influences the development of the law and government policy;
- promotes good practice;
- fosters better relations between communities.

▌ Ministry of Justice (MoJ)

Britain's criminal justice system has two core elements—the court system and the treatment of offenders—both of which are now the Justice Secretary's responsibility.

The court system and civil law

The day-to-day business of running British courts is performed by an MoJ executive agency, Her Majesty's Courts Service. The Justice Secretary is personally responsible for promoting more general reforms of civil law and the legal aid system.

The government's principal legal advisers are the Attorney General and Solicitor General—both members of either the Lords or Commons. In Scotland their roles are performed by the Advocate General for Scotland (who assumed the roles previously held by the Lord Advocate and the Solicitor General for Scotland).

Subordinate to the Attorney General are the Director of Public Prosecutions (DPP), who runs the Crown Prosecution Service (CPS)—the state-owned legal service that brings prosecutions on behalf of the Crown—and the DPP for Northern Ireland, along with the Director of the Serious Fraud Office (SFO). At present there remains an as yet unresolved debate about the future role of the Attorney General stemming from controversy about the perceived over-politicization of the 750-year-old post under Mr Blair's government. Lord Goldsmith was seen to be torn between party loyalty and legal protocol in advising ministers on the legitimacy of invading Iraq, and in his later decision (subsequently overturned by the SFO) not to press charges against BAE Systems over its controversial overseas business dealings.

Criminal law

The Justice Secretary has overall responsibility for criminal law and introducing Bills to change it. This work is delegated to the following two principal agencies:

- National Probation Service (NPS)—oversees supervision of individuals serving community-based sentences for criminal offences or periods in prison during which they are permitted to live in the community. Each year NPS supervises 175,000 offenders (90 per cent male), a quarter of whom are 16–20-year-olds. There are forty-two county-based probation services in England and Wales, spread across ten regions (corresponding with those of local police forces). Since 2001 the NPS has come under the National Probation Directorate in the HO and been supervised by an independent HM Inspectorate of Probation.

- **National Offender Management Service (NOMS)**—body that runs all 135 English and Welsh prisons (in Scotland this role is retained by the Prison Service, which had it beforehand). Formed in April 2008, NOMS oversees *all* jails—whether publicly or privately funded/owned—and its chief executive office has been left with ultimate responsibility for administrative mistakes arising from its conduct. The Prison Service still exists—but only as one 'unit' of NOMS, with responsibility for publicly funded jails.

Recent and future developments in the prison system

NOMS employs the 50,000-plus wardens, officers, and governors who administer prisons on the ground. Since the Criminal Justice Act 1991, management of many prisons has been contracted out to the private sector—as has transportation of defendants held in custody to and from court.

The first four newly built prisons handed over to private managers were the Wolds (Humberside), Blakenhurst (Worcestershire), Doncaster, and Buckley Hall (Rochdale). By April 2012 there were fourteen privately managed jails, under the auspices of major independent security providers including G4S Justice Services, Serco, and Sodexo Justice Services. But, given its wholesale privatization of many public services, it was perhaps unsurprising when the Coalition outlined plans to go further. In July 2011 Mr Clarke announced the biggest mass privatization of prisons in British history—putting nine jails out to tender and closing two others (Latchmere House resettlement unit in Richmond, west London, and Brockhill Prison, Redditch) in a drive to save £4.9m upfront from the MoJ budget and £11.4m a year thereafter. The following March a public spat erupted between the governor of three South Yorkshire prisons and his local probation trust after it emerged the latter had formed an alliance with G4S to take over his jails. G4S's prison expansion plans were ultimately to prove short-lived, however: in November 2012 the company failed in a series of bids to take over additional jails and lost its existing contract to run the Worlds prison in South Yorkshire, which was due to return to the public sector in July 2013.

Complaints about the prison and probation services are handled by the Prisons and Probation Ombudsman for England and Wales (PPO). HM Prison Inspectorates—one for each of England, Scotland, and Wales—are charged with inspecting prisons every three years. Individual prisons and young offenders' institutions also have 'boards of visitors'—groups of local people appointed by the Home Secretary to relay complaints from prisoners in the same way as Healthwatch groups operate in the NHS (see p. 179).

Since the early 1990s prisons have seldom been out of the news. Typically, stories tend to be negative, focusing on overcrowding, riots, and periodic breakouts. To provide spare capacity, successive governments have done everything from adapting military camps to act as temporary prisons to commissioning a 'prison ship', *HMP Weare*, moored off Portland, Dorset. During his time as a tough-talking Home Secretary in Mr Major's government, Michael Howard vowed to cut the number of community sentences and send more people to jail, particularly violent offenders. But his famous cry of 'Prison works!' set him on a collision course with then Director General of the Prisons Service, Derek Lewis, who warned of dangerous overcrowding. In January 1995 the simmering prisons crisis came to a head during a succession of riots and breakouts, first at Everthorpe Jail, Humberside, then Parkhurst. A damning report into the state of the system saw Mr Howard sack Mr Lewis that October—but not without facing tough questioning from Jeremy Paxman in a now legendary interview for BBC2's *Newsnight*, during which he was asked twelve times if he had 'threatened to overrule' Mr Lewis.

Overcrowding has remained a serious concern for recent governments. In May 2007 the prison population reached 80,500—within a whisker of its maximum capacity. At the time a further 300 prisoners were being held in police and court cells. Lord Falconer, then Lord Chancellor, appealed to the courts to limit their use of custodial sentences for people convicted of minor offences, and it emerged ministers were considering releasing 3,000 inmates early to free up cells for more serious offenders. To add to their blushes, Lord Phillips, the Lord Chief Justice, declared that the country's jails were 'full' and the rate of prison sentencing would soon 'outstrip the capacity of the prisons'. By the time Labour left office in May 2010 the prison population had climbed to a record high of 85,201—nearly twice the level under the previous Tory government.

In June 2010 the Scottish Parliament unilaterally reduced prisoner numbers north of the border, through a new Criminal Justice and Licensing Bill introducing a presumption against sentences of three months or less alongside a commitment to tougher community sentences. The Bill also raised the age of criminal responsibility in Scotland from 8 to 12—two years higher than in England and Wales, where Mr Brown's government had kept it at 10.

The Coalition's aim of cutting the prison population has taken longer than expected to materialize: in June 2012 it emerged that inmate numbers had actually risen by 1,500 since May 2010. Mr Clarke blamed this, in part, on a spike in jail sentences following England's August 2011 urban riots (see p. 497)— arguing that tougher sentencing had been needed 'to restore public order' after that event, with MoJ figures showing that four out of ten of the 1,715 convicted rioters were repeat offenders.

Rehabilitation of offenders

Convicted offenders receive sentences that are either *custodial*—detention in prison or a young offenders' institution—or *non-custodial* (for example, conditional discharge, community service, probation, fines, or compensation order).

The latter are supervised in England and Wales by the NPS, and in Scotland by council-employed social workers.

Other than in the exceptional cases when royal pardons are issued on the advice of the Justice Secretary (see p. 21), prisoners are only generally granted early release in recognition of 'good behaviour' in custody. This system is known as **parole**. Although the application process is relatively simple, parole itself is complex, in that prisoners' eligibility depends on various factors—most notably the nature and severity of their offences. Those eligible for parole may apply six months before their earliest possible release date (normally specified at the time of sentence). A file on the prisoner will be compiled and three members of the Parole Board—the body that advises the government on applications—will meet to decide whether to grant the prisoner's wishes.

A swift decision may be taken for more minor offenders to allow them parole 'on licence'—under which they may be released early, subject to the condition that they do not reoffend. If they do reoffend within the remaining period of their original sentence they may end up serving the remainder of that term in jail after all, in addition to any further conviction period. Full Parole Board hearings tend to be called only for the most serious offenders.

Due, in part, to concerns about prison overcrowding, in practice parole has become all but automatic for most offenders. The Criminal Justice Act 1991 toughened the procedure. The conditions he introduced to guide future decisions included that:

- Prisoners other than the most serious offenders (rapists and murderers) serving *four years or more* should be released on Parole Board recommendation after serving half their sentences, and normally automatically after serving two-thirds.

- Final decisions on the early release of prisoners serving *more than four but less than seven years* should be taken by the Parole Board.

- Prisoners sentenced to life imprisonment for certain kinds of murder—those of police officers, terrorism, and child killings—would tend automatically to serve at least twenty years. Early release of such 'mandatory life prisoners' could only be authorized by the Home Secretary in consultation with the Parole Board and judiciary.

- Those sentenced to life for offences other than murder would normally be released by the Home Secretary after a period set by the judge at their trial. The Board would still have power, though, to order continued confinement beyond this period if necessary to protect the public. Such sentences—known as 'indeterminate sentences for public protection' (IPP)—have caused headaches for recent governments. In February 2008 three Court of Appeal judges and the Lord Chief Justice ruled that the Board was not sufficiently independent of ministers to approve IPPs at their request, and that Justice Secretary Mr Straw had acted 'unlawfully' in his prior treatment of such prisoners. Among the high-profile prisoners repeatedly refused release on grounds of public safety were late Moors murderer Myra Hindley and serial killer Rose West. Peter Sutcliffe, the 'Yorkshire Ripper', was told by a High Court judge in July 2010 he would never be released. Others, including Tracey Connelly, mother of child domestic abuse victim Peter Connelly ('Baby P'), are serving indefinite sentences.

see also local
government,
p. 528

In addition to the 1991 Act, the Crime (Sentences) Act 1997 further toughened the sentencing regime by putting greater emphasis on the idea of prisoners *earning* parole—restyling them 'early release days' and introducing the idea that they could be gained and lost.

It also introduced:

- automatic life sentences for those convicted twice of serious sexual or violent crimes;

- mandatory minimum prison sentences for drug dealers and serial burglars.

In opposition, the Conservatives consistently called for increased funding for additional prison places. On re-entering government, however, Mr Clarke performed an apparent volte-face, announcing a 'rehabilitation revolution' intended to cut the jail population. Pledging to 'shut the revolving door of crime and reoffending', he unveiled a new scheme analogous to that introduced by Mr Brown to find work for the long-term unemployed, under which private firms like A4E would be paid by results for turning repeat offenders (particularly those previously jailed for petty crimes) into 'law-abiding citizens' and prisoners would work for their keep while in jail.

Until 2006, Scottish parole policy was more lenient than those elsewhere in Britain—with prisoners serving four to ten years released on the Board's say-so after serving half their sentences, and only those incarcerated for more than ten years needing the Home Secretary's consent. But under the Custodial Sentences and Weapons Act 2007 (passed by the Scottish Parliament) conditions for early release were toughened. Automatic early release without conditions for prisoners serving less than four years was replaced with a new licensing system. Anyone released early who breaches his/her licence terms is now returned to jail. In addition, sentencing judges who consider a defendant to be of particular public risk can stipulate that he/she waits longer than the usual halfway mark before qualifying for parole. The Board also has powers to increase this custodial period at a later date, should the circumstances arise. The Management of Offenders (Scotland) Act 2005, meanwhile, ended unconditional early release for sex offenders sentenced to between six months and four years, subjecting them to a new licence and supervision system.

In Northern Ireland special circumstances apply in terrorism cases, in recognition of the unique nature of 'The Troubles'. Until 1995 terrorists sentenced to five years or more were usually paroled only after serving two-thirds of their terms, but this has since been harmonized with the rest of Britain—that is, eligibility after serving half a sentence. Terrorists convicted of another offence before the end of their original sentence must complete this before their next starts. In response to the positive progress of the Northern Ireland peace process at the time, a one-off arrangement was made allowing inmates of the Maze Prison out on licence for Christmas 1999 and New Year 2000.

≣ Topical feature idea

The Coalition has embarked on a huge shake-up of the pension system—downgrading 'gold-plated' pensions previously enjoyed by public sector workers and raising the retirement age for both men and women. The state pension age for men and women—previously 65 and 60 respectively—will be equalized between 2016 and 2018. What do public and private sector workers in your area think about the recent changes to pensions for teachers, doctors, and civil servants, and what do women feel about the increase in retirement ages? How will these changes affect their decisions about when to retire?

✳ Current issues

- **Welfare reform:** the Coalition is committed to reducing Britain's welfare bill as part of its programme to cut the country's Budget deficit and perceived 'dependency culture'. According to the ONS, 8.2 per cent of British adults of working age are currently 'economically inactive' (neither employed/self-employed nor officially unemployed), although critics argue many are students or pensioners. The Coalition has introduced a £26,000-a-year benefits cap and an all-in-one payment, the Universal Credit, to replace the existing blizzard of benefits and tax credits.

- **Privatization of the police and prisons:** Home Secretary Theresa May is on a collision course with police after imposing 20 per cent cuts to their budgets, reforming their pensions, and giving the go-ahead to the outsourcing of frontline and back office services to private companies. Meanwhile, former Justice Secretary Kenneth Clarke announced a mass prison privatization programme shortly before leaving office in September 2012.

- **Controversy over Work Capability Assessments:** rigorous tests were introduced under Gordon Brown's government to assess the ability to work of people claiming Employment and Support Allowance—but four out of ten claimants who appealed against decisions to strip them of benefits won. Under the Coalition the tests have become even tougher, leading campaigners and commentators like *Guardian* columnist Polly Toynbee to accuse ministers of 'bullying' the sick and disabled.

? Review questions

1. What is the difference between a 'contributory' and a 'non-contributory' benefit?

2. Outline the history, aims, and responsibilities of the Home Office. To what extent have these changed and been extended since its inception?

3. To what extent has the welfare state remained true to its founding principle to look after British citizens—regardless of their means—from the cradle to the grave?

4. Outline the recent developments in UK pension policy, explaining the main types of state-funded pension and some of the alternatives.

5. Which government department—the Home Office or the Ministry of Justice—has greater jurisdiction over criminal justice matters in the UK? Outline the specific responsibilities in relation to crime, policing, and the courts of each department.

→ Further reading

Golding, P. and Middleton. S. (1982) *Images of Welfare*, Oxford: Mark Robertson. **Classic historical overview of evolution of welfare policy and public attitudes towards claimants, backed by authoritative analysis of media portrayals**.

Hansen, R. S. (2001) *Citizenship and Immigration in Post-war Britain: The Institutional Origins of a Multicultural Nation*, Oxford: Oxford University Press. **Accomplished evaluation of socio-economic and cultural impact of immigration since 1945.**

Ishkanian, A. and Szreter, S. (2012) *The Big Society Debate: A New Agenda for Social Welfare?*, Cheltenham: Edward Elgar Publishing. **Bang up-to-date examination of impact of Coalition's 'Big Society' approach to addressing social concerns of 'Broken Britain', focusing on translation of rhetoric into Iain Duncan Smith's wide-ranging welfare reforms.**

Lowe, R. (2004) *Welfare State in Britain Since 1945,* 3rd edn, London: Palgrave Macmillan. **Third edition of standard work on evolution of welfare state, incorporating analysis of recent trends in welfare provision, such as tax credits and Welfare to Work.**

Reiner, R. (2000) *The Politics of the Police*, 3rd edn, Oxford: Oxford University Press. **Fully revised third edition of standard text on origins, history, and present-day make-up of British police. Includes detailed analysis of current issues, including those arising from Macpherson Report into Stephen Lawrence case.**

Sanders, A. (2006) *Criminal Justice*, London: LexisNexis UK. **Critical analysis of British criminal justice system, focusing on all aspects of crime and punishment including habeas corpus, penal system, and sentencing procedures.**

🌐 Online Resource Centre

www.oxfordtextbooks.co.uk/orc/Morrison3e/
Visit the Online Resource Centre that accompanies this book for web links and regular updates.

9

The European Union (EU)

Even before the uncertainty wrought by the 'eurozone' sovereign debt crisis that has dominated debate about it for several years, the European Union (EU) was already a subject that divided British politicians, public, and, for that matter, media into two equally vociferous camps. On the one side are 'Europhiles'—those who see closer economic and political integration as a logical, common-sense, and desirable state of affairs that can only enhance mutual understanding and, ultimately, prosperity across the European continent. Ranged opposite them are the 'Eurosceptics'. While some are merely critical of the EU's current composition (seeing it as overly bureaucratic, undemocratic, and lacking accountability), others view the very idea of the Union as an anathema, arguing that it threatens individual nations' rights to sovereignty and self-determination.

As befits such a contentious issue, Europe generates extensive (if not always well-informed) coverage in the British press. Although EU press officers are forever complaining about how difficult it is to interest editors and reporters in writing meaningful news stories about its work, the number of column inches devoted to supposed diktats from 'Brussels' (to cite the commonly used shorthand) has steadily increased since the dramatic parliamentary scenes of the early 1990s surrounding the passage of the 'Maastricht Treaty' (see p. 296). The furores have often verged on the farcical. In 1998 *Daily Mail* readers were greeted by near-hysterical headlines in response to the European Commission's attempt to force British chocolate manufacturers such as Cadbury to redefine their products as 'vegelate', reflecting the high percentage of vegetable fats they contained in comparison to cocoa butter. More recently, in 2005 *The Sun* launched a 'Save our Jugs' campaign in protest at a supposed attempt by 'EU killjoys' to force busty barmaids to cover up their cleavages. The actual proposal (dropped in light of the opposition) was a draft 'Optical Radiation Directive' designed to protect workers from builders to park-keepers from excessive exposure to the sun. It made no mention of barmaids' breasts.

What, then, *does* EU membership mean for Britain, and how did it come about?

▶ Britain's twisty path to EU membership

The European 'Common Market' (as it was widely known in Britain until the 1970s) began its slow emergence in the post-war period, as the continent struggled to rebuild itself after six years of bruising conflict. But although it shared many of the same economic interests as its neighbours, for a long time Britain's attitude towards them was lukewarm at best. Buffered by the existence of its Commonwealth of dependent nations on the one hand and its emerging 'special relationship' with the USA on the other, it was reluctant to be too tied to the activities of its Continental cousins.

By 1961, however, the positive economic impact membership of the European Economic Community (EEC) appeared to be having for its member states encouraged the UK, under then Conservative Prime Minister Harold Macmillan, to apply for membership alongside Denmark, Ireland, and Norway. At the time its application was blocked by France's then President, Charles de Gaulle, who twice obstructed it (in 1963 and 1967) because he argued Britain was not sufficiently 'European' to join.

In the ensuing disagreement with fellow member states, De Gaulle precipitated one of the biggest constitutional upheavals in the history of the embryonic EU by refusing to send representatives from France to meetings of any of the three Communities from 1965–6 (an affair known as the 'empty chairs crisis'). His action led, in 1966, to the passing of the Luxembourg Compromise—an informal understanding that agreements between member governments must in future be made *unanimously*, rather than by *majority vote*, as had been the case before.

Following de Gaulle's resignation in 1969 negotiations began in earnest for Britain's accession to the new Community, and the country was taken into it by Edward Heath's government in 1973. Ireland and Denmark joined at the same time.

Yet any hopes that the country's accession would finally end years of squabbling between Britain and its European neighbours—not to mention the internecine fighting over the European Community (EC) in the UK's main political parties—were short-lived. By the time of the next general election in 1974, divisions were so marked within Harold Wilson's Labour Party and the country at large that Labour pledged to hold a referendum on the issue if returned to power. This it did, on 5 June 1975, but only after Mr Wilson had waived the decades-old convention of collective responsibility (see pp. 101–2), allowing members of his Cabinet who opposed his pro-European stance to campaign actively for 'no' votes. These included then Industry Secretary Tony Benn and Employment Secretary Michael Foot, who blamed rising unemployment figures on Britain's membership of the EC. They argued free trade between Britain and its Continental neighbours was allowing cheap imports to flood high-street shops, undermining the profits of British-based manufacturers and leading to job cuts.

Despite the best efforts of the 'no' lobby, Wilson got his way decisively enough to lay to rest the EC membership debate for the time being (although not, it transpired, forever). Two months after weathering a humiliating defeat on the issue by members of his own party at a one-day Labour conference, his 'yes' campaign clinched more than two-thirds of votes cast in the referendum, on a 64 per cent turnout.

Mr Wilson's triumph was pyrrhic: Britain's troubled admission into the EU marked the beginning of what has continued to be, at best, a love–hate relationship with the Union. At various points during its membership the country has refused to toe the line—negotiating 'opt-outs' from clauses to treaties that bind most, if not all, of its peers (John Major's refusal to sign the Social Chapter of the 'Maastricht Treaty' and David Cameron's unwillingness to endorse the new Fiscal Compact approved by all other member states save the Czech Republic in December 2011 being famous examples) and struggling to win parliamentary approval for various others. In 1992 Mr Major's government was almost brought down by its own backbenchers over Maastricht—an episode explored in depth later in this chapter—while more recently Tony Blair and Gordon Brown both resisted the clamour for a referendum on the 'Lisbon Treaty', a similarly controversial agreement that many Eurosceptics (and some Europhiles, like Kenneth Clarke) argued was essentially the same document as the ill-fated 'EU Constitution' (see p. 296). Although in coalition with the predominantly Europhile Liberal Democrats (whose leader, Nick Clegg, is both a former member of the European Parliament (MEP) and 'Eurocrat'), David Cameron's Conservatives remain a largely Eurosceptic party. Prior to gaining power they formed a breakaway right-wing political grouping in the European Parliament. Since doing so, they have refused to cede any further powers to the EU without a referendum—and at time of writing were calling for a cap on the Union's budget spending to reduce Britain's contributions in line with the austerity measures ministers were introducing domestically.

Aside from Sweden and Denmark, the UK is the only EU state to have held out against joining the euro, while its refusal to sign the Schengen Agreement (see Table 9.1 below) is the reason why Britons are still expected to show their national passports when crossing internal EU borders—including returning to their home country—while citizens of fellow member states are not.

▌ Evolution of the EU

So how did today's EU come about? What happened to transform it from a loose confederation of states cooperating over trade in core post-war raw materials (principally steel and coal) into a sprawling supranational alliance exercising a degree of control—often contentiously—over everything from employment rights to economic migration?

Its growth and evolution can best be charted with reference to the succession of key treaties and summits that paved the way for it to become the hugely influential entity it is now. Providing a detailed explanation of every agreement signed during the six decades since the concept of a 'European Union' was first committed to paper would require a chapter in itself. Instead, the most significant developments in the evolution of the EU are outlined in Table 9.1.

Of all the treaties listed, the British government found it particularly difficult to ratify 'Maastricht' (see below), but it was not alone in encountering hurdles. In June 1992 the people of Denmark—who were given a direct say in a national referendum—rejected it. The Danish government finally squeaked it through eleven months later, after being forced to negotiate 'opt-outs' from two of its key provisions: economic and monetary union (EMU) and the move towards a common European defence policy.

▌ From 'three pillars' to one EU

A key sticking point of the Maastricht Treaty for individual member states was its underlying emphasis on fostering a 'supranational' approach to major policy areas over and above the EU's traditional drive towards Europe-wide free trade. Where several countries—notably Britain, Sweden, and Denmark—wanted to limit the EU's influence to the economic sphere (ideally preferring an 'intergovernmental' approach to even that based on bilateral negotiated agreements between independent member states), the likes of France and Germany were keen to roll out the Union's responsibilities to encompass everything from criminal justice and drugs policy to defence and security. In so doing, they also appeared willing to surrender varying degrees of national sovereignty—giving EU institutions the power to determine policies governing these areas with limited input from national parliaments.

The process of negotiating the Maastricht settlement led to the emergence of three broad areas of policy to be overseen, subject to the principle of subsidiarity (see p. 276), by the European Parliament (EP), European Commission (EC), Council of the European Union (Council of Ministers), and European Court of Justice (ECJ). These areas, known as the 'pillars' of the EU, corresponded with the three strands of its mission from that point on: the European Communities pillar (covering economic, social, and environmental policies); the Common Foreign and Security Policy (CFSP) pillar; and the Police and Judicial Cooperation in Criminal Matters (PJCC) pillar. With the advent of the Lisbon Treaty (see p. 278), the pillars were abolished—to be replaced by a single, consolidated structure for the EU.

Table 9.1 Chronology of the evolution of the European Union (EU)

Agreement	Year	Main provisions
The Treaty of Paris	1951	Established earliest forerunner of EU: European Coal and Steel Community (ECSC). Membership initially limited to France, Germany, Italy, Luxembourg, Belgium, and Netherlands. Treaty initiated joint production of two materials most central to war effort (coal and steel) and fledgling European assembly, which met for first time in Strasbourg in September 1952.
The Treaties of Rome	1957	Often erroneously referred to in singular, these twin treaties spawned two organizations later to coalesce into modern EU: European Economic Community (EEC) and European Atomic Energy Community (EURATOM). Their joint aim was to foster trading links between member nations by ending tariffs imposed by one nation on imports from another and removing other distortions in market, as well as:
		1. introducing Common Agricultural Policy (CAP)—encouraging free trade in agricultural products within EEC, while guaranteeing farmers' incomes in relation to competition from third-party countries through subsidies, as consolidated in 1962 by formation of European Agricultural Guidance and Guarantee Fund (EAGGF);
		2. creating 'common market' for free movement of goods, services, and capital between member states (in practice only free trade in goods followed until Single European Act 1986).
Merger of three European Unions	1965	In 1967 ECSC, EURATOM, and EEC merged into single European Community (EC). This consolidated alliance was framed around four core institutions: European Commission (the EC's 'Civil Service'); European Assembly (later renamed European Parliament); European Court of Justice; and future Council of Ministers.
Launch of European Monetary System (EMS)	1979	Designed to relax, if not abolish, exchange rates between member states, this eventually led to launch of euro (see pp. 289–92).
Enlargement	1981	Greece admitted into EC.
The Single European Act and further enlargement	1986	First full-scale revision of original 1957 European Treaties, encapsulating in one document structure of new-look EC and paving way for following extensions of community:
		1. greater economic integration;
		2. strengthened supranational institutions;
		3. practical moves towards single European currency and linked exchange rates in form of economic and monetary union (EMU).
		In same year Spain and Portugal entered EC.

(continued)

Table 9.1 (*continued*)

Agreement	Year	Main provisions
The Treaty on the European Union ('Maastricht Treaty')	1992	EC formally renamed 'European Union' ('EU'), adding new areas of responsibility. Although signed in February 1992, had to be formally ratified by each state, and passage was far from smooth in Britain (see p. 274 and p. 290). It:
		1. introduced EU-wide commitment to move towards full EMU in three stages—ultimate ends being either single currency or 'common' one (native currencies retained, in parallel with EU one);
		2. established single European Union from existing communities;
		3. set up framework for potential common foreign and security policy;
		4. increased cooperation on domestic issues, particularly criminal justice;
		5. established principle of **subsidiarity**—system defining EU institutions as 'subsidiary to' those of individual member states and safeguarding their ability to run own internal affairs without consulting EU unless they could not achieve national objectives unilaterally;
		6. introduced concept of 'EU citizenship'.
The Corfu Treaty	1994	Allowed Austria, Finland, and Sweden to join EU in January 1995 and paved way for Norway's accession (it subsequently declined to join).
The Amsterdam Treaty	1997	Arose out of 1996 intergovernmental conference convened by heads of EU states. Extended rights of EU citizens in relation to:
		1. consumer protection;
		2. fight against crime and drugs;
		3. environmental protection.
		Treaty also introduced Charter on Fundamental Workers' Rights.
		Summit had attempted to persuade member states to agree EU-wide immigration and asylum policy, but Britain, Ireland, and Denmark opted out, leaving rest to form Schengen Group, which UK declined to join at 2000 Nice Summit. Its name referred to deal known as **Schengen Agreement**—signed in two stages, in 1985 and 1990—abolishing border controls between participating nations.
The Helsinki Summit	1999	This removed existing system under which notional target dates set for accession of specific countries to EU membership. From now on any country meeting qualifying conditions would be eligible for swift entry. Entry talks quickly began with Slovakia, Malta, Lithuania, Bulgaria, Latvia, and Romania. Turkey also entered talks soon after, despite having previously been rejected in 1997.

Table 9.1 (*continued*)

Agreement	Year	Main provisions
Agenda 2000, *For a Stronger and Wider Europe*	2000	Commission discussion document setting out blueprint for onward development of Community in twenty-first century. Many provisions intended to prevent future disagreements between members like those provoked by discussion of EMU, proposed common defence policy, and CAP. Also signalled attempt to set firm rules for acceptance of new countries. Among its stipulations were:
		1. any new country wishing to join EU must meet economic and political criteria for membership and adopt *acquis communitaire*—laws and policies of EU—before being accepted (as Cyprus had just been admitted, new regulations kicked in with accession negotiations for ten additional states that entered in 2004);
		2. redefining CAP and 'structural funds' used to ensure equitable socio-economic infrastructure across Europe;
		3. expressing then Commission's view on proposed accession to EU of countries in central and eastern Europe;
		4. proposing new budgetary framework for EU, with initial proposals for Community-wide budget 'not exceeding 1.27 per cent of EU's GNP'.
The Nice Treaty	2000	'Proclaimed' EU Charter of Fundamental Rights (a conflation of principles outlined in preceding European Convention on Human Rights, devised in 1950 by Council of Europe—see pp. 314–15). Charter's fifty-three 'Articles' not legally binding at time, but expressed shared set of aims, including:
		1. equality between men and women;
		2. fair and just working conditions;
		3. workers' rights to collective bargaining and industrial action;
		4. public rights to access EU documents;
		5. right of elderly to life of 'dignity'.
		Nice Summit also aired many concerns since key to political discussion about EU—including implications of accepting twelve prospective additional members, who later joined.
		Consensus emerged that EU's main governing institutions would have to change over time for following reasons:
		1. arrival of twelve potential new members would mean they needed votes in Council of Ministers, own EU commissioners, seats in European Parliament, and judges;
		2. reunification of Germany, following fall of Berlin Wall in 1990;
		3. impact of EU enlargement on asylum, immigration, and economic migration.

(*continued*)

Table 9.1 (*continued*)

Agreement	Year	Main provisions
The Göteborg Summit	2001	Focused on perceived conflict between EU membership and Irish Constitution, particularly in relation to province's neutrality. At around same time Ireland narrowly voted 'no' in referendum on EU membership. Another controversy stemmed from realization of larger member states that enlargement might result in reductions in funds they received from EU.
White Paper on EU Governance	2001	Produced in response to mounting distrust of unelected EU policymaking institutions, this paved way for more democratically accountable EU by: 1. involving individual states, especially smaller ones, more openly in decisions; 2. introducing 'better policies and regulations'; 3. moving towards system of 'global governance'; 4. 'refocusing' EU's core institutions. These ideas were underpinned by clearer list of principles that EU pledged to embody in future: 1. openness—encouraging its institutions to work together more; 2. participation—encouraging all members to take active part in decision-making; 3. accountability—giving clearer definitions of roles of EU institutions; 4. effectiveness—ensuring policies appropriate to current socio-economic climate and promptly implemented once decided upon; 5. coherence—making sure policies easily understood; 6. proportionality; 7. subsidiarity—ensuring 'action' by EU in relation to member states only taken when strictly necessary.
Enlargement of the Union	2004	Czech Republic, Estonia, Hungary, Latvia, Lithuania, Poland, Slovakia, Slovenia, Malta, and Greek Cyprus joined EU.
Enlargement of the Union	2007	Romania and Bulgaria joined.
European Union Reform Treaty ('Treaty of Lisbon')	2007	Almost as contentious as 'Maastricht', this followed short-lived 'EU Constitution'—abandoned after being rejected in French and Dutch referendums. 'Lisbon Treaty' also rejected by Ireland (initially) but eventually came into force in December 2009. Its main provisions were to: 1. make Charter of Fundamental Rights legally binding; 2. extend role of directly elected European Parliament; 3. introduce permanent president of European Council in place of current 'rotating presidency' and formally recognize Council as fifth EU governing institution; 4. give EU as a whole legal status of single entity capable of signing international treaties with other institutions or bodies.

▐ The main EU institutions

Journalistically, the best EU stories invariably arise out of conflict and confrontation. Notwithstanding ongoing wrangles over the Union's future direction and scope, many contentious issues emerge from the day-to-day deliberations of the EU's five principal governing institutions listed above:

- European Commission (EC);
- European Parliament (EP);
- Council of the European Union (Council of Ministers);
- European Court of Justice (ECJ);
- European Council.

Each institution is chaired by its own president, whose method of election or appointment varies from one to another.

The European Commission

Formed in 1951 and based in Brussels, the **European Commission** is the Civil Service and executive (government) of the EU rolled into one. It employs 25,000 staff working at various levels across more than thirty 'departments and services' or 'Directorates-General'.

Each Directorate-General is headed by one of twenty-seven commissioners—one from each member state, appointed for a five-year period. Meetings are chaired by one of their number, elected president by the European Parliament (on the recommendation of the European Council/Summit). The president chairs meetings of the Commission much as a prime minister sitting in Cabinet. Although the Council of Ministers, composed of representatives from each member state's government, takes the final decisions on major political developments and structural changes in the EU (subject to 'emergency brake' intervention by the European Council in exceptional cases), the Commission is the primary institution responsible for *initiating* policy. It does this in much the same way as national policy is originated through Cabinet government, with commissioners sitting around a table devising and debating ideas for prospective legislation.

What makes this process more controversial in relation to the Commission than the workings of the British Cabinet is that none of the commissioners is elected: all are 'proposed' (nominated) by the governments of their native countries. The fact they are chosen by democratically elected politicians arguably gives them some degree of legitimacy, but they are not directly answerable to the European citizens whose lives their proposals affect. This perceived lack of accountability was famously described in a 1980s pamphlet as a 'democratic deficit' by the British Liberal Democrat MEP Bill Newton Dunn.

The Commission issues its policy proposals in three broad guises: *regulations*, *decisions*, and *directives*. Both 'regulations' and 'directives' must be scrutinized by the European Parliament and Council of Ministers before they can be enacted, but this is where the similarity between them ends. The former are EU-wide laws similar to British primary legislation that, once passed in Council, will automatically apply in all member states. The latter, in contrast, are broader 'end results' that must be achieved in each state, but it is left up to individual members to decide for themselves how to do this by, if necessary, introducing new or adapting existing national legislation. 'Decisions' are binding laws (akin to private Bills in the UK—see p. 67) used to impose conditions or confer rights on individuals or authorities in a particular state—for example, forcing a government department or quango to issue new guidelines to local authorities on kerbside recycling.

Not that policies devised by the Commission are automatically a done deal: elected members of the European Parliament (MEPs) have ample opportunity to scrutinize and even reject them, and ultimate say-so for new regulations rests with the Council of Ministers. Moreover, although it has far greater political clout than the British Civil Service—the job of which is merely to implement government policy 'on the ground' once Parliament has approved it (see p. 105)—the Commission also fulfils this basic administrative function. The EP may also dismiss the Commission in exceptional circumstances (although, curiously, it is prevented from removing individual commissioners and must instead sack all of them). This scenario has arisen more than once in recent years. In March 1999 the Commission under then President Jacques Santer resigned en masse following publication of a damning report into its alleged nepotism. Although it stopped short of suggesting that any commissioner was directly involved in corrupt practices, the 144-page report, by five independent 'wise persons', singled out former French Prime Minister Edith Cresson for her 'dysfunctional' organization and favouritism in staff appointments.

Although not elected, commissioners are invariably experienced politicians and/or public figures who have previously served in senior positions in their home countries. Until the EU's membership expanded from fifteen to twenty-five states in the 2004 enlargement, the countries with the biggest populations—Britain, Germany, France, and Italy—had two each, with smaller states having just one. Among those who served in this capacity were former Labour leader Neil Kinnock, who was Commissioner for Transport, and ex-Conservative Home Secretary Sir Leon Brittan, one-time Commissioner for External Trade Relations. Former Northern Ireland Secretary Lord Mandelson became Britain's first single Commissioner in 2004 (overseeing trade), but after being recalled to the British Cabinet in Gordon Brown's second reshuffle in October 2008 he was replaced by Baroness Ashton of Upholland. Following implementation of the Lisbon Treaty in December 2009, the Commission was dissolved and reconstituted, and Lady Ashton was elevated to the newly created role of

High Representative for Foreign Affairs and Security Policy (and one of seven vice-presidential positions). Her swift promotion was interpreted by some in the media as a consolation prize for Britain in the wake of the EU's 'snub' to former Prime Minister Mr Blair's designs on the first 'EU presidency'. Having been formally approved by the EP, the new Commission took office in 2010.

Enduring controversy over the Commission's composition, powers, and privileges has led to repeated attempts to reform it. For many years its mammoth expenses bill was cited as one of the main causes of concern for EU taxpayers, and terms such as 'Brussels bureaucrats' and 'gravy train' were frequent bedfellows in the British tabloids. This issue was somewhat addressed in the 1999 report and subsequent reforms—some instigated by Lord Kinnock, who, in his role as Commission vice-president, tried to clean up its act by establishing an internal audit service and ethics committee. But concerns about the perceived power it wields—and the apparent dominance of certain countries in its decision-making—led to several further reforms being proposed in the 'Lisbon Treaty'. These were to have included a reduction in the number of commissioners, with only two-thirds of member states being represented at any one time from 2014, with seats distributed fairly on a rotating basis. However, Ireland's initial rejection of Lisbon in its 2008 referendum prompted the European Council to take the executive decision to retain the existing 'one member, one commissioner' system for the time being, by way of a peace offering to it and other smaller nations. The Council's ability to do this was itself formalized by Lisbon, which gives it the right to unilaterally alter the number of commissioners at any time, subject to unanimous approval by its members.

The Commission's present composition is outlined in the table entitled 'The current composition of the European Commission', to be found on the Online Resource Centre.

The European Parliament (EP)

Although the **European Parliament** has the appearance of a legislature, until recently it had considerably less influence on EU law-making than either Commission or Council of Ministers. Traditionally it has tended to be consulted on decisions, rather than taking them itself, in the manner of a giant House of Commons committee rather than a legislative assembly per se. For this reason, it was for many years caricatured as a supine talking shop. However, Maastricht gave it the ability to *reject* legislation it dislikes, according it 'joint' legislative status with the Council in certain areas, under a process known as *co-decision*. Briefly, this works as follows: the Commission will pass a proposal for a new regulation or directive to the EP, which then expresses its opinion at a 'first reading'. If the Council approves of this opinion the 'law' is passed, but if not it will deliver its own verdict to the EP, together with an explanation of its thinking. The EP then enters a 'second reading' stage, at which it can either approve the Council's changes (in which case the law is passed), amend them, or reject the law outright. All the while, the Commission will also be giving its opinion on suggested amendments, and if it rejects any, the Council must vote to approve the amended law unanimously, rather than by a majority. If, on the other hand, a stalemate exists between the EP and Council which lasts more than three months, the presidents of the two institutions may convene a *conciliation committee*, made up of equal numbers of MEPs and Council members, to broker a compromise.

→
see also
local
government,
p. 379

This equal-weighted, if drawn-out, approach to law-making—renamed the 'ordinary legislative procedure' under Lisbon—used to exist in relation to only a few areas, such as health, culture, science, sport, and some aspects of asylum policy. But Lisbon extended it to most others, including agriculture, transport, and decisions over how to allocate European structural funds. The EP also has powers to legislate in relation to the smooth operation of the 'eurozone' (see pp. 291–2) and, crucially, to veto the EU budget. And (subject to agreement with the Council) it may also take action over other aspects of economic policy: in July 2010 the EP passed legislation capping bankers' bonuses. Since January 2011 upfront cash bonuses have been limited to 25 per cent of the total (or 20 per cent for 'particularly large' bonuses), with 40–60 per cent deferred. In a move designed to deter excessive risk-taking by bankers, the rules also stipulated that at least half the total bonus should be paid as 'contingent capital'— meaning it would be the first money to be called upon in the case of future debt or liquidity problems. In April 2012 new proposals were unveiled by the EP to limit future bonuses to no more than bankers' fixed salaries—prompting some banks to raise basic pay levels in anticipation—but at time of writing it remained unclear whether (or when) any such further changes would be introduced.

Despite its title, when originally christened in 1958 the EP's representatives were not elected at all, but appointed, one by each member country. But since 1979 the EP has been a fully elected institution. By the time of its first election the number of representatives—today known as **members of the European Parliament (MEPs)**—had increased from 142 to 410.

The EP's current membership numbers 754, although it will fall back to 751 in 2014. Elections are held every five years and prior to 1999 were conducted on a 'first-past-the-post' (FPTP) system analogous to that used in UK general elections (see pp. 121–2). The European Parliament Act 1999 changed this by introducing proportional representation (PR), generally based on the party list system. Parties are awarded a number of seats proportional to their share of the vote.

Britain is currently divided into twelve European electoral regions (including Northern Ireland, which uses its own version of PR). Each region returns between three and ten MEPs, depending on its population size. There are seventy-two British MEPs altogether (down from seventy-eight since the recent enlargements): fifty-nine elected in England, six in Scotland, four in Wales, and three in Northern Ireland.

Like the Commission, the EP has its own president (elected by absolute majority in a secret ballot of members for renewable terms of two-and-a-half years), and its principal base is in Brussels, where it sits for three weeks a month. For the other week its members travel to Strasbourg in neighbouring France, convening in an identical chamber.

As in Britain's Parliament, MEPs sit in political groupings reflecting their ideological affiliations, rather than regional or national delegations. The minimum number of MEPs needed to form a group is:

- twenty-nine if they all hail from a single member state;
- twenty-three if they come from two member states;
- fourteen if they come from four or more member states.

There are currently seven political groupings, although at time of writing twenty-nine MEPs remained 'non-attached' (independent). These included five from Britain—among them one United Kingdom Independence Party (UKIP) member, Mike Nattrass, and two from the far-right British National Party (BNP), Andrew Brons and its leader, Nick Griffin. The groupings sit at designated points around the 'hemispherical' (semicircular) parliamentary chamber, according to their notional position on the Left–Right political spectrum. Communist MEPs will sit to the far left of the central seat occupied by the EP president, while fascists and extreme right parties like France's Front National (allied to the BNP in an 'unofficial' grouping called the Alliance of European National Movements (AENM)) will occupy seats on the far right.

To be recognized as a legitimate grouping (and, since 2011, entitled to additional funding), an interparty alliance needs to number at least twenty-five MEPs. The current political groupings are:

- European People's Party (EPP) (265 members as at August 2010);
- Progressive Alliance of Socialists and Democrats (S&D) (184);
- Group of the Alliance of Liberals and Democrats for Europe (ALDE) (85);
- The Greens/European Free Alliance (Greens/EFA) (55);
- European Conservatives and Reformists (ECR) (54);
- European United Left/Nordic Green Left (EUL/NGL) (35);
- Europe of Freedom and Democracy (EFD) (31).

While Britain's Labour Party remains part of the socialist grouping (despite its recent drift to the centre-ground), after much internal debate the Conservatives finally made good on a long-standing promise to pull out of the centre-right EPP after the June 2009 European elections. Mr Cameron, who had made this pledge a central plank of his 2005 campaign for the party's leadership, announced the formation of the ECR—a Eurosceptic alliance including several parties the views of which have invited disdain in the liberal media. Of these, Poland's Law and Justice Party, which draws much of its support from ultra-conservative Catholics, has been accused of homophobia, while Latvia's Fatherland and Freedom Party counts among its members a number of former recruits to Hitler's Waffen SS. The Tories' decision to quit the EPP earned it barbs from centre-right European leaders including then French President Nicolas Sarkozy and German Chancellor Angela Merkel, and it looks set to remain a point of contention in coming months and years as the EU moves to consolidate the Lisbon reforms while shoring up the embattled eurozone in the teeth of the sovereign debt crisis (see pp. 292–5).

Administration of the EP's functions is overseen by yet another layer of EU bureaucracy: a 'bureau' run by the president, fourteen vice-presidents, and five 'quaestors' (civil servants responsible for accounting matters directly affecting the MEPs themselves). All these officials are elected, like the president, for two-and-a-half years at a time.

The Council of Ministers

The **Council of Ministers of the European Union** is the single most powerful EU institution. Comprising departmental ministers from each of the twenty-seven member states, its precise composition varies according to the issue being debated on a given day. If, for example, the Council is debating health policy, a health minister from each member state will attend, while discussions about crime, policing, and security issues will involve interior ministers (in Britain's case, the Home Secretary or another Home Office minister).

The Council has ten 'configurations', reflecting the broad policy areas under its jurisdiction:

- General Affairs;
- Foreign Affairs;
- Economic and Financial Affairs;
- Justice and Home Affairs;
- Employment, Social Policy, Health, and Consumer Affairs;
- Competitiveness;
- Transport, Telecommunications, and Energy;
- Agriculture and Fisheries;
- Environment;
- Education, Youth, and Culture.

Although policy ideas are often proactively proposed by the Commission, all but the most minor must be formally approved by the Council to make them 'law'. To this end, it is supported by a related institution, the Committee of Permanent Representatives (COREPER), made up of civil servants seconded from each member state or each state's EU ambassador (itself backed by a further 150 committees and working groups).

All meetings of the Council are chaired by a senior politician (normally the president or prime minister) from the country currently holding the rotating EU presidency. Britain last held the presidency in 2005. In view of the need for continuity emphasized by this rota, the Council has its own dedicated civil service: the General Secretariat of the Council.

Qualified majority voting (QMV)

The voting system used in the Council is complex and, as such, warrants its own section, given its importance in determining the direction of EU policy.

The unanimous approval of member states is normally required to pass major decisions with implications for the future of the EU—such as whether to admit additional countries into the Union. The annual confirmation of the EU's budget also traditionally requires unanimity. Since Maastricht, however, an increasing number of (often significant) decisions have been agreed through a process known as **qualified majority voting (QMV)**. As its name suggests, the premise of QMV is for agreement on a policy to be reached without the need for every member state to approve it—that is, on a majority basis. This majority system is 'qualified', however, in two respects:

- Member states are not accorded an equal say in the Council—rather, the number of votes allocated to each is weighted to reflect its population size, giving some countries greater clout than others.

- A simple majority system (like that which determines whether Acts are passed in the UK Parliament) would require only one more 'yes' vote than the total number of 'no' votes—but under the Nice system (still in force at time of writing) approval by QMV requires the backing of 74.8 per cent of weighted votes in the Council (258 out of 345), representing 62 per cent of the EU's population (on the request of a member state). The present definition of 'qualified majority' will be revised from 2014 to denote a 'double majority': for a decision to carry from then on it will need the backing of at least 55 per cent of member states and 65 per cent of the EU's population. To block a motion a minority must then comprise at least four states. However, there will initially be scope for these changes to be waived in certain cases: between 2014 and 2017 any member state may request that the current system be used.

Of the bigger countries, France, Britain, Germany, and Italy presently have the most votes, with twenty-nine apiece. The least populated country, Malta, has just three. The overall breakdown of vote allocations under QMV is spelt out in the table entitled 'Allocation of voting power under qualified majority voting (QMV)', to be found on the Online Resource Centre.

Perhaps unsurprisingly, QMV has its critics. Some smaller states argue that at times they have policies imposed on them—regardless of their views—by more heavily populated ones. Eurosceptics, meanwhile, see the absence of a 'one member, one vote' system as evidence that individual countries are increasingly being subsumed within an embryonic 'European superstate', rather than treated as a confederation of independent—and equal—countries.

Given the inequitable allocation of votes between member states, the fact that some decisions need only a simple majority to be passed can prove especially controversial. In the past it has been possible for a handful of the most highly populated countries to muster sufficient votes to approve a policy by rallying support from half of the member states. It was for these reasons (as well as the need to give fair representation to newer members) that the changes due to come in from 2014 were agreed.

The European Court of Justice (ECJ)

Established in 1952, the **European Court of Justice (ECJ)**—officially the 'Court of Justice of the European Communities'—is the EU's supreme legal institution. Unlike other bodies it is based in Luxembourg City, but like them it has its own president (appointed by their fellow judges on a renewable three-year term).

Again like the other key EU institutions, the Court comprises twenty-seven members: one judge per member state. For practical reasons, a maximum of thirteen judges will usually hear a case at any one time, sitting as a 'Grand Chamber'. The judges are assisted by eight 'advocates-general'—lawyers tasked with presenting to them impartial 'opinions' on individual cases. Judgments are made in a collegiate way and must be unanimous.

Each judge is nominated by the member state from which he/she hails, on a renewable six-year term. Five advocates-general are nominated by the biggest EU member states—Britain, France, Germany, Italy, and Spain—with the other three rotating in alphabetical order between the remaining twenty-two. Poland has consistently argued that, because its population is only marginally smaller than Spain's (and its representation under QMV the same), it should have an automatic right to nominate an advocate-general too. This has yet to materialize.

The Court may be required to pass judgment in a variety of circumstances—for example, if there is evidence a member state has not implemented a treaty or directive, or a complainant alleges that a governmental institution, non-government organization (NGO), or commercial business has in some other way broken EU law.

Areas of EU law covered include:

- free trade and the movement of goods and services in the EU single market;
- employment law and the European Social Chapter (see p. 295);

- competition law (cartels, monopolies, mergers, and acquisitions);
- public sector regulation.

In practice, it is unusual for a case involving an individual or small group of individuals to go before the ECJ itself. And even when a case *is* heard by the Court, this will often be by three or five judges, rather than thirteen. Only in exceptional cases (such as when an EU commissioner is alleged to have seriously failed to fulfil his/her obligations) will it ever sit as a 'full court', and even then only a quorum of fifteen judges—rather than the full complement of twenty-seven—is needed.

In lesser cases, hearings are convened by a junior body established in 1988 to deal with the growing number of routine complaints being generated as the EU extended its influence: the General Court (until Lisbon, 'Court of First Instance'). Like its more illustrious counterpart, this also boasts twenty-seven judges, one per member state, and a president appointed by them for renewable three-year terms. Unlike the ECJ, however, it has no advocates-general, so a judge from among its own number is sometimes nominated to fulfil this role. A 'judge-rapporteur' will also be appointed to oversee proceedings and draft a provisional judgment—to be deliberated on by the judges—after hearing representations from complainant and respondent.

The General Court's responsibilities encompass the following policy areas:

- agriculture;
- state aid;
- competition;
- commercial policy;
- regional policy;
- social policy;
- institutional law;
- trademark law;
- transport.

It has the authority to impose various penalties, as outlined in the table entitled 'Forms of ruling that can be made by the European Court of Justice (ECJ)', to be found on the Online Resource Centre.

Judgments by the General Court are subject to a right to appeal to the ECJ. In addition to the General Court, two further courts exist to deal with more specific cases: the Civil Service Tribunal, which handles complaints about maladministration by EU employees, and Court of Auditors (which oversees its accounts).

For individual member states the extent to which European law can be said to take precedence over national legislatures, judiciaries, and (where relevant) constitutions is a subject of intense interest and ongoing debate. In recent years, however, a series of landmark Court judgments have pointed towards a growing sense that the EU holds supreme. In 1999 Mr Blair's government faced a compensation bill of up to £100m after the ECJ ruled that Margaret Thatcher had broken European law by passing a 1988 Act of Parliament intended to ban Spanish trawlermen from using British registered boats to fish in UK waters—a practice known as 'quota-hopping'. The final judgment in this case, known as *Factortame* (after the name of one of the 100-plus Spanish fishing companies that brought the original action), only came after a decade of legal ping-pong between London and Luxembourg.

Several 'test case' rulings have focused on the scope of EU employment law—and in particular the extent to which commercial companies and other non-government organizations can be bound by it. In the case of *M. H. Marshall v. Southampton and South-West Hampshire Area Health Authority* (1986) a Ms Marshall sued her employer after being dismissed from her job on reaching the then state retirement age for women (60). She argued this contravened EC Directive 76/207 (focusing on non-discrimination), because men were not expected to retire until the age of 65 and the Directive created rights that could be enforced 'horizontally' between individuals. The ECJ ruled against this interpretation—stipulating that directives generally only applied 'vertically' (that is, through the aegis of the specific individuals or organizations at whom they were directed). However, there was a silver lining for Ms Marshall: as the health authority employing her was 'an organ of the state' (meaning it was bound by the Directive on a vertical basis) she still won her case.

Some judgments have proved so momentous that new legal concepts have been named after them: in 1991 a group of Italian workers who lost their jobs when their employer became insolvent successfully sued the country's government for failing to implement EC Directive 80/987, which would have guaranteed them compensation. The ECJ's ruling in favour of the workers established the principle of member states being liable for compliance with EU law by all bodies based on their soil, including private companies. This has been christened the '*Frankovich* Principle' (after the surname of one victor).

But not all ECJ judgments have gone claimants' way, and some outcomes suggest a rather less clear-cut balance of power between UK courts and the EU. In *Van Duyn v. the Home Office* (1974), the ECJ found in favour of Britain after a Dutch national, Yvonne Van Duyn, sued under the Treaty of Rome for being denied entry to the country because she was a practising Scientologist. The Court ruled that member states could bar individuals on the basis of their 'personal conduct' if this conflicted with national 'public policy' objectives, and the UK's public policy was to prevent the spread of Scientology. More significantly, in 1993 the German judicial system successfully asserted its supremacy over the EU in internal constitutional matters. In *Brunner v. the European Union*

Treaty the German Constitutional Court ruled that it was for it alone to determine whether European laws, and the powers conferred on individual Union institutions, were compatible with Germany's constitution. And, in a warning similar to Mr Cameron's recent refusal to cede any further powers to the EU without consulting the British public first, it ruled that the country would not be bound by any interpretation of the Treaty that extended the Union's overall remit (or 'kompetenz'), or any laws subsequently adopted by the EU that increased its existing powers—unless German law decided that such laws should apply.

European Council

For many years referred to as the 'European Summit' (to avoid confusion with the Council of Ministers), the **European Council** finally gained official status as a governing institution of the EU only with the ratification of the Lisbon Treaty. Composed of the heads of state or government of all twenty-seven member states of the EU, it meets up to four times a year, usually in the Justus Lipsius Building in Brussels, headquarters of the Council of Ministers.

Since the Lisbon Treaty came into force on 1 December 2009 the Council has been chaired by a full-time, 'permanent' **president of the European Council** selected by members of the Council. The inaugural president, re-elected unopposed for a second term of two-and-a-half years on 31 May 2012, is former Belgian Prime Minister Herman Van Rompuy. Previously, chairmanship of the Council rotated between member states, with individual heads of government taking it in turns to hold it for six months at a time, in tandem with their parallel presidency of the Council of Ministers (see pp. 284–5). While the European Council has no legislative power (unlike its near-namesake), a member state may complain formally to the Council if it disagrees with a decision taken in the Council of Ministers, under a procedure known as the 'emergency brake'. The Council may then choose to settle the matter by holding its own vote—giving it what some observers see as the ultimate veto over disputed EU policy. Since Lisbon, it has also been charged officially with mapping the overall future strategic direction of the Union.

▌ Evolution of the euro

The concept of moving towards some form of single European currency has been quietly fermenting for decades. But what started out as the seed of an idea in the minds of European commissioners in the late 1960s took some thirty years to reach fruition. The following section focuses on the more decisive stages in the development of the euro project.

The exchange rate mechanism (ERM) debacle and 'Black Wednesday'

In an effort to control inflation, encourage trade, and stabilize exchange rates between individual EU member states' currencies—in doing so kick-starting the process of introducing a single currency—in 1979 the EU introduced the exchange rate mechanism (ERM). The ERM was based on the idea of fixing narrower margins between which member states' currencies would be permitted to fluctuate in value in relation to those of other members—effectively 'pegging' one country's exchange rate to another's. Before its introduction, bilateral exchange rates between EU states were based on the European currency unit (ecu)—a 'virtual' European currency traded in stock markets—the value of which was equivalent to a weighted average of those of the individual EU members' currencies. As a condition of EU membership, states were required to contain fluctuations in the value of their currencies within a 2.25 per cent margin either side of their bilateral exchange rates (except Italy, which was allowed a variance of up to 6 per cent).

The Maastricht Treaty envisaged the European monetary system (EMS) moving towards full monetary union in three stages, as set out in the table entitled 'The three stages of Economic and Monetary Union (EMU)', to be found on the Online Resource Centre.

Britain was characteristically slow to sign up. It finally did so in 1990, when John Major was Chancellor, but pulled out dramatically on 16 September 1992, after a panic-stricken day of stock market speculation and interest rate hikes, by his successor, Norman Lamont.

'Black Wednesday'—as it came to be known—arose out of the unsustainable position in which the British currency (the pound sterling) had found itself during the months after the country signed up to the ERM. Throughout much of the 1980s Margaret Thatcher's Chancellor, Nigel Lawson, had 'shadowed' the German Deutschmark when deciding whether to raise or lower interest rates to maintain sterling's value. By September 2002 this had had the effect of valuing sterling unsustainably high compared to the US dollar. Because many British exports were valued in dollars, not sterling, the UK was potentially losing significant income from overseas markets by allowing the gap between the dollar and the pound to widen. But with Britain pegged to the ecu in the ERM, there was limited room for the Chancellor to devalue sterling in the way he otherwise might have done to remedy this.

The approaching crisis reached its tipping point when US speculators, including billionaire George Soros, began frenziedly borrowing pounds and selling them for Deutschmarks in mid-September, in the belief that sterling was about to be devalued and they could therefore profit by repaying their loans at deflated prices. This prompted Mr Lamont to raise interest rates from 10 to 12 per cent on 16 September (with the promise of a further increase, to 15 per cent, later the same day), in an effort to stop sterling's value falling too far by tempting speculators to buy pounds. But, apparently disbelieving him, speculators continued selling pounds in anticipation of a slump in its value.

With sterling's value plummeting as a result, at 7 p.m. Mr Lamont pulled Britain out of the ERM—freezing interest rates for the time being at 12 per cent, rather than raising them to the promised 15 per cent. During the course of one day, he had spent £27bn of Britain's gold reserves propping up the pound. By the time the Conservatives lost to Labour five years later, official Treasury estimates calculated that the ultimate cost to the taxpayer of 'Black Wednesday' was £3.4bn. The Tories' previous reputation for economic competence was dealt a body blow by the events of that day, from which it took years to recover.

Launch of the euro and growth of the eurozone

The **euro** has existed in 'non-physical' form—that is, in the guise of travellers' cheques, electronic transfers, etc.—since 1 January 1999, but it officially came into being on 1 January 2002, when the **European Central Bank (ECB)** in Frankfurt began issuing notes and coins in the twelve EU member states that had signed up to join. At the time there were only fifteen EU states, and membership of the euro has since been extended to include five of the additional twelve countries admitted through enlargement: Malta, Cyprus, Slovenia, Estonia, and Slovakia. Of the 'original' fifteen EU members, Britain, Sweden, and Denmark are the only three to have resisted joining. Both Swedish and Danish populations have rejected the single currency in national referendums (the latter twice), and the former has since circumvented any pressure from 'eurozone' states to make a fresh attempt to join them by failing to adhere to the 'convergence criteria' that countries are expected to meet before being accepted into the euro.

The main convergence criteria, designed to promote price stability across participating states, require applicants to achieve the following:

- inflation rate no more than 1.5 per cent higher than that of the three lowest-inflation member states of the EU;

- ratio of no more than 3 per cent between their annual government deficit and gross domestic product (GDP) at the end of the preceding tax year;

- ratio of gross government debt to GDP no greater than 60 per cent at the end of the preceding tax year (it is sometimes acceptable to approach this target);

- membership of the successor to the original ERM—'ERM II'—for at least two consecutive years without at any point simultaneously devaluing their currency;

- nominal long-term interest rates no more than 2 per cent higher than that of the three lowest-inflation EU member states.

At time of writing, the seventeen countries in the eurozone were (in alphabetical order): Austria, Belgium, Cyprus, Estonia, Finland, France, Germany, Greece, Ireland, Italy, Luxembourg, Malta, the Netherlands, Portugal, Slovakia, Slovenia, and Spain. In addition, Denmark has recently made tentative steps towards joining the euro by becoming a member of ERM II in preparation, and there is talk of a further referendum.

For its part, Britain remains a refusenik. Mr Major's government negotiated an 'opt-out protocol' before belatedly signing the Maastricht Treaty, removing any obligation on its part to move from stage two to stage three of EMU. On entering office Mr Blair (widely seen as a Europhile, compared to the more cautious Mr Brown) promised to hold a referendum before committing the UK to the single currency. He repeated this pledge at various points during his ten years in power and is thought always to have been broadly supportive of the idea of joining one day. But in 1997 Mr Brown announced that, before surrendering the strength of sterling to the untested vagaries of the euro, he would need to be convinced Britain had met 'five economic tests'. These 'tests'—actually questions to determine whether the UK economy would benefit from entry—are outlined in the table entitled 'Gordon Brown's "five economic tests" for Britain's entry into the euro', to be found on the Online Resource Centre.

Critics argued that these questions—which effectively kept Britain out of the euro for the duration of the New Labour government—were at best susceptible to obfuscation and at worst unanswerable. In reality, many claimed, they were introduced to enable Mr Brown to place continual delays in the way of a referendum—arguing at any point in time that one or more tests had yet to be satisfactorily met.

The eurozone 'sovereign debt crisis'

Because several EU member states have yet to join the single currency, the Union has often been described as a 'two-speed' Europe. Until recently many observers argued that, whatever their preferences, a time would one day come when Britain and all other member states outside the euro would be forced to join—if only to retain their influence at the negotiating table over other issues affecting the Union. Former French President Jacques Chirac and German Chancellor Gerhard Schroeder each made several speeches when in office emphasizing the need for Britain to commit more fully to the EU by entering the euro.

However, tumultuous recent events in the 'eurozone' sparked by sovereign debt crises in several member states—notably the so-called 'PIGS' economies of Portugal, Ireland, Greece, and Spain (see pp. 293–4)—have sharpened opposition to joining within the British political establishment and cast doubt on the future of the euro itself. Sparked, in part, by the 2008–9 banking collapse (see pp. 213–16), there have been so many twists and turns in this escalating emergency that it is impossible to give a definitive account of it in a book of this kind. Moreover, at time of writing events continue to be so fast-moving that any attempt to do so would inevitably appear out of date by the time it is published. Nonetheless, it would be remiss not to include a broad overview of the origins of the crisis and its most immediate ramifications.

In May 2010 the euro was plunged into the biggest crisis in its history after first Greece, then a succession of other EU member states using the single currency, became the subject of intense concern over the extent of their 'sovereign debt': the individual budget deficits they had built up in the wake of the global financial meltdown and (in some cases) their previous levels of government borrowing.

Trouble began in Greece, where a package of austerity measures unveiled by the government provoked a wave of wildcat public sector strikes and violent demonstrations. Financial analysts Standard & Poor's swiftly reduced the status of the country's government bonds to 'junk' (the highest level being 'AAA'). In an effort to contain Greece's downturn—preventing it from having a knock-on effect on the euro and, by extension, the economies of other EU states—on 2 May the 'eurozone' countries teamed up with the International Monetary Fund (IMF) to offer the country an unprecedented €110bn (£93bn) loan bailout, on condition it imposed harsh domestic spending cuts. Within a week, though, a further massive cash injection was required to stabilize the euro as a whole. This saw Europe's finance ministers collectively approve a loans package worth £624bn aimed at ensuring financial stability across Europe by shoring up the sixteen states by that point struggling to service their debts. In one of his last actions as Labour Chancellor, Alistair Darling signed off the deal—committing the UK to providing between £9.6bn and £13bn to support a new £95bn 'stabilization mechanism' designed to stop individual countries' economies collapsing.

In the ensuing weeks, governments in a succession of other eurozone states, including Spain, Portugal, and Italy, began implementing similarly tough austerity measures. But as international money markets indicated a new wariness towards the previously unassailable euro, the crisis came closer to home, as Ireland was forced to accept a joint €85bn (£71bn) bailout by the IMF and the eurozone countries.

The following two years saw a succession of other bailouts—and further waves of painful austerity in member states forced to accept them. In unprecedented scenes, two countries paralysed by their deepening debt problems, Greece and Italy, ended up forming governments led by so-called 'technocrats': unelected officials with extensive professional experience of working in the financial sector but no democratic mandate. In Italy Mario Monti, a veteran economist and former EU commissioner for competition, supplanted the disgraced Silvio Berlusconi as prime minister in November 2011, while around the same time Luca Papademos, erstwhile vice-president of the European Central

Bank, took over in Greece until the belated formation of a new centre-right-led elected coalition seven months later. Central to the often fraught negotiations among member states—including Britain and others not in the euro—was the question of how far the country with the strongest economy, Germany, was willing to go in propping up those in crisis in an effort to avoid a break-up of the eurozone. At various stages the idea was mooted that Greece (the state in the weakest financial position, at least initially) might be forced to 'default' on its debt or even withdraw from the euro altogether and re-adopt its own currency. This would allow it to devalue in the hope of boosting export areas, such as tourism and shipping, in which it had a 'comparative advantage'—defined in economics as goods or services a country can afford to produce at lower marginal costs than its competitors. With escalating crises in Spain, Portugal, and Italy, however, at time of writing Germany seemed determined to prevent this happening, if only to avoid other states following suit and the eurozone as a whole collapsing.

At the height of the sovereign debt storm, in December 2011, eurozone members led by Germany and France proposed a twin-pronged strategy for limiting the likelihood of future financial crises on the scale of that which had begun three years earlier. The first element would be a new **Fiscal Compact** which, if enacted, would effectively allow the ECB to vet individual member states' national budget plans. Officially entitled the Treaty on Stability, Coordination, and Governance in the Economic and Monetary Union, the Compact requires all signatories to introduce into their domestic laws formal requirements that future governments keep their annual budgets in balance or surplus. Any state breaking this pledge would be fined 0.1 per cent of its GDP by the ECJ. At time of writing it was still unclear whether the Compact would come into force, however, as it first needed to be formally ratified by at least twelve eurozone states prior to a deadline of 1 January 2013. Following the May 2012 election of Francois Hollande, France's first Socialist president in nearly two decades, this was looking less certain, given his stated intention of renegotiating the treaty. And by September that year ECB president Mario Draghi also appeared to have adopted a more emollient attitude towards debt-ridden EU nations, by offering to buy up government bonds issued by struggling member states in an effort to artificially lower their borrowing costs. Officially, the new programme— saddled with the characteristically bureaucratic-sounding title Outright Monetary Transactions (OMT)—had the endorsement of both market analysts and indebted states, including Germany.

The second element of this eurozone firewall was a proposed EU 'financial transaction tax' (FTT), which, if implemented in the form proposed by the Commission, would come into force on 1 January 2014 and see a charge of 0.1 per cent imposed against the exchange of shares and bonds and 0.01 per cent against derivatives contracts transacted between financial institutions in all signatory states. It was the proposal to raise some 57 billion euros a year through such a tax, more than the planned Compact, that prompted Mr Cameron to stage his equally celebrated and derided 'walkout' from negotiations in December 2011. He put his refusal to sign up to the FTT down to concern about the disproportionate impact it was likely to have on the City of London, and described his move as a 'veto'—though critics, including Labour, were quick to point out that it was, at best, an 'opt-out', as the treaty introducing the Compact was still likely to go ahead, having been signed by all other EU states apart from the Czech Republic. The future of a full-blooded EU-wide (or even eurozone-wide) FTT remains uncertain, however (see p.), in light of recent proposals to water it down to a stamp duty-style levy which may end up only being introduced in states that individually choose to adopt it.

▌ Towards an EU 'superstate'?

Of all issues to divide the main British political parties in recent years, none has been more damaging than what many see as the gradual shift from an EU based on mutual cooperation between sovereign nations towards a 'federal' union more akin to the USA's. By the late 1980s the perception that many mainland European countries (in particular France and Germany) wanted to create a 'European superstate' provoked staunch resistance from Mrs Thatcher and other Eurosceptic ministers to almost any prospect of further UK involvement. Famously, during a Commons debate on the charismatic European Commission President Jacques Delors's plans to accelerate further EU integration, she declared 'no, no, no' to his vision.

Although as Leader of the Opposition Mrs Thatcher had supported the 'yes' campaign for Britain to remain in the then EEC, a decade into her premiership she saw things quite differently. By then the pace of integration had stepped up a gear, and the likes of Mr Delors and German Chancellor Helmut Kohl were championing ever-closer ties between member states, with the contents of the Maastricht Treaty a particular bone of contention. High-profile resignations by pro-European Cabinet colleagues, such as Chancellor Nigel Lawson and Foreign Secretary Sir Geoffrey Howe, did little to dent her resolve. It was the Tories' growing internal rift over Europe as much as the Poll Tax riots that led to her being challenged for the party's leadership in 1989 by a 'stalking horse' candidate, the obscure backbencher Sir Anthony Meyer, and her ultimate downfall in her ill-fated defence against the 1990 challenge by Michael Heseltine (see p. 96).

Despite producing a more mild-mannered replacement, the ensuing leadership election failed to heal party wounds. Mr Major did much to placate his Eurosceptic colleagues in his first months in Downing Street. In particular, he negotiated British opt-outs to various clauses in the Maastricht Treaty—notably the Social Chapter (later signed by Mr Blair's government, which enshrined new rights for EU workers, including the Working Time Directive barring employers from forcing staff to work more than forty-eight hours a week).

But such fillips to the Right could only delay an inevitable confrontation over Maastricht (which effectively *had* to be signed if Britain were to remain in the EU). By May 1992, having secured a narrow fourth successive Tory victory in an election earlier that month with a majority of just eighteen MPs, Mr Major found himself held to ransom by a hardcore of Eurosceptic backbenchers, known collectively as the 'Maastricht rebels' (see p. 52). Only by temporarily withdrawing the whip from these MPs, building a fractious alliance with the Ulster Unionists and Democratic Unionists, and threatening his party with a further election, which it would almost certainly have lost, did Mr Major manage to force through the European Communities (Amendment) Bill on a wafer-thin majority. Among those actively rebelling from the backbenches were bullish former Employment Secretary Lord Tebbit and a certain Mrs Thatcher. In addition to the usual suspects, such as stalwart right-wingers Bill Cash and Teddy Taylor, the rebels included no fewer than three future ministers in Mr Cameron's government: David Willetts, Dr Liam Fox, and Iain Duncan Smith.

As the Tories' Eurosceptic resolve has hardened, old divisions have also resurfaced in the Labour Party. The publication in 2004 of a draft 'EU Constitution'—or Constitutional Treaty—ostensibly did little more than draw together in a single (if mammoth) document various earlier agreements, such as the 1986 Act and Maastricht. But those already wary of earlier shifts towards a more centralized EU power structure saw in it a clear attempt to consolidate the Union, leading to greater **federalism**—a reduction in status of the sovereign governments of member states akin to the limited devolution accorded to individual states in the USA.

Ironically, the Treaty emphasized the concept of subsidiarity—the antithesis of federalism, which defines member states as paramount and the EU as only a 'last port of call' should individual countries' self-determination falter. It also set out, for the first time, the practical steps states could take if they wished to withdraw from the EU altogether. Nonetheless, under mounting pressure from the Tories and his own backbenchers, Mr Blair promised a referendum on the constitution if he were to win a third term in the 2005 election.

It was his handling of the issue from his 2005 victory onwards—not to mention that of his successor, Mr Brown—that was to cause the greatest disquiet among not only Tory but also Labour MPs. Having taken cover from the collapse of the constitution proposals following their rejection by both France and the Netherlands in national referendums, both Mr Blair and Mr Brown refused to follow through on their earlier pledge with the advent of the Lisbon Treaty. This was despite the fact that, even according to many of its supporters, in content if not name it was substantially the same document.

After months of pressure from his own backbenchers and a Commons debate lasting twelve days, Mr Brown formally settled the issue in February 2008 with a slim victory in support of ratifying Lisbon on a three-line whip (to the fury of

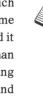

Eurosceptic papers like the *Daily Mail*, the front-page headline of which described the outcome as 'The day they betrayed British democracy'). Some twenty-nine Labour MPs defied the party whip by backing a referendum, and it was only Mr Clegg's decision to whip Lib Dem MPs into abstaining (rather than opposing the government) that carried the day for the prime minister. In doing so, Mr Clegg angered some in his own ranks: three frontbenchers resigned and fifteen voted for a referendum, despite his using a three-line whip to discipline them. Oddly, the Lib Dems had spent much of the previous week in Parliament demanding a referendum on Europe—but on Britain's ongoing membership of the EU, rather than the constitutional issue in particular.

While Lisbon ultimately had a smoother passage than the abortive constitution, Britain was not the only country to have trouble ratifying it. On 13 June 2008 the only EU nation granted a referendum, the Irish, rejected it by 53.4 to 46.6 per cent (paving the way for a failed last-ditch attempt by Tory peers to delay its passage through the Lords). Facing the threat of isolation or, worse, expulsion from the EU, Ireland finally approved Lisbon in October 2009. But it was not until December that year—eighteen months after it had been signed in principle by EU leaders—that the Treaty finally came into force.

Today substantial questions (and divisions) remain as to the future direction of the EU and Britain's continuing place within it. With a largely Eurosceptic Tory-led government returned to power in May 2010, and some eurozone leaders urging more profound steps be taken towards European integration in order to save the euro, the next few years are likely to decide the nature and extent of the UK's long-term membership of the EU. At time of writing there was a growing clamour from the Tory backbenches for a decisive 'in/out referendum' to resolve, once and for all, whether Britain should remain in the Union in light of its removal from the increasingly convergent trajectory followed by eurozone countries. While Labour remained committed to EU membership, the party's new policy chief, Jon Cruddas, was said to be broadly in favour of a referendum to settle the issue, with several prominent Lib Dems taking a similar view. Whatever the final outcome of this debate, Mr Cameron (who describes himself as a 'practical Eurosceptic') has already taken firm steps towards limiting the extent of further British integration into the Union, by legislating to impose a 'referendum lock' preventing future UK administrations signing treaties that would change the country's relationship with the EU without first obtaining a mandate through a public vote.

▶ Other issues facing the EU

Other potentially explosive issues facing Britain's EU membership are explained in Table 9.2.

Table 9.2 Major issues facing Britain's membership of the EU

Issue	Explanation
Common Agricultural Policy (CAP) and the British rebate	CAP takes bigger annual chunk of EU's budget than any other area—equivalent to 44 per cent of spending each year. Mrs Thatcher negotiated generous annual rebate for Britain from CAP and other EU subsidies in late 1980s, in recognition that Britain received less than states more reliant on agriculture, like France. In December 2005 Mr Blair accepted £1bn-a-year cut in Britain's £3.6bn rebate following row with then French President Mr Chirac that threatened to paralyse negotiations over EU budget. His opponents argued increased subsidies from richer western European countries were needed to assist then new member states—particularly former Soviet countries.
Common Fisheries Policy (CFP)	Long-standing policy designed to protect fish/seafood stocks in European seas by using 'quota' system for fishing rights, supposedly fairly allocated among relevant member states. In mid-1990s there were frequent confrontations between Britain and Spain over 'quota-hopping'—alleged practice by Spanish trawlers fishing in British waters of registering boats under third country's 'flag of convenience' to enable them to exceed their country's quota. Many UK trawlermen forced to scrap boats because of strict quotas introduced in waters they fished.
Common defence policy	Concept of greater cooperation over defence formally introduced in Maastricht Treaty. In Britain Eurosceptic Defence Secretary Michael Portillo vowed in patriotic Conservative conference speech that Britain would never surrender right to maintain independent Armed Forces. Idea of EU 'Rapid Reaction Force' designed to intervene swiftly in event of member state being threatened or invaded very much on table.
Economic migration	Expansion of EU to encompass former Eastern Bloc countries has seen increase in economic migration from poorer to richer countries, fostered by the free movement of labour (as well as goods, services, and capital) enshrined in various treaties. This has strained community relations and public services in some areas—creating tensions between migrants and indigenous peoples. In 2007 Britain became first member state to introduce new restrictions on migrant workers from two newest EU entrants, Bulgaria and Romania.

☰ Topical feature idea

There has been extensive discussion in the British news media of late about the issue of migrant workers competing with UK nationals for scarce jobs in industry, construction, and the service sector. With Britain in a 'double-dip recession' and thirty or forty people chasing every vacancy in the towns covered by your newspaper, tensions have been rising between local people and migrants who have recently moved in—largely from former Eastern Bloc countries admitted to the EU during enlargement. Your editor wants you to write a balanced background feature explaining the underlying issues that have sparked recent demonstrations by unemployed workers and outbreaks of violence between some locals and migrants. To whom would you go to obtain quotes reflecting both sides of the debate? What would you ask them? How would you go about finding statistics to demonstrate the scale of inward migration locally?

✱ Current issues

- **The sovereign debt crisis in the eurozone:** in spring 2010 several EU member states were forced to introduce swingeing austerity measures because of rising concern on international money markets about their ability to service their national debts. Greece was loaned €110bn by the International Monetary Fund and had its credit rating downgraded by Standard & Poor's to 'junk bond' status, as its government announced massive spending cuts in the face of angry street protests and death threats. Spain, Portugal, Ireland, and other countries in the eurozone have followed suit.

- **Turkey's accession to the EU:** negotiations over Turkey's accession to the EU began seriously in 2004, but the country's questionable human rights record and historical tensions with other member states, including Germany, have so far conspired to slow progress, and the present sovereign debt crises are threatening to thwart it further..

- **The prospect of an 'in/out' UK referendum:** Britain seems more isolated than ever in Europe after 'opting out' of the upcoming Fiscal Compact and mooted financial transaction tax (FTT). As eurozone countries try to solve the sovereign debt crisis, the prospect of fuller integration is looming larger—prompting MPs in all the main parties to argue for an 'in/out' referendum on EU membership.

? Review questions

1. Outline the roles, structures, and composition of the main European Union institutions. Which is the most powerful and why?

2. How does qualified majority voting (QMV) work, where and how often is it used, and can it be described as fair and democratic? If not, why not?

3. What were the main stages leading up to full economic and monetary union (EMU)? What are the arguments for and against Britain joining the euro?

4. Is the EU a federal superstate in the making, or one that has stayed true to its stated aim of preserving subsidiarity? To what extent, if any, is national sovereignty threatened by recent developments in European integration?

5. List some of the main issues affecting the future of the EU, explaining why they are significant to the UK's membership of the Union.

→ Further reading

Bomberg, E. and Stubb, A. (eds) (2012) *The European Union: How Does it Work?*, Oxford: Oxford University Press. **Concise introductory text focusing on demystifying key EU institutions and their sometimes arcane governing procedures**.

Daniels, P. and Ritchie, E. (1996) *EU: Britain and the European Union*, London: Palgrave Macmillan. **Analysis of relationship of Britain's main governmental institutions with EU**.

Jones, A. (2007) *Britain and the European Union*, Edinburgh: Edinburgh University Press. **Invaluable introduction to EU, its history and institutions, with particular emphasis on changing relationship between EU and UK**.

McCormick, J. (2008) *Understanding the European Union: A Concise Introduction*, London: Palgrave Macmillan. **Leading introductory text to history, institutions, and treaties of EU. Latest edition includes comprehensive assessment of Lisbon Treaty and impact of EU enlargement**.

@ Online Resource Centre

www.oxfordtextbooks.co.uk/orc/Morrison3e/
Visit the Online Resource Centre that accompanies this book for web links and regular updates.

10

International relations

We live in an era in which terms like 'globalization', 'development', and 'fair trade' are part of most people's everyday cultural vocabularies. More than at any time in its history, Britain's fortunes are tied to those of its neighbours in Europe. But its involvement in international affairs stretches well beyond the European Union (EU). Until recently, the country was involved in at least three ongoing conflicts— in Afghanistan, Iraq, and Libya. UK-based multinationals like Shell and BP retain oil and mineral interests across Africa, Latin America, and the Middle East. And then there are those last vestiges of the once sprawling British Empire, in the guise of Northern Ireland, the fifty-three-nation Commonwealth, and a handful of island protectorates, including Gibraltar, the Falklands, and Diego Garcia.

At the same time as Britain is flexing its military and economic muscle, it has become one of the biggest players in the fight to eradicate global poverty, contributing nearly £7bn a year in overseas aid to developing countries in Africa, Asia, and South America, and leading the way at recent G8 and G20 summits for binding multilateral agreements on debt relief. The country has also played a significant—if so far limited—role in brokering international agreements on issues ranging from climate change to human rights abuse.

▌ The Foreign and Commonwealth Office (FCO)

The Foreign and Commonwealth Office (FCO)—commonly known as the 'Foreign Office'—is the government department overseeing Britain's overall foreign policy. It was formed in 1968 from the merger of the existing Foreign Office (dating from 1782) and the then separate Commonwealth Office. At its head are several ministers, the most senior being the Foreign and Commonwealth Secretary, or 'Foreign Secretary'.

The FCO's main roles are to:

- maintain diplomatic and/or consular relations with 188 different countries;
- maintain diplomatic missions with a further nine countries;
- act as the UK's main broker in drawing up international treaties, common defence policies, and economic sanctions;
- use its overseas embassies to act as local focal points for diplomatic relations between Britain and the countries concerned;
- help to promote the UK as a trading partner with other countries through its embassies.

When Labour regained power in 1997 its newly installed Foreign Secretary, the late Robin Cook, vowed to pursue an 'ethical foreign policy', putting diplomacy and human rights campaigning ahead of narrow national interests and warfare. But in 2001 he was replaced by Jack Straw, who had earned a reputation as a tough-talking Home Secretary in the government's first term. Within months, the FCO was dealing with the fallout from the 11 September terrorist attacks on New York. In 2006, under then Foreign Secretary Margaret Beckett (the first woman to hold the post), the FCO announced ten new 'strategic priorities' for the next five to ten years—an approach broadly upheld by the Coalition. These are outlined in the table entitled 'Ten-year strategic objectives of the Foreign and Commonwealth Office (FCO)', on the Online Resource Centre.

Unlike most government departments, the FCO has only one executive agency: Wilton Park International Conference Centre organizes summits on international social problems, attended by academics, business people, and other relevant professionals. There are also several independent think tanks with close links to the FCO, the most famous being the Royal Institute of International Affairs, founded in 1920 and based at Chatham House, St James's Square, London (commonly known simply as 'Chatham House'). It is from Chatham House that the oft-cited 'Chatham House Rule'—beloved of (and cursed by) editors in equal measure—originates. This is a 'gentleman's agreement' allowing journalists access to candid discussions and debates held by private or public organizations in return for their agreement to respect the anonymity of participants. Reporters are normally permitted to use some or all information gained from such meetings, but on the strict condition that they do not attribute it to named individuals. The precise wording of the 'Chatham House Rule' is as follows:

> When a meeting, or part thereof, is held under the Chatham House Rule, participants are free to use the information received, but neither the identity nor the affiliation of the speaker(s), nor that of any other participant, may be revealed.

The civilized, if rather quaint, rule reflects the overall culture of the FCO, which is often criticized for its antediluvian procedures and maintaining a cosy 'old boy' approach to business more redolent of a Graham Greene novel than the harsh realities of twenty-first-century *Weltpolitik*. In August 2005 Andrew Mackinlay, a Labour member of the Commons Foreign Affairs Select Committee, leaked details of a report by management consultancy Collinson Grant, which suggested it was hugely overmanned and needed reform to address the following weaknesses:

- 'slowness to act';
- lack of delegation in its management structure;
- poor accountability;
- overmanning—with at least 1,200 jobs, £48m a year could be saved.

Of the recent controversies involving the FCO, none has been more damaging than the debacle over Iraq. There is insufficient space here to detail the circumstances leading to the US-led invasion of the country over Saddam Hussein's alleged stockpiling of weapons of mass destruction (WMDs) or the subsequent failure to locate any such arms. It is fair to say, however, that the spectre of this ongoing conflict—not to mention the threat of terrorism, as brought home to Britain in the multiple bombings of 7 July 2005—is reflected in the wording of the FCO's current statement of 'priorities'.

Many other recent issues faced by the FCO—and played out in the media—have also stemmed in large part from Britain's involvement in the 'War on Terror' (although this expression was pointedly dropped by the UK government, if not the USA, after Tony Blair left Downing Street). These have included Britain's belated intervention to secure the release of UK-based terrorist suspects held in the US Guantanamo Bay detention camp on Cuba, from which the first four finally returned to their families in 2007—five years after being captured by the US military in Afghanistan. During Gordon Brown's premiership, meanwhile, a row broke out over Foreign Secretary David Miliband's admission—contrary to previous assurances by ministers—that a British territory had been used for so-called 'extraordinary rendition' by the USA. This is the process by which suspected terrorists have been flown to third-party countries to be interrogated by agents working on behalf of the Central Intelligence Agency (CIA). The process has been criticized as 'torture by proxy' by human rights organizations, which argue that, by allowing prisoners to be questioned in countries known for their strong-arm tactics, the USA has given tacit approval to interrogation practices banned in its own country. In a speech to the Commons in February 2008 Mr Miliband revealed he had been told by then US Secretary of State Condoleezza Rice only after the event that US planes, each carrying a single suspect, had stopped on the British island of Diego Garcia in the Indian Ocean. One had been en route to Guantanamo Bay; the other to Morocco.

For his part, Foreign Secretary William Hague has signalled a new, more 'clear, focused, and effective' approach to international diplomacy, emphasizing the need for Britain to be proactive in Europe and build strong relations with emerging 'economic superpowers'—principally the so-called 'BRIC' states: Brazil, the Russian Federation, China, and India. In a swipe at Labour's legacy, he has argued that the UK came to be seen by some as a state that only engaged with them in the event of disaster or when it needed their support for crucial votes (an oblique reference to the elusive 'second resolution' Mr Blair had sought from the UN to legitimize the 2003 invasion of Iraq). Mr Hague has since announced an accelerated timetable for withdrawing British combat troops from Afghanistan, setting out his intention to complete this task by 2014.

However, despite initially appearing to favour a less 'gung-ho' approach to foreign affairs than their Labour predecessors, the Coalition was soon accused of reverting to type. In 2011 Messrs Cameron and Hague were among the most proactive voices calling for military intervention to impose a 'no-fly zone' over Libya to prevent dictator Muammar Gaddafi's forces bombing their own people. And bellicose rhetoric has characterized their approach to dealing with everyone from Syrian despot Bashar al-Assad and Iranian president Mahmoud Ahmadinejad to the Argentine leader, Christine Kirchner, following her decision to revive her country's claims to sovereignty over the Malvinas (to Britain, the Falkland Islands). The Coalition itself was also split over moves by Mr Hague and then Justice Secretary Kenneth Clarke to introduce closed court hearings for handling sensitive information judged to be potentially prejudicial to British national security—a throwback to the 'Big Brother' policies for which Labour had come under fire from civil liberties campaigners. In the end the government scaled back on these plans somewhat, by dropping a clause from the resulting Bill demanding that sensitive inquests should be held in secret.

The Diplomatic Service

A 'subdepartment' of the FCO, this is staffed by seconded administrators and is responsible for manning the embassies and consulates through which Britain discharges its diplomatic relations with their host countries. It employs some 20,000 officials and is headed not by a government minister, but a career civil servant. Despite the fact he/she is a salaried official, not an elected MP, this civil servant has a title similar to a certain type of minister: 'Permanent Under-Secretary of State at the FCO'.

Personnel employed by the service at all levels enjoy 'diplomatic immunity'—freedom from prosecution under the laws of the countries in which they are based. They may, however, be expelled for committing an offence, and may well be tried back in Britain.

▌ The Ministry of Defence (MoD)

What with the continuing military operations in Iraq and Afghanistan, controversies over the treatment of service personnel at home and abroad, and periodic outbursts about both these and other issues by retired senior officers, the Ministry of Defence (MoD) has grabbed more recent headlines than virtually any other government department. When Mr Blair was elected in 1997 he made a now infamous speech declaring himself part of the 'first generation' able to 'contemplate that we may live our entire lives without going to war or sending our children to war'. Yet, by the time he stepped down ten years later, he had taken Britain into no fewer than four conflicts: to prevent ethnic cleansing by Serbia's Slobodan Milošević in Kosovo (1999); intervening in the civil war in Sierra Leone (2000); supporting the US-led invasion of Afghanistan (2001); and 'liberating' Saddam's Iraq (2003). In addition, UK planes were heavily involved in the sustained bombing of Iraq by Bill Clinton's US administration in 1998.

Formed in 1964 from the amalgamation of four other departments of state—the War Office, Admiralty, Air Ministry, and Ministry of Aviation—the MoD is, ironically, most often in the news in times of conflict. Once diplomacy has broken down and Britain has declared war on another nation, the FCO tends to fade out of the picture, to give way to the department charged with coordinating the military. Although its original aim was (as its name suggests) to provide a first line of 'defence' for Britain against foreign aggressors, in practice it is more likely to see action at times when the UK is doing the attacking.

The principal roles of the MoD in its present form are outlined in the table entitled 'Principal roles of the Ministry of Defence (MoD)', to be found on the Online Resource Centre.

In recent years the MoD's raison d'être has changed in light of global developments, principally the end of the Cold War and the rising terrorist threat. The current operation in Afghanistan notwithstanding, so-called 'conventional warfare'—involving ground troops, tanks, helicopters, planes, and ships—is becoming less common. For a time during the 1980s—before the collapse of the Berlin Wall and the break-up of the Soviet Union—the consensus was that future wars would generally be fought 'by remote', with computerized missile systems replacing traditional armaments. While nuclear strikes have yet to occur, today's field weapons are increasingly sophisticated, and the number of soldiers required to fight conflicts continues to diminish as their equipment becomes capable of doing more of the work for them. In response to the new challenges and opportunities presented by modern warfare, the Labour government published two major reviews of defence expenditure: the 1998 Strategic Defence Review and a 2003 White Paper, entitled *Delivering Security in a Changing World*.

The Coalition published its own 'strategic defence and security review' in October 2010—prompted as much by the swingeing departmental spending cuts ordered by George Osborne's Treasury as any genuine desire by then Defence Secretary Liam Fox to break with Labour's policy priorities. At the time, the review sparked fury among some senior military figures (and near-hysterical newspapers headlines) after it emerged that ministers would be pressing ahead with existing contracts signed by Labour for two new naval aircraft carriers— despite being unable to afford any aircraft for them to carry for another eight to ten years. Further opprobrium was heaped on Dr Fox, particularly in the pages of the ever-patriotic *Sun*, when he confirmed he was scrapping an order for a new generation of both Harrier Jump Jets—the iconic aircraft used to devastating effect during the Falklands War—and Nimrod spy planes (although his successor, Phillip Hammond, reversed the former decision in 2012). The review also put off a final decision on how, when, and whether to renew Britain's independent Trident nuclear deterrent until after a 2015 general election— thereby neatly averting a potentially incendiary row with the Lib Dems.

More personally worrying for service personnel was the early announce- ment of 42,000 redundancies in the MoD and Armed Forces, followed in July 2012 by confirmation that the British Army alone would be cut from 102,000 to 82,000 by 2020—its lowest headcount since the Napoleonic Wars, and half its size at the height of the Cold War era. Altogether, some seventeen units and thirty-six battalions are to be scrapped, with a number of centuries-old regimental names—known as the 'golden thread'—perishing in the process. Among the casualties, ironically, will be the historic title of the 3rd Battalion of the Yorkshire Regiment: 'the Duke of Wellington's'. Critics argue that such real-terms shrinkage threatens to leave the UK in the position where it could never again mount a military operation on the scale of Iraq or Afghanistan.

Civil Service oversight of MoD policymaking

The Chief of the Defence Staff—effectively the permanent secretary of the Armed Forces as a whole—is supported by a Vice-Chief of the Defence Staff and the following heads of the three individual Armed Forces:

- First Sea Lord/Chief of the Naval Staff;
- Chief of the General Staff;
- Chief of the Air Staff.

Aside from the ongoing criticisms of levels of defence expenditure—the MoD's annual budget is said to be less than the £100bn spent by the Treasury on 'res- cuing' Northern Rock from collapse (see p. 198)—the ministry has weathered numerous other storms in recent years. At the height of the Iraq War then

Defence Secretary Geoff Hoon was accused of failing to provide adequate equipment for British troops. Mr Hoon, like Mr Blair, had also been repeatedly criticized for his apparent eagerness to invade Iraq on the basis of questionable intelligence about Saddam's WMD threat—and his unwillingness to apologize for the ensuing loss of life when it later emerged that no such weapons existed. Years after the event, during his January 2010 appearance before the Iraq Inquiry convened by Mr Brown to identify lessons from the ill-starred conflict, Mr Hoon sought to blame this 'scandal' on his former boss, claiming that during his time as Chancellor he had forced 'difficult cuts' on the MoD.

The MoD has also been castigated in the press for failing to maintain barracks and domestic quarters for personnel to a civilized standard, and for selling off large amounts of military accommodation to private landlords— only to end up renting it back from them. In March 2008 it emerged that British taxpayers were paying a private housing company £29m a year to rent 8,200 marital homes that were lying empty for lack of any Forces families to move into them.

▌ The Department for International Development (DfID)

Until the 1997 election the fields of humanitarian aid and investment in developing countries were the responsibility of a minister in the Foreign Office, the Minister for Overseas Development. When Mr Blair was elected, however, this post was incorporated into the Cabinet. Its first incumbent was Clare Short, a passionate advocate of overseas aid and sustainable development, who resigned from the Cabinet over her reservations about the post-war reconstruction of Iraq. When the Coalition took power, the Department for International Development (DfID) was one of very few to have a proportion of its budget (relating specifically to overseas aid) ring-fenced in the teeth of impending public spending cuts.

Today, DfID works directly with 150 developing countries—principally in Africa, parts of Asia, Latin America, and the Far East. Its annual budget is more than £4bn and it has two headquarters: in London and East Kilbride, near Glasgow.

DfID's so-called 'Millennium Goals' to help eradicate child poverty and improve access to education and health care for women and children in developing countries are outlined in the table entitled 'DfID Millennium Goals', on the Online Resource Centre.

▌ Britain's role in the United Nations (UN)

In addition to the EU, Britain is a member of several major international organizations with differing, if sometimes overlapping, remits. Of these, perhaps the most significant is the **United Nations (UN)**—a global body set up after the Second World War with the stated aim of promoting peace, preventing future conflicts, and achieving international cooperation on economic, social, cultural, and humanitarian issues. From the outset the UN has been committed to solving disputes between nations by peaceful means, wherever possible, and when it sends troops into a country this tends to be in a 'peacekeeping' capacity—to police borders, protect aid routes, etc.—rather than engage in active hostilities against any party.

Formally established in October 1945, the UN set out to avoid the perceived errors of its precursor, the League of Nations. The League—born out of the First World War—had imposed crippling reparations on Germany, in so doing contributing to the dire economic woes that were to foster the rise of Nazism. Initially founded by fifty-one states, today the UN embraces 193 participating nations—with the then newly created state of South Sudan welcomed into its fold in July 2011. The most senior UN official is its Secretary-General (at time of writing Ban Ki-Moon). In theory, UN membership is open to every recognized state in the world, but in practice individual countries have been periodically excluded—or have chosen to exclude themselves—in disputes over the legitimacy of their governance (or, occasionally, that of the UN itself).

The UN is based in New York—a fact that has periodically led some member states (particularly those with a history of disagreeing with the USA) to argue that the US government wields a disproportionate influence on its decisions. In October 2006, Hassan Turki, deputy leader of Somalia's Islamic Courts, one of several parties wrestling for control of the war-ravaged country, declared he did not recognize the UN—dismissing it as an 'American interest group'.

The UN Security Council

The term 'United Nations' was coined during the Second World War itself, when Winston Churchill and US president Franklin D. Roosevelt used it in speeches to refer to the Allies: the countries opposing Hitler. But the UN was only born in earnest after the UN Conference on International Organization convened in April 1945, and a formal UN Charter was drafted and signed by the majority of its founding states on 24 October. Giving substance to Churchill's famous remark that 'history is written by the victors', of these fifty-one nations the five who had played arguably the most significant role in defeating Hitler were awarded permanent seats on a newly formed UN Security Council—the body charged with allocating peacekeeping forces around the world, ratifying economic sanctions, and in extreme cases authorizing military action.

According to the UN Charter, its role is to:

- investigate any situation threatening international peace;
- recommend procedures for peaceful resolution of a dispute;
- call on other member nations to completely or partially interrupt economic relations as well as sea, air, postal, and radio communications, or to sever diplomatic relations;
- enforce its decisions militarily, or by any means necessary.

The five permanent members of the UN Security Council are the USA, Britain, France, the Republic of China (later renamed the People's Republic of China), and the Soviet Union (now the Russian Federation). They are joined at any one time by a further ten members, elected by the UN's 'parliament', the General Assembly, for two-year terms. These are chosen from among the remaining 187 UN countries on a rotational basis. For the two-year periods commencing 1 January 2011 and 1 Jan 2012 respectively, and thereafter 1 Jan 2012 and 1 Jan 2013, the temporary members of the UN Security Council were as outlined in the tables entitled 'The temporary membership of the UN Security Council (2011–13)' and 'The temporary membership of the UN Security Council (2012–14)', available on the Online Resource Centre.

As a mark of its seniority, each permanent member has the right to veto votes on prospective UN actions. It was this fact that presented the biggest stumbling block to Britain and the USA's campaign to win support for the invasion of Iraq. Both then French president Jacques Chirac, and his Russian counterpart, Vladimir Putin, made it clear they had no intention of supporting any such further resolution authorizing military strikes without conclusive proof that Saddam was stockpiling weapons of mass destruction (WMDs)—the ostensible pretext for military action. Their immovability blocked the passage of the 'second resolution' the USA and UK sought, forcing them to abandon pursuing it and go it alone.

The UN General Assembly

The primary purpose of the UN's second governing body is to approve its annual budget and appoint non-permanent representatives to the Security Council. It also receives reports from the UN's various other subsidiary bodies, and wields considerable influence over policy areas including international aid and climate change.

Unlike the Security Council, the Assembly gives each UN member state an equal say at meetings. It convenes for regular annual sessions, lasting from September to December, but can be assembled for emergency meetings at other times. Meetings are chaired either by the serving Secretary-General or by a president, elected by Assembly members on a yearly basis. Votes are passed if a two-thirds majority of those present is achieved.

Other UN bodies and agencies

Like every major organization, national or international, the UN requires administrators. The UN Secretariat employs 8,900 staff, the majority based at the UN headquarters in New York. Others are stationed in its regional headquarters in Addis Ababa, Bangkok, Beirut, Geneva, Nairobi, Santiago, and Vienna. The Secretariat's responsibilities are divided, like those of the British Civil Service and European Commission, into separate departments overseeing discrete policy areas—ranging from the 'advancement of women' to the office of the UN High Commissioner for Refugees.

Other significant agencies of the UN and their responsibilities are outlined in Table 10.1.

▶ Life after the Cold War—Britain's ongoing role in NATO

Founded in 1949, the **North Atlantic Treaty Organization (NATO)** is (unlike the UN) a *military* alliance, established against the backdrop of the emerging Cold War between East and West, and the ensuing nuclear arms race, to protect the security of Western powers. NATO comprises twenty-eight member states—principally the USA, Canada, and western Europe, although since the collapse of the Soviet Union it has also embraced several former 'Eastern Bloc' nations.

NATO's origins lay in an earlier agreement, the 1948 Treaty of Brussels, which founded the Western European Union—a smaller-scale forerunner composed entirely (as its name suggests) of western European countries. In fact its only signatories were Britain, France, and the Benelux countries: Belgium, the Netherlands, and Luxembourg. As the Western European Union began deliberating, its members concluded that, for any military counterweight to the Soviet Union to be effective, it would need to embrace America. Hence the decision was taken to open its doors to the USA, and on 4 April 1949 the North Atlantic Treaty was signed in Washington DC. Along with the USA and Canada, Portugal, Italy, Norway, Denmark, and Iceland were admitted at the same time. Greece and Turkey joined in 1952. Perhaps unsurprisingly, given the nature of the then current global political climate, West Germany had to wait longer, but it finally signed up on 9 May 1955. East Germany was effectively absorbed in 1990, following the reunification of Germany a year earlier.

Given the rapid expansion of NATO and its hostility to Stalin's growing empire in the East, it was only a matter of time before the Soviet Union retaliated by establishing an equivalent organization. On 14 May 1955 it signed the

Table 10.1 Subordinate bodies of the UN

Body	Role and remit
International Court of Justice (ICJ)	Comprising fifteen judges, elected for nine years, ICJ sits in Peace Palace in The Hague, Netherlands. Hears cases referred by member states and adjudicates between warring parties.
	Several countries—including USA, France, Germany, and China—have refused to be bound by rulings.
	Most famous cases have included protracted trial of late Serbian dictator Slobodan Milošević on sixty-six charges of genocide and 'crimes against humanity', and recently opened hearings into similar charges against Bosnian Serb leaders Radovan Karadžić and Ratko Mladić.
	(Membership of Court for nine years beginning March 2007 can be found in table entitled 'The membership of the International Court of Justice (ICJ)', to be found on Online Resource Centre.)
The United Nations Economic and Social Council (ESOCOC)	Promotes cooperation between UN states on economic and social policy—all fifty-four members elected by General Assembly for three-year terms. Has president, elected for one-year term from among smaller and 'middle-ranking' states represented on the ESOCOC. Historically meets once a year for four weeks, in July, but since 1998 has also convened in April to liaise with finance ministers heading key committees of World Bank and International Monetary Fund (IMF). ESOCOC consults with 2,000 non-government organizations (NGOs) and oversees numerous agencies, including UNESCO, UNICEF, WHO, UNDP, ILO, and UNHCR.
United Nations Educational, Scientific and Cultural Organization (UNESCO)	Formed to promote cultural understanding through education, science, and arts. With 193 member states and six associate members it has more notional participants than UN itself.
	Based in Paris, with thirty other offices.
United Nations Children's Fund (UNICEF)	Formerly 'United Nations International Children's Emergency Fund', this provides urgent food and health care to children whose countries have been devastated by natural or man-made disasters. A voluntary agency, reliant for income on governments and private donations.
World Health Organization (WHO)	Established on first World Health Day, 7 April 1948, WHO coordinates international efforts to monitor outbreaks of deadly diseases like malaria, cholera, typhoid, and AIDS, sponsoring vaccination programmes and medical research. Among its famous pronouncements is 'Breast is Best' advice to mothers in developing countries to encourage use of breast milk to rear infants, rather than formula, which relies on clean water supplies to make it safe. UN-affiliated NGOs like UK-based Baby Milk Action have repeatedly come into conflict with multinational Nestlé over its alleged promotion of powdered milk.
United Nations Development Programme (UNDP)	Executive board within Assembly, funded by voluntary donations, and world's largest source of aid for investment in industrial and agricultural development.

(continued)

Table 10.1 *(continued)*

Body	Role and remit
The International Labour Organization (ILO)	Based in Geneva, Switzerland, ILO promotes opportunities for individuals to 'obtain decent and productive work, in conditions of freedom, equity, security, and human dignity'. Focus has been increasingly on unequal plight of women in developing countries.
	Meets three times a year—in March, June, and November—and holds International Labour Conference in Geneva each June.
	The ILO boasts governing body comprising representatives from twenty-eight governments, fourteen workers' groups, and fourteen employers' groups. Ten seats held permanently by USA, UK, Brazil, China, France, Germany, India, Italy, Japan, and Russian Federation; remaining ones elected by member states on three-year basis.
The Office of the United Nations High Commissioner for Refugees (UNHCR)/The United Nations Refugee Agency	Established in 1950, coordinates international efforts to protect refugees and relieve situations that might lead to indigenous peoples fleeing their countries. Employs 6,300 staff in 110 countries.

Warsaw Treaty of Friendship, Cooperation, and Mutual Assistance—better known as the 'Warsaw Pact'. This came to encompass all Soviet countries, except Yugoslavia. But, in belated recognition of the redundancy of the Warsaw Pact following the collapse of Communism in the East, on 12 March 1999 former members Hungary, Poland, and the Czech Republic joined NATO. Bulgaria, Estonia, Latvia, Lithuania, Romania, and Slovakia followed suit in March 2004, with Albania and Croatia acceding on 1 April 2009.

NATO remains based in Brussels, but as with the UN this has not stopped some countries accusing it of being in the USA's pocket. In 1958 French President Charles de Gaulle provoked its first constitutional crisis by proposing a new tripartite NATO 'directorate', headed jointly by the USA, Britain, and France. Writing to US President Dwight D. Eisenhower and then British Prime Minister Harold Macmillan, he accused them of undermining NATO's collective decision-making process through their cosy 'special arrangement'.

The North Atlantic Treaty

The foundation stone of NATO was the North Atlantic Treaty. Perhaps its most defining (and oft-cited) clause is Art. V, which sets down the principle of 'collective defence'. Its precise wording is as follows:

> The Parties of NATO agreed that an armed attack against one or more of them in Europe or North America shall be considered an attack against them all. Consequently they agree that, if such an armed attack occurs, each of them, in exercise of the right of individual or collective self-defence will assist the Party or Parties being attacked, individually and in concert with the other Parties, such action as it deems necessary, including the use of armed force, to restore and maintain the security of the North Atlantic area.

A recent invocation of Art. V came in the aftermath of the 11 September attacks on New York, when the USA argued that the terrorist strikes on the World Trade Center amounted to a military attack on the country and therefore required a joint response from NATO members. There was some dispute about whether the usual rules applied, given that precise nationalities of all the terrorists were not immediately known—making any decision to target a specific country in retaliation problematic. Having asserted an Al-Qaeda link, the USA argued that the Taliban in Afghanistan was principally answerable, since its then leader, Mullah Omar, was believed to be harbouring leaders of the Al-Qaeda movement, including Osama bin Laden.

In the event, action in defence of the USA was authorized on 4 October 2001 (despite rowdy scenes in some NATO meetings), and the alliance participated in two subsequent operations: Operation Eagle Assist and Operation Active Endeavour. The former was a series of precautionary sorties over US skies, performed by planes from thirteen NATO states. The latter was to become an ongoing naval operation in the Mediterranean Sea designed to intercept the passage of WMDs. Since Operation Active Endeavour commenced, it has involved twelve NATO members and five partner countries (Russia, Egypt, Tunisia, Morocco, and Ukraine).

Previous attempts to invoke Art. V have also failed. In 1982 Margaret Thatcher's government attempted to persuade NATO to do so in response to the Argentine invasion of the Falklands, but because those islands are located thousands of miles from the UK (in the South Atlantic) the invasion was not deemed to be an attack on Britain.

Art. V is far from defunct, though. In April 2012, the Turkish prime minister, Recep Tayyip Erdoğan, threatened to call on NATO to use Art. V to protect his country's borders from military incursions by Syria. More intriguingly, in the weeks running up to NATO's June 2011 adoption of a new 'Policy on Cyber Defence'—intended to protect member states from the perceived threat of 'cyber-terrorism' by everyone from rogue states to nuisance hackers—General Stéphane Abrial of its Supreme Allied Command Transformation used a *New York Times* editorial to outline circumstances in which the alliance might invoke Art. V against so-called 'hacktivists'. His intervention followed a series of 'security breaches' relating to senior NATO officials, including the creation of a bogus Facebook profile for its Supreme Allied Commander Europe, Admiral James Stavridis.

The North Atlantic Council (NAC)

NATO's principal governing body, the North Atlantic Council (NAC), meets twice a week: on Tuesdays for informal lunch meetings, and on Wednesdays for formal decision-making sessions. Its composition varies: on some occasions so-called 'permanent representatives' (PermReps)—salaried career diplomats from each state—will meet, but when major issues are due to be debated, member states usually send their foreign or defence ministers.

The most senior official in NATO, as in the UN, is its civilian Secretary-General, currently former Danish Prime Minister Anders Fogh Rasmussen, whose job it is to chair meetings of the NAC and to act as the alliance's public figurehead.

The Secretary-General is supported by a Deputy Secretary-General.

The Military Committee

NATO's status as an alliance focusing on security and defence-related issues means some of its operational decisions require direct input from military personnel. To facilitate this, the Organization has its own Military Committee, which (unlike the NAC) comprises members of the Armed Forces rather than civil servants. Each member state sends to its meetings a military representative (normally a chief of staff). The Committee has a permanent chairman and several subsets: an Allied Command Europe, Allied Command Atlantic, Allied Command Channel, and Regional Planning Group (for North America), each under its own 'supreme commander'.

The NATO Parliamentary Assembly

Not actually part of NATO's official structure—but created in 1955 to complement and liaise with it—the NATO Parliamentary Assembly is a fairly informal annual convention of parliamentarians/legislators (MPs) from each member state, that meets to discuss common policy issues.

▌ The Council of Europe

Founded in 1949, the **Council of Europe** predates by two years the European Union (with which it and its institutions are often confused). As such, it has the distinction of being the longest-running organization dedicated to promoting European integration and cooperation. Recognized under international law, it has forty-seven member states (twenty more than the EU to date).

Its prime purpose is to foster the adoption of common legal standards and human rights among its members. To this end, its most famous institution is the

European Court of Human Rights (ECtHR) in Strasbourg, and by far its most celebrated achievement the European Convention on Human Rights (ECHR), which the Court upholds and has brought the Council into frequent conflict with recent British governments (see pp. 10–12).

Moves to establish some form of European political and social confederation, of which the Council became the first expression, arose out of the anti-Nazi alliance forged in the Second World War. In a famous speech at the University of Zurich in 1946, Winston Churchill (at the time Britain's Leader of the Opposition, following his defeat by Labour in the 1945 election) called for the formation of a 'United States of Europe', with France and Germany at its head. Although he pointedly stopped short of suggesting Britain should be a part of this alliance—instead saying it should join with the USA in embracing it—his coining of the term is conveniently forgotten by many of his fans on the right of today's Conservative Party. In due course the Council was established by the Treaty of London, on 5 May 1949, and a 'Statute' outlining its statement of principles was signed by ten countries: Belgium, Denmark, France, Ireland, Italy, Luxembourg, the Netherlands, Norway, Sweden, and Britain.

Article 1 of this Statute declared:

> ❝The aim of the Council of Europe is to achieve a greater unity between its members for the purpose of safeguarding and realising the ideals and principles which are their common heritage and facilitating their economic and social progress. ❞

Its overall list of aims and objectives are set out in the table entitled 'The aims and objectives of the Council of Europe', which can be found on the Online Resource Centre.

▌ International trade and economy

Promoting peace is one key area of international cooperation in the modern world; the other is fostering free trade and financial investment between nations. Over and above the EU, the UN, and the Council of Europe, several key bodies were founded in the second half of the twentieth century to achieve these and related goals.

From G8 to G20

The **G8—or Group of Eight**—is not a formal body like many of the others in this list, but rather a forum comprising the world's biggest industrialized nations and military superpowers. Its membership is as follows: Canada, France, Germany, Italy, Japan, the Russian Federation, the UK, and the USA. The most recent country to join was Russia and, even today, the group sometimes convenes in its absence. On such occasions it reverts temporarily to the title 'Group of Seven' (G7).

The G8 has its origins in the seismic economic turmoil created in Europe by the 1973 oil crisis involving the USA, Japan, Britain, and other western European countries on the one hand, and the Arab members of the Organization of the Petroleum Exporting Countries (OPEC), plus two of their allies, Egypt and Syria, on the other. At the time these countries were refusing to ship oil to the West in protest over its support for Israel in the Yom Kippur War. In response, the USA convened the 'Library Group'—an informal meeting of financial experts from the USA, Britain, France, Japan, and West Germany—and in 1975 then French President Valéry Giscard d'Estaing called a summit in Rambouillet that led to the formation of a Group of Six (G6), comprising the future members of the G8 minus Canada and, obviously, Russia. Canada joined the following year.

Since then the G6 and its successors have held annual meetings at different locations in participating countries, under a rotating presidency. Although the group has no economic or constitutional powers per se, it is one of the most influential talking shops in global politics. At the G8 Summit in Gleneagles in July 2005, Mr Blair used his chairmanship to secure a £29bn boost to international aid and cancel the debt of the eighteen poorest African nations. Despite

criticisms from some campaigners, Sir Bob Geldof and Bono described the date of the agreement as 'a great day'.

More recently, Russia's ongoing membership of the G8 was briefly called into question in light of the initially belligerent foreign policy of President Dmitry Medvedev. When the country invaded Georgia in August 2008—ostensibly to protect the neighbouring territory of South Ossetia in the Caucuses from Georgian aggression—it invited widespread condemnation. There were calls from some quarters for its G8 membership to be suspended.

Since the 2008–9 global financial crisis, the G8 has been eclipsed in influence (and media coverage) by the **G20**, which announced in September 2009 its in-

tention to formally supplant the G8 as the world's main economic council of wealthy nations. This expression of confidence came five months after its most significant and heavily publicized meeting to date: a conference hosted by Mr Brown in London at which, in the teeth of mass marches by everyone from climate change protestors to the Stop the War Coalition, it reached what appeared to be firm agreement on measures to stabilize the global economy. These included an international 'Financial Stability Board', a crackdown on 'tax havens', and reform of the global banking system, bringing hedge funds and private equity firms under global regulation for the first time. In practice, though, these have yet to materialize in any tangible way.

Although the summit (and Mr Brown's chairmanship) was widely hailed a success, there has been criticism since of the sluggish implementation of its promised reforms.

The International Monetary Fund (IMF)

Like many other supranational organizations, the International Monetary Fund (IMF) was formed in response to the Second World War. It was founded in July 1944, when the representatives of forty-five governments met at Bretton Woods, New Hampshire, and its remit from the outset was intrinsically economic: to restore and maintain stability in the world's financial sector and prevent widespread recessions through mechanisms including exchange rate agreements and short-term monetary aid packages. Indeed, one of its key roles in the ensuing decades has been to provide loans to countries experiencing temporary financial blips. This money is borrowed from a pool contributed to on a rolling basis by member states.

The IMF today counts 188 countries among its members. All UN states, apart from North Korea, Cuba, Andorra, Monaco, Liechtenstein, and Nauru, are included. Kosovo joined it in 2009 and a long excluded country, Tuvalu, acceded in June 2010. Its headquarters are in Washington DC—a fact that has led to repeated accusations by some that it is effectively a puppet of the USA (a similar charge is often levelled against the World Bank).

As with most banks, including the Bank of England, the IMF has a board of governors. While every member state has a presence on the board and may vote on resolutions, as with the EU Council of Ministers some countries wield more power than others. The extent of an individual state's say on the board is governed by its 'quota' of the votes available. This relates as much to the amount of money it has contributed to the IMF in the past as its population size. Each state also has a corresponding right in relation to how much it is permitted to borrow, should it need to, from the bank's pool of finance—entitlements known as 'special drawing rights' (SDRs).

Both Britain and the USA do relatively well out of the IMF. Britain wields more than 4 per cent of the available votes, while the USA commands nearly 17 per cent. In terms of borrowing ability, the USA has access to 42,122 million SDRs and Britain 10,739—compared to just 3.1 for the Pacific island of Palau. In 1976, Labour Chancellor Denis Healey had to ask the Fund for an emergency loan to enable his government to plug a huge hole in its public finances (see p. 197).

The IMF has seen its fair share of controversy. Perhaps giving succour to criticisms that the USA and certain European countries wield a disproportionate influence on its decisions, the governing board has in the past approved significant loans to dictatorships friendly to the West. Pinochet's Chile and Musharaf's Pakistan are two of the states helped out by the Fund, despite being boycotted by other institutions and non-government organizations (NGOs) because of their alleged human rights abuses. The Fund has also been heavily criticized for imposing strict 'conditionalities' on developing countries that approach it for assistance. The most common conditionality is a 'structural adjustment programme' that essentially obliges the country seeking aid to privatize state-owned utilities and other industries as a prerequisite for its loan. Similarly contentious are the IMF's habits of charging high interest to countries judged at risk of defaulting and recalling loans at short notice—practices that helped precipitate severe financial crises in Argentina and Bolivia in the 1990s.

In May 2012, then recently appointed IMF head Christine Lagarde sparked widespread condemnation from politicians across Europe—and thousands of angry postings on her Facebook page—by using an interview with Britain's *Guardian* newspaper to criticize residents of recession-hit Greece (see pp. 293–4) for 'trying to escape tax', and contrasting their plight with those she judged worthy of 'more help', such as poor schoolchildren in Niger. It subsequently emerged that Ms Lagarde's £298,675-a-year salary is tax-free.

The World Bank

Also based in Washington DC, the World Bank was formally established on 27 December 1945. Its remit has evolved over the decades and now principally revolves around the so-called 'Millennium Development Goals' designed to eliminate child poverty and promote sustainable development in poorer countries. The Bank has five constituent parts, of which the following are the most powerful:

- The *International Bank for Reconstruction and Development* (IBRD)—originally formed to fund the rebuilding of countries devastated by the Second World War, but now primarily devoted to providing loans through secure bonds to developing countries to relieve poverty and build infrastructure. The bonds it issues are rated 'AAA' (indicating they are as secure as possible). This is guaranteed by the fact they are backed by member states' share capital.

- The *International Development Association* (IDA)—provides long-term, interest-free loans to the world's eighty-one poorest countries for help with education, health care, sanitation, clean water, and environmental protection. Since its inception it has made loans totalling nearly £80bn (on average, £4bn–14bn a year).

The World Bank, like the IMF, has encountered increasing hostility from some development charities because of the stringent conditionalities it requires before agreeing to assist struggling states. Some see the criteria it expects them to meet before recognizing them as stable business environments as an attempt to impose a Western-influenced neo-liberal economic model on nations whose indigenous institutions and sociocultural make-up do not sit easily with it. The 'five key factors' stipulated by the Bank as necessary for promoting economic growth are listed in the table entitled 'The five key objectives of the World Bank', to be found on the Online Resource Centre that accompanies this book.

In terms of the USA's influence on the Bank, a high-profile row occurred in March 2005 when then President Bush nominated his erstwhile Deputy Defence Secretary, ardent 'neoconservative' Paul Wolfowitz, to its presidency. Mr Wolfowitz was criticized during his short-lived tenure (including by his own colleagues) for trying to skew the Bank's policies on issues such as family planning and climate change towards a right-wing agenda. But by far the most significant controversy arose when it emerged he had abused his position to award a disproportionate pay rise and promotion to Shaha Riza, a former bank employee with whom he had had an affair. Mr Wolfowitz resigned in June 2007 after admitting his actions to the board of governors—although he maintained he had 'acted ethically and in good faith'.

The World Trade Organization (WTO)

Established on 1 January 1995, the World Trade Organization (WTO) replaced the General Agreement on Tariffs and Trade (GATT) originally set up after the Second World War to foster free trade and industrial harmony between member states. It is based in Geneva.

Although, theoretically, it promotes fair trade between nations, the USA has often been accused of ignoring or bypassing its rulings: the UK/EU tried to protect the Caribbean states by supporting the price of their banana exports recently, but the USA complained about this. In the end the WTO backed the USA.

More recently, America itself tried to impose tariffs on its imports of foreign steel, inflating their market price relative to domestically produced steel. Other UN nations have complained that this amounts to protectionism—a claim the WTO is investigating.

The Organisation for Economic Co-operation and Development (OECD)

Based in Paris and formerly called the 'Organisation for European Economic Co-operation' (OEEC), the OECD comprises twenty-nine industrialized member countries. It was formed in 1948, initially to help implement the Marshall Plan for the reconstruction of war-ravaged Europe, but changed its name in 1961 when the decision was taken to admit non-European members.

The OECD's primary aims are to promote global free trade, together with representative democracy, and to this end (along with the G8 and World Economic Forum) its focus is the encroachment of **globalization**—the term denoting the increasingly interdependent nature of the global economy.

As with most supranational organizations, the OECD is run by a ruling council, and has a Secretary-General and its own secretariat (Civil Service).

The World Economic Forum (WEF)

The World Economic Forum (WEF) is a not-for-profit foundation based in Geneva, the aim of which is to improve the distribution of economic opportunity throughout the world by fostering interaction between governments, businesses, academic institutions, and the arts. Its members meet each year at the Davos Symposium in Switzerland. Two hundred government leaders, 800 chief executives, and 300 assorted experts, scientists, artists, and media representatives take part in its summits.

▶ End of empire—the Commonwealth and the British Council

The British Empire may have long since collapsed, but two more benign aspects of its legacy continue, in the institutional guises of the Commonwealth and the British Council.

The Commonwealth of Nations (the Commonwealth)

Today's Commonwealth is comprised of fifty-three countries—most (but not all) former British colonies. It takes its name from a remark by Lord Rosebery, then Foreign Secretary (and future prime minister), who, on visiting Adelaide in 1884, described what remained of the UK's then crumbling empire as 'the Commonwealth of nations'. The Commonwealth's current membership is outlined in Table 10.2.

The Commonwealth's main purpose is to foster cross-cultural understanding and collaboration between some of the world's developed economies and the large number of developing nations that are also members. The broad policy areas over which it seeks to reach consensual agreement are:

- democracy;
- economics;
- education;
- gender;
- governance;
- human rights;
- law;
- treatment of small states;
- sport;

Table 10.2 Current membership of the Commonwealth

Country	Year joined
Antigua and Barbuda	1981
Australia	1931
Bahamas	1973
Bangladesh	1972
Barbados	1966
Belize	1981
Botswana	1966
Brunei Darussalam	1984
Cameroon	1995
Canada	1931
Cyprus	1961
Dominica	1978
Fiji Islands	1970 1997
The Gambia	1965
Ghana	1957
Grenada	1974
Guyana	1966
India	1949
Jamaica	1962
Kenya	1963
Kiribati	1979
Lesotho	1966
Malawi	1964
Malaysia	1957
Maldives	1982
Malta	1964
Mauritius	1968
Mozambique	1995
Namibia	1990
Nauru	1968
New Zealand	1931
Nigeria	1960 1999
Pakistan	1949 1989 2004
Papua New Guinea	1975
Saint Kitts and Nevis	1983
Saint Lucia	1979
Saint Vincent and the Grenadines	1979

(continued)

Table 10.2 (*continued*)

Country	Year joined
Samoa	1970
Seychelles	1976
Sierra Leone	1961
Singapore	1965
Solomon Islands	1978
South Africa	1931 1994
Sri Lanka	1948
Swaziland	1968
United Republic of Tanzania	1961
Tonga	1970
Trinidad and Tobago	1962
Tuvalu	1978
Uganda	1962
United Kingdom	1931
Vanuatu	1980
Zambia	1964

- sustainability;
- youth.

In addition, in 1971 the Commonwealth formally committed itself to upholding the following list of core values, by signing the Singapore Declaration, which was further cemented in 1991 with the drafting of the Harare Declaration:

- world peace and support for the United Nations;
- individual liberty and egalitarianism;
- opposition to racism;
- opposition to colonialism;
- eradication of poverty, ignorance, disease, and economic inequality;
- free trade;
- institutional cooperation;
- multilateralism;
- rejection of international coercion.

While the Queen remains head of the Commonwealth (see p. 320), she is now head of state of only sixteen of its member states (known as the 'Commonwealth realms'): Antigua and Barbuda; Australia; the Bahamas; Barbados; Belize; Canada; Grenada; Jamaica; New Zealand; Papua New Guinea; Saint Kitts and

Nevis; Saint Lucia; Saint Vincent and the Grenadines; the Solomon Islands; Tuvalu; and the UK itself. Australia narrowly voted to retain her as its sovereign in a referendum in 1999.

There have been significant ructions in the Commonwealth in recent times. South Africa rejoined in 1994 after a thirty-three-year absence following the election as president of Nelson Mandela. In contrast, Pakistan was temporarily expelled in 1999, following the military coup of then President Musharaf. Zimbabwe, meanwhile, withdrew voluntarily after previously being suspended in light of President Robert Mugabe's dubious human rights record.

Like most other supranational organizations, the Commonwealth has its own governing and administrative institutions, as listed in the table entitled 'Commonwealth institutions and their functions', to be found on the Online Resource Centre.

The British Council

The British Council is a registered charity that receives core grant aid from the FCO but earns half of its total income from teaching English, running British exams, and managing training and development contracts. It is the UK's main agency for maintaining cordial, mutually beneficial cultural relations with other nations, and, to aid it in this role, it has some 254 offices and teaching centres in 110-plus countries.

Among the technological, scientific, and artistic initiatives sponsored by the charity is the UK's entry to the Venice Biennale, which showcases the work of a leading contemporary visual artist every two years. In recent years Britain has been represented by such 'Brit Art' luminaries as Chris Ofili, Gilbert and George, and Tracey Emin. The British Council supports student exchange programmes between the UK and numerous other nations through its Central Bureau for Educational Visits and Exchanges.

Although generally perceived as a benign organization, the Council has encountered notable diplomatic difficulties in recent times. Since 1994 it has operated in Russia under an interim intergovernmental agreement focusing on the fields of education, science, and culture. But the cordial relations between the charity and the Russian authorities were abruptly cooled when, in May 2007, the British government demanded the extradition by Russia of Andrei Lugovi. Mr Lugovi had been identified as the prime suspect in the murder of Alexander Litvinenko, a former lieutenant-colonel in the Russian Federal Security Service who was poisoned with the radioactive chemical polonium-210 while staying in London in November 2006.

Having already closed all its branches in Russia, other than in Moscow, St Petersburg, and Ekaterinburg, the British Council was ordered to shut up shop everywhere except the capital in December 2007. Justifying its actions, the Russian Foreign Ministry alleged the Council was 'operating illegally' and had 'violated tax regulations, among other laws'.

☰ Topical feature idea

The number of British troops and civilian MoD personnel killed during the war in Afghanistan had reached 414 by May 2012. As the number of fatalities has risen in recent years, there have been growing rumblings of unease among military 'top brass' and backbench MPs about the prospect for any clear-cut military 'victory', and calls from Afghan President Hamid Karzai and numerous international observers for formal peace talks to be opened with the Taliban. How many British troops with links to your area have been killed or injured in Afghanistan? What do they, their friends and families, and local politicians feel about Britain's continued military presence in the country?

✳ Current issues

- **Ministry of Defence funding:** with Britain still involved in overseas conflicts, and the death toll among troops continuing to mount, the Coalition sparked huge controversy by laying out plans for a drastically 'streamlined' Armed Forces in its October 2010 strategic defence and security review. However, not all Conservative voices have been united in condemning the cuts. Even before the review was published, some commentators, such as *Guardian* columnist Simon Jenkins, have called for its budget to be axed entirely—arguing it is unnecessary in a post-Cold War age.

- **Prioritizing overseas aid spending:** the Department for International Development has managed to sidestep the deep spending cuts faced by other ministries, thanks to a Conservative election pledge to ring-fence its overseas aid budget. Despite this, in June 2010 International Development Secretary Andrew Mitchell warned the World Bank, United Nations, and twenty-eight other bodies through which £3bn a year of UK aid funding is channelled that to continue qualifying for it they needed to provide proof of value for money.

- **Future of global financial regulation under G20:** at the height of the 2008–9 global financial crisis, the G20 leaders agreed in principle to establish several new international regulatory institutions and move towards tougher rules on bank lending. However, recent summits have seen finance ministers from the world's twenty biggest economies shy away from introducing any new cross-border taxes, and firm reforms of global banking regulation remain to be implemented.

? Review questions

1. What are the main government departments responsible for overseeing Britain's participation in international affairs? Which is most significant?

2. Outline the founding principles of the UN, and the specific roles and responsibilities of its main institutions. How true would it be to say that the UN is in the pocket of the USA?

3. Outline the founding principles of NATO, and the roles and responsibilities of its main institutions. How has NATO adapted in the post-Cold War era?

4. What are the main supranational bodies responsible for overseeing the global economy and promoting free trade? Which are most influential?

5. What are the modern-day roles of the Commonwealth and the British Council?

→ Further reading

Brown, C. and Ainley, K. (2005) *Understanding International Relations*, London: Palgrave Macmillan. **Useful introduction to international relations and diplomacy.**

Evans, G. and Newnham, R. (1998) *The Penguin Dictionary of International Relations*, London: Penguin. **Indispensable A–Z of international relations jargon, covering terms ranging from 'ambassador' to 'weapons of mass destruction'.**

Jackson, R. and Sorensen, G. (2012) *An Introduction to International Relations: Theories and Approaches*, Oxford: Oxford University Press. **Succinct introduction to main political theories surrounding international relations.**

Young, J. and Kent, J. (2003) *International Relations Since 1945: A Global History*, Oxford: Oxford University Press. **Concise single-volume analysis of international relations during and since the Cold War, including overview of topics ranging from conflict in Middle East to evolution of European Union.**

Online Resource Centre

www.oxfordtextbooks.co.uk/orc/Morrison3e/

Visit the Online Resource Centre that accompanies this book for web links and regular updates.

11

Origins and structure of local government

The history of government in Britain can be rationalized into two phases: gradual unification beneath first a single monarch and then a centralized Parliament, and the more recent trend towards handing back much of the sovereign power accrued by the centre to regional and local administrations.

When the process of nation-building first began in the UK, competing kings vied with each other to extend their realms to encompass first England, then Wales, Scotland, and, in due course, Ireland. Ironically, by the time these countries were formally consolidated into a single 'United Kingdom', in the 1707 Acts of Union (see p. 10), the monarchy's power was already waning, and it was not long either before Parliament would begin ceding a significant amount of self-rule to 'the provinces'.

That said, the evolution of local government in Britain has been as much a bottom-up as a top-down process. Medieval monarchs had a vested interest in appointing locally based courts and creating titled landowners to maintain loyalty and public order among their subjects. Conversely, pressure for jurisdiction over issues as diverse as public health, road maintenance, and refuse collection to be handed to locally based individuals, guilds, and, in due course, elected councils came from the artisans and merchants whose trade and enterprise fostered the emergence of the first towns. Their motive was self-interest: without adequate sanitation, water supplies, and housing, they would have no peasants to till the land or textile workers to spin their yarn; devoid of well-kept highways, they would have no trade routes through which to export their wares to ports and markets; without local law courts to assert their ownership rights, guarding them against theft and robbery, they would have no protection for their property or wealth. Over time, these early moves towards local government were to become increasingly sophisticated and multifaceted. Today there are 433 UK local authorities—353 in England, twenty-two in Wales, and thirty-two in Scotland. Plans by Labour to cut Northern Ireland's tally from twenty-six to eleven, originally mooted for 2011 and then 2015, were finally abandoned by the Coalition in June 2010 because of ongoing disagreement within the Northern Ireland Executive.

What follows is the story of how Britain's highly developed local government framework came about.

▶ The first 'British' local authorities

Long before the emergence of anything that could be described as a 'council'—the term by which we refer to local authorities today—it suited those in power at the top of British society to maintain a rudimentary 'local government'. Even the absolutist monarchs of the early medieval period promoted this—if only to maintain a stable administration of land ownership, to collect taxes to fund wars and public building works (and food surpluses and tributes to sustain their luxury lifestyles), and to prevent anarchy at grass-roots level by upholding the rule of law (see p. 6). To this end the Saxon kings set up 'shire courts' across the countryside—local bodies with executive, legislative, and judicial powers rolled into one—and their Norman successors established a feudal system based on this, with vassals (peasants) kept in check by lords of the manor who, in time, became the squires of the seventeenth, eighteenth, and nineteenth centuries.

By the twelfth century, demographic changes had led to the emergence of the first true towns, as the population began to cluster around the newly flourishing markets and ports. With urbanization taking root, the individuals and groups whose activities provided the bedrock of their local economies—artisans, merchants, and guilds—began to see the virtue of establishing a strengthened form of local autonomy to protect their rights to land, property, and free-flowing trade routes. Their pleas were rewarded with the granting of the first 'letters patent' and 'Royal Charters'—special privileges, approved on the advice of the Privy Council, conferring the status of an 'incorporated body' (a self-governing entity) on first cities, then 'municipal boroughs' (smaller towns recognized as having legitimate claims to run their own affairs on a commercial and legal basis). These areas were run by nominally elected 'municipal corporations'.

Both cities and boroughs continue to exist to this day, albeit largely in name, as their powers have been brought in line with those of other forms of local council. In rural areas, however, the shire courts were more short-lived. Struggling to maintain the same degree of order over the local subjects as their urban equivalents—notably in the aftermath of the Black Death, which killed up to 60 per cent of the British population in the 1340s—they were eventually replaced by a new, solidified local regime: the Justices of the Peace (JPs). Unlike the shire courts, JPs' authority arose out of Acts of Parliament rather than common law and, over time, they were assisted in their work by their local 'parishes'. These bodies—comprising representatives of the local community elected by their propertied peers—were a form of embryonic local government structure, based initially around ecclesiastical parish boundaries, but they ultimately evolved into the civil parish council structure that remains in place, in diluted form, today. This is further discussed later in this chapter.

The emergence of the modern idea of local authorities

It was in the early nineteenth century, at the height of the Industrial Revolution, that a combination of commercial, political, and simple logistical pressures combined to foster the emergence of the first true local authorities.

By the close of the eighteenth century, there were some 800 boroughs, most governed by a local major (mayor) and council. Unlike today's elected mayors and councillors, who theoretically can hail from any background, class, or occupation, these were elected exclusively from among the wealthiest local merchants, industrialists, and landowners. The electorate (to the extent there was one) was limited to other equally moneyed individuals and a handful of marginally less affluent tradesmen. Such public services as existed—street lighting and road maintenance, for example—tended to be delivered largely to make conditions better for commerce.

No new charters were granted in the eighteenth century, so major emerging industrial towns and cities like Manchester and Birmingham had to make do with more limited autonomy, in the form of 'improvement commissioners' approved by Parliament. In rural areas, meanwhile, the by-then-established JP/parish combination continued to hold sway. JPs and parish councils met four times a year in so-called 'quarter sessions', which tended to take place in public houses. They collected 'rates'—a form of local taxation based on the 'rateable' (or rental) value of land and property, which continued in one form or another until the late twentieth century—from local households to pay for the following core officials:

- parish constables;
- surveyors of the highways;
- overseers of the poor.

The origins of today's local government system lie in the key Acts listed in Table 11.1.

Table 11.1 Chronology of main Acts instrumental in the emergence of local government

Act	Effect
Great Reform Act 1832	Extended right to vote in parliamentary elections to all 'ten-pound households' (those with property worth £10 or more). Abolished most 'rotten boroughs' (see p. 117).
Municipal Corporations Act 1835	Abolished pre-existing government structure in urban areas, reforming constitutions of existing municipal boroughs to standardize election methods and modus operandi. Extended voting rights in municipal elections to *all* local ratepayers—regardless of value of their properties—to prevent corporations that ran them becoming self-perpetuating oligarchies. Some 178 boroughs reformed this way, with further sixty-two towns incorporated under the Act, after petitioning Crown for borough status.
Public Health Acts 1848, 1872, 1875	First of these reforms prompted by sweeping cholera epidemics of 1840s. Central government began allocating more money to local areas for building houses and improving sanitation (domestic hygiene and sewage disposal) to combat spread of disease. Two new forms of local authority emerged, responsible for promoting sanitation in towns and country areas respectively: *urban sanitary districts* and *rural sanitary districts*. They were administered in towns by boroughs, new local boards of health, and improvement commissioners, and in rural areas by voluntary Poor Law unions (charities often run with Church involvement).
Local Government Act 1888	Set up more formal system of **county councils** to assume roles previously undertaken by JPs in quarter sessions. County (rural) areas with populations of 50,000-plus given county borough status, meaning they could continue running their own affairs, retaining privileges granted to extant municipal boroughs. Other rural areas renamed county councils. Some towns with smaller populations, such as Worthing, West Sussex, granted municipal borough status, giving them same powers of self-government as larger towns.
Local Government Act 1894	Renamed sanitary districts in towns and country areas not yet granted borough status by Crown urban and rural district councils (forerunners of today's district councils).

By 1894 the following five types of local authority—which continued in more or less the same form for the best part of eighty years—were established outside London:

- county councils;
- county borough councils;
- municipal borough councils;
- urban district councils;
- rural district councils.

▶ The rolling reorganization of local government

Since the 1970s there have been four significant reorganizations of local government:

- 1974: introduction of the two-tier structure in England and Wales;
- 1986: abolition of metropolitan counties in major urban areas;
- 1990s onwards: phased introduction of unitary authorities;
- 2000 onwards: gradual introduction of directly elected mayors in major towns and cities.

The following section examines each of these developments in more detail.

Because the evolution of local government in London and Scotland followed different trajectories from the rest of the UK, they will be looked at separately.

The 1974 reorganization

Perhaps the largest-scale restructure of the local authority framework in England and Wales (excluding London), the 1974 reorganization has its origins in the conclusions of a Royal Commission on Local Government set up in 1965 by Richard Crossman, then Minister for Housing in Harold Wilson's Labour government.

When it reported in 1969, the Commission (chaired by Lord Redcliffe-Maude) recommended that the thousand existing local authorities should be replaced by a rationalized system of sixty-one 'local authority areas', of which fifty-eight would be 'all-purpose authorities'. These would effectively be unitary authorities (see pp. 333–4), taking responsibility for all areas of local service provision. Conurbations (major urban centres where two or more towns and cities had merged to form single built-up areas) like Manchester and Birmingham would have their own two-tier *metropolitan* authorities, in recognition of their larger populations and community needs.

Labour lost the 1970 general election and the Commission's recommendations were deemed too revolutionary by Ted Heath's incoming Conservative administration. In the event, it was not until John Major's tenure as prime minister in the 1990s that unitary authorities finally began appearing. However, Heath's government recognized the need for some reform, and duly instituted this in the guise of the Local Government Act 1972, which took effect in 1974. This introduced the following:

- A **two-tier structure** of county councils and district councils, which remained the norm until the mid-1990s and still exists in some areas today. Many of the new districts subsequently applied for Royal Charters, entitling them to call themselves borough councils or city councils (like the boroughs and cities of old). This move led to the amalgamation of some district and county councils, reducing the overall number of local authorities to thirty-nine counties and 296 districts in England, with an 8:37 split in Wales.

- An alternative two-tier 'metropolitan county' local authority structure in six pilot conurbations: the West Midlands, Merseyside, Greater Manchester, West Yorkshire, South Yorkshire, and Tyne and Wear. (A breakdown of the towns and cities encompassed by each is contained in the table entitled 'The composition of metropolitan county/borough areas', to be found on the Online Resource Centre.) Each conurbation was split for administrative purposes into several 'metropolitan borough councils', each taking charge of financing and running most day-to-day local services—for example, rubbish collection, housing, and environmental health. The conurbations would each be overseen by a single 'metropolitan county council', in charge of services affecting the area as a whole, such as strategic town and country planning, main roads linking neighbouring towns, public transport, emergency services, and civil protection.

The new two-tier structure saw the end of long-standing counties like Cumberland, Westmorland, and the three different parts of Lincolnshire, and the introduction of new ones like Avon, Cleveland, Cumbria, Humberside, Clwyd, Dyfed, and Gwent. Some of these were never wholly accepted by local people, and have subsequently vanished (Avon was merged with neighbouring Somerset as part of the post-1992 unitary authority settlement). The reorganization also saw certain cities stripped of their pre-existent 'municipal borough' status. These included Nottingham, Bristol, Leicester, and Norwich—although by way of compensation they were allowed to retain the nomenclature 'city', not to mention 'lord mayors' (senior officials who perform ceremonial duties and in other towns are called simply 'mayors').

Under the rationalized two-tier structure, **district councils, borough councils,** and the new metropolitan borough councils were equivalent to each other, and were each given the same responsibilities—largely providing the most localized, 'door-to-door', services such as rubbish collection. Likewise, county councils and metropolitan county councils became responsible for providing countywide services, with social care and education being the biggest spending areas. A full breakdown of the responsibilities of the current types of local authority is outlined in Table 11.2, and a list of the central government departments at Whitehall responsible for overseeing each local authority service area is given in Table 11.3.

Northern Ireland's local government reorganization took a different form, and happened at a different pace. In 1973, twenty-six district councils emerged, but many functions were transferred from local to central government at Westminster.

The 1986 reorganization

The Tory Party's 1983 election manifesto described the six metropolitan county councils it inherited on regaining power in 1979—alongside the then Greater London Council (GLC), under the leadership of Ken Livingstone—as a 'wasteful and unnecessary tier of government'. It promised to abolish them and return their functions to the second-tier metropolitan borough councils that still existed 'beneath' them (which they redesignated 'metropolitan district councils').

To this end it passed the Local Government Act 1985, which, as well as establishing metropolitan boroughs, set up new police authorities. Tyne and Wear was unusual, in that its police provision fell under the Northumbria Police Authority. Metropolitan areas also gained their own fire and civil defence authorities and passenger transport authorities, and some acquired joint boards responsible for handling their waste disposal services. This happened in Merseyside and Greater Manchester (except Wigan), although in the West Midlands, for example, joint arrangements between neighbouring boroughs were established on an ad hoc and purely voluntary basis. In other areas commissioning and/or running public transport services and waste disposal services continued to fall under the auspices of county councils.

Other than introducing these new, service-specific types of local authority, in all other respects the effect of the 1986 changes was to replace the previous metropolitan two-tier structure with what were effectively the first unitary authorities—all-purpose councils, responsible for fulfilling the roles split in other areas between districts/boroughs and counties. Opponents of the move saw in it a clear attempt by the Conservatives to diminish the authority of metropolitan

Table 11.2 Breakdown of council services offered by different types of local authority

District councils, borough councils, metropolitan borough councils, and unitary authorities	County councils and unitary authorities
Environmental health (sanitation, drainage, pollution, food hygiene)	Education (schools and further education)
Development control (planning permission)	Social services (care for elderly, mentally ill, and vulnerable children)
Housing and the homeless	Highways (road-building, maintenance, and on-street parking)
Refuse collection (now incorporating waste for recycling)	Refuse disposal (landfill sites)
Car parks	Emergency planning
Council Tax and uniform business rate (UBR) collection	Cultural and leisure services (libraries, museums, sports centres)
Local strategic planning	Countywide strategic planning
Licensing	Passenger transport (buses, trams)

Table 11.3 Links between local authority service areas and Whitehall departments

Service area	Department responsible
Antisocial behaviour	Home Office; Department for Communities and Local Government (DCLG)
Car parks	Department for Transport (DfT)
Children's services (schools, child protection)	Department for Education; Department of Health (DH); DCLG
Council Tax and uniform business rates (UBR) collection	DCLG; HM Treasury
Cultural and leisure services	Department of Culture, Media, and Sport (DCMS)
Further education	Department for Business, Innovation, and Skills (BIS)
Emergency planning	Department for the Environment, Food, and Rural Affairs (Defra)
Environmental health (sanitation, drainage, pollution, food hygiene, waste management)	Defra; Home Office; Ministry of Defence (MoD)
Highways (road-building and maintenance)	DfT
Housing and the homeless	DCLG
Licensing	DCMS
Passenger transport (buses, trams)	DfT
Police	Home Office
Social services (care for the elderly, mentally ill, and vulnerable children)	DH
Town and country planning	Defra

councils by reducing them to lower-level, more localized administrations on the one hand, and hiving off responsibilities formerly overseen by the scrapped metropolitan counties to new bodies with clearly defined and limited scope on the other. Mr Livingstone and other left-wing council leaders, including Sheffield City Council and South Yorkshire County Council's David Blunkett (a future Labour Home Secretary), saw the diluted powers as an assault on their socialist policies by a right-wing government fearful of major populated areas becoming 'states within states'. Referring to this notion explicitly at one point in the late 1980s, Sir Cyril Irvine Patnick, Tory MP for Sheffield Hallam, famously described Mr Blunkett's domain as 'the People's Republic of South Yorkshire'.

The 1990s introduction of unitary authorities

The most significant restructuring of local authorities since the 1974 reorganization began in 1992, with the start of a process of phased change designed to rationalize local government across much of England and Wales. The aim of introducing a **unitary structure** was to improve the efficiency and transparency of local administration by reducing service duplication, slashing bureaucracy, and establishing a simplified, uniform council structure across the country. Unitary authorities, which to date number fifty-five in England, thirty-two in Scotland, and twenty-two in Wales, are defined in law as being 'any authority which is the sole principal council for its local government area'.

Despite the bold claims made in favour of the new unitary system, critics argue it has only added to the confusion, by ushering in a patchwork landscape of local government, with unitary authorities in many areas sitting directly alongside councils that have retained the two-tier structure. Counties in which both unitary and two-tier authorities coexist are described as having a **hybrid structure**. Examples include Lincolnshire, where Lincoln City Council (a unitary authority) sits beside Lincolnshire County Council and borough/district councils in nearby towns such as Grantham and Gainsborough. In East Sussex, Brighton and Hove Council is a unitary authority, while down the road Lewes District Council and Eastbourne Borough Council retain the classic borough/district responsibilities, with East Sussex County Council providing 'countywide' services. The chronology that the phased introduction of unitary authorities followed is outlined in the table entitled 'Chronology of the phased introduction of unitary authorities', to be found on the Online Resource Centre.

In addition to hybrid counties, the unitary authority system has produced other quirks. A growing number of unitary authorities encompass entire counties—notably the Isle of Wight, Rutland, County Durham, and Cornwall. The Isles of Scilly, meanwhile, have a unique form of council that, though not officially designated as such, is treated as *sui generis* ('in a class of their own').

▌ City councils and the meaning of 'city status'

Between Henry VIII's reign and the end of the nineteenth century cities were generally synonymous with ecclesiastical seats of power and, more specifically, the presence of Church of England cathedrals and diocesan bishops. But even in the Tudor period this was not always the case: in practice, city status could be conferred by the sovereign through letters patent (a legal instrument issued by a monarch), the granting of a town's Royal Charter, or even, over time, accepted custom and practice.

In the nineteenth century the Church of England actively sought to increase the number of its urban dioceses, creating more cities in the process. These included Ripon, Liverpool, St Albans, and Britain's most south-western city,

Truro. And not all towns designated as cities had prior royal borough status: Ely, for example, was a humble urban district when recognized as a city. In addition, by the close of the nineteenth century cities had begun to spring up in places that did not have cathedrals—for example, Birmingham, which successfully petitioned Queen Victoria in 1889 on the basis of its large population and history of effective local government under its charismatic Liberal mayor, Joseph Chamberlain. It was around this time that Scotland gained its first cities by letters patent and Royal Charter—prior to 1889, major medieval towns like Edinburgh and Perth were often referred to by the term 'civitas' and, although the word 'city' had been coined for them by the eighteenth century, their status remained unofficial.

Today 'city status' no longer depends on the presence of a cathedral, or any significant ecclesiastical influence. Neither are cities always major population centres: with a mere 2,000 inhabitants, Britain's smallest city, St David's in Pembrokeshire, has a population significantly lower than most towns.

For much of the twentieth century it was the Home Secretary's job to advise the monarch on which towns should be made into cities. This happened to Lancaster in 1937, Swansea in 1969 (marking the investiture of the Prince of Wales), and Sunderland in 1992 (to celebrate the fortieth anniversary of the Queen's accession to the throne). More recently, however, the rules have been bent somewhat. In December 2000 three new cities were created, in Brighton and Hove, Wolverhampton, and Inverness, as part of a 'Millennium City' competition launched by the Labour government. The Queen created a further five in 2002 to mark her Golden Jubilee—Stirling, Preston, Newport, Lisburn, and Newry. She repeated this for three more—Chelmsford, Perth, and the north Wales town of St Asaph, which boasts Britain's smallest cathedral—on the advice of the Deputy Prime Minister, Nick Clegg, in the run-up to her Diamond Jubilee. This brought the overall number of UK cities to date to sixty-nine.

Just as the criteria used to determine whether a town qualifies for city status are nebulous, so, too, is the degree to which becoming a city has any tangible effect. A **city council**—the moniker adopted by local authorities covering places with official city designation—is not a type of council or administration in itself; the term is really no more than an honorary title. In terms of their functions, city councils are actually other standard types of local authority in all but name. Some operate as unitary authorities (Brighton and Hove, York, and Stoke-on-Trent); others are metropolitan boroughs or districts (Birmingham, Wolverhampton). Most, however, remain district or borough councils in a two-tier structure.

There are several curious exceptions. Confusingly, seven English cities—Chichester, Ely, Hereford, Lichfield, Ripon, Truro, and Wells—are actually no more than civil parishes, in terms of their administrative status. This means that, technically, they fall within the remit of parish councils—the lowest tier of local government (see the next section). Similarly, in three Welsh cities (Bangor, St David's, and St Asaph) the city status applies to local community councils (the equivalent of parish councils in Wales and Scotland). In two English cities (Bath and Salisbury), meanwhile, city status is the preserve of so-called 'charter trustees'—an arcane form of local administration intended to be a temporary stopgap for towns when their borough status has been removed by the Crown prior to the formation of a parish council. A full rundown of designated cities, together with details of the type of local authority in each place, is listed in the table entitled 'Local authorities with city status and the types of council in each case', to be found on the Online Resource Centre accompanying this book.

Parish councils, town councils, and community councils

As stated above, the lowest tier of local government is represented by elected parish councils in England, and community councils in Wales and Scotland. Civil parish councils—not to be confused with the pre-existing *ecclesiastical* parishes established by the Church—were created under the Local Government Act 1894 to oversee social welfare and basic civic duties in villages and small towns, and act as the collective 'voices' of their local communities. Historically, some parish and community councils in larger villages and small towns have called themselves town councils. Those that do so tend to have their own town mayors—not to be confused with the more official (if also largely ceremonial) mayors of borough and city councils, or the directly elected mayors now found in some towns and cities (see pp. 406–7). Councillors take turns to spend a year as mayor, on rotation, with a formal 'mayor-making ceremony' often held in the town hall to mark the handover from one to another. The role of mayor is largely ceremonial (opening church fetes, switching on Christmas lights), although he/she also tends to chair full council meetings during his/her year in office.

Under the 1972 Act, all parishes with more than 150 inhabitants were compelled to have their own parish council—a stipulation that has significantly increased their number. Those with smaller populations are only required to hold **parish meetings**—regular gatherings open to all local registered electors. Unlike the meetings that might be held in towns and villages with formal parish councils, those convened in lesser populated parishes have statutory powers to act as de facto parish councils. In such circumstances a clerk and chairman are elected to preside over business.

Today many of the limited day-to-day powers once exercised by parish, community, and town councils are wielded by higher-level local authorities: county and district/borough councils or unitary authorities. But parish councils are still allocated budgets by those authorities—dubbed 'parish precepts'—which, unlike revenue raised by higher-level councils, cannot be capped by central government (see pp. 372–4). Therefore, in areas in which parish councils are more proactive, parish precepts can be high: Thurston Parish Council in Suffolk, for example, put its share of the Council Tax up by 214 per cent in 2008/9. In most areas, however, the precept is usually only sufficient to pay the rent for the town council buildings in which it holds its monthly meetings, and minor local improvements such as replacement street lights, park benches, or new goalposts for the village football pitch.

Parish councils do, however, play a significant advisory role. For example, they have a statutory right to be consulted formally by, and represented on, public inquiries into major planning applications affecting their localities. In fact, often the first time a reporter—and, by extension, his or her news organization—hears of a potentially controversial planning proposal or other council-related issue will be by attending a meeting at which it is thrashed out by his/her local parish council. And far from being mere talking shops, in truth there has been something of a resurgence in the importance of parish councils in recent years. Labour experimented with new models of service delivery, involving partnerships between neighbouring authorities and delegation of certain responsibilities to voluntary and lower-level statutory bodies, including parish councils.

In recent years the two most influential partnership initiatives were:

- local area management (LAM);
- quality parish councils.

Local area management (LAM)

LAM refers to the promotion of 'joined-up' service delivery and shared 'best practice' between neighbouring local authorities, including parish, community, and town councils. Some parish, town, and community councils have joined forces with their local district/borough, county, or unitary authorities to form 'local strategic partnerships' (LSPs) or 'local area partnerships' (LAPs). These are semi-formal alliances, designed to streamline services within individual local authority boundaries by drawing together public, private, and voluntary sector organizations to pool their resources, reduce their collective costs, and improve efficiency. LSPs are set up under the terms of local area agreements (LAAs), approved by the Department for Communities and Local Government (DCLG). At time of writing, LSPs, LAPs, and other forms of collaboration between local authorities looked to be more necessary than ever, in light of the two-year Council Tax freeze (see p. 373) and multibillion-pound public spending cuts announced in George Osborne's June 2010 Budget. Their emphasis on collaboration between public, private, and voluntary ('third') sector partners also appeared well suited to the vision of bottom-up, community-run local services envisaged by David Cameron's 'Big Society'.

Quality parish councils

Introduced by Labour in 2003, 'quality parish councils' are parish, community, or town councils that have been granted 'quality' kitemark status in recognition of their efficiency in overseeing the limited local services they have up to now provided. Their 'reward' has been additional responsibilities (matched by variable rises in budget) commensurate with their efforts to:

- represent, and actively engage with, all parts of their communities, providing vision, identity, and a sense of belonging;
- be effectively and properly managed;
- articulate the needs and wishes of their communities;
- uphold high standards of conduct;
- commit themselves to working in partnership with principal local authorities and other public service agencies;
- deliver, in proportion to their size and skills, services on behalf of principal local authorities when this represents the best deal for local communities;
- work closely with voluntary groups in their communities;
- provide leadership to their communities through their work on parish plans;
- act with their partners as information points for local services.

In practice, quality parish councils have, as a bare minimum, played a greater role than previously in organizing community-based activities, such as youth groups, childcare, home support, and transport for the elderly and disabled. More proactive ones have gone further, taking over responsibility for delivering on the ground many of the services funded by their principal local authority (or authorities), such as libraries or buses. They are also expected to draw up and publish a parish plan, outlining medium- and long-term proposals for their area. In many ways, quality parish councils were a prototype of the 'Big Society' initiatives outlined below.

Service users as 'service owners'—the dawn of the 'Big Society'

With the advent of the Coalition came a new emphasis—part philosophical, part pragmatic—on the idea that lower-tier authorities like parish, town, and community councils, and ultimately communities themselves, should become more involved in the 'ownership', management, and/or delivery of their own local services. The so-called 'Big Society' idea was a product of the thinking of a number of 'blue-sky' policy advisers, including Mr Cameron's (now former) Director of Strategy, Steve Hilton, and Phillip Blond, Director of the centre-right think tank ResPublica and writer of an influential 2009 pamphlet entitled *Red Toryism*. The

'Big Society' proposed a return to a more traditional brand of grass-roots, communitarian conservatism (in a broadly similar vein to Lord Glasman's musings on 'Blue Labour'—see p. 153). In hard policy terms, the Coalition has since introduced four so-called 'community rights', allowing community groups and lower-tier councils (known collectively as 'relevant bodies') to bid to take over running local services they deem to be poorly run, or physical assets they would like to maintain themselves. For a fuller explanation of 'community rights', see Chapter 13.

▌ Evolution of local government in London

London's autonomy has always been exercised in a distinct way from the rest of Britain, although at times its local government structure has resembled that of the major English conurbations described earlier in this chapter. Today London operates under a unique two-tier system, with responsibilities for service provision split between the **Greater London Authority (GLA)**, headed by the capital's elected mayor, and thirty-three second-tier councils (a system akin to the pre-1986 metropolitan county/borough structure abolished by Mrs Thatcher's government).

Of these thirty-three councils, thirty-two are London boroughs, elected in similar fashion to the metropolitan boroughs that still operate in the other conurbations, but the last is a unique entity run by an unreformed medieval-style City old boys' network. The City of London Corporation—officially, the 'Mayor and Commonalty and Citizens of the City of London'—is Britain's oldest surviving local authority. It covers the 'Square Mile' containing the capital's central financial district and, although democratically accountable like other local authorities, has long attracted criticism for the anachronistic nature of its electoral processes and its peculiar customs (see p. 346).

The City of London was the only corporation to escape the axe when the Municipal Corporations Act 1835 abolished all others, and it continues to be presided over by a non-partisan administration of a kind that prevailed more widely before the emergence of formal political parties (see Chapter 5). At its head is the Lord Mayor of London, his attendant aldermen, and a Court of Common Council, beneath which is a range of committees responsible for specific areas of local policy. Again uniquely, the City of London Corporation was allowed to retain a system of *non-residential voting* (often referred to as the 'business vote') after this was abolished elsewhere in 1969. This concession was, in part, in recognition of its tiny resident population (some 7,400 at the time of the 2011 census). (A fuller explanation of the voting system used here and elsewhere in London is given in Chapter 14.)

Vocal critics of the Corporation—which many see as a self-perpetuating, privileged cabal—include Labour backbencher John McDonnell (an unsuccessful candidate for the party's leadership following first Tony Blair's, then Gordon Brown's, resignations). In the debate over the City of London (Ward Elections) Act 2002, which significantly increased the size of the business franchise in the capital, he said of it:

> ❝ The corporation is a group of hangers-on, who create what is known as the best dining club in the City . . . a rotten borough. ❞

A timeline of the evolution of local government in London is presented in Table 11.4.

Modern-day local government structure in London

As with devolution for Scotland, Wales, and Northern Ireland, Labour advocated the re-establishment of a single overarching local authority for London long before winning the 1997 election. The 1986 abolition of the Greater London Council (GLC), under its then leader Ken Livingstone, had been seen by some in the party as an act of war by the Conservative government. Others had viewed it as an error of judgement that needed redressing for more pragmatic reasons should their party regain power.

In its 1997 manifesto Labour pledged to introduce a new form of 'elected city government', topped by an EU-style elected mayor. A year after regaining power, the promised vote was held, and 72 per cent of London's electorate voted in favour of the proposed GLA. A year later the Greater London Authority Act 1999 formally paved the way for the establishment of the new authority and, with more than a hint of déjà vu, Mr Livingstone was duly elected London mayor in March 2000.

Mr Livingstone's return to power in the capital was hardly smooth. As had happened (with variable success) in Wales and Scotland, the Labour leadership attempted to parachute in a cherry-picked candidate, in defiance of his support among the party rank and file. But its official choice, former Health Secretary Frank Dobson, was no match for the former GLC leader, who resigned his parliamentary seat and the Labour whip to fight for the mayoralty as an independent. In the event, he returned to the party fold before his 2004 re-election, by which time Mr Blair had reluctantly endorsed him as Labour's prospective candidate.

Although the GLA has become a model for certain other towns and cities that have since adopted elected mayors (see Chapter 13), initially its method of conducting business was unique among British local authorities. In a manner akin to the way the US president shares power with that country's parliament (Congress), the London mayor is elected separately to the twenty-five-strong London Assembly with which he shares power over the GLA. As with the US president, it is the mayor's job to propose policy and set out a prospective annual budget to cover the cost of the services he/she proposes

Table 11.4 Timeline of the evolution of local government in London

From	Legislation	System
1835	Municipal Corporations Act 1835	The small, ancient, self-governing City of London remains unreformed by legislation covering the other major city corporations and does not expand into the growing metropolitan area surrounding it. Area now known as Greater London is administered by parishes and hundreds in counties of Middlesex, Essex, Kent, Surrey, and Hertfordshire, with very little coordination between them. Special areas, such as the Liberty of Westminster, are exempt from county administration. In other areas, ad hoc single-purpose boards are set up.
1855	Metropolis Management Act 1855	Metropolitan Board of Works created to provide the infrastructure needed in the area now known as Inner London. Its members are nominated by the vestries and boards.
1889	Local Government Act 1888	County of London created from the area of responsibility of the Metropolitan Board of Works. A London County Council shares power with the boards and vestries, but the City of London is outside its scope. Croydon and West Ham (and, later, East Ham) become county boroughs outside the County of London, but also outside control of newly formed Surrey and Essex county councils.
1894	Local Government Act 1894	Rest of England, including area around 'County of London' and county boroughs (but not within it), divided into urban districts and rural districts. In Greater London area, they are consolidated over next seventy years into municipal boroughs and urban districts, with no rural districts remaining. Many districts later become populous enough to apply for county borough status, but are rejected. Royal Commission on the Amalgamation of the City and County of London attempts, but fails, to facilitate the merger of the City and County of London.
1900	London Government Act 1899	Metropolitan boroughs created within County of London, their functions shared with London County Council. Existing vestries, boards, and liberties in the area are abolished.
1965	London Government Act 1963	Enlarged Greater London replaces County of London, the county boroughs, and all local government districts within twelve-mile radius. The mostly strategic Greater London Council shares power with thirty-two London boroughs and City of London.
1986	Local Government Act 1985	Greater London Council abolished and London boroughs work as unitary authorities with strategic functions organized by joint boards and quangos. Residual Inner London Education Authority remains for inner area, but is abolished during national reform of education.
2000	Greater London Authority Act 1999	Regional Greater London Authority, consisting of Mayor of London and London Assembly, assumes strategic function, sharing power with London boroughs and City of London.

to provide in the coming financial year. The Assembly must then approve or amend these proposals, in the manner of Congress, and its committees and subcommittees (like their Congressional equivalents) may scrutinize the mayor's actions in office and the performance of services provided by the GLA. The parallels between the London mayoral and US parliamentary systems have gone further in recent years, in light of changes to the political composition of both. Just as President Barack Obama (a Democrat) spent the second half of his first presidential term fighting to get the more contentious aspects of his legislative programme through a Republican-dominated House of Representatives, Mr Livingstone had to work with Conservatives following the 2004 elections (nine members to Labour's seven). The re-election of his successor, the Conservative Boris Johnson, in May 2012 promised a period of renewed tension between the mayor's office and a Labour-led Assembly.

The GLA is the top tier of local government in London, with individual boroughs continuing to provide day-to-day services for Londoners. The division between the roles of the GLA and boroughs is explained in Table 11.5; of the major roles fulfilled by the GLA, the majority are overseen by the agencies listed in Table 11.6.

Table 11.5 Breakdown of local authority responsibilities in London

Greater London Authority (GLA)	London boroughs
Transport	Schools and further education (FE)
Policing	Social services
Fire and rescue	Waste collection
Congestion charging	Highways repair and maintenance
Environmental policy	Libraries and local leisure and cultural services (museums, theatres)
Strategic development and planning	Development control

Table 11.6 Main agencies of the Greater London Authority (GLA)

Agency	Responsibilities
Transport for London (TfL)	Manages most aspects of London's transport system, including public transport (London Underground, Docklands Light Railway, London Buses), main roads, and traffic management (incorporating the congestion charge zone)
Metropolitan Police Authority (MPA)	Oversees Metropolitan Police Service
London Fire and Emergency Planning Authority (LFEPA)	Administers London Fire Brigade and coordinates emergency planning

The London Development Agency (LDA), which held responsibility for strategic development planning and rejuvenation of infrastructure across the capital, was abolished in March 2012, and its powers transferred direct to the Mayor's Office.

▶ Local government in Scotland

As with several other aspects of public affairs—notably its legal and education systems, the latter of which is explored in Chapter 15—Scotland has a different local government framework to the rest of Britain.

Until the 1974 reorganization the country effectively had a single-tier form of local administration. The Local Government (Scotland) Act 1929 had replaced the pre-existing parish councils with a nationwide network of district councils with significantly increased autonomy and budgets. This structure, refined by the Local Government (Scotland) Act 1947, distinguished between smaller and larger 'burghs', which were a form of local unit derived from medieval administrative boundaries. The latter—burghs with populations greater than 20,000—were handed more power.

All this changed with the passage of the Local Government (Scotland) Act 1973, which ushered in a two-tier system along the lines of that implemented in England and Wales. The district councils remained, albeit with slightly refined borders and some variation in their levels of responsibility, but the higher-tier authorities introduced were named 'regional councils', as opposed to county councils. Three notable exceptions—the Western Isles, Shetland, and Orkney—were, however, effectively given unitary status even at this early stage, in recognition of their perceived homogeneity.

When Mr Major's government began its phased reorganization of local authorities in the early 1990s, Scotland was again treated as an exception. In a 'Big Bang' approach that ministers avoided elsewhere, unitary authorities were introduced across the country in one fell swoop. While rationalizing a patchwork system, this 'one-size-fits-all' strategy caused controversy in some areas—not least because of the wildly varying population sizes covered by individual councils. The unitary authority for Inverclyde (an area with relatively few inhabitants) followed the same boundaries as the extant district council, while that of Clackmannanshire embraced the whole of that county—and that of Highland a sprawling 30,650 km swathe of north-west Scotland, encompassing chunks of the former counties of Inverness-shire, Ross and Cromarty, Caithness and Nairnshire, as well as the whole of Sutherland.

Today there are thirty-two 'council areas' covered by unitary authorities in place across the country. In May 2012 a report by the Reform Scotland think tank recommended reducing the number of councils to nineteen, and giving them extra responsibilities by abolishing the existing health and police boards. In justifying its proposals, it cited the 'crisis' in Scottish local government high-lighted by poor turnout in that month's local elections.

◗ Emergency services at the local level

→
see also
central
government
pp. 253–4.

While ambulance services are today part of the National Health Service (NHS), with trust status akin to that accorded to hospitals, the other core emergency services are overseen by discrete forms of authority.

Origins of the British police force

Until the early nineteenth century Britain had no countrywide police force. Instead local law and order fell to town magistrates to maintain, and before then, ad hoc arrangements had existed. Perhaps unsurprisingly, London was the first UK city to adopt its own police force. In 1749 the author Henry Fielding and his brother, Sir John, set up a group of semi-professional law enforcers known as 'The Bow Street Runners'. Operating out of Henry's house at 4 Bow Street, these early police officers wore civilian clothes and did not patrol the streets routinely like their modern-day equivalents. Rather, they acted to intercept criminals and bring them before the courts on the authority of local magistrates, who had become increasingly frustrated at their inability to prevent offenders absconding and enforce punishment without the help of an arresting force.

Shortly afterwards, an embryonic Thames Police was formed, partly based on the model established by the Fielding brothers. It was not until some eighty years later, however, when Sir Robert Peel was Home Secretary, that the first true constabulary was formed in the guise of the Metropolitan Police, based at Scotland Yard. Established in 1829 and variously dubbed the 'Bobbies' and the 'Peelers' after their founder, the 'Met' were funded by a local tax—'the police rate'—which citizens were obliged to pay in addition to the 'poor rate' (used to fund limited handouts for the poorest members of society and to finance work-houses). In due course similar innovations followed in the emerging borough council areas and with the introduction of a new breed of county magistrates.

Today the UK Police Service, although notionally a nationwide organization, is actually divided into thirty-nine local forces in England and four in Wales. Scotland has had eight regional forces since 1967, but in June 2012 the Scottish Parliament formally approved the merger of all police and fire forces north of the border into single services from as early as 2013, as a result of Whitehall-directed budget cuts. Northern Ireland has its own dedicated police force, dubbed the Police Service of Northern Ireland, which replaced the erstwhile

Royal Ulster Constabulary (RUC) in November 2001. Most forces in England, Scotland, and Wales have historically respected county boundaries, although there have long been some exceptions: a single force, Sussex Police, covers the two counties of East and West Sussex, while the south-westernmost force is Devon and Cornwall Police. In 2006, then Home Secretary Charles Clarke proposed merging a number of forces (among them the five existing East Midlands forces, which would be turned into a single 'super-force'), bringing down the total number in England and Wales to just twenty-four, in an effort to streamline the Service and better equip the country to fight terrorism. His plans—heavily criticized by both the Police Federation (the union representing police officers) and the Association of Chief Police Officers (ACPO)—were shelved by his successor, John Reid, later that year, although a White Paper published in December 2009 signalled the then Labour administration's determination to cut £500m from the police budget by 2014 by, among other things, encouraging them to collaborate in areas such as forensics and procurement (recruitment, commissioning, and investment). More recently, individual police forces in certain regions have voluntarily entered into negotiations about possible mergers. At time of writing, talks were ongoing between the Durham and Northumbria forces.

Police force accountability: from authorities to commissioners

Other than in London, where the Metropolitan Police Authority was handed executive control over the Met by ministers in the Greater London Authority Act 1999, UK police forces all come under the overarching control of the Home Secretary (or, in Scotland, the Deputy First Minister). Until 1995 forces were regulated by police committees answerable to their local county councils or unitary authorities, but the advent of the Police and Magistrates' Court Act 1994 saw these replaced by a new second tier: the police authority. The change, consolidated by the Police Act 1996, reduced the involvement of councillors from relevant local authorities in favour of a mixed membership intended to represent local residents and the business community better.

Police committees were made up entirely of officials—usually two-thirds councillors and one-third magistrates, while the typical composition of a police authority involved nine councillors, three magistrates, and five 'independent' members co-opted from the local civilian and business communities.

A police authority would raise its revenue by levying precepts (annual budget requests) on its local billing authority, which were then included explicitly in local Council Tax bills (see Chapter 12). Their responsibilities included maintaining effective and efficient forces for their areas (with the Home Secretary and/or Home Office Inspectorate empowered to 'act in default' if they failed); appointing and holding to account their local chief constables and assistant chief constables; and convening regular open public meetings along the lines of those held by local authorities, at which their members were expected to answer questions on their activities.

As of 15 November 2012 the role of police authorities is due to be assumed by new US-style directly elected **police and crime commissioners (PCCs)**, in a highly contentious move condemned by some, including Sir Hugh Orde, president of the Association of Chief Police Officers, as 'politicizing' the police. The specific duties of PCCs, as set out under the Police Reform and Social Responsibility Act 2011, are as follows:

- setting the strategic accountability and direction for policing;
- working with partners to prevent and tackle crime;
- invoking the voice of the public, the vulnerable, and victims;
- contributing to resourcing of policing response to regional and national threats;
- ensuring value for money.

As well as the controversy flowing from the introduction of commissioners—many of whom stood for election on explicitly party-political platforms—there was considerable colour. In the run-up to the closure of nominations for the positions, an eclectic array of politicians, former police officers, and even celebrities were rumoured to be considering running for office—among them former Labour deputy leader Lord Prescott (who eventually stood in Humberside), serving Mayor of Middlesbrough Ray Mallon, and Nick Ross, ex-presenter of BBC1's *Crimewatch* programme. Colonel Tim Collins, one of the most senior Army officers to serve in the Iraq War, began the race as Tory candidate for Kent, before pulling out in May 2012 because of his inability to commit to attending all the required selection meetings.

The new commissioners were established in only forty-one of the existing forty-three English and Welsh police force areas. The City of London (as with so many special liberties) was exempt from the arrangement on historical grounds, while the role of commissioner for the capital as a whole was automatically assumed by the mayor, Mr Johnson.

Northern Ireland's Police Service continues to be overseen by an independent Police Board.

The role of chief constables

Chief constables have always had statutory responsibilities separate from those of their governing committee or authority. It is their role to deliver the policies agreed by their police authority on the ground. This entails appointing all officers in their force below the rank of assistant chief constable, producing an annual report on their performance in the preceding twelve months (covering specific categories of offence, along with other areas highlighted as being of local concern, like violent crime), and disciplining officers for misconduct.

In operational terms it is the job of the chief constable and his/her assistants to manage the force's budget, hire and fire other officers, and ensure that personnel are suitably allocated to maintain adequate patrols across the force area. But over the past twenty years, as both population levels and the range of responsibilities faced by the police have increased out of proportion with rises in the number of officers, successive governments have tried to remove some of the burden of more mundane patrol duties from the professionals by bolstering them with semi-trained back-up officers recruited by police authorities from the local community. These include part-time volunteers known as 'special constables' or 'specials' and semi-trained policemen and women introduced by the Blair government called **police community support officers (PCSOs)**.

As of the last detailed survey, conducted in October 2007, some 13,500 PCSOs were employed across England and Wales—including 3,700 in London alone. In November that year they were given enhanced powers—partly in response to complaints by senior police officers that their trained staff were overstretched due to increased paperwork generated by legislation designed to make the stop-and-search and arrest procedures more transparent. Although they are entitled to paid overtime, a minimum of twenty-one days' annual leave, and various other benefits, PCSOs earn significantly less than fully trained officers. Starting salaries for professional police constables (PCs), the lowest rank, are around £22,000; in contrast, a PCSO will initially earn about £16,000. This fact—combined with evidence that police recruitment has been failing to keep pace with government targets in recent years—has led to many critical newspaper headlines about perceived underfunding of the police service.

In addition to PCSOs, Labour introduced another layer of partially trained, community-based officials, in the guise of 'neighbourhood wardens'. A type of glorified Neighbourhood Watch coordinator, these uniformed individuals, employed by councils or housing associations, were an initiative of the DCLG's Neighbourhood Renewal Unit. They were introduced to patrol, and be otherwise readily available, in areas with large numbers of elderly and/or vulnerable residents—particularly those notorious for property crime, graffiti, and antisocial behaviour (ASB). After 2005 both PCSOs and wardens began working alongside fully qualified police officers on the one hand, and groups of volunteers on the other, in a new breed of de facto police force called a *neighbourhood policing team* (also known as 'safer neighbourhood teams' and 'safer, stronger community teams'). Around 3,600 were subsequently set up across England and Wales.

PCSOs today have considerable clout. They are authorized to issue summary fixed-penalty notices on members of the public for offences ranging from littering and cycling on footpaths to failing to keep their dogs under control. Under the authority vested in them by Labour's 'Respect' agenda, they may also require names and addresses from people they apprehend for antisocial behaviour—for example, fighting or swearing in the street. These details may subsequently be used by police or local authorities to apply to magistrates' courts for permission to impose **antisocial behaviour orders (ASBOs)** on individuals. ASBOs are civil penalties in the first instance, but individuals who breach their conditions—for example, by failing to respect curfews or remaining resident at prohibited addresses—may be prosecuted for criminal offences. The Crime and Disorder Act 1998, which introduced ASBOs, defines antisocial behaviour as conduct that:

> 66 caused or was likely to cause alarm, harassment or distress to one or more persons not of the same household as him or herself and where an ASBO is seen as necessary to protect relevant persons from further anti-social acts by the defendant. 99

Towards the end of Labour's reign, the ASBO concept was extended to tackle lower-level problematic behaviour, through *acceptable behaviour contracts* (ABCs). These were agreements that young people identified as having previously acted in an antisocial way were asked to sign, with input from their parents or guardians, pledging to change their ways and/or take specified action to make amends.

In addition to being able to impose orders and contracts on named individuals, both neighbourhood wardens and PCSOs were given power (like ordinary police officers) to apply to councils for *dispersal orders* to cover locations judged to be antisocial behaviour 'black spots'. Groups of two or more people alleged to be causing 'harassment, alarm, or distress' may be forcibly broken up and/or moved on from a location under the terms of such orders. Failure to comply can lead to fines of up to £2,500. As with ASBOs, breaching the terms of a dispersal order may lead to prosecution.

Police could also obtain and enforce *designated public places orders* (DPPOs)—a variation on the dispersal order concept designed to clear specific streets, squares, or alleyways of drink-related antisocial behaviour. Anyone caught drinking in these locations who refuses to surrender his/her alcohol is liable for a £50 fixed penalty, or for arrest and a fine of up to £500.

Despite the widespread ridicule with which news of some ASBOs was greeted in the media (a man was banned from his own home after being given one for playing his music too loudly, while several have been imposed on grumpy pensioners for relatively minor 'offences' such as cursing at their neighbours), they proved hugely popular among law enforcement agencies and many local communities blighted by unruly behaviour. According to Home Office figures, 18,566 ASBOs were issued in total between their introduction in April 1999 and January 2011. Embarrassingly for ministers, though, some 10,380 of these had been breached by their recipients at least once. Despite this, Labour had continued to use the popularity of the orders as a springboard to expand the scope of its ASB crackdown, by increasing the range of 'misdemeanours' for which summary penalties could be issued by police and local authorities, and giving parish and community councils powers to impose them.

In May 2012, however, Home Secretary Theresa May outlined the latest of several sets of proposals from the Coalition to replace them with alternative measures, which she argued would be both easier to police and more demanding of those who received them. The two principal orders due to supersede ASBOs were as follows:

- **criminal behaviour order (CBO)**—the imposition of a 'ban' on forms of behaviour designated as ASB, with the ability to 'force' people to undertake programmes, such as drug or alcohol rehabilitation courses, designed to improve their conduct;
- **civil crime prevention injunction (CCPI)**—a 'fast-track' ASBO to be used for lower-level ASB, and which can be imposed more quickly (within days or hours of an 'offence' being committed) while requiring a lower standard of proof than ASBOs.

A range of other measures was also set to be tried out in the government's three chosen pilot areas—Manchester, Brighton and Hove, and West Lindsey in Lincolnshire—including *community protection notices* (CPNs) to penalize people judged to be blighting their local community, for instance by leaving piles of refuse in their gardens or driveways.

The police complaints process

Allegations of misconduct initially follow the same process as other complaints about the local police force. This process is outlined in Figure 11.1.

All cases involving deaths in police custody or at the hands of officers in the community—for example, the shooting of a drug dealer—are automatically passed to the **Independent Police Complaints Commission (IPCC)**. Even when matters are handled locally by the chief constable or the police authority, the IPCC may intervene if dissatisfied with the choice of investigating officer. Alternatively, it will approve his/her appointment by issuing an 'appropriate statement'.

Taking disciplinary action is a matter for the local commissioner in relation to the most senior officers, or the chief constable in relation to all others. The authority has to follow a formal disciplinary procedure, and can impose sanctions on senior officers (including chief constables). If a chief constable indicates he/she is *unwilling* to take action where the IPCC has become involved, the Commission can *direct* him/her to do so. Disciplinary charges imposed on officers are heard by chief constables (unless it is they, or an assistant chief constable, who are accused) and punishment can include cautions, demotions, or in certain cases dismissal. There is a right of appeal from the chief constable's decision—and this must go to a police disciplinary appeals tribunal. In the last resort, members of the public left unhappy by the way a complaint has been dealt with may apply to the courts for a private summons to prosecute the officers concerned (as was attempted unsuccessfully by the family of

Figure 11.1 Flow chart outlining the police complaints process

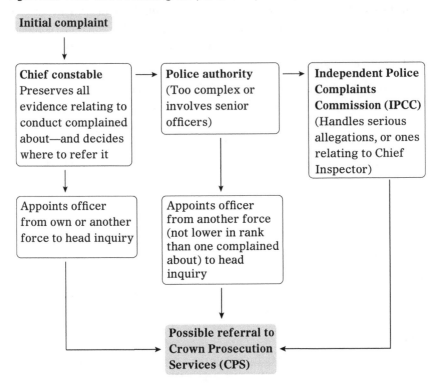

Mr De Menezes, prior to their successful private prosecution of the Met for breaching health and safety legislation).

In recent years there has been some controversy over the stringent 'standard of proof' required before disciplinary charges may be brought. This is illustrated by the stark contrast between the wording of the 'civil' standard—which applies in most employment-related situations—and the 'police' standard. The former is worded thus:

> ❝Is it more likely than not, on the balance of probabilities, that the police officer committed the disciplinary offence? ❞

The latter reads:

> ❝Did the police officer commit the disciplinary offence, beyond all reasonable doubt? ❞

Fire and rescue authorities

In contrast to the police (which, although divided into local forces, all fall under the umbrella of one national police service), technically speaking fire and rescue services—or 'fire brigades' as they once were—are entirely locally based. In common with the police, they are managed by a separate authority, but unlike it they do not have their own discrete body. Instead, in two-tier areas, the 'fire and rescue authorities' are usually county councils, but for fire services based in unitary areas, 'combined' fire authorities are established. In metropolitan areas, fire services are overseen by separate fire and civil defence authorities (as in London). Table 11.7 is a timeline outlining the history of Britain's fire services.

An important distinction between fire services that fall under county councils and combined fire authorities (and fire and civil defence authorities) is that the former are supervised by county council committees and have their budgets managed by them, while the latter two determine their own budgets like

Table 11.7 Timeline for emergence of UK fire services

Year	Event
Before 1938	Ad hoc volunteer fire brigades set up by local parish and town councils and fire insurance companies (latter only fought fires in houses belonging to their policyholders—indicated by a 'fire mark' plaque fixed to exteriors of homes).
1938	Fire Brigades Act makes it compulsory for county borough councils, non-county borough councils, and urban district councils to provide fire brigades.
1939–45	All fire brigades combined for duration of Second World War into one National Fire Service.
1947	Fire Services Act returns all fire brigades to local authority control, this time under auspices of county councils (designated 'fire authorities').
1963	London Government Act updates above by creating GLC in London.
1972	Metropolitan county councils designated as fire authorities in relevant areas by the Local Government Act.
1985	Local Government Act abolishes GLC and metropolitan counties, and creates seven 'fire and civil defence authorities'. In six metropolitan areas these comprised councillors nominated by each new metropolitan borough council, with numbers based on size and political balance of each authority. In London one councillor was nominated from each of thirty-two boroughs, plus one from City of London.
1992	Rolling reorganization of local government ushers in new combined fire service authorities in unitary areas.
2000	Formation of Greater London Authority sees pre-existing fire and civil defence authority replaced by new London Fire and Emergency Planning Authority (LFEPA).
2004	Fire and Rescue Services Act harmonizes fire service provision across England, introducing new Fire and Rescue National Framework (including services for which they may charge) from that July, and devolved responsibility for fire services to Wales (this had already happened in Scotland and Northern Ireland). Reserve powers introduced enabling government, if necessary, to set up new independent bodies to oversee negotiations over firefighters' pay and conditions.
2012	Police and Fire Reform Act (Scotland) agrees to merge all Scottish fire services into single service from as early as 2013.

police authorities. They are, however, answerable to the Secretary of State for Communities and Local Government.

It is the Communities Secretary's role to check each year the establishment schemes in place in each fire service area—that is, the level and precise nature of provision it makes available to local people. In law, all fire services must:

- equip and train a firefighting force;
- make arrangements for dealing with calls for help;
- gather information about local 'risk' buildings—for example, high-rises, timber-framed structures, or ones housing large numbers of elderly or disabled people;
- give advice on fire protection to the business community, local schools, etc.;
- make sure that any local water companies maintain an adequate supply of water at a pressure suitable for firefighting;
- draw up mutually beneficial 'reinforcement schemes'—that is, pool their resources—with neighbouring fire services to help them to deal with major fires.

Fire services are also called on to deal with other emergencies in addition to blazes. These so-called 'special services' are divided into two broad categories: humanitarian (for example, serious road accidents and floods) and non-humanitarian (less urgent calls, such as a request to help a resident gain access to their home after leaving their keys inside). Whereas firefighters would once willingly answer calls to scale trees in pursuit of errant cats, it has become increasingly commonplace for today's fire services to charge for such 'non-essential' operations.

Under the Fire Precautions Act 1971, various types of premises are now barred from operating without an official fire service seal of approval in the form of a fire certificate. These are issued, after an inspection, by the fire authorities. The types of premises affected include:

- offices;
- sports grounds;
- hotels;
- theatres.

Other Acts passed to increase fire safety include:

- the Public Health Act 1936—which stipulated that fire escapes must be provided in buildings such as hotels and theatres;
- the Fire Safety and Safety of Places of Sport Act 1987—which introduced tough new seating standards in the aftermath of the 1985 Bradford City Football Club tragedy (including a cut in attendance limits at UK football grounds).

Emergency planning and civil defence

The aspect of 'emergency services' provision in which local authorities have historically been most directly involved is the broader category of contingency planning and civil defence. The notion of 'civil defence' in particular—namely, the idea that councils might be expected to help to protect citizens against enemy attack or other forms of security emergency—arose in the aftermath of the Second World War. As a policy, it was initiated by the post-war Labour government, but has remained largely a notional responsibility in 'peacetime'—perhaps its most tangible application being the plans for a hypothetical nuclear attack expected to be updated by local authorities at various junctures during the Cold War. Notable exceptions included the strategies employed to safeguard London's population from terrorist bombs during the Troubles and the measures that had to be implemented following the Real IRA's attack on a Manchester shopping centre in 1996. In this age of increased security threats, however, it is not hard to imagine a time when renewed importance may be attached to civil defence departments.

As recently as 2004, a new Civil Contingencies Act effectively replaced the entire body of existing emergency planning legislation on the statute book. The most significant aspect of the shake-up, ordered by then Secretary of State for Transport, Local Government, and the Regions John Prescott, was the new requirement placed on so-called 'responder' organizations in each local area to appoint a full-time **emergency planning officer** (sometimes known as a 'civil contingencies officer', 'civil protection officer', or 'resilience officer') to coordinate the measures that would be implemented in the event of a civil emergency. As well as security threats, civil emergencies might include any number of natural or man-made disasters: for example, floods, major fires, landslides, or nuclear accidents. Responder organizations are divided under the Act into 'Category 1' and 'Category 2'. The list of bodies in each category is outlined in the table entitled '"Responder" bodies that are required to appoint emergency planning officers', which can be found on the Online Resource Centre that accompanies this book.

The history of local government's involvement with civil defence began with the passage of the Civil Defence Act 1948, under which the Home Secretary was empowered to direct local authorities to take 'appropriate measures' to ensure the civil defence requirements for their populations were met. These were further defined by the Civil Defence (Planning) Regulations 1974, which gave county councils the power to 'make plans to deal with hostile attacks' and, in certain circumstances, to prepare for war, in consultation with boroughs/districts. It was only in the 1990s, after the end of the Cold War, that the term 'emergency' was explicitly redefined to cover peacetime disasters such as floods. Finally, in 2001, responsibility for civil defence shifted from the Home Secretary to a new Cabinet Office Coordination Unit.

A further type of agency involved in preparing for civil emergencies is the recently formed 'regional resilience board'. Sometimes referred to as 'regional control and resilience boards', these are joint bodies drawing together representatives from local police forces, fire service authorities, and council civil defence departments to oversee overall emergency planning for entire regions. The 2004 Act also required responder organizations to set up collaboratively more localized versions of the regional boards—'local resilience forums' (LRFs)—based in each police area. Each is expected to produce a community risk register that is specific to their area, outlining particular localities, buildings, businesses, or residential areas that are seen to be particularly vulnerable. They are overseen at national level by a new executive agency in the Cabinet Office: the Civil Contingencies Secretariat.

The government's much-vaunted new 'resilience' strategy for the country was prompted, in large part, by the 11 September 2001 terrorist attacks and the 2004 Madrid bombings (not to mention persistent fears of an avian flu pandemic, which have been periodically publicized by the media since 2003). But this new state of preparedness failed to prevent the 7 July 2005 attacks on London. And more embarrassing still for ministers was the organizational chaos and buck-passing between local authorities, the Environment Agency, and central government that greeted the widespread winter floods that devastated parts of Britain in 2007 and 2009.

At the top of the chain of command for emergency planning is an ad hoc government committee, codenamed 'Cobra' and headed by the prime minister, which meets in a Cabinet Office briefing room whenever necessary. (Despite its James Bond-style title, the acronym actually stands for something rather humdrum: 'Cabinet Office Briefing Room A'.) Among the emergencies for which Cobra has recently been convened were the 2007 foot-and-mouth outbreaks and the terrorist attack on Glasgow Airport—all of which occurred within weeks of Gordon Brown's becoming prime minister. When the premier is unavailable, his/her place is taken by the Home Secretary. This happened at the time of the

7 July bombings, because then Prime Minister Tony Blair was at a G8 summit in Gleneagles when the news broke.

▶ Empowering local authorities in the age of the 'Big Society'

While community groups and lower-tier authorities now have enhanced powers to hold higher-tier ones to account—and even take over the running of services if they are dissatisfied with those they are receiving—a 'flip side' of the Coalition's 'Big Society' drive has been to bestow greater freedoms on local government itself. The Localism Act 2011 introduced a 'general power of competence' for all local authorities—from town and parish councils through districts, counties, and unitaries, to fire and rescue authorities. In an effort to cut 'red tape' and encourage more entrepreneurial thinking by officers and councillors at a time of harsh budget cuts, ministers aimed to move away from what they saw as a 'can't-do' culture, in which councils 'can only do what the law says they can', to a 'can-do' one that frees them up to 'do anything—provided they do not break other laws'. As an example, the Act spells out its hope that councils will find increasingly innovative ways of working together to 'drive down costs' and do 'creative, innovative things to meet local people's needs'.

▶ Local government associations

The Local Government Association (LGA) was established in 1997 to give a collective voice in Whitehall policymaking to all 388 English local authorities. A self-styled 'voluntary lobbying organization' (as opposed to a trade union or association), it is based close to Parliament, at Smith Square, in the former Transport House: historic headquarters of the Labour Party. In addition to representing district/borough councils, county councils, metropolitan borough councils, and unitary authorities, the LGA also speaks on behalf of subscribing police authorities, fire authorities, national park authorities, and passenger transport authorities. Councils in Wales are represented by a Welsh Local Government Association (WLGA), which is a subset of the LGA.

In 2007/8 the LGA published the strategic objectives summarized in the table entitled 'Local Government Association (LGA) strategic objectives', to be found on the Online Resource Centre.

In addition to the central LGA, there are thirteen regional **local government associations**, the remits of which broadly follow the boundaries of the government's English regions.

☰ Topical feature idea

At a time of wide-scale government spending cuts, and an impending Council Tax freeze, media attention is focusing increasingly on the quality of services provided by local authorities, and perceived disparities—or postcode lotteries—between one area and another. Two aspects of service delivery likely to face greater scrutiny are the perceived overlap and duplication between upper- and lower-tier councils in two-tier areas, and the wide variations in the range and nature of services provided by the same types of council in different areas. How is local government organized in the catchment of your news organization? What types of local authority are present, where do the responsibilities of one end and the other's begin, and how might finite resources be better harnessed to improve services, making them more accountable, in these tough economic times?

✳ Current issues

- **The future of unitary authorities:** one of the Coalition's first actions in relation to local government was to abandon already advanced plans for unitary authorities to be introduced in Norwich and Exeter. Nearly two decades after John Major introduced the gradualist unitary programme, a question mark remains over its future.

- **Election of elected police and crime commissioners:** to make police forces more accountable to those they serve, the Coalition recently replaced police authorities with US-style directly elected commissioners. However, critics have raised fears that replacing police authorities with single individuals could be a recipe for political interference and/or corruption.

- **Poor transparency of some council provision:** an ongoing concern for some local government observers (not to mention councillors) has been the proliferation of local strategic partnerships and other collaborations between neighbouring councils and/or external bodies over service delivery. Critics warn that 'outsourcing' increasingly significant chunks of council business to quango-style bodies overseen by unelected boards is undermining the accountability of service providers to the public.

? Review questions

1. When did the first local authorities emerge, and what was their initial role and purpose?
2. What were the main reforms instigated in the 1974 reorganization of local government?
3. Outline the current local government framework in England and Wales. What are 'two-tier areas', 'unitary authorities', and 'hybrid structures'?
4. In two-tier areas, what is the division of responsibilities between district/borough and county councils?
5. How is the UK police force structured, and how and by whom can local chief constables be held to account?

→ Further reading

Atkinson, H. and Wilks-Heeg, S. (2000) *Local Government from Thatcher to Blair*, Cambridge: Polity Press. **Comprehensive account of the succession of local government reforms passed by the Thatcher, Major, Blair, and Brown administrations.**

Stallion, M. and Wall, D. S. (2000) *The British Police: Police Forces and Chief Officers 1829–2000*, London: M. R. Stallion. **Exhaustive handbook to the UK police service, from its inception to the new millennium, including profiles of every force past and present and introductory essays.**

Stevens, A. (2006) *Politico's Guide to Local Government*, 2nd edn, London: Politico's Publishing. **Fully updated second edition of the comprehensive guide to every aspect of local government, including the interplay between local and central administrations.**

Stewart, J. (2003) *Modernising British Local Government: An Assessment of Labour's Reform Programme*, London: Palgrave Macmillan. **Meditative examination of the impact of the Local Government Act 2000, focusing on the tension between the idea of increasing localism and complaints of diminishing council accountability.**

Wilson, D. and Game, C. (2006) *Local Government in the United Kingdom*, 4th edn, London: Palgrave Macmillan. **Revised fourth edition of the standard text on contemporary local government in Britain. Covers all the major recent developments, including the introduction of unitary authorities and elected mayors.**

Wilson, D., Ashton, J., and Sharpe, D. (2001) *What Everyone in Britain Should Know about the Police*, 2nd edn, London: Blackstone Press. **Fully revised second edition of the informative core text charting developments in the UK police service from its origins in the early nineteenth century up to the present day, with a focus on recent changes from the idea of the traditional 'Bobby on the beat' to today's target-led—and frequently armed—officers.**

 Online Resource Centre

www.oxfordtextbooks.co.uk/orc/Morrison3e/
Visit the Online Resource Centre that accompanies this book for web links and regular updates.

12

Financing local government

Some of the most newsworthy and politically contentious local government stories arise from the way in which it is financed—and how the funding it raises is spent. Above-inflation rises in councillor allowances, all-expenses-paid 'fact-finding' junkets for members and officers, hikes in Council Tax bills, and the impact of government cuts on the delivery of grass-roots services are among the bread-and-butter headline material.

▌ Revenue versus capital finance

Local authorities need money for two types of spending: to build infrastructure (offices, roads, traffic crossings, schools, and housing), and to operate and maintain these facilities on a day-to-day basis. The cost of building things falls under **capital expenditure**. Cash spent staffing, lighting, heating, and repairing them is **revenue expenditure**.

▌ Revenue expenditure and how it is financed

Revenue spending is financed through the council's *income*: the grants it receives from central government, taxes it raises/has allocated to it locally, and any upfront fees or penalties it charges for services (for example, parking permits and library fines). Each income stream is examined in detail below, starting with the source of funds underpinning all others—the government grant system.

The reformed government grant system

The overwhelming majority (75 per cent as of 2012/13) of local authority revenue finance derives from government grants. Until relatively recently the bulk of this came in the form of the **revenue support grant (RSG)**—or **general block grant**—which individual councils were left to spend at their discretion, focusing on particular local funding needs. After Labour's return to power in 1997, the process by which central government grants were allocated to local authorities became steadily more baffling. At the same time, the importance of the RSG progressively diminished as more and more government money became 'ring-fenced' and directed to specified areas of spending—notably schools. This process—known as 'passporting'—saw, over time, a steady decline in the size of the RSG, to the extent that by 2010/11 it represented only around 4 per cent of councils' annual revenue budgets in England. By far the biggest portion—65 per cent—was allotted to councils in the form of discrete, increasingly sizeable chunks, many of which had to be spent in prescribed ways dictated by ministers. Local authorities' own reserves and annual grants given to the police between them made up a further 5 per cent. Perhaps surprisingly, given the controversy it generates in the media, the Council Tax today accounts for barely a quarter of revenue income.

The formation of the Coalition, with its focus on ending 'big government' and increasing localism (see pp. 354–5), meant the days were numbered for Labour's top-down approach to local finance. Within months of entering office, Conservative Communities Secretary Eric Pickles had announced plans to abandon all but a handful of the passported grants—reviving the tradition that councils be allowed to decide for themselves where to spend money allocated to them by Whitehall. They were also given powers to 'repatriate' the national non-domestic rates (NNDR)—or uniform business rates (UBR)—paid by companies located in their areas, rather than continuing to have them siphoned off into a centralized pot of money to be redistributed around the country as ministers saw fit. Mr Pickles announced that by the start of the 2014/15 tax year £4 billion worth of grants previously distributed to authorities in prescriptive ways would be absorbed into a single 'unhypothecated' (non-passported) grant—rationalizing the number of separate grants allocated to local government, in one fell swoop, from ninety-plus to fewer than ten.

Types of revenue grant

Central government calculates—traditionally each year—how much money it thinks individual councils need to provide services for their communities, up to a standard 'national level'. Under Labour the grants ministers allocated on this basis were known collectively as 'formula grants'. They comprised:

- revenue support grant (RSG)/general block grant;
- redistributed NNDR/UBR;
- principal formula police grant (PFPG).

Though the precise ways the three different formula grants were calculated differed, the principle underpinning them all was that a substantial proportion of the government's overall revenue funding pot should be allotted to councils on the basis of their comparative levels of 'need'. In other words, more money would be distributed to councils covering areas with high levels of socio-economic deprivation or those facing other peculiar demographic challenges, such as a disproportionately elderly and/or infirm population. This approach to funding supplanted the system inherited by Labour, which had adopted a more straightforward 'per capita' ('per head') model for funding councils—allocating grants broadly on the basis of the relative *size* (rather than *nature*) of local populations.

While the Coalition is expected to retain the first and third of the above grants (for the time being), NNDR/UBR is already being reformed to allow local authorities to retain some or all of the money they generate from local businesses to spend in their areas—effectively removing it from the 'pool' previously collected by the Treasury. The way this tax has customarily been calculated, and the changes proposed in the Coalition's Local Government Finance Bill 2012, are explained later in this chapter.

Meanwhile, the Coalition is giving even shorter shrift to Labour's other favoured funding channels. In addition to formula grants, Tony Blair's government introduced two types of *non-formula* grants, which had the effect of tying councils' hands by forcing them to spend certain annual lump sums on particular service areas that ministers judged to be high priority. The two categories non-formula grants fell into were as follows:

- **specific grants**;
- area-based grants (ABGs).

To complicate matters further, specific grants were divided into two subcategories: **ring-fenced grants** and **unfenced grants** (sometimes called *targeted grants*). The former—as their name suggested—were 'hived off' for very particular ends. One of the most famous ring-fenced payments (retained by the Coalition at time of writing) is the **Dedicated Schools Grant (DSG)**, which councils were forbidden from spending on anything other than staffing and maintaining schools or providing related services like special needs teaching. As well as being reserved for schools generally, the DSG has at times been prescribed even further, with ministers stipulating it must go towards specific running costs, such as buying textbooks or improving extra-curricular activities. But such 'micro-passporting' has often caused conflict between central and local government—including a high-profile contretemps between several councils and then Education Secretary Alan Johnson in 2005 after it emerged they had used part of their DSG to subsidize other services.

'Unfenced' grants, by contrast, were allocated to councils to spend however they saw fit—albeit within certain parameters dictated by ministers. Unlike the

RSG, unfenced grants were not calculated on the basis of a formula related to local demographic and socio-economic factors; rather, they were residual pots of money to be spent on services judged equally worthy of central government funding nationwide. An example of a long-standing unfenced specific grant was the Housing and Planning Delivery Grant (HPDG). Although councils could only spend it on services related to housing/planning, in practice they used them in any of a number of different ways.

Labour's stated aims for specific grants were to:

- help councils achieve a specific purpose—for example, reducing Council Tax or introducing uniform standards of domestic upkeep or disabled access provision;
- subsidize poorer areas where the 'Council Tax base'—the number of households eligible to pay it—was too low to meet the cost of local needs;
- cut costs of services that were either spread unevenly across the country (for example, flood barriers) or of benefit to the country generally (e.g. roads);
- fund services for which ministers had laid down statutory requirements— for example, the Mental Illness Specific Grant (MISG), introduced under the Community Care Act 1990 to provide community-based support for people with mental health problems.

By the time Labour left office the lion's share of revenue grants for local government were passported, and there was a bewildering array of individual payments—many targeted for highly specific purposes. The lack of manoeuvre councils had to determine for themselves how best to spend the resources at their disposal spurred Mr Pickles to introduce the radically simplified system explained below.

As for the area-based grant (ABG), this was a later addition to local authorities' financial armouries. Introduced in 2008/9, it was drawn from the budgets of various ministries other than the Department for Communities and Local Government (DCLG) itself, including the Department for the Environment, Food, and Rural Affairs (Defra) and Home Office. ABG was designed to encourage councils to work with 'partner' organizations, such as charities, businesses, and neighbouring authorities, to improve services across the shared localities where they operated. The idea was that by forming partnerships authorities would achieve efficiency savings and avoid duplicating/overlapping with other service providers.

Though the above definition of ABG's purpose bears a superficial resemblance to the Coalition's 'Big Society' approach to local service delivery (see pp. 338–9), in fact it was the first of Labour's extensive menu of revenue grants to be abolished outright. Since 31 March 2011, money previously allocated through ABG has been rerouted through a new non-formula, unfenced **Local Services Support Grant (LSSG)**, which councils now receive in twelve monthly instalments a year. To give some idea of the impact of this one reform, the LSSG currently draws from seven 'funding streams' (sources) whereas, by the time it ended in 2010/11, the ABG drew on sixty-one. While councils are likely to welcome any simplification of their notoriously complex revenue settlements, it remains to be seen whether LSSG will be worth as much as the ABG in the long run—and it is this bottom line, more than anything, that will determine its popularity. With councils across the piece being asked to cut costs to the tune of nearly 30 per cent over four years, commencing in 2011/12, while simultaneously freezing Council Tax bills (see p. 373), it is unclear whether the initial 'transition grant' built into the LSSG will be sufficient to counteract the need for dramatic service cuts. Even according to Mr Pickles's own figures, the short-term cash boost, introduced in 2011/12 could only limit the 9.9 per cent core funding cut projected for that year to 8.8 per cent.

Following the changes introduced by the Coalition so far, then, the new breakdown of revenue grants from central government is as follows:

(a) *Formula*

- revenue support grant (RSG);
- principal formula police grant (PFPG).

(b) *Non-formula*

- local services support grant (LSSG);
- specific grants:

(i) ring-fenced grants—DSG and new public health grant (PHG) (see p. 360);

(ii) unfenced—including **early intervention grant (EIG)**.

Of the new specific grants, EIG has already proved the most contentious—largely because of the huge expectations placed on it. Education Secretary Michael Gove has specified it be used to fund multiple costly, complex, and politically sensitive services, ranging from the (previously ring-fenced) Sure Start budget (see p. 468) through free preschool education for disadvantaged two-year-olds to drug and alcohol misuse prevention projects for teenagers.

Calculating core grants—how RSG and PFPG are decided

Since 2006/7, levels of both RSG and police grant awarded to individual authorities have been worked out using a calculation which involves subtracting the relative resource amount (RRA) for each area from its relative needs formula (RNF).

The **relative needs formula** is a formula based on detailed information about the population size, social structure, and other characteristics of a council area. By taking into account precise local factors, like the number of pensioners and school-aged children living in an area and its relative economic prosperity, ministers aim to allocate funds that fairly and accurately reflect that area's needs and the cost of servicing them to its local authorities. Within the RNF, separate formulae are used to decide how much should be allocated to individual authorities to cover the likely expenses associated with each 'major service area': education, social/children's services, police, fire, highways maintenance, environmental, protective and cultural services (EPCS), and capital financing.

The **relative resource amount**, in contrast to RNF, is a *negative* figure. It is based on the logical assumption that an area with a large number of Council Tax-paying households—particularly those in higher tax bands, indicative of a relatively affluent population—needs less financial help from central government than a poorer one. RRA is essentially subtracted from the previously calculated RNF to give a figure more accurately reflecting what an individual area should be allotted in formula grants.

The resulting grant is shared between local councils in proportion to their levels of responsibility—with 'upper-tier' county councils and unitary authorities gaining more than 'lower-tier' district/borough councils and police and fire authorities.

Over and above the core chunk of formula grants allocated in this way, a small percentage tends to remain in an overall 'formula pot' to be distributed between council areas on a purely per head basis. This has traditionally been the same for all local authorities delivering the same services—that is, all district/borough councils receive identical per capita amounts—and is known as 'central allocation'. In addition, Labour introduced a procedure known as 'floor-damping' to ensure every council—no matter how poorly it fared from a grant settlement compared to others—received at least a *minimum* year-on-year increase in formula grant. Four different 'floor levels' were set (one for each type of authority). During the last year for which funding settlements were agreed by that government (2010/11), counties and unitaries were guaranteed a 1.5 per cent increase in grant, whatever their perceived 'relative needs' and 'relative resource amounts'. Early indications from the Coalition were that the days of floor-damping might be numbered. The total value of formula grants allocated by the British government to English councils for 2012/13 was £27.8bn—down from £29.4bn the previous year—with councils outside London expected to draw on their reserves to the tune of £501 million to help make up the difference.

The end of passporting—and return of virement?

Labour's efforts to constrain local authorities' ability to spend revenue income where they pleased did not end with specific grants. It was once commonplace for councils that found themselves with unexpected shortfalls in one spending department during a financial year to transfer money from another's budget, in a process known as **virement**. But in recent years repeated extensions of the passporting regime have rendered all but the most modest shuffling of books impossible. Chancellor George Osborne effectively signalled the return of virement by announcing the abolition of all but two ring-fenced grants in his October 2010 Comprehensive Spending Review (CSR) (see p. 246). But the astute political timing of his gesture (ahead of the announcement of swingeing spending cuts) wasn't lost on the BBC's political editor, Nick Robinson, who evoked the following 'old Whitehall saying' on his blog:

> Governments with money centralize and claim the credit, those without decentralize and spread the blame.

Figure 12.1 gives a full breakdown of the sources of local government revenue finance in England in 2012/13—at which point Mr Pickles's funding overhaul was only partially complete. Figure 12.2 summarizes the overall percentages of English local authority revenue spending that year in each service area.

While the way the overall revenue finance 'cake' is divided to prioritize particular service areas tends to be fairly uniform across Britain, it is worth noting that devolution has seen widening disparities open up between central government's approach to funding councils in different nations. In 2012/13, 33 per cent of the Welsh local government budget was earmarked for education, 19 per cent for social services, and 9 per cent for policing—broadly on a par with spending allocations in England. However, while the percentages of income Welsh authorities derived from Council Tax, redistributed UBR, and police grant (plus floor funding) were comparable to those received by English ones (at 23.9, 15.8, and 4 per cent respectively), the remaining 56.4 per cent was made up not of passported grants but an old-style RSG, allowing individual councils to allocate money at their own discretion. Though it strikes a stark contrast to the present picture in England, in many ways the breakdown of funding sources in Wales is likely to be the shape of things to come when the Coalition completes its process of removing ring-fencing in the coming years.

Local taxation and evolution of the Council Tax

The idea of local taxation dates back to a time when medieval churches charged 'tithes' to parishioners renting their land, and lords of the manor used bailiffs to extract taxes from peasant farmers. But as early as 1601 it began to become a more systematic affair, with the emergence of 'rates'—a property tax based on the 'rateable' (rental) value of an individual's home, which was to remain in place (with modifications) for four centuries.

The rates were a tax levied on domestic properties, rather than the individual citizens who occupied them. The broad assumption was that the bigger a property and the higher its rateable value, the better off its occupants were likely to be. But over time the rating system (to use its full title) produced peculiar anomalies that led to growing calls for reform. Before its eventual abolition by

Figure 12.1 Breakdown of regular local authority revenue income in England for 2012/13

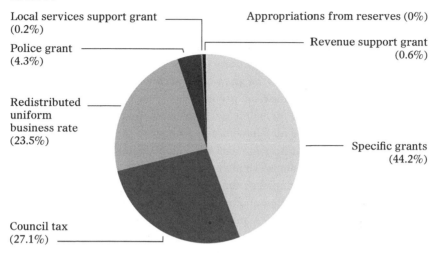

Local services support grant (0.2%)

Appropriations from reserves (0%)

Police grant (4.3%)

Revenue support grant (0.6%)

Redistributed uniform business rate (23.5%)

Specific grants (44.2%)

Council tax (27.1%)

Source: Department of Communities and Local Government (DCLG) © Crown copyright 2012

Figure 12.2 Breakdown of annual local authority revenue spending patterns for 2012/13

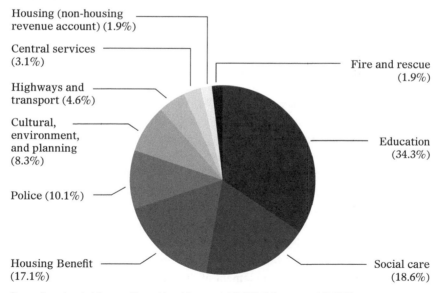

Housing (non-housing revenue account) (1.9%)

Central services (3.1%)

Fire and rescue (1.9%)

Highways and transport (4.6%)

Cultural, environment, and planning (8.3%)

Education (34.3%)

Police (10.1%)

Housing Benefit (17.1%)

Social care (18.6%)

Source: Department of Communities and Local Government (DCLG) © Crown copyright 2012

Margaret Thatcher's government in 1990 (1989 in Scotland), the most oft-cited illustration of its unfairness was that of the elderly pensioner living alone, on a fixed income, in a house for which he/she had spent his/her lifetime paying—next door to several sharing professionals whose combined incomes were far greater. Because rates were property-based, both 'households' might be charged exactly the same, meaning each professional would be paying significantly less than the pensioner.

Although there was widespread agreement that rates needed reforming, their immediate successor was short-lived. Ushered in by the Local Government Finance Act 1988, the Community Charge—dubbed the 'Poll Tax' by its opponents—sought to address the grievances of ratepayers 'punished' for living alone by shifting the onus from property onto people. In future individual residents would be billed for using local services—forcing everyone to pay their way. But, while this may have seemed fairer in theory, in practice the new 'head tax' soon became even more unpopular than the rates. While various rebates and exemptions were introduced to take account of the inability of certain groups (for example, the unemployed) to afford it, working people living in the same area ended up paying identical sums—regardless of any differences in their incomes. A multimillionaire tycoon might be charged exactly the same as his/her cleaner. In addition, some low-income groups previously excluded from local taxation altogether were suddenly included for the first time. Full-time students, for example, became liable (albeit with a 75 per cent discount).

Such was the furore over the Community Charge that it has been widely viewed as the tipping-point in the loss of confidence in Mrs Thatcher among Conservative MPs that ultimately led to her resignation in 1990 (see p. 96). The tax also proved extremely costly to administer, due in part to the fact that many of its opponents seemed prepared to forgo their right to vote, by dropping off the electoral roll, rather than allowing themselves to be tracked down by the billing authorities. Others openly refused to pay, leading to costly litigation by councils (much of which never bore fruit). In the end, ministers were forced to increase grants temporarily to allow for a gross reduction in Community Charge bills of £140 a person, funded by a 2.5 per cent increase in VAT. In 1990/1 the Poll Tax paid for 44 per cent of local expenditure, but this was halved to 22 per cent following the cut (compared to 25 per cent for today's Council Tax).

Following the biggest peacetime protests ever seen in Britain (at least prior to the 2003 'Stop the War' marches on the eve of the Iraq invasion), Mrs Thatcher's successor, John Major, abandoned the charge—replacing it with **Council Tax**. This 'hybrid' tax reinstated the property link, but unlike rates related it to market or *capital* values, rather than rateable ones. To placate critics of the rates, it also retained an element of 'individual' liability introduced by the Community Charge. Each household was billed on the assumption it comprised two adults (meaning bills did not increase for three or more). But to avoid returning to a time when households occupying identical properties paid exactly the same—regardless of how many working adults lived in each—a range of reductions and exemptions for single people and low-income groups was introduced to make the system fairer, as outlined in Table 12.1.

Table 12.1 Council Tax exemptions and reductions

Exemption/reduction	How it works
Single person discount	25 per cent off a full Council Tax bill.
'Reductions for Disabilities' scheme	Lowers bills of homes in Bands B–H if they have been adapted for disabled occupants. Exists to ensure houses not unfairly overvalued because of expensive modifications.
Exemptions	Apply to severely mentally impaired, carers, full-time students, and certain categories of dwelling, such as student halls of residence.
Unoccupied dwelling discount	Discount of up to 50 per cent—although councils allowed to charge more in 'ghost towns'.
Council Tax Benefit	Traditionally writes off Council Tax bills for unemployed and certain other people on low incomes and other benefits, but due to be abolished by Coalition in favour of new localized schemes for helping those on low incomes, to be devised by individual councils. This less comprehensive system, which relies on local discretion, expected to save up to £500m as part of government's deficit-reduction programme.
'Transitional relief'	Provided during transition from Community Charge to Council Tax for those whose local tax bills suddenly leapt as result.

Although designed to deal with many of the anomalies and inequities preserved by previous local tax regimes, the new benefits and exemptions system inevitably ushered in its own. Full-time students might have been exempt from Council Tax in theory, but in practice those renting from private landlords invariably found themselves having to pay it on the homeowner's behalf—or seeing their rent artificially inflated to cover the cost. Students sharing houses with one or more employed adults also lost their exemptions by default, because the household automatically became liable for the tax.

Perhaps most controversial has been the 50 per cent reduction traditionally available to households with two or more properties, whose additional homes are generally unoccupied. In Wales and south-west England, in particular, the 'ghost towns' created in picturesque areas favoured by wealthy city-dwellers as holiday home locations have been exacerbated by the relative cheapness of keeping such properties empty for much of the year, in light of the Council Tax discounts they receive. Under Labour, in certain areas blighted by this trend councils were given limited discretion to charge more than 50 per cent, to deter property owners from leaving them unoccupied. A 2003 statutory instrument gave individual billing authorities the power to determine classes of discount in their areas for the first time, in recognition of the 'ghost town' issue (not to mention the risk of such properties being broken into). Unoccupied but furnished properties—those most likely to be used as second homes—became liable for reduced discounts of 10 per cent, while some long-term empty homes faced losing their reductions altogether. In April 2008 Newcastle City Council used this new power to scrap its 50 per cent reduction for unfurnished and uninhabitable homes—charging them full Council Tax for the first time.

Whether motivated by morality or a desire to boost council incomes in straitened times, the Coalition has shown early signs of taking an even tougher line towards what Communities Minister Andrew Stunell has described as the 'scourge' and 'national scandal' of empty homes. The Local Government Finance Bill has dispensed with the long-running 'empty dwelling exemption'—a provision entirely exempting from Council Tax, for up to twelve months, homes undergoing or judged to require major repairs to make them habitable—in favour of a discount, the level of which should be decided locally. More significantly, it is introducing a new 'empty homes premium', enabling councils to charge owners of dwellings left empty for two years or more up to one-and-a-half times as much as other homeowners.

For all these changes, Council Tax is still seen by many as regressive. Newspapers frequently feature stories about the financial problems it causes for pensioners and others on modest fixed incomes, who do not fall into convenient categories making them eligible for reductions—for example, people on Employment and Support Allowance (see pp. 242–4). Some have even been fined or jailed for 'refusing' to pay. In September 2005 Sylvia Hardy, a 73-year-old retired social worker from Exeter, was imprisoned for refusing to pay £53.71 in Council Tax arrears on time. She told Exeter magistrates' court defiantly that she was following the example of other individuals in history who had fought to change 'unjust laws'.

Such has been the concern about the unfair impact of Council Tax on low-income households that for many years in opposition the Liberal Democrats argued for replacing it with a 'local income tax'—a system, based on the calculations used to determine national Income Tax bands, that should more closely match a household's Council Tax bill with its ability to pay. In Scotland, where the Scottish Parliament has the power to make changes to local taxation, the Scottish Nationalists have long pledged to introduce a local income tax, though this has yet to materialize—six years into their reign at Holyrood. Table 12.2 outlines arguments for and against a property-based (rather than people-based) local tax.

Council Tax banding

Council Tax bills in England, Scotland, and Wales are based on a system that divides domestic properties into one of eight 'bands' (nine in Wales)—A–H (A–I), respectively—according to their notional capital values. In Wales these bands were most recently revised in 2005, to take account of changes in property prices in the fourteen years that had elapsed since the original ones were set on

Table 12.2 Arguments for and against property-based and people-based local taxes

Property-based tax	People-based tax
Cheap to administer and collect, and provides predictable source of income.	Boosts local finances because number of bills sent out hugely increases to reflect fact all adults—rather than households—are charged.
Difficult for people to avoid paying rates or Council Tax because property, unlike people, is immobile.	Some argue it is fairer, because burden of paying for local services spread across all adults—including those who might otherwise be 'invisible' to taxes based on property values. 'Head tax' does not need to be 'one size fits all': local income tax would reflect individuals' ability to pay.
Simple, clearly understood system.	Fosters greater local authority accountability, because all adults charged and can voice views on use of their money at local elections.
Fair in theory, in that people occupying larger dwellings likely to be better off.	Because individuals have to fill in forms accepting liability for taxes like Community Charge, there is huge disincentive to register. When introduced in Britain, many councils collected barely half what they were owed—and those unable or unwilling to pay lost voting rights by dropping off electoral roll.
Property taxes can be disincentive to home improvement, because major refurbishment/extension likely to hike bills.	Straight head taxes like Community Charge also mean low-income groups like students, pensioners, and working people on modest wages pay same as vastly richer ones—unless explicit exemptions and reductions introduced.

1 April 1991. Controversially, however, neither England nor Scotland has had its bands changed since they were originally set—meaning they remain exactly the same as on 1 April 1993 (by which time even the original valuations were outdated). Despite pledging in its 2005 election manifesto to revise the bands if re-elected, Labour dropped the policy on returning to power. Cynics saw its reluctance to tackle the issue anywhere but in Wales as an example of political back-pedalling, motivated by a fear it would lose future votes in marginal constituencies where people whose house prices had significantly risen since the early 1990s might be moved into higher bands. In fact, according to Local Government Association research, the number of households likely to lose out in a revaluation was the same as the number that would have benefited (around 4 million).

Whatever the merits of retaining existing bands, it is undeniable that the property values to which they relate are anachronistic today, in light of the substantial rises in house prices seen across much of Britain. In England the highest Council Tax band (H) currently applies to all homes valued at more than £320,000 in 1991, while in Scotland (where bands are set by Scottish assessors) the top rate starts at just over £212,000. As stated previously, only in Wales has there been any rebanding since 1993: as of 1 April 2005 a new top band (I) has applied there for properties worth more than £424,000. Homes built since the dates when the bands were set are given nominal values based on what they would have been worth had they existed on 1 April 1991 (1 April 2003 in Wales). The lowest Council Tax band (A) is set for homes worth £40,000 or less in England, £44,000 in Wales, and £27,000 or less in Scotland, while the 'average band' (D) applies to those worth between £68,000 and £88,000 in England, £91,000 and £123,000 in Wales, and £45,000 and £58,000 in Scotland.

The introduction of revised banding in Wales has led to complaints that the country is no longer on an equal footing with the rest of Britain. Moreover, despite the fact the price ranges covered by each Welsh band were all adjusted upwards to reflect the general surge in property values since 1993, the revaluation was not simply a question of mapping properties in the old Band A into the new one. Instead, it produced clear winners and losers. Because values in some areas had risen significantly further than others—with some previously cheaper homes overtaking in value those that were once more expensive—around a third of households found themselves moving into higher bands than before. Most jumped at least one band, while some leapfrogged three or more. Only 8 per cent of homes moved down.

At present around one in four homes fall into the lowest band in England and Scotland as a whole, although in north-east England this proportion rises to 60 per cent. The current Council Tax bandings in England, Scotland, and Wales are outlined in Table 12.3.

How individual bills are calculated—and who collects the money

As explained above, domestic properties are charged Council Tax in line with the bands into which they are placed based on their actual or notional capital values in April 1991 (2003 in Wales). But who actually puts them in these bands, and determines the nominal 1991/2003 values of homes built in the years since they were originally set?

Table 12.3 Current Council Tax bands and values in England, Scotland, and Wales

Band	England	Scotland	Wales
A	Up to £40,000	Up to £27,000	Up to £44,000
B	£40,001–£52,000	£27,001–£35,000	£44,001–£65,000
C	£52,001–£68,000	£35,001–£45,000	£65,001–£91,000
D	£68,001–£88,000	£45,001–£58,000	£91,001–£123,000
E	£88,001–£120,000	£58,001–£80,000	£123,001–£162,000
F	£120,001–£160,000	£80,001–£106,000	£162,001–£223,000
G	£160,001–£320,000	£106,001–£212,000	£223,001–£324,000
H	£320,001 and above	£212,001 and above	£324,001–£424,000
I	N/a	N/a	£424,001 and above

Responsibility for valuing homes rests with the Valuation Office Agency (VOA), an executive agency of HM Revenue and Customs (and, ultimately, the Treasury), but it is for individual billing authorities to maintain lists of valuations. Based in eighty-five regional offices, the VOA's day-to-day work is undertaken by a team of *listing officers*, who compile and update lists of properties grouped in each band in their area. Overall responsibility for running each district office falls to a local *valuation officer* (sometimes known as the district valuer). It is his/her job to hear any formal appeals initiated by households unhappy with their property valuations.

Although the Council Tax banding system has never been reset in England and Scotland since the government's original mass valuation, homes originally placed in one band can still be moved into a different one under certain circumstances. A property might go up or down for any of the reasons outlined in Table 12.4.

Over the years considerable vitriol has been aimed at the VOA, not least by those whose homes are in higher bands. When the valuations were initially set in 1991 an urban myth circulated that agents employed by the VOA to help valuation officers in the mammoth task of valuing millions of homes for Council Tax purposes for the first time did so simply by driving past houses and awarding them notional market values purely based on their locations and outer appearance—so-called 'second-gear valuations'.

Local authorities that charge Council Tax to help finance their services fall into two broad categories, depending on their degree of involvement in collecting the money:

- **Billing authorities** (or collection authorities)—councils that actually send out bills to households and collect the proceeds to be distributed between themselves and other authorities in their area. In two-tier areas the billing

Table 12.4 Ways in which properties can change Council Tax bands between revaluations

Band change	How it happens
Neighbourhood changes or alterations to buildings	Property falls in value because part of it has been demolished, or state of its locality has changed significantly (e.g. sewerage works has been built)
Non-domestic use of property	Householder has started/stopped using his/her home for business purposes
Rise in value due to material change to property	Home can increase in value because of an extension or other major alteration—although increase in band will not occur unless/until property sold
Home adaptations	Changes made to adapt home for disabled person (e.g. ramps, stairlifts, etc.)
Incorrect original valuation	Mistake made with original valuation—to determine this, new occupants of property must appeal to listing officer within six months of moving in

authority is the district/borough council, while in unitary areas it is the unitary authority.

- **Precepting authorities**—all types of council entitled to issue 'precepts' (instructions or orders) to their local billing authority asking for a share of Council Tax proceeds. In two-tier areas this applies to the billing authority itself, county council (in its role as both top-tier council and local fire authority), and local police authority. In unitary areas there are still three precepting authorities: the unitary, police, and fire authorities. Every annual Council Tax bill received by a paying household should include a breakdown of the shares allocated to each precepting authority over the financial year. The largest portion goes to the top-tier council (unitary or county). Parish councils also issue precepts for the modest local services they provide, so precepting authorities are grouped into 'major' (county/district/unitary) and 'minor' (parish).

When Council Tax bills for each band for the coming tax year have been determined by local precepting authorities, they will express their precepts publicly in terms of an 'average rate' of Council Tax and the 'average rise' in the value of this rate faced by local taxpayers in comparison to the previous year. As indicated earlier, the 'average rate' is that applying to a Band D property. It is determined by the following formula:

$$\frac{\text{Total amount the authority intends to spend} - \text{Total non-Council Tax revenue}}{\text{Council Tax base (number of eligible households)}}$$

How central government 'controls' Council Tax bills

Ministers have powers to prevent local authorities charging excessive Council Tax by introducing formal ceilings to stop bills rising above specified levels. This process—**capping**—was introduced by the Tories in the Rates Act 1984, and used increasingly during the 1980s and 1990s to restrict bill increases by supposed high-spending councils (often Labour ones in poorer areas, which argued they faced above-average costs in housing, education, and social care). New Labour was generally reluctant to cap authorities, although it retained reserve powers allowing it to do so under certain circumstances, and capped increasingly towards the end of its thirteen-year term. In 2008/9 ministers threatened to cap Portsmouth City Council and seven police authorities—Bedfordshire, Cheshire, Leicestershire, Lincolnshire, Norfolk, Surrey, and Warwickshire—after each announced Council Tax rises above the 5 per cent ceiling it had urged them to respect. David Williams, Portsmouth's chief executive, argued the cost of rebilling taxpayers in his area would be £90,000, while only £40,000 would be refunded to 'overcharged' households—causing a deficit of £50,000. Ultimately, only Lincolnshire—which increased its precept by 78.9 per cent—was actually capped, although the other authorities faced limits on precept increases in future.

Such examples aside, Labour's approach to holding down Council Tax bills largely remained that of using reserve powers to target specific authorities, rather than favouring the across-the-board capping occasionally used by the Conservatives. In November 2007 David Cameron revealed the Tories were considering readopting a version of this 'universal' approach. Under his proposals a so-called 'trigger threshold' would be introduced to limit bill rises. In true 'Big Society' fashion, this would be a government-dictated level, above which authorities in England could not raise Council Tax without first obtaining local electors' permission in a referendum. Mr Pickles belatedly confirmed the level of rise for which councils would be required to obtain the public's consent in December 2011. In 2012/13—the year the rule was introduced—referendums only needed to be held by authorities proposing rises of 3.5 per cent or more, but the 'threshold' for prompting votes was due to be reviewed annually by ministers thereafter. Before the 'referendum lock' was introduced, critics had argued that giving the public a direct say in whether Council Tax bills should rise was tantamount to asking turkeys to vote for Christmas—making it capping by another name. But when the new system was actually introduced, it had a rather different (unintended) consequence, with some authorities threatening to raise bills to just below the threshold, thereby avoiding referendums—a response then Housing Minister Grant Shapps condemned as a 'democratic dodge' on Radio 4's *Today*.

A similarly rebellious response greeted Mr Osborne's announcement in June 2010 that he would be 'freezing' Council Tax rates across England for two years (a decision prompting an immediate call from the LGA for the projected £625m loss of revenue to councils to be reimbursed by central government). Though the Coalition has repeatedly cited the (ongoing, at time of writing) 'freeze' as an example of how it is working to ameliorate the impact of financial pressures on hard-pressed households at a time of job cuts, falling real wages, and rising utility and fuel bills, its claim to have prevented rises across the board is somewhat disingenuous. The fact that the freeze was not imposed as a formal cap meant that, in practice, authorities remained at liberty to raise Council Tax if they so wished. One authority that quickly broke ranks was Brighton and Hove Council, whose minority Green Party administration opted to forego a handout from a fund set up by ministers to compensate those that played ball—worth some £650 million a year in total over four years. The council's leadership argued it could generate more income by raising Council Tax up to the 3.5 per cent limit, and believed this was necessary to protect frontline services from the deeper cuts that would otherwise be needed. Shortly afterwards, eighteen other councils indicated they were minded to do likewise. In the event, Labour and Conservative opposition councillors in Brighton ultimately voted down the Greens' proposal in February 2012, following a vigorous 'no' campaign led by local evening newspaper, the *Argus*. Nevertheless, a survey by the Chartered Institute of Public Finance and Accountability published the following month found that 15 per cent of councils were still wavering over whether to accept government compensation or go ahead and raise Council Tax—with many again planning rises to just below the level that would prompt referendums. At the same time, some 43 per cent of households were facing at least a small increase due to rising precepts from police and fire authorities.

A further way in which recent governments have sought to keep Council Tax at reasonable levels is by banning authorities from issuing supplementary precepts—last-minute increases to the sums they request from their billing authorities because of previously unforeseen changes to their budgetary predictions for the coming year. This was outlawed in 1982.

The 'gearing' effect

Notwithstanding central government's ability to 'cap' bills, Council Tax has traditionally been the one device available to authorities to generate significant income, over and above their annual grants, to finance costly expenditure. Therefore, any decision by ministers to *reduce* contributions to a council (either by cutting or freezing grants) has tended to push them into increasing bills significantly to make up for resulting shortfalls. Similarly, if a council suddenly faces unforeseen revenue demands, but its contribution from government is already set, it will again turn to the Council Tax. The disproportionate rise in bills that can result is known as the 'gearing' effect.

To cite a theoretical example, if a council raises a total revenue income for the coming year of £100m—approximately £25m from the Council Tax—but ends up needing £101m to meet its final spending demands, it will need to raise Council Tax by significantly more than the 1 per cent shortfall to achieve this, in the absence of other viable funding streams. In fact, its average Council Tax bills would have to rise by 4 per cent:

$$\text{Projected Council Tax increase} = \frac{\text{£1m}}{\text{£25m}} = 4 \text{ per cent}$$

National non-domestic rates (NNDR)/Uniform business rates (UBR)

In addition to their responsibilities for valuing domestic properties, listing and valuation officers are also charged with administering the 'equivalent' tax for local businesses. While this may sound straightforward, **uniform business rates (UBR)**—otherwise known as **'national non-domestic rates'** (NNDR)—have proved almost as controversial as the Council Tax. Introduced alongside the Community Charge in 1990, UBR's initial tax bands were based on a revaluation instigated at the time (aligned to rateable values in 1991) but have since been revalued every five years. The most recent revaluation took place in 2010, based on rateable values at 1 April 2008.

How UBR has traditionally worked—and why it is so unpopular

Like both the long-standing domestic rates system and the previous local business tax before it, UBR is based not on a property's capital value but its **rateable value**. Listing officers keep rating lists covering all business premises in their area. When first introduced in 1990, UBR caused uproar among many occupants of commercial and industrial land and buildings because of the huge increases in the values of those premises that had occurred since 1973, when the previous business tax—the 'general rate'—had been set.

UBR has customarily worked as follows. Business premises are valued by the local listing officer (in Scotland, the assessor), based on how much they could have been let for at the relevant date. The amount they are actually charged in UBR annually will then depend on a centrally determined calculation made by the Communities Secretary, known as the 'national multiplier' ('poundage' in Scotland). The multiplier is the number of pence in each pound of the rateable value ascribed to a given business premises that its owner is liable to pay for that year. It is set at two levels: a 'standard' rate for middle-range and bigger companies, and a 'small business' rate for those that meet the necessary criteria to be defined as such by the Department for Business, Innovation, and Skills (BIS) and Treasury. Whichever category it falls into, the multiplier is normally held below the level of inflation for business properties with 'average' values.

UBR is therefore determined by the following formula:

$$\text{Rateable value of property} \times \text{National multiplier}$$

To cite a hypothetical example, a business whose premises has a rateable value of £50,000 would be expected to pay £25,000 in a year when the multiplier was set at 50p.

As of April 2008, empty business premises became liable for UBR—although, as with all bills, companies may appeal against their ratings.

Separate multipliers are currently set for England and Wales. Scotland, in contrast, retains a different system of business rates, which is largely the same as that which first came into existence there in 1854. Although the 1988 Act amended the existing Scottish system as it did elsewhere in Britain, it remains distinct to this day. Until recently, when the Scottish Government began 'pooling' business rate revenue and redistributing it from the centre, one of its primary differences from the English and Welsh UBR was the fact it was still a 'local tax'—that is, one both collected and spent in each area.

And this has long been the single most contentious aspect of UBR. As with Council Tax, UBR bills have traditionally been sent out to businesses by local billing authorities, with revenue generated initially collected by them. But having been 'raised' locally, UBR revenue is then gathered up by central government and redistributed to councils according to a population-based formula, taking into account variations in local socio-economic factors in a similar way to the RSG. In effect, this has led to certain areas of the UK 'sub-sidizing' others: with, for example, the City of London generating millions of pounds through UBR which is then gathered up and redirected to poorer areas by ministers.

Such state-directed micromanagement of local finance sits uneasily with a government committed to rolling out bottom-up localism. To this end, the Local Government Finance Bill working its way through Parliament at time of writing includes proposals to 'repatriate' UBR for local communities—allowing councils to retain an (as yet unspecified) 'large share' of the money raised from businesses in their areas to safeguard and improve local ser-vices. The Coalition's distaste for 'one of the most centralized' council fund-ing regimes 'in the world' has been matched by its awareness of an increasingly urgent need to promote growth in the stalling British economy—and it is the pursuit of jobs and industrial expansion that is now being used as the main justification for localizing UBR. As the Bill now makes clear, the hope is that allowing councils to keep a substantial portion of the UBR paid in their areas will incentivize them to proactively push for local business investment, tak-ing advantage of other 'Big Society' changes introduced by ministers to foster partnerships and fast-track planning applications (see pp. 475–6). In the vari-ous consultation and briefing papers issued by Mr Pickles's office on this sub-ject he has argued that, if anything, councils currently have a *disincentive* to 'go for growth' in their areas—encumbered as they are by red tape and a war-iness about increasing traffic and having to finance infrastructure to support investment without the means to do so. The proposed changes—which, in the-ory, will give many authorities short-changed by the previous regime access to extra funds—were due to be introduced from the 2013/14 tax year.

Any system has its winners and losers, though, and critics of Mr Pickles's pro-posals fear that in this case the latter are likely to be those councils (and areas) least able to stand on their own two feet. Authorities with 'weak business rate bases'—those that tended to do relatively well out of the old regime, because they received money rerouted from other areas—will receive 'top-ups' from central government, at least in the short term, to compensate them for their losses. Over time the idea is that this initial safety net will be replaced with money redistributed to poorer areas from a new levy to be introduced on the proceeds of additional UBR income received by more prosperous authorities. But not everyone is convinced this will be enough to make up for what the 'losers' have lost. In January 2012, Neil McInroy, chief executive of the Centre for Local Economic Strategies, explained what he termed 'the Barnsley Question' (an oblique reference to the 'West Lothian Question'—see pp. 31–2) in an interview with *Public Finance* magazine:

❝Barnsley doesn't have a good business rates base, whereas Westminster City Council has the business rates of a medium-sized country.❞

Moves towards greater 'localization' of UBR are not all about raising *more* money, however. The Localism Act 2011 empowers councils to offer 'discounts' on UBR. This would have the effect of cutting the sums from UBR coming back into the locality—a 'deficit' the authority would be expected to make up for from other resources available to it. In addition, the Act watered down the generally unpopular Business Rates Supplement Act 2009, introduced by Labour to give counties and unitaries a measure of local determination over income generated from businesses in their areas by allowing them to impose additional levies on companies, provided the proceeds were directly used to promote economic development. Since 2011 supplements can only be levied if local business communities first approve them in formal ballots (referendums in all but name).

The means used to distribute the proceeds of UBR is far from the only controversy surrounding it. Another long-standing debate has revolved around the way it is calculated—which, at time of writing, ministers appeared to have no intention of changing. The practice of charging businesses according to the rateable values of the physical premises they occupy, rather than their profits, has been seen to unfairly penalize companies operating large factories or warehouses, which are charged significantly more than businesses based in single offices—irrespective of which generates the most revenue. Restructuring of the British economy over recent decades has seen many businesses offering IT support or legal and financial advice (the 'service sector') generate huge profits—despite the fact they often run their affairs from modest premises, with small overheads. In contrast, the decline of the manufacturing sector has seen turnovers plummet for old-style industries producing large consumer goods using expensive plants and costly machinery.

These examples aside, like the Council Tax, UBR does offer reductions and exemptions for certain kinds of business property. In addition to those left un-occupied for prolonged periods, exemptions include:

- agricultural land and buildings;
- places of public worship—for example, churches and mosques;
- properties used by the disabled;
- fish farms;
- sewers;
- public parks;
- road crossings over watercourses—that is, traffic bridges;
- properties built in specified 'enterprise zones'—designations intended to rejuvenate deprived areas;
- properties occupied by visiting Armed Forces.

Other sources of local authority revenue income

In addition to the Council Tax and grants, local authorities derive income from:

- council house rents;
- leisure service use—for example, swimming pools, sports centres, library fines, etc.;
- the collection of trade refuse;
- car parking tickets, fines, etc.;
- income from private contractors;
- the European Social Fund (ESF), which provides grants to companies, voluntary groups, and communities in deprived areas to improve training and employment prospects.

The annual budget timetable at local level

As with most other organizations, the financial year for councils runs from 1 April to 31 March. While capital expenditure (see p. 380) has traditionally been planned on three- to five-year cycles, only recently have ministers sought to move revenue expenditure onto the same footing by introducing three-year grant settlements.

The process by which local spending is decided and budgeted for is outlined in Table 12.5.

Stories about councils being forced to make redundancies and/or slash budgets for essential services because of real-term reductions in government grants have long been a staple of British newspapers. But in October 2008, as the full impact of the global banking crisis unfolded (see pp. 213–16), it emerged that at least a hundred councils were facing a highly unusual threat to their solvency. The LGA revealed that up to £1bn of taxpayers' money had been collectively invested by councils and police authorities in collapsed Icelandic banks. One authority alone, Kent County Council, had invested £50m, while Transport for London (TfL) had deposited £40m, and the Metropolitan Police £30m. While a few had been remarkably canny (Brighton and Hove Council decided not to trust the banks' promises), others were named and shamed. For example, Winchester City Council had invested £1m in Heritable, a subsidiary of Iceland's national bank Landsbanki, barely a fortnight before its parent company's collapse—apparently ignoring early warning signs that the country's institutions were on the brink.

In March 2009 the Audit Commission published a report in which it criticized seven councils for 'negligently' ignoring official warnings by continuing to invest in Icelandic banks even after their credit ratings had been downgraded below acceptable levels. It found £32.8m had been deposited between the

Table 12.5 Local authority budget-setting timetable

Time	Stage
April	Council holds provisional meeting early in financial year to draw up overall 'budget strategy' for next one.
Late April/early May	Follow-up meeting held to decide levels of Council Tax needed to help finance expenditure for coming year.
Late May/early June	Full council meeting follows earlier meetings of main financial committee (until recently, policy and resources committee) or cabinets of new-style councils (see p. 401). Council leader or elected mayor must obtain formal endorsement of cabinet for major budgetary decisions.
July–September	Once overall budget strategy is determined, broad revenue estimates for following years must be ironed out.
October–December	Government normally announces following year's formula grant allocations, forcing authorities to make significant adjustments to budgeting for coming financial year. Usually last stage at which individual departments can increase requests for revenue funding from authority's 'pot'. To do so they must submit **supplementary estimates**, outlining reasons for higher-than-expected outgoings.
January–February	Council usually confirms and publishes final draft estimates for revenue spending.
February	Full council has 'final say' at special meeting, deciding levels of spending and Council Tax for next financial year (approximate budgets normally approved, subject to later modifications).

reclassification of the Landsbanki and Glitnir banks as 'adequate' on 30 September 2008 and their collapse barely a week later, on 7 October. Among the biggest investors were the South Yorkshire Pensions Authority, which deposited £10m in one go on 2 October, and Kent County Council, which paid in £8.3m in two chunks on October 1 and 2. Though not directly related to the issue of investment in banks, the Coalition's wide-ranging review of local finance has led to a loosening of the rules concerning councils' ability to acquire corporate bonds. While the 2003 regulations which introduced prudential borrowing (see Table 12.6) also allowed authorities to invest surplus funds in bonds and shares (albeit at their own risk), it also stipulated that should they invest money in an individual company this transaction would be treated as 'capital expenditure' for accounting purposes. This rule—intended to discourage 'speculative' investments—has now been amended to explicitly allow councils to invest in individual companies' bonds (though not shares). Justifying the change, ministers argued that bonds issued by firms with triple-A credit ratings were often 'a safer investment option than a collective scheme with a lower rating'. The rule change also altered the definition of *income* generated through the sale or redemption of bonds—specifying that only those acquired before 1 April 2012 would be treated as 'capital receipts' (see p. 381) on being sold/reaching maturity.

▌ The local authority capital budget

The main sources of local government capital finance are outlined in Table 12.6.

Capital borrowing

Although capital projects are funded in discrete ways significantly different from those used to finance revenue spending, they do incur a financial cost to local Council Tax payers. One regular outgoing councils are compelled by central government to factor into their annual revenue budgets is a 'minimum revenue provision' to cover systematic repayment of any outstanding debt. This is usually equivalent to 2 per cent of housing debt and 4 per cent of that incurred for other capital purposes in a given year. In addition to paying back the debit itself, councils must also make provision for any interest on their long-term capital borrowing—the 'revenue implications of the capital programme'. These repayments of capital interest from the revenue account are known as the **debt charge**.

Despite the fact it incurs interest and can take years to pay off, borrowing money to finance capital investment is often seen as politically desirable by both central and local government. The rationale is that, by taking out loans, authorities are 'spreading the costs' of their spending over a number of years—meaning it is not only local taxpayers living in the area at the time a decision is taken to invest in a project who shoulder the burden, but anyone moving into the area during its lifetime. In addition, borrowing avoids authorities having to fund expensive projects entirely upfront, enabling them to fast-track construction of schools, libraries, and other amenities they would otherwise take decades to afford.

Similar arguments have been made by recent governments in favour of councils forming co-funding alliances with the private sector—public–private partnerships (PPPs) or private finance initiatives (PFIs)—to finance capital projects that would otherwise take years to finance through public funds alone (see pp. 230–1).

▌ Financial transparency at local level

For journalists, some of the best (and most accessible) stories can be found in authorities' publicly available accounts. Under s. 15 of the Audit Commission Act 1998 press and public have the right to both inspect and copy these accounts,

Table 12.6 Main sources of capital finance available to local authorities

Source	How it works
Prudential borrowing	'Prudential borrowing' introduced in Local Government Act 2003 to replace 'credit approvals'—limits agreed by government—in place since 1990, when emphasis switched away from controlling council *spending* to limiting *borrowing*. Today's prudential borrowing is determined in three ways:
	1. Each council may borrow up to 'affordable' figure in line with Prudential Code endorsed by Chartered Institute of Public Finance and Accountancy.
	2. Low-interest loans for specific projects from central government, through **Public Works Loan Board (PWLB)**— body operating within UK Debt Management Office, a Treasury executive agency.
	Councils borrow money and repay it from their own resources without government support. They calculate how much they can afford to borrow according to code drawn up by the Chartered Institute of Public Finance and Accountancy (CIPFA).
	3. US-inspired **Tax-Increment Financing (TIF)** due to be introduced in England and Wales from 2013/14—allows councils to borrow money for infrastructural capital investment against additional future income expected to be generated through UBR from companies likely to be attracted by that investment. Also being developed in Scotland.
Supported capital expenditure (supported borrowing in Scotland)	Councils may borrow to finance capital spending with support of central government, which provides funds to help them repay loan and service interest. Most finance comes from DCLG but other departments also contribute, including Department for Education, Department of Health, and Home Office.
Capital receipts	Money raised through councils' sales of capital assets. This is divided into *usable* part and *reserve* part. Council must set latter aside for use in specified ways, including paying back existing debts. Former can be used to supplement prudential borrowing to invest in new buildings, land, etc.
	Communities Secretary determines percentage of usable capital receipts at any time. In 1998 agreed percentage was 50 per cent—except receipts from council home sales, only 25 per cent of which could be used for capital spending. 2003 Act revoked stipulation that proportion of housing receipts must be set aside by councils for debt reduction, introducing centralized 'pooling' arrangement under which 75 per cent of capital receipts from council home sales under 'Right to Buy' scheme (see pp. 503–6) and 50 per cent of other housing-related receipts are redistributed from authorities with less housing shortage to those in greater need.
	Authorities in 'demonstrable financial difficulty' may apply to DCLG for 'direction' allowing them to use capital receipts for 'specified revenue expenditure'. Items like redundancy payments, equal pay awards, and pension fund contributions have in past been redefined in this way as capital expenditure.

(continued)

Table 12.6 (*continued*)

Source	How it works
Capital grants	These traditionally come from government departments, public bodies distributing National Lottery money, or hybrid arrangements combining borrowing with grants (e.g. Transport Supplementary Grant, Single Regeneration Budget, New Deal for Communities, City Challenge, etc.). Coalition moving to 'less bureaucratic' approach, with more limited grants drawn from Supported Capital Expenditure budget.
European Union (EU) grants and loans	Money from EU pots, including European Regional Development Fund (for specific infrastructure projects and industrial development, usually in deprived areas); European Social Fund (training/employment initiatives aimed at young people); and structural funds. Currently EU 'Convergence' funds available to areas, like Cornwall, where GDP is less than 75 per cent of Union's average.
Private sector investment	Often 'in kind' offers—such as development land—and/or funding for capital works like road access or traffic management from private company, in exchange for ability to recoup investment at later date by running profit-based business related to land concerned (so-called *planning gain*—see pp. 481–2).
	Favourite means of encouraging private capital investment today is through PFI/PPP deals (see also pp. 230–1). These see private companies footing much of initial construction cost, enabling projects to progress quicker than if reliant solely on public funds. In return, companies paid back—with interest—over period of years, in arrangements similar to mortgages. Final costs to taxpayers significantly higher than if projects funded upfront by councils. Recent PFI-funded projects include Brighton and Hove's award-winning solar-powered £14m Jubilee Library.
Local lotteries	Councils permitted to run own lotteries under conditions outlined in National Lottery Act 1993.
Local strategic partnerships (LSPs)	Labour's £36m Community Empowerment Fund to encourage community and voluntary organizations to cooperate in LSPs to tackle social deprivation supplanted by Coalition's *Total Place*—a 'Big Society' scheme to boost cooperation between councils and agencies over wider geographical areas, to avoid duplicating services by adopting 'whole area' approach to delivering them. Local authorities may currently invest up to 15% of the money they save to pay their employees' pensions in infrastructure projects such as roads and housing (equivalent to £22.5bn of the £150bn collectively held by them in this way). At time of writing the Coalition was consulting on plans to double the amount they can invest in these ways, to £45bn.

and all books, deeds, contracts, bills, vouchers, and receipts relating to them. On completing their audited accounts for the previous tax year (usually by June), all authorities must make them formally available for public inspection for twenty working days, advertising this in advance. Anyone inspecting council accounts may address questions about them to the district auditor, although these must relate to the period inspected and not be about council policy. Those unhappy with items listed in the accounts may lodge a formal grievance with the auditor, in the form of a written 'notice of objection'.

Several notable court judgments have flowed from the 1998 Act—most upholding the public's right to disclosure. In December 2009 the case of *Veolia ES Nottinghamshire Ltd v. Nottinghamshire County Council* saw the High Court uphold the council's decision to open the files on confidential documents relating to its signing of a commercial waste management contract. Citing a line in the Act compelling authorities to disclose 'all the financial movements or items of account of the council's funds', it confirmed the Act contained no exemption for commercially confidential information (unlike the law governing access to council meetings—see pp. 419–22).

However, while the Act has certainly made it easier for Council Tax payers to inspect their councils' balance sheets, the media's attempts to assert similar rights have not always gone unchallenged. In 2004 ITV West (previously HTV West) narrowly won a High Court judgment forcing Bristol City Council to recognize its status as a 'person interested'—allowing it access to information relating to payments made to a former officer sacked in 1998 for gross misconduct. Justice Elias ruled in the company's favour on a technicality, saying it was only in its status as a local 'non-domestic rate taxpayer' that it qualified.

The Act also redressed the balance in previous legislation towards a particular aspect of local financial transparency: the ability of local electors to access details of council payrolls under s. 17(1) of the Local Government Finance Act 1982. Prompted by the 1985 case of *Oliver v. Northampton Borough Council*, the Act precluded public access to accounts or documents containing personal information about authority employees.

Since entering office, the Coalition has embarked on a major push to promote more financial transparency by local authorities—with everything from senior staff salaries to all items of spending and contracts worth £500-plus to be published by them online (see p. 417).

☰ Topical feature idea

Figure 12.3 reproduces an extract from the audited 2010/11 accounts statement of Tamworth Borough Council. It focuses on the authority's estimates of the likely costs of specified financial 'uncertainties' it has factored into its budget forecast for the year ahead. How would you use this table as the starting point for generating stories about the financial difficulties facing the council? Which is the strongest potential story here, and why? How would you develop it into a newsy background feature, and who would you interview?

Figure 12.3 Extract from Tamworth Borough Council's Annual Statement of Accounts 2010/11

Assumptions made about the future and other major sources of estimations of uncertainty

The statement of accounts contains estimated figures that are based on assumptions made by the authority about the future or that are otherwise uncertain. Estimates are made taking into account historical experience, current trends and other relevant factors. However, because balances cannot be determined with certainty, actual results could be materially different from the assumptions and estimates.

The items in the Authority's Balance Sheet at 31 March 2011 for which there is a significant risk of material adjustment in the forthcoming financial year are as follows:

Item	Uncertainties	Effect if Actual Results Differ from Assumptions
Icelandic deposits recovery	Level of recovery dependent on run off estimates from the Administrators for KSF & Heritable. Glitnir deposits dependent on Icelandic Supreme Court appeal ruling.	For Glitnir—subject to appeal could mean an increase in the assumed recovery level from 29 per cent (as included within these accounts) to 100 per cent of deposit equating to c. £2.13m.
Pensions	Estimation of the net liability to pay pensions depends on a number of complex judgements relating to the discount rate used, the rate at which salaries are projected to increase, changes in retirement ages, mortality rates and expected returns on pension fund assets. A firm of consulting actuaries is engaged to provide the Authority with expert advice about the assumptions to be applied.	Adjustment to the level of liability on the balance sheet. During the year the overall liability reduced from £39m to £22m—see note 39 on page 112.
Property, Plant and Equipment	Assets are depreciated over useful lives that are dependent on assumptions about the level of repairs and maintenance that will be incurred in relation to individual assets. The current economic climate makes it uncertain that the Authority will be able to sustain its current spending on repairs and maintenance, bringing into doubt the useful lives assigned to assets.	If the useful life of assets is reduced, depreciation increases and the carrying amount of the assets falls. It is estimated that the annual depreciation charge for Council dwellings would increase by £33k for every year that useful lives had to be reduced.

This list does not include assets and liabilities that are carried at fair value based on a recently observed market price.

© Tamworth Borough Council

✳ Current issues

- **Return of general block grants:** after years of criticizing Labour's increasingly prescriptive approach to local finance, the Coalition is handing back to councils powers to decide how to spend most of their revenue income, removing ring-fencing from all but two grants and gradually absorbing £4 billion worth of payments into a single 'unhypothecated' lump sum.

- **Lowering Council Tax**: Chancellor George Osborne used his 2010 Budget to announce a Council Tax 'freeze' for at least two years, and Eric Pickles swiftly announced that local authorities would in future have to hold referendums before raising it above predetermined 'thresholds' set by government annually. In 2012/13, the first year of the new regime, votes had to be held if councils wanted to raise bills by 3.5 per cent or more.

- **'Repatriation' of NNDR/UBR:** the Local Government Finance Bill 2012 allows councils to 'repatriate' revenue generated by business rates paid by companies in their areas, as an incentive to them to promote economic growth. 'Poorer' authorities will be compensated by a 'top-up' from central government initially, and a levy on additional UBR income raised by 'richer' areas in future years.

? Review questions

1. What is the difference between 'revenue' and 'capital' expenditure? Outline the main sources of each available to local councils.

2. How does the government determine how much money to give an individual local authority in grants each year, and how does it control where that money is spent?

3. How is the Council Tax calculated generally, and how does this translate into bills sent to households? List some of the exemptions and reductions.

4. What are the arguments for and against a property-based local tax?

5. Who sets and collects the uniform business rate (national non-domestic rate) and why has it traditionally been controversial?

→ Further reading

Betty, S. (2011) *The PFI; 'Teething Problems or Fundamentally Flawed?': A critical analysis of the UK's Private Finance Initiative*, Bury St Edmunds: Lambert Academic Publishing. **Critical overview of impact, positive and negative, of PFI revolution in UK capital financing.**

Fischel, W. A. (2005) *The Homevoter Hypothesis: How Home Values Influence Local Government Taxation, School Finance, and Land-Use Policies*, Cambridge, MA: Harvard University Press. **Globe-spanning sociological text examining impact of**

homeowners on concentration and quality of local services, and emergence of
'stakeholder-led localism'.

Hollis, G., Davies, H., Plokker, K., and Sutherland, M. (1994) *Local Government Finance:
An International Comparative Study*, London: LGC Communications. **Again targeted
at local professionals, this offers useful comparisons between Britain's system of
local government finance and those applied elsewhere, primarily in mainland
Europe.**

Midwinter, A. F. and Monaghan, C. (1993) *From Rates to the Poll Tax: Local Government
Finance in the Thatcher Era*, Edinburgh: Edinburgh University Press. **Thoughtful
exploration of turbulent Thatcherite reforms of local government finance, focusing
on replacement of rates by Community Charge.**

 ## Online Resource Centre

www.oxfordtextbooks.co.uk/orc/Morrison3e/

Visit the Online Resource Centre that accompanies this book for web links and
regular updates.

13

Local government decision-making

The previous two chapters examined the nature of councils, how they evolved, and the funding systems underpinning them. But what form do their chains of command take and how do they take decisions?

▌ Councillors and officers—who's who?

The work of local authorities is divided between two sets of individuals: councillors and officers. Like central government, councils comprise a series of spending departments, the duties of which spread across the range of services for which they are responsible. These departments—covering areas like education, housing, and social services—are each administered by paid civil servants who are expected to be politically neutral. *Appointed* to their posts on merit, like anyone else given a job, these are the **officers**.

While officers are concerned with process, decisions to put money into one service area rather than another—and precise choices about how those services are run—are based on political judgements taken by elected **councillors**, whose role is to 'govern' authorities in a manner akin to that in which decisions affecting the whole UK are taken by members of Parliament (MPs). Like MPs, councillors (also known as 'members') each represent their own equivalent of a constituency. In the case of county councillors these are known as electoral divisions (or 'county divisions'), while in unitary authorities and district/borough councils they are usually called wards (see p. 425).

What kind of person becomes a councillor?

The seminal 1972 Bains Report defined the duties of local councillors as:

- directing and controlling the affairs of the local authority;
- taking key policy decisions defining the objectives of the council and allocating the resources required to attain them;
- keeping under review the progress and performance of local services.

This vision of the operation of local government was echoed fourteen years later by the 1986 Widdicombe Report, which stressed the importance of the 'complementary relationship' between 'part-time councillors' and 'full-time officers with professional expertise'. The issue was also tackled by a 1990 Audit Commission discussion paper, *We Can't Go on Meeting Like This*, outlining a threefold role for councillors. Four years later, a report by Robert Gifford, then leader of Milton Keynes District Council, identified four 'typical' profiles for councillors. The main conclusions of these seminal papers are listed in the table entitled 'Two models for effective councillors', to be found on the Online Resource Centre.

Although councillors may be likened to MPs in that they are accountable to voters, there is a fundamental difference between the two: unlike MPs, councillors are not salaried. The work they do is therefore voluntary and, for those trying to juggle it with their day jobs, necessarily 'part time'.

The fact councillors are unsalaried has given rise to considerable controversy, not least because it leads to many councils being dominated politically by the retired and wealthy—those with the time and money to devote themselves to unpaid work for their local communities. Because most councils and committees have traditionally met for business during normal working days, any employed person able to stand as a councillor has tended to be in a managerial post or running his/her own company—in other words, free to set his/her own hours or negotiate time off for meetings.

This combination of militating factors has also discriminated against women, fewer of whom have historically held such senior posts (many being housewives, with all of the attendant childcare responsibilities). Ethnic minorities have also been under-represented historically—even in areas with large immigrant popu- lations. Hardly surprising, perhaps, that the media so often portrays town halls as the preserve of pushy pensioners and white, middle-aged, middle-class men. Recent moves to introduce more evening sittings in some areas—particularly in and around London, where many people work unsocial hours and commute long distances—have done something to address these issues, but not enough to satisfy critics.

In 1986 the government-appointed Widdicombe Committee found that eight out of ten councillors were male, and 59 per cent hailed from one of three socioeconomic groups: professionals, employers and managers, and 'intermediate non-manual' jobs, together representative of only 23 per cent of the overall population. The average councillor at the time was aged 45, with none under 24. The oldest was 85. The Committee made eighty-eight recommendations—although most concerned moves to democratize the *political* composition of councils and their committees. Many were implemented by the Local Government and Housing Act 1989.

A succession of surveys by the Local Government Association and the Improvement and Development Agency (IDeA) suggest little has improved since. The results of the 2010 census (the most recent to date) show that, while the proportion of women councillors had risen by half—from 19 per cent in 1986 to 31 per cent in 2010—this had stalled at the same level since 2008. The average age of councillors, far from being brought down, had *increased* to 60. Ethnic minorities also continued to fare poorly: only 4 per cent were non-white (compared to 8.4 per cent of Britain's population).

Almost as contentious as the question of how to make councillors more representative of multicultural twenty-first-century Britain is the issue of how much work should be expected of them, given their 'unpaid' status. Various attempts have been made to quantify exactly how much time is spent by the average member on council duties, both inside and outside 'official hours' (principally meetings). Widdicombe compared his own research with that contained in an earlier study, published in 1964. At that time the average number of hours councillors spent on duties was fifty-two a month; by 1986 this had risen to seventy-four. According to a 1998 Green Paper, it had increased to ninety-seven by 1992.

The most comprehensive survey of councillors' hours to date, however, was undertaken by Ken Young and Nirmala Rao for the Joseph Rowntree Foundation in 1994. Covering a sample of 1,682 councillors in fifty-three local authority areas, *The Role of Local Government Councillors in 1993* found:

- councillors spent seventy-four hours a month on average on council business (as cited in the Widdicombe Report);
- one in five councillors felt their hours were 'about right';
- the majority felt their most rewarding duty was 'representing' their wards, with only a small minority preferring policymaking or 'carrying out their party's programme';
- councillors spent 56 per cent of their time in council itself, whether attending meetings or liaising with officers;
- most councillors were happy with the long-standing committee and full council decision-making system (see pp. 398–401);
- there was widespread scepticism about the idea of adopting Westminster-style cabinets, but considerable support for introducing Commons-style scrutiny committees (see p. 402).

The last two observations (if not the others) would ultimately feed into the root-and-branch reorganization of councils' internal chains of command instigated by Labour in the Local Government Act (LGA) 2000 (see pp. 401–2).

Councillors' allowances and expenses

Introducing more 'flexible' working hours is not the only way in which councils have sought to increase participation by younger working people, women, and minorities. In a radical attempt to widen participation, some are increasingly bending the rules to offer more generous allowances in lieu of formal 'wages'.

Although councillors are unsalaried, there has been a recognized system of allowances and expenses in place for some time. Allowances are designed to give elected members modest payments for attending meetings, while they may also claim expenses to reimburse themselves for the cost of return travel to meetings by car, bicycle, or public transport. Expenses are also available to cover other outgoings that arise out of their official duties, such as paying for overnight accommodation, meals bought during the course of such business, and subsidizing postal costs and domestic telephone bills for phone calls related to their pastoral work with local electors. Councillors aged under 70 are also now eligible to join the generous Local Government Pension Scheme. There are two main types of allowance:

- **Basic allowance**—flat-rate annual payment, usually paid monthly, for *all* councillors representing a specific authority.

- **Special responsibility allowance**—additional payment received by councillors who hold posts of greater responsibility. The size of allowances varies according to how much responsibility they have: council leaders receive the biggest special responsibility allowances, while members of subcommittees and committees are paid much smaller ones.

Those with dependent children and/or other relations may also claim a separate carers'/dependants' allowance.

Each English council is free to set its own allowance levels, subject to certain restrictions. Since the LGA 2000, every council has been required by law to establish an **independent remuneration panel** comprising at least three individuals—none of whom are themselves councillors. It is the panel's task to review (and adjudicate on) any application by the authority to increase or otherwise amend its allowances. In Scotland, Wales, and Northern Ireland, the system is administered more centrally, with councillors' allowances in each of the devolved countries set by a single independent panel. The powers of the panels are limited, however: for instance, councillors are not legally obliged to accept their recommendations to cut or freeze allowances.

Recent surveys point to wide disparities in the generosity of allowances paid by different local authorities—with certain councils offering payments comparable to full-time salaries. According to figures published by local authorities in March 2011, a number of council leaders earned £50,000 or more in the 2010/11 tax year, while average annual allowances for other councillors topped £10,000 in many areas, and £20,000 in London—defying the pay caps and cuts endured by most council employees. The district of Rochford in Essex had seen the biggest increase in the previous five years—surging by 158 per cent. In general, councils paying more argue they are trying to encourage a more representative cross-section of the community to stand. Others, such as Plymouth City Council, have argued that to perform their council work properly members need to treat it as a full-time job—and to be able to do this, those without independent means require allowances comparable to a living wage.

Devolved administrations have proved considerably more generous with allowance settlements: in 2010 the Independent Remuneration Panel for Wales recommended a rise in basic allowances from the £11,000-plus many councillors had previously received to £13,868, with council leaders (many already 'earning' £40,000 or more) licensed to claim up to £57,785. Alive to public disquiet about the then recent MPs' expenses scandal—not to mention the pay cuts and freezes many workers have been enduring under the Coalition's austerity drive—some authorities, including Cardiff City Council, refrained from claiming their full entitlements. Meanwhile, in January 2010 the Convention of Scottish Local Authorities (Cosla) voted to back a one-year freeze on basic allowances (which already averaged £15,000—twice the level in England at the time). In Northern Ireland, where by August 2010 around two-thirds of members of the Legislative Assembly (MLAs) (each earning at least £42,000) also retained seats as local councillors, controversy has focused less on the size of members' allowances, which averaged £9,500 in 2009, than on their (still unresolved) 'double-jobbing' status, and the fact they have been able to continue claiming for council duties while sitting at Stormont.

Meet the experts—the role of local government officers

The number of officers employed by councils varies widely and is ultimately decided by the level of resources councillors allocate to finance them. Every council is obliged to provide certain statutory services and its administration is therefore split, like Whitehall's, into different departments—each run by an expert professional.

There are two main types of council spending department: *service* and *central*. As the term implies, the former are concerned with delivering services—housing, education, social services, etc. Central departments are those concerned with *administering* the council's functions—principally its legal and financial departments, and those devoted to corporate activities, such as public relations (PR) and marketing.

Officers, like Whitehall civil servants, must be *politically neutral*—whatever their levels of seniority. Those in senior grades are also *politically restricted* (see p. 121). Despite being required to avoid political bias, however, officers are expected to provide councillors with policy advice based on their knowledge and experience. Their roles are to:

- *advise*—defined by the Widdicombe Report as giving 'politically impartial' information and support to aid councillors in their decision-making;
- *support* the executive, non-executive, and scrutiny arms of the council— helping *all* councillors, not only the most senior ones.

Each department is headed by its own equivalent of a Whitehall permanent secretary. Among the most influential are the leading civil servants in the biggest spending areas: directors of social services and chief planning officers.

Higher up still are three officials whose role is to oversee the workings of the council as a whole, as follows.

- **Chief executive** (or 'head of the paid service')—the council's main policy adviser, manager, and coordinator. Chief executives often perform the role of 'acting returning officer' at elections, on behalf of the official returning officer—normally, the council chairperson or mayor (see p. 429).
- **Monitoring officer**—reports to members any acts of maladministration or failures by officers or councillors to uphold the council's code of conduct (see pp. 411–12). They are normally also their councils' chief legal officers and should be trained lawyers, and must ensure councils act within their statutory remits at all times (that is, not ultra vires).
- Chief financial officer (treasurer/director of finance)—oversees administration of his/her council's finances, and must be a member of a recognized accountancy body. He/she may also be referred to as 'director of central services' or 'section 151 officer' (referring to the statutory provision from which his/her authority derives).

Under the LGA 2000 chief executives are formally barred from being appointed as monitoring officers. In addition, like any other officer, chief executives, monitoring officers, and chief financial officers are all subject to a statutory disciplinary procedure that could ultimately lead to their dismissal in the case of misconduct.

To streamline administration of its affairs, improve efficiency, and avoid duplication, each council now has a 'chief officers' management team'. This is a group of senior officers, headed by the chief executive, that meets weekly or fortnightly to discuss policy ideas that might be put forward for councillors' consideration at meetings, and/or issues relevant to more than one department.

Despite largely managing to sidestep the 'politics' of local government, officers are far from immune to controversy. Recent years have witnessed a succession of negative news stories about the eye-watering salaries it is possible for senior council figures to earn—and, like the chief executives of NHS trusts, it is not uncommon for chief executives to be paid much more than the prime minister (see p. 169). Partly in response to these furores, Coalition Communities Secretary Eric Pickles has introduced a new rule requiring councillors to vote on and publish formal policy statements on pay scales for their officers. In addition to publicizing details of the allowances and expenses claimed by their members, all councils must also now do the same in relation to senior managers, and following a 2011 ruling by the Information Commissioner (see p. 598), it is Mr Pickles's intention that they go even further—by publishing the names and salaries of all staff earning £58,200 or more. Following Mr Pickles's criticism of some councils for paying salaries that would make Premiership football managers 'blush', a growing number of neighbouring local authorities have opted to start 'sharing' their chief executives to reduce their managerial wage bills and protect frontline services.

New models for service delivery—subcontracting and outsourcing

Until the 1980s most local services—from refuse collection and street cleaning through to building, equipping, and maintaining schools and care homes—were carried out directly by council employees. But over the past thirty years there has been a fundamental shift in the role of councils from being direct *providers* to *enablers*. Whereas everyone from local parking attendants to account clerks would once have been local authority employees, today they are just as likely to be on the payroll of a private company, voluntary organization, or agency. Rather than delivering services through the aegis of their own officers and departments, councils are charged with financing, coordinating, and 'commissioning' them—and the private and voluntary sectors have as much chance of winning contracts to provide them as authorities themselves. In the 'Big Society' era this trend is being accelerated—with local taxpayers now entitled to take over running their services directly, under the Coalition's new 'community rights' to 'bid' and 'challenge', and some councils are already experimenting with wholesale outsourcing (see pp. 396–7).

The system that originally ushered in this contract-based approach to local service delivery was known as 'compulsory competitive tendering' (CCT). Introduced in the Local Government, Planning, and Land Act 1980, this forced councils to put services out to tender—inviting competing bids from public, voluntary, and/or private sector organizations. The idea was that the most 'cost-effective' bid would be successful, cutting waste and bureaucracy and giving local people better value for money—while having the added benefit of curbing union influence, following the mass strikes of the 1970s and early 1980s.

CCT initially applied largely to 'blue collar' areas of service provision, such as building maintenance and construction work, but was extended by the Local Government Act 1988 to cover refuse collection, street cleaning, and school catering. A further extension was introduced by the Local Government Act 1992, which enabled councils to outsource 'professional' and/or 'support services', such as information technology (IT), marketing, and PR. Those wishing to continue providing services in-house were required to set up arm's-length 'companies' to compete for contracts on an equal footing with the private and voluntary sectors: 'direct labour organizations' (DLOs) for building projects, and 'direct service organizations' (DSOs) for services.

Many councils decided to group together several DSOs and/or DLOs under a senior officer—known as 'contract services divisions'—giving them more professional overall management structures and producing some of the economies of scale enjoyed by large commercial companies. When Labour returned to power in 1997 it scrapped CCT, only to replace it with a new system of procurement (itself now defunct), called Best Value (BV) (see also p. 416). A new statutory obligation was introduced, requiring councils to hire the 'most suitable' provider (whether public, private, or voluntary), choosing those best placed to deliver 'economic, efficient, and effective' services (the '3 Es') (see p. 541).

In theory BV meant services should only be contracted out to the private sector in future if doing so demonstrably offered local people a better deal. There was a perception that some councils had previously outsourced work purely to cut costs, and what had often resulted was an inferior alternative delivered by a company concerned more with remunerating shareholders than providing a high-quality service for local taxpayers. The 1998 Green Paper accused CCT of 'neglecting' service quality and producing 'uneven and uncertain' efficiency gains, 'antagonism' between rival providers, and 'significant costs for employees', including high staff turnover and demoralization. Despite such statements, Labour still expected councils to put contracts out to tender and, although price was no longer the biggest factor in determining successful bids, many argued that using 'BV' criteria to award (and remove) contracts amounted to CCT in all but name.

Cameron's 'Big Society'—what role for councillors and officers now?

A central plank of the Conservatives' May 2010 election campaign was that of the 'Big Society'. Although derided by critics for lacking tangibility, the philosophy underpinning David Cameron's approach to government appears to be an eagerness to devolve as much power as possible from Whitehall (and, indeed, local authorities) to citizens themselves. This delegation of power, and responsibility, to the grass roots manifested itself in several ways in the early days of the new government: the loosening of 'red tape' Mr Cameron saw as stymieing business investment and the planning process; the 'freeing' of schools and hospitals from direct government control (see pp. 444–54 and 176–82); and inviting ordinary members of the public, working alone, in groups, or in partnership with charities or private companies, to set up and run their own local services.

The idea of community-run bus services or road-sweeping patrols may sound fanciful, but in a speech in July 2010 Mr Cameron signalled his hope of returning to a (to some, imaginary) golden era of active 'volunteerism'. He talked of transforming the 'third sector' (charities and voluntary organizations) into the 'first', and 'turning government upside-down'. While Opposition MPs dismissed this rhetoric as a smokescreen for further cuts and/or a buck-passing exercise enabling ministers to shift the blame for service reduction onto councils—then Shadow Work and Pensions Secretary Yvette Cooper dismissed the 'Big Society' as a 'big con'—for now this new bottom-up approach to commissioning and delivering local services is here to stay. Mr Cameron used his speech to launch a new Big Society Bank (see p. 396), to which people could apply for start-up funding—financed by money held in dormant British bank accounts. He also named four local authority areas as trailblazing 'Big Society communities': Liverpool, Eden Valley in Cumbria, Windsor and Maidenhead, and Sutton.

Among the (largely Conservative-led) authorities keen to take its 'licence to contract out' to a logical conclusion was the London Borough of Barnet, which, after rebranding itself 'One Barnet', began shedding a swathe of services. This bold experiment—which swiftly saw the authority dubbed 'Easy Council' (a reference to budget airline EasyJet)—encountered the first of a series of major hurdles when, in June 2011, local bloggers exposed the fact it had spent £1.3 million buying in services from private security firm MetPro without first conducting basic financial or security tests, or even putting the contract out to tender. 'Blue-sky Big Society thinking' has caused problems for other authorities too. Labour's narrow recapture of Bury Council in the May 2011 local elections saw advanced plans to downgrade itself to little more than an 'enabling' authority put on ice. Around the same time, Tory-run Suffolk County Council was forced into a 'period of reflection' over radical plans to outsource virtually all local services, after uncomfortable backbench councillors mounted a rebellion. Suffolk's controversial plan, branded a 'new strategic direction' by its most enthusiastic cheerleader, then chief executive Andrea Hill, had prompted criticism from politicians at local and national level—with its own previous leader, Bryony Rudkin, condemning it as 'a circus act with no safety net'.

In future, more typical examples of 'Big Society' outsourcing are likely to come about through the exercise by groups of concerned citizens of the following new 'rights':

- 'Community right to build'—a new entitlement giving groups of citizens the right to bypass the normal planning process to construct small-scale, site-specific capital projects, such as community centres, libraries, or even pubs (see also p. 380).

- Neighbourhood planning—a right for communities to decide for themselves what developments should be built in their areas, rather than leaving this to councils.

- 'Community right to challenge'—the right for community groups, voluntary organizations, parish councils, or council employees to challenge councils to allow them to take over running services they feel they could deliver more effectively.

- 'Community right to bid'—the right of such groups to enter bids to purchase and take over running council-owned assets they judge to be important for their areas.

Of these, community rights to bid and challenge are of most relevance here. They are open to everyone, from groups of interested local residents or existing council employees who wish to form their own mutuals, to charities, voluntary groups, and parish councils (an echo of the enhanced powers hitherto conferred on 'quality parish councils'). The right to challenge allows 'relevant bodies' like those listed above to proactively confront councils at any time about services they regard as inadequate, and ask to take them over. In one sense, the right to bid is a more straightforward (if still unorthodox) extension of the existing process used to outsource local services, which allows communities to compete with other organizations for contracts. Where it differs, however, is in the fact that it would allow 'neighbourhood forums' (i.e. citizens themselves) or other community bodies not only to take over responsibility for running the services but also to acquire the associated capital assets (for example, libraries, children's centres, village shops or pubs). In considering bids, councils are expected to give such bodies a fair, even preferential, hearing before otherwise disposing of assets or deciding who should run a service. However, if a number of bids are received from rival groups the normal procurement process will need to be followed.

Sceptics argue that, at a time of severe austerity and with many people struggling to find paid work to make ends meet themselves, there is little appetite among most to take over running their own services—let alone on a voluntary basis, as many such projects would demand. But by May 2012, so confident was Communities Minister Andrew Stunell that communities up and down the country would be eager to do so that he announced the launch of a new 'Communities in Action' map to flag up examples of 'local projects that are making a real difference' for all to see (and, where suitable, emulate). In April 2012, meanwhile, the government launched **Big Society Capital**—a new, state-sponsored but independently run, financial institution designed to (in its own words) 'develop and shape a sustainable social investment market', by giving charities, community groups, and other third sector (voluntary) organizations the funds required to tackle 'major social issues'. By lending money to a range of recognized *social investment finance intermediaries* (SIFIs)—banks, trusts, and other bodies with track records of financing social enterprises—the fund directs low-interest loans and grants to groups and individuals working at the coalface.

No such gestures, however, have placated critics of the 'Big Society'—who portray it as, at best, a well-meaning but inadequate attempt to replace top-down state direction with bottom-up community control and, at worst, a smokescreen for an ideological mission to cut back 'the state' and mask the true scale of spending cuts. In a book due to be published after his retirement in December 2012, entitled *Faith in the Public Square*, outgoing Archbishop of Canterbury Rowan Williams criticized the 'Big Society' concept as 'aspirational waffle designed to conceal a deeply damaging withdrawal of the state from its responsibilities to the most vulnerable'.

→ see also central government, Chapter 8.

Politicization of council officers—the rise of political assistants

While local government officers are expected to be politically neutral, as early as the Widdicombe Report it was recognized that senior councillors might benefit from access to professional political advice from central government-style special advisers (see pp. 111–12). It envisaged 'political assistants' being hired in the following circumstances:

- for councils with chief executives who were 'by disposition' managers rather than politicians;
- where a council is 'hung', with three parties all holding the balance of power.

The terms under which such assistants were to be employed are listed in the table entitled 'Conditions of employment for political assistants', to be found on the Online Resource Centre.

In addition, elected mayors under the executive models introduced by the LGA 2000 would be entitled to appoint their own political assistants. Successive London mayors Ken Livingstone and Boris Johnson hired several 'spin doctors', in addition to policy gurus like US public transport expert Bob Kiley, the former's adviser on part-privatization of London Underground. Though many such advisers are effectively independent consultants, journalists should be wary when dealing with a council or its leadership through advisers, rather than press officers. As political appointees, they are not expected to give objective views of their paymasters' policies and achievements. Indeed, as an active Conservative and former party vice-chairman, Kulveer Ranger, the current mayor's Director of Environment and Digital London, is arguably a political appointee. In an earlier role, as Johnson's transport adviser, Ranger promoted various green initiatives, including trials of electric cars and the commercially sponsored Barclays Cycle Hire scheme ('Boris bikes'), which allows Londoners to pick up and drop off bicycles at any of 315 'docking stations' scattered around the City of London and eight other boroughs.

▶ Local government hierarchies before the LGA 2000 and under 'alternative arrangements'

Before the LGA 2000 one fundamental truth applied to all councillors, irrespective of whether the parties to which they were affiliated held overall power on their local authorities: they each had a *direct say* in at least some policy decisions taken by their councils. Policy proposals were initially referred to specialist subcommittees or committees of councillors covering the relevant areas, and had to be approved by them before ever being presented for final approval to full council. If rejected at this first hurdle, the full council would never get to discuss them. If reworded, diluted, consolidated, or otherwise amended, the version of the policy voted on by the full council had usually been substantially shaped by the committee or subcommittee. Because every councillor (whatever his/her party) sat on at least one committee, he/she had a direct input, however minor, into the policymaking process. Committee decisions were normally couched as 'recommendations'—that is, subject to final approval by full council. Councils also reserved the right to reject their rulings or **refer back** items for further reconsideration. Committees therefore constituted an important part of the day-to-day policymaking function of their councils—a 'bottom-up' approach to policymaking, as illustrated by the flow chart in Figure 13.1.

In addition to giving all councillors a direct (and, on paper, equal) say in decisions, the pre-LGA 2000 local authority set-up preserved a simple hierarchy of councillors not dissimilar to that seen among MPs in the Commons. A party that won sufficient seats in a local election to secure an 'overall majority' on the council would become 'the government' in all but name, and its leader would automatically be appointed **leader of the council**—effectively, local 'prime minister'. Beyond this, there were no visible divisions in 'status' between members of the ruling party (or group) and other councillors. The pre-LGA 2000 model remains relevant to this day, as it still applies to local authorities covering populations of 85,000 or fewer—where it is referred to as 'alternative arrangements' (see p. 400)—and is likely to become more widespread again shortly, in light of reforms being introduced by Mr Pickles (see p. 407).

Under this old-style model, there are/were three types of committee:

Figure 13.1 Flow chart depicting the decision-making process in 'old-style' local authorities and district/borough councils operating under 'alternative arrangements'

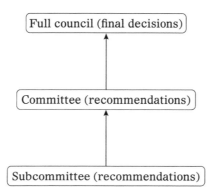

- *standing (statutory) permanent committees*, set up to discharge a specific function (for example, to take decisions on planning, education, environmental services);
- *ad hoc committees*—often given briefs directly related to the above, but set up to consider specific issues in greater detail than is possible on standing committees;
- *area-based committees*—formed to look at policy governing specific geographical areas under a council's control; they sometimes contained members of the local community beside councillors, and even had delegated budgets.

As in Parliament, the political composition of committees and subcommittees generally reflected the balance of power on the full council at any one time. If the Conservatives were in overall control, most committee chairpersons would be Tories and overall membership would be broadly proportionate to the distribution of seats between parties on the full council. Where no political group had overall control, standing committees sometimes had no permanent chair; instead, different chairpersons were elected to serve on a meeting-by-meeting basis.

Other conventions governing old-style committees included:

- Non-councillors could be 'co-opted' to serve on them, either temporarily or on an ongoing basis. These de facto members did not have voting rights—unless they were church representatives sitting on an education-related committee.
- Mayors, council chairpersons, and leaders were *ex officio* members of *all* committees. Significantly, this gave them rights both to attend *and* vote on these committees.

- Councils had to avoid any perceived or real conflicts of interest by ensuring committees with related functions had different memberships.
- In addition to committees, councils often set up working parties comprising both councillors and officers to consider policy options in detail, and their proceedings were not always open to the public.

Despite the influence of committees, like governing parties at Westminster, ruling groups tended to come up with many of the policy ideas debated in full council. Indeed, assuming they had big enough majorities after a local election, they could normally muster sufficient votes to drive through their proposals—whatever a committee might think of them. The leader was also usually appointed chairperson of the single most powerful council committee: the **policy and resources committee**. Because this controlled the council's purse strings, it had to approve any major policy decisions likely to involve significant resources, and could veto those it considered too costly. Many smaller councils have now abolished these committees, but some have retained equivalent 'boards' or 'panels'.

In other ways, ruling groups had little real 'executive power' in the sense that the government and prime minister do nationally—a clear contrast to their position in most local authorities following the LGA 2000 reforms. Leaders could appoint cabinets of senior colleagues, but these had no authority to make executive policy decisions behind closed doors, as commonly occurs both at Westminster and in councils that have adopted new-style executive arrangements. Moreover, in practice, the limited majorities attained by ruling groups in many local elections meant coalitions were commonplace—forcing the largest party to compromise many of its policy ideas.

Besides district/borough councils covering fewer than 85,000 people, the only authorities permitted to retain 'alternative arrangements' until recently were those, like Brighton and Hove City Council, that had held unsuccessful referendums to introduce directly elected mayors (see pp. 406–7). Even then this was on condition that they adopted committee-based systems with sufficient scrutiny powers to carry out the same functions competently. Under Labour there was a tacit recognition in these areas that it was probably only a matter of time before they would be forced to adopt a post-LGA 2000 executive model.

However, the Coalition's Localism Act 2011 now permits them to bypass it for good—with authorities that have previously switched to the newer system also being allowed to 'move away from an executive form of governance' if they so wish. In order to do so, councillors on the authority concerned must first pass majority resolutions favouring the move; revise their constitutions to incorporate the proposed change of arrangements; make this information available for public inspection; and publish the same proposals in one or more newspapers in their areas. On 23 May 2012 South Gloucestershire Council became one of the first authorities to revert to a committee-led system, after its ruling Conservative group was outvoted by a coalition of Labour and Lib Dem members in favour of the move.

▶ Local government hierarchies since the LGA 2000

The main difference between the 'old-style' system and its principal replacements is that, under the post-LGA 2000 structures, the balance of power between 'ordinary councillors' and those in ruling groups has shifted radically in favour of the latter. Whereas, once, all councillors were active participants in the local legislative process, today's council leaders—or, where adopted, elected mayors—hold disproportionate power. Their cabinets, too, have moved from being largely nominal entities to ones equipped to take executive decisions that the rest of the council has little chance of overturning.

The three types of executive management introduced by the LGA 2000 were:

- leader of the council and cabinet/executive;
- directly elected mayor (DEM) and cabinet/executive;
- DEM and council manager.

The third option was formally scrapped by Labour in the 2007 Act, after the experience of the only council to adopt it—Stoke-on-Trent—became an object lesson for the disproportionate powers that could be accrued by some individuals under the LGA 2000. Under this system, executive decision-making powers were vested in only one person other than the elected mayor: the council manager (an unelected officer). Following repeated claims that this model was leading to a culture of secrecy in Stoke, in October 2008 local electors voted to replace it with a leader-and-cabinet model.

Nonetheless, until the Localism Act 2011 councils continued to be encouraged by ministers to adopt one of the other LGA 2000-style models. To do so they must go through the following two-stage consultation process before introducing their chosen system:

1. Issuing an explanation to the public of the three models of executive structure.
2. Carrying out a more detailed formal consultation among local people.

Once a decision has been taken to adopt a particular model, the council must agree the wording of a formal constitution with the Communities Secretary. Any subsequent attempt to change it requires the constitution to be rewritten in consultation with ministers.

Under both surviving LGA 2000 models, the leader or mayor's position is of paramount importance. All councils adopting one of these systems are further divided hierarchically into the following functions: *executive*, *non-executive*, and *scrutiny*. As is the case nationally, the term 'executive' refers to the powers exercised by senior councillors—cabinet members plus the leader/mayor. Like the prime minister and his/her Cabinet, these individuals may initiate policy in private—even taking final decisions on some matters—without needing to consult committees and subcommittees, as happened under the old-style system.

The terms 'scrutiny' and 'non-executive' both apply to committees and sub-committees. Each describes one of the two roles undertaken by committees under the post-LGA regimes.

Non-executive committees

Committees overseeing regulatory matters like planning and licensing have delegated powers to take some decisions—rejecting or approving matters brought before them. The range of matters referred to non-executive committees is limited, however, compared to those deliberated over by committees under the old-style model. A planning subcommittee/committee, for example, might take a decision to reject or approve an application brought before it—without the need for it to be referred to the full council or cabinet for final approval—but this would only apply to *minor* applications (for example, relating to an extension to someone's house). The outcome of such applications will already largely have been dictated by the authority's existing planning rules, as previously agreed by the full council and set by higher tiers of government. More major applications—for example a bid by Tesco to open an out-of-town superstore—will have to be approved by full council.

Scrutiny committees

'Overview and scrutiny' (or simply 'scrutiny') refers to the function accorded to committees and subcommittees charged with examining specific council policy proposals and/or the workings of individual spending departments—for example, children's services, social services, or transport. Their powers, then, are more akin to those of Westminster-style select or general committees (see pp. 49–50) than old-style local authority ones: like parliamentary committees, they can propose policy amendments, call witnesses, and publish reports, but have little power to reject or overturn executive decisions. All local authorities—including those operating under alternative arrangements—are required to establish an overarching **overview and scrutiny committee** comprising councillors drawn from parties in proportion to the distribution of seats on the council. In practice, the majority have split their scrutiny function among several subject-specific subcommittees/panels, with some even referring to these as 'select committees' in reference to their parliamentary antecedents.

Criticisms of the 'new' systems

One of the Blair government's principal arguments for the new-style hierarchies was a desire to speed up council decision-making, by reducing the ability of committees and subcommittees to delay final policy decisions. But the stark division between the influence on policymaking exerted today by cabinet members, compared to 'ordinary' councillors, has sparked severe criticism of these reforms—not least from veteran councillors who, after years of public service, have found themselves with less direct say than previously in the running of their councils. The new-style models have been widely viewed as introducing 'two tiers' of councillors, as at Westminster: a powerful 'frontbench', and a sometimes vocal but often toothless 'backbench'.

Some criticisms of the post-2000 committee changes are arguably justified—not least those levelled by frustrated journalists who yearn for a return to the more knockabout meetings and policy stand-offs of old. However, many scrutiny committees have had tangible input into councils' policy initiatives. In July 2009 the London Borough of Hounslow's children and young people scrutiny panel was awarded £90,000 by the Department of Health to commission new services to tackle speech and language difficulties among poor children in its area. A month earlier, a credit union was set up to provide low-cost loans to poor households across North Yorkshire after a scrutiny review launched by county councillors brokered a partnership between public, private, and voluntary organizations—bringing to an end a decade of campaigning by locals.

Table 13.1 gives an overview of arguments for and against the LGA 2000 hierarchical models.

Table 13.1 Arguments for and against the LGA 2000 management models

For	Against
Allowing leaders, elected mayors, and cabinets to take some executive decisions unilaterally makes local legislative process faster—and more effective—than when committees had to approve everything.	New models create 'two-tier' internal council structures, in which frontbenchers have more influence on policymaking than backbenchers, and sometimes are the *only* councillors with obvious powers.
Introducing elected mayors engages public more closely with local democracy—giving it direct say in decisions over council leadership. In this sense, it is more democratic and councils are more accountable than under old system.	By giving small groups of individuals executive powers 'elective dictatorships' can form, making councils *less* democratically accountable.
LGA 2000 laid down process by which local electorates could demand referendums on introduction of elected mayors—bottom-up local democracy in action.	Introducing three alternative models for council leadership has led to patchwork landscape of local authority hierarchies. This confuses voters and can lead to inconsistent local representation.

Types and levels of council decision

Under the new-style executive models, the full council (which used to have to approve virtually all policies before they were implemented) is now only concerned with the most significant decisions. These proposals—defined as those affecting two or more wards/electoral divisions and likely to incur 'significant' expenditure—are called **key decisions**. An example might be the approval of a Council Tax rise or a planning application by developers keen to build a new road (which, by definition, will affect several wards). Each month, in the interests of transparency to local electors, every authority is required to publish a **forward plan** of all key decisions it intends to take over the coming four weeks, with its cabinet/executive also agreeing its own.

Whatever internal decision-making framework they favour, there are certain other terms common to the proceedings of all local authorities:

- Specific roles/powers delegated to councils by statute—and by councils to their own committees, subcommittees, and cabinets—are known as **prescribed functions**.

- Whenever final decisions are taken on matters before committees, full councils, or cabinets/executives, these are known as **resolved items**. Scrutiny committees or panels may, however, 'call in' items resolved in cabinet and/or refer them back for rethinks (as with old-style committees).

Figure 13.2 illustrates the top-down decision-making process that defines the chain of command in post-LGA councils.

The 'leader and cabinet' model

Of the three new executive management options introduced by the LGA 2000, that with most similarities to the existing system is the 'leader and cabinet' model. As under the old-style council hierarchy, the leader is normally the head of his/her party—usually that securing the most seats in a local election. He/she heads a **cabinet** (or 'executive') made up of close confidantes on the council, normally drawn from his/her own party or (where no single party has overall control) a coalition grouping.

But this is where any similarities between old-style and new-style leader and cabinet systems end. 'New-style' cabinets/executives are much more like those formed by prime ministers than the earlier council, more informal, ones. Until recently it was left to individual councils' discretion to decide whether they wanted 'weak' or 'strong' leaders. Under the former approach, the council as a whole selects its leader and individual cabinet members, and all executive decisions must be taken *collectively* by cabinet. The 'strong leader' approach, in contrast, allows the leader (once elected by his/her fellow councillors) to

Figure 13.2 Flow chart depicting the decision-making process in post-LGA 2000 councils

choose the cabinet members, delegating Westminster-style policy portfolios to each. As of December 2010 this variant became mandatory for all councils with leaders and cabinets (other than those still using alternative arrangements)—with county councils, London boroughs, metropolitan districts, non-metropolitan districts/boroughs, and unitary authorities introducing them successively in a programme of phased reform under the Local Government and Public Involvement in Health Act 2007. This Act also stipulated that executive leaders should serve automatic terms of four years—an approach dubbed 'strong leader-plus'—whereas the 2000 changes had allowed councils to appoint them for one year at a time.

Controversially, although individual cabinet members are generally expected to consult with frontbench colleagues, in some cases they may take executive action with little input from any other councillors—'backbench' or 'frontbench'. The same applies to the leader. Of still greater concern to some critics is the fact that, although most cabinets now meet publicly at least some of the time, they are only obliged to do so in relation to policy matters they have agreed to resolve collectively. In other words, matters delegated for decisions to individual cabinet members (or, in some cases, unelected officers) may be resolved in secret. Under the Localism Act 2011 cabinets retain their ability to meet in private.

The committee system has therefore gone from being a *proactive* agent in policymaking to a largely *reactive* one. Meanwhile, meetings of the full council—which still nominally has the final say over whether policies are approved—are often portrayed as 'rubber stamps' for decisions already finalized behind closed doors in cabinet. Similar charges are made of the second of the three models.

The 'directly elected mayor and cabinet' model

As explained in Chapter 11, there is a long-standing tradition among district/ borough councils and metropolitan district councils of appointing mayors. The office of **mayor** has customarily been ceremonial—with elected councillors taking it in turns to spend a year in the role, before passing on their chain of office to a colleague. While serving as mayor, the individual will adopt the role of returning officer in the event of a local, general, or European election, and officiate over civic duties (opening fetes, visiting schools, etc.), as well as chairing meetings of full council, in most cases. Like the Commons Speaker, mayors (temporarily) drop their party allegiances and right to vote on policy matters for the duration of their office. Some authorities, however, choose to divest mayors of their council chairmanship roles by electing separate speakers to perform that duty. In May 2012 Sylvia Gillard was elected speaker of Bedford Borough Council.

Directly elected mayors occupy different positions to ceremonial ones. First, unlike both council leaders and old-style mayors, they are not themselves councillors: instead they are voted in by their local electorates in separate ballots run *alongside* council elections. When Conservative Boris Johnson thwarted Ken Livingstone's bid for a mayoral comeback in May 2012, the separate election for the London Assembly saw Labour increase its grip on City Hall, securing twelve members to the Tories' nine. In this respect, the post of elected mayor bears more similarities to that of US president than British prime minister. While no Labour premier could remain in post long after an election in which the Tories won more seats, the same is not true of presidents: since the second half of his first White House term, Barack Obama has so far had to horse-trade with a Republican-dominated House of Representatives (though the Democrats retain a majority in the Senate).

Before being permitted to introduce elected mayors, councils must first hold referendums of the local electorate. Conversely, if 5 per cent of that electorate decides it favours a mayoral system, it may *demand* a referendum—whatever the council's own view.

Labour's hope was that *all* English councils would have initiated consultations about their proposed executive frameworks within six to nine months of the LGA 2000's passage—with many favouring the mayoral option. In practice it took until February 2002 for most to publish proposals, and when they did 80 per cent opted for the leader and cabinet model.

At time of writing, only sixteen councils had introduced elected mayors. The Greater London Authority Act 1999 made the GLA the first to adopt one, while four of the capital's borough councils have since done so: Hackney, Lewisham,

Newham, and Tower Hamlets. Other major towns and cities to do so include Middlesbrough, Mansfield, Leicester, and Bedford—with Doncaster voting to retain its DEM in May 2012 despite repeated controversies surrounding holders of the office.

Supporters of DEMs initially put down the slow overall pace of reform to the fact that, under Labour, whenever a referendum was lost another could not be held by the same council for five years. Of the forty-seven such referendums held to date, thirty-four failed to secure a majority in favour of elected mayors. In addition, campaigns have been launched at various points in four local authority areas to abolish the post: successfully in Stoke-on-Trent (see p. 401), but also in Doncaster, Lewisham, and Hartlepool (where, in 2009, Hartlepool United Football Club mascot 'H'Angus the Monkey'—alias Stuart Drummond—became the first DEM to win a third term. However, in November 2012, Hartlepool voted to abolish the role of elected mayor.). The fifteen councils operating an elected mayoral system as of October 2012 are listed in the table entitled 'Local authorities with directly elected mayors', to be found on the Online Resource Centre. To boost take-up, Labour published new proposals in July 2008 making it easier for local electors to trigger referendums, by enabling those campaigning for 'yes' votes to recruit supporters through online petitions. The plans were announced shortly after the failure of a campaign by the *Birmingham Mail* newspaper to marshal the 36,000 electors required to kick-start a local mayoral contest.

The Coalition has since mounted its own drive to persuade cities to adopt elected mayors. To this end, on 3 May 2012 Liverpool elected its first DEM (former Labour council leader Joe Anderson) and the ten other biggest cities outside London held local referendums, after Mr Pickles used a clause in the Localism Act 2011 to force votes in those areas. In the event, the Coalition's 'Big Bang' gamble backfired: nine out ten referendum cities, including Birmingham and Nottingham, rejected the idea, with only Bristol approving it. As an exercise in 'direct democracy', the referendums hardly set electorates on fire either: average turnout rates for the polls, held on the same day as English local elections, were below 29 per cent. To date only one Welsh local authority, Ceredigion County Council, has ever held a referendum on whether to adopt a DEM. It rejected the idea.

⊟ Topical feature idea

As for the Localism Act 2011, councils operating under post-LGA 2000 leader and cabinet executive arrangements have been allowed to abandon the system to return to an earlier form of collective decision-making by subcommittees and committees (which is still used by those covering populations of 85,000 or under).

How are authorities in your area responding to these reforms by the Coalition government? Is the executive decision-making system used locally in recent years likely to change—and, if so, how and when? Why not conduct a vox pop to find out how much local electors know about the current system of governance and any plans to change it?

✳ Current issues

- **The future of directly elected mayors:** the Coalition entered power committed to revolutionizing local democracy, in part through a mass roll-out of Labour's drive to introduce US-style directly elected mayors in English towns and cities. Following 'no' votes in nine out of ten cities balloted in May 2012, however, the future of DEMs now looks uncertain.

- **Curbs on pay of senior council officers:** Mr Pickles has said that in future few senior officers can expect to earn more than £100,000. Councils must now vote on/publish formal policy statements on pay scales for officers, and make details of senior staff salaries available on their websites and via a postcode search on the <http://www.direct.gov.uk> information portal.

- **The rise of the 'Big Society':** the Coalition is going further and faster than previous governments to encourage councils to outsource services to the private and voluntary sectors—with new 'community rights' allowing groups of citizens to bid to take over local assets when they come up for auction, or even challenge authorities to hand services over to them if they think they could run them better.

? Review questions

1. Outline the main differences between the responsibilities of 'officers' and 'councillors'. Who has most power and who is more accountable?

2. Describe the main changes to internal local authority hierarchies introduced over the past thirteen years. Which model is most democratically accountable?

3. What are the differences between the traditional roles of mayors and those of directly elected mayors? How does a town or city go about introducing the latter?

4. Who has power to take executive action under the three forms of local authority leadership that now exist? Why were the LGA 2000 changes so contentious?

5. How are councillors currently remunerated? What are the arguments for and against increasing their payments and/or introducing salaried councillors?

→ **Further reading**

Boynton, J. (1986) *Job at the Top: Chief Executive in Local Government*, London: Financial Times/Prentice Hall. **Concise, authoritative text examining emergence and growing influence of council chief executives and other senior officers.**

Cooper, K. and Macfarland, C. (2012) *Clubbing Together: The Hidden Wealth of Communities*, London: ResPublica. **Report by 'Red Tory' think tank ResPublica on how community-based social activities, clubs, and societies can foster Big Society-style projects delivering public benefit**.

Hodge, M., Leach, S., and Stoker, G. (1997) *Local Government Policy: More than the Flower Show—Elected Mayors and Democracy*, London: Fabian Society. **Pamphlet arguing for merits of directly elected mayors, prior to their introduction by Blair government and embrace by Coalition.**

Norman, J. (2010) *The Big Society: The Anatomy of the New Politics*, Buckingham: University of Buckingham Press. **Fiercely intellectual critique of ideas, ideology, and historical traditions underpinning David Cameron's 'Big Society' concept, published as volume in popular 'Look Inside' series.**

 Online Resource Centre

www.oxfordtextbooks.co.uk/orc/Morrison3e/
   Visit the Online Resource Centre that accompanies this book for web links and regular updates.

14

Local government accountability and elections

Between them, British local authorities are responsible for spending more than £65bn a year in taxpayers' money. Perhaps understandably, the decisions they make on behalf of those whose interests they represent are subject to increasing scrutiny.

Councils are accountable to local citizens by:

- publishing their own standing orders, codes of conduct, and constitutions;
- submitting their accounts to independent audits and publishing performance data;

- allowing press and public to attend their meetings and to access agendas and reports;
- giving local people a say through the ballot box at local authority elections.

This chapter focuses on the ways in which today's councillors (and officers) are held to account.

▌ Local government post-Nolan—the new era of transparency

As with central government, councils have long been expected to adhere to systems, rules, and procedures in conducting their business. But the extent to which they were required to *demonstrate* their integrity and openness underwent a profound shift following the succession of high-profile parliamentary scandals that led to the findings of the Nolan Inquiry (see pp. 54–5).

The immediate effect of Lord Nolan's recommendations, published in 1996, was to compel all public officials—starting with MPs, but extending down to local councillors and officers—to uphold 'Seven Principles of Public Life': selflessness, integrity, objectivity, accountability, openness, honesty, and leadership (see p. 55). But he and the prime minister who commissioned his inquiry, John Major, had a desire to go further—an aspiration shared by the latter's successor, Tony Blair, who consolidated the reforms in the Local Government Act 2000. Today the processes introduced to police the behaviour of MPs at national level also underpin accountability in local government.

Emergence of council constitutions

As mentioned in the previous chapter, under the LGA 2000 every local authority is now obliged to draw up—and agree with the Communities Secretary—its own **council constitution**. Within reason, this constitution can take any number of forms—whether a broad mission statement or a more detailed breakdown of the council's responsibilities and services. The very fact that individual councils are free, in theory, to devise their own wording reflects an acknowledgement by government that the particular issues different councils face in running their affairs vary. Since 19 December 2000, however, *all* constitutions have had to contain all of the components listed in Table 14.1.

Section 37 of the LGA 2000 specifies that copies of councils' constitutions must be available for inspection by the public 'at their principal offices' within

Table 14.1 Compulsory components of a council constitution

Component
1. Summary and explanation of purpose and content of constitution.
2. Description of composition of council, scheme of ordinary elections for members of council, and their terms of office.
3. Breakdown of principal roles and functions of councillors, including rights and duties of individual members.
4. Scheme of allowances for councillors.
5. Description of local inhabitants' rights and responsibilities, including their rights to vote in local elections and access information about local services and council, committee, subcommittee, and cabinet/executive meetings.
6. Description of council's roles.
7. Rules governing conduct and proceedings of meetings of authority.
8. Description of roles/functions of council chairperson (or mayor), leader/directly elected mayor, cabinet/executive, individual cabinet members, and individual officers with delegated executive powers.
9. Description of operational arrangements for overview and scrutiny committees, their terms of reference, membership, and any rules governing them.
10. Provisions in council's executive arrangements with respect to appointment of committees of executive.

(continued)

Table 14.1 (*continued*)

Component
11. Membership, terms of reference, and functions of committees and subcommittees, and any rules governing conduct of their meetings.
12. Description of roles of authority's standards committee and any parish council subcommittee of standards committee (plus details of membership).
13. Description of roles and membership of any area committees of authority.
14. Description of any joint arrangements made with other councils.
15. Description of officers' roles, including those of senior management.
16. Roles and functions of chief executive, monitoring officer, and chief finance officer.
17. Code of conduct for local government employees issued under Act, plus any details governing their recruitment, disciplinary procedures, etc.
18. Any protocol established by authority in respect of relationships between its members and officers.
19. Description of arrangements council has in place for access of public to members, and officers to meetings of full council, cabinet/executive, committees, subcommittees, and joint committees.
20. Description of arrangements the authority has in place for access of public to members, and officers to information about decisions made—or to be made—by any of above meetings.
21. Register stating names and addresses of every executive member, wards/divisions they represent, and names of every member of each executive committee.
22. Description of rules and procedures for management of authority's financial, contractual, and legal affairs, including procedures for auditing.
23. Authority's financial rules and regulations, and those governing procedures regarding contracts and procurement (including authentication of documents).
24. Rules and procedures for legal proceedings brought by and against authority.
25. Description of register of members' interests of all full and co-opted members of authority, and procedures for publicizing, maintaining, and updating it.
26. Description of rules and procedures for reviewing and revising authority's constitution and management structure.
27. Copy of authority's standing orders and code of conduct.

'all reasonable hours'. Personal copies must also be supplied by them to anyone on request—subject to the payment of a 'reasonable fee'.

The foundation stones of council constitutions

What, then, of the various technical terms highlighted in the government's criteria for the content of constitutions? The concept of **'standing orders'** is one that should be familiar to anyone who has worked for an organization of any size, whether in the public, private, or voluntary sectors. It refers to the overall system of rules and guidelines governing the day-to-day conduct of council business. Like the constitution as a whole, individual councils set their own standing orders—meaning they can be as detailed or as vague as they wish.

Some authorities may choose to incorporate into their standing orders rules governing the propriety of councillors and officers—for example, the requirement that those with financial interests in a matter due to be discussed by a committee in which they are involved must declare this fact and remove themselves from its meetings. Others may confine their standing orders to mundane procedural issues (as a bare minimum, most contain a breakdown of the customary order of business at council, committee, and cabinet meetings).

The remaining terms singled out by the LGA 2000 in instructing councils how to frame their constitutions all refer to the post-Nolan preoccupation with enforcing national standards of ethical conduct by public officials. Most councils have long had agreed **codes of conduct** specifying lists of 'dos' and 'don'ts' by which their members must abide. Following the sleaze allegations of the 1990s, however, a new onus was placed on those in public life at all levels to clean up their acts—in particular, keeping their 'outside interests' separate from duties they performed on the public's behalf.

Given the unpaid nature of councillors' work and the fact many juggle their duties with earning livings elsewhere (not always in the same town or city), the potential conflicts of interest in local government are arguably more multifarious than those faced by MPs. The councillor who is a member of his/her authority's planning committee and also sits on the board of a company with development interests in the area poses an all-too-familiar conundrum—and for this reason most councils have long had in place clear rules compelling members to make a **declaration of interest** in relation to any outside pecuniary interest. There has also been some criticism that councillors in this position are relegated to weaker positions than others—particularly those who stand for election on 'independent' tickets related to particular causes, such as defending a local service from closure, rather than conventional party-political platforms. It was partly in response to this concern that Coalition Communities Secretary Eric Pickles inserted a clause into the Localism Act 2011 to 'clarify' the rules on so-called 'predetermination'—the notion that, whatever their personal interests in particular local matters, individual councillors should come to council discussions demonstrating 'an open mind'. While any councillor henceforth exposed for withholding details of (or otherwise misrepresenting) a financial interest would be liable for criminal prosecution, the rewritten rulebook would generally allow them greater freedom to 'play an active part' in local debate, free from the threat of 'legal challenge'. Journalists had previously complained of a reluctance among councillors to speak to them ahead of meetings for fear of 'fettering' their discretion by doing so: that is, breaching their code of conduct or prejudicing potential future judicial reviews of council decisions.

The Local Government Act 1972 introduced the idea of local registers of interests, but as these were voluntary, councils were under no legal obligation to comply. It was the LGA 2000 that finally standardized the process, requiring *every* council to publish a reworded constitution reflecting Lord Nolan's 'Seven

Principles'. Declarations of interest, meanwhile, must now be made at the point someone first stands for election. As with MPs and peers, they are required to enter all interests on registers of members' interests (see p. 54) within twenty-eight days of being elected, which—given that new ones can emerge at any time—must be updated within twenty-eight days of any such changes occurring. Councillors must also declare relevant interests at the start of meetings in which they are due to participate if they have personal involvement in any agenda items. They should also remove themselves from such meetings—but only while the relevant item is discussed. The main types of interest defined by law are:

- employment or business interests;
- contributions to election expenses;
- shareholdings of £25,000 or more, or ownership of more than 1 per cent of issued share capital, in a company with a place of business or land in the council's area;
- a business interest in contracts between the authority and any other;
- land owned, leased, or held under licence for more than twenty-eight days in the authority's area;
- membership or management of a public authority, company, charity, trade union, or professional association.

Beyond this, it is the precise 'nature and extent' of a councillor's interest that determines whether it falls into one of two categories that might affect their ability to carry out their duties in an impartial and/or trustworthy way. Where previously interests would have been seen as either 'pecuniary' or 'non-pecuniary', the LGA 2000 redefined them as either:

- *personal*—any matter considered by the council the outcome of which might reasonably be regarded as affecting the 'well-being or financial position' of him/herself, a relative, friend, or organization in which he/she has an interest;
- *prejudicial*—a matter which a member of the public with knowledge of the facts might reasonably regard as so significant that it is likely to prejudice the councillor's judgement of what is in the public interest.

Regulating standards

Who, then, polices these rules? As explained in the last chapter, each authority has a designated monitoring officer, whose job is to ensure the council as a whole—and its constituent parts—act within the law and do not overreach their powers. The introduction of codes of conduct and registers of interests—coupled with the onus placed on officers, as well as councillors, to act accountably—was initially accompanied by a greater emphasis on objective scrutiny. To this end, the LGA 2000 compelled each council to appoint its own **standards committee**, like that at Westminster, to monitor its officials' actions and raise concerns about unethical conduct. Its independence was theoretically assured by the fact that, in addition to two or more councillors, it must include at least one individual who was neither a member nor an officer of that or 'any other relevant' authority.

The roles of standards committees were to:

- promote and maintain high standards of conduct by members and co-opted members;
- assist members and co-opted members of the authority to observe its code of conduct;
- advise the authority on the adoption or revision of a code of conduct;
- monitor the operation of the code of conduct;
- advise, train, or arrange to train members and co-opted members of the authority on matters relating to the code of conduct.

On a day-to-day basis, they often devolved many of their functions to a subcommittee of the authority, but its composition and precise remit must be formally agreed with the involvement of local parish councils.

At the other end of the scale, the conduct of English councils, their members, and officers was, for more than a decade, overseen by a quango, Standards for England (formerly the Standards Board for England), until its abolition in the Localism Act 2011. Councillors made aware of apparent misconduct by a colleague were expected to make formal 'written allegations' to it. Mr Pickles used the 2011 Act to scrap the existing 'standards regime' in its entirety—criticizing Labour's system for forcing councils to 'spend time and money investigating trivial complaints', and so 'undermining people's faith in local democracy'. Instead, each authority must now draw up a new code governing the conduct of its councillors, using the full force of criminal law to prosecute them for wrongdoing on the rare occasions such action becomes necessary. In the absence of a more independently policed standards framework, however, it remains to be seen how future breaches will come to light in the first place.

In Wales allegations of councillor misconduct continue to be handled by its overarching Public Services Ombudsman for Wales, while errant members of Scottish authorities may be disciplined by the Standards Commission for Scotland. At time of writing, the Northern Ireland Assembly was still finalizing a new 'ethical standards framework' for councils as part of a prolonged consultation over its Local Government (Reorganization) Bill.

While the various standards regulators have only minimal legal powers, helpfully for the media, they normally disclose the fact a complaint has been made, issuing full details of their eventual decisions and any sanctions imposed.

From 'Beacon Councils' to the National Indicator Set—the growth of performance data

The growing emphasis placed on promoting high ethical standards among public officials emerged hand in hand with what critics decried as a spiralling government obsession with centrally directed performance targets, league tables, and ratings systems to grade the quality of their work. First up under New Labour were 'Beacon Councils'—authorities singled out as examples of best practice in particular areas of service delivery. Then came Best Value performance indicators (BVPIs), which defined four key 'dimensions of performance' (criteria, to the layperson) against which the effectiveness of specific local services would in future be measured: 'strategic objectives', 'service delivery outcomes', 'quality', and 'fair access' for all local citizens.

The early Blair years saw an explosion of BVPIs—some covering local services as a whole; others specific aspects of individual ones, ranging from local street cleaning to childcare provision. Early BVPIs focused on 'service delivery' (the actual standard of local services from the public's perspective) and 'corporate health' (a category containing a further eighteen indicators, relating to everything from 'customers and the community' to 'partnership working'). Eventually there were more than ninety.

The advent of BV (see p. 394) marked merely the beginning of a new era of monitoring, auditing, and evaluating councils' performance. In December 2002 a system of service-by-service performance ratings was introduced: *comprehensive performance assessment* (CPA). Overall responsibility for monitoring the effectiveness of individual councils in England and Wales (including police authorities)—and taking action when necessary—was handed to a central government quango, the Audit Commission, which discharged this role through a network of district auditors (each overseeing a specific authority area). Scottish councils were to be held to account by Audit Scotland, while Northern Irish ones would have their books pored over by officers from the Northern Ireland Audit Office (NIA).

Initially covering only 'top-tier' local authorities (county councils and unitaries), CPA was subsequently extended to encompass districts/boroughs, and fire and rescue authorities. One of the main differences between BV and CPA was that the new set of data was made public, allowing local taxpayers and the media to judge the performance of their councils in specific service areas against those of other authorities, in much the same way they might view hospital league tables or school exam performance data.

Taxpayers could visit the Commission's website at any time to access their council's CPA 'scorecard', while its annual reports would 'name and shame' the best and worst of the previous year, judging them not only on their absolute star rating, but also a value-added basis, known as 'direction of travel'. But CPA was far from the last word in New Labour's quest to find the perfect rating system—spawning, in turn, *comprehensive area assessment* (CAA) (a CPA derivative designed to record taxpayers' experience of services in their 'areas', rather than those provided by individual councils) and *National Indicator Sets* (NIS) (a more sophisticated version of the same, giving everyone instant online access to all of this information via a single website—http://oneplace.direct.gov.uk).

In keeping with its distaste for Labour's centrally directed 'target culture', the Coalition stopped updating oneplace in June 2010, and scrapped the NIS system entirely in March 2011. However, in a move decried by some critics as contradictory, Mr Pickles made good on another of the Conservatives' stated aims—to make councils more accountable to local people for how they spend taxpayers' money—by stipulating that they lay bare everything from waste disposal and recycling rates to food hygiene reports and pub licensing decisions on their own websites. They must also publish details of all items of expenditure, contracts, and tenders worth £500 or more, all payments to councillors, and all staff salaries of £58,200 and over (see p. 393).

While the abandonment of Labour's blizzard of performance data was welcomed by many authorities, and representative bodies like the County Councils Network, there was a less universal thumbs-up for Mr Pickles's sudden abolition of the Audit Commission—the quango set up to vet local authorities' balance sheets by a previous Tory government in 1983. Even more contentious was his decision to scrap its research role and outsource its auditing function to a network of independent providers. When the first tranche of contracts was announced, in March 2012, critics of the 'privatization' of public sector auditing felt their warnings had been vindicated: DA Partnership, an employee-owned offshoot of the Commission touted by ministers as an example of the new forms of community-based company they wanted to promote as part of the 'Big Society', secured only one of the ten regional franchises on offer. The remaining nine were carved up by private consultancy firms Ernst & Young, KPMG, and Grant Thornton. The latter—which won four contracts, with a combined value of £41.3m—had pledged to take on 300 of the Commission's existing 2,000-strong staff, but even this proved controversial, with some 500 employees taking industrial action in February that year over concerns about their pension rights being eroded during the takeover.

The last resort—the role of Local Government Ombudsmen

Of course targets, league tables, and publication of performance data can only take things so far. What should people do if they feel they have suffered an injustice at the hands of their local authorities—or if they believe they have lost out because a council has, say, taken an incorrect decision on their eligibility for services?

In relation to English authorities, for nearly forty years the answer has been to lodge a formal complaint with the **Local Government Ombudsman (LGO)**—officially, the **Commission for Local Administration in England**. The remit of the two ombudsmen employed by the service is to investigate allegations of maladministration—the negligent or incompetent running of local services. They are not there simply to consider complaints relating to decisions about which people are unhappy, however, *unless* those decisions show evidence of maladministration. Since 1988 complainants have been able to take their cases direct to the ombudsmen without the need to use their local councillors as intermediaries (a principle enshrined in the Local Government Act 1974, which had first established the service). This change had an immediate impact on the number of complaints made: in the first year alone they soared by 44 per cent.

England's twin ombudsmen each oversee patchwork spreads of geographical areas and specific authorities:

- One covers all London boroughs except Lewisham; Manchester, York, Trafford, and High Peak; unitary authorities in Essex, Kent, East Sussex, Surrey, Buckinghamshire, and Gloucestershire; authorities in Berkshire, Suffolk, the south and west of England, and several councils in central England.

- The other deals with Lewisham, Birmingham, Coventry and Solihull; county and district authorities in Essex, Kent, East Sussex, Surrey, Buckinghamshire, and Gloucestershire; and eleven councils in West Sussex, Surrey, Hertfordshire, Cheshire, Derbyshire, Nottinghamshire, Lincolnshire, Warwickshire, and the north of England (except for High Peak BC, Trafford BC, and the cities of Manchester and York).

Handily for journalists (and public), 'annual reviews' of the overall performance of individual English councils in dealing with complaints made about them to the ombudsman are published on its website at http://www.lgo.org.uk/CouncilsPerformance.

In Wales, since 2006 local government maladministration has been policed by the overarching Public Services Ombudsman for Wales, while in Scotland a Scottish Public Services Ombudsman was introduced in 2003. The Northern Ireland Ombudsman, meanwhile, has been in place since 1969.

Complaints processes to these bodies are subject to various conditions. Those applying in England are indicative of those in the devolved countries, as outlined in the table entitled 'The conditions for filing complaints with the Local Government Commissioner', to be found on the Online Resource

Centre.

As more people become aware of the ombudsmen, so the number of complaints investigated each year continues to rise. Their powers have also been extended, allowing them to handle two new categories of complaint: those made by adults arranging and/or funding their own social care (see p. 546), and criticisms by pupils and parents about school performance in fourteen local education authority areas. Recent years have also seen a notable increase in the number of complaints about the administration of the benefits system at local level—significantly, at a time when unemployment has generally been rising, while the Coalition has been simultaneously redefining entitlement criteria and reducing payments for some claimants. Understandably, journalists are always keen to learn about cases being heard by the ombudsmen as they come up, because they tend to concern major complaints and be highly newsworthy. At times, however, these stories can be frustrating: while ombudsmen's final adjudications are always made public, because the identities of those involved are usually kept anonymous, the resulting reports are rarely as revealing as press or public might hope.

Punishing errant councillors and officers

In exceptional circumstances, individual councillors and senior officers found culpable of major financial or managerial irregularities have in the past been personally *surcharged* by the Audit Commission on behalf of their authorities. The most infamous example of wilful misconduct of this kind was the 'homes for votes' scandal of July 1987, which saw then leader of Westminster City Council Dame Shirley Porter and her colleague, David Weeks, conspire to sell off 500 council houses a year to potential Tory voters living in marginal wards, in order to engineer Conservative victories in forthcoming elections. The mass sell-off—dubbed 'Building Stable Communities'—was made possible by the Thatcher government's 'Right to Buy' scheme (see pp. 503–6), but Dame Shirley's motives were exposed after an investigation by district auditor John Magill, who condemned her actions as 'disgraceful and improper gerrymandering'. After a legal battle lasting for much of the 1990s, the Tesco heiress was ordered to repay £27m to the council, plus interest and legal costs. Having initially claimed she had little more than £300,000 to her name, in 2004 she finally relented—reimbursing £12m. The surcharging power was repealed by the LGA 2000 but, like MPs, councillors and officers can still be prosecuted for serious offences like fraud.

▌ Access to council meetings and business—the 'old' system

Until recently the rights of press and public to attend meetings of councils, their committees, and subcommittees were straightforward and widely understood. Though authorities often refer to the Local Government Act 1972 in their published papers, it was the Local Government (Access to Information) Act 1985—arising out of a private member's Bill introduced by Conservative backbencher Robin Squire—that enshrined their right to attend *all* such meetings, unless information due for discussion was 'confidential' or 'exempt'. The former category refers to specified classes of information supplied by government departments, or matters disclosure of which is prohibited under statute or by the courts. An example might be details relating to national security or crime prevention prohibited by either the Official Secrets Act or anti-terror laws. 'Exempt' information includes:

- details judged 'personal' and/or 'commercially sensitive'—for example, those relating to the terms of contracts disclosure of which might have a negative impact on the authority's future ability to negotiate value for money for local taxpayers;
- matters 'in the process of being negotiated'—for example, details of contractual negotiations with competing companies the council is considering hiring to provide services;
- issues 'protected by legal privilege'—for example, when a council's members are discussing confidential legal advice given to it in relation to litigation by or against it, or contractual matters they are seeking to resolve through the courts.

Under these arrangements councils tended to use one of two methods for excluding the press and public from meetings (or more usually *sections* of meetings). Most commonly, councils divided their meetings into a 'part one' and 'part two'—with all confidential and/or exempt items (commonly known as 'below the line') held back until the second half. Alternatively, they might hold votes to exclude press and public for the duration of single, specified agenda items. The vote had to be formally proposed, seconded, and carried by members at the meeting—and *reasons* given to those excluded (usually citing the Schedule to the 1985 Act under which the exclusion was being sought). If the motion failed, the matter concerned had to be heard publicly, and copies of supporting reports instantly circulated to members of the press and public present.

In addition to granting the press and public automatic access to its meetings, councils were also required to provide information in *advance* of the proceedings, and after the event to publicize the outcomes of any votes and debates. At the meetings themselves, clerks had to ensure they went further, in the interests of accessibility, than simply unlocking the doors to the press and public galleries. Most of these access provisions, which apply to open meetings to this day, are listed in Table 14.2.

In the past councils were frequently accused of going against the spirit of these access requirements (if not the letter). The not uncommon practice of holding meetings on controversial issues in very small rooms—or barring entry because of 'overcrowding'—was once famously condemned as 'bad faith' by then Lord Chief Justice Lord Widgery. Admission for press and public to meetings of other bodies, including NHS trusts and non-principal local authorities (parish and town councils), are guaranteed by the Public Bodies (Admissions to Meetings) Act 1960.

Table 14.2 Access-to-meetings requirements expected of local authorities

Requirement	What it means
Public registers	Each authority must keep lists of names and addresses of all councillors, and details of committees on which they serve. Any powers delegated to officers must be listed.
Copies of agenda papers	Orders of business and all reports prepared by officers for consideration at meetings—and submitted during open parts—must be made available on the day. No matters must be heard unless listed on agendas at least three days beforehand—only exception is when urgent issues arise that could not have been predicted. In such circumstances, they should be mentioned during 'matters arising', towards end of agenda.
Access to **background papers**	All reports presented for public inspection should list any background papers used to help draft them. Press and public may also examine these (although they may be charged 'reasonable fee' for doing so).
Minutes of previous meetings	Copies of minutes of open meetings should be made available automatically to press and local electors on request. **Minutes** are records of proceedings that *actually* take place at meetings—including items debated that were not on original agenda—and official record of all decisions taken. They normally resemble detailed 'summing up' of what each person said, rather than verbatim record. Minutes of local authority meetings will usually be sent to journalists, along with agendas for subsequent meetings.
'Reasonable accommodation'	This must be provided for both press and public, and normally means there should be sufficient numbers of seats and, whenever possible, press benches. At meetings expected to be unusually popular (e.g. planning committee or full council meeting at which decision is due to be made about major housing development), 'overflow rooms' should be provided. If oversubscribed, audio and/or video feed of proceedings should be made available to those forced to sit or stand outside meeting room, enabling them to see/hear proceedings.

Other measures councils have been encouraged to take to improve their communication with—and accountability to—press and public include appointing public relations and/or press officers (a move suggested in the Bains Report). The remit of such paid PR people would be strictly to promote *council* initiatives and policies, rather than to generate positive publicity for specific *political groupings*. Councils were also expected to give journalists access to individual councillors—particularly committee chairmen or cabinet members—to obtain quotes justifying political decisions, and even senior officers, should they require technical explanations.

In practice, by the mid-1990s many local authorities still had no press office, although more recently a common complaint levelled at them by journalists has been that they place too much emphasis on proactive media management, designed to deflect criticism of their actions and promote council policies, and too little on serving the needs of journalists. Controversy has also surrounded the plethora of taxpayer-funded newspapers, magazines, and newsletters published by councils, ostensibly to inform residents about the services they provide. Editors and owners of commercial newspapers have accused some authorities of undercutting them by courting paid external advertising, and professionalizing their publications by recruiting experienced journalists on generous salaries to write them, while broadening their coverage to encompass non-council-related articles. By 2010 *East End Life*, a weekly published by the London Borough of Tower Hamlets, was being posted free of charge through the letterboxes of 81,000 homes, while its long-established independent rival, the *East London Advertiser*, was selling just 6,800 copies at a 50p cover price.

In their defence, some councils have argued that they feel forced to publish their own news sheets because of the unwillingness of their local press to run positive stories, or ones concerning worthy but dull information they need to pass on to local people. However, mounting concern about the use of public money for such purposes prompted successive Communities Secretaries to liken council publications to the Soviet-era state-owned newspaper 'Pravda' and 'propaganda sheets'. In 2011 Mr Pickles clamped down on the practice by introducing a new 'publicity code' banning councils from: publishing newspapers in direct competition with the local press; producing them more often than once a quarter; or including in their pages anything unrelated to the services they provided or commissioned. He later warned that authorities that flouted the ban—including the London boroughs of Tower Hamlets and Greenwich—could be penalized by judicial review.

▌Access to local authority business—the 'new' system

The LGA 2000 introduced significant new limitations on the extent to which press and public would be allowed access to meetings of local authorities adopting one of the 'new-style' executive arrangements (see pp. 401–6). While full council, committee, and subcommittee meetings remain as public as ever under these regimes, access to others has become more restricted. Because many final decisions are now effectively taken by cabinets and related bodies with delegated powers, critics argue that—contrary to their rhetoric—councils have become *less* transparent than previously. Initially cabinets were not obliged to meet publicly at all, but the LGA 2000 was modified by government guidance issued in 2002 requiring them to convene openly whenever discussing key decisions (see p. 404) to be taken by their members collectively. Controversially, however, key decisions delegated to individual cabinet members, or in some cases officers, may still be taken in private.

The main requirements for openness in council decision-making under the LGA 2000 (as modified by the later guidance and the Local Government and Public Involvement in Health Act 2007) are listed in Table 14.3.

The principal differences between the old-style and new-style systems in relation to openness to press and public scrutiny are twofold. Because many significant decisions about policy formulation and implementation are now taken in cabinet—or even individually, by elected mayors, leaders, or cabinet members (and sometimes officers) with delegated executive powers—by holding such meetings in private councils can prevent the public finding out about their plans until after the event. For example, in February 2010 Woking Borough Council finalized the £68m purchase of a local shopping centre in a closed meeting—only revealing the fact in a statement afterwards on its website. The buyout relied on a loan from the Public Works Loan Board (PWLB) that will take the borough's taxpayers fifty years to repay. Such practices are occurring, say critics, at a time when meetings that *are* still open to the public—those of subcommittees, committees, and even the full council—are being reduced to talking shops (see pp. 405–6).

Criticisms aside, the press and public continue to have a right to the following:

- three days' notice of meetings open to the press;
- agendas and minutes of council meetings;
- registers of planning applications;
- records of payments to councillors;
- the council constitution, code of conduct, and standing orders;
- a statutory register of members' interests;
- copies of any reports into allegations of maladministration by the Local Government Commissioner (Local Government Ombudsman);
- the council's annual accounts, annual audit (including the right to inspect certain items), performance indicators, and future performance plans;

Table 14.3 Changes to access-to-meetings criteria under the 'new-style' system

	Change
1.	Full council, committee, and subcommittee meetings to continue meeting in public, subject to 'access to information' requirements under 1985 Act.
2.	Executive/cabinet bodies *not* required to meet publicly unless discussing key decisions they are due to resolve collectively. They must, however, publish more minor decisions after taking them, and monthly forward plans outlining all upcoming key decisions in advance.
3.	Decisions of mayors/individual executive politicians are subject to 1985 Act—but 'records' of their decisions must be published after they are taken.
4.	Overview and scrutiny committees—and other scrutiny bodies—to meet in public, subject to existing 'access to information' requirements.

- general financial information;
- the council's full annual report (including comparative data indicating how well it has performed as against 'similar authorities').

The order of business in local authority meetings

All meetings of councillors—whether committee, full council, or executive—follow the same format as they did under the old system, as outlined in Table 14.4.

▶ Local elections

Until 1974 local elections were held throughout the first week in May, but the Local Government Act 1972 stipulated that they take place on the first Thursday in May (unless the Home Secretary fixed another day). The Act also

Table 14.4 Order of business in council, committee, and subcommittee meetings

Order of business	What happens
Publication of agenda	**Agenda**—document outlining matters to be discussed at meeting and proposed order of business—prepared by council's chief executive, secretary, or director of administration—and publicized in advance.
Approval of minutes	Meeting opens with formal approval of minutes of previous meeting of same body.
Questions	Usually written down in advance by specific councillors, these are put to committee chairpersons. At full council meetings for local authorities that have adopted a post-LGA 2000 constitution, questions put to elected mayor, leader, or relevant cabinet member.
Public questions	Observers on public benches given chance to question committee chairpersons (optional).
Petitions	Any petitions from electors (e.g. in protest over proposed site of new landfill site) presented to full council by local councillors representing relevant ward or electoral division. Actual debates on these issues held at relevant later committee meetings.
Consideration of reports	In full council, reports from committees are considered, while committees consider those of subcommittees. Debates often arise over politically controversial matters. Councillors with strong objections to given proposal may ask for matter to be amended or 'referred back' to committee (or cabinet).
Notices of motion	Individual councillors should table these in advance if they wish them to be debated. They usually cover issues not formally listed on agenda. In LGA 2000-style councils, any notices impinging on executive issues must be referred to executive/cabinet for final decision.

clarified—for the first time—that *all* councillors must be directly elected. Up to this point archaic offices had remained in certain areas—for example 'aldermen', who were elected only by other councillors.

All councillors are now elected for four years—except those voted in at by-elections caused by deaths of sitting councillors, or their resignation or disqualification from office in mid-term. Councillors elected in by-elections sit for the remainder of the terms of the members they replace, and stand for re-election at the same time as their colleagues. If a councillor dies or otherwise leaves office after the September of a year preceding an election, his/her seat remains vacant until polling day—it is considered too near the general poll to call a by-election.

Local authority constituencies

Councillors, like MPs, have their own constituencies (albeit covering far smaller geographical areas than parliamentary ones). Unlike Commons seats, however, those used in council elections are represented by up to three councillors at a time.

The terms used to refer to council constituencies differ from one type of local authority to another:

- 'County divisions'—or **electoral divisions**—are the constituencies in county elections in England and Wales. Some unitaries also use electoral divisions. They tend to be geographically bigger, and represent more people, than those for other types of council.
- **Wards** are the constituencies in districts/boroughs, metropolitan boroughs, London boroughs, and most unitary authorities in England and Wales. All Scottish local authorities have wards.

In general, whether a ward or electoral division is represented by one, two, or three councillors is determined by its population size. Most urban wards contain roughly the same number of electors and, as they are based in towns, have fairly high populations. They are generally represented by three councillors. In rural electoral divisions and wards in mixed rural/urban areas, population levels can be significantly more varied—meaning some have only one councillor, while others are designated 'multimember divisions or wards', with up to three.

Since 31 December 2010 there have been 9,434 wards and electoral divisions in the UK, each covering an average population of 5,500. The table entitled 'The numbers of wards and electoral divisions in the UK', to be found on the Online Resource Centre, gives an overview of the number of wards and electoral divisions in each of the four countries of England, Wales, Scotland, and Northern Ireland.

Local authority election cycles

The precise election cycle followed by a local authority—that is, the years in which it holds its elections—depends on which type of council it is. Present cycles are listed in Table 14.5.

As illustrated above, local election cycles can be confusing for electors. This is especially true for those living in two-tier areas, who face elections more often than most, given that they are covered by not one but two councils: a district/ borough and county. In some areas, where district/borough and county elections are occasionally held in the same year, the process can be particularly confusing.

Among the many other changes it heralded, the LGA 2000 envisaged councils' patchwork election cycles gradually being rationalized over time. The Act tried to facilitate this by recommending that they all adopt one of the following three models:

- whole-council elections *every four years* at the same time;
- half the council stands for election *every two years*;
- one-third of the council stands in *three out of four years*.

Table 14.5 Electoral cycles for different types of English council

Type of local authority	Electoral cycle
County council	Every four years, with whole council retiring at same time. Elections last held in 2009, and due in 2013, 2017, etc.
London borough councils	Every four years—with whole council retiring simultaneously. To avoid conflicting with county polls, London boroughs hold elections in different years. Last were in 2010.
Metropolitan borough councils	Three out of every four years—one-third of councillors retire each time (usually one councillor per ward). Elections never take place in these areas in same year as county council polls. Current cycle began in 2010.
District/borough councils	Choice of elections *either* in three out of every four years—one-third of council retires each time—*or* all councillors in one go. If districts/boroughs opt for 'three-out-of-four-year' cycle, electoral calendar is same as that for metropolitan boroughs. If they opt for 'Big Bang' polls every four years these are held midway between those of counties—in 2015, 2019, etc.
Unitary authorities	Choice of elections *either* in three out of every four years *or* all councillors in one go—special arrangements made in areas with hybrid council structure (one or more unitary authorities coexisting with two-tier system—see p. 334). When new unitary authority is created from amalgamation of pre-existing district and county, statutory order may be passed stating new council should initially sit for *less than four years*—to stop elections clashing with future county ones.
Parish, town, and community councils	Every four years—whole council retires at same time, in 2015, 2019, etc. Each parish council must have at least five councillors—actual numbers fixed by local district council. Some parishes follow ward-based system (like their parent authorities).

Because it was left up to individual councils to decide when (and whether) to reform, little has come of the Act's recommendations. In January 2004, following a lengthy consultation, the Electoral Commission warned in a report that public confusion about electoral cycles was contributing to the general malaise afflicting local democracy, by further eroding turnouts already dwindling due to widespread political apathy. It cited research conducted on its behalf in April 2003 by MORI, which found a quarter of British people did not know whether elections were due to be held in their areas that May. Only one in six were able to say how often elections were held locally. The findings prompted the Commission to make the following recommendations (yet to be acted on by ministers):

- all councils in England should hold whole-council elections every four years;
- county councils and the Greater London Authority (GLA) should hold elections in different years from boroughs/districts, unitaries, metropolitan boroughs, and London boroughs.

Quite apart from their baffling nature, the present local electoral cycles have produced curious quirks. Because individual district/borough councils are permitted to choose whether to follow a whole-council election model or one in which votes are held in three out of every four years there are some counties in which, in any one year, elections may be held for a borough, district, county, and potentially even neighbouring unitary authority. By the same token, two district/borough councils sitting side by side in the same county may choose to adopt different cycles, meaning that—despite having the same council functions—they only hold elections on the same day as each other a maximum of once every four years.

Who can stand as a councillor?

As at general elections (see Chapter 4), any citizen of the UK, Irish Republic, or a Commonwealth country who lives in Britain and is over the age of 18 on the day he/she is nominated may stand as a candidate—provided he/she can prove one of a range of verifiable connections with the area in which he/she is standing, and is not disqualified in law for any of the reasons listed in Table 14.6. There is no requirement for an election deposit.

Unlike at general elections, candidature is also open to European Union (EU) citizens who meet the same criteria. To be nominated, a prospective councillor has to obtain the signatures of both a *proposer* and *seconder*—both of whom must be registered to vote in the relevant local authority area. Candidates must also be able to prove that *at least one* of the following is true:

- he/she is a legitimate elector listed on the local electoral register—the list of registered voters kept by the local electoral registration officer;

Table 14.6 Disqualifications for candidacy as a councillor

Category of person	Details of disqualification
Some bankrupts	Prospective candidates barred if they are undischarged bankrupts subject to bankruptcy restriction order made by Insolvency Service (executive agency of Department of Business, Innovation, and Skills). This means they have been found to have acted dishonestly or in otherwise 'blameworthy' way. In Northern Ireland anyone adjudged bankrupt is barred, while in Scotland anyone whose estate has been sequestered is banned.
Certain recent convicts	Those convicted of a criminal offence with minimum penalty of three months in prison during five years before election.
Electoral fraudster	Anyone convicted of corrupt or illegal election practice in previous five years.
Politically restricted officials	Those working for council for which they intend to stand, or holding a post with any other authority that is politically restricted (e.g. senior officer position in which they are expected to work closely with elected councillors and give dispassionate advice free from any personal political bias—see p. 121). Civil servants working for Whitehall departments above 'Grade 7' may only stand in local elections with permission of their employers (most senior ones are banned).

- he/she has been resident in the area for the twelve months before the nomination process;
- his/her 'principal or only place of work' has been in the area for the whole preceding year;
- he/she has owned property in the area for the whole of the preceding year.

The ability of EU citizens to stand as councillors, and the rather fluid test of 'residency' in a council's area, make the qualifications for local authority candidates seem less stringent than those for prospective MPs. Unlike in general elections, this liberal attitude extends to peers entitled to sit in the Lords, who, although barred from standing for the Commons, may become councillors. Labour peer and former minister Lord Bassam was, for a time, leader of Brighton and Hove Council in the 1990s.

Who can vote in local elections?

Only people whose names are on the electoral register for a given council area are entitled to vote. To be eligible for inclusion on the register, a person must be:

- aged at least 18 or due to turn 18 during the twelve-month period covered by the register (provided he/she is 18 by the date of voting);

- a UK, Commonwealth, Irish Republic, or other EU citizen;
- qualified on the basis of normal residency, service in the Armed Forces or as a merchant seaman, or a declaration as a voluntary mental patient;
- not barred because he/she:
  - is a foreign national from outside the EU and Commonwealth;
  - is a convict detained in prison or a mental institution;
  - has been convicted within the previous five years of corrupt or illegal practices.

As with general elections, it is the electoral registration officer's responsibility to ensure that every household completes a *compulsory* electoral registration form. Anyone moving from one council area to another may have his/her name added to the electoral register at the start of a given month under a system of 'rolling registration' introduced in 2000.

The local election process

The procedure governing local elections is summarized in Table 14.7.

Of the various other rules governing the legitimate conduct of local elections, most notable are those limiting the sums candidates are allowed to spend on campaigning. The spending cap was most recently raised in March

Table 14.7 Local election procedure in Britain

Stage	Procedure
Notice of election	Must be published *at least twenty-five days before an election.*
Nomination papers submitted	To be handed in *by noon nineteen days before the election.*
Publication of candidates list	Must be published *by noon on the seventeenth day before the election.*
Candidate withdrawals	This can happen *no later than sixteen days before the election.*
Appointment of officials	Each council appoints returning officer to preside over election count (normally mayor or chairperson of council, but role may be taken on day by 'acting' or 'deputy returning officer', usually chief executive—see p. 392). It is his/her responsibility to appoint presiding officers and poll clerks to attend polling stations during day, supervise counting of votes, rule on whether any ballot papers have been 'spoiled', and publish finished results.
Polling stations open	Usually based at local schools and community centres, these open from 8 a.m. to 9 p.m. for local elections.
Votes cast	When electors (or their proxies) arrive at polling station to vote, their names are checked against register before ballot papers issued. If electors apply for postal votes, they must send them to designated place, not the polling station.

2005, by statutory instrument, at the Electoral Commission's request. Those standing as councillors may now spend £600 on campaign expenses, while mayoral candidates are entitled to spend up to £2,000 (both sums are broadly equivalent to 5p per elector). The decision to more than double spending limits (council candidates had previously been forced to keep their expenditure below £242) was partly a belated response to the impact of the Representation of the People Act 1983, which, for the first time, required candidates to declare the financial value of 'benefits in kind' such as free use of stationery, offices, or other facilities. To ensure limits are not exceeded, agents must send inventories of their candidates' expenses to their returning officer after the poll.

Moves towards improving local election turnout

Dwindling engagement in local elections has long concerned UK governments. Compared to many EU countries, the turnout in Britain's local polls is extremely poor: in a 2000 survey by the then Office of the Deputy Prime Minister (ODPM) it came bottom of the European league, with an average turnout of just two out of every five electors (a drop of 37 per cent since 1987). Between 2 million and 4 million people are estimated to be absent from the electoral register at any one time—whether intentionally (to avoid Council Tax) or because of apathy towards the democratic process.

The Labour government, aided by the Commission, mooted several changes to boost turnout, but up to now these have only been implemented in a piecemeal way:

- introducing anonymous registration for those reluctant to have their names listed;
- opening polling stations at supermarkets, workplaces, colleges, doctors' surgeries, etc.;
- allowing voting over a period of a few days, rather than just one;
- introducing universal postal voting;
- electronic voting—via email, Internet, text messaging, etc.;
- holding annual elections for at least a portion of each council, to make councils more accountable to electors by forcing them to campaign for votes continually.

The most 'successful' local elections—such as the 2008 and 2012 votes for London mayor and the GLA—are often viewed through the prism of what is happening on the national and global political stages, rather than as true tests of public opinion about the merits of the candidates and parties locally. The results of 'mid-term' local elections—those held partway through Parliaments, by which time voters are often disenchanted with serving governments—frequently send 'shots across their bows', and are consequently styled 'protest votes' by political commentators and pollsters. The 2008 local elections were an object lesson in protest voting. Barely a week after Mr Brown's government had meekly pledged to compensate low-earners hit by the abolition of the 10p starting rate of Income Tax (many its own grass-roots voters), Labour polled its worst result for more than forty years. It scored barely 24 per cent, coming one point behind the Lib Dems, and 20 per cent shy of the Tories—a share that would have sent it to a crushing defeat in a general election.

The task of reviewing the electoral arrangements of English councils—and overall structures and boundaries—was until recently the responsibility of a committee of the Boundary Committee for England, but in 2010 it was a replaced by a new dedicated **Local Government Boundary Commission for England (LGBCE)**. This is charged with carrying out electoral reviews of all councils every few years to ensure the number of electors represented by each councillor is broadly the same nationwide. It may also undertake discrete reviews for individual councils, such as newly established unitary authorities. There are separate local boundary commissions for Scotland and Wales, and a Local Government Boundaries Commissioner for Northern Ireland.

≣ Topical feature idea

Figure 14.1 summarizes the Local Government Ombudsman's official 2011 annual review for Christchurch Borough Council, Dorset, taken from the organization's website. What questions are raised by the number of complaints forwarded by the LGO for formal investigation, and the areas about which they were lodged? What questions arise out of the two rulings of maladministration and injustice against the council, and how would you set about finding out more about these decisions? Who would you approach for interviews?

✳ Current issues

- **The 'end' of target culture:** the National Indicator Set (NIS), the latest of several systems introduced by Labour to rate the performance of local service areas, has been abolished by the Coalition. Instead, councils must voluntarily 'throw open their books' by publishing their own performance data and details of all spending, contracts, and tenders worth more than £500.

- **Abolition of Labour's standards regime:** as part of its strategy of moving away from national and regional oversight of local government to more localized regulation,

Figure 14.1 Local authority report: Christchurch BC, for the period ending 31 March 2011

Enquiries and complaints received	Benefits & Tax	Corporate & Other Services	Education & Childrens Services	Environmental Services & Public Protection & Regulation	Highways & Transport	Housing	Other	Planning & Development	Total
Formal/ informal premature complaints	0	0	0	0	0	0	0	0	0
Advice given	0	0	0	0	0	0	0	0	0
Forwarded in investigative team (resubmitted)	1	0	0	1	0	2	0	1	5
Forwarded to investigative team (new)	0	0	0	0	0	0	0	3	3
Total	1	0	0	1	0	2	0	4	8

Investigative team

Decisions	Reports: maladministration and injustice	Local settlements (no report)	Reports: Maladministration no injustice	Reports: no Maladministration	No Maladministration (no report)	Ombudsman's discretion (no report)	Outside jurisdiction	Total
2010/11	2	0	0	0	7	8	1	18

Source: Local Government Ombudsman, © Commission for Local Administration in England, 2008

the Coalition has scrapped Labour's Standards for England quango and the framework it oversaw. Its annual cost to the taxpayer had been £7.8m, although it handled only approximately 1,000 complaints a year. Councils are now being left to police themselves—using the criminal law, rather than civil rules and regulations, to punish errant councillors.

- **Attempts to increase turnout at local elections:** the Coalition began life pledging to move further and faster than Labour towards addressing the historical decline in voting in local elections—rolling out electronic voting (or 'e-voting') and postal ballots, and opening polling stations in supermarkets and shopping centres—but progress seems to have stalled.

? Review questions

1. Outline the electoral cycles for district/borough councils, county councils, and unitary authorities. Why might a district council have an election in a year when a neighbouring borough council does not?

2. What are the qualifications for candidates and electors in local elections? Who oversees the electoral process, and to whom besides this individual might one complain about it?

3. In what ways besides elections can councillors be held accountable for their actions? What mechanisms exist to punish them for misusing their positions?

4. Outline the changes to the ways in which the performance of councils in service delivery is assessed, exposed, and regulated.

5. What rights do the press and public have to attend and access information from meetings of councils, and their committees and subcommittees? How were the access rights changed by the Local Government Act 2000?

→ Further reading

Barron, J., Crawley, G., and Wood, T. (1991) *Councillors in Crisis: The Public and Private Worlds of Local Councillors (Public Policy and Politics)*, London: Palgrave Macmillan. **Detailed case study-led examination of balancing act undertaken by councillors between public duties and private lives, based on empirical research**.

Johnston, R. and Pattie, C. (2006) *Putting Voters in Their Place: Geography and Elections in Great Britain*, Oxford: Oxford University Press. **Thoughtful examination of geographical differences in voting/turnout patterns in local, national, and European elections. Examines emergence of safe seats and roles of marginal wards and constituencies in winning polls**.

Knowles, R. (1993) *Law and Practice of Local Authority Meetings*, 2nd edn, London: ICSA Publishing. **Updated second edition of indispensable guide to statutory rules and regulations governing access for press and public to council meetings**.

Pratchett, L. (2000) *Renewing Local Democracy? The Modernisation Agenda in British Local Government*, London: Frank Cass. **Thoughtful assessment of impact of 'New Labour' reform agenda, focusing on attempts to increase public participation in local democracy through mayoral elections and new forms of voting**.

 Online Resource Centre

www.oxfordtextbooks.co.uk/orc/Morrison3e/
Visit the Online Resource Centre that accompanies this book for web links and regular updates.

15

Local authorities and education

If any other policy area has the capacity to compete with the health service for headlines it is education. Whether it is local unrest over changes to school catchment areas, anger over disruption caused by striking teachers, reports about soaring undergraduate student debt, the annual rows over 'grade inflation' when General Certificate of Secondary Education (GCSE) and A level results are published, or the frantic scramble for university places through the clearing system each summer, the trials and tribulations of parents and pupils are seldom far from the media spotlight.

The involvement of local education authorities (LEAs) in this huge policy area stretches across all four 'phases' of the education process: primary, secondary, further (or tertiary) education (FE), and higher education (HE). These phases are explained in Table 15.1.

In addition, LEAs have a statutory responsibility to ensure suitable pre-school education is available across their areas, through nurseries, registered childminders, and other forms of recognized early-years childcare. This chapter examines each layer of state education in detail, beginning with perhaps the most important—and certainly the most controversial: the school system.

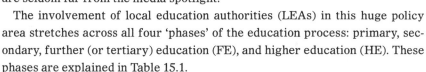

▌ The origins of state schools and comprehensive education

Until Victorian times many British children had little or no formal education. The offspring of the aristocracy and the bourgeois middle classes that emerged during the Industrial Revolution fostered the growth of a burgeoning private education system for those who could afford it. But for the large number of poorer households, paying the high fees these schools charged was out of the question. Poor parents were forced either to teach their children themselves

Table 15.1 Structure of the British education system

Phase	Structure
Primary phase	Education in subjects of 'primary' importance (e.g. English language, maths, basic history, and science). Takes place in **primary schools** (ages 5–11), or at infant school (5–7) and junior school (7–11). In some areas children attend first school (5–8/9) then middle school (8/9–12/13).
Secondary phase	Education for 11–16-year-olds (or 13–16-year-olds in some areas) in core subjects like English and maths, with increasing specialization in other areas after children take 'options' at 13/14. Compulsory secondary education in England, Wales, and Northern Ireland leads to final assessment between 14 and 16, through GCSEs and/or vocational diplomas. GCSEs awarded through mix of exams and coursework across eight grade bands: A*–G. In England GCSEs in English, maths, and sciences to be replaced by new English Baccalaureate Certificate (Ebac) from 2017.
	Scotland's GCSE equivalent is Standard Grade (levels 1–7). Standard grades take up first half of four-year National Qualification (NQ) programme, encompassing Scottish equivalent of gold standard pre-degree qualification in rest of UK, A levels (Scottish Higher).
	School-age qualifications and most of those taught in sixth forms/at FE level in England regulated by **Office of the Qualifications and Examinations Regulator (Ofqual)**, which also oversees vocational qualifications in Northern Ireland. These qualifications accorded a 'level' on National Qualifications Framework (NQF)—form of 'credit transfer' system for accredited UK courses and exams. In Northern Ireland, school-age qualifications regulated by Council for the Curriculum, Examinations, and Assessment (CCEA), in Wales in-house by Department for Children, Education, Lifelong Learning, and Skills (DCELLS), and in Scotland by Scottish Qualifications Authority (SQA).
Further education (FE) phase	'Sixth-form' education in chosen subjects to A level in England, Wales, and Northern Ireland, Advanced Subsidiary (AS) Level (taken during first year of standard two-year A level course), vocational diploma, or International Baccalaureate (IB) (qualification widely taught outside UK).
	In Scotland pupils study for intermediate-level certificates, followed by Scottish Highers.
	'Catch-up' tuition for less academic/those seeking to retake GCSEs/Standard Grades also offered at this stage. BTEC National Diplomas, foundation degrees, and other practical, trade-based post-GCSE certificates also often taught in school sixth forms, and at further education (FE), technical, or tertiary colleges.

Table 15.1 (*continued*)

Phase	Structure
Higher education (HE) phase	University education to degree—Bachelor of Arts (BA) and Bachelor of Science (BSc)—and postgraduate—Master of Arts (MA), Master of Science (MSc), Doctor of Philosophy (PhD)—level for those gaining requisite A levels or equivalent qualifications.

or rely on piecemeal philanthropy from any local churches, charities, or guilds—groups of wealthy merchants and tradesmen—prepared to fund local schools for the working classes. In the absence of a state system, the opportunity for children from many families to gain an education varied hugely from place to place—an early 'postcode lottery'.

By the late nineteenth century, however, there was a growing clamour for the government to provide some form of across-the-board schooling for the nation's children. Campaigns by civil rights movements like the Chartists and Radicals had brought social inequality into sharp focus. Morality aside, there was also a belated recognition that allowing 'the masses' to remain uneducated might limit Britain's potential to compete economically.

The foundation stone of the modern 'state school' system—or 'maintained sector'—was the Elementary Education Act 1870, which introduced nationwide *elementary schools*. The term 'elementary' is key: even at this stage, poorer children were only offered the most basic level of teaching, and only up to 13 years of age—what would later be termed secondary school level. Neither was even this limited schooling guaranteed to be within the financial grasp of all parents: local school boards elected to manage the system on the ground, setting up new schools in areas devoid of provision by a church or guild, charged families up to 9d a week to send their children. While boards had discretion to waive fees for the poorest households, they could only do so for limited periods. It was only with the Education Act 1891 that elementary education became free for most pupils, and not until 1918 that every last fee was abolished. This reform was initiated by county councils, which, as of 1901, were designated *LEAs*.

The path towards introducing secondary schools was even more protracted: not until after the Education Act 1944 did a nationwide system open to all children—regardless of their parents' ability to pay—come into being. When the 1870 Act had been passed the compulsory age for children to stay at school was just 10 (despite the fact elementary schools were prepared to teach them up to 13). The leaving age was increased incrementally—first to 11, then 13, then 14—by three subsequent Acts, in 1893, 1899, and 1918. But it was only Tory Education Minister Rab Butler's 1944 Act that introduced secondary schooling for all in England and Wales (a provision extended to Northern Ireland in 1947).

Despite the widespread welcome given to the new universal free secondary schools, the Butler Act was highly contentious. Its most controversial innovation was the introduction of not one, but three types of secondary school:

- **grammar schools**—for the most academically gifted;
- secondary modern schools—a more standard alternative for the less able;
- technical schools—offering practical, vocationally orientated education rather than academic.

Whether a child was admitted into one or other would depend on their performance in a new exam they would sit at elementary school leaving age—the '11-plus'. This system came to be known as *selection*. A chronology of key education Acts can be found in the table entitled 'Timeline of major UK school reforms', to be found on the Online Resource Centre.

The ideological divisions caused by the introduction of selection, and the repeated efforts of later Labour governments to scrap grammar schools, are discussed later in this chapter. One such government, however—Harold Wilson's first administration, elected in 1964—went further than most towards abolishing the tripartite secondary school framework ushered in by Butler, in favour of a more egalitarian system. Under the Conservative governments of the late 1950s and early 1960s, the number of non-selective secondary schools had gradually increased to cater for the post-war 'baby boom' generation. These schools—focusing on a broad-based academic education—eventually came to be known as **comprehensive schools** after Labour Education Secretary Anthony Crosland issued a policy instruction entitled 'Circular 10/65' in 1965, instructing LEAs to begin dismantling the 'two-tier system' preserved by grammars. These schools came to be known variously as 'high schools', community schools (see p. 445), and, in Scotland, 'academies' (not to be confused with their modern-day namesakes—see pp. 446–51).

The number of grammar schools has since fallen dramatically, thanks to a slow process of attrition that began in the late 1960s. Between then and the late 1970s successive Labour and Conservative governments engaged in a game of educational ping-pong over the future of grammars, with Mr Wilson initially instructing LEAs to start dismantling the system, only for his Tory successor, Ted Heath, and the latter's Education Secretary (one Margaret Thatcher) to reverse this directive after winning the 1970 election. When Labour was re-elected in 1974 it swiftly overturned Mrs Thatcher's instructions, but a sluggish response by certain LEAs meant that, by the time she became prime minister in 1979, a number still remained.

In their mid-1960s heyday, there had been several hundred grammar schools, including 179 'direct grant' schools—fee-paying grammars that agreed to take between a quarter and half of their pupils from poorer families in return for state subsidies. Today there are 164, spread over ten LEA areas, including Devon,

Kent, and Lincolnshire. The Conservatives' traditional support for selection gave grammars a reprieve in the 1980s, but few new ones were established.

Nonetheless, the great selection debate has repeatedly resurfaced. Mrs Thatcher (an ex-grammar school pupil) would do more to encourage selection than simply saving the 11-plus. In 1980 she introduced the 'assisted places scheme'—a means by which pupils from lower-income families who passed entrance exams for private and public schools were entitled to state financial aid with tuition fees, according to a sliding scale.

Labour scrapped assisted places when it returned to power in 1997. Yet the 11-plus remains in many areas where it survived the axe in the 1970s, thanks to the more consensual way in which the party broached the issue of grammar schools under Tony Blair. Rather than abolishing them (and infuriating new-found middle-class supporters), the School Standards and Framework Act 1998 instead gave parents in areas where they remained a direct say, through ballots, in whether the 166 then still standing should be kept or scrapped.

By the time Labour legislated to ban the building of any further grammar schools, there were 164 left in England and sixty-eight in Northern Ireland. Labour's failure to make good on its long-standing pledge to abolish grammars—despite its huge Commons majority—infuriated many of its backbenchers. These rumblings of unease grew louder when it emerged that ministers were planning to *introduce* a degree of selection in academies and specialist schools (see p. 447).

But it was not only Labour's leadership that had trouble containing its backbenchers over the grammar school question. In 2006, then newly elected Tory leader David Cameron provoked a fight with party traditionalists—portrayed in some media as his 'Clause 4 moment' (see pp. 149–52)—by announcing that a future Conservative government would not found new grammars. The following May, after months of infighting over the issue, he accused his critics of 'clinging on to outdated mantras that bear no relation to the reality of life', adding that most parents did not 'want children divided into successes and failures at 11'. He was later forced to make a significant concession to rebels, however, after the party's Europe spokesman, Graham Brady, resigned over the issue. Mr Cameron reassured diehard '11-plus' supporters that a Tory government *would* sanction more grammars in areas where they already existed and there was enough demand.

Sure enough, within two years of entering office Mr Cameron was accused by critics of selection of expanding the grammar school system by stealth. By subtly rewording the *School Admissions Code*—the rulebook governing the allocation of school places to children in the state sector—Coalition Education Secretary Michael Gove paved the way for Kent County Council to approve the first expansion of a grammar school in fifty years. The rewritten code, which came into effect on 1 February 2012, contains a clause allowing oversubscribed state schools (whatever their category) to expand beyond their existing boundaries. This prompted Kent councillors, buffeted by growing demand from parents, to vote in favour of allowing a new 'satellite school' to be built in the

Sevenoaks area as an overflow for pupils unable to access existing grammars in Tonbridge and Tunbridge Wells.

▌The 1988 Act—and the birth of 'independent' state schools

Just as it turned its back on forty years of consensus over health policy by introducing the NHS 'internal market' (see pp. 166–9), in 1988 Mrs Thatcher's Conservative government initiated the most profound change in the state education system since comprehensive schools were first established. The Education Reform Act 1988 marked the culmination of the 'Great Debate' of the early Thatcher years—revolutionizing how many primary and secondary schools were managed by liberating them from LEAs and giving parents and teachers a greater say in their day-to-day running than ever before. It also polarized political opinion between those who viewed the transfer of power from councils to citizens as a triumph of full-blooded 'localism' over bureaucratic interference, and defenders of the faith who saw in it a recipe for postcode lotteries and the fragmentation of the universal ideal. Debate over how far to increase school autonomy continues to dominate the education agenda in England to this day (see pp. 444–55).

Until 1988 the designation 'independent schools' was used as an umbrella term for private sector fee-paying schools: 'private schools' and older, more expensive, 'public schools' like Eton. What the 1988 Act did was apply the concept of independent *governance* for the first time to schools in the public sector. Schools would be offered the opportunity to 'opt out' of LEA control—in much the same way as GPs were invited to become independent fund-holders (see p. 168). Schools opting out would be renamed 'grant-maintained (GM) schools', and given autonomy to take their own decisions on admissions, staffing, and spending, funded by direct grants from central government. The Tories were handing them de facto independent status (albeit without freedom to charge fees) in the name of a new form of localism that would give direct power to ordinary citizens, rather than councillors elected to discharge it on their behalf. The underpinning philosophy—a foretaste of Mr Cameron's 'Big Society' vision (see pp. 338–9)— was that decisions on running vital public services like education and, progressively, health and social care should be placed in the hands of those who 'knew best' (the individuals who *used* and/or staffed them) rather than politicians or bureaucrats. The main provisions of the 1988 Act are outlined in Table 15.2.

The Local Management of Schools (LMS) scheme that supported GM schools proved hugely divisive. The element of selection introduced by some popular schools to simplify their admissions procedures and cherry-pick 'academic' applicants was seen to favour children with educated, professional parents,

Table 15.2 Main provisions of the Education Reform Act 1988

Reform	Effect
Introduction of grant-maintained (GM) schools	Primary and secondary schools with 300-plus pupils allowed to 'opt out' of LEA control, becoming GM schools. Initially, entitlement was 'reward' for high-performing schools (those with high numbers of pupils attaining five or more A–C GCSEs), but eventual aim to extend to most state schools. GM schools could set staff pay/conditions and decide own admissions policies (some began to select). They received direct government grants towards running costs and could apply for capital funding for new equipment/buildings and repairs.
Local Management of Schools (LMS)	Day-to-day financial decisions and full autonomy over staff recruitment delegated to head teachers of GM schools, working with boards of governors. LEA-run schools also given greater leeway than before, with head teachers redefined more as managers than educators and, with governors, given limited autonomy to hire and fire staff—though LEA remained employer.
Introduction of **National Curriculum (NC)**	NC dictated not only key subjects all schoolchildren must be taught (or offered) at various stages, but core skills/content covered (e.g. basic spelling and punctuation in English). Curriculum to cover broadly same content throughout England and Wales, up to and including GCSE level, with exams at 'key stages' 1, 2, and 3 (ages 7, 11, and 14), through **National Curriculum assessments (Sats)**.
	Welsh Assembly has authority to make slight adjustments in Wales—with Welsh language compulsory in all state schools, alongside English.
Launch of key stages (KS)	Formal stages introduced by which each pupil is expected to attain certain educational objectives. Normally established through testing and/or continuous assessment.
Emergence of parent choice	First signs of 'choice' introduced in school admissions process, with parents allowed to specify which local school they wanted children to attend.
First school league tables	Publication of school exam results—seen by ministers as providing objective information on performance of local schools for parents considering where to send children. Attention today focuses on comparative data relating to truancy, exclusions, and performance in external exams—primarily GCSEs, and benchmark of how many children achieve five 'good' passes (A*–C). Since 2007, A*–C grades recorded by all schools for league table purposes—excluding academies—have had to include English language and maths, following criticism that many top grades obtained by children studying 'easier' subjects.
Introduction of city technology colleges (CTCs)	New generation of specialist schools established, geared to needs of industry and technology sector, with private companies invited to sponsor them. Most would later become academies.

and discriminate against those from disadvantaged backgrounds. Critics argued it would worsen existing inequalities between schools, leading to gradual polarization between high-performing ones dominated by the affluent middle classes and 'sink schools' in poorer areas. The ability of head teachers and governors to set their own pay scales to attract the 'best' staff was seen to compound this problem: by headhunting high-performing teachers from LEA-run schools, or ones with poorer results, they would make their own schools yet more 'successful', while further impoverishing those already struggling. To top it all, government money followed the high-performing schools—rewarding them with bonuses and extra freedoms, and fast-tracking grant allocations for GM head teachers by enabling them to bypass cumbersome application procedures used by 'one-size-fits-all' LEAs.

Although it would adopt its own version of LMS after regaining power, Labour initially opposed the 1988 reforms. All the more embarrassing for Mr Blair when in 1995 it emerged he was sending his eldest son, Euan, to the London Oratory, a Roman Catholic GM school—and Harriet Harman, Labour's then health spokesperson, was revealed to be sending one of her sons to the same school and her other to a grammar.

To some opponents the idea of introducing 'parent choice' into the GM schools equation set the final seal on an emerging 'two-tier' state system. If parents were allowed to choose between rival schools in their area, who in their right mind would opt for the one with worse results and less money to spend on pupils? As these 'successful' schools became richer and more successful, less popular ones were likely to fall further behind and become 'poorer'. Moreover, successful schools would realistically have only limited ability to expand to take in growing numbers of applicants, and their vested interest in favouring those most likely to succeed might tempt them to become more selective. All the while, children forced to attend less popular and/or 'failing' schools would suffer. A summary of arguments for and against schools opting out of LEA control can be found in Table 15.3.

The first school to gain grant-maintained status was Skegness Grammar School, in 1988. By the time GM schools were finally abolished (in name at least) in 1998, there were nearly 1,100 nationwide—three out of five at secondary level.

City technology colleges and the rise of specialist schools

Although pedants might point to the post-war technical schools as early examples of secondaries specializing in specific disciplines—in their cases, practical subjects like carpentry—the birth of **specialist schools** per se came much later. Reviving the notion that some children are more predisposed towards vocational subjects than academic ones—and that more needed to be done to tailor the skills and qualifications with which 16–18-year-olds left school to the

Table 15.3 Arguments for and against state schools being allowed to 'opt out'

For	Against
Parents know what is best for their children. Giving them direct input into running schools enables them to customize teaching to suit individual children's needs, replacing 'one-size-fits-all' approach of bureaucrats.	Allowing schools to become self-governing worsens inequalities in state system. Given control of own budgets and teacher recruitment, they poach 'best' from elsewhere—widening gap between 'successful' and 'failing' schools.
Giving head teachers and governors (parents, teachers, and members of local community) more power gives them sense of 'ownership' of school. Ownership increases determination to drive up standards.	Giving schools control of own disciplinary procedures, staff recruitment, and budget decisions breeds huge inconsistencies in nature/quality of provision across sector. It is also thin end of the wedge: how long before they demand right to select brightest pupils—or use 'social selection' to do so by back door?
LEAs unwieldy and bureaucratic, and slow to take decisions. Putting power in hands of governors and head teachers speeds up decision-making by 'cutting out middleman'.	LEAs run by elected councillors and therefore accountable to all members of community at ballot box. School governors accountable to no one but parents of children already attending those schools, and only have responsibility to those families. Who will stop them taking decisions that adversely affect other schools?

demands of industry—the 1988 Act saw the Conservatives introduce a new generation of 'technical schools'.

From the outset these secondary schools-cum-sixth-form colleges—**city technology colleges (CTCs)**—were distinct from anything before them. Inspired by the US experience of involving business and industry sponsors through 'charter schools', CTCs saw private companies become involved not only in funding buildings and equipment, but, more controversially, in day-to-day decisions about how they were run. Rather than focusing entirely on teaching practical subjects, as an alternative to the National Curriculum, they still offered pre-16 children all the usual subjects. *In addition* to this, however, they were equipped with particular specialisms in the sciences, maths, the emerging field of information technology (IT), and other related disciplines.

But the defining characteristic of CTCs was the extent of private sector involvement. In capital terms, private sponsors helped finance upfront the expansion and refurbishment of existing schools—and the construction of new ones—in return for long-term leaseback agreements that would make their investments profitable over time. This was one of the first tangible manifestations of the Tories' new 'big idea' for funding expensive public sector projects, the private finance initiative (PFI) (see pp. 230–1). But the sponsorship arrangements went deeper than this: companies investing in CTCs were given seats on their governing boards. To the horror of some, certain schools went so far as to 'rebrand' themselves—incorporating the names of sponsoring companies into their official titles and logos. The first CTCs were set up at the tail end of the 1980s in Kingshurst, Birmingham, and Nottingham. But the most controversial early opening—and the first to incorporate the name of its sponsor so brazenly— was Dixons Bradford CTC, funded by the high-street electrical retailer. The college, which opened in 1990, later converted into an academy. At time of writing only three CTCs remained, the rest having done likewise (see p. 447).

The purpose of CTCs was not solely to provide an education more geared to the changing demands of industry and oncoming technological revolution. By granting them a degree of independence commensurate with that offered to GM schools, ministers were giving head teachers a more decisive say in running their schools—with the quid pro quo that underperformance would be questioned by their increasingly influential governing boards. These boards— far from being the talking shops of old, there to be 'consulted' by LEAs but otherwise ignored—gave parents, teachers, local residents, and business-people a direct say in school management for the first time.

In a further echo of the old tripartite system, Mr Gove confirmed in March 2011 that he was establishing a new swathe of 'technical schools' for children aged 14 and over. These **university technical colleges (UTCs)**, sponsored by the private sector, would be used to train future generations of plumbers, electricians, and mechanics—ending what ministers decried as 'dead-end' vocational courses in favour of hard skills better suited to reviving Britain's flagging industrial fortunes. To inculcate a work ethic among students, UTCs will abandon customary 9 a.m.–3 p.m. school timetables for 'business hours', and classes will be held an extra two weeks a year beyond the length of the usual school calendar.

The growth of school autonomy: foundation schools, free schools, and the rise and rise of academies

Mr Blair's election in 1997 owed much to his rallying cry of 'education, education, education'—and his pledge to improve school standards and opportunities for children from all backgrounds. Labour had opposed both CTCs and the principle of schools 'opting out' of LEA control in opposition. But, as in the NHS, it was not long before Mr Blair and his ministers were converted into champions of specialist schools, PFI—which they renamed public–private partnerships (PPPs)—and the concept of school autonomy.

New Labour arguably left the state school landscape more fragmented than it found it. The School Standards and Framework Act 1998 converted all existing GM schools into **foundation schools**. Its immediate effect was to bring them back under a measure of LEA control—to the extent that, rather than continuing to be funded direct by government, they would receive grants channelled through their councils. In practice, however, the sums allocated to each foundation school would largely be determined by Whitehall, and in many respects they would retain an independence akin to that wielded by GM schools before them. The land and buildings occupied by foundation schools would be owned by their governing boards (unless ownership were handed, or the school had historically belonged, to a charitable foundation), and, though banned from selecting, they gained control over their own admissions policies. They could also hire and fire their own staff, rather than relying on councils to recruit on their behalf.

The most controversial extension of autonomy was the second. If schools were to be allowed to decide which pupils to admit and exclude, critics argued, would this not reintroduce selection by the back door? How were LEAs and ministers to prevent popular schools discriminating between applicants on the basis of their prior academic records, social backgrounds, or even appearance? A layer of complication was added to the debate when, in Mr Blair's final months in office, the Education and Inspections Act 2006 introduced **trust schools** into the equation. Trust status—a term borrowed, like 'foundation', from the NHS—has since been offered to foundation schools choosing to set up charitable trusts to manage their affairs. These trusts employ their own staff, manage their own assets, and set their own admissions policies. Within a year, 300 foundation schools had either converted into trusts or were doing so. A number have since been formed through the merger of two or more schools or takeovers of 'failing' schools by more successful ones. Trust schools were not generally offered any additional funding as incentives to convert—nor were they allowed to 'opt out' of local authority control to any greater extent than foundation schools—but in December 2007 then Schools Secretary Ed Balls offered 'sweeteners' to encourage high-performing schools to team up with less successful ones, including the promise of £300,000 cash injections to smooth over the process. The idea of multiple schools 'clubbing together' under the same head teacher and governing board was extended further by Labour in later years, through the introduction of 'federations'—a form of shared governance, like trust status, open to both primary and secondary schools.

Alongside foundation schools, the 1998 Act retained two other principal types of secondary school: community schools and voluntary schools. '**Community school**' is the umbrella term for all 'ordinary' state primaries and comprehensives: councils continue to own and maintain their infrastructure, determine admissions policies, and recruit staff. Before the 1998 Act, standard primary and comprehensive (or 'high') schools had for some time been known as 'county schools'. Some community schools have since been renamed community *colleges*, reflecting the fact that, in addition to teaching the National Curriculum, they also offer adult education and training (normally through evening classes) like that provided elsewhere by FE and tertiary colleges.

Voluntary schools are (as their name suggests) stalwarts of earlier times, normally linked to either the Church of England or Roman Catholic Church. They are divided into two types: *voluntary aided schools* and *voluntary controlled schools*. The former operate from premises owned by either a church or charitable foundation, but receive all their revenue funding and up to 50 per cent of their capital outlay from central government, in return for teaching the National Curriculum and offering free school places. As with foundation schools, however, their governing boards may determine their admissions and staffing policies. The principal difference between aided and controlled schools is that, in the latter case, the LEA controls their admissions and staffing procedures in return for providing all of their funding. Although the term 'voluntary school' is not generally used in Scotland, since the Education Act 1918 it has been commonplace for secondary schools to specify a denominational bias, with a number labelling themselves 'RC schools'.

The emergence of academies—and return of specialist schools

The most significant additional change to school designations under New Labour was its conversion to the twin ideas of specialization and independent management *within* the state sector. The Learning and Skills Act 2000 introduced 'city academies'—schools with state-of-the-art buildings and facilities, part-funded by commercial companies, targeted at poorer postcode areas. They were allowed both to specialize in key subjects geared to the demands of their local communities, and manage their own affairs (including admissions). Some traditionalists saw in this policy a direct contradiction of the party's initial opposition to CTCs, and betrayal of the ideals of state schooling being entirely funded and managed both within and *by* the public sector. Pragmatists like Mr Blair and then Education Secretary David Blunkett saw it as a way of pumping much-needed teaching resources into deprived areas more quickly than if government financed the investment single-handedly, while equipping previously disadvantaged youngsters with the skills demanded by modern industry.

In their early years, **academies** (as they were later renamed) had much in common with CTCs. Buildings and amenities received significant boosts from private capital, in return for complex PFI/PPP leaseback arrangements and often a stake for sponsoring companies in the running of the schools. For some this was to be an 'arm's-length' arrangement—a presence on the governing board and consultation over expansions or mergers—but for others it became more hands on. Towards the end of Labour's tenure, private investors often became directly involved in the day-to-day staffing of ancillary functions like administration, security, maintenance, and/or catering at academies such as William Hulme's Grammar School in Manchester. Pupils attending academies (as with CTCs) often work longer days than children in other types of school, and/or between different term dates. Unlike CTCs, however, they have not tended to specialize in scientific, business, or technological subjects: if their local communities lack adequate sports facilities, or if there are specific demands for people with skills in the arts and media, these factors have generally determined their specialisms.

Perhaps the most controversial 'privilege' granted to academies under Labour was their qualified exemption from one of the sacred cornerstones of the party's traditional education policy: its opposition to selection. From the outset, academies were permitted to select up to 10 per cent of pupils on the basis of 'aptitude' in their specialist subjects. The choice of this word—pointedly distinguished from 'ability' by ministers—has been the cause of considerable controversy (not to mention bemusement). Labour appeared to be walking a tightrope between offering some head teachers the autonomy they craved to introduce limited selection, and distancing itself from the Conservatives' customary support for selective schools. In drawing what many saw as an artificial distinction between a pupil's 'potential' to do well in a subject (their 'aptitude') and their proven 'ability' in it, however, ministers left many head teachers nursing headaches. In 2003 the House of Commons Education and Skills Select Committee recommended that tests be scrapped, arguing the government had failed to provide a clear definition of 'aptitude'. Ministers countered that the aim of introducing limited selection was to identify pupils who 'would benefit from' accessing a specialism.

Arguments about autonomy aside, the rise and fall of CTCs, and their subsequent metamorphosis into academies, was in many ways just the latest manifestation of a decades-old debate about the wisdom of dividing pupils into 'academic' and 'practical', and gearing education towards the *needs of industry* as well as the *aspirations of young people* keen to develop their intellects in a wider sense. In earlier times this debate led to the schism between Left and Right over grammar schools (see pp. 438–40); more recently, it has been played out in arguments over the introduction of new qualifications covering vocational disciplines. Since September 2008, 14–19-year-olds have had the option of studying for vocational diplomas covering subjects as varied as health and social care, creative media, and engineering, in addition to—or instead of—GCSEs and/or A levels.

Indeed, the specialization reintroduced under the academies programme is far from confined to those schools today. During the second and third Labour terms it became so prevalent in the state sector that some 3,000 secondary schools (nearly nine out of ten) now specialize in one or more subjects—meaning the oft-used label 'specialist school' is less a separate category than an umbrella term embracing all schools with a specialism (whatever other 'box' they fall into). A council-run community school is just as likely to specialize as one that is independently managed. Achieving specialist status under Labour earned schools significant injections of capital and revenue to support the development of their curriculums. Those seeking specialist status first had to raise around £50,000 in sponsorship. If granted their wish, they then qualified for an extra £100,000-plus each year in capital grants from government, plus an additional £130 per pupil, to help put their specialist ambitions into practice. Applications were normally successful if the chosen specialism either related to genuine areas of outstanding achievement by the school's pupils or filled gaps in provision of facilities for the local community (for example, playing fields or concert facilities).

In return for this funding boost, specialist schools were expected to make their improved amenities available to neighbouring schools and community groups. Like academies, many specialist schools were permitted to select one in ten pupils on the basis of their aptitude in a relevant subject, but only if they specialized in one or more of the following subjects: languages, the performing and visual arts, and sport. Schools that could, over time, demonstrate improvements in academic performance in their specialist subjects were able to apply for 'high-performing specialist school' status. By the time Labour left office, 900-odd schools (or 30 per cent of those with specialisms) had achieved this.

Shortly after the Coalition entered power it effectively ended the process of recognizing specialisms, though existing specialist schools continue to operate. Preoccupied with his ambitious plans to roll out his version of Labour's academies system (see next section) and a new free schools programme (see pp. 451–4), Mr Gove removed the need for schools to formally apply to be designated (or redesignated) 'specialist'; rerouted funds for specialist schools through the mainstream Dedicated Schools Grant (see p. 360); and abolished the quangos which previously channelled money to them—the Specialist Schools and Academies Trust (SSAT) and Youth Sports Trust (YST).

Mr Gove's academies 'revolution'

Labour's original academies programme was meant to prioritize 'failing' comprehensives—principally those in deprived areas—using public–private partnerships to funnel capital injections into rejuvenating their existing facilities or building new schools from scratch. After a sluggish start, the number of academies grew steadily—from seventeen in the first year to 203 by the time the party lost the 2010 election. In its third term, academies' greatest advocate, then Education Minister Lord Adonis, invited private schools struggling to meet recruitment targets in the face of growing competition in the 'true' independent sector to consider converting into academies. Several, including Belvedere School in Liverpool and Bristol Cathedral School, subsequently did. Meanwhile, applications for academy status were increasingly being granted to less obviously 'struggling' schools and/or those in more affluent areas.

But the arrival of Conservative Education Secretary Mr Gove heralded not only a dramatic acceleration in the roll-out of academies but also a significantly more liberal attitude towards the kinds of school that qualified. Within weeks of taking office he wrote to the head teachers of every primary and secondary school in England, inviting them to convert. Under the ensuing Academies Act, rushed through the Commons before the summer recess, schools rated 'outstanding' in their latest Ofsted reports could be 'fast-tracked' by September 2010—though any currently falling under the auspices of a foundation, trust, charity, church, or other faith group would need their consent before converting. In the event, only around thirty-two new academies opened ready for the autumn term.

If take-up initially appeared sluggish, this was to change dramatically. In a pincer movement designed to massively boost the number of academies, Mr Gove reiterated that all 'outstanding' schools should consider themselves 'pre-approved' for academy status, while the 2010 Act gave him new powers to effectively *force* 'failing' schools (those placed in 'special measures' by Ofsted—see p. 463) to convert, without consulting their governing LEAs. A further liberty granted to 'outstanding' schools (and 'good' schools with one or more 'outstanding' features) was an exemption from the customary requirement for prospective academies to first secure sponsors. An explicit distinction was thus made between the *sponsored academies* of old—a status that continues to be accorded to 'failing' schools required to adopt academy status—and a new generation of 'successful' *converter academies* that proactively opt out of LEA control in pursuit of greater independence.

Mr Gove's reforms had the desired effect. With heads of outstanding schools required to demonstrate only a commitment to work with other (less high-performing) local providers to raise standards, and those struggling at the bottom left with no option but to find sponsors and convert, the result was an unprecedented surge in academy numbers. By 1 September 2012 there were 2,309 in existence—a tenfold increase on the number open by the time Labour left office. More than half of all secondary schools either had academy status or were in the process of converting. So rapid had been the expansion under the Coalition that in April that year an independent commission was convened by the Royal Society for the Encouragement of Arts, Manufactures, and Commerce (RSA), under the chairmanship of former Ofsted chief inspector Christine Gilbert, to investigate the potential impact on the schools system as a whole of impending 'total academization'.

Indeed, the mass roll-out of academies has not been without its controversies. As a mark of their new-found financial freedoms, the 2010 Act included a provision enabling academies to boost their revenue budgets by acquiring direct access to the 10 per cent of central government funding for each state school (academies included) currently still spent by LEAs collectively on their behalf. This provoked immediate criticisms from LEAs and teachers' unions, who pointed out that its effect would be to dilute the communal 'pools' of funding reserved for council-wide school services, including help for pupils with special educational needs (SEN) not attending academies. In June 2011 Mr Gove agreed to review his new funding formula for LEAs after twenty-three councils threatened legal action over his plans to cut the value of the collective pool by £148m that year and £265m in 2012.

There has also been resistance from some 'failing' schools the government has ordered to convert. Downhills Primary School in Haringey, north London, became a media cause célèbre early in 2012 after teachers, parents, and local MP David Lammy (a former pupil) united in protest against Mr Gove's instruction for it to become an academy, following a critical 2010 Ofsted report in which it was ordered to make 'significant improvement'. Under pressure from Mr Gove, the school reluctantly agreed to a further Ofsted inspection, but when it was subsequently placed in 'special measures' its head, Leslie Church, had little option but to resign, and the school relented to the minister's wishes. In Brighton and Hove, meanwhile, Whitehawk Primary School, another struggling school which tried to hold out against becoming an academy, was so desperate for a third-party backer when it finally yielded that it was forced to consider the bizarre option of seeking sponsorship from the very LEA from which it was meant to be 'freeing' itself.

Making good on his promise to allow heads of newly established academies significant additional freedoms, Mr Gove has given them permission to form partnerships with other public and private sector organizations, and (like those already established) to lengthen their school days/terms and set their own pay and working conditions. Perhaps most contentious, however, has been his decision to 'disapply' the National Curriculum his own party introduced in the 1980s for this new wave of academies—exempting them from teaching the same core subjects, in broadly the same ways and stages, as all other forms of state school. Significantly, the academies established under Labour, though allowed some freedom to deliver the curriculum as they saw fit, were still broadly expected to frame their teaching around it.

A further controversy is the fact that, unlike LEA-run schools, academies are automatically designated charities—a status conferring on them various privileges, including generous tax breaks. More contentious still is the fact that, unlike other charitable organizations, they have 'exempt' charity status, meaning they are not regulated by the quango charged with ensuring charities do not abuse their privileges: the Charity Commission.

Although the academies programme has its opponents, though, more than a decade after its introduction there is some evidence to suggest acquiring academy status can improve individual schools' performance—even if this does not conclusively translate into raising standards across the board (as its advocates often claim). In September 2009, at the end of his final academic year as Schools Secretary, Mr Balls announced that GCSE results for academies had improved by more than twice the national average rate in the preceding twelve months. Since converting, one of Labour's flagships, Harefield Academy in Hillingdon, west London, had seen a fivefold increase in GCSE A*–C pass rates—rising to 45 per cent from just 8 per cent when it was a floundering comprehensive. But critics have pointed to less rosy examples, and the fact that Labour's academies were exempt from the Freedom of Information Act 2000 until January 2011 (September 2010 in the case of those set up under the Coalition)—making it impossible to judge how well they had performed

Table 15.4 The main types of state school as of 2013

School type	Description
Community school/college	Primary and secondary ('comprehensive') schools run directly by LEAs. Community colleges offer evening classes for adults as well as daytime teaching.
Foundation	Largely self-governing schools but with funds directed via LEA by government.
Trust	Foundation schools that have formed independent trusts to manage finances/policies at 'arm's length'.
Free	Fully self-governing primary/secondary providers set up by parents/teachers/communities in location without sufficient 'good quality' schools. Have charity status.
Academy	Fully 'independent' state schools, sponsored by business/charity/other school, which can deviate from National Curriculum and have charitable status. Can select up to 10 per cent of pupils on 'aptitude'.
Special	Dedicated schools for children with 'special educational needs'.
Voluntary aided/controlled	Schools operating from church/charity-owned premises. Aided schools set own policies and employ own staff, but controlled are part-run by LEAs.
Faith	Schools set up by faith groups in the round, including non-Christian ones like Muslim, Hindu, and Jewish.

compared to other secondary schools, as their pupils might have been achieving top grades in 'easier' subjects.

Table 15.4 outlines the main types of state school today.

Extending self-determination—the arrival of free schools

Rolling out academies is but one element of the Coalition's mission to reshape the school system in the service of its 'Big Society' localism agenda. Shortly after inviting all state head teachers in England and Wales to apply for academy status in 2010, Mr Gove wrote a second letter—this time to LEA chief executives and children's services directors—setting out the process by which charities, universities, and other interested parties (including groups of teachers, governors, and/or parents) could found their own schools in areas where there was perceived to be a lack of 'good quality' extant state provision. Like academies, **free schools** were to be run independently of LEAs and allowed to draw up their own curriculums. They would also have to admit children of all abilities and be non-selective, and not charge fees. The resulting programme, a hybrid of a profit-based 'free school' model that originated in Sweden and the US charter school approach that originally inspired academies, aims to:

- respond to parental demand in areas where there is felt to be a lack of 'good quality' schools in place, by making it easier and quicker for new ones to be established;

- promote hands-on involvement by parents, teachers, and local business-people in developing the ethos, teaching methods, and outcomes of their schools, to foster greater community involvement in place of what the Coalition portrayed as intrusive and controlling state intervention.

Mindful of early scepticism about the logistical hurdles some parents might face with the nitty-gritty of setting up their own schools (particularly those with full-time day jobs), Mr Gove added that, as well as central government funding, ministers would offer project managers professional guidance through the New Schools Network—a charity established to promote social mobility through flexible models of state education. He also revealed that council planning policies would be relaxed to enable school-building programmes to be fast-tracked, with £50m immediately diverted from Labour's Harnessing Technology Grant fund to provide upfront capital finance for free schools.

While some critics predicted Mr Gove's offer would be met with silence (he himself forecast he'd be lucky to see sixteen launched in the first year), demand quickly picked up, with twenty-four start-ups opening their doors in September 2011. By that October the Department for Education (DfE) had approved another fifty-five free schools and thirteen 'self-starter' UTCs, with a further eight and three of each respectively in the pipeline within the same time frame, subject to final ministerial approval. By February 2012 some 330 applications had been received from groups hoping to establish free schools from September 2013—prompting Rachel Wolf, FSN director, to warn ministers that to meet demand they would need to relax their strict requirement for applicants to secure sites for new schools through the DfE's capital arm, Partnerships for Schools (PfS). With 102 more ministerial approvals given that July, at time of writing the total number of free schools set up or in the pipeline numbered around 200.

Among the high-profile free schools to open to date is the West London Free School, Hammersmith—brainchild of a 400-strong consortium of parents headed by journalist Toby Young (whose father, late Labour peer and eminent sociologist Lord Young, had ironically been one of the architects of the comprehensive system). By summer 2012 the school was able to boast of receiving nine applications for each of the 120 places available in that September's intake. Other prominent free school backers have included glamour model Katie Price (though her consortium's bid was rejected) and Oscar-winning actress Dame Helen Mirren, who fronted a successful campaign for a new secondary school in the socially deprived neighbourhood of Wapping, east London.

Opponents of the scheme, initially including Labour, warn of the danger of creating a two-tier schooling system—with 'pushy middle-class parents' exploiting the new freedoms to set up schools dominated by children from similar households, while families in poorer areas (where new and better schools were needed) might lack the skills and confidence to mobilize in the same way.

Others argued it would be folly to establish free schools in areas where there was no shortage of 'good' providers already—simply because some people wanted them—when their introduction might generate surplus places, and jeopardize the viability of existing providers. In April 2012 the National Union of Teachers (NUT) warned that, contrary to assurances from ministers, in practice free schools were increasingly being approved in areas with no shortage of spare places—and threatened to have a 'negative impact on existing good or outstanding local schools'. Among the towns and cities adversely affected by the policy was Bristol, where the opening of a free school had left four head teachers struggling to fill 300 empty places, at a cost to the LEA of £450 a year per place. The NUT alleged the popularity of newly opened Sandymoor Free School in Halton, Merseyside, was likely to lead to the closure of two local schools, with a loss to the local council of £3m. And, in a counterproductive step even by ministers' own standards, academies were also said to be suffering—with one in Beccles, Suffolk, facing a 15 per cent cut in its budget because of the loss of potential pupils to a neighbouring free school.

Thorniest of all, however, has been the ongoing question of whether free schools should ultimately be allowed to operate *more* 'freely': in essence, like fully fledged private companies. Free schools are already permitted to employ US-style *educational management organizations* (EMOs) to take care of their day-to-day management—and these may operate for profit. The Lilac Sky Schools group oversees schools in Bristol, Taunton, and Bradford, while Breckland Free School in Suffolk employs the for-profit Swedish provider, Internationella Engelska Skolan. However, in Sweden, where free schools were pioneered in the early 1990s, they are permitted to generate profits directly—and, more alarming to some, exempted from requirements to maintain their own counsellors, nurses, or even libraries. Concerns that Mr Gove had been nurturing a private desire to move towards profit-making free schools—despite earlier news stories suggesting that the Lib Dems had forced him to drop any such aspiration—were revived when, in his May 2012 evidence to the Leveson Inquiry (see p. 93), he let slip that they might be allowed to 'move toward' becoming fully fledged commercial concerns if the Tories won the 2015 election. His words, condemned by unions but backed by Sir David Bell, a former chief schools inspector and permanent secretary at the DfE, came against a growing backdrop of concern about the long-term effectiveness of the free school model, even in Sweden. A report by the Organisation for Economic Co-operation and Development (OECD), published in December 2010—just as Mr Gove was inviting the first round of bids for British free schools—had found that Swedish schoolchildren dropped from ninth to nineteenth for literacy, and seventeenth to twenty-fourth in maths, in a league table of fifty-seven countries between 2000 and 2009. Critics claimed that part of the reason for the decline was cost-cutting at profit-making free schools, where in some cases children had been taught by unqualified teachers and trainees.

As with academies, free schools are increasingly (though not always) set up by charities, conferring on them various privileges—including tax breaks—not enjoyed by other state schools.

Reviewing the curriculum—the future of teaching

In June 2012 Mr Gove announced a wide-ranging review of the primary school curriculum, placing renewed emphasis on the teaching of traditional subjects, primarily the 'three Rs'—'reading, writing, and (a)rithmetic'—and rote-learned facts and figures about British history and culture. His back-to-basics approach brought him into conflict with the Tories' Lib Dem Coalition partners later that month, though, when the *Daily Mail* splashed on leaked plans for GCSEs to be supplanted by old-style exam-based qualifications, modelled loosely on the 'Ordinary Level' (O level) regime that had preceded them (before being abolished by one of Mr Gove's idols, Mrs Thatcher). The paper reported that 16-year-olds could be sitting the 'tough' new exams as early as 2016, with less

academic students offered less demanding ones in the mould of the much-reviled Certificates of Secondary Education (CSEs) offered to weaker pupils instead of the original O levels. Mr Gove later dropped any plans to reintroduce a 'two-tier' system (reportedly under pressure from the Lib Dems), but confirmed his determination to restore 'rigour' to exams after the increasing grade inflation he believed had arisen out of a 'race to the bottom' between rival exam boards competing for schools' business. Ironically, Mr Gove's aversion to competition in the exam sector (and the rationale underpinning it) was precisely the opposite approach to that being adopted contemporaneously in the NHS, where the principle of rival providers competing for business was being rolled out breathlessly even as he spoke (see pp. 178–82).

In September 2012 Mr Gove and Mr Clegg jointly unveiled firmer Coalition proposals—which centred on plans to scrap GCSEs in English, maths, and science and replace them with a new, continental-style English Baccalaureate Certificate (Ebac) from 2017, with other 'core' subjects (including geography, history, and languages) set to follow later. They also confirmed there would be a single exam board overseeing the new qualification. In a separate but related move, the Coalition was planning to bring forward measures introduced by Labour's Education and Skills Act 2008 to raise the school leaving age to 17 in 2013 and 18 in 2015. Mr Gove plans to reach the 18 target two years earlier.

The Coalition's announcement of its plans to call time on GCSEs came as ministers were still struggling to extricate themselves from a more than usually testing furore over that summer's exam grades. The perennial media circus surrounding GCSE 'results day' erupted into a full-blown row between schools, Ofqual, and, by extension, government when it emerged that students sitting English language exams in the summer had been marked more harshly than those taking exactly the same papers earlier in the academic year. Some were left facing the prospect of having to delay going into tertiary education for up to a year as they resat exams in pursuit of the all-important C grades others had already received for work of exactly the same standard. The dispute intensified when the *Times Educational Supplement* published a leaked letter sent by Ofqual to one exam board, Edexcel, apparently urging it to mark that summer's papers more harshly than those sat earlier in 2012. And, in a twist that deepened the sense of injustice felt by pupils affected in England, the Welsh Government intervened to confirm it would be using its devolved power to act as exams regulator in Wales to regrade 2,386 papers previously marked down as D and C grades by Cardiff-based board WJEC. Though he expressed sympathy for English pupils left with Ds where they had been expecting Cs, Mr Gove stoutly refused to pressure Ofqual to do likewise.

The rise of faith schools

Another debate that has bubbled consistently in recent years concerns the future of **faith schools**—an umbrella term used to describe those run by particular religious communities. The term 'faith school' has traditionally been used interchangeably with 'voluntary school', as discussed earlier in this chapter. In this context, however, it also denotes schools run by non-Christian faith groups, including the Muslim, Sikh, Hindu, and Jewish communities. There are around 7,000 faith schools in England, Wales, and Northern Ireland, and a growing number in Scotland. A breakdown of the split between different religions in England and Wales is given in the table entitled 'A breakdown of faith schools by religion/ denomination in the UK', which can be found on the Online Resource Centre.

Faith schools were championed by Mr Blair, whose eldest son, Euan, attended one. He and other advocates argued they had above-average attendance rates compared to standard primaries and comprehensives, and high achievement rates. They were also praised for instilling firm discipline and respect among pupils. Mr Blunkett famously said he wanted to 'bottle' the essence of faith schools and use it as a template for reform elsewhere. Yet faith schools have generated vocal opposition. Although most are subsidized by the state, non fee-charging, and obliged to follow the National Curriculum, critics like the National Secular Society regard the idea of children being educated at schools with prescriptive underlying world views as a form of brainwashing incompatible with one of state education's primary roles—to foster freedom of thought and expression. Others, including some politicians and teaching unions, argue that maintaining single-faith schools— whether inside or outside the state system—promotes ghettoization and undermines efforts elsewhere to foster multiculturalism. Some also object to their being allowed to exercise limited selection, albeit faith-based rather than academic, unlike most other state schools. In March 2008 the NUT proposed requiring *all* state schools to become 'multifaith' institutions, offering faith-based instruction, a choice of religious holidays, and varied prayer facilities.

Alleged self-segregation is not the only criticism to be levelled against faith schools: the ability of academies to vary their curriculums has, say some, enabled those sponsored by religious groups to introduce 'unorthodox' approaches to certain subjects. Concern that some Christian schools were minded to teach 'intelligent design', or 'creationism'—the idea that the natural world was created by God, rather than being the product of evolution—as valid theory in science lessons led, in January 2012, to the DfE warning that it would withdraw funding from those that attempted to do so. Amongst those who had campaigned for a crackdown on creationist teaching were the biologist Richard Dawkins, naturalist Sir David Attenborough, and the British Humanist Association.

Specialist versus special schools—avoiding confusion

Despite the similarity of the terminology, specialist schools are not to be confused with **special schools**, which specialize not in particular disciplines but teaching children with learning difficulties, such as dyslexia or autism, or mental or physical disabilities. Before 1997 these were commonly known as 'special needs schools'.

To be judged eligible to attend a special school a child must be 'statemented'—awarded a 'statement of special education need'—by his/her LEA, following a diagnosis by a GP or specialist and (in some cases) a formal academic test. Recent years have seen a growing trend for such pupils to be integrated into mainstream schools, to avoid segregation from their peers and help them attain skills and qualifications that will give them career prospects comparable to other children's. Some mainstream primaries and secondaries now have their own 'special units', while others integrate disabled children and those with learning difficulties into general classes. However, the disparate approach adopted by different LEAs has created a widening postcode lottery.

The question of 'integration versus segregation' continues to be politically sensitive, with many councils having closed down dedicated special schools recently, often for financial reasons rather than because they have a strong policy in favour of the former approach. During the 2010 election campaign, Mr Cameron was barracked in front of television cameras by the father of a boy with spina bifida, who accused the Tories of planning to 'segregate' disabled children by promoting a return to separate schools. Mr Cameron, whose late son, Ivan, had suffered from cerebral palsy and epilepsy, had used his party's manifesto to condemn what he described as Labour's 'ideologically driven closure of special schools' and end the 'bias' towards pushing them into mainstream ones.

▎ The dwindling role of LEAs

LEAs have had their powers progressively eroded—caught between the pincer movement of growing self-determination for schools and direct intervention in cases of underperformance by the Secretary of State (see p. 463). But the single most significant recent reform of local education occurred in the Children Act 2004, passed in the wake of the Victoria Climbié child abuse case (see p. 524). The media inquest into this gruesome tragedy led to a sweeping reorganization, under the 'Every Child Matters' agenda. This saw old-style education departments hand their oversight of schools to across-the-board 'children's services' departments, and chief education officers replaced by new all-encompassing 'directors of children's services' in each LEA area. The aim was to join up a range of services affecting children, that were seen to have become fragmented, in an effort to better safeguard child welfare and make it less likely that warning signs of abuse would be missed in future.

Although they played an overarching role in implementing the 2004 Act, LEAs have seen significant reductions in their powers in relation to schools. Today they tend to be less the principal state education providers in their areas than enablers and coordinators, and in light of the Coalition's determination to drive forward the academy and free school programmes their influence is only likely to diminish further. A full list of the powers retained and lost by LEAs in recent years is contained in the table entitled 'Powers retained and lost by local education authorities (LEAs)', to be found on the Online Resource Centre.

Despite the gradual erosion of their status as 'providers' LEAs continue to be responsible for ensuring that each school-aged child in their area has access to an education. In addition, they still have an input into many of the areas examined below—notably monitoring school admissions policies and drawing up catchment boundaries.

Monitoring school standards—and the great 'parent choice' debate

Besides selection, the other great issue to have dominated debate about state schooling in recent years is that over 'parent choice'. This is the long-standing notion that families should be free to send their children to whichever local school they choose. Dividing lines were sharpened, however, in the 1980s and 1990s with the introduction of two key innovations designed to inform parents better about the relative academic merits of different schools in their areas: school league tables and a national inspectorate, the Office for Standards in Education (renamed the **Office for Standards in Education, Children's Services, and Skills (Ofsted)** in April 2007).

League tables of school exam results were introduced under the 1988 Act, but took a while to catch on with parents. The more decisive agent of choice was arguably the introduction of systematic school inspections. Until 1992 school standards were enforced by two bodies: Her Majesty's Inspectorate of Education and LEAs themselves. But the Education (Schools) Act 1992 and School Inspections Act 1996 established Ofsted in England and Estyn in Wales, providing more consistent nationwide frameworks. (In Scotland, school inspections remain the province of the HM Inspectorate, while Northern Ireland has an Education and Training Inspectorate.)

Ofsted is headed by a Chief Inspector of Schools, and has traditionally been tasked with conducting regular inspections of all English state schools. Its first visits to each school were carried out within four years of its inception, but thereafter they became six-yearly until Labour made them more frequent, giving shorter notice periods to allow schools less scope to 'clean up their acts' at the last minute.

Today Ofsted inspects the following providers:

- nursery and primary schools;
- secondary schools;
- special schools;
- service children's education—for offspring of those in the Armed Forces;
- pupil referral units—schools for children 'who cannot attend' normal schools, such as pregnant teenagers, those with specific medical problems, and pupils excluded from mainstream schools for problematic behaviour;
- some independent schools, excluding members of the Independent Schools Council (ISC) and Focus Learning Trust, which are inspected by the Independent Schools Inspectorate (ISI) and School Inspection Services (SIS).

Ofsted reports have traditionally rated schools 'outstanding', 'good', 'satisfactory', or 'inadequate'. After an inspection a school is expected to act on any recommendations the report contains, as outlined in the table entitled 'Process for responding to recommendations in an Ofsted report', to be found on the Online Resource Centre.

Perhaps unsurprisingly, the arrival of league tables and Ofsted intensified competition for places at high-performing schools. By highlighting 'the best' and naming and shaming 'the worst' they helped create a thriving market for places at successful providers and an exodus of middle-class families from those deemed 'failing'. There was no starker illustration of this pattern than the East Brighton Centre of Media Arts (COMART)—a struggling comprehensive that went through not one but two name changes, and a costly PFI building programme, before finally closing in summer 2005. Based in one of Brighton's most deprived areas, Whitehawk, the school consistently had the worst GCSE and truancy rates in Brighton and Hove. Better-off parents voted with their feet—reducing its social mix and overall pupil numbers, and sending its standards plummeting further.

Critics argue that 'parent choice' has parallels with 'patient choice' in the NHS, which has seen successful hospitals oversubscribed and failing ones avoided. While a growing number of 'failing' schools are closing, 'successful' ones gain greater financial rewards and freedoms—enabling them to headhunt the most experienced staff and improve further. Devoid of these privileges, underperforming schools can become locked in a downward spiral. Many fear this is a fate awaiting unpopular community schools (and, indeed, some hitherto popular ones—see p. 447) in areas where the Coalition's academy and free school programmes are being rolled out.

From a journalistic viewpoint, particularly for local media outlets, Ofsted reports provide 'easy hit', newsworthy stories that can usefully fill space or airtime. As inspections have become more frequent and the process better understood, however, the regulator itself cannot be relied on to send out reports proactively to newspapers or television and radio stations, so it is usually up to journalists to chase them. Reporters should also be wary about relying on a school's own account of its inspection and Ofsted's findings: as with most things in journalism, it is best to go straight to the horse's mouth for the full story. Handily, though, all Ofsted reports are available in downloadable PDF form on its website.

Another area of controversy related to the growing national obsession with league tables is testing. Ministers have consistently clashed with head teachers and unions over the sheer volume of assessment that schoolchildren now face—and the pressure this puts on both pupils and teachers. Opposition to the culture of testing intensified in summer 2008 when ETS Europe, the commercial company contracted to oversee marking of the key stage 2 and 3 tests for 11- and 14-year-olds, presided over a marking fiasco. Results for some schools suffered severe delays, and there were reports of exam papers lying uncollected (and unmarked) in head teachers' offices weeks after exams had been sat. Ministers launched an independent inquiry, headed by Lord Sutherland, and in August ETS Europe had its £156m five-year contract terminated by the now defunct QCA. It had been paid £39.6m for 2008 alone.

In October 2008 Mr Balls scrapped National Curriculum assessments (Sats) for 14-year-olds, instead promising a new US-style 'report card' for each primary and secondary school child from 2011, giving an overall grade from A to F covering not only his/her exam results and performance but his/her attendance and/or truancy rate, behaviour, and health. In July 2011 Mr Gove confirmed he would be implementing the recommendations of an independent review into Sats by Lord Brew, a professor of politics at Queen's University, Belfast, by introducing more rigorous testing of core skills like maths, grammar, and spelling, and improving assessments of children's creativity.

Other recent trends to monitor and improve standards have seen more direct state intervention to help struggling schools. Before leaving office, Mr Balls offered schools with fewer than 30 per cent of pupils achieving five GCSE A*–C passes extra money to channel into top-up tuition via a National Challenge for Schools programme. In a further sign of a shift towards 'carrots' and away from 'sticks', in April 2008 new *school improvement partners* (SIPs) were introduced in many areas of England—individuals or organizations with relevant expertise that provide an outside consultancy role to schools to help them improve standards.

Determined to move towards a situation in which most state schools could be described as 'good' or 'outstanding', Mr Gove has since shaken up the Ofsted regime. From January 2012 he introduced a new inspection framework, exempting schools judged outstanding in their most recent reports from being inspected at regular intervals—a condition which up to that point had applied to all providers, whatever their ratings. In future, outstanding schools would only be inspected as and when certain 'triggers' took effect—principally, when Ofsted was contacted by teachers or parents concerned about deteriorating standards. But barely a month after the new system came into effect, new chief inspector, Sir Michael Wilshaw, qualified the exemption by stating that up to a quarter of outstanding schools—those that had failed to achieve that rating in the teaching category—would face reinspection, as before, within the next four-year cycle.

In a contentious speech, in which he accused his predecessors of having 'tolerated mediocrity for far too long', he outlined a range of other proposals to be included in a consultation paper on changes set to be implemented that autumn. These included going a stage further than Labour had in reducing the amount of advance warning given to schools of impending visits—by introducing 'no-notice' inspections. Most controversially, he announced plans to abandon the long-standing 'satisfactory' label entirely, in favour of a new threefold rating system: 'outstanding', 'good', and 'requires improvement'. The inference that schools currently rated 'satisfactory' were effectively being redefined as 'unsatisfactory' raised the hackles of many head teachers. Chris Keates, general secretary of Britain's largest teaching union, the National Association of Schoolmasters Union of Women Teachers (NASUWT), publicly condemned these proposals for 'trashing the reputation of Ofsted and removing anything that parents can rely on by which to judge a school'.

▌ The future of school catchment areas

The flip side of 'failing' schools becoming unpopular is that 'successful' ones become *oversubscribed*. The trends in school applications fostered by extending 'parent choice' have had an inevitable impact on *catchment areas*—the geographical patches within which families need to live to be eligible to send their children to particular schools. Pressure on popular schools to admit more pupils—potentially at the expense of maintaining high standards—has seen some councils take drastic steps to 'ration' places, to keep their numbers sustainable and improve the social mix and performance of other institutions.

In 2008 Brighton and Hove Council began allocating places for oversubscribed secondary schools in the city's 'Golden Triangle' by lottery (or 'random allocation'). Many families living in this area had paid high prices for houses in the expectation of being automatically entitled to send their children to one of these high-performing schools. Under the lottery the schools' catchments were extended to cover areas until now devoid of comprehensives, and children from outlying districts became as likely to be admitted as those living on their doorstep, as once applications to attend one of the affected schools exceeded the number of places available, a lottery was used as a tie-breaker. Brighton's experiment was soon emulated elsewhere, and after Labour introduced a new admissions code allowing town halls and head teachers of oversubscribed schools to determine who should be offered places by drawing names out of a hat, lottery systems of one kind or another were gradually adopted by up to one in three English LEAs. The government's guidelines—meant to stamp out 'selection by mortgage'—also banned schools from interviewing parents, considering their backgrounds, or excluding people financially by, for example, stipulating that they buy uniforms from expensive suppliers. However, a report published by the British Educational Research Association in September 2010 found that, contrary to expectations, the Brighton experiment had failed to produce any visible improvement in 'social mix' at the schools concerned. The report did not criticize the lottery system per se, but rather the fact that the council had redrawn catchments in such a way that even the enlarged area from which applications had since been accepted principally embraced middle-class neighbourhoods, with poorer ones in peripheral areas still excluded.

In May 2011 the Coalition announced plans to find alternative ways of giving children from poorer families access to the best schools. A new draft admissions code announced by Mr Gove would ban LEAs from using lotteries—terminating all those currently in place—and instead permit academies and free schools (but not other state providers) to reserve places for children entitled to free school meals and those whose families earned less than £16,190 a year. Schools would also have to prioritize children in care and those whose parents were in the Armed Forces, and ensure twins and triplets were taught in the same class—though, controversially, the new code would also allow class sizes to rise above the notional 30-pupil limit he had inherited (already too high for some).

▌ Bridging the educational divide—other recent developments

One tactic Mr Brown favoured for bolstering the state sector (and breaking the perceived divide between state and independent schools) was to instruct the Charity Commission—the quango responsible for regulating the conduct of registered charities—to impose new conditions on independent schools seeking to retain their charitable status. Having a charity label entitles organizations to significant tax breaks not enjoyed by companies. The biggest condition was a requirement to earn this privilege by opening up their playing fields and other facilities to state schools and community groups. Shortly after being announced, these moves were criticized by Chris Parry, short-lived head of the Independent Schools Council, as provoking a new 'Cold War' between private and state sectors. Undeterred, ministers pointed to other developments, including a recent invitation to independent schools to sponsor academies (accepted by the £18,000-a-year Wellington School, the head teacher of which was Mr Blair's biographer, Anthony Seldon), and share amenities and expertise with the new trusts, as proof of their desire for partnership.

One innovation introduced by the Coalition, at the Lib Dems' behest, is the **pupil premium**—a pot of money designated to provide extra one-to-one tuition to children from disadvantaged backgrounds, in an effort to intercept potential educational inequalities from an early stage in their schooling. Starting in April 2011, £488 was allotted to each pupil receiving free school meals out of an initial £625m budget (rising to £1.25bn in year two). The money was distributed to schools to spend on behalf of these pupils as they saw fit, with LEAs taking charge of the purse strings for those being taught in 'non-mainstream' settings. As of the 2012/13 financial year the premium was extended to pupils who had received free school meals at any point in the previous six years.

Despite such initiatives, Coalition ministers have been accused of placing several educational roadblocks in the way of children from lower-income households. Among their most controversial decisions was the abolition of the education maintenance allowance (EMA)—a £30-a-week allowance introduced by Labour for 16- to 18-year-olds in continuing education, which several studies had credited with enhancing the career prospects of those from poorer households by incentivizing them to attain further qualifications and/or training. More explosive still was the Lib Dems' wholesale abandonment of a pre-election 'pledge' to the National Union of Students to move towards scrapping undergraduate tuition fees, in favour of a Conservative-driven policy allowing universities to raise their annual fees from a £3,290 limit to £9,000. By July 2011, 58 per cent of universities were planning to charge the new 'top rate' for at least some courses from September 2012, with one in three proposing to do so across the board—prompting critics to argue that many talented prospective students from poorer households would either be forced to abandon hope of studying for anything other than strictly vocational courses (i.e. those better placed to 'guarantee' them employment) or deterred from applying altogether.

Ensuring fairness—the role of schools adjudicators

Ofsted is not the only body to have been introduced in the 1990s to police the state school system. The 1998 Act saw the establishment of a second: the **Office** of the Schools Adjudicator (OSA). Like Ofsted (which employs a number of inspectors), the office has more than one adjudicator: in fact it has ten, led by a 'chief adjudicator'.

There are many misconceptions about OSA—the most common being that it is there to rule on complaints by parents about their children's failure to get into their chosen school. In fact, that role is taken by independent appeals panels. OSA, in contrast, has statutory duties to:

- determine objections to admission arrangements and appeals from schools against directions from the local authority to admit a particular pupil;
- resolve local disputes on statutory proposals for school reorganization or on the transfer and disposal of non-playing field land and assets;
- decide on competitions to set up new schools where the local authority has entered the contest with its own proposals;
- decide on requests to vary already agreed admission arrangements.

In the last resort, deciding individual cases still in dispute after OSA has made its judgment falls to the Secretary of State. As the powers of LEAs to control state education in their areas has diminished with the emergence of new types of self-governing school, conversely his/her role has been resurgent—leading some to argue that, far from being about localism, many of the Coalition's policy initiatives, from academies to free schools, are actually a form of centralization and ministerial micromanagement. Direct intervention by the Education Secretary can now take any of the forms outlined in Table 15.5.

Table 15.5 Modern-day powers of the Education Secretary

Power	Effect
Intervention 'in default'	Prevents unreasonable uses of power by LEAs and 'acts in default' when they fail.
Managing the availability of school places	Directs LEAs to reduce surplus places in schools, by merging/closing unpopular ones, or to increase provision where there is high demand.
Intervening in 'failing schools'	Places 'failing' schools under 'special measures' (two-year period during which he/she closely observes their progress) and instigates 'Fresh Start' if they fail to improve—replacing existing head teacher and all other teaching staff. In 2000 Mr Blunkett introduced 'fresh starts' for schools where fewer than 15 per cent of pupils achieved five or more A–C GCSE passes. When Labour left office, schools where fewer than 30 per cent of pupils achieved five A–Cs were judged 'underperforming' but Mr Gove raised bar to 35 per cent.
Tackling inequalities of educational opportunity	Education Secretaries intervene, if necessary, to improve educational opportunities for poorer children; in 2007 Alan Johnson ordered LEAs to ensure good social mixes in their schools.

Other issues affecting schools

Besides the customary slew of stories about damning Ofsted reports, catchment areas, and league tables, there has been significant coverage in recent months about public spending cuts in relation to schools.

More contentious still was Mr Gove's abandonment of Labour's £55bn programme for refurbishing or rebuilding every secondary school in England: 'Building Schools for the Future' (BSF). This initially saw £3bn devolved direct to LEAs to spend on improving and maintaining their school buildings, with the aim of renewing the school in greatest need in each locality with money from the fund by 2011. Every LEA was told to start work on at least one major building project by 2016. Mr Gove cancelled the bulk of the programme with immediate effect in July 2010, initially stating that 715 schools previously earmarked for redevelopment would no longer undergo work, and 123 prospective academy projects would be reviewed on a case-by-case basis. In an early embarrassment for the Coalition, however, he had to revise the list of schools spared from the chop not once but five times—eventually admitting that of those he had earlier led to believe had been saved, at least thirty rebuilds would not now go ahead. However, in May 2012 Mr Gove announced his own (more modest) version of BSF: the Priority School Building Programme. Under this scheme 261 English schools in urgent need of redevelopment will be awarded grants out of an overall pot of £2bn over the five years to 2017.

The school system remains such a hotbed of political disagreement that it is impossible to list all the issues arising out of it here. However, another key aspect of Mr Gove's reforms has been a renewed emphasis on school discipline. Among his main innovations have been the introduction of a scheme to fast-track former members of the Armed Forces into teacher training; a change to the rules governing physical contact, enabling teachers to use 'reasonable force' to restrain disruptive pupils; and a call on school heads to reintroduce mandatory uniforms where they have previously adopted more relaxed dress codes.

The role of LEAs in further education

Councils have had an on–off relationship with the FE sector over recent decades. Like schools, FE colleges—then known as 'technical colleges'—were both managed and financed by county councils up to 1988. But the sweeping reforms under the 1988 Act included liberating FE and sixth-form colleges from LEA control, giving them 'semi-independent' status *within* the state sector, analogous to that granted first to GM schools and CTCs, then foundation and trust schools, academies, and free schools.

Labour initially did little to challenge FE colleges' new-found autonomy. In 2001 it established the *Learning and Skills Council* (LSC) to finance the sector across England and Wales. In 2005 the Scottish Further Education Funding Council was transformed into a joint body charged with overseeing the funding of the country's forty-three FE colleges and nineteen HE institutions: the Scottish Further and Higher Education Funding Council (SFC).

By way of answering some of the criticisms levelled at FE colleges under the self-governing regime introduced by the Tories, in the Learning and Skills Act 2000 Labour extended Ofsted's scope to cover FE. From September 2001 all FE and sixth-form colleges began being inspected on four-year cycles. This decision was, in part, an attempt to address growing concerns about lack of transparency in the management of some colleges, shorn of direct LEA scrutiny. For example, in 1998 Stoke-on-Trent College received a bottom grade for management from government inspectors following a succession of scandals that led to an £8m deficit, and the dismissal of a principal accused of bullying staff and running a pub in Wales while on extended sick leave. Under Mr Brown's government, the tone of FE policy began shifting away from college autonomy. By the time Labour left office, ministers had drawn up plans to return the UK's 385 English and Welsh FE colleges to some form of LEA control and the LSC had been closed. Reflecting its enthusiasm for self-governing educational institutions, however, the Coalition has restored autonomy to FE colleges, with their governing bodies—'boards' or 'corporations'—regaining primary autonomy over their day-to-day management and LEAs providing only a *strategic* role, as with a growing number of schools. Similarly, 'outstanding' FE colleges are now exempt from automatic Ofsted inspections in the same way as top-rated schools. In a rare example of a real-terms spending increase at a time of swingeing cutbacks, in May 2010 Chancellor George Osborne announced a modest £50m boost for investment in FE building projects. Shortly afterwards, Business Secretary Vince Cable used a speech at London South Bank University to call for an end to artificial distinctions between further and higher education—signalling his intention to increase funds for technical, part-time, and adult courses in FE and have more HE-level courses taught in tertiary colleges.

▌ The role of LEAs in higher education

LEAs play an increasingly limited role in **higher education (HE)**. They are, however, still responsible for providing mandatory awards—*education maintenance grants*—to students undertaking full-time degree courses at universities or other HE institutions. As of September 2012, students whose parents had a joint income of £25,000 or less were entitled to 'full' grants of £3,250 a year and to have their tuition fees paid for them. Those with parents earning up to £42,600 (down from £50,000 previously and, before that, £60,000) still received partial grants.

Over and above the mandatory undergraduate grants for students from poorer backgrounds, LEAs also retain the power to make discretionary awards to those who follow courses that do not benefit from this system—for example, vocational postgraduate degrees.

Funding and monitoring fairness in higher education

HE funding in England is the responsibility of the **Higher Education Funding Council for England (HEFCE)**. There is a separate *Higher Education Funding Council for Wales* (HEFCW), while both FE and HE in Scotland are the province of a *Scottish Funding Council*. In Northern Ireland, funding comes direct from the Assembly's Department of Employment and Learning.

The principal roles and purpose of HEFCE are to:

- distribute public money for teaching and research to universities and FE colleges delivering HE courses;
- promote high-quality education and research in a 'financially healthy' sector;
- play 'a key role' in ensuring accountability and promoting good practice.

To this end, HEFCE has its own board and committees with the following remits:

- quality assessment, learning, and teaching;
- widening participation;
- research;
- business and the community;
- leadership, governance, and management.

The task of ensuring HE institutions operate 'fairly'—particularly in relation to admissions policies—falls to the **Office for Fair Access (OFFA)**, led by a 'Director for Fair Access'.

OFFA's primary job is to ensure institutions that opt to charge tuition fees above the 'standard level' produce 'access agreements' detailing how they intend to ensure they do not exclude people from disadvantaged backgrounds. In practice many universities have sought to do this voluntarily, by offering bursaries and scholarships targeted at high achievers from low-income households, those with disabilities, and people from under-represented minority groups.

OFFA arose, in part, out of the perceived continuing bias of some 'top' universities towards children from independent school backgrounds. Concern about this issue has been rumbling since Mr Brown publicly condemned Magdalen College, Oxford, in 2000, for failing to offer Laura Spence, a pupil at Monkseaton Community High School in Whitley Bay, North Tyneside, a place to read medicine—despite the fact she had achieved ten A* passes at GCSE and was predicted to gain five As at A level. In the event, Ms Spence (who secured straight As) won a £65,000 scholarship to Harvard.

As recently as July 2011, however, it emerged that five schools were sending more pupils to Oxbridge each year between them than 2,000 others combined. These included just one state provider, Hills Road Sixth-Form College, Cambridge, and four top public schools—among them Eton (attended by Mr Cameron), Westminster (where Nick Clegg was educated), and St Paul's (Mr Osborne's alma mater). The figures were published by the Sutton Trust, an educational charity formed to promote greater equality of opportunity in the British school system. Labour's mission had been to raise more income for investment in HE so half of British 18-year-olds could be lured into it by 2015. But OFFA's job has become harder, argue critics, since the government introduced 'top-up fees' in England and Wales in 2006/7 and the Coalition's decision to allow universities meeting certain safeguards to triple their fees from September 2012.

▌ The growth of free preschool education

LEAs today have limited direct involvement in providing preschool or nursery education. Before 1997 the Conservatives left it up to individual councils whether to fund free nursery education for children from lower-income backgrounds. Given the choice between squeezing more money out of already tight budgets and leaving it to 'the market' to provide where there was sufficient demand, many authorities voted with their feet. A 1986 audit found that free provision ranged from zero to a maximum of 27.5 places per 100 children—hardly a ringing endorsement of council investment. Many LEAs today run at least some nurseries themselves, but most are provided by the private and voluntary sectors. In addition, money directed to enable children from poorer backgrounds to access preschool education tends to come directly from central government, rather than via councils.

In the early 1990s the Conservatives made limited inroads into funding free nursery care for preschool children. 'Nursery vouchers'—virtual money used to 'buy' access for children aged 4 and over to preschool education and/or childcare worth up to £1,100—were introduced in 1996, but abandoned by Labour. Vouchers had baffled many parents: although billed as an extension of 'parent choice', they could not compensate for the fact that—however willingly families shopped around for desirable nurseries—in many areas there simply were not enough places available.

Labour's solution was to launch its first National Childcare Strategy, focusing on two immediate priorities:

- increasing the number of childcare places available;
- guaranteeing all 4-year-olds a nursery place from April 1998 onwards.

Provision has been gradually extended. From April 2004 LEAs were obliged to guarantee free nursery places to all 3- and 4-year-olds for up to twelve and a half hours a week, for thirty-three weeks a year. As of September 2010, free weekly provision for 3-year-olds was extended to fifteen hours. While Labour's pre-election plans to extend universal provision to 2-year-olds was indefinitely shelved, a Lib Dem-led Coalition policy to provide this for 260,000 children in poorer areas was set to go ahead from 2013.

Improving access and accountability in preschool education

While responsibility for 'early years education' rests with the devolved administrations in Scotland, Wales, and Northern Ireland, in England a new programme was established in 1999 to drive through the government's aims of guaranteeing high-quality provision for children from low-income households: **Sure Start**. Although its primary focus is welfare and educational development, Sure Start has extended its support to the whole of a child's family.

The 'Sure Start' concept arose out of New Labour's conviction that early-years education was crucial to a child's social and emotional well-being, and families prevented from accessing it were missing out on vital development tools. Ministers' decision that preschool teaching should be a core entitlement, rather than an optional 'add-on' accessible only to the middle classes, was based on a body of research into its impact in later life and the outcomes of experiments in similar schemes pioneered in Scandinavian countries.

Sure Start aimed to:

- increase the availability of childcare for all children;
- improve health and emotional development for young children;
- support parents as parents and in their aspirations towards employment.

Sure Start operates through a network of children's centres, often based in community centres and church halls. Staffed by multidisciplinary teams comprising health visitors, teachers, and social workers, they have become focal points for liaison between families and other support services such as Jobcentre Plus and expert antenatal and postnatal advice for new parents.

Where Sure Start ensures that everyone has *access* to preschool education, Ofsted monitors the *standard* of that provision. Its remit was recently increased to cover nurseries, nursery schools, playgroups, and childminders. At time of writing, the Coalition was committed to retaining Sure Start, although Labour had accused it of effectively abandoning the programme by ceasing to ring-fence the LEA grants traditionally used to fund it.

≡ Topical feature idea

In July 2010 Michael Gove announced that more than 700 planned school refurbishments and rebuilds scheduled under Labour would no longer proceed—with nine facing the chop in a single West Midlands borough, Sandwell. At the time councillors, teachers, and parents were in uproar. But in May 2012 Mr Gove announced that six dilapidated schools in the Birmingham area would benefit from a new £2bn Priority School Building Programme, including three in Sandwell. How would you develop this 'good news story' into a detailed background feature? Where would you go, who would you interview, and what would you ask them?

Figure 15.1 Article from the *Birmingham Mail*, 24 May 2012

Six crumbling Birmingham schools set for revamp, Michael Gove has announced

By Jonathan Walker

Birmingham Mail

24 May 2012

Web link: http://www.birminghammail.net/
news/birmingham-news/2012/05/24/
six-crumbling-birmingham-schools-set-for-
revamp-michael-gove-has-
announced-97319-31039573/

SIX crumbling Birmingham schools will be rebuilt or refurbished, Education Secretary Michael Gove has announced.

But many others have been told their bid for funding has been rejected.

Mr Gove has finally named the schools to benefit from the government's new building programme following months of delays.

The scheme, called the Priority School Building Programme, replaces a previous policy called Building Schools for the Future, which was cancelled by the Government in 2010.

This decision meant plans to refurbish or rebuild 13 Birmingham schools were stopped in their tracks.

Birmingham City Council had applied for 19 schools to be included in the replacement scheme. Publishing the list of winners, Mr Gove finally revealed that six have been successful.

Hallmoor School in Kitts Green and Heathlands Junior and Infant School in Castle Bromwich will each receive a share of a £400 million Government fund to pay for urgent work to their buildings.

Castle Vale Performing Arts College, Kings Norton High School, Plantsbrook School in Sutton Coldfield and Turves Green Boys' School, in Northfield, have received permission to press ahead with Private Finance Initiative schemes, in which private developers help fund work in return for long-term payments and maintenance contracts.

In the Sandwell area, where nine building projects were cancelled in 2010, the Government is backing three school refurbishments, at Hall Green Primary School, Harvills Hawthorn Primary School and the Phoenix Collegiate, all in West Bromwich.

Nationally, 587 schools applied for the programme but only 261 bids, fewer than half, were successful.

Mr Gove said: 'I know that many schools will be disappointed not to be included in the programme. We have had to take difficult decisions in order to target spending on those schools that are in the worst condition.

'In order to ensure that the process was robust and fair, a qualified surveyor has visited every school for which an eligible application was received to verify the condition of the buildings.'

Source: Birmingham Post and Mail

✳ Current issues

- **Mass expansion of academies programme:** the number of academies has increased sevenfold under the Coalition, and it is committed to extending the programme further—freeing hundreds more schools from council control and giving them greater discretion over the extent to which they stick to the National Curriculum.
- **Emergence of 'free schools':** a key Tory manifesto commitment was to allow parents and teachers in areas devoid of good secondary schools to set up their own. Several dozen 'free schools' are now in existence, with more coming—but opponents claim the scheme is already damaging existing schools, including ones judged 'good' or 'outstanding' by Ofsted, by leaving them with spare capacity and reduced budgets.
- **Introduction of pupil premiums:** in negotiating the coalition agreement, the Conservatives agreed to introduce the 'pupil premium' proposed in the Lib Dems' manifesto. This top-up funding is paying for additional tuition for low-achieving children from poorer backgrounds, ensuring that wherever they attend school they receive extra help to stop them falling behind.

? Review questions

1. Outline the structure of state education in Britain, identifying the main differences between England, Wales, Scotland, and Northern Ireland.
2. How have the designations of different types of state school changed since 1997?
3. Describe what is meant by 'localism'. What are the main types of self-governing state school, and how do their levels of autonomy differ?
4. What are the main issues surrounding higher education in relation to student access? How have Labour and the Coalition sought to address them?
5. Outline the role of Ofsted and local league tables. What impact have they had on the relative popularity of different schools, and what are the main issues arising out of the Coalition's reform of the inspection regime?

→ Further reading

Ball, S. J. and Junemann, C. (2012) *Networks, New Governance, and Education,* Cambridge: Polity Press. **Thoughtful and timely examination of impact of policies inspired by 'Third Way' and 'Big Society' thinking on education sector in England.**

Crook, D., Power, S., and Whitty, G. (2000) *The Grammar School Question: A Review of Research on Comprehensive and Selective Education*, London: Institute of Education. **Examination of comparative qualitative and quantitative data relating to selective and non-selective state schools**.

Mansell, W. (2007) *Education by Numbers: The Tyranny of Testing*, London: Politico's Publishing. **Informed overview and critique of recent governments' increasing reliance on targets, league tables, and academic testing**.

Phillips, R. and Furlong, J. (2001) *Education, Reform, and the State: Twenty-Five Years of Politics, Policy, and Practice*, London: Routledge Falmer. **Critical overview of major trends and debates in educational reform in UK over past quarter-century**.

 Online Resource Centre

www.oxfordtextbooks.co.uk/orc/Morrison3e/
Visit the Online Resource Centre that accompanies this book for web links and regular updates.

16

Planning policy and environmental protection

Health care and education may be the policy areas closest to the hearts of the British public, but if there is one subject (besides tax and bill rises) guaranteed to get them even more agitated it is planning. Newspapers are crammed with stories about planning controversies every day: from rows about out-of-town superstores sucking the lifeblood from town centres to protests by 'NIMBY' ('not in my backyard') residents about proposed sites for New Age traveller camps or drug treatment centres.

But away from the placard-waving and alarmist headlines, planning is serious business. Without planning policy there would be no schools, hospitals, offices, care homes, supermarkets, or village shops. Before a developer can start work on a site, or a company, school, or NHS trust gets anywhere near opening new premises or altering existing ones, planning consent must be obtained. And decisions by councils about whether to grant consent are dictated by overarching guidelines—some set by central government, others by themselves—designed to provide infrastructure and promote economic growth while limiting its impact on the natural environment.

Compared to other council responsibilities—particularly highways, transport, and public health—'town and country planning' has emerged relatively recently. Its three underlying principles are to:

- ensure that all development is supported by appropriate infrastructure—for example, roads, traffic crossings, bus routes, leisure facilities;

- make sure any environmental impact is sustainable;

- ensure development is located on land unlikely to be affected by factors such as flooding.

Table 16.1 Role of the Communities Secretary in relation to planning

Role	Responsibilities
Guidance	Publishes guidelines on how planning authorities should discharge their responsibilities by issuing 'planning policy statements' (PPSs) (until recently 'planning policy guidance notes' (PPGs)). Under Labour these were supplemented by more specific regional strategies, produced by Government Offices for the Regions, but the Coalition has given councils and communities more say in shaping development in their areas.
Setting ground rules	Draws up fixed rules about types of land suitable for development.
Arbitration	Acts as final arbiter in disputes between individuals and authorities, appointing independent inspectors to convene inquiries to determine disputed applications.
Ruling in last resort	Can 'call in' controversial planning applications to give final ruling where inquiry fails to resolve issue.

Up to now a single Town and Country Planning Code has governed all forms of development in England and Wales, established by nine principal Acts:

- Town and Country Planning Act 1947;
- Town and Country Planning Act 1968;
- four separate Acts passed in 1990;
- Planning and Compensation Act 1991;
- Planning and Compulsory Purchase Act 2004;
- Planning Act 2008.

The planning process is divided into two levels:

- *Forward planning*—strategic development plans drawn up by individual planning authorities (district/borough councils and unitaries) at area level. These map out long-term planning strategies for each area, guiding councils' day-to-day planning decisions.
- *Development control*—authorities' decisions whether to approve individual applications to undertake material changes to existing land/buildings or carry out physical development (construction, alteration, or demolition).

The role of the Communities Secretary in relation to planning is outlined in Table 16.1.

Forward planning

Between 1991 and 2008 there were three varieties of local authority development plan, the names of which varied according to the types of council that drew them up. All three—structure plans (counties), local plans (districts/

boroughs), and unitary plans (metropolitan and unitary areas)—were eventually replaced by a more *regional* approach to development planning. As with most issues concerning local government, here and there the system produced exceptional quirks. In most hybrid counties—those in which two-tier structures sat alongside one or more unitary authorities—countywide development plans, encompassing the elements of structure, local, and unitary plans, tended to be produced by *joint strategic planning authorities*. In London, in addition to unitary plans produced by individual boroughs, the Greater London Authority (GLA) continues to oversee a joint strategic planning authority for the whole city today.

The 2004 Act began the process of introducing a simplified system, which ministers claimed would speed up and harmonize development planning across the UK—initially giving the eight regional assemblies the power to take strategic decisions for huge swathes of the country by publishing *regional spatial strategies* (RSSs). This system was further shaken up in 2010, when regional development agencies (RDAs) briefly took over the 'regional planning body' role and began publishing *regional plans*. As of March 2012, however, regional planning ceased, following the Localism Act. Exemptions apply (for the time being) to the capital, which is still covered by an overarching London Spatial Development Strategy, and the devolved nations, which have their own single spatial plan.

While regional planning has been scrapped, the Coalition has retained some innovations introduced by Labour—building on them to give councils and, more particularly, community groups much more say in future development decisions. The principal planning strategies produced by individual councils remain *local development documents* (LDDs). When RSSs were still in place these were effectively 'watered-down' local and unitary plans, because authorities were unable to deviate from the strict guidelines set at regional level. And they were further constrained by the terms of *local development schemes*—broad statements of intent by authorities about their long-term planning strategies, which dictated the terms within which specific plans were proposed. In abolishing RSSs—which he dismissed as 'Soviet-style top-down planning targets'—and the unelected and unaccountable RDAs that had long been a bête noire of many elected local politicians, Communities Secretary Eric Pickles confirmed his intention to make councils' strategic plans less 'bureaucratic' and much more 'bottom-up', reflecting the Coalition's 'Big Society' agenda.

In November 2010 he announced that communities themselves would be able to propose new long-term **neighbourhood plans**, which, if approved by 51 per cent of voters in a local referendum, would have to be implemented by their councils in the same way as if councillors had devised them. Theoretically, neighbourhood plans allow small numbers of engaged local citizens to decide for themselves where (and whether) they want new homes, shops, and offices built—as well as what the resulting developments will look like and which developers will build them. In the first year of the new policy, four waves of council areas piloted it, including Exmoor in Devon and Milton Keynes. One so-called 'vanguard authority' was the Royal Borough of Windsor and Maidenhead, which by April 2012 was reporting that it had plans under way in six different neighbourhoods, including improvements to Windsor and Eton (location of Mr Cameron's alma mater).

Hand in hand with neighbourhood plans comes a new 'community right to build' (see also p. 396), which was formally launched in April 2012. As its name suggests, this entitles local citizens and other community groups to build their own amenities—for instance shops, housing, community halls, and playground facilities—where there is a demonstrable 'need for development'. The great virtue of the new system, in theory, is that it circumvents the need for communities in desperate need of low-cost homes for key workers to go through the normal planning process (see next section)—effectively fast-tracking their applications. As with neighbourhood plans, however, development can only take place subject to the rest of the local community first approving it in a referendum, and the council, too, giving final approval—so it remains to be seen whose proposals will take precedence should the community's wishes conflict with those in existing council plans. Money enabling community groups across England to build in this way is being drawn from a new fund administered by the Homes and Communities Agency, worth £175 million over three years, with separate arrangements applying in London.

At the same time as announcing its move away from regional to hyper-local 'neighbourhood' planning, the Coalition confirmed it was abandoning Labour's centrally determined 'national policy statements' (NPSs). With them went the top-down 'housing quotas' and other targets ministers had previously used to parachute developments into particular areas (see p. 510).

The abolition of RDAs and NPSs initially left a vacuum in terms of the role they had previously played in channelling rejuvenation funds to areas facing particular economic challenges. To answer concerns about this, Mr Pickles established a new generation of **local enterprise partnerships (LEPs)**, which, like the groups responsible for drawing up neighbourhood plans, would be staunchly 'local' alliances of councils and businesses. Despite this, he left open the option for councils and business leaders to form alliances at regional level should they feel this was justified and/or necessary.

The future of large-scale developments

Labour's last three years in power witnessed a renewed emphasis on planning for major infrastructural projects—an outcome of the 'fiscal stimulus' which characterized the administration's response to the 2007–8 banking collapse (see pp. 213–16). To this end, the Infrastructure Planning Commission was established in April 2009 to fast-track major construction programmes, including nuclear power stations and wind farms—if necessary overruling regulations preventing building on greenfield and greenbelt sites (see pp. 482–6). Its members—though bound by NPSs—were independent of government, and held public hearings. By taking the final say on infrastructural planning away from the Secretary of State it also theoretically replaced politically motivated judgements with impartial decisions. No such selling points were sufficient to save it from the chop and it was abolished in 2011.

It wasn't long, however, before the Coalition also stood accused of paving the way for governments to override local decision-makers by imposing major developments on them. A new National Planning Policy Framework announced in June 2011 by Planning Minister Greg Clark introduced a 'presumption in favour of sustainable development'. Billed as a way of boosting economic output by fast-tracking the construction of new homes and business premises through removing costly and obstructive 'red tape', this sparked an immediate outcry from interest groups as varied as *The Daily Telegraph* newspaper (a long-time Conservative Party cheerleader) and the studiously apolitical National Trust. To placate the environmental lobby, which raised the spectre of large tracts of English countryside being bulldozed, ministers emphasized the use of the word 'sustainable'. However, critics argued that, however green they might be, the 'presumption' that major projects should be approved would have the effect of severely blunting the ability of councils (let alone community groups) to obstruct developments judged commercially desirable. Examples of such projects include the high-speed rail link planned between London and Birmingham (dubbed 'HS2'), and hotly debated proposals for a third runway at Heathrow Airport—both opposed by several of the government's own backbenchers because of the negative environmental impact they could have on their constituencies.

▌ Development control

Although long-term development plans impact significantly on British families and businesses, it is specific planning applications that typically arouse the strongest emotions. This is invariably reflected in the nature of press coverage about planning issues: while most people would struggle to remember the last time there was a notable debate about their council's planning scheme, most will be familiar with local disputes about the proposed locations of new sewage works and landfill sites.

As explained previously, the procedure used by councils to determine individual planning applications is known as 'development control'. The right to build on a site from scratch or make major structural alterations to an existing development is known as **planning permission**. Minor building alterations require no permission, or only a 'one-stop' decision from the council to give consent. But most 'new-build' applications, however big or small, require permission in two stages.

1. **Outline planning permission/consent**—consent 'in principle' for a development. Obtaining outline permission is often used by major developers to 'test the water' with proposals they may not pursue once they have investigated further to gauge their commercial (and political) viability—for example, proposed shopping centres. Plots of land are often sold to prospective developers with outline permission already in place. Outline permission lasts five years from the date granted, but if developers have not proceeded to the next stage within three it lapses.

2. *Detailed (full) planning permission/consent*—once outline permission is obtained and a developer decides to proceed with a development, he/she applies for detailed consent. With any major scheme the outline planning process will usually have highlighted 'gaps' in detail the developer now has to fill—for example, a detailed proposal for an out-of-town retail park will need to address concerns about transport, access, and environmental impact. It will also need to specify the exact location, dimensions, and make-up of the proposed development—including how many shops and parking spaces the development will include. Like outline permission, detailed permission lapses if not acted on within five years.

When deciding whether to grant planning permission, authorities have three options:

- *Unconditional consent*—approving the application with no alterations.
- *Conditional consent*—approving it subject to provisos (for example, better site access or improved or new traffic crossings). Developers will often be given outline permission with attached conditions and expected to satisfy these before being granted detailed consent.
- *Refusal*—outright rejection.

Before any planning authority can decide whether to grant permission for a proposed development, it is generally expected to follow a detailed process designed to give every 'interested party'—those likely to be most directly affected by its approval—a chance to air their views. This procedure is detailed in Table 16.2.

Small-scale planning applications—and changes of use

While a tight rein is kept on more ambitious development plans because of their potential to affect large numbers of people, it is not always necessary to obtain formal permission for minor material alterations to land or buildings. Under the Town and Country Planning (Use Classes) Orders 1987 and 1995, land and

Table 16.2 Stages of the development control application process

Stage	Process
Completing an application	Official forms obtained from local authority responsible for development control (district or borough council in two-tier areas, unitary authorities, or metropolitan/London borough councils).
Entering on the register	Application appears in formal register of applicants, and immediate neighbours immediately notified by council. Parish and/or community councils also fully consulted.
Advertising application	Certain kinds of application advertised in local press to enable others who 'may be affected' to comment.
Public consultation and exhibition stage (major applications only)	Public exhibitions organized for major developments, often involving detailed plans and models, either at council offices or local libraries.
Subcommittee, committee, and full council decisions	Routine/small-scale planning applications (e.g. extensions to domestic garages) normally determined at subcommittee or committee level, purely on basis of published regulations.
	Major applications affecting two or more wards, or likely to incur 'significant' cost, treated as key decisions (see p. 404), and determined by both cabinet and full council.
Appealing	If application refused, applicant has six months to appeal to Secretary of State. Each stage of application must be determined within two months (unless granted extension). If not, applicant may apply for ruling from central government on 'non-determination' grounds.
'Calling in'	Secretary of State may 'call in' controversial planning applications for final decision—normally when bid raises 'unusual issues' or ones of national or regional importance; arouses 'more than local opposition'; or it becomes 'unreasonable' to expect council to adjudicate alone.

property are split into 'classes', and material changes of use 'within the same class' will normally not need consent; neither will certain changes between 're-lated' classes (provided they entail no major building work).

For example, a greengrocer's shop may be changed to a newsagent's with no need for permission, because both are class A1 business premises and there-fore considered sufficiently similar. Restaurants, meanwhile, can be changed into shops without permission, because both are within the same overall 'class order' (the former A1 and the latter A3). The same is not always true in reverse, however—changing a shop into a restaurant may also involve making further applications, including obtaining a liquor licence. Neither is it possible to change from an A- to a B-class establishment without permission. The table entitled 'Changes of use allowed without acquiring planning permission', on the Online Resource Centre, outlines the changes currently allowed without for-mal permission.

In addition to the above permitted changes of commercial use, the 1995 Order allows home extensions to go ahead without planning consent—provided they comply with specified conditions. Councils have discretion, however, to pass an 'Article 4 Direction' removing some of these permitted development rights—particularly if the extension is likely to have a negative impact on the view and/or quality of light enjoyed by a neighbouring property. Planning consent is not usually required to lop or cut down a tree—provided it is not subject to a tree preservation order (TPO) or in a conservation area. If the former is violated, the council may prosecute.

Applications for planning permission are *always* required for material changes of use involving amusement centres, theatres, scrapyards, petrol filling stations, car showrooms, taxi firms, car hire businesses, and youth hostels—all of which are categorized as *sui generis*.

Planning appeals and inquiries

It is possible for either an unsuccessful applicant or his/her executor to appeal to the Planning Inspectorate over a council's rejection of a planning application—provided he/she does so within six months of the date on the decision letter. If permission is refused, or only conditional consent granted, applicants may lodge appeals for free. There is one inspectorate each for England and Wales.

Appeals are decided in one of three ways:

- planning inspector's consideration of written representations by both parties, alongside a brief site visit;
- formal hearing with both parties present;
- full **planning inquiry**—by far the lengthiest and most costly option.

At present, four out of five appeals are determined by the 'written method', 16 per cent by hearings, and 4 per cent after inquiries. Though third-party objectors have no right of appeal against successful applications, they may mount legal challenges—and these can sometimes result in inquiries (as well as court cases). Plans to build nine wind turbines in west Devon, approved after an initial inquiry in 2006, were later subjected to a second after an alliance of local residents calling itself the Den Brook Judicial Review Group persuaded the Secretary of State to overturn the decision due to fears about noise pollution.

In Scotland the Planning (Scotland) Act 2006 altered the previous appeal system—which saw them referred directly to the Scottish Government's Directorate for Environmental and Planning Appeals—to bring decision-making closer to the ground. In Northern Ireland the planning appeal process remains the responsibility of the Planning Appeals Commission.

The most high-profile planning inquiries tend to be those concerning applications that generate the most public opposition. Stansted Airport has been the subject of two recent inquiries, both related to the expansion plans of its owner, BAA (forcibly abandoned after the High Court upheld a Competition Commission ruling in February 2012 that BAA must sell Stansted). The company's plans for a fifth terminal at Heathrow—finally realized in 2008—were also subject to an inquiry that lasted nearly four years, starting in May 1995.

Even after an inquiry, the Secretary of State occasionally intervenes to make a final ruling, based on the inspector's recommendations. This was the case in the decade-long debacle over Brighton and Hove Albion Football Club's ultimately successful application to build a new 22,000-seater stadium near the village of Falmer in East Sussex, which prompted two separate inquiries.

The only way in which the Secretary of State's 'final decision' in these exceptional cases may be challenged is in the High Court, by a judicial review based on a point of law. Both appellant and planning authority may apply to the inspector for the other side to pay its costs should the judgment go their way. In the Brighton stadium case, then Secretary of State John Prescott's decision to back the proposal in October 2005 led to a pledge by its main opponents—Lewes District Council, Falmer Parish Council, and the South Downs Joint Committee—to mount a challenge. But after his successor, Hazel Blears, reaffirmed his verdict in July 2007, they reluctantly dropped their resistance.

The procedure surrounding planning inquiries is outlined in the table entitled 'Procedure for planning inquiries', to be found on the Online Resource Centre.

Inquiries can be a fertile source of stories for journalists, often providing high drama during hearings and a long run of follow-up angles. If a reporter attends an evidence session and registers as an interested party, he/she should automatically receive a copy of the inspector's full report when it is ready—ensuring he/she is kept abreast of the final decision.

▶ Other issues affecting major developments

Although notionally highly rigorous, the convoluted consultation procedure surrounding planning applications has often been dismissed as a mere paper exercise in local democracy. Despite its supposed transparency, councils (and developers acting under their instructions) have been criticized for doing too little to publicize 'consultations'—sticking poorly photocopied notices to trees and lamp posts, rather than proactively leafleting homes or knocking on doors. The planning process was memorably lampooned in Douglas Adams's *The Hitchhiker's Guide to the Galaxy*, in which the hero, Arthur Dent, awoke to find a bulldozer about to demolish his house to make way for a bypass, about which he had only found out by taking a torch into a disused toilet bearing a sign with the legend: 'Beware of the Leopard!'

In real life, if a proposed development is lawful, the odds have historically been stacked in favour of major projects—especially where they are likely to bring new jobs and other economic benefits—and councillors have frequently been criticized for being won over by grandiose gestures and promises of prestige.

Planning obligations (contribution/gain)

Developers have increasingly sought to persuade local authorities to look kindly on their applications by offering them 'sweeteners', such as additional infrastructure the council would otherwise struggle to afford. For example, a company seeking permission to build a new luxury apartment complex might offer to build social housing elsewhere in the area at a reduced price in the hope of inducing councillors to back its principal project. This offer of a 'benefit in kind' is known variously as **planning obligations, planning contribution, and planning gain**. Gain is also intended to avoid major new developments putting an unnecessary strain on existing infrastructure by ensuring developers make the necessary changes to accommodate them.

Although it had operated informally for some years beforehand, the concept of planning gain was legally recognized in the early 1990s. Until then it had been the convention for developers only to provide infrastructure—roads, crossings, and community amenities—*within* the bounds of the housing estate or business development they were building. All external roads, access points, traffic crossings, etc. tended to be financed by the council. Since 1991 it has become commonplace for developers to provide both 'on-site' and any 'off-site' gain required to enable the proposed development to function properly—for example, to give people access to the development, and even transport them there. Although this saves councils money and 'penalizes' developers, the quid pro quo is that applicants can use the incentive of off-site planning gain as a 'carrot' to wave before councils more liberally than in the past. In this sense, planning contribution is arguably a 'gain' for both developer and council.

In England and Wales planning gain was formalized in law by the 1990 Act (as amended by the 1991 Act), in the guise of 'section 106 agreements'. The Scottish equivalent is the 'section 75 agreement' introduced by the Town and Country Planning (Scotland) Act 1997. These rules specify that, having already granted outline permission for a site, councils can subsequently require developers to sign legally binding contracts obliging them to provide community infrastructure, avoid damaging existing facilities, or even transfer ownership of development land to the authority or another body for 'safekeeping'. Examples include:

- developers giving an area of woodland to the council, together with a fee to cover future maintenance;
- developers being required to plant specified numbers of trees and maintain them for a stipulated period—or only use some of the land for a particular amenity purpose;

- a requirement for a developer to build a specified quantity of social housing in a particular location, provide funds for a school or other community facilities local to a housing estate it has constructed, or create a park, playground, or nature reserve.

Developers cannot be *forced* to sign section 106 agreements. In practice, however, they are often happy to do so—not least in relation to controversial developments otherwise likely to become the subject of protracted legal challenges by disgruntled locals—because they offer as much protection to them as to councils.

Planning gain has undeniably helped finance much that is worthwhile. Recent examples have included the £2.5m invested by London's Canary Wharf (a privately owned estate) in the Tower Hamlets Further and Higher Education Trust—a grant-giving body designed to provide educational opportunities for people from deprived backgrounds. And it is not only commercial businesses that get involved in negotiations over planning gain: in June 2008 then Environment Secretary Hilary Benn wrote to every local authority asking it to consider 'volunteering' to become the location of a deep geological disposal facility for waste from Britain's nuclear power stations. The prize should they agree? More local jobs and 'other benefits', including improved infrastructure and services.

Indeed, ministers have looked for even more imaginative ways of helping councils profit from commercial development. In its 2006 White Paper (the first of two that formed the basis of the 2008 Bill) Labour proposed a new 'planning gain supplement'—a tax of up to 20 per cent on profits made by landowners selling off land for development. The idea was that 70 per cent of the proceeds would be pumped back into the local area to finance the schools, roads, and community amenities needed to support the government's huge house-building programme. But, following extensive lobbying by the building industry, which argued that less land would be available for housing as a result, the plan was shelved. The 2008 Bill also promised a new tax on development land—the 'community infrastructure levy'—which failed to materialize.

Greenfield versus brownfield sites—and the decline of the greenbelt

An enduring conflict facing planning authorities is their struggle to balance the perceived need for certain developments—homes, schools, hospitals, and shopping centres—with their legal and ethical obligations to protect the environment. At a basic level, councils have to take decisions daily about whether to approve applications to build on **greenfield sites**—locations that have either never been built on before or have remained 'natural' for prolonged periods. Obvious examples of greenfield land include agricultural fields, parks, and public gardens. The alternative to the greenfield site—and that favoured by

New Labour—is the **brownfield site**. This is a plot of land, normally in a town centre or suburb, that was previously developed. It may be the location of an abandoned office block or car park, or a largely derelict scrap of land devoid of extant buildings.

Between the 1960s and 1980s successive governments liberalized planning laws to make it easier for developers to build on 'out-of-town' or 'edge-of-town' greenfield sites, in recognition of the pressure on space in tightly developed town centres (many of which had originally developed in unplanned, organic ways). By the late 1990s, however, a backlash had begun against such developments, with town centre businesses complaining of losing custom to the then new breed of out-of-town superstores, and growing social and infrastructural problems afflicting housing estates in outlying areas—many the preserve of benefit claimants and the unemployed.

In its first few years in office Labour sought to redress the balance, introducing guidelines to encourage councils to lure developers into town centres. The aim was twofold: to regenerate eyesore urban sites while providing homes and amenities in the heart of the community (in so doing integrating previously marginalized groups, and making it easier for them to obtain work and contribute meaningfully to society).

But times change—and so do government priorities. The soaring house prices of the 1990s and 'Noughties' boom years saw many British people—including modestly paid 'key workers', like nurses and teachers—unable to climb onto even the lowest rung of the property ladder. The limited space offered by brownfield sites for development on the scale the government believed necessary to tackle the national shortage of affordable homes led to sweeping quotas being imposed on many regions and local authorities. This trend saw more developments targeted at rural areas, including the **greenbelt**—'fallow' land formally preserved by councils around towns and cities, to prevent urban sprawl and protect wildlife.

Introduced in 1935 by the then Greater London Regional Planning Committee, the notion of a ring of land indefinitely protected from urbanization quickly became fashionable in smaller centres. It was eventually formalized by central government—first in the Town and Country Planning Act 1947 and then Planning Policy Guidance Note 2 (PPG2, introduced in 1995). As of the 1993 structure and local plans—in the event, the last to be drawn up—around 13 per cent of the English countryside was designated greenbelt, covering fourteen discrete areas.

Planning Policy Guidance Note 2 specifies that greenbelts should:

- check the unrestricted sprawl of large built-up areas;
- prevent neighbouring towns merging into one another;
- assist in safeguarding the countryside from encroachment;
- preserve the setting and special character of historic towns;
- assist in urban regeneration, by 'recycling' derelict and other urban land.

Once an area has been designated greenbelt it is expected to safeguard:

- opportunities for access to open countryside for the urban population;
- opportunities for outdoor sport and outdoor recreation near urban areas;
- attractive landscapes and enhanced landscape near where people live;
- improvement of damaged and derelict land around towns;
- secure nature conservation areas;
- land in agricultural, forestry, and related uses.

For many years greenbelts were treated as sacrosanct by councils, but the pressure to meet central government targets under Labour councils increasingly compromised their long-held resistance to expansion into these zones.

Between 1996 and 2010 developers proposing to build new supermarkets on the outskirts of towns, or within easy reach of a town, were forced to satisfy both a 'needs test' and 'impact test' to be eligible for consent. The former required them to prove a new superstore was 'needed' in that location, given lack of choice for consumers elsewhere, while the latter was meant to limit any negative impact on trade in nearby town centres. Towards the end of Gordon Brown's premiership, however, a new planning policy statement was issued scrapping the needs test—a move that, according to the Association of Convenience Stores, had led to a notable rise in the number of out-of-town stores when adopted in Scotland. In place of the needs test, then Planning Minister John Healey announced a 'tougher' impact test, though his Tory opposite, Caroline Spelman, said this amounted to 'tying the hands' of councils by preventing them blocking superstores on grounds that there was already sufficient grocery provision in their areas. Once in power, however, the Coalition declined to reintroduce the needs test in its own planning framework.

Greenbelts are not the only designation used to protect land from development. Some rural and coastal areas are regarded as so exceptional that they qualify for designation under the National Parks and Access to the Countryside Act 1949 as:

- an **area of outstanding natural beauty (AONB)**—a locality deserving special protection to conserve and enhance the natural beauty of its landscape, meet the need for quiet enjoyment of the countryside by the public, and protect the interests of those who live and work there;
- a **national park**—an area with additional statutory protection against development, commercial exploitation, and habitation;
- a **site of special scientific interest (SSSI)**—an area judged to have special or unique natural features—further subdivided into *biological SSSIs* (those with rare or unusual flora and/or fauna) and *geological SSSIs* (those of particular physiographic interest).

Until recently AONBs, national parks, and SSSIs were designated by the Countryside Agency, but this job now falls to **Natural England**. According to its mission statement, this quango is committed to 'conserve, protect, and manage the natural environment for the benefit of current and future generations'. It seeks to promote:

- a healthy natural environment;
- enjoyment of the natural environment;
- sustainable use of the natural environment;
- a secure environmental future.

Despite its remit, Natural England has not been afraid to challenge some 'sacred cows' since its inception in October 2006. In 2007 then chairman Sir Martin Doughty used its first anniversary speech to argue that 'the sanctity of greenbelt land should be questioned' in light of perceived need to find space for 3 million more homes by 2020 (see p. 509).

There are currently forty AONBs in England and Wales: thirty-five wholly in England, four entirely in Wales, and one straddling the border. Nine exist in Northern Ireland, with another two (Erne Lakeland and Fermenagh Caveland) proposed. The smallest AONB is the Isles of Scilly (designated in 1976), which is just 16 km², and the largest is the Cotswolds (covering 2,038 km²). Although they notionally qualify for greater protection than mere greenbelts, in practice councils are not required by law to preserve AONBs and have little power to do so, other than by applying standard planning controls more vigorously.

Perhaps because of this, significant development has continued on or alongside AONBs, prompting vociferous protests from countryside pressure groups, most notably the Campaign to Protect Rural England (CPRE), fronted by best-selling author Bill Bryson. In 2006 it highlighted the plight of three. Dorset AONB was threatened by major road plans, while the Kent Downs faced the encroachment of proposals by Imperial College, London, to build thousands of new homes and offices. Brighton's stadium debacle (see p. 480) was particularly sensitive because of the scheme's proximity to the Sussex Downs AONB (now a national park).

National parks are a higher form of designation afforded greater statutory protection than AONBs. Protected by their own national park authorities, there are fifteen in total—ten in England, three in Wales, and two in Scotland, where AONBs do not exist (the nearest equivalent being *national scenic areas* or NSAs). The existing national parks are listed in Table 16.3.

In addition to AONBs, national parks, SSSIs, and greenbelts, successive governments have tried to conserve much of Britain's woodland in the teeth of ever-increasing demands for development land. The quango responsible for preserving woods for public benefit is the Forestry Commission, headed by a chairman and ten regional commissioners. The freedom people have long

Table 16.3 National parks

National park	Established
Peak District	1951
Lake District	1951
Snowdonia (Welsh: *Eryri*)	1951
Dartmoor	1951
Pembrokeshire Coast (Welsh: *Arfordir Penfro*)	1952
North York Moors	1952
Yorkshire Dales	1954
Exmoor	1954
Northumberland	1956
Brecon Beacons (Welsh: *Bannau Brycheiniog*)	1957
The Broads	1988
Loch Lomond and the Trossachs	2002
Cairngorms	2003
New Forest	2005
South Downs	2008

enjoyed to ramble through the UK's forests unimpeded is so prized that woe betide any government that interferes with it. The Coalition found this out to its cost after its then Environment Secretary, Caroline Spelman, published proposals to sell off 258,000 hectares of woodland to promote a new 'mixed model' of ownership between public, private, charitable, and community sectors. Visions of 'no entry' signs and ticket booths springing up along public footpaths and bridleways achieved the seemingly impossible by uniting in opposition everyone from the Labour Party to *The Daily Telegraph* and moneyed middle-class activists in 'true blue' Tory heartlands. By February 2011 the policy was considered so politically damaging that Ms Spelman dropped it—and in an uncomfortable Commons statement she took personal responsibility for the farrago, conceding the government had 'got this one wrong'.

Land-banks and the great supermarket stranglehold

A planning issue that has come to prominence recently, and one which relates to the wider controversy about out-of-town developments, is the growing practice by some big developers and their clients of accumulating 'land-banks'. This term refers to the practice of purchasing pockets of land—and often obtaining outline planning permission to develop them—without actually commencing building for prolonged or indefinite periods. The use of land-banks is viewed as unscrupulous by many: although developers argue they are merely guaranteeing themselves 'first refusal' to build on the sites, the fact they are 'sitting on' them without doing so is seen as anti-competitive behaviour designed to stop others getting in first. In some cases, land-banks have proved even more controversial, with developers or their clients buying up land only to sell it on to third parties—and writing clauses into the sales agreements to prevent it being developed by rival companies.

Of all alleged 'land-bankers', the one most often cited is supermarket giant Tesco. Perceived threats to the historic town centre marketplace of St Albans posed by a dormant land-bank purchased by the company prompted the forma-tion of a media-savvy 'St Albans Stop Tesco Group' and captured national head-lines in 2007.

New Age traveller and gypsy sites

During the 1990s a familiar staple of local newspapers was the periodic dis-putes between 'New Age traveller' and/or gypsy communities looking for land on which to camp—often temporarily, but sometimes for longer periods—and sedentary households concerned about the mess, noise, and damage to their own property prices they alleged were caused (whether consciously or unwit-tingly) by such encampments. Labour responded to the growing number of dis-putes by the time it entered office by introducing clear rules requiring local authorities to provide adequate land for camps. Over time, some £150m was paid to councils to facilitate the construction of designated traveller sites.

In May 2010 the Coalition scrapped the £30m set aside by Labour ministers to establish new sites that year, and three months later announced a major revi-sion of the previous government's rules on establishing encampments. However, in describing most travellers as 'law-abiding', Mr Pickles said coun-cils would be allowed to use some money from the New Homes Bonus scheme being introduced to encourage affordable house-building to establish addi-tional authorized traveller sites in suitable locations.

Otherwise, the Coalition's approach to accommodating travellers has been loose—requiring councils only to 'make their own assessment' of need in their areas, plan for necessary sites 'over a reasonable timescale', and protect green-belt from 'inappropriate development'. At the same time it has urged councils to promote 'private traveller site provision' wherever possible—encouraging travelling communities to buy their own land, instead of 'squatting' on other people's—while increasing their powers of 'enforcement' to block or remove 'unauthorized' encampments. A vivid illustration of this no-nonsense approach to traveller camps was Basildon Council's successful eviction of a 1,000-strong commune from Dale Farm, which made international headlines in late 2011 and early 2012. Though the travellers had purchased the six-acre plot of land on which they were camped, it was located within a greenbelt and they had built up their settlement extensively without obtaining prior planning permission (though, to complicate matters, consent had been secured for a camp comprising thirty-four legal pitches at neighbouring Oak Lane). After a decade-long legal battle, culminating in several High Court hearings and interventions by both the United Nations and Council of Europe in defence of the travellers' human rights, the council won its case, and the community was forcibly removed amid scenes of violence on both sides.

Compulsory purchase orders and planning blight

Sometimes plans are approved for developments on such a mammoth scale—or with such a significant likely impact on surrounding environments—that it is necessary for land and buildings that might otherwise stand in their way to be 'cleared' before work proceeds. Examples of such projects include airport runways, roads, waterways (canals), harbours, or new towns (see pp. 497–8). In such cases it is sometimes necessary for councils to force homeowners and businesses to move, so their premises can be bulldozed. In this case, a **compulsory purchase order (CPO)** may be served, in a process outlined in the table entitled 'The compulsory purchase order (CPO) process', to be found on the Online Resource Centre.

CPOs are not the only means by which councils sometimes find themselves facing compensation claims from property owners because of planning decisions. Should a property's value drop because a council approves a controversial application, it might be regarded as 'blighted'. In such cases, owners can effectively force councils to buy their properties—a type of 'CPO in reverse'. The process for lodging a planning blight claim is outlined in the table entitled 'The procedure for making a claim against planning blight', to be found on the Online Resource Centre.

▌ Other quirks of the planning system

Authorities now have the power to decline to consider planning applications on the grounds that the Secretary of State has refused a 'similar' one, on appeal, within the preceding two years. In addition, there are various ways of *enforcing* planning controls, as well as monitoring to ensure developments granted are lawful, as listed in the table entitled 'Other forms of planning notice', to be found on the Online Resource Centre.

Building regulations

Even when formal permission is not required for a 'new-build' or to adapt an existing structure, **building permission** (under **building regulations**) invariably will be. The reason for such regulations is to ensure buildings are structurally sound. An inspector (normally from the council) will visit the property during work to ensure it meets specified regulations.

Other than in inner London (which has its own system), the standard of regulations is the same across England. It derives from the Public Health Act 1961, which stopped councils making their own building by-laws and returned that power to ministers, and the Health and Safety at Work Act 1974. The process for applying is as follows:

- plans for the building work must be submitted to the planning authority;
- if they comply with the basic regulations and are not in any other way defective, prima facie, they must be approved; if not, they must be rejected.

Building regulation cases are usually overseen by trained inspectors, rather than councillors, because of their technical complexity. Councils can order buildings without building consent to be demolished or remedial work to be undertaken by their owners. Alternatively, they can carry out the work themselves—at the owner's cost.

Listed buildings and conservation areas

Although buildings of historic or architectural interest are not immune to demolition if they fall into severe disrepair, their owners can obtain substantial help with their upkeep by having them 'listed'.

Buildings are listed—on the advice of **English Heritage**—if they have:

- 'architectural interest'—for example, the recently renovated Grade II* Morecambe Bay Hotel in Lancashire, regarded as a classic example of Art Deco;
- 'historical interest'—reflective of a particular period or movement;
- links to nationally important people or events—Charleston, the Grade II listed country home of the Bloomsbury Set, near Lewes in East Sussex;
- 'group value' as an architectural or historical unit, or a fine example of planning—for example, the Regency Brunswick Square in Hove.

There are three 'grades' of **listed building**:

- *Grade I*—buildings judged 'exceptional';
- *Grade II**—fractionally lower down the pecking order than Grade I, these include the Shakespeare Memorial Theatre in Stratford-upon-Avon;
- *Grade II*—buildings judged 'particularly important'.

Decisions to list buildings must be approved by the Culture Secretary under the Listed Buildings Act 1990. Although there has traditionally been a reluctance to list post-war buildings, in 1988 a rolling 'thirty-year rule' was introduced, stipulating that any structure deemed sufficiently interesting for one of these reasons, and at least three decades old, could be listed.

When buildings are listed the lists themselves must be published and notified to councils, their owners, and occupiers. Once listing has taken place, any alteration or addition to a building entails the owner obtaining listed building consent in addition to other permissions. Among the new constraints will be limitations on the types of material they are permitted to use—and an obligation to keep the property in a good and characteristic state of repair. Unauthorized work on listed buildings will see councils issue enforcement notices requiring it to be reversed.

One of many controversies to arise out of Chancellor George Osborne's 2012 Budget was his decision to levy VAT on alterations made to listed buildings. This did not go down well with the custodians of such buildings, including English Heritage and the National Trust, at a time when they were already struggling to maintain those in their care in the face of other rising costs (and falling visitor numbers). Vociferous critics of the policy included twenty-three cathedral deans, who warned that adding this 20 per cent surcharge to the cost of refurbishments 'seriously jeopardizes the sustainability of our great buildings'.

If councils wish to protect 'non-listed' buildings threatened with demolition or serious alteration, they may serve building protection notices—a process referred to as 'spot-listing'. This covers the building for six months, during which time the Culture Secretary must decide whether to list it formally.

One further way of protecting groups of buildings—or whole areas of a village, town, or city deemed to have 'special architectural or historic interest'—is to designate them as **conservation areas**. Introduced by the Civic Amenities Act 1967, these offer particular protection for buildings from unsympathetic and/or inappropriate cosmetic alterations. Special attention is paid to conservation areas whenever a planning application arises within them. 'Permitted development rights', which allow changes of use of buildings without the need for planning permission, do not apply to those in conservation areas. Planners can also make 'Article 4 directives' to increase their control over the insertion of replacement doors and windows.

Councils must advertise in a local paper notice any application in a conservation area that might affect its 'character or appearance'—giving the public twenty-one days to object. It is a criminal offence to lop or cut down trees in conservation areas.

☰ Topical feature idea

Reproduced in Figure 16.1 is an extract from the list of planning applications submitted during the week commencing 11 June 2012 to the City of Bradford Metropolitan District Council. How would you go about making sense of this and deciding whether any of the items listed have news potential for the *Bradford Evening Telegraph* newspaper on the basis of the scant information reproduced here? Which details would you follow up and how?

Figure 16.1 A list of planning applications submitted to the City of Bradford Metropolitan District Council during the week beginning 11 June 2012

Planning Applications

■ **Construction of single storey garage**

122 Toftshaw Lane Bradford West Yorkshire BD4 6QS

Ref. No: 12/02490/HOU | Received: Fri 15 Jun 2012 | Validated: Fri 15 Jun 2012 | Status: Pending Consideration

■ **MOT Station in part of existing garage**

Euroway Commercials Limited 21A Commondale Way Euroway Industrial Estate Bradford West Yorkshire BD4 6SF

Ref. No: 12/02461/CLP | Received: Thu 14 Jun 2012 | Validated: Thu 14 Jun 2012 | Status: Pending Consideration

■ **Discharge of condition 3 attached to approval 11/05758/FUL (Installation of replacement windows including 14 arched windows, four windows with top openers and the replacement of eight fixed windows) to provide window details**

20 - 30 Baptist Fold Queensbury Bradford West Yorkshire BD13 2AF

Ref. No: 11/05758/SUB01 | Received: Thu 14 Jun 2012 | Validated: Thu 14 Jun 2012 | Status: Pending Consideration

■ **Works as per submitted schedule of work for T1 to T45.**

St Josephs Catholic College Cunliffe Road Bradford West Yorkshire BD8 7AP

Ref. No: 12/02457/CPN | Received: Wed 13 Jun 2012 | Validated: Fri 15 Jun 2012 | Status: Pending Consideration

■ **Change of use from B8: Storage/Distribution to A1: Shop/Retail creating indoor markets stalls**

Fairfield House Toller Lane Bradford West Yorkshire BD8 8LX

Ref. No: 12/02417/FUL | Received: Tue 12 Jun 2012 | Validated: Wed 13 Jun 2012 | Status: Pending Consideration

■ **1) Amend the new car park entrance to be an entrance and exit. 2) Provide a new footpath from the new car park to the back door of the offices. 3) Change the gabion retaining wall to the Redi-Rock proprietary system.**

Denso Marston Limited Marston House Otley Road Charlestown Baildon West Yorkshire BD17 7JR

Ref. No: 12/00992/NMA01 | Received: Tue 12 Jun 2012 | Validated: Tue 12 Jun 2012 | Status: Pending Consideration

■ **Submission of details of traffic calming to comply with condition 3 of permission 11/03517/MAF dated 14 October 2011: Construction of a new through age Academy (3-19) with associated external works and amended access to the highways, incorporating** accommodation for 1200 11-16 pupils, 240 student sixth form provision, a 440 place primary provision and a 39 place nursery. BB98 and BB99 guidelines for these numbers establish a target overall area for the Academy accommodation of approx 14600 sqm. Subsequent to completion of the new school, the existing school and ancillary buildings are to be demolished unless noted as retained. Highway works to include amended access to highways and new laybys to be added to Rhodesway.

Dixons Allerton Academy Oaks Lane Bradford West Yorkshire BD15 7RU

Ref. No: 11/03517/SUB03 | Received: Mon 11 Jun 2012 | Validated: Mon 11 Jun 2012 | Status: Pending Consideration

- **T1 Sycamore - Deadwood, remove epicormic growth and thin by 5%. Reduce limbs to give a 1.5m clearance to house ridge. T2 Sycamore - Deadwood and thin by 5%. T3 Sycamore - Deadwood and thin by 5%. T4 Oak - Remove epicormic growth.**

  1 Branshaw Garden Keighley Road Oakworth Keighley West Yorkshire BD22 7EP

  Ref. No: 12/02429/TPO | Received: Mon 11 Jun 2012 | Validated: Mon 11 Jun 2012 | Status: Pending Consideration

- **Two illuminated fascia box signs and vinyl on glass**

  39 Queensway Keighley West Yorkshire BD21 3PY

  Ref. No: 12/02412/ADV | Received: Mon 11 Jun 2012 | Validated: Wed 13 Jun 2012 | Status: Pending Consideration

- **Demolition of building**

  20 - 32 Great Horton Road Bradford West Yorkshire

  Ref. No: 12/02394/PN | Received: Mon 11 Jun 2012 | Validated: Fri 15 Jun 2012 | Status: Pending Consideration

Source: City of Bradford Metropolitan District Council http://www.planning4bradford.com/

✳ Current issues

- **Introduction of neighbourhood plans and community right to build:** as part of the Coalition's 'Big Society' localism reforms, local communities are being handed control of strategic planning for their areas, while community and voluntary groups are being allowed to bid for their share of a £175m pot of money, enabling them to build their own amenities.

- **Ban on 'garden-grabbing':** the practice of developers buying up land on which there have previously been houses with gardens and concreting over them to provide room for high-density urban and suburban accommodation ('garden-grabbing') was banned by Communities Secretary Eric Pickles in June 2010. He was able to block such development by withdrawing the brownfield site classification of domestic gardens, thereby allowing councils to preserve more green spaces.

- **Row over planned third runway at Heathrow Airport:** the Conservatives remain divided over how to increase England's airport capacity, with Mr Cameron and other ministers favouring a third runway at Heathrow, and London Mayor Boris Johnson advocating a new airport entirely, on 'Boris Island' in the Thames Estuary. Having only entered Parliament in 2010, Zac Goldsmith, MP for Richmond Park and North and ex-editor of *The Ecologist* magazine, told BBC2's *Sunday Politics* programme he would not be willing to stand as a Tory candidate if the party entered the next election with a manifesto advocating Heathrow's expansion.

? Review questions

1. Outline the application and decision-making process for standard planning proposals. What is the difference between 'outline' and 'detailed' consent?

2. What is 'planning contribution' (or 'planning gain')? Who benefits from the 'gain' concerned—local authority or developer? Give some examples.

3. What devices are available to local authorities and other public bodies to force property owners to comply with planning regulations?

4. What is the difference between building regulations and listed building consent?

5. Outline the planning appeals process, and explain to whom appeals should be made in England, Wales, Scotland, and Northern Ireland.

→ Further reading

Bryan, H. (1996) *Planning Applications and Appeals*, Oxford: Architectural Press. **Helpful guide to handling complexities of planning process**.

Cullingworth, J. B. and Nadin, V. (pending) *Town and Country Planning in the UK*, 15th edn, London: Routledge. **Fifteenth edition of standard text giving comprehensive overview of local planning process. Updates core sections to take into account impact of recent reforms**.

Hall, P. (2002) *Urban and Regional Planning*, 4th edn, London: Routledge. **Fourth edition of classic text charting history of town and country planning in Britain up to and including New Labour years**.

Smart, G. and Holdaway, E. (2000) *Landscapes at Risk? The Future for Areas of Outstanding Natural Beauty in England and Wales*, London: Spon Press. **Insightful look at challenges facing AONBs in era when land in increasingly short supply. Examines new economic pressures being tackled by AONB managers trying to preserve them**.

Online Resource Centre

www.oxfordtextbooks.co.uk/orc/Morrison3e/
Visit the Online Resource Centre that accompanies this book for web links and regular updates.

17

Local authorities and housing policy

One of the most politically sensitive issues in Britain is housing—particularly the lack of 'affordable' homes for those on low incomes and others without the means to clamber onto the property ladder. Councils have traditionally been responsible for the following aspects of housing policy:

- building and maintaining their own housing stock;
- liaising with housing associations, other voluntary bodies, and private companies to promote developments that bring low-cost or social housing to their local rented sector, and affordable homes to the private market;
- granting planning permission for appropriate public, private, and voluntary sector housing schemes in locations best suited to meet demand;
- providing night shelters, temporary accommodation, and, where necessary, longer-term support for the homeless;
- assessing claims for Housing Benefit/Local Housing Allowance and administering it locally.

Until the mid-1980s councils played a more direct role in providing social housing for the poor and unemployed, by building flats and houses and making them available for rent at subsidized rates. But during Margaret Thatcher's premiership the council housing stock began to steadily diminish, as long-term tenants were given the right to buy their homes at discounted prices, and councils' ability to build more to replace them was curbed in favour of an expanded role for the voluntary and private sectors.

Today 2 million homes remain in council ownership nationwide and about the same number are managed by voluntary housing associations (see pp. 506–7). But, perhaps ironically, in September 2009 the National Housing Federation predicted that by 2011 around 2 million families would be on waiting lists for rented social homes.

The amount of 'capacity' available in the social housing sector varies from area to area. In some areas the number of surviving 'council homes' is piecemeal; in others non-existent. Much of the rented accommodation currently available to low-income tenants is today owned by private agencies, professional and semi-professional landlords, and a new generation of amateur 'buy-to-let' developers. Meanwhile, as successive governments have asserted the public's 'right' to aspire to own their homes, the political focus has switched, at least in part, away from 'social' and towards 'affordable' housing: making houses and flats on the private property market more accessible to ordinary working people.

◗ From prefab to new town—a potted history of social housing

Providing fit and proper public housing has been one of the prime purposes of local government since embryonic council services emerged in the nineteenth century (see Chapter 11). Eliminating overcrowding and poorly constructed housing—in so doing, integrating proper sanitation and sewerage systems and improving hygiene—was a vital part of the fight against diseases such as cholera, dysentery, and typhoid fever undertaken by early public health authorities.

Public housing and the prefab

Between the world wars there was a period of major public housing activity. A campaign dubbed 'Homes Fit for Heroes' arose out of concern about the poor physical health of many young servicemen from lowly backgrounds recruited to bolster the ranks in the trenches and, under the Housing Act 1919, a start was made on clearing the worst slums. New planned estates were constructed in their place, largely in existing urban areas. But it was not until after the Second World War that a proper house-building boom began, as the struggle to provide shelter for people rendered homeless by Hitler's bombing campaigns became a national emergency.

Ironically, the Blitz (though it could hardly be described as a blessing) helped clear the way for development. The large areas of wasteland created by the bombings of Britain's major cities offered ample scope for extensive housing projects, and it was not long before the new spirit of collectivism channelled into the 'war effort' was being harnessed to build cheap, functional homes for those returning from the battlefront, and the many families left dispossessed by air raids.

Displaced families needed housing at a time when materials were in short supply, so the 'prefab' was developed—literally, a prefabricated, single-storey compact house, made not from conventional bricks and mortar but anything from shipping containers to surplus aluminium aircraft parts. Prefabs could be manufactured off-site and erected quickly. Their lifespan was intended to be limited, but they fared so well that they survived into the 1970s and can be viewed in building museums to this day.

Prefabs were not the only weapon in the post-war Labour government's bid to provide new housing. In October 1945 Lord Reith was appointed chairman of a 'new town housing committee' charged with devising a workable solution to the growing problem of city overspill. His suggested solution was to draw inspiration from the British New Town movement of Victorian philanthropist Ebenezer Howard, who created the garden cities of Letchworth and Welwyn, both in Hertfordshire: government-backed development corporations would acquire land for construction within 'designated areas'. The resulting New Town Act 1946 designated Stevenage (again in Hertfordshire) as Britain's first official 'new town', and within a decade there were ten more.

The rise of high-rise living

Population growth during the 1950s 'baby boom' inevitably led to increasing demand for housing and, by the end of the decade, ministers had empowered councils to clear away many of the jerry-built prefabs, demolish the last inner-city slums, and commence a mammoth house-building programme.

Under a series of Acts, beginning with the Housing Act 1957, councils embarked on extensive slum-clearance schemes, using compulsory purchase orders (CPOs) (see p. 488) to obtain enough land sufficiently quickly to facilitate the construction of suitable alternative housing. But no sooner had they done so than they faced an immediate dilemma that echoes to this day in the decision-making of urban planners: how were they to accommodate a rapidly rising population without resorting to similar tactics to their forebears—namely cramming homes together in high-density Victorian-style terraces or overcrowded estates? Their solution was to build upwards, rather than laterally, as in the past—in so doing, creating the first generation of high-rise tower blocks.

Although a number of multistorey blocks still exist in and around major towns, there has been a growing backlash against them since the 1970s by planners, politicians, and public. Tight terraces and sink estates might have been shoddily built and poorly served by infrastructure, but at least many such homes had their own backyards or small gardens, facilitating interaction and cooperation between neighbours. Neither were residents forced to share the entrances into their blocks or take temperamental lifts up ten or twenty floors before reaching their own flats. Many tower blocks were initially of sturdier construction than the social housing that preceded them, but over time their sheer height and overall scale engendered major long-term structural weaknesses. The lack of accessible shared social spaces and amenities—especially for those living on higher levels—contributed to serious social problems like drug-taking, vandalism, violent crime, and general isolation. Today, like the sprawling slums before them, tower blocks are viewed by many as ghettoes for a forgotten 'underclass', cut off from mainstream society.

Tower blocks have also witnessed ugly scenes. Broadwater Farm in Tottenham, north London, was depicted as one of the worst places to live in Britain in Alice Coleman's influential 1985 book about the perils of one-size-fits-all urban planning, *Utopia on Trial*. Later that year it witnessed one of the most notorious riots of the 1980s and, in an echo of that time, was the starting point for a protest march prompted by the police shooting of local man Mark Duggan which, in turn, sparked the mass outbreak of civil lawlessness in August 2011 (see p. 266).

The great 'new town' boom

Given the limited capacity of tower blocks to cater for rapidly rising population levels and the social deprivation increasingly associated with them, by the 1960s both central and local government were, unsurprisingly, looking for alternative solutions to providing low-cost housing on a mass scale for those unable to buy their own homes.

A consensus quickly emerged that there should be a further roll-out of new towns and, in the decade from 1960, ten more were founded. By far the most famous to emerge from the ensuing English new town programme was Milton Keynes in the Midlands—founded from scratch in 1967. In other cases, the term 'new town' proved a misnomer: the ancient cathedral city of Peterborough in Cambridgeshire was designated one in 1967, with Northampton acquiring the status a year later. In effect, these designations gave the towns—along with Warrington—a licence to expand, boosted by government investment, on a scale out of step with elsewhere.

The advantages of new towns over other housing solutions were manifold. By effectively starting out with a blank slate, urban planners had free rein to design roads, estates, and other infrastructure in a more ergonomic, 'human-centred' way—making maximum use of space and integrating vital community facilities to enhance quality of life for those who would be living there. The housing itself tended to be built on a more domestic scale, with two- to three-storey homes arranged along clear street patterns, backed and/or fronted by individual gardens and focal spaces.

But new towns had their downsides: established urban areas rarely provided enough building space for them, so they tended to be developed in largely rural locations, becoming satellite or dormitory towns from which residents had to commute, often considerable distances, to the established urban centres where they worked. Efforts were, however, made to ensure that new towns were as self-sufficient as possible, with their own shops, sports and leisure centres, cinemas, and, in time, employment opportunities. In some cases, new towns became so populated that new local authorities were set up to cater for their services.

Despite the demonstrable benefits of new towns for families on modest incomes previously excluded from the property market, in practice they brought limited gains for those at the bottom. During the 1970s and 1980s, a growing divide opened between poorer households fortunate enough to live in new towns, in which there had been sufficient investment in new council housing, and the large number of council tenants in older towns still confined to tower blocks.

Between 1947 and 1970, twenty-one new towns were established in England, and the new town experiment has been extended over time to the rest of Britain, with Scotland acquiring six, and Wales and Northern Ireland two each. Table 17.1 lists all thirty-two existing new towns, together with their populations.

▌ The Housing Revenue Account (HRA)

Every council maintaining its own stock of social housing is required by law to record all income and expenditure relating to it on a separate balance sheet to that used for its general revenue funds (see Chapter 12). This is called the *Housing Revenue Account* (HRA). The HRA is split into two halves: one covering revenue income and spending; the other capital payments. Most income generated by the HRA takes the form of rent, but councils may also charge one-off fees for arrears or damage to property, and the account can accrue interest. The primary purpose of the capital component of the HRA is to record all income generated from house and flat sales under 'Right to Buy' (see pp. 503–6). The way in which HRAs operate is currently the subject of a government review.

Council tenants' rights and how they qualify

Council tenancies have traditionally boasted significant advantages over the standard shorthold tenancies available when renting in the private sector, including:

- secure tenure;
- no deposit;
- rent set at a level substantially below the market average;
- the right to buy their home at a discount (see pp. 503–6).

Table 17.1 A list of new towns currently designated in Britain

New town	Population
Basildon	102,400
Bracknell	52,243
Central Lancashire (Preston, Chorley, and Leyland)	365,000
Corby	53,000
Craigavon	57,685
Crawley	99,727
Cumbernauld	51,300
Cwmbran	47,254
Dawley	11,399
Derry	107,300
East Kilbride	73,820
Glenrothes	38,927
Harlow	80,600
Hemel Hempstead	83,000
Irvine	33,090
Letchworth	33,600
Livingston	50,826
Londonderry	83,652
Milton Keynes	230,000
Newton Aycliffe	25,504
Newtown	12,783
Northampton	194,400
Peterborough	161,800
Peterlee	30,093
Redditch	79,216
Runcorn	61,252
Skelmersdale	38,813
Stevenage	79,790
Telford	138,241
Warrington	158,195
Washington	60,000
Welwyn Garden City and Hatfield	97,546

Unsurprisingly, social housing is much prized among those on low incomes. To ensure they allocated their limited housing stock as fairly and equitably as possible, councils traditionally kept a *housing register* (or 'housing waiting list'). Anyone over 16 who met certain eligibility criteria could apply to join it, with certain applicants prioritized—for example, minors, the elderly, and those with long-standing connections to the area. This system was changed by the Homelessness Act 2002, which introduced a 'points system' to prioritize applicants. It stipulated that 'reasonable preference' should be given to anyone falling into a set of specified categories, although other long-standing factors favouring certain households over others must also be taken into account.

These are outlined in the table entitled 'Criteria for prioritizing social housing applicants', to be found on the Online Resource Centre. Those granted council homes normally begin with a one-year 'introductory tenancy'. Assuming they 'pass' this de facto probation period, they are usually then awarded a 'secure tenancy', *unless* they are evicted for:

- not paying their rent;
- causing nuisance to neighbours;
- using the property for illegal activities such as drug dealing;
- moving out of their homes or subletting them.

The continuation of tenancies 'for life', although for many years seen as a justified perk of council housing, has become increasingly controversial as home shortages have worsened, particularly in oversubscribed areas of the southeast, where private accommodation is disproportionately pricey. Recent governments have faced growing pressure to prioritize Britain's limited social housing stock, if necessary by terminating tenancies for people whose financial positions significantly improve during their occupancy (enabling lower-income households to replace them). In October 2010 George Osborne scrapped secure tenancies for new social housing tenants in favour of fixed-term contracts. This followed David Cameron's earlier pledge to introduce greater 'flexibility' to encourage unemployed tenants to move to other areas in pursuit of work, and to move those whose incomes increased over time across to the private rented sector—freeing up housing for the most needy. Ministers also launched a 'Freedom Pass' scheme, allowing English social housing tenants to swap homes with those in other areas, to facilitate economic mobility. How these reforms play out in practice remains to be seen, particularly in light of Mr Osborne's further announcement that social rents will in future rise to up to 80 per cent of levels charged in the private sector—all while Housing Benefit is being capped. Confirming these changes in his October 2010 Comprehensive Spending Review (CSR), Mr Osborne added that the budget set aside by Labour for building more affordable housing would be slashed by 60 per cent, piling further pressure on an already squeezed social housing sector. In the wake of the CSR, charities like Citizens Advice and Shelter warned of an impending rise in homelessness.

Some councils use their discretion to explicitly *disqualify* certain people from applying for social housing, for example those who have left a previous tenancy owing money—making the job of finding homes for 'qualifying' applicants easier. Others introduce harsh sanctions for those judged to be in breach of their social housing contracts. Burnley Borough Council, Lancashire, writes into its tenancy agreements a clause allowing the social housing provider to evict tenants for antisocial behaviour (a sanction authorized by the Housing Act 1996). Recent governments have also climbed onto the conditionality bandwagon: in spring 2008 Labour Housing Minister Caroline Flint mooted the idea of requiring new council tenants to sign 'commitment contracts' promising to look for work. But the concept of 'earned' tenancies has been embedded by the Coalition, with individual local authorities given greater licence to distinguish between more and less 'deserving' cases. In December 2011 *The Guardian* reported plans by Westminster City Council to require unemployed people hoping to qualify for social housing and related benefits to sign 'civic contracts' pledging to undertake voluntary work in their local community as a precondition. The idea (since replicated elsewhere) was one of a raft of proposals the Tory-run council said it was putting in place to end the 'something for nothing culture' and better reward those who 'play by the rules'—language which could have been lifted word for word from a speech by a Coalition minister. Among the other ways Westminster is now rationing the points it allocates to prospective social tenants is to give more to nurses, volunteer police officers, Territorial Army members, ex-service personnel, and those who foster or adopt children— while deducting them from adults whose children persistently play truant from school and those penalized for antisocial behaviour (see pp. 347–8).

However brutal these measures may seem to some, there are signs of an emerging consensus on the need for tougher rationing of social housing among political parties in Parliament. In June 2012 ministers published new guidelines pressing councils to move employed people looking for social homes higher up their housing lists. In recognition of both the increasing appetite of its own core working-class voters to penalize 'undeserving' welfare recipients and the scarcity of social resources as a result of the Coalition's austerity policies, Labour has signalled that it, too, may be open to introducing harsher points-based qualifications if returned to government. Significantly, in Westminster itself the Labour opposition group abstained in the crucial vote on whether to introduce the new conditions, rather than voting against them.

Other local authority housing responsibilities

Councils not only have to provide *new* houses and flats for rent, but are required to maintain and improve existing social housing—as well as monitoring the state of private sector accommodation in their areas. Many have now combined their housing and environmental health departments, following a series of court actions brought against landlords under various Public Health Acts. The 1990 Act outlined councils' duty to inspect existing buildings in their areas to detect 'statutory nuisances'—defined as including premises prejudicial to health, as well as menaces like smoke, dust, fumes, rubbish, and noise pollution. The Act gave local authorities powers to 'eliminate' the statutory nuisance.

Councils may also take action over houses deemed 'unfit for human habitation'. Most of this work relates to the private sector. When assessing if a house is 'unfit', housing authorities look at its state of repair, freedom from damp, natural lighting, ventilation, water supply, drainage, and sanitation. The Housing Act 1985 gave councils the power to serve 'repair notices' on owners of unfit homes. Alternatively, they may carry out specified repairs to bring dwellings up to a habitable standard themselves, charging owners afterwards. In exceptional circumstances they can serve 'closure notices' (ordering owners to cease using a dwelling for that purpose) or 'demolition notices'. Today they can go further—buying unfit houses outright and taking them into their own stock. Sometimes it is necessary to act against an entire 'area', requiring or undertaking improvements or demolition. Demolished areas are known as 'clearance areas'. Before a clearance order can be made, the authority must arrange rehousing for all tenants and finance the work. The Housing, Grants, Construction, and Regeneration Act 1996 enables councils to pay discretionary relocation grants to displaced people to help them to buy at least a part-share in a new home in the same area.

The Local Government and Housing Act 1989 also empowered councils to declare whole districts 'renewal areas' for up to ten years. These normally encompass a minimum of 300 dwellings, at least 75 per cent privately owned, and where a third of the inhabitants are receiving benefits. Once a renewal area is designated, the authority may acquire the land by agreement or through a CPO, providing new housing, improving existing stock, and disposing of property to a suitable third party for future management.

Privately owned accommodation can also benefit from council help. Under the Housing Act 1996 means-tested, mostly discretionary, grants were introduced to help private homeowners unable to afford essential adaptations themselves. More recently, various new 'green' grants—funded by central government—have also been introduced to help tenants and homeowners improve their energy efficiency, to reduce both their fuel bills and carbon footprints. The Queen notoriously tried to take advantage of this scheme, as revealed by a Freedom of Information request made by *The Independent* newspaper in 2010 (see pp. 591–2).   The main types of grant are listed in the table entitled 'Local authority grants available to private homeowners', to be found on the Online Resource Centre.

▌ Thatcherite housing policy and the decline of the council home

As with many areas of policy, such as health, education, and the utilities, the Thatcher government had a profound effect on the availability of social housing in Britain. Less than a year after gaining office in 1979 the Conservatives embarked on a radical overhaul of the extant council house framework—giving long-standing tenants the chance to buy their homes at knock-down prices and compelling local authorities to sell to them. Within the decade, responsibility for building and maintaining social housing had moved decisively away from local authorities, towards new not-for-profit organizations independent of direct democratic control—**housing associations (HAs)**—overseen by a similarly unaccountable national quango: the Housing Corporation. Things would never be the same again.

'Right to Buy' and the privatization of council housing

One of the defining election-winning policies of the Thatcher era—and in many ways the death knell for traditional council housing—was the 'Right to Buy' (RTB) programme ushered in by the Housing Act 1980 in England and Wales, and the Tenants' Rights (Scotland) Act 1980 north of the border. Under this scheme some 5 million 'long-term' council tenants were offered the chance to purchase their homes at a discount on the price they were estimated to be worth on the open market.

Tenants eligible for RTB could initially claim the following discounts:

- Households who had occupied their homes for at least three years were allowed to buy at a 33 per cent discount for a house, or 44 per cent discount for a flat.

- Those who had rented from a council for more than twenty years received a 50 per cent discount on either a house or a flat.

The Housing Act 1985 increased the value of discounts significantly, as follows:

- Tenants living in houses for more than two years could claim a 32 per cent discount plus 1 per cent for each complete year by which the qualifying period exceeded two years (up to a 60 per cent maximum).

- Those resident for two years or more in a flat could claim 44 per cent plus 2 per cent for each complete year by which the qualifying period exceeded two years (up to a maximum of 70 per cent).

Between 1980 and 1995, 2.1 million homes previously in the local authority, HA, or new town social sectors were transferred to private ownership. Since then social housing has continued being sold off at a rate of around 60,000 a year—with the result that some areas, including Leicester and parts of Argyll and Bute in Scotland, now have little or no council-owned stock left.

RTB—lauded by Mrs Thatcher in the Tories' 1983 election manifesto as the 'the biggest single step towards a home-owning democracy ever taken' and 'the transfer of property from the State to the individual'—was understandably popular with aspirational working-class voters. By the time of the party's 1987 general election victory even Labour had dropped its formal opposition. On the face of it, the policy also provided a welcome boon to hard-pressed councils, liberating them from responsibility for financing the upkeep of often aged and creaky accommodation, and raising millions of pounds in capital receipts that (theoretically) could be spent in other areas of need. According to social policy think tank the Joseph Rowntree Foundation, proceeds from council home sales between 1987/8 and 1989/90 generated £33bn—more than the windfalls from privatizing BP, British Telecom, British Gas, British Airways, and Rolls Royce put together.

But critics maintain RTB has had a devastating impact on the ability of councils and HAs to provide homes for future generations without the financial means to rent or buy privately. Perhaps its most controversial feature was the strict controls imposed by the government on councils' ability to spend the capital receipts generated by sales on improving or increasing their remaining social housing stock. Initially, they were limited to spending only 20 per cent of this income on housing, rising to 25 per cent following the Housing Act 1989. But what the 1989 Act gave with one hand it took with the other: it stated that the three-quarters of receipts remaining must be spent not on building new schools, care homes, or roads, but paying off their debts. These rules were later modified (see p. 381), but there has continued to be criticism of the strictures they place on councils.

As part of its tightening up of the social housing regime (see pp. 512–15), the Coalition has resolved to re-embrace RTB—with the nominal guarantee that, this time round, councils will not only be permitted but required to ensure the income they generate from selling homes is ploughed directly into building new ones for those who still need them. The former Housing Minister Grant Shapps pledged that for each additional council home sold a new one would have to be provided at 'affordable rent'. The 'catch', however, was that councils selling off homes would only be allowed to use 30 per cent of their receipts from RTB sales to fund new ones—forcing them to find the balance from a combination of the 'affordable rent' (of up to 80 per cent of market value) they were charging on other properties, borrowing, and 'cross-subsidy' from their 'own resources'. All the signs are, though, that the revived scheme will go down a treat with aspirational tenants. Those eligible will be able to buy their homes at £75,000 below the market price—a numerical reduction which effectively trebles the discount cap that applied in most of England (and quadruples that in London) by the end of Labour's tenure.

Nonetheless, the mass sell-off of council homes continues to be blamed by some for the transformation of picturesque villages and coastal towns in the West Country and Wales into 'ghost towns'. The lack of social housing in such areas has priced many locals out of the property market, with buy-to-let and absentee holiday home-buyers pushing up both private rents and sale prices way beyond the means of native people employed in traditional rural and seaside jobs. In Tenby, Pembrokeshire, the price of the average house had risen to

£200,000 by 2010, and 40 per cent were second homes. However, as of July that year the Welsh Assembly Government was granted devolved powers to ban RTB purchases in situations where allowing them would have a detrimental effect on housing stock. At a wider national level, the Coalition's favoured solution to shortages of affordable housing is for local communities to take it into their own hands to promote development—by allowing them to fast-track applications for small-scale housing projects (see p. 475).

Between 1997 and 2010 Labour took incremental steps towards restoring local authorities' ability to build new housing stock—with, for example, ministers giving the go-ahead to the construction of 2,000 new council homes across England in September 2009, amid warnings that a further 200,000 families were headed for housing waiting lists. Nevertheless, with the Office for National Statistics (ONS) predicting that Britain's population is likely to top 65 million by 2020, the country continues to lack the sustained investment in housing some say is needed. At time of writing, the Scottish Government was reviewing the future of RTB north of the border, with Shelter Scotland urging it to scrap the policy to safeguard social homes needed to address the country's acute housing shortages. Arguments for and against 'Right to Buy' are explored in Table 17.2.

Despite its manifest attractions for aspiring homeowners of limited means, RTB contained caveats designed to deter people from cashing in. If a house was sold within three years of being bought by a tenant part of the discount had to be repaid—pro rata the time that had elapsed since its purchase. The general

Table 17.2 Arguments for and against 'Right to Buy'

For	Against
RTB offers low-income households who could never otherwise afford their own home a chance to buy one. It is progressive policy promoting opportunity, aspiration, and ownership among poor.	Under RTB councils historically only allowed to spend fraction of capital receipts from council house sales on building more. This leaves fewer available for poor people who need them in future.
Council tenants have traditionally had to rely on local authorities for repairs and essential maintenance—often waiting months or years. Enabling them to buy their homes liberates them from shackles of local bureaucracy—giving them flexibility to pay for repairs when needed, and motivating them to maintain properties to high standards.	Distribution of council housing has historically been unequal, with some more proactive about promoting RTB than others. Tenants' ability to buy their homes therefore subject to 'postcode lottery'—with those on low incomes forced to rent from private landlords because of lack of rentable social housing.
RTB raises significant revenue for local government that can be used to repay debts. Less debt means healthier finances, as more money left for essential services—and savings may feed through into lower Council Tax.	Selling council housing enables councils to offload punitive repair costs onto (former) tenants. While initial sale prices may be attractive, disrepair of some homes leaves those purchasing them with high ongoing depreciation costs.

thrust of the government's approach, however, was to do everything possible to persuade tenants to purchase housing and councils to part with it. If local authorities appeared to be doing too little to promote the scheme the Secretary of State could appoint a commissioner to investigate and, if necessary, enforce it. Some Labour authorities, like Norwich City Council, actively tried to sabotage it and ended up footing the legal bill for unsuccessful fights to preserve their housing stock.

Ministers also introduced 'RTB mortgages', administered by councils—although in time these were replaced by 'rent-to-mortgage' schemes introduced under the Leasehold Reform, Housing, and Urban Development Act 1993. The price fixed for a house or flat comprised two elements:

- *initial capital payment*—a form of part-mortgage paid in regular instalments at the same or a similar level to the rent for which they would previously have been liable;
- *deferred financial commitment*—a lump sum that accrued no interest but was repayable on the sale of the property, the death of the purchaser, or by a voluntary payment that could be made at any time.

These models were the forerunners of the shared ownership schemes commonplace today, under which 'tenants' buy shares in properties from HAs, with the help of normal home loans, paying rent on the remainder.

From HAs to social landlords

The 1957 Act had formalized councils' responsibilities as primary providers of social housing, but when the 1985 Act supplanted it as the 'principal' housing law on the statute book, this mantle was passed to new not-for-profit HAs. Coming at the same time as Mrs Thatcher's government was waging war on the Greater London Council, metropolitan borough councils, and 'loony left' authorities elsewhere, the decision to dilute the powers of local housing departments was viewed by some as another assault on the autonomy of elected councillors. Councils, it seemed, were caught in a carefully orchestrated pincer movement—between households keen to buy up their council homes on the one hand, and newly emancipated HAs (backed by Whitehall) on the other.

Sometimes called the 'third arm of housing', Britain's 1,800 HAs—today known as *registered providers*—are regulated by the *Tenant Services Authority* (TSA) and funded by the *Homes and Communities Agency* (HCA). Together these replaced the Housing Corporation, in November 2008. In Scotland HAs are regulated directly by the Scottish Government, in Wales by the Welsh Assembly, and in Northern Ireland by the *Northern Ireland Housing Executive*. Most HAs are registered as industrial and provident societies. All have volunteer management committees elected by their membership. Some have no professional staff, while others are large, with substantial workforces.

Councils may loan money or provide guarantees to registered HAs, in return for interest. They normally have the right to nominate up to half of council home tenants in their areas to HA schemes.

The primacy of HAs was cemented by the introduction of 'Tenants' Choice' in the Housing Act 1988, under which councils were pressurized to promote them as alternative social housing providers. But rather than simply giving tenants the right to move into HA properties, the Act sought to facilitate the transfer of housing stock itself into association hands. In truth even some Labour-run authorities (whatever their ideological objections) were attracted by the prospect of offloading their homes, given the high running costs and other complexities associated with repairs and maintenance. By July 1996, fifty-one local authorities had transferred their entire stocks to HAs—totalling 220,000 properties.

Further emasculation of councils followed. The 1993 Act and the detailed regulations flowing from it introduced the concept of 'tenant management organizations' (TMOs). Groups of council tenants living in a designated area were permitted to set up TMOs to take over day-to-day management of their housing and its associated finances—effectively *replacing* councils and forming de facto HAs. The National Federation of Tenant Management Organizations had more than 100 member TMOs by September 2010.

Another development came with the Housing Act 1996, which introduced the label 'social landlord'—an umbrella term used to define a variety of different models of shared social housing management. Whatever precise form they take, social landlords are overseen, like HAs, by the TSA. They include a new type of not-for-profit 'housing company'—often partnered with, but not directly controlled by, local authorities and tenants themselves—and 'housing co-ops' (a variation on TMOs).

The outcome of this flurry of reforms was precisely what the Conservatives had set out to foster: 'a more pluralist and more market-oriented system'. A symbolic final seal was set on the logical direction of the party's policies when the Local Government and Housing Act 1989 explicitly freed councils from any obligation to retain their own social housing stock.

The rise of owner-occupancy and the 'affordable housing' debate

Recent surveys—produced separately for England, Scotland, Wales, and Northern Ireland—suggest that, despite years of spiralling house prices and the well-reported financial obstacles faced by first-time buyers, Britain has come some way towards becoming that great 'home-owning democracy' heralded by Mrs Thatcher back in 1983. Figures 17.1 and 17.2 provide a comparison between the breakdown of dwelling types in England in 1961 (the year records began) and 2010/11 (the most recent year for which data is available). Information from the census of 31 March 1961 revealed that, of the

Essential public affairs for journalists

Figure 17.1 Where English residents were living as of 31 March 1961

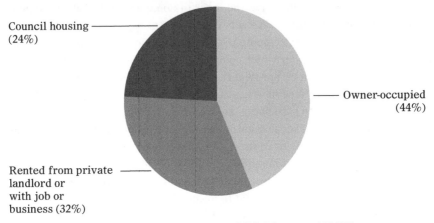

Council housing (24%)

Owner-occupied (44%)

Rented from private landlord or with job or business (32%)

Source: Department for Communities and Local Government (DCLG) © Crown copyright 2012

Figure 17.2 Where English residents were living as of 2010/11

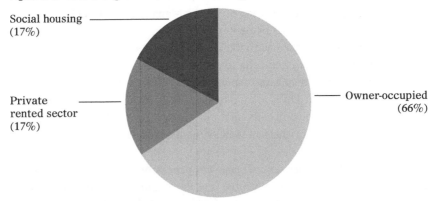

Social housing (17%)

Owner-occupied (66%)

Private rented sector (17%)

Source: Department for Communities and Local Government (DCLG) © Crown copyright 2012

13.83 million dwellings in which English inhabitants were then living, 6.1m (44 per cent) were owner-occupied houses and flats, with 4.4m (32 per cent) rented from private landlords or as part of the residents' job or business, and 3.38m (24 per cent) council housing. Half a century later, the United Kingdom Statistics Authority's English Housing Survey found that, out of a total of 21.8m dwellings the number of owner-occupied properties had soared to 66 per cent of the total (14.4m)—though, in light of the ongoing economic crisis this had fallen from 17.5m two years previously. The proportion rented from local authorities (and other social landlords) had fallen by more than one-third over the fifty-year period—bringing it nearly neck and neck with the private rented sector for the first time, at 17 per cent (3.8m, compared to 3.6m). Significantly, the social housing share was down by 700,000 on 2009, when it was 4.5m, with fewer than one in ten low-cost homes being traditional council houses or flats. At time of writing private rented accommodation was widely expected to have overtaken social housing as a proportion of the overall market by 2013.

Despite the growth in home ownership, however, many people—particularly those on low incomes and single public sector professionals living in southeast England—found it next to impossible to enter the property market during the Noughties housing boom. As a consequence, recent years have seen much government rhetoric, and numerous policy initiatives, geared towards helping out those who neither qualify for conventional social housing nor can afford their own homes. Particular emphasis has been placed on the plight of 'key workers'—public servants like teachers and nurses (especially those living in areas like inner London, where prices are disproportionately high).

To guarantee the market provided more 'affordable' houses, Labour ministers aimed to build 3 million new homes by 2020, at a projected cost of £8bn. In theory, by targeting the homes at areas with shortages of affordable private sector homes this would have both provided bricks and mortar upfront and forced prices down across the board. A 2007 Green Paper outlined a raft of new priorities and top-down targets, including a pledge to build 70,000 new homes a year (45,000 in the social sector) and speed up the planning process to prevent councils stalling.

The sheer scale of development proposed for some areas generated fierce opposition. In the south-east, where 200,000 new houses were due to be built, councils and local residents alike objected to the 'quotas' they were presented with by ministers. The newly designated South Downs National Park was targeted for thousands of homes (many in flood plains), to the fury of parish councils and environmental campaigners. There was also considerable controversy over ministers' pledge to give preferential permission to sustainable housing developments, or 'eco-towns'. Criticisms have included the fact that, to establish these supposed paragons of environmental friendliness, large tracts of as-yet-undeveloped countryside would need to be surrendered to house-building. Green campaigners also argued that some sites earmarked for such developments were in rural areas bereft of public transport infrastructure—a factor likely to lead to above-average levels of car ownership among those who ended up living there, making a mockery of their 'eco' credentials. Campaigns against the mass house-building programme were launched from the south-west to the north-east.

In contrast, some experts claimed the government's plans were too modest. In October 2007 the National Housing and Planning Advice Unit predicted typical UK house prices would spiral to nine-and-a-half times the average salary by 2026 unless ministers increased supply even more dramatically. By 2016, they argued, 270,000 new homes would need to be built each year to avert a crisis in home ownership among low and middle earners—as opposed to the 240,000 a year planned at the time.

Whatever the true picture, by autumn 2008 the arguments for and against the onset of a fresh 'new town' era were looking increasingly academic: the economic downturn, coupled with a collapsing housing market, saw many developers involved in the government's plans bringing their house-building programmes to an abrupt standstill. Although the mortgage market has since stabilized, the number of approvals in the year to June 2008 slumped by 70 per cent, according to the British Bankers' Association (three years later the Bank of England reported it was still falling—albeit by a tenth of that amount). Top-down housing targets were abandoned in July 2010 (to wails of protest from Opposition MPs and the House-Builders' Federation) by Coalition Communities Secretary Eric Pickles. In future, he said, it would be up to individual councils, and the communities they served, to determine 'the right level of local housing provision in their area' (see p. 361). To allay fears that abolishing quotas and *regional spatial strategies* (RSSs) might leave a short-term policy vacuum, while councils worked out their ongoing approaches to strategic planning, Mr Pickles urged them to decide swiftly whether to abandon or retain targets previously imposed on them so 'communities and landowners know where they stand'. As critics pointed out that, even before targets were scrapped, house-building in England had fallen to its lowest levels since the 1920s, in August 2010 Mr Shapps unveiled a New Homes Bonus scheme, designed to incentivize councils to build affordable housing by offering them extra funding for doing so. For every new home built the government would match the Council Tax raised on the premises for the following six years. But Mr Shapps's Labour opposite, John Healey, said that in practice existing government grants to councils were likely to be raided to finance it—meaning ministers would be 'robbing Peterborough to pay Poole'.

▌ Housing policy and the homeless

Councils have a statutory duty to house the 'unintentionally homeless' and those threatened with homelessness 'within 28 days of being made aware of their predicament' under the Housing (Homeless Persons) Act 1977 and the Homelessness Act 2002. Under the Housing Act 1996, however, the ambit of 'homelessness' was narrowed to allow councils to take into account available accommodation across the UK and even 'elsewhere'. The aim of this reform was to help out councils presented with disproportionately high numbers of homeless people (particularly asylum-seekers) because it would be unreasonable for them to be expected to house all applicants in their own areas. Ensuing regulations also tightened the law regarding the eligibility of asylum-seekers for help with housing: anyone who did not claim asylum-seeker status at the port of their arrival was rendered ineligible (barring refugees and those granted 'exceptional or unconditional leave to remain in the UK'). The Act also introduced a two-year limit on the provision of accommodation in certain cases and a review of all cases after that.

The types of homeless people treated as priority cases are those:

- with dependent children;
- made homeless by an emergency or disaster (flood, fire, etc.);
- vulnerable because of old age, or mental or physical disability;
- who are pregnant.

When assessing applications from homeless people for permanent housing and while waiting for flats to become available, councils often use short-stay, hostel, and/or 'bed and breakfast' accommodation (in reality, often little more than dingy bedsits or studio flats within multi-occupancy dwellings).

The overriding controversy over councils' responsibilities towards the homeless, however, relates to the Act's rather wide-ranging definition of 'unintentional homelessness'. Under the law the 'intentionally homeless' include people evicted from private sector accommodation for falling behind with rent, and even those fleeing home 'voluntarily' to escape domestic abuse. Nonetheless, if 'intentionally homeless' people fit into priority categories, councils must provide them with advice, assistance, and temporary accommodation.

The Coalition has gone further in diluting the responsibility of councils towards the homeless—allowing them to abandon their 'duty of care' once they have successfully steered people into private sector accommodation for a year.

Tony Blair's government made a high-profile effort to tackle street homelessness during its first term. Under a Rough Sleepers Unit headed by bullish 'Homelessness Tsar' Louise Casey he launched the Rough Sleepers Initiative, initially in central London but then across several other cities with high levels of homelessness, including Bristol and Brighton. Its stated aim was initially to provide places in short-term hostels and leased spaces in 'move-on' accommodation, before rerouting street-sleepers to permanent homes, high-dependency specialist care homes, and special accommodation for people with drink/drug problems. The initiative officially ended in March 2002, having (according to ministers) largely achieved its aims.

Not everyone was convinced by its figures. 'Spot counts' of rough sleepers were periodically carried out on the streets of target towns and cities—but controversy erupted in December 2002 when volunteers working with the homeless in Waterloo and Westminster alleged they had been moved out of the London boroughs two nights before a count, to gerrymander their figures downwards.

▌ Local authorities and Housing Benefit (Local Housing Allowance)

In addition to providing social housing and shelter for the unintentionally homeless, councils administer Housing Benefit (HB) on behalf of the Department for Work and Pensions (DWP). Since April 2008 HB—a payment equivalent to all or part of the rent charged to low-income tenants living in private, public, or voluntary sector accommodation—has been calculated on the basis of a **Local Housing Allowance (LHA)** formula.

There are two types, depending on individuals' circumstances:

- *standard Housing Benefit*—paid to employed people on low earnings;
- *certificated Housing Benefit*—for those on Jobseeker's Allowance (JSA), Income Support, Incapacity Benefit, and other benefits related to an inability to work.

The principal difference between the new and old methods of calculating HB payments relates to the method used to assess how much eligible claimants receive. HB used to involve individual properties being inspected by housing officers to determine their (notional) rental values, with successful claimants then receiving payments commensurate with what their council felt the accommodation was worth. LHA has simplified this process, by offering claimants blanket rates for different levels of property (from one-bedroom flats to four-bedroom houses) based on 'middle-of-the-range' market rents for each category in their neighbourhoods (known as *broad market rental areas* (BMRAs)).

Anti-poverty campaigners argue the 'new' calculation method, introduced by Labour in its third term, means sums received by even those granted full help with rental costs, and living in modest properties, often fall well short of what landlords actually charge them. Disability groups, meanwhile, have complained that LHA discriminates against severely disabled people who require two-bedroom homes because of their need to accommodate live-in carers. In November 2009 a benefits tribunal found against Walsall Council in a case brought by the mother of a severely disabled woman, who argued the new regulations had unfairly left her with a weekly £70–5 rent shortfall on the two-bedroom home they shared.

Discontent over cutbacks to HB/LHA was gathering momentum at time of writing, thanks to the Welfare Reform Act 2012, which will see all benefits incorporated into an all-encompassing Universal Credit (UC) from October 2013 (see p. 245), and the introduction of caps. As well as bringing in a £280-a-week limit for a one-bedroom flat and one of £400 a week for a four-bedroom house, the Act formalized an across-the-board annual benefits cap for households of £26,000, including HB—putting paid to the type of story, beloved of the *Daily Mail*, about welfare-dependent families receiving tens of thousands of pounds a year to live in palatial homes in central London that most waged households could never afford. The way LHA itself is calculated has also become less generous: Labour set payments at 50 per cent of the BMRA, but the Coalition has reduced the ratio to 30 per cent. And more may be to come. From April 2013 social tenants living in properties with a spare room stand to lose £40 a month, and those with two spare rooms £70—a move designed to 'free up spare capacity' for those on waiting lists, but one that housing charities have warned will inevitably lead to people being forced out of their homes and, in extreme cases, made homeless. And in a speech in June 2012, Mr Cameron mooted going even further to bring down England's HB bill after the 2015 election—withdrawing the benefit entirely from up to 380,000 under-25-year-olds and forcing them to support themselves or move in with their parents.

Some proposals have been shelved (if not permanently abandoned). George Osborne's 2010 CSR had included plans to save £2bn a year by cutting the amount of HB claimable by single people under 35 to the cost of a room in a shared property, rather than their own flat, and slashing entitlements for those claiming JSA for more than a year by 10 per cent—forcing jobseekers still without work to either dig into their £65-a-week living expenses to cover their rent or uproot themselves and their families and move elsewhere.

see also central government, p. 239

Ahead of the 2012 Act receiving royal assent, some London boroughs revealed they were already seeking out 'bed and breakfast' accommodation in cheaper outlying suburbs in anticipation of a rise in evictions—prompting Labour frontbencher Chris Bryant to condemn the government's reforms as 'social cleansing'. Influential backbencher Jon Cruddas likened them to a latter-day 'clearances'—a reference to moves to corral paupers and the unemployed in the eighteenth and nineteenth centuries. Even Boris Johnson, the Conservative Mayor of London, told a radio presenter he would not allow poor people to be shunted out of the capital 'on my watch'. Ministers retorted that such claims were scaremongering—arguing cuts in HB/LHA would merely induce claimants to move into more modest rented properties (of which they said there were plenty) and/or landlords to charge less, as the private rental market corrected itself.

But since the Act came into effect some of the fears appear to have been borne out. Investigations by *The Guardian* and BBC Radio 4's *Today* programme respectively have demonstrated that in London and Oxford (the second most competitive rental market in England) there is a severe shortage of surplus private rented properties priced at or below the new LHA levels the owners of which will accept benefit claimants. Given these findings it came as little surprise to critics of the government's reforms when in

April 2012 *The Guardian* reported that Westminster and Hammersmith councils had begun shipping social tenants priced out of their homes elsewhere, while Labour-run Newham Council had approached a Stoke-based HA asking it to accommodate 500 families it argued had been forced to leave the London borough due to the HB cap (which came into force that month). Newham's move prompted ministers to accuse Labour of 'playing politics' with social tenants. But, responding to Mr Shapps's insistence that there were more than 1,000 affordable rental properties within a five-mile radius of Newham available on the Rightmove lettings website as of April 2012, *Guardian* journalist Polly Curtis conducted her own experimental search. While she found 339 four-bedroom houses available in the area at or below the new £400 cap level, not one of the half-dozen agents she called randomly to enquire about the properties said they were willing to accommodate claimants.

In June 2012, meanwhile, *The Guardian* reported a warning by England's HAs of a chronic lack of space in social homes for the estimated 100,000 people who had already received letters telling them they needed to find smaller properties if they were to continue receiving benefits that would cover the cost of the roofs over their heads. Iain Sim, chief executive of Coast & Country, one of the largest providers in north-east England, told the paper that while there were 2,500 properties on his books with at least one spare room which could be freed up if 'underoccupiers' moved out, he only had sixteen one-bedroom flats available to house those who did. Around the same time, a government-commissioned study by the Centre for Regional Economic and Social Research at Sheffield Hallam University found that four out of ten private landlords in London, and a third of those elsewhere in England, were planning to stop accepting benefit claimants within the year.

Others have cast doubt on the entire premise for the Coalition's reforms: principally the idea that workless benefit claimants are being unfairly subsidized at the expense of 'hard-working families' struggling to pay their own way unaided. In a 2010 article in *Inside Housing*, trade journal of the social housing sector, Helen Williams, assistant director of the National Housing Federation, argued that, far from being a mass of feckless, work-shy scroungers, three-quarters of the 4.7 million households claiming HB were either retired, disabled, or full-time carers. Of the remaining 24 per cent, half were in work. Figures from homelessness charity Shelter and the Department of Work and Pensions itself backed up this assertion, with the former demonstrating that fewer than one in eight HB claimants were unemployed.

Though the administration of housing-related benefits is set to change with the advent of UC, at time of writing it remained the province of councils.

Alongside LHA they also administer Council Tax Benefit, which normally equates to a full Council Tax rebate for those qualifying for LHA. However, in his 2010 CSR Mr Osborne localized this system for everyone other than pensioners, and ordered councils to cut the reliefs they paid. At the time, Andy Sawford, chief executive of the Local Government Information Unit, predicted some authorities might scrap the benefit for specific groups, such as the long-term unemployed, to protect others.

▍ Forcing down market rents—the case for 'rent controls'

Controversy about housing shortages and benefit cuts has led to a revived debate about a long-standing policy for protecting low-income tenants, abandoned by the Thatcher government nearly a quarter of a century ago: 'rent controls'. Under the rent control regime—which ran from 1915 until its abolition in 1988—council-employed rent officers could intervene directly in their areas to limit the cost of rents to the unemployed and low-paid. The axing of controls was accompanied by the introduction of six-month 'assured shorthold' tenancies for both landlords and renters. At the time ministers argued that, however noble the intention behind them, controls had had the effect of stifling investment in the private rental sector, in so doing encouraging 'slum landlords' to let out substandard accommodation at bargain-basement rents to the poor. The reintroduction of rent controls was one of the signature policies to which Labour's Ken Livingstone shackled his ultimately unsuccessful campaign to be reinstated as London mayor in May 2012. Though yet to be formally adopted by any of Britain's major parties as national policy, at time of writing controls were rumoured to be among several radical ideas being considered by then newly appointed head of Labour's policy review, Mr Cruddas.

☰ Topical feature idea

Figure 17.3 is an extract from an article in the *Exeter Express and Echo* on 27 August 2011. It focuses on a council initiative to free up surplus rooms in underoccupied council houses and flats, to find space for the 17,471 individuals on its waiting list by offering households cash payments as an incentive to move into smaller properties. The story reflects similar schemes introduced elsewhere in the face of dwindling social housing stock and lengthening queues for low-cost homes. How would you develop the story into a balanced background feature? Who would you interview and what would you ask them?

Figure 17.3 Article from the *Exeter Express and Echo*, 27 August 2011

Council tenants offered cash incentives to move

No byline

Exeter Express and Echo

27 August 2011

Web link: http://www.thisisdevon.co.uk/
Council-tenants-offered-cash-incentives/
story-13215133-detail/story.html

COUNCIL house tenants are being offered cash for moving to properties with fewer bedrooms.

The city council is hoping the scheme will free up family accommodation and enable families on the housing register to move into properties that meet their requirements.

As the Echo recently revealed, the number of people in need of housing in Exeter is at an all-time high.

Recent figures showed there were 8,108 households in the city on the housing waiting list—17,471 people. And finding homes for them has been described as the biggest challenge now facing the city council.

Of the households on the list, 487 are classed as being in bands A and B, which means that they are in urgent need of accommodation.

The figures showed a sharp rise from the 6,500 households on the list just over a year ago.

Members of the council's scrutiny community committee will be asked on September 6 to back a scheme that will see tenants who downsize—giving up two or more bedrooms— to receive a maximum payment of £2,000.

Those who give up one bedroom will get a maximum payment of £1,500. Currently the incentives stand at £1,500 and £1,000 respectively.

The scheme was first introduced in 2007. Over two years, 102 people took advantage of the cash incentives paid to downsizing tenants, freeing up a total of 121 bedrooms that weren't really being used.

However, the original scheme's budget was exceeded and the incentives had to be suspended.

Larger family homes were still required and a revised policy was drawn up, offering tenants a reduced payment. This change resulted in fewer tenants coming forward to downsize.

Councillor Rob Hannaford, lead councillor for Housing and Community Involvement, said: 'Nothing's changed—we still desperately need larger family homes and we're hoping that by increasing the cash incentive more people will come forward offering to downsize.'

The total amount paid to downsizing tenants depends on any rent arrears or any repairs recharges on the property after the tenant has moved.

The payments are only made to tenants moving between city council properties and do not include moving into new council schemes like Knight's Place or Rowan House.

Source: Exeter Express and Echo

✴ Current issues

- **Housing targets replaced by New Homes Bonus scheme:** Communities Secretary Eric Pickles has scrapped Labour's centrally dictated house-building targets. His decision came as a relief to councils struggling to find suitable land but was criticized by housing campaigners, who said many households would continue being priced out of the property market. Former Housing Minister Grant Shapps later announced a New Homes Bonus Scheme to incentivize councils to build homes.

- **Expansion of eco-friendly home-building schemes:** the Coalition wants to ensure that by 2016 all new homes built in Britain are carbon-neutral. Its definition of 'zero carbon' is based on the outcome of a four-year consultation instigated by Labour. Appropriate housing schemes are now being offered grant support from the Homes and Communities Agency.

- **The impact of cuts in Housing Benefit (Local Housing Allowance):** the Welfare Reform Act 2012 has introduced a £26,000-a-year cap on the total value of benefits that can be claimed by a single household and formalized annual caps for specific types of property. The Coalition has also cut the rate at which LHA is calculated, from 50 to 30 per cent of average rents in each postcode area. Already some councils in London have been trying to rehouse poorer tenants in other towns and cities—reviving accusations of 'social cleansing'.

? Review questions

1. What is the difference between 'social housing' and 'affordable housing'?

2. Who are the main providers of social housing in Britain today and how did this multi-agency system come about?

3. Explain what is meant by the term 'Right to Buy'. How and when was it introduced, and what are its benefits for council tenants?

4. What is the Housing Revenue Account (HRA)? Outline how it works.

5. What is meant by 'unintentional homelessness' and what responsibilities do local authorities have to house the unintentionally homeless?

→ Further reading

Jones, C. and Murie, A. (2006) *The Right to Buy: Analysis and Evaluation of a Housing Policy*, London: Wiley-Blackwell. **Thorough and balanced evaluation of legacy of Thatcher government's 'Right to Buy' policy. Policies set in context of New Labour's housing reforms**.

Lund, B. (2006) *Understanding Housing Policy*, Cambridge: Policy Press. **Up-to-date appraisal of issues in social and low-cost housing, focusing on decline of local authority housing, and growth in involvement of housing associations, co-ops, and other providers**.

Malpass, P. (2005) *Housing and the Welfare State: The Development of Housing Policy in Britain*, London: Palgrave Macmillan. **In-depth historical critique of the evolution of housing policy in Britain since the Second World War**.

Mullins, D., Pawson, H., and Gilmour, T. (2010) *After Council Housing: Britain's New Social Landlords*, London: Palgrave Macmillan. **Up-to-date examination of evolving 'mixed economy' of low-cost housing in UK, containing thoughtful comparative analysis of different types of social landlord.**

 **Online Resource Centre**

www.oxfordtextbooks.co.uk/orc/Morrison3e/
Visit the Online Resource Centre that accompanies this book for web links and regular updates.

18

Children's services and adult social care

One of the most intricate, sensitive, and (occasionally) explosive aspects of local policy delivery is 'social services'—an umbrella term referring to the provision of everything from foster care and adoptive parents for vulnerable children to residential and nursing homes for the elderly and disabled. Today 1.5 million people in England rely on support from social services, including 400,000 children.

Although the term 'social services' may not be used as often in the media as 'NHS' or 'health service', stories relating to its work—and scandals arising from its failings—are seldom far from the news agenda. Controversies have ranged from complaints about errant social workers failing to identify cases of domestic child abuse until it is too late (Victoria Climbié's death at the hands of her foster parents and the 2008 'Baby Peter' case) to screaming headlines about prematurely discharged mental patients running amok (the 1992 murder of musician Jonathan Zito by schizophrenic Christopher Clunis).

Most of these stories, however, have arisen out of atypical circumstances and, with the exception of specialist sections such as *Society Guardian*, Britain's media is often accused of neglecting the complexities of this 'difficult' policy area in favour of sensationalism. But given some of the current demographic and social trends in the UK—the liberalization of the adoption laws, rising diagnoses of mental illness, and a rapidly ageing population—only a foolish editor would be unwilling to engage with the underlying issues that determine the direction of policy (and occasionally give rise to some of the more dramatic situations about which we often hear).

Until the early twentieth century such social welfare services as existed were provided on an ad hoc basis by charities and voluntary foundations, or in workhouses or infirmaries funded by parishes under the Poor Law. But social reform under the modernizing governments of David Lloyd George and

Clement Attlee saw the introduction of more widespread and coordinated social care provision, paralleling the nationwide establishment of the National Health Service (NHS) and welfare state. The main landmarks included a seminal report by the 1968 Inter-Departmental Committee on Local Authority and Allied Personal Services (the 'Seebohm Report'), which led to the decision, two years later, to form discrete social services departments by merging the pre-existing health and welfare and children's departments under the Local Authorities Social Services Act 1970. The new departments, run by county councils, worked closely with existing housing departments (a district/borough service area) and the NHS.

Until 2004, when children were given their own dedicated department following the Climbié case, social services departments were responsible for three broad policy areas:

- child protection (often known as 'children and families');
- domiciliary and residential care for the elderly and disabled;
- care for those with mental health problems.

▌ Child protection

Historically child protection has been overseen collaboratively by social (now children's) services departments, in partnership with various other organizations:

- local education departments (normally within the same local authority);
- police child protection units;
- NHS trusts and primary care trusts (PCTs) (now GP consortia—see p. 178);
- National Society for the Prevention of Cruelty to Children (NSPCC);
- registered adoption agencies.

Until 2004 these various bodies liaised through an area review committee (ARC), which determined the child protection procedures each should follow and conducted reviews of cases when those processes failed to prevent 'non-accidental injury' from taking place. Information on vulnerable children was shared between them through a local child protection register maintained by the ARC.

The Children Act 2004—passed in the wake of the Climbié case—abandoned ARCs in favour of **children's trusts**: all-in-one bodies bringing together representatives of every statutory agency involved in promoting child welfare, and comprising multidisciplinary teams of experts, including social workers, health visitors, paediatricians, and child psychologists. Local child protection registers were replaced by individual **child protection plans**, drawn up by professionals following an initial conference to assess a child's degree of risk.

The sweeping changes, ushered in under the 'Every Child Matters' banner (see pp. 524–8), saw all services relating to children—from schooling to social care—combined under the discrete heading 'children's services', headed by new directors of children's services. Adult social care remains within the remit of social services, albeit under new directors of adult services.

Children's social services are required to:

- promote the general welfare of children;
- encourage the upbringing of children by their families (wherever possible);
- pay regard to the wishes and feelings of the child;
- work in partnership with parents in the best interests of the child;
- provide accommodation for children over whom no one has 'parental responsibility' (see pp.)—taking on the role of 'corporate parent' if the child is lost or abandoned, or if the person responsible is unable to provide care;
- advise, assist, and befriend any child who leaves local authority care—and provide financial assistance and support to find accommodation.

The following two sections primarily focus on the web of regulations and guidelines currently governing child protection policy in England and Wales, as derived from two key Acts:

- Children Act 1989;
- Children Act 2004.

The 1989 Act and the definition of 'parental responsibility'

The Children Act 1989 sought to harmonize the existing body of public and private law on the care, protection, and safe upbringing of children, giving it a more cohesive focus. It came into force in England and Wales in 1991 and Northern Ireland in 1996.

As had long been the case, the Act's presumption was that the best place for children to be brought up was at home with their parents or guardians—unless there was serious concern for their welfare should they remain there. To this end, councils were given a 'general duty' to 'keep a child safe and well' and provide suitable support services to help them remain with their families. The Act's definition of 'family' was quite fluid—referring to any adult(s) with 'parental responsibility' for a child in law. It defined 'parental responsibility' as 'all the rights, duties, powers, responsibilities and authority which by law a parent of a child has in relation to the child and his property'.

The main categories of 'children in need' defined in the Act were those who are:

- disabled—blind, deaf, dumb, or with a mental disorder or physical impairment;
- unlikely to have—or have the opportunity to have—'a reasonable standard of health or development' without the help of services from a local authority;
- unlikely to progress in terms of health or development;
- unlikely to progress in health or development without the help of local authority services.

The Act entitles any parent, guardian, or carer who feels his/her child might be eligible for services to contact the relevant department for a 'needs assessment'. This assessment, carried out by a qualified social worker, should take into account not only the child's needs, but also those of his/her parent(s) or guardian(s). For example, the child might require remedial educational support or therapy, but the adult with parental responsibility might qualify for financial assistance, counselling, or (depending on circumstances) respite care—a short break from caring, perhaps involving a stay away from home, while the child is looked after by professionals. Since 2000, assessments have been conducted in a 'multi-agency' way, under the Department of Health's Framework for the Assessment of Children in Need and their Families. This means that, in addition to providing for a child's immediate physical, mental, and emotional needs, a more holistic plan must also be put in place—catering for any ongoing specialist social, financial, or educational requirements.

The range of services available under the 1989 Act includes:

- short break services;
- holiday play schemes;
- care at home—including help with washing, dressing, and mobility;
- some aids and adaptations—for example, stair lifts, hoists, wheelchairs;
- financial help—for example, to pay for fares to hospital visits.

Services can be arranged by councils on behalf of children and families, with some provided in-house, and outside agencies and charities usually contracted to deliver others. Alternatively, the parent/guardian may request the use of a *direct payment* scheme. This involves cash payments being made direct to families, giving them the freedom to 'shop around' for services of their choice rather than being left to make do with the 'one-size-fits-all' approach traditionally used by councils. Direct payments (also known as *self-directed support*)—based on a similar principle to 'patient choice' being rolled out in the NHS—were piloted in the context of care packages for the elderly as early as 1996, but have recently been extended, controversially, to severely mentally impaired adults (see pp. 541–2).

see also central government, pp. 176–7

In addition to setting out the range of day-to-day services available for children in need, the 1989 Act addressed the thorny issue of councils' role in the wider question of child welfare. In particular, it defined the circumstances in which social (now children's) services should intervene to ask family courts to decide where (and with whom) a child 'at risk' of neglect or abuse by his/her parents, guardians, or other relations should live. The Act set out four types of court order—collectively known as 'section 8 orders' (see Table 18.1).

From time to time the level of intervention by councils permissible under the above orders is insufficient to deal with the care needs of a child; at other times, an order may be breached, again putting the child at unacceptable risk. In such circumstances it may be necessary for the council to consider taking children 'into care'—away from the adult(s) with parental responsibility for them. The procedure for doing this and the range of care options available to children once removed from home is discussed in the section on care orders, fostering, and adoption later in this chapter.

The 1989 Act only applies to England and Wales, although most of its provisions are reflected in the Children (Scotland) Act 1995. The one significant difference is that under Scottish law legal proceedings surrounding child welfare follow a distinct process, known as the 'children's hearings system', first established in the early 1970s, which determines any compulsory supervision measures a minor may need. The 1995 Act's one notable strengthening of existing procedures was in its emphasis on the role of 'safeguarders'—that is,

Table 18.1 Types of 'section 8 order' under the Children Act 1989

Order	Effect
Contact order	Requires person with whom child is to live to allow him/her to visit or stay with another named person (e.g. another parent) or for that person and child to have other specified contact.
Prohibited steps order	Prohibits certain 'steps' related to role of person with parental responsibility for a child to be taken without express prior agreement of court (e.g. to prevent parent with whom child does not live taking him/her away on holiday in circumstances in which there is thought to be danger of this parent absconding with child). During some family proceedings (particularly those relating to serious custody disputes between separated couples) court may make child a *ward of court*. This is where court itself, rather than council, takes child into care temporarily. Again, this is normally used to prevent one parent leaving country with child unlawfully.
Residence order	Specifies that child must live with named person, often outlining other specific arrangements.
Specific issue order	Determines 'specific question' that has arisen, or may arise, in relation to care of child (e.g. where he/she should go to school, if parents or guardians disputing custody each want him/her to attend one near their homes).

individuals with relevant professional backgrounds (normally lawyers, social workers, or teachers) appointed to act as the 'voice of the child'.

The 2004 Act and the 'Every Child Matters' agenda

The 2004 Act focused less on introducing additional duties of care or legal powers for local authorities and courts than on radically shaking up the 'culture' of child protection. Its main emphasis was on improving communication between professionals and early intervention, following the horrific case of Victoria Climbié.

In 2000, 8-year-old Victoria died of hypothermia, with 128 separate injuries to her body, after two years of systematic torture and abuse at the hands of her great aunt, Marie Thérèse Kouao, and the latter's boyfriend, Carl Manning, in their London bedsit. She had been sent to Britain in the hope of a better life by her parents, who both lived on the Ivory Coast. During the months before her death Victoria was systematically beaten, burnt with cigarettes and scalding water, tied up, and forced to sleep in a bath with only a bin liner over her naked body. Police, social workers, and even the NSPCC failed to treat the warning signs sufficiently seriously—bringing a child protection investigation to a premature end on the basis of a paediatrician's mistaken diagnosis that scars on her skin were caused by scabies.

After Victoria's treatment was finally exposed both Kouao and Manning were jailed for murder at the Old Bailey, several social workers at Haringey Council were sacked, and three major investigations were prompted—by the local authority, Independent Police Complaints Commission (IPCC), and in a public inquiry chaired by former Chief Inspector of Social Services Lord Laming. The last, which reported in January 2003, made seventeen recommendations for the reform of child protection procedures. The most significant are explained in the table entitled 'Main recommendations of the Laming Inquiry', to be found on the Online Resource Centre.

The government's response was to publish a now famous Green Paper, *Every Child Matters*. It dwelt on four key 'themes' in relation to the issue of child protection:

- increasing the focus on supporting families and carers—'the most critical influence on children's lives';
- ensuring that necessary intervention took place before children reached crisis point, and protecting them from falling through the net;
- addressing underlying problems identified in the report into Victoria Climbié's death—weak accountability and poor integration;
- ensuring that people working with children are valued, rewarded, and trained.

Following a widespread public consultation and a further paper, *Every Child Matters: The Next Steps*, many of Lord Laming's recommendations came into effect under the 2004 Act. They revolved around five 'Every Child Matters' outcomes, which set out to enable all children to:

- be healthy;
- stay safe;
- enjoy and achieve;
- make a positive contribution;
- achieve economic well-being.

To drive forward these outcomes the government created children's trusts—multidisciplinary teams comprising professionals of all types involved in promoting children's 'well-being'. To improve coordination of children's services on the ground these trusts would bring together various professionals at a single location in the local community, such as a children's centre or school. Between them they would be expected to:

- carry out joint needs assessments for children in need;
- reach shared decisions on priorities relating to children's well-being;
- identify all available resources suited to improving children's well-being;
- carry out joint plans to deploy those resources and avoid duplication/ overlap.

Even before trusts were in place everywhere, plans were unveiled in June 2008 for their remit to be widened to encompass aspects of youth justice previously overseen by the Police Service and Prisons Service Agency. Then Children's Secretary Ed Balls increased collaboration over the care of the 2,900 under-18s in young offender institutions, privately run secure training centres, and local authority secure units between the Youth Justice Board, established earlier by Labour, and children's trusts. His stated aim was to replace the pre-existing, more punitive approach to youth justice with an early-intervention strategy designed to 'catch' potential career criminals early and prevent repeat offending. The policy— branded *Integrated Resettlement Support* (IRS)—arguably marked a return to the 'tough on crime, tough on the causes of crime' (as opposed to simply 'tough on crime') view espoused by Tony Blair in his days as Shadow Home Secretary.

To steer Labour's changes to child protection policy, an independent **Children's Commissioner for England** was appointed in March 2005, in the shape of Professor Al Aynsley-Green, a former national clinical director for children in the Department of Health (since succeeded by Maggie Atkinson, a former head of children's services at Gateshead Council). The Commissioner's remit is to:

- promote awareness of the views and interests of children among all sectors;

- work closely with organizations that take decisions affecting all aspects of children's lives, including the police, schools, hospitals, and voluntary groups;
- have regard to the framework of the five 'Every Child Matters' outcomes and the rights of children under the 1989 UN Convention on the Rights of the Child.

In the run-up to the Commissioner's appointment, consultation among children found that their main concerns included bullying, personal safety, and pressure in education (especially exams). Many also stressed problems they faced coming from deprived and minority social backgrounds.

A further significant reform instigated in the wake of *Every Child Matters* was the introduction of discrete children's services departments, and the requirement for them to develop an integrated children's system to coordinate needs assessments, planning, early intervention, and periodic reviews of service provision. As of April 2006 social care services for under-16s were removed from the general social services arena and combined with education provision under this new all-embracing umbrella. The Act also stipulated that every county council or unitary authority—except those with 'excellent' ratings under comprehensive area assessment (see p. 416)—must publish periodic *children and young people's plans* (CYPPs), to which every agency should contribute. These should detail all services for children and young people in their area, and the shared objectives of partner organizations for improving them.

The council-run boards demanded by Lord Laming were introduced in the guise of **local safeguarding children's boards (LSCBs)**. These are charged with coordinating the various agencies involved in delivering services and monitoring the effectiveness of their work. The Act defined three levels of action to be taken by boards, as outlined in Table 18.2.

To further facilitate a more joined-up approach to providing care and support to children in need, a new database, ContactPoint, was launched in 2009 enabling

Table 18.2 Three levels of responsibility of local safeguarding children's boards

Type of responsibility	Meaning
Activities	Preventing maltreatment—or 'impairment of health or development'—by introducing better mechanisms to identify abuse or neglect, and providing clear, accessible contact points for children seeking to report them.
Proactive work	Offering outreach activities for specific groups—e.g. children 'in need' but not suffering abuse or neglect.
Reactive work	Responding more quickly and effectively where children are suffering neglect/abuse by family members, other adults known to them, other young people, professional carers, or strangers.

communication and expertise to be exchanged between different agencies involved in a child's care. Controversially, its aim was to record the following basic details for each child in England up to his/her 18th birthday:

- name, address, gender, date of birth, and unique identifying number;
- name and contact details of his/her parent/carer;
- contact details for services working with the child, including educational setting (for example, school) and GP practice, but also other services, where appropriate;
- a means of indicating whether a practitioner is a lead professional and if he/she has undertaken an assessment under a new *common assessment framework* (CAF).

Months before the £224m database had even been launched it was already generating controversy. Despite reassurances from ministers that only professionals involved in the care of children would be able to access it—and then only subject to passing advanced Criminal Records Bureau (CRB) checks to ensure they had no convictions for offences involving children—the Conservatives and several charities expressed concern about potential security breaches. They cited the experience of the succession of then recent data leaks by government departments relating to everything from the personal details of Child Benefit claimants to the domestic arrangements of military personnel (see p. 108). Eyebrows were also raised about the fact young people's details would remain on the database until they reached 25.

The Coalition switched off ContactPoint in August 2010. However, as a sign of their determination to address failings in the system to improve the efficiency of statutory agencies in intercepting future cases of abuse and neglect, ministers ordered a swift review of child protection by Eileen Munro, professor of social policy at the London School of Economics. Published in April 2011, this argued for the abandonment of a top-down, target-driven approach to protecting children, in favour of locally driven strategies based on past experiences and expert judgements of professionals. It made the following recommendations, the bulk of which were swiftly accepted by ministers:

- the specific legal requirement for assessments of children's needs to be completed within rigid, centrally determined timescales should be scrapped;
- local child protection services should be adapted to the specific needs of their areas, and liberated from 'nationally prescribed ways of working', with professionals trusted to redesign services on the basis of informed research and feedback from local families;
- the punitive approach to *serious case reviews* (SCRs) should be dropped, with more emphasis placed on learning from how and why mistakes were

made and why professionals behaved as they did, rather than simply naming and shaming those responsible, with Ofsted's ability to evaluate SCRs removed;

- the introduction of a new 'duty' for all local services to make an 'early offer of help' to families who may not (yet) meet the criteria for intervention under child protection legislation, to prevent their circumstances escalating to a point where they do;
- improved Ofsted inspections of children's services, to put more weight on feedback from children and families themselves and observing social workers in action;
- experienced social workers should continue to work some of the time on the front line, so their expertise is passed down directly to junior levels;
- each children's services authority should appoint a Principal Child and Family Social Worker to regularly report the views and experiences of frontline staff to management.

The one recommendation on which ministers resolved to consult more widely before deciding whether to implement it concerned Ms Munro's suggestion about improving SCRs. To begin the process of enabling councils to adopt many of her other recommendations, though, it confirmed that future council funding settlements would include provision for a (non-ring-fenced) early intervention grant (see p. 362).

Care orders

The reforms described so far illustrate the extent to which social services and the various agencies working to promote child protection have become increasingly interventionist, due in part to pressure from the media, the general public, and families themselves. But sometimes they are required to be more proactive still, in the interests of a child they believe to be at serious risk of abuse or neglect if he/she remains in the care of a parent/guardian. The Climbié case highlighted what can happen if early warning signs are not noted or acted upon by professionals. Similar allegations were levelled at the authorities more recently over the death of 17-month-old Peter Connelly (known initially as 'Baby P') after eight months of abuse at the hands of his stepfather and a family lodger in Haringey—just streets away from where Climbié had perished. The scandal led to the sacking of Haringey's director of children's services, Sharon Shoesmith, and the resignation of the council leader and cabinet member for children and young people.

While it lambasts the system for any failure to identify abuse, the media is equally quick to criticize conscientious social workers who, fearing a child is living in an abusive environment, intervene overzealously to remove them.

Perhaps the most infamous example of heavy-handed intervention occurred in Cleveland in 1987, when 121 cases of suspected child abuse were diagnosed by two Middlesbrough-based paediatricians, Marietta Higgs and Geoffrey Wyatt. Several children were removed from their families by social services in the ensuing investigation, using a power introduced under the Children and Young Persons Act 1969, a 'place of safety order'. In the end twenty-six children from twelve families were found by judges to have been wrongly diagnosed and cases involving another ninety-six alleged victims were dismissed by the courts.

More recently, several newspapers—notably the *Daily Mail*—castigated Portsmouth City Council for being too ready to take children into care following the death of a 17-month-old girl, Anna Hider, who drowned in her foster parents' swimming pool, allegedly while they were entertaining guests. But the pendulum swung back the other way yet again when news broke in April 2009 of a vicious attack by two brothers, aged 10 and 11, on two other boys in Edlington, south Yorkshire. An SCR concluded the violent sexual assault might have been prevented had some thirty-one chances to intervene with the families not been missed by nine different agencies over a fourteen-year period. The case review launched by Doncaster Council marked the tipping point in a five-year period during which seven children had died in and around the town—despite being on the 'at risk' register.

Recent Acts have seen successive governments attempt to walk the tightrope between guaranteeing high standards of child protection and preventing cavalier intervention by social services and other agencies. Since the 1989 Act the principal means by which local authorities have been able to take children into care for indefinite periods—often against the will of their parents or guardians—is by applying to a family court for a **care order**. Under these circumstances parents/guardians must still be allowed 'reasonable access' to the child (unless the court explicitly prohibits this) but the local authority assumes parental responsibility in law and has the power to determine the *degree* of any contact. Occasionally, the need to safeguard a child's welfare is perceived to be so urgent that a council can apply to a court for a fast-tracked order to remove him/her from a threat at home. This is known as an **'interim care order'** or **emergency protection order**. Initially granted for up to eight days, but renewable for a further week, these may only be granted if a court judges there to be 'reasonable cause to believe that the child is likely to suffer considerable harm' if left in situ. Since the Family Law Act 1996 the emphasis has been on removing 'the source of danger', rather than the child (for example, applying for a 'non-molestation order' against a named individual will lead to his/her removal—potentially averting the need to uproot a child from home unnecessarily).

Councils also have the power to apply for a lesser action known as a 'supervision order'—a device enabling them to 'supervise' parents or guardians in a closer way than normal to ensure children potentially at risk are properly cared for. Under the 1989 Act a court may only make a supervision order if it is satisfied:

- a child is suffering, or likely to suffer, significant harm if one is not granted;
- the harm, or likelihood of harm, is attributable to the care given (or likely to be given) to the child not being what it is 'reasonable to expect a parent to give' or the child's being 'beyond parental control' (persistently truanting from school, and/or acting antisocially or criminally).

Under supervision orders it is council's duty to 'advise, assist, and befriend' children and approach the court for variations of the orders—converting them into care orders if they prove insufficient in practice. Likewise, councils may apply to the court for orders to be lifted should it no longer be necessary. Where requests for orders specifically relate to children's non-attendance at school or their parents' refusal to send them, a local education authority (LEA) may apply for a specific 'education supervision order'.

Fostering and other forms of local authority care

There are various ways, then, in which children can be removed from their homes, should professionals and courts be sufficiently concerned for their welfare. But where do these boys and girls—known as 'looked-after children'—actually *live* while under council protection?

Whether children are under emergency protection or full care orders, they will normally be accommodated in one of two ways:

- in a registered community children's home;
- with foster parents (sometimes known as 'foster homes').

Children's homes

As with other forms of residential accommodation for vulnerable groups, today's children's homes may either be run directly by councils or any number of other 'registered providers', from private companies to specialist charities like Barnardo's. Although far removed from the grim Victorian orphanages and homes of yesteryear, many of those operating today still contain shared dormitories, as well as individual rooms. They tend to take both boys and girls, rather than being single sex, and can house a hundred or more children at any one time (although most limit their intake to double figures).

The roles of children's homes are to:

- keep young people safe;
- give them consistent boundaries and routines;

- give them assistance in accessing education;
- promote their health and well-being;
- provide quality of life—for example, games, leisure activities, external trips.

Children's homes—like adult care homes—used to be inspected by their local authorities, but this role has been taken by a succession of quangos in recent years, and is currently the responsibility of the Office of Standards in Education, Children's Services, and Skills (Ofsted—see pp. 457–60). In Scotland all social care, including that for children, is regulated by the *Scottish Commission for the Regulation of Care* (SCRC), while the *Scottish Social Services Council* (SSSC) is charged with raising standards in both adult and child social care. In Wales these functions are discharged by the *Care and Social Services Inspectorate Wales* (CSSIW) and the *Care Council for Wales* respectively, while in Northern Ireland all health and social care is regulated by a single body: the *Regulation and Quality Improvement Authority* (RQIA).

In July 2012 serious questions were raised about both the quality of care in children's homes and the manner in which responsible councils allocate vulnerable juveniles to them, following publication of a highly critical report by deputy children's commissioner Sue Berelowitz. The report—commissioned after nine men were jailed in Rochdale for grooming and sexually abusing young girls, including one in care—found that the high turnover of young people in children's homes provided a 'constant flow of vulnerable children for perpetrators to exploit'. It also highlighted the difficulty of tracking down those who go missing from care because of the absence of any clear statistics on the subject.

Ms Berelowitz's report came a month after an all-party parliamentary group set up to investigate the plight of children who vanish from care homes revealed that 46 per cent of juveniles are placed by councils miles (if not hundreds of miles) away from their native communities and support networks, with large concentrations of homes clustered in coastal resorts in north-west and south-east England. Condemning the 'very serious weaknesses' exposed in both reports, then Children's Minister Tim Loughton ordered councils to revise their placement policies to ensure juveniles were placed in homes near their local areas whenever possible. Ministers also announced they were establishing an expert group to devise a way of drastically improving data-gathering to address significant disparities between official council figures for the number of children who go missing from care for twenty-four hours or more and incidents relating to vulnerable juveniles recorded by police.

Foster parents

Fostering can be arranged on a long-term or short-term basis by children's services, often with the help of an independent foster agency. It is usually seen by councils as preferable to keeping a child in a community children's home because the involvement of designated foster parents places them in a familiar, domestic-style setting, rather than an impersonal institution. Children placed in long-term foster care will normally be located with 'parents' who have at least one child of their own. They may continue living in this environment for a number of years, although if they leave home at 16 their foster carers will no longer have any legal rights over them. If their stay is very long term, however, their foster parents may apply at some stage to adopt them. Assuming this application is successful, the foster parents will then become their legal parents.

There are various forms of foster arrangement, the main ones of which are explained in the table entitled 'Different types of fostering arrangement', to be found on the Online Resource Centre. The strict vetting procedure for prospective foster parents is outlined in Table 18.3.

As with adoptive parents, there is currently a national shortage of foster carers. According to some estimates, at least 10,000 more are needed to provide for all the youngsters waiting to be placed. In December 2011 the Fostering Network reported that 59,000 children in care were still waiting for foster placements—up from 49,700 in 2005. Some campaigners have blamed the shortfall on the financial burdens of fostering. In 2007 the same charity called for foster carers to be paid professional salaries. A survey published at the start of its campaign found that three-quarters of foster carers received less than the minimum wage, and four out of ten nothing at all.

Despite this, all foster carers qualify for an allowance to cover the basic costs of clothing, feeding, and otherwise providing for children. If a fostering arrangement has been negotiated through an agency, it will set the level of this

Table 18.3 Vetting procedure for foster parents

Procedure	What happens
Background investigation	Children's social services staff provisionally approve prospective foster parents following investigation into their family lives, and medical and criminal backgrounds. Anyone convicted of causing or permitting bodily harm to a child barred from fostering. Anybody living in same house as someone with such background usually prohibited, as are those who have had orders made against them to remove child from their care.
Regular spot checks	Social workers retain right to see foster children regularly on request and can remove them from care without notice if they believe this is in child's interests. Such actions can prompt foster parents to apply to court for residence order, asserting right to keep child with them.
Training for foster parents	Prospective foster parents required to attend classes on statutory responsibilities of foster carers. Although not yet compulsory, many also study for formal qualifications: in England and Wales, National Vocational Qualification (NVQ) Level 3 in Caring for Children and Young People; in Scotland, Scottish Vocational Qualification (SVQ) can be pursued.

allowance, usually dependent on the child's age, with carers of older children qualifying for more. As of April 2007, in recognition of the wide disparities in foster allowances from agency to agency, the government introduced guaranteed minimum levels for the first time in relation to different age groups—as outlined in the table entitled 'The national minimum weekly fostering allowance for England (2007/8)', to be found on the Online Resource Centre.

In 2003 the government introduced a new Income Tax allowance for foster parents, allowing them to 'earn' up to £10,000 a year from foster allowances tax-free. At the same time a new National Insurance-backed scheme called 'Home Responsibility Protection' was introduced to ensure long-term foster parents would not retire on anything less than the state pension—a contributory benefit—even if they had made too few NI contributions to qualify under normal rules.

see also central government, p. 238

The adoption process

The distinction between fostering and **adoption** is that, while the former is theoretically a temporary arrangement, the latter is permanent. At any point up to 4,000 children across the UK are looking for adoptive parents. By law children can only be adopted through an adoption agency—either a children's services authority or government-approved registered adoption society (a voluntary adoption agency). Most agencies cover a radius of around fifty miles from their offices. Not all arrange placements themselves, but they may carry out adoption assessments to ensure that prospective adoptive parents are suitable.

Who, then, is entitled to adopt? Until recently, the right was largely restricted to married heterosexual couples, with those under 40 more likely to be successful than older applicants (who would be of mature age by the time their adopted children had grown up). But much of this changed with the Adoption and Children Act 2002, which opened adoption up to single people, as well as one partner in an unmarried couple (whether straight or gay). The law was further tweaked in 2005 to enable unmarried couples to apply to adopt jointly— effectively giving them the same rights as married ones. For gay couples the procedure is usually quicker if they are in civil partnerships, but provided they live together they normally stand as much chance of success as straight couples. Qualifying conditions for adopters are listed in Table 18.4.

There are two different types of adoption process, depending on whether the natural parent(s) of the child have given their consent for him/her to be adopted:

- *Single-stage adoption*—placement made with full cooperation of the child's natural parents. This is the procedure followed when, for example, the child was conceived during rape or by a girl below the age of consent (16) who feels unable to take on the responsibility of bringing him/her up. In such cases a straightforward adoption order will be made by the court, without any opposition, because the mother fully endorses the procedure.

- *Two-stage adoption*—when a child's natural parent(s) object to his/her (or their) child being adopted, an agency will have to apply to a court for a *freeing order*—removing the child from his/her parents' custody against their will. At this stage the child's parents are often not identified in court.

The usual adoption procedure for applicants follows a similar, if slightly more rigorous, route to that for fostering, as explained in Table 18.5.

Growing adoption waiting lists—the number of children placed with adoptive families fell by 15 per cent between March 2009 and 2010—have prompted a wide-ranging review by the Coalition of what Education Secretary Michael Gove decried in February 2011 as 'politically correct' and overbureaucratic 'edicts' preventing prospective parents from adopting because they were too old or from different ethnic backgrounds to their intended adoptees. Mr Gove, who was adopted himself, went on to launch new, liberalized guidance for councils to speed up the process for those awaiting placements—particularly black children, who take up to twice as long to be placed as those from other ethnic groups—while improving scrutiny of the 76 per cent of agencies then recently rated 'good' or 'outstanding'. It was nearly a year before Mr Cameron formally

Table 18.4 Criteria for prospective adopters

Criterion	Meaning
Age	Must be over 21 and able to prove they are happy to make space in their lives for child, and are patient, flexible, energetic, and determined to make difference to child's life. No official upper age limit, although agencies may sometimes favour younger people.
Criminal checks	Must not have been convicted of any serious offence against child. More minor offences must be looked into but may not preclude adoption.
Relationship status	Couples who are married or in civil partnerships, single people, or one partner in unmarried couple (heterosexual, lesbian, or gay) may adopt in England, Wales, and Scotland. Unmarried couples may also apply to adopt jointly. In Northern Ireland a ban remains on gay and/or unmarried couples adopting.
Good health	Prospective adopters must have medical examinations and health issues (including hereditary conditions) should be explored.
Ethnic/cultural background	People of all ethnic backgrounds may adopt. Preferential treatment often given to prospective parents of same racial and/or religious identity as child (influenced by research into well-being of minority-adopted adults who grew up with families who did not match their ethnic identities).
Disability access	People with disabilities may adopt, subject to conditions set down on case-by-case basis.

Table 18.5 The adoption process

Procedure	What happens
Initial meeting(s)	Following application through agency, prospective adopter(s) meets social worker, together and individually (if in a couple), on several separate occasions.
Background investigation	Prospective adoptive parents' personal backgrounds investigated and they are asked why they wish to adopt. Confidential enquiries made through their local children's services department and police.
Personal references	Supplied by at least two friends of adopter(s), and prospective adopter(s) has GP medical examination.
Independent adoption panel	Hearing by panel (linked to agency through which prospective adopter(s) has applied) considers case and decides if they should progress to final stage: opportunity to meet panel in person.
Provisional care agreed	Once adopter(s) approved in principle, child put into their provisional care (children's services authorities or adoption panels must be notified if done through approved adoption society, rather than council).
Adoption order confirmed	Decision made by family proceedings court, sitting in private, three months after notification to authority.

set out government plans to introduce a 'foster-to-adopt' system and a 'faster, fairer' vetting process, focusing on measures to make it easier for white parents to adopt black children and forcing social workers to consult the *national adoption register* to fast-track placements if they failed to find adoptive families locally within three months. However, despite announcing his proposals with some media fanfare, the prime minister indicated they might not be introduced until 2015.

Childminding

'Childminding' is the term used to describe a type of day care provided for children outside nursery, preschool, or school. Registered childminders look after children in their own homes, normally while the parents/guardians are at work. Under the Care Standards Act 2000 regulation of childminding is overseen by Ofsted, rather than councils as previously.

Ofsted's role is to:

- provide a register of professionals paid for looking after under-5-year-olds on an area-by-area basis;
- inspect the homes of anyone applying to be registered as a childminder to ensure there are adequate facilities, including toilets and play equipment.

Registration, when granted, is subject to various conditions covering facilities to be provided; number of staff, and their qualifications/experience of working with children; and the maximum number of children who may be minded at one time (particularly babies and those aged under twelve months). If registration conditions are breached at any point, registration can be revoked or modified to reduce the maximum number of children to be minded.

The Protection of Children Act 1999

Introduced following a series of high-profile scandals about the abuse of children in residential care homes, the Protection of Children Act 1999 saw the launch of a statutory list of all people considered unsuitable to work with children. The Consultancy Service Index, a list along these lines, had been kept by Secretaries of State since 1993, but the 1999 Act (in Scotland the Protection of Children (Scotland) Act 2003) formalized the process by enforcing it as a statutory list, to which all existing names were added.

It requires childcare organizations to inform the government if:

- they transferred or dismissed someone who had harmed a child or put one at risk;
- an individual evaded disciplinary action along these lines by resigning or retiring.

▌ Adult social services and the rise of community-based care

Although children's services account for the bulk of councils' social care budgets—and attract the most media coverage—councils retain significant responsibilities in relation to both the elderly and adults of working age with enduring physical and mental illnesses or disabilities.

Until relatively recently much of the care provided for people falling into these categories was delivered in institutional environments—long-stay residential care homes (like adult versions of children's homes) or nursing homes for those who could no longer wash or dress themselves or perform other basic functions without assistance.

People with mental disorders severe enough to prevent them continuing to live at home were often transferred for prolonged periods into NHS-run mental hospitals or specialist secure asylums managed by their local authorities. The oldest of these facilities had been established in the early 1800s and many continued in more or less uninterrupted use for the best part of 200 years. But under Margaret Thatcher and John Major a revolution occurred that was to transform the culture of social care for both the mentally ill and all other categories of adult 'service user'.

This transformation came in the form of the National Health Service and Community Care Act 1990, which restyled patients as 'clients' and ushered in the now-notorious policy of 'Care in the Community'. In simple terms its aims were to:

- place greater emphasis on **community care**—providing support services for elderly people and those with mental and physical illnesses and disabilities in their homes, with a view to enabling them to remain in a community setting for longer periods, while reducing the pressure on acute wards and residential facilities;
- make the delivery of social care more cost-effective and increase choice for service users through greater involvement of providers from the private and voluntary sectors, including charities.

Although few opposed the idea of empowering the vulnerable to continue living in their own homes in *theory*, many were alarmed by the way the NHS and councils began implementing the Act in practice. Long starved of funding for the so-called 'Cinderella service' of mental health, and with many homes and asylums severely underoccupied (and therefore uneconomical to maintain), many councils and trusts used the freedom granted by the Act to shut down half-empty units—discharging inpatients to return to 'the community' irrespective of the strength of their personal support networks or ability to fend for themselves.

Tabloid newspapers reported a slew of scare stories about assaults, and even killings, by prematurely discharged mental patients. Perhaps the most infamous case was the 1992 murder of musician Jonathan Zito by a paranoid schizophrenic released from mental hospital just weeks earlier under 'Care in the Community'. Mr Zito's death prompted the establishment of the Zito Trust by his wife, Jayne, which continues to campaign for changes to mental health policy in the best interests of patients and public. Other high-profile cases included the 1996 murders of Lin Russell and her 6-year-old daughter, Megan, by Michael Stone on a country lane in Kent. Stone, who had a severe personality disorder, had been out of prison and receiving a package of community care since 1992.

At the time of the murders it was not only the 1990 Act that was criticized in the media but also the Mental Health Act 1983, which, opponents claimed, contained a loophole preventing mental health professionals providing care for people suffering from untreatable conditions, such as Stone's, even when they asked for help (Stone had repeatedly pleaded to be admitted to Broadmoor). The *British Medical Journal* subsequently cast doubt on this suggestion, yet criticisms of Stone's case remain. Much more recently, in July 2010, it emerged that the fugitive gunman Raoul Moat, who led police on a week-long manhunt after murdering his ex-partner's boyfriend and shooting both her and a police constable, had asked Newcastle City Council social workers to refer him to a psychiatrist months before his rampage.

Table 18.6 Main provisions of Community Care Act 1990

Measure	Meaning
Emphasis on 'Care in the Community'	Councils to promote domiciliary (home) care, day care (attendance at day centres and activity groups), and respite services (short breaks for carers and/or cared-for) to allow people to live in own homes.
Emphasis on practical support to promote self-reliance	Ensuring all agencies and authorities involved in providing services prioritize practical support.
Detailed needs assessment	Carrying out 'proper assessment' of individuals' needs, followed by good case management by appointed key workers (normally social workers or occupational therapists).
Promoting partnerships	Developing flourishing independent/private sector alongside good public services.
Long-term care planning	Preparing strategic plans for community care arrangements, working with NHS authorities; publishing these, and keeping them under review, in consultation with bodies in public and voluntary sectors. Collaboration between NHS and councils to improve non-hospital services had first been introduced under National Health Service Act 1977, when joint consultative committees (JCCs) were set up, comprising representatives from all relevant statutory agencies.

But not every aspect of the renewed emphasis on community care has proved negative. For many elderly and disabled people the channelling of social services funding into care packages tailored to their individual needs, and home adaptations designed to make their domestic environments more comfortable and user-friendly, has proved liberating—enabling them to spend crucial extra years living near friends and family that would have been 'lost' had they been prematurely admitted to residential homes.

The responsibilities with which social services authorities are charged under the 1990 Act in relation to community care are listed in Table 18.6.

Nonetheless, the scale of the 'Care in the Community' controversy proved so damaging and long-lasting that when Labour returned to power in 1997 it swiftly scrapped the initiative (although, in practice, the 1990 Act remains the main legal basis underpinning adult social care). Community care is still the government's preferred option for caring for the elderly and disabled, at least until such time as they require full-time nursing, although the balance has been redressed somewhat between domiciliary and residential care arrangements.

New Labour's biggest reforms included:

- Health Act 1999—introduced new forms of NHS structure and partnerships with the private health care sector, formally abolishing the joint consultative committees established in 1977.

- National Carers' Strategy—built on the Carers (Recognition and Services) Act 1996, which gave statutory recognition to the work of unpaid relatives or friends looking after people receiving community care in their homes. It enabled these informal carers to access their own support.

Community care—what the state provides

Social services authorities have a duty to assess the needs of people requiring care due to their age, infirmity, or disability. If an assessment indicates someone requires services the council must determine their needs and inform them of the details of their assessment and their right to appeal. Some authorities have been accused of raising the bar in relation to 'eligibility criteria' because of budgetary concerns, but courts have ruled it appropriate for councils to take their financial resources into account when setting those criteria.

The principal community care services provided by councils, whether delivered by them, voluntary organizations, or private agencies, include:

- home help (assistance with washing, dressing, and cleaning the home);
- hot meals ('meals on wheels');
- help with shopping and financial management;
- advocacy (advice and support with accessing other services, paying bills, etc.);
- telephone access;
- cheap travel (disabled and OAP bus passes, free transport to appointments);
- free and accessible parking through the 'disabled badge holder' scheme;
- day care (access to day centres for structured activities, day trips etc.);
- respite care;
- home modifications and aids to daily living (stairlifts and hoists are usually provided by housing departments on social services' advice; wheelchairs and other mobility aids are often accessed through the NHS or charities).

In addition, training and employment can be provided for disabled people in sheltered workshops, while day nurseries and centres are available for their children.

These days 'packages' of community care are put together by a client's key worker (case worker). Because most social care professionals now work in multidisciplinary teams designed to improve coordination between social services, the NHS, and the other agencies, this may be a social worker, community psychiatric nurse (CPN), or occupational therapist (OT). The latter's expertise lies in assessing individuals' capacity to perform basic tasks for themselves and providing support in carrying them out where needed.

Key workers have a statutory duty to produce—and regularly update—a 'care plan' individually tailored to each client's needs. This should be made available in writing to the client and/or his/her carer, on request, and cover the following ground:

- services to be provided (and by whom), when and where this will happen, and what is intended to be achieved by providing them;
- contact point for dealing with problems about service delivery;
- information on how to ask for a review of services provided if the client's or carer's circumstances change.

Specific concern about the plight of people with serious mental health issues led to the introduction, in 1991, of a more rigorous care plan procedure, known as the 'care programme approach' (or 'care plan approach'). This is broken down into four stages:

1. initial assessment of the client's needs;
2. consultation with all professionals involved, any informal carer, and (depending on their degree of mental capacity) the client themselves;
3. appointment of a key worker;
4. coordination of services agreed on the basis of the initial assessment by that professional.

As with residential care (see pp. 542–46), the quality of homecare for the elderly has come in for sustained criticism recently. In March 2012 consumer group *Which?* described much of the provision offered to older people in their homes as 'disgraceful', referring to a litany of missed visits by professionals, soiled beds, and food being left out of reach as illustrations of typical complaints detailed in diaries kept by thirty service users and carers that January. Though the organization declined to 'name and shame' specific service providers, it highlighted the growing issue of disinterested private care agencies. In a separate survey half the respondents said prearranged home visits had been missed in the previous six months—with six out of ten receiving no prior warning. Four months later a survey of 739 companies providing domiciliary care by the UK Homecare Association, which represents providers, concluded three-quarters of councils were 'rationing' home visits for budgetary reasons by demanding they be completed within half an hour. One in ten were imposing time limits of just fifteen minutes.

The role of home carers

Britain's rapidly ageing population, coupled with the growing emphasis on community-based care, has led to a huge rise in the number of carers—defined as people who spend at least part of their lives looking after elderly and/or disabled relatives or friends in their or the other person's home. According to Carers UK, as of July 2012 there were 6.4 million unpaid carers in Britain. Action for Children estimated 175,000 or more of these were aged 18 or under, while 2011 census figures show 230,000 are aged between 16 and 24.

Long-running campaigns by support groups set up to help carers have led to belated recognition of their work, initially through the 1996 Act (entitling them to limited respite care), and the ten-year National Carers' Strategy established by Mr Blair in 1999. Renewed by Gordon Brown in 2008, this made the commitments listed in the table entitled 'The main points of Labour's ten-year "National Carers' Strategy"', to be found on the Online Resource Centre.

In practice, although it has undeniably improved the situation for some, the strategy was just that. Recent studies suggest carers still feel isolated, undervalued, and bewildered by the often labyrinthine network of services and providers theoretically available to them, and the bureaucratic, jargon-laden processes involved in accessing them. Of the 400 carers interviewed in a survey of carers' views in summer 2006 for the Princess Royal Trust for Carers' 'Duty to Care' campaign, more than half confessed to having felt like walking out on the person for whom they cared. Fifty-six per cent said they felt 'depressed', seven out of ten 'stressed', and 86 per cent 'frustrated'.

Choice in community care—the rise of direct payments

As if negotiating the maze of options available to those in community care—and the mountains of paperwork that accompany them—was not already mind-boggling enough, recent governments have put service users and carers more directly in the driving seat as part of their 'choice' agenda (see p. 164). The Tories introduced this concept, in the Community Care (Direct Payments) Act 1996. This enabled cash payments to be made by councils to dependent individuals, enabling them to 'buy' their own services from providers of their choice. This approach was not mandatory and authorities were required to ensure any individual to whom they paid money had the capacity to take informed decisions about their needs and to locate and access suitable services. In some cases—when there was evidence that the money had been spent on things other than services related to the client's needs (for example alcohol or gambling)—councils could halt direct payments and even require money paid thus far to be refunded.

In 'policy and practice guidance' issued in 2000, Labour made it clear it intended to retain some form of direct payment system, stating it wanted to see 'more extensive use made' of it. In January 2006 a White Paper entitled *Our Health, Our Care, Our Say* outlined plans to roll it out further, taking in groups of clients whose conditions, until then, were seen as impeding their capacity to make decisions for themselves. These included:

- young disabled people whose parents have managed direct payments on their behalf and whose payments may have to stop when they reach 18;
- people with dementia, where the use of direct payments is not set out in a 'power of attorney (PoA)' agreement—a legally binding document detailing the individual(s) authorized to handle the affairs of their estate;
- people with more profound learning disabilities.

Variously known as 'individual budgets', 'personal budgets', and now once again 'direct payments', this approach has divided campaigners for the elderly and mentally ill. While some have welcomed the flexibility it allows capable service users to seek out the medical and psychological support (not to mention social and leisure opportunities) best suited to them, others argue that vulnerable individuals in dire need of care and/or treatment risk losing out on help to which they are entitled because of the complexity of negotiating the system and managing their own accounts. An in-depth 2008 evaluation of the impact of individual budgets (as they were then known) in thirteen pilot areas found that, while working-age people with mental health difficulties had responded positively to them on the whole, they were causing 'anxiety and stress' to elderly service users—many of them concerned that, after a lifetime spent under a top-down NHS and social services model, they were suddenly being expected to shop around for support.

see also central government, pp. 176–7

Care homes, nursing homes, and the rise of the private sector

When it is agreed that a person is no longer well and/or capable enough to continue living in his/her own or carer's home, arrangements will normally be made for him/her to move into either a long-term residential care home or one with nursing provision (a 'nursing home'). The former is usually a 'low dependency' environment, in which residents can enjoy relatively independent lifestyles in the company of other people of similar age or with comparable physical and/or mental health needs. A nursing home, in contrast, is targeted at individuals with more severe physical and/or mental impairments—often the very old or those at advanced stages in the progression of their conditions—who require care provided or supervised by a registered nurse.

Broadly speaking, the process followed when an elderly person reaches the point of requiring residential accommodation is as follows:

- they are assessed by a key worker in a multidisciplinary team and placed in a home that best suits their needs (local authority, voluntary, or private);
- where a private home is chosen, the ability of the person to pay 'the full economic cost' of their care is assessed—taking into account the value of

property in their name, which might be sold to contribute to care home fees.

Since the late 1980s there has been a marked increase in the amount of residential care provided by private companies, rather than social services. In many areas there are no longer any homes maintained by the council directly: all are owned and managed by the private or voluntary sectors. Under the Tories' 'mixed economy of care', residents in private homes could claim a 'social security residential care allowance', which they had to pass to the owner, and a small 'personal allowance', to keep for themselves.

But those in council-run homes were not entitled to the former—a fact that meant the final 'bill' presented for the care of individuals admitted to them often appeared superficially higher. This was used by ministers as leverage to argue that councils were being 'excessive' with their charges. Opposition leaders at the time said this charge was being used as a pretext to expand the private sector and undermine councils, particularly when a special transitional grant (STG) was made available to them, on condition that they spent 85 per cent of the money provided on arranging private sector residential placements.

In tandem with the expansion of private sector provision and rising fees that followed, Mr Major's government risked infuriating the 'grey vote' with new moves to divide the cost of residential care between state and individual. Under the 1990 Act anyone with assets of £16,000 or more—including the homes in which they lived until being admitted into residential care—was expected to pay for themselves up to the point at which that money was exhausted (at which stage the state would take over). In practice this meant many people—particularly widows and widowers whose homes were entirely in their possession—being 'forced' to sell houses and flats for which they had spent much of their working lives paying. The 'capital/assets limit' remains in place, but has been raised incrementally since to £23,250 today.

So politically combustible had this issue become by 2010, with increasing diagnoses of age-related conditions requiring long-term care, such as Alzheimer's disease and dementia, that then Health Secretary Andy Burnham announced plans for a new 'National Care Service'—to improve homecare provision and stop individuals forced to move into residential/nursing care having to sell their homes to pay the fees. His unrealized plans (which he touted as a twenty-first century legacy for Labour, comparable to the NHS it bequeathed in the twentieth) were lambasted by the Tories, who used a high-profile poster campaign to accuse him of planning a 'death tax' on grieving families. They were referring to Mr Burnham's favoured option—revived during his subsequent Labour leadership bid—to finance the proposed new service using a 10 per cent levy on all estates (paid after death). At the time, the Tories' proposed alternative was to charge people a one-off 'voluntary' payment of £8,000 at 65—a fee critics pointed out would be beyond the means of many. In July 2011 an independent inquiry headed by Oxford economist Andrew Dilnot made the following two key recommendations:

- that the present threshold in savings or other assets above which the state will offer individuals help with the cost of their social care be more than quadrupled, to £100,000;
- a cap of £35,000 should be imposed on the amount any individual should be expected to pay towards the cost of social care in his/her lifetime.

At the time of its publication there was a growing mood among the major parties to try to forge a consensus about the best way of tackling the care deficit. And yet a year later, in July 2012, Age UK and other charities warned of a worsening crisis in care home provision, as private providers were shorn of previously guaranteed funding in the wake of ongoing budget cuts and the uncertainty over future government policy. Mr Lansley promptly confirmed ministers' intention to legislate before 2015 to cap social care costs, but Labour responded by saying he had effectively abandoned cross-party talks.

Another source of tension that emerged in the 1990s was that between social services departments and the NHS over how to provide for people not yet considered in need of residential care but who experience frequent, sometimes prolonged, periods of ill health necessitating hospital treatment. Hard-pressed acute hospitals—already struggling with long waiting lists—increasingly became the subject of news reports as they combated 'bed-blockage' ('bed-blocking'): the need to cater for vulnerable patients too sick to be sent home, but for whom residential care spaces were either not yet deemed necessary or unavailable.

Given that more than half of over 65-year-olds now have a disabling condition requiring long-term care and Britain's population is ageing fast, it is no wonder bed-blocking remains a serious issue as councils struggle to find enough care home places to meet demand—particularly for those with unusual and/or debilitating ailments. Yet critics argue that the government's answer has merely been to intensify the pressure, by getting tough with councils found 'guilty' of contributing to bed-blocking, rather than concentrating on boosting the number of residential care places. Under the Community Care (Delayed Discharges etc.) Act 2003 NHS hospitals may fine local authorities up to £120 a day for every 'blocked' bed—a rule condemned by the Local Government Association. The Act was motivated, in part, by a 2001 Audit Commission report that found two out of three patients in English hospitals at any one time were aged over 65—with around 5,000 people on any given day unnecessarily stuck on acute wards. To discourage hospitals from discharging patients prematurely, then Health Secretary Mr Lansley announced in June 2010 that those having to readmit the same individuals within a month of sending them 'home' would receive no extra funding for additional treatment.

→ see also central government, p. 184

Regulating social care

The regulator charged with ensuring high-quality care standards are provided throughout England is the **Care Quality Commission (CQC)**. In the social care field it is responsible for inspecting day centres, care homes, domiciliary care agencies, nurses' agencies, children's homes, and residential special schools.

→ see also central government, p. 185

All residential care and nursing homes must be formally registered under the Registered Homes (Amendment) Act 1991 (previously the Registered Homes Act 1984), but since 2004 the 18,500 listed homes have also had to register separately with the CQC. On inspection, all care organizations (including agencies) are rated under a star system. The meanings of these classifications are as follows:

- no stars—poor;
- one star—adequate;
- two stars—good;
- three stars—excellent.

Following an inspection (or subsequent investigation) the CQC may use its statutory powers either to demand an organization meets specified 'conditions to improve', to bring it up to agreed national minimum standards, or in extreme cases force its immediate closure. In addition, instances of abuse or neglect may be referred to the police and/or Crown Prosecution Service (CPS). The Commission is especially vigilant in relation to adults with serious mental/physical disabilities or impairments that put them at greater risk of abuse—in line with the 'Protection of Vulnerable Adults' (POVA) scheme introduced in July 2004. As with children in social care, anyone directly involved in caring for vulnerable adults must undergo periodic CRB checks and there are bans preventing those who have harmed such people in the past from continuing to work with them.

Although the CQC has theoretically tightened regulation of the increasingly disparate social care 'market', serious concerns have been repeatedly raised about the rigour with which its inspections are carried out. In June 2008 an investigation by Radio 4's *Today* programme found that many of the Commission's own inspectors were unhappy with the frequency and quality of its care home inspections. More than 200 employees of the then Commission for Social Care Inspection (CSCI)—now absorbed into the CQC—participated in an anonymous questionnaire, with one commenting: 'I wouldn't leave my dog in 90 per cent of our care homes.'

Criticism of the regulatory regime for social care has been sharpened following a slew of deeply critical reports published in 2011 and 2012 exposing the poor quality of residential and inpatient provision for the elderly. The first to attract media attention collated the outcomes of ten investigations into inadequate care by English NHS trusts and two GP practices carried out by health service ombudsman Ann Abraham. In October 2011 the CQC concluded that more than half of the 100 hospitals it inspected to check on care standards for older people were 'failing', with one in five not adequately catering for their 'dignity' or nutritional needs—two benchmarks emphasized in revised standards introduced a year earlier. Its findings prompted Mr Lansley to fast-track inspections for 500 nursing homes, inviting Age UK to recruit past and present service users to participate. Two months later the first ever 'National Audit of Dementia'—drawing data from 210 hospitals in England and Wales—identified 'problems across practically every aspect of care for patients admitted to hospitals' with the condition. It pinpointed the impersonal manner of many staff, poor training and supervision, and patients' feelings of being ignored as key issues—despite the fact that separate figures suggested one in four hospital beds was occupied by people with dementia.

Long-term care homes have come in for even harsher criticism. So much so that in February 2012 a commission set up by Age UK, the NHS Confederation, and the Local Government Association (LGA) published a report entitled *Delivering Dignity*, in which they collectively issued 'a call to arms to the whole health and social care system'—recommending residents be directly involved in day-to-day management decisions, ageist language be stamped out, and a new rating system be introduced to inform future CQC inspections. The report's overarching emphasis was on improving the quality of the care home experience, by moving beyond a utilitarian approach to running homes—whereby efficiency was measured purely in terms of the speed with which tasks like washing, dressing, and feeding were performed—to one in which residents took centre stage and were enabled to lead more active and fulfilling lives in residential environments. Other recommendations included the establishment of a Care Quality Forum to raise standards of professionalism in older people's care, and improved training for not only frontline care workers but also managers.

'Sectioning' the mentally ill

Since the Mental Health Act 1983, councils have had limited powers to detain mentally infirm adults not in residential care in specialist hospitals and units—a process known as 'sectioning' after the appropriate sections in this and subsequent Acts. The procedures by which they may do so are outlined in Table 18.7.

The Mental Health Act 2007

Before it finally received royal assent in July 2007 Labour's Mental Health Bill (originally published more than four years earlier) endured one of the rockiest rides of any piece of legislation in recent memory. At the heart of the Bill were

Table 18.7 Powers of social services in relation to the mentally infirm

Power	Effect
Application for compulsory observation	Approved mental health practitioners (AMHPs)—may apply for person to be admitted to hospital for up to seventy-two hours for compulsory observation under s. 136 of Mental Health Act 1983. AMHPs may either be social workers, nurses, occupational therapists (OTs), or psychologists. Application must be supported by two *responsible clinicians* (RCs)—formerly responsible medical officers (RMOs). These may be social workers, nurses, OTs, or psychologists—not only GPs and/or psychiatrists, as previously. In 'emergencies' applications may go ahead with one RMO's endorsement.
Appointment of 'nearest relatives'	Applications for people to be admitted to mental hospital are normally subject to consent by nearest relative. If AMHP believes consent is being withheld 'unreasonably' he/she can apply to courts for order appointing someone else to assume 'nearest relative' rights.
Application to extend observation	Observation order may be granted for up to twenty-eight days by hospital psychiatrist under s. 2. Following this (or sometimes from outset), six-month renewable treatment period may be agreed under s. 3. The RC agreeing to detention under s. 2 or 3 must be a qualified doctor. This may be renewed after initial six months, subject to approval by mental health review tribunal (MHRT) and with patient/nearest relative given right to appeal. Further renewal may be made after twelve months and thereafter yearly.
Application for warrants	If AMHP believes mentally disordered person is being ill-treated or neglected on private property he/she may make application to magistrate for warrant to search premises.
Assumption of the role of 'guardian'	Social services can be appointed 'guardians' to mentally ill people unlikely to respond to hospital treatment but needing protection. Private individuals can be appointed, too—with council's consent.

two key proposals that provoked fury among mental health and human rights campaigners, and a high-profile campaign by *The Independent on Sunday*:

- new powers enabling doctors to detain people with serious mental health conditions who might pose potential risks to themselves or others, primarily for the protection of the public—rather than to receive treatment;

- authority for clinicians (doctors and psychiatrists) to 'impose' treatment on the severely mentally ill, regardless of their wishes and even if they were judged to have the mental capacity to make their own decisions.

At various stages the Bill was opposed by campaign groups across the gamut—most notably the Mental Health Alliance, a coalition of seventy-eight organizations, including Mind, the King's Fund, and various bodies representing practitioners. In the end it was watered down, although the ability of doctors to prescribe enforced medication remained in the final version.

The Act's other main features are listed in the table entitled 'Other main provisions of the Mental Health Act 2007', to be found on the Online Resource Centre.

Prior to the final passage of the 2007 Act, Labour introduced a marginally less controversial reform in the guise of the Mental Capacity Act 2005, which sought to enshrine the rights of people with severe mental health issues to exercise power over their own care that legally had previously only existed in common law. The Act covered only England and Wales, but similar provisions had earlier been made under the Adults with Incapacity (Scotland) Act 2000.

The Act also introduced:

- a new *Independent Mental Capacity Advocate Service* (IMCAS) for England and another for Wales from 2007;

- new criminal offences of 'wilful neglect' and 'ill-treatment';

- ability of service users to nominate 'substitute decision-makers' to their nearest relatives under a new lasting power of attorney (LPA);

- a new *Court of Protection* with extended powers.

≡ Topical feature idea

Figure 18.1 is a news story from the *Oxford Mail* newspaper focusing on a 'bed-blocking' crisis in Oxfordshire hospitals caused by a lack of care home places and community support for elderly and disabled people. Your news editor asks you to explain the background to this story in a feature, 'humanizing' it by finding some service users prevented from returning to their own homes or moving into care because of budget cuts to social services. How would you go about contacting service users in this position? What other sources would you consult to provide a rounded picture of the impact of recent reforms and austerity measures?

Figure 18.1 A human interest news story from the *Oxford Mail*, 18 April 2012

Plan to free up beds in wards

Oliver Evans

Oxford Mail

18 April 2012

Web link: http://www.oxfordmail.co.uk/news/
yourtown/oxfordshire/9653866.Plan_to_free_
up_beds_in_wards/

A NEW deal is to be struck to help solve Oxfordshire's bed-blocking crisis.

Latest figures show nearly 200 people are taking up hospital beds in the county when they are medically well enough to go home.

The bed-blocking problem is mostly caused when people—mainly the elderly or disabled—are unable to go back home without extra care being put in place or home adaptations to allow them to live independently.

But under a new plan, the number of people being helped after hospital discharge in the county looks set to double.

Health bosses will only be paid for every person they help, rather than getting cash up-front as presently.

The county council hopes the move will swell the number of people helped from 1,800 now to 3,250 in the next year and 3,750 after that.

Managers will then get a bonus if they exceed this. No costs have yet been agreed.

The 'reablement' service provides home visits to help people who have suffered an illness or injury with tasks like getting out of bed.

Oxfordshire has consistently recorded the worst results for bed-blocking in the country.

Oxfordshire county councillor Arash Fatemian said the new scheme introduced 'a very significant incentive' to solve the problem.

He said Oxford Health NHS Foundation Trust—which runs the service on behalf of the county council—must show it has helped each patient lead an independent life.

He said: 'If it does not do so, it will not be paid.'

Mr Fatemian, cabinet member for adult services, said: 'By getting more people into the service we should see a knock-on reduction in delayed transfers of care from acute and community hospitals.'

Trust spokesman Wendy Samways said: 'People using reablement experience greater improvements in physical functioning and improved quality of life compared with using standard home care.'

Campaigners and health bosses welcomed the news as a step towards preventing patients from enduring long, stressful stays on wards.

Age UK spokesman Rachelle Kennedy said: 'It is very encouraging to see concrete commitments and targets from the council.'

A spokesman for Oxfordshire Clinical Commissioning Group, which is leading efforts to tackle bed-blocking, said: 'Supporting more people to remain at home should have a knock-on effect to reduce unplanned admissions to hospital and reduce the delays that some people are experiencing when being discharged from hospital.'

Paul Brennan, director of clinical services at Oxford University Hospitals NHS Trust, said: 'We welcome this new approach.

'We hope that it will mean that patients are able to access reablement services more quickly and so move to more appropriate care settings for them, freeing up beds for other patients.'

But Mary-Jane Sareva, of East Oxford, whose late father Frank, 80, refused to leave hospital after being offered a community hospital bed, was sceptical.

She said: 'The county council has reduced so much care for people at home. I don't have the confidence the care packages will be appropriate.'

The council is cutting £37m from its £195m social care bill between 2011 and 2015.

Latest snapshot bed-blocking figures, for February, show 194 county people were waiting longer than they should.

A total 5,784 bed days were lost that month—the highest in England—compared to 4,029 in April last year and 6,335 in October.

Of the 194, some 138 were waiting for community NHS care, a care home bed or support to live in their own homes. A further 38 could not leave hospital because they had not been assessed.

Courtesy of the Oxford Mail

✳ Current issues

- **Expansion of self-directed support:** Labour began a large-scale move away from the traditional means by which social care in the community had been funded (a top-down approach, with professionals applying for funds on behalf of the service users for whom they were responsible). It introduced a system giving service users themselves and/or their carers direct control of their own budgets—leaving them to 'shop around' for suitable services. The Coalition is moving further and faster in this direction, giving direct payments to those needing care to ensure they are able to seek out and apply for their own respite care more easily.

- **Review of long-term care:** one of the most heated issues in the 2010 election campaign was the question of how to fund future long-term care for the elderly and/or seriously ill/disabled. For twenty years or more, individuals moving into long-term care have been expected to sell their homes to pay for it (unless there is someone else still living there), but in its manifesto Labour proposed a National Care Service, funded by some form of estate levy that was likely to take account of individuals' ability to pay. The Coalition is planning an imminent White Paper to address this issue.

- **Review of child social work:** a 'fundamental review' of child protection practices was launched by the Coalition on entering office, in an effort to identify and recommend ways of ensuring that child social workers can spend more time dealing directly with children. Following the scandals in local authority areas such as Doncaster, where a series of serious case reviews remained hidden from councillors and the public until a local newspaper exposed them, all local safeguarding children's boards have also been told they must publish the overview reports and executive summaries of future serious case reviews.

? Review questions

1. What is the definition of 'children in need'? Outline the main responsibilities of local authority social services departments in relation to such children.

2. What were the main reforms arising from the Victoria Climbié Inquiry and the 'Every Child Matters' agenda? What are 'children's trusts'?

3. What is the difference between adoption and fostering? Outline the processes for adopting or fostering, and the range and types of people entitled to adopt or foster under British law.

4. What is meant by the term 'community care'? What are the main types of support available to the elderly and mentally ill under this policy?

5. Outline the purpose and powers of the Care Quality Commission.

→ Further reading

Blackman, T., Brody, S., and Convery, J. (eds) (2001) *Social Care and Social Exclusion: A Comparative Study of Older People's Care in Europe*, London: Palgrave Macmillan. **Thoughtful and informative comparisons between different approaches taken by six states—including Britain—to providing social care for the elderly**.

Leff, J. (1997) *Care in the Community: Illusion or Practice?* London: Wiley-Blackwell. **Critical evaluation of impact of Conservative Party's 'Care in Community' policies on mentally ill and those who treat them**.

Philpot, T. (2007) *Adoption: Changing Families, Changing Times*, London: Routledge. **Examination of British adoption laws, focusing on real-life stories and recent changes to open up process to same-sex and unmarried couples**.

Stanley, J. and Goddard, C. (2002) *In the Firing Line: Violence and Power in Child Protection Work*, London: Wiley-Blackwell. **Thoughtful insight into pressures faced by child social workers and other professionals in identifying and protecting children in need, containing recent case studies**.

 Online Resource Centre

www.oxfordtextbooks.co.uk/orc/Morrison3e/
Visit the Online Resource Centre that accompanies this book for web links and regular updates.

19

Transport, environment, and 'quality of life' issues

As we have seen from previous chapters, the bulk of local authorities' time and money is spent raising and allocating funds, administering the planning process, and managing (if not always directly delivering) core services like schools, housing, and social care. But beyond these complex and costly areas, councils are responsible for various other things: maintaining roads; licensing pubs and nightclubs; inspecting hotels and restaurants; and running museums, theatres, and libraries. This broad sweep of service areas—covering everything from public transport to environmental health and trading standards—is where the basic utilitarian needs represented by the core spending areas listed above make way for those that might broadly be described as about 'quality of life'.

▌ Highways and public transport

A prime motivator behind the emergence of local government was the promotion of production and trade and the need to service the rapidly evolving agricultural and manufacturing economy ushered in by the Industrial Revolution. To this end, embryonic nineteenth-century councils became preoccupied with two broad areas of policy designed to facilitate economic expansion:

- *Highways and transport*—specifically, the movement of workers and goods from country to town and between markets, and the maintenance of proper roads.

- *Public health*—the provision of housing and sanitation of sufficiently high quality to cater for the workers on whose labour the new economy was founded. Today this is split between council housing (see Chapter

17), environmental health, and waste management functions, and their recently revived responsibility for overseeing public health and for scrutinizing local health services in their areas.

→ see also central government, p. 180

For hundreds of years the only highways of a decent navigable standard were the remains of Roman roads and others built from the Tudor era onwards by local parish councils. But the growth of commerce and long-distance trade in the eighteenth century meant industrialists and merchants soon recognized the need for their goods to be transported speedily and safely. This prompted a dramatic boost in private investment in highways.

The main developments early in the history of highways and public transport are outlined in the table entitled 'Timeline of emergence of road-building in Britain', to be found on the Online Resource Centre.

Types of road and the highways authorities responsible for them

Construction and maintenance of Britain's labyrinthine road network is today divided between multiple authorities. Minor roads and those linking two or more towns together are usually maintained by relevant councils (counties, unitaries, or metropolitan boroughs), but the longest and widest (A-roads and M-roads—or motorways) are normally overseen by the Secretary of State for Transport. Upkeep of these primary roads falls to the **Highways Agency (HA)**, an executive agency of the Department for Transport (DfT). While highway maintenance may sound like the dullest possible subject for a news story, inadequate street lighting, potholes, and general road disrepair are among the most common causes of complaints to councils (which in itself is arguably newsworthy). The main road designations and authorities responsible for them are outlined in Table 19.1.

New highways are usually either the result of deliberate local and/or central government road-building schemes—in which case they are automatically 'adopted' by the relevant authority once built—or incidental outcomes of new house-building programmes. In the latter case, a scheme's developer will normally sign a formal agreement with the planning authority to ensure it can hand over responsibility for the roads when the development is complete. Such agreements are backed with 'bonds' issued by banks or building societies to ensure that, if the developer enters receivership or defaults, the roads will be finished without costing local taxpayers.

In some circumstances, however, highways—normally footpaths or bridleways—may be closed or diverted to enable development. There are two main ways in which this is done:

- If a highway is being closed because it is no longer used, the authority must apply to magistrates for an 'extinguishment order' under the Highways Acts.

- A highway can sometimes be *realigned* to run around, rather than through, a development, by granting a 'public path diversion order' under the terms of various Town and Country Planning Acts.

Developers must conduct detailed research before embarking on their plans, to ensure they have applied for any necessary extinguishment or diversion orders. This is done by consulting a 'definitive rights of way map' maintained by the highways authority.

Roles of Secretary of State and Highways Agency

Because of their major infrastructural significance, motorways are designated 'special roads' by government. In relation to both motorways and trunk roads, the Secretary of State is ultimately responsible for:

Table 19.1 Types of road and authorities responsible for them

Road type	Definition	Authority
Trunk roads (M- and major A-roads)	Major roads linking towns/cities and/or connecting them to ports/airports. Normally divided into at least dual carriageway layout, biggest are multilane motorways. M25 will shortly become eight-lane motorway, with one stretch (junctions 12 to 14) boasting ten.	Secretary of State for Transport, and Highways Agency.
County roads (A-roads)	Major arterial roads (almost all A-roads) linking smaller towns, normally within boundaries of single county.	County councils, unitary authorities, metropolitan borough councils, and London boroughs.
Secondary roads (B-roads), and public bridleways and footpaths	B-roads and smaller roads in both rural and urban areas, particularly those linking villages, hamlets, and smaller settlements. Bridleways and footpaths often little more than dirt tracks, following lines of medieval/Roman/more ancient routes and paths through fields and woodland.	Councils (as above).
Private roads	Highways contained within boundaries of private estates like Canary Wharf, east London, or City of London.	Private estates and related businesses (e.g. Canary Wharf)—unless road formally adopted by relevant council under Private Street Works Act 1892.

- *overall policy*—whether/where to build new M/A-roads, use of tolls and other forms of road-pricing, and balance between road-building and investment in passenger transport via the rail network and airports;
- *planning, improvement, and maintenance*—the logistics of building, repairing, and maintaining major roads, and implementing policies on the ground;
- *financing and controlling* the trunk road and motorway programme through taxation.

In practice many important decisions have traditionally been taken in the recently abolished regional government offices, with most maintenance and improvement overseen by the HA, which, in turn, subcontracts hands-on engineering work to other companies—for example UK Highways. In addition, although county councils have long undertaken road maintenance on behalf of the government, this, too, is franchised out to private contractors.

There is also an increasingly complex system by which primary, secondary, and unclassified roads can be 'designated' to lower-tier authorities to take control of their day-to-day maintenance, to ensure smooth traffic flows and tackle congestion and pollution from noise and petrol fumes. In this way the Secretary of State can 'designate' responsibility for maintaining motorways and major A-roads to London boroughs, while county councils do likewise to borough/district councils. When roads are designated downwards, this is known as 'de-trunking'.

The HA, established in 1994, is overseen by its own board, under a chief executive earning £180,000 a year. It boasts seven regional control centres and another twenty-eight outstations from which its traffic officers operate. Its official statutory responsibility is to oversee the 'operation and stewardship of the strategic road network in England on behalf of the Secretary of State', as well as:

- managing traffic;
- tackling congestion;
- providing information to road users;
- improving journey times, road safety, and reliability;
- minimizing the impact of the road network on the environment.

The agency, working with the Secretary of State and individual councils, is responsible for organizing wide-ranging consultations when major road projects are planned. The main stages in this process are outlined in the table entitled 'Main stages in the consultation process for major road projects', to be found on the Online Resource Centre.

In practice, road projects often go far from smoothly. Numerous high-profile protests have occurred in recent years against major projects, the most famous being the campaign against the 'Newbury Bypass'—a nine-mile stretch of dual carriageway built around the market town of Newbury, Berkshire. From

January to April 1996 some 7,000 protestors—ranging from hardcore environ-mentalists to middle-aged professionals and pensioners—picketed a 360-acre site in an effort to thwart the building programme, which involved felling 120 acres of ancient woodland. In the end the work went ahead, but not before the cost of policing the protest (dubbed 'Operation Prospect') had topped £5m, and that of hiring private security firms to erect fences and patrol the perimeter had reached £24m.

Other notable protests include those over the construction of the A30 between Exeter and Honiton in Devon, which saw a network of tunnels and tree houses built at a camp near Fairmile. These protests made a media celebrity out of 'Swampy' (aka self-proclaimed eco-warrior Daniel Hooper), whose later antics included a one-off stint as a panellist on BBC1's current affairs comedy quiz show, *Have I Got News for You*.

Recent national reforms of traffic policy

Road-building continues to be a sensitive issue across Britain, not least because there is little evidence continuing expansion of the network has done much to ease congestion. Studies suggest funnelling government spending away from public transport and into road-building programmes *increases* traffic jams—by encouraging more people to drive. A study by transport consultant Halliburton published in 2002 predicted an increase in congestion in the M25 corridor of a third by 2016 unless radical steps were taken to persuade people to use public transport, like charging tolls or introducing a luxury bus service around the motorway.

Concern about road policy is arguably one of the rare issues to unite sup-porters and opponents, albeit from different perspectives: to environmental campaigners congestion represents a cause of serious pollution and long-term ecological damage, while motorists and long-distance hauliers view traffic jams as a huge source of discomfort and frustration. Ministers have launched a number of initiatives in recent years to address congestion and pollution, as listed in the table entitled 'Major government traffic and transport initiatives since 1997', to be found on the Online Resource Centre.

Despite this, many road and rail users agree Britain has some way to go before it can boast anything like the 'integrated transport policy' first promised by then Deputy Prime Minister John Prescott in 1999.

Local traffic management, road-pricing, and congestion charging

The term 'traffic management' was, for long years, synonymous with little more than road crossings, signs, lights, and 'lollipop ladies'—in short, the bread-and-butter mechanisms used to direct traffic from A to B, help pedestrians cross it, and 'warn' motorists about everything from changes in speed limits to steep slopes, sharp bends, and bumpy road surfaces. To a large extent, councils remain preoccupied with these and other humdrum concerns—many of which continue to excite the attention of local newspapers and television news outlets. The more workaday responsibilities of highways departments include planning, installing, and monitoring the effectiveness of:

- traffic lights;
- roundabouts;
- sleeping policemen (speed bumps) and other 'traffic calming' measures;
- zebra crossings, pelican crossings, and crossings manned by 'lollipop ladies';
- road signage;
- one-way systems;
- 'park and ride' schemes—free bus services to and from town centres;
- dedicated bus and taxi lanes and cycle lanes/paths.

In recent years traffic management has entered a new phase, as pedestrians' and motorists' frustration with mounting congestion has sparked growing calls from both environmentalists and the business community for radical action to address the unsustainable growth in private car ownership. Environmentalists' prime concern remains the pollution caused by carbon monoxide exhaust fumes and the noise generated by heavy traffic. Business leaders, meanwhile, are increasingly alarmed by the impact of lengthy traffic delays on the smooth running of the economy. A 2005 survey by the Institution of Civil Engineers (ICE) estimated traffic was costing UK businesses up to £20bn a year because so many employees were arriving late for work. Similar figures have been quoted by the Confederation of British Industry (CBI).

Faced with the prospect of roads becoming even more clogged, and the associated negative impact on people's quality of life, successive governments have looked to other countries for inspiration as to how to lure people out of their cars and onto passenger transport. Given the high cost of travelling by rail and the severe congestion on many train routes—particularly in south-east England—the 'carrot' of public transport has historically failed to persuade sufficient numbers to leave their cars at home. As a result, policymaking has gradually shifted towards adopting more of a 'stick' approach, focusing on mechanisms borrowed from overseas, like congestion charging and road-pricing (tolls).

Congestion charging

Originating in Singapore, where it was introduced in 1975, congestion charging is the system by which flat-rate fees are charged to drivers entering specified 'congestion charge zones' (usually in or around urban centres) between specified hours on given days. In Britain the most famous example of congestion charging to date (though not the first—an honour which falls to Durham) was introduced by former London Mayor Ken Livingstone in February 2003, initially within a limited central zone defined by the capital's inner ring road. This zone was extended to cover much of west London in February 2007, although in December 2010 Mr Livingstone's successor, Boris Johnson, scrapped the extension as a 'Christmas present' to local people. The charge operates between 7 a.m. and 6 p.m., Monday to Friday, and was initially set at £5 a day. It is currently between £9 and £12 a day for most qualifying vehicles, depending on which method drivers use and how far in advance they pay. Drivers may now pay by credit or debit card over the phone, by mobile phone text message, via a dedicated website, or over the counter in shops equipped with PayPoint facilities. Those who fail to pay are fined.

The congestion charge has won praise from both business leaders and green lobbyists, with various reports suggesting it has cut jams in central London by up to 20 per cent. It has won fans in the medical community, too: according to a 2008 study in *Occupational and Environmental Medicine* magazine, its impact on pollution may have already 'saved' up to 1,888 extra 'years of life' among London's 7 million residents. Perhaps unsurprisingly, however, it has infuriated many motorists—including shift workers required to arrive at (or leave) work in central London at unsocial hours, when little or no public transport is available.

On its launch, the charge became the subject of a high-profile campaign by stage actors, including Tom Conti and Samantha Bond ('Miss Moneypenny' in the Pierce Brosnan James Bond films), who cited the plight of low-paid shift workers, but also argued that the timings of the daily charge period would adversely affect the size of audiences for West End performances by penalizing theatregoers for entering the zone in the early evening.

Nonetheless, its perceived success has seen major international cities from New York to Stockholm imitating it, and before leaving office Labour (initially sceptical of Mr Livingstone's plans) had committed itself to rolling it out elsewhere. In June 2008 then Transport Secretary Ruth Kelly approved what would have been the biggest congestion charge scheme introduced anywhere in the world, in the form of a dual–ring zone around Greater Manchester, covering an area twelve times bigger than the original London zone. However, in December 2008 the plan was thrown into disarray when local residents roundly rejected it by 79 to 21 per cent in a referendum. Advanced plans for other cities, including Bristol, to adopt charges have stalled for now, following then Coalition Transport Secretary Philip Hammond's decision in June 2010 to suspend the Transport Innovation Fund used to co-finance schemes, in a drive to find departmental savings of 25–40 per cent.

In addition to congestion charging, in February 2008 Mr Livingstone introduced a 'low-emission zone' (LEZ)—an area encompassing all 610 square miles (1,580 km²) of Greater London. The worst polluting lorries, buses, and coaches were fined £200 per day for entering the capital between 7 a.m. and 6 p.m. on weekdays, excluding public holidays, with drivers starting journeys late in an evening and ending them early the following morning forced to pay for two days, not one. On entering office, Mr Johnson, who had condemned the charge as 'the most punitive, draconian fining regime in the whole of Europe', moved to suspend it, but in practice it has continued (a fact for which the mayor has occasionally sought to 'blame' the European Union (EU)—see also Chapter 9). In January 2012 the LEZ emissions standards were even made stricter, with new classes of vehicle affected, including larger vans, minibuses, motor caravans, motorized horseboxes, and 4x4 utility vehicles registered as new before 1 January 2002. Meanwhile, individual councils—including some in the capital—have experimented with even more novel ways of penalizing 'gas-guzzling' vehicles. In January 2007 Richmond became the first of nine London boroughs to introduce higher-rate residents' parking permits for owners of 'Chelsea tractors' and other cars with larger engines. Although the scheme was replicated elsewhere, after years of protest from residents and motoring organizations like the AA the council finally scrapped the scheme in July 2010.

Road-pricing

Congestion charging may be flavour of the month among councils seeking to battle traffic problems (and raise the odd million for local investment), but the idea of forcing motorists to pay upfront to use roads is hardly new. In Britain 'road-pricing' was first mooted by John Major's Conservative government, which outlined proposals to introduce a network of privately financed toll roads on major routes, modelled on systems used in France and other mainland European countries. To date Britain has only one private toll motorway—a twenty-seven-mile stretch of the M6 between Coleshill, Warwickshire, and Cannock, Staffordshire, which opened in December 2003. In July 2004 then Transport Secretary Alistair Darling announced plans for two fifty-mile 'pay-as-you-go' expressways between Wolverhampton and Manchester. But these remain unrealized, and are likely to remain so in light of figures published by the Campaign for Better Transport in August 2010, revealing the private company operating the route, Midland Expressway Ltd, had been running it at an annual £25m loss.

Labour remained ambivalent about private toll roads overall, in light of research into the so-so impact of road-pricing. In January 2005 an answer to a parliamentary question to the DfT revealed congestion on and around the M6 had *increased* since the opening of the existing toll road. Junctions to the south had seen traffic levels rise by up to 10,000 vehicles daily, with those to the north witnessing 5,000 extra a day. Ministers' focus has also been sharpened by the scale of public opposition to increased road-pricing. In February 2007, 1.7 million people signed an online petition objecting to more tolls—prompting outgoing Prime Minister Tony Blair to reply, stressing his government's mind had not yet been decided. It never was.

Perhaps the most significant statement of policy direction on roads by a recent British premier occurred in March 2012, when David Cameron risked igniting a row as incendiary as that over the Coalition's short-lived plans to 'privatize' England's forests (see p. 486) by outlining radical proposals to address an 'urgent' need for more private investment in Britain's highways network. Among the ideas he floated were more tolls—beginning with the introduction of charges to help fund improvements to the A14 between the Suffolk port of Felixstowe in the M1–M6 interchange—and handing stretches of the road system over to sovereign wealth funds, pension providers, and other commercial companies on long-term leases, to encourage them to invest. Claiming congestion on Britain's roads cost its economy £7bn a year, he announced the DfT would publish the results of a feasibility study into 'new ownership and financing models' for improving the network that autumn. In the meantime, speculation grew about the precise form new road-funding schemes might take under any new 'privatization' or 'public–private partnership-based' arrangements. One idea suggested by the Civil Engineering Contractors' Association was that private firms managing roads might be paid 'shadow tolls' by the government on the basis of how much traffic they attracted to their new/improved highways—obviating the need to charge motorists themselves.

'Speed' cameras

The days of roadside safety cameras—used to photograph number plates of vehicles exceeding official speed limits on roads, and to award their drivers fixed penalties for speeding—are fast fading. In July 2010 Oxfordshire County Council became the first major local authority to stop funding them. Its decision to end its contributions to the collaborative Thames Valley Safer Roads Partnership, which encompassed several counties, led to speed camera enforcement in Oxfordshire ceasing immediately. Other areas have since followed suit, including Warwickshire and London, where 75 per cent of all 754 speed cameras had been switched off by June 2012. Across Britain as a whole 1,522 of the 3,189 cameras were no longer being actively used.

While councils and police forces have decided to dispense with speed cameras for largely pragmatic reasons—regarding their retention as a costly luxury, given the relatively small sums generated by fines—there have been conflicting reports about the impact of this 'policy' on road safety. According to figures published in *The Sun* newspaper in June 2012, the number of accidents in which speed was a factor in Avon and Somerset had actually fallen since sixty-nine of the area's cameras were shut down in April the previous year. In contrast, statistics released to *Highways* magazine and the *Salisbury Journal* in the February 2012 figures showed accidents in which people were injured rose by nearly a quarter in Wiltshire between June and August 2011; this followed the closure a year earlier of the Wiltshire and Swindon Road Safety Partnership and the camera switch-off that accompanied it.

Other aspects of highways and transport policy

Lighting

Street lighting tends primarily to be the preserve of councils. As with parking policy (see pp. 564–5), however, district/borough councils are often responsible for maintaining and repairing roads and pathways delegated to them, along with the budgets required to contract out the necessary work. Quality parish councils (see p. 338) have also increasingly taken over the maintenance of individual roads in smaller towns, villages, and other rural settlements.

Public transport

Since the National Bus Company (Britain's publicly owned nationwide bus provider) was privatized in the 1980s, followed by the subsequent deregulation of local routes and introduction of dedicated passenger transport authorities in metropolitan areas, councils have played a diminishing role in providing public transport. As in many policy areas, they have largely been reduced to the status of 'enablers'—monitoring the provision of bus, tram, Underground, and river boat services by the free market, and stepping in as 'providers of last resort' where unacceptable gaps and/or inconsistencies in services emerge.

Under the Local Government Act 1972 the then newly established metropolitan county councils were charged with providing bus services through 'passenger transport executives' designed to promote 'integrated' local transport. But in 1985 this changed, when Margaret Thatcher's government replaced metropolitan counties with metropolitan boroughs and scrapped the Greater London Council (GLC), introducing independent passenger transport authorities in these areas. The most famous of these was London Transport—now Transport for London (TfL) (see pp. 563–4). At the same time, councils' responsibility for providing transport links to and from airports and docks was transferred to new joint boards. The one abiding legacy of the 1972 Act was the transfer of highways and transport responsibilities from boroughs/districts to county councils. This remains the case to this day, except in unitary areas.

The effective privatization of local transport was formalized in the Transport Act 1985, with councils expected to provide directly only 'socially necessary' services—for example those linking villages and smaller towns—and only then when the market failed to do so. A year later the system was formally deregulated, allowing any number of bus companies to compete on specific routes—known as 'registered bus routes'—provided they first obtained 'public service operator's licences' from the **Traffic Commissioners**. Trams, like those operating in urban centres from Manchester to Croydon, had to be similarly licensed.

Under the present licensing regime there are seven regional Commissioners. Their responsibilities are to:

- license operators of delivery lorries or heavy goods vehicles (HGVs), and operators of buses and coaches—known as 'public service vehicles' (PSVs);
- register local bus services;
- grant vocational licences and take action against drivers of HGVs and PSVs if necessary.

The Traffic Commissioner for Scotland has additional powers that in England and Wales are exercised individually by officers in council highways departments. These include determining appeals against taxi fares and removing improperly parked vehicles in Edinburgh and Glasgow.

One effect of deregulating local bus services was to undermine councils' ability to subsidize public transport. While in some areas introducing competition did improve services by pushing down fares, in others the loss of council-run buses deprived residents of heavily subsidized tickets that found no replacement in the privatized marketplace. Among the most celebrated local services were the cut-price buses ushered in by Mr Livingstone in the days of the GLC and the record-breaking 2p fares introduced by future Home Secretary David Blunkett while leader of Sheffield City Council in the 1970s.

Contracting out bus services has also been blamed for the increasing isolation of some communities, particularly those based in remote villages and hamlets, because—shorn of state subsidies—private companies have been reluctant to maintain, let alone initiate, unprofitable routes. On occasion, poorer suburbs have also been left isolated by private operators' refusal to continue running services there—normally in response to outbreaks of vandalism, or verbal and/or physical violence towards drivers. In June 2006 one of Britain's biggest private bus operators, Stagecoach, briefly suspended services to Hull's Orchard Park estate after receiving sixteen separate reports of missiles being thrown at buses in four days.

While bus licensing has long since passed to the Commissioners, county councils, unitary authorities, and metropolitan boroughs retain responsibility for issuing licences to taxi operators and minicab firms, including Hackney carriages outside London (where they are licensed by the Commissioner of the Metropolitan Police).

Although deregulation of the buses may have produced a patchy service in many areas, with some now very poorly served, recent years have seen the introduction of generous **concessionary fare schemes** for those who meet certain criteria, such as students, the disabled, and old-age pensioners (OAPs). Councils fund the schemes by subsidizing local bus operators the equivalent of the full fares they are 'losing' by implementing them. As of April 2006 all councils have had to provide a bare minimum of free off-peak bus fares for pass-holders. And since April 2008 registered OAPs and the disabled have been entitled to free off-peak travel anywhere in England and Wales, rather than simply their local authority area, as had been the case before. 'Off-peak' is defined as between 9.30 a.m. and 11.00 p.m. (avoiding morning rush hours). Both Scotland and Northern Ireland recently introduced equivalent schemes. There has been some speculation that the Coalition might remove subsidies to councils that help them maintain concessionary fares for better-off pensioners, as part of a wider drive to save money by means-testing certain benefits which currently apply universally—including the 'Winter Fuel Allowance' (see p. 238), but for the time being it remains.

While major transport infrastructural projects have traditionally been over-seen by central government, in recent years there has been a trend towards devolving autonomy for these to local and regional authorities, particularly in metropolitan areas. However, by June 2010 this short-lived era appeared to be nearing an end following the Coalition's abolition of regional development agencies (RDAs) (see pp. 474–5) and decision to individually review all trans-port projects yet to secure planning permission and/or funding. Among the initiatives axed (together worth £5.2bn) were phase one of an oft-delayed Tees Valley Metro system linking Teesside to Darlington, which has since been revived on a smaller scale in the absence of Whitehall funds. In Leeds a long-delayed network of electric 'trolleybuses' powered by overhead cables was delayed for a second time by the Coalition in December 2011, pending the out-come of a 'value for money' audit.

Transport for London (TfL)

Transport for London (TfL) is a quango charged with managing (if not directly running):

- London buses, Croydon Tramlink, and Docklands Light Railway (DLR);
- London Underground (the 'Tube') network;
- Transport for London Road Network (TLRN);
- London River Services—licensed passenger ferries along and across the Thames.

It is also responsible for:

- delivering the Integrated Transport Strategy published by the mayor in July 2001, and revised in 2004 and 2006, in consultation with the Greater London Assembly (GLA);
- regulating taxis and minicabs;

- helping coordinate Dial-a-Ride and Taxicard schemes providing door-to-door services for people with mobility problems;
- installing and maintaining traffic lights across London;
- promoting safe use of the Thames for passenger and freight movement.

To help deliver the strategy for London in 1998 a Transport Committee for London was set up by the GLA to replace the four pre-existing bodies responsible for overseeing the Tube, buses, taxis, main roads through the capital, and the DLR (a privately owned company).

While all this may sound harmonious, at times the process of taking decisions about the future of London's transport network has been anything but. Between 1997 and 2001 Mr Blair's government was locked in a tortuous stalemate with Mr Livingstone and London Transport Commissioner Bob Kiley over his insistence on 'part-privatization' of the Underground. Despite widespread criticism about the shambolic sell-off of the national rail network, ministers went to huge lengths to persuade the mayor to accept a public–private partnership (PPP) (see pp. 230–1), which saw a near-identical model adopted for the Tube, with franchises to run services on individual lines contracted out to competing private companies, while the tracks, signals, stations, and even rolling stock remained in the hands of a separate authority (in this case, TfL). With the Underground, the proposed management/ownership split was actually three-way, rather than two-way, as with rail—with companies contracted to carry out the £13bn, fifteen-year programme of improvements on the Underground infrastructure given a stake in it too. More recently, TfL was involved in protracted negotiations over Crossrail—the upcoming £16bn overland train link that, once completed, should connect thirty-seven stations, from Heathrow Airport and Maidenhead in the west to Canary Wharf and Shenfield, Essex, in the east, bringing twenty-four overland peak-time rail services an hour through the heart of London. Crossrail was finally approved in September 2007, after a decade of deliberation, and work commenced on the biggest engineering project in Europe, with the construction of 21 km twin-bore tunnels stretching under central London in spring 2012.

Car parking

Responsibility for administering and policing car parking is broadly divided between councils, as outlined in Table 19.2.

Until relatively recently, parking responsibilities were split fairly clearly in two-tier areas between boroughs/districts and counties, with the former managing off-road car parks and the latter on-street parking. In many areas these distinctions are blurred today, with some districts entering into agency agreements with neighbouring counties, and vice versa, effectively contracting out these functions to the other. To confuse the public further, while fixed-penalty fines tend to be administered by county councils or unitary authorities, the actual issuing of

Table 19.2 Types of council responsible for car-parking services

Type of parking	Local authority
On-street and residents' parking	Traditionally county councils and unitary authorities, but now administered by all types of council (subject to local arrangements)
Open-air car parks on public or council-owned land	Traditionally district/borough councils and unitary authorities, but now depends on local arrangements
Multistorey car parks	Private firms like National Car Parks Ltd (NCP)
Car parks at hospitals, colleges, universities, and business premises	Run by organizations themselves, increasingly using private contractors

penalty notices—the action of placing them on parked vehicles—has traditionally been performed by traffic wardens employed by the police. This recently changed, with council-employed parking attendants taking over the role in most areas—and themselves being redesignated 'civil enforcement officers' in 2009.

As with traffic management, parking issues have a habit of raising motorists' blood pressure—and, consequently, provide raw material for endless news stories. A common misconception is that wardens and attendants are paid commissions or 'bonuses' related to the number or value of fixed-penalty notices they issue. In fact, the government legislated to prevent this happening in the Traffic Wardens and Parking Attendants Act 2005. So combustible has the car-parking issue become in recent years, nonetheless, that ticket recipients may now appeal to a National Parking Adjudication Service (NPAS).

A particular parking management 'scandal' to receive media attention recently has been Westminster City Council's highly controversial decision to introduce a blanket charge of up to £4.80 an hour at evenings and on Sundays—a move condemned by an unlikely alliance of local residents and businesses, West End theatres, religious leaders, and London's *Evening Standard* newspaper. A High Court ruling in December 2011 forced the council to put the so-called 'nightlife tax' on hold until after the August 2012 London Olympics, but at time of writing opponents were holding their breath for its reintroduction.

Waste management and environmental health

Public health has been on the local agenda for longer than almost anything else. A rundown of major Public Health Acts and other relevant legislation is given in the table entitled 'Chronology of public health legislation in the UK', to be found on the Online Resource Centre.

The task of ensuring that housing, businesses, and local amenities in each area conform to basic hygiene and safety standards today falls to district/borough and unitary environmental health departments. Of their myriad responsibilities by far the most costly and complex are those related to the effective organization of waste management services—an area so broad it requires the active involvement of every type of council.

Waste collection, recycling, and waste disposal

There are two overriding aspects to waste management, each handled by different authorities in two-tier areas:

- *waste collection*—districts/boroughs, unitaries, and metropolitan boroughs;
- *waste disposal*—counties, unitaries, and metropolitan boroughs.

Waste collection

Household and business waste collection has traditionally been carried out in the form of weekly door-to-door services. In recent years, however, a growing number of councils have introduced fortnightly collections to save money, while the nature of 'rubbish collecting' itself has changed, with more emphasis on recycling, rather than the simple disposal of refuse at 'tips' (landfill sites).

As with most areas of local service delivery, waste collection is periodically put out to tender (see pp. 393–4), with the result that many 'bin men and women' are now employed not by councils directly but private contractors hired on their behalf. Having started out with kerbside recycling points at supermarkets, parks, and other public amenities, many collection authorities in England and Wales now operate at least a fortnightly door-to-door recycling service. The operator contracted to collect the normal 'black bin' household and/or business waste (food waste, plastics, etc.) may not be the same one picking up the ('green bag') recycling.

Despite dramatically increasing its levels of recycling, Britain was slow to embrace it compared to most European countries. As a result, Labour ministers considered increasingly fiendish ways of cajoling or forcing householders and businesses to recycle more waste. Most controversial was the mooted introduction of 'pay-as-you-throw' fines for people who chucked away too much, with commensurate 'rebates' for those who made most use of their green bins. Then Environment Secretary David Miliband announced plans to give councils powers to charge for excessive black bin waste in May 2007, as part of the government's drive to force councils to recycle at least 40 per cent by 2010 and 50 per cent by 2020. Under the Climate Change Act 2008 trials of bin taxes began in 2009 in five pilot areas, policed by new quangos, known as 'joint waste authorities', which in future would potentially be able to set new taxes. Not content to wait for the outcome of the pilots, some councils launched pay-as-you-throw schemes off their own backs: in September 2006 Woking Borough Council was accused of snooping on households after installing electronic chips capable of weighing 'residual' (non-recyclable) waste in wheelie bins. But on entering office, Coalition Communities Secretary Eric Pickles abandoned the concept—announcing plans to 'incentivize' households to recycle, rather than punish those that did not, by rewarding the diligent with vouchers to be used in local shops, restaurants, or leisure centres. This idea was based on a popular pilot run by Windsor and Maidenhead Council—earmarked by Mr Cameron as a standard-bearer for his 'Big Society' approach to running local services (see p. 395).

Whether carrot or stick wins out in the end, British councils are facing an uphill struggle to meet European Union recycling targets over the coming decade: a 1999 directive stipulated that the amount of biodegradable waste dumped at UK landfill sites (equivalent to 18.1m tonnes in 2003–4) should be cut to 13.7m tonnes by 2010, 9.2m tonnes by 2013, and 6.3m by 2020. Failure to meet these targets would see the government fined £180m a year by the European Commission. Britain met its first target by the end of 2010, but it remains to be seen whether it will achieve the tough reductions set for 2013 and 2020.

Waste disposal

The Environmental Protection Act 1990 required all waste disposal authorities to form arm's-length local authority waste disposal companies (LAWDCs) to dispose of refuse on their behalf—a form of direct service organization (DSO) (see p. 394). In turn, these were required to 'hire' waste disposal contractors (in practice, either the company itself or another franchisee) to:

- provide waste transfer and landfill sites to which householders can take large items (for example, electrical goods) for landfill or destruction;
- dispose of items collected from local people's homes by collection operators;
- recycle or sell waste for scrap.

Contractors running waste disposal sites on behalf of councils must obtain waste management licences (WML) from the Environment Agency (EA) in England and Wales. In Scotland applications are made to the Scottish Environmental Protection Agency (SEPA), and in Northern Ireland to the Department of the Environment (Environment and Heritage Service).

Because the EU has toughened its recycling targets, the issue of straightforward rubbish dumping has become acutely politically sensitive over the past two decades. Faced with rapidly dwindling capacity at Britain's existing landfill sites, successive governments have sought to deter councils from continuing to dump waste in the age-old tradition. Perhaps the most contentious mechanism they have used is the Landfill Tax. Introduced in the Finance Act 1996, this was initially levied on councils, waste disposal companies, and other organizations involved in dumping rubbish, at a standard rate of £7 a tonne and a reduced rate of £2 a tonne. In its 1999 Budget Labour raised the standard rate to £10 a tonne and introduced a 'Landfill Tax accelerator' designed to increase it by a further £1 a tonne each year until 2004. In his 2002 Pre-Budget Report then Chancellor Gordon Brown announced further stepped rises, with the medium- to long-term aim of charging £35 a tonne. For 2012/13 the two rates were:

- *standard rate*—£64 a tonne (rising by £8 a tonne per year until at least 2014) for household waste that may decay and/or contaminate land;
- *reduced rate*—£2.50 a tonne for rocks and soils, ceramics and concrete, unused minerals, furnace slag, ash, low-activity inorganic compounds, and water.

To dilute the impact of the tax on site operators, Mr Major's Environment Secretary, John Gummer, introduced a Landfill Tax credit scheme designed to reward them with a 90 per cent tax credit against any donations made to environmental bodies registered with the scheme's regulator, Entrust. This was, however, capped at 20 per cent of their Landfill Tax liability. Labour later introduced a Landfill Allowance Trading Scheme (LATS), overseen by the Department for Environment, Food, and Rural Affairs (Defra) (under the Waste and Emissions Trading Act 2003), to allow individual waste disposal authorities with surplus landfill space to 'sell' it to those in 'deficit', in the manner of carbon trading.

Rows over the Landfill Tax and recycling targets are not the only reasons the issue of waste disposal is so constantly in the news. In 2005 an investigation for BBC1's *Real Story* programme found that 500 tonnes of supposedly recycled waste from UK households had actually been dumped by contractors in Indonesia—raising concerns that British citizens might be salving their consciences over recycling at the expense of developing countries. Around the same time, EA figures revealed that half the 8m tonnes of green waste generated each year in Britain finished up overseas.

Air quality, noise pollution, fly-tipping, and dog fouling

The council officials charged with inspecting domestic and business premises to ensure they meet statutory environmental health standards are **environmental health officers**. One of their main duties is to investigate complaints relating to waste collection and disposal—or, rather, *lack* of collection and disposal in cases when, for example, a property owner or occupier fails to leave out his/her rubbish in the correct place for removal by the collection authority. They also investigate reports of 'fly-tipping'—the practice of dumping rubbish on someone else's doorstep, often used by residents or businesses to offload refuse on neighbours after missing their own collection days. Complaints will often arise from a neighbour who reports an unpleasant smell or the unsightly presence of overloaded bin bags days before they are (or were) due to be collected. In extreme cases, rotting waste that has been inadequately stored or left out for days between collections may attract vermin, necessitating direct intervention by environmental health 'pest controllers' to remove them. The cost of ridding an area of vermin will normally be passed straight to the offending party—and the council may also choose to prosecute under environmental health legislation. Conviction usually leads to a fine.

Another menace accorded greater priority in recent years is dog fouling. After years of campaigning by environmental groups and others concerned about the potential danger contact with dog mess poses to young children, so-called 'poop scoops' and dog litter bins have become a common feature of most parks and public rights of way. Yet many areas remained so blighted by it that some councils went so far as to use CCTV cameras to spy on errant dog owners who fail to clean up after their pets until this practice was banned by the Coalition. Councils' ability to do this (using anti-terror measures introduced in the Regulation of Investigatory Powers Act 2000) sparked a media outcry when it emerged in June 2008. In January 2011 Home Secretary Theresa May confirmed that they would no longer be permitted to snoop on residents for 'bin crimes' or other such minor infringements—except in cases when alleged offences carried custodial sentences. Even then this would only in future be possible if councils first obtained formal approval from a magistrate. In practice, however, reports of such 'spying' have persisted.

see also
central
government,
pp. 260–3

Other menaces continue to be the subject of strict statutory powers. In response to growing pressure on Britain to conform to EU directives, the Pollution Prevention and Control Act 1999 made councils responsible for exercising 'local authority pollution prevention and control' (LAPPC) in relation to so-called 'Part B' industrial installations in their areas. These include smaller power plants, glassworks, waste disposal sites, sewerage works, and municipal and hospital incinerators. More major polluting installations—for example, oil refineries, nuclear power stations, steelworks, and large chemical plants— were designated as 'Part A1' and placed under 'integrated pollution prevention and control' (IPPC) orders overseen by the EA, SEPA, or the Northern Irish Department of the Environment. There is also a third category of process ('Part A2'), which relates to medium-range installations. This, like Part B, is policed by local authorities in the following way:

- Applications for a process to be carried out must be made to the relevant authority (if refused, appeals can be lodged with the Environment Secretary).

- If an enforcing authority believes an operator has breached an authorization, it can serve an enforcement notice specifying the nature of the breach, the steps that need to be taken to rectify it, and a deadline for that work to be completed.

- If it feels external factors are creating an imminent risk of serious pollution (even if unconnected with the process itself), it can serve a prohibition notice.

Another newsworthy issue recently has been the growing intolerance of 'noise pollution'. In certain circumstances authorities may now seize offending equipment, such as stereos or drills. The Noise Act 1996 empowered them to send officers to investigate sources of excessive noise at night and 'measure' noise levels. Wherever it exceeds statutory limits, warning notices may immediately be served on those responsible. Failure to comply is a criminal offence and officers may subsequently enter properties without warrants to seize offending equipment. Prosecution often also follows.

Noise pollution has also been a notable target of government crackdowns on 'antisocial behaviour' (see pp. 347–9). The use of antisocial behaviour orders (ASBOs) to tackle it has generated highly newsworthy, occasionally outlandish, outcomes. In March 2005 Andrew Gordon and his 18-year-old son, Phillip, were banned from their own home in Dunfermline for three months under the Antisocial Behaviour (Scotland) Act 2004 because of noise and disruption caused by drinking, cursing, fighting, and drug-taking at the house when Mr Gordon was away.

Action taken against 'unpleasant' smells has also made numerous headlines. One contentious case involved an award-winning vegetarian cafe in Greenwich, which was ordered to stop serving cooked food in June 2008 after neighbours complained about the smell.

Environmental health officers also oversee various other areas, as listed in Table 19.3.

Environmental health and food safety

One of the most widely understood duties of environmental health officers (or 'inspectors') is the role they play in promoting food safety by ensuring restaurants, cafes, pubs, and shops serving food are preparing, cooking, and storing meat and other items of suitable quality and under appropriate conditions. This role—memorably satirized in the classic 'Basil the Rat' episode of BBC1 sitcom *Fawlty Towers*—covers all aspects of food hygiene, including its sale, importation, preparation, transportation, storing, packing, wrapping, displaying, serving, and delivery.

The Food Standards Act 1999 set up a Food Standards Agency (FSA) to oversee hygiene and animal husbandry issues at a national level, while building on existing legislation to introduce two criminal offences for businesses failing to meet minimum standards: rendering food 'injurious to health' and selling food

Table 19.3 Additional responsibilities of environmental health officers

Responsibility	Definition
Litter	Councils, 'statutory undertakers' (companies contracted to run local services), and other public landowners legally bound to keep their land free of litter. If council designates specific 'litter control area', it is an offence for anyone to throw, drop, or dispose of litter on land owned by public body in that area.
General health risks	If measures for preserving public health fail and diseases like dysentery, smallpox, typhoid, or foot-and-mouth break out, authority must inform NHS and local community physician or Director of Public Health.
Maintaining public areas	These range from public parks and playgrounds to cemeteries.
Vermin control	Taking action to tackle infestations of rodents, insects, etc.—if necessary charging private individuals after event, if infestation relates to privately owned land or property.
Contaminated land	Management of land contaminated by industrial processes or military tests involving radiation is still covered by 1990 Act. Borough/district councils or unitary authorities responsible for identifying and registering contaminated land in their areas. If serious problem noted, authority must designate 'special site' and notify EA/SEPA, which takes responsibility for enforcing actions taken. Enforcing authority serves remediation notice on person or business responsible, specifying action needed to remedy problem. In Northern Ireland contaminated land issues overseen by Department of Health under Radioactive Contaminated Land Regulations (Northern Ireland) 2006.
Air quality	Following types of emission prohibited under Clean Air Act 1993 (which built on provisions of Clean Air Act 1956, introduced to eliminate winter smog): • dark smoke' issuing from chimneys; • excessive smoke, grit, dust, and fumes from chimneys; • excessively high chimneys; • excessive exhaust emissions; • smoke emissions in designated 'smoke control areas'. Environment Act 1995 required councils to review present and likely future air quality in their areas. Where air not meeting desired standard, councils given powers to designate 'air quality management areas' covered by air quality action plans.
Statutory nuisances	1990 Act empowers councils to serve 'abatement notices' on those responsible for statutory nuisances prejudicial to health. In addition to vermin and noise pollution generated by premises, vehicles, machinery, or equipment in street (e.g. by roadworkers), these include smoke, gas, fumes, dust, steam, or effluvia, and accumulations of rubbish.
Public lavatories	Providing sufficient public conveniences to hygienic standard, including accessible toilets, baby-changing facilities, etc.

'unfit for human consumption'. The Act also introduced new, all-encompassing council environmental services departments, specifying that environmental health officers had the responsibility for:

- inspecting and seizing suspicious food;
- issuing improvement notices to owners of food businesses;
- serving emergency prohibition notices to close down businesses in the case of perceived serious health risks;
- liaising with the National Health Service (NHS) whenever they feel it necessary to take action in relation to potentially communicable disease risks;
- issuing additional enforcement notices dictated by central government in instances of sudden crisis—for example, the ban on the sale of beef on the bone as a consequence of the bovine spongiform encephalopathy (BSE—or 'mad cow disease') crisis in the late 1980s and early 1990s.

The aforementioned 'outbreak' of BSE presented one of the biggest instances in recent memory of environmental health issues affecting the wider public health arena. The alarm generated by the first diagnoses of BSE in cattle in November 1986, and subsequent identification of symptoms of Creutzfeldt–Jakob disease (CJD) in several Britons, became of international concern—leading to a ten-year ban on the export of UK beef on the bone to EU countries, from 1996 to 2006.

Other examples of recent environmental health scares have included a succession of outbreaks of foot-and-mouth disease in British livestock. The major one occurred in 2001, leading to a mass cull of sheep and cattle—including tens of thousands of healthy animals—in what was widely portrayed in the media as a panicky, unnecessarily costly government reaction. Two localized outbreaks occurred in 2007, attracting more measured responses. Under the law, where a landowner suspects an outbreak of a communicable (infectious or contagious) disease among his/her animals, he/she must inform the police, council, and Defra. Once an outbreak has been confirmed, the movement of animals 'from the land' or 'within and beyond the local area' is prohibited, other than through a licence granted by an inspector.

More usually, environmental health officers are called in to individual business premises to remove samples of food for laboratory analysis on receiving public complaints about food poisoning, unpleasant tastes or odours, or outdated food labels. Among the more commonplace—if potentially dangerous— food safety issues arising is the identification of bacteria such as *E. coli* or salmonella. In one of the most notorious examples of overreaction by government to the latter, in 1988 Junior Health Minister Edwina Currie provoked widespread alarm (and her own resignation) by erroneously telling reporters:

&& Most of the egg production in this country, sadly, is now affected with salmonella. 🢒🢒

Food safety authorities also oversee the regulation of slaughterhouses in accordance with EU rules and inspect the quality of meat bought from them. They are also authorized to provide their own public slaughterhouses, cold stores, and refrigerators.

Environmental health officers are not the only officials involved in policing outbreaks of diseases like foot-and-mouth, *E. coli*, and salmonella: trading standards officers (employed by unitary authorities and county councils) and other Defra-approved contractors also have duties in such instances, albeit primarily in relation to animal welfare. Trading standards departments (the wider role of which is discussed in the next section) inspect livestock for signs of illness or poor treatment, and help enforce UK and EU legislation relating to safe and humane animal transportation. Meanwhile, a 2007 EU directive introduced a requirement for formal 'competence assessments' to be carried out by agencies appointed by Defra on anyone intending to transport livestock, horses, or poultry over distances of more than 65 km.

The future of public health at local level

Amid the wholesale franchising out of most local services advocated by the Coalition, it came as a surprise when ministers announced plans to give councils *additional* powers in relation to one area of policy: public health. The initiative—which revives the tradition that existed prior to the NHS of councils being held responsible for promoting healthy lifestyles and combating threats to public health—was formalized with the publication of a new national Public Health Outcomes Framework in January 2012. Under the new rules councils will be held responsible for everything from encouraging local people to lose weight and give up smoking, promoting breastfeeding, and cutting tooth decay in children, to reducing rates of heart disease, strokes, cancer, and serious falls among over-65-year-olds. From April 2013 funding for local initiatives to achieve these ends will be drawn from a new **public health grant** (see p. 362)—one of only two ring-fenced payments by central government into their revenue budgets to survive the Coalition's reforms of council finance—initially worth £5.2 billion a year.

❚ Trading standards and the new licensing laws

While environmental health officers are responsible for verifying the *safety* of food sold to the public, wider consumer protection issues relating to its sale and presentation fall to **trading standards officers** to police. Under the Food Safety Act 1990 there are two main criminal offences relating to trading standards:

- selling food 'not of the nature or substance or quality demanded by the purchaser';
- 'falsely describing or presenting food'—usually without advertisement or labelling.

In addition to these food-related responsibilities, trading standards officers are responsible for ensuring businesses comply with government policy in several other areas.

General consumer protection

Consumer protection involves monitoring the accurate description of goods, use of credit, and product safety for items such as household tools, appliances, and children's toys. Trading standards departments are also responsible for ensuring trade is carried out 'fairly' in their areas, under terms set out by the Office of Fair Trading (OFT) (see pp. 209–11). So time-consuming and costly can this work be that some authorities have even established dedicated consumer advice departments to pool resources with their local Citizens Advice Bureaux (CABs) and the Consumers Association.

The Fair Trading Act 1973 introduced a Director General of Fair Trading, with the authority to ask anyone in the course of business 'acting in a way detrimental to the interests of consumers' to give assurances as to his/her future conduct. If he/she fails to do so, the Director General can take individuals to county courts or the Restrictive Practices Court, which has the power to accept an assurance that he/she will not repeat the offence—or make an order. Civil claims under the Sale of Goods Act 1979 must be brought by individuals through county courts.

Weights and measures

Each authority must appoint a 'chief inspector of weights and measures' to ensure all traders in its area comply with authorized weights and measures (the 'metric system' of metres and litres used throughout the EU, rather than the previous 'imperial system' of yards and ounces).

The history of Britain's reluctant conversion to metric standards is almost as long and tangled as its relationship with the EU itself. It began in earnest with the passage of the Weights and Measures Act 1963, which formally redefined yards and pounds in terms of metres and kilograms, and abolished archaic imperial measurements such as 'scruples', 'rods', and 'minims'. In 1965, under pressure from industry, the then President of the Board of Trade committed Britain to adopting the metric system fully within a decade, and by 1968 a Metrication Board had been established to promote it. The pledge was reaffirmed on its entry into the European Economic Community (EEC) in 1973.

Despite several concrete moves, such as the decimalization of the UK's currency in 1971, subsequent governments further delayed full implementation of metrication and it was only with the advent of two EU directives—in 1995 and 2000 respectively—that Britain was finally ordered to introduce the metric system across the board, first for packaged and then bulk-sold goods (for example, fresh fruit and vegetables sold on market stalls).

This diktat did not stop some traditionalists resisting. The first few years after the introduction of metrication in fruit and vegetable markets was marked by high-profile court cases that captured the imagination of the popular press—with so-called 'metric martyrs' continuing to label their goods in pounds and ounces in defiance of EU law. In September 2007 the enduring public defiance finally scored a pyrrhic victory when the EU Commissioner responsible for the single market, Gunther Verheugen, announced they would be permitted to continue labelling their items in imperial measures after all—provided they also did so in metric measurements. The EU subsequently relaxed its stance even more, allowing most traders to continue using only imperial measures, but some councils still insisted on prosecuting those who did so. A victory of sorts for the metric martyrs finally came when, in October 2008, the then Department for Innovation, Universities, and Skills (DIUS) issued new guidelines urging councils to take only 'proportionate' action against refuseniks in future.

In addition to checking that goods are itemized in metric measures, inspectors regularly vet market stalls and shops to ensure food is not sold in 'short weight'—that is, that scales are being used correctly and that consumers are being sold the correct quantities of goods. Short weight is a criminal offence. Weights of manufactured goods are checked at factories, while those of loose food, fuel, and beer are checked at the point of sale.

Sunday trading

The Deregulation and Contracting Out Act 1994 marked the first major liberalization of Britain's retail laws, which up to that point had been among the strictest in Europe—with most shops commonly opening only between 9.30 a.m. and 5.30 p.m., and few allowed to trade on Sundays out of respect for Christian worshippers. The 1994 Act gave individual traders freedom to decide their own opening hours and other employment practices on weekdays and Saturdays. A Bill introduced by the Tories to remove all remaining restrictions—particularly those relating to Sunday opening—initially collapsed on its second reading in the early 1990s, but change was finally introduced in the Sunday Trading Act 1994, which stipulated that:

- 'large shops'—those with internal sales areas of 280 m² or more—could open for up to six hours between 10 a.m. and 6 p.m., but must remain closed on Easter Sunday and Christmas Day (if the latter falls on a Sunday);

- smaller shops could open as and when they chose to;
- certain measures were introduced to protect the rights of shop workers who did not wish to work on a Sunday—especially those who wished to attend church.

Coalition Chancellor George Osborne came in for criticism from church leaders and supporters of the 'Keep Sunday Special' campaign when he used his March 2012 Budget to announce plans for emergency legislation to relax Sunday trading laws for eight weeks from 22 July to enable larger shops across England and Wales to open longer than the traditional six hours during the Olympics and Paralympics.

Trade descriptions

It is a criminal offence under the Trade Descriptions Acts of 1968 and 1972 for 'false descriptions' to be ascribed to goods or 'false indications' given of their sale prices—for example, for labelling not to include VAT as part of the cover price.

Licensing of pubs and clubs, and drinking by-laws

The Licensing Act 2003, which finally came into force in February 2005, ushered in so-called 'twenty-four-hour drinking' by allowing pubs and bars to apply to vary their existing liquor licences so they could open until later than the customary 11.00 p.m. closing time on weekdays and Saturdays and 10.30 p.m. on Sundays. Nightclubs and restaurants were given the option of applying for 'late licences' allowing them to stay open beyond their usual 2 a.m. shutdown. In liberalizing the drinking laws, Labour's stated aim was to tackle Britain's rising epidemic of 'binge-drinking' by ending the frantic 'last orders' culture, which often saw drinkers racing to buy two or more drinks just before closing time to get the most out of the limited time available. The hope was that this more relaxed approach to buying and drinking alcohol would foster a Continental-style 'cafe culture', with a steadier stream of drinkers drifting in and out of bars at different times, and fewer of the sudden explosions of violence and rowdy behaviour traditionally witnessed at 'chucking out' times.

The 2003 Act also introduced significant changes in the way licences were issued and policed. Until 2005 local magistrates' courts were responsible for awarding and varying liquor licences, but the Act transferred this duty to local authorities. Councils would henceforth work together with police to ensure the terms of licences were adhered to, obtaining formal orders from magistrates to revoke them if breached.

The new licensing laws had a mixed reception from licensees, public, and police alike. One of the main complaints made by landlords and nightclub owners in the early days related to the complexity of the revised system. Rather than having to apply simply for a personal licence to serve alcohol between stated hours on stated days, and a single public entertainment licence giving them the freedom to stage occasional events, such as concerts or stand-up comedy, they were now required to apply for both the former and a separate premises licence or temporary event notice for each occasion when they planned to stage any entertainment—whether a live acoustic band or karaoke competition.

Following a high-profile run-in between the Musicians' Union, various other groups representing performers, and the Department of Culture, Media, and Sport (DCMS)—the ministry charged with implementing the reforms—the Act was tweaked to avoid any unintended consequences, such as deterring pubs from putting on shows or plays. In rationalizing this aspect of the law, however, ministers unwittingly made it easier for licensed premises to put on all manner of other performances: lap dancing, for example, was recategorized alongside other forms of more innocuous public entertainment, meaning premises no longer needed to apply for separate 'sexual encounter' licences, as before, to stage it. Perhaps unsurprisingly, there has since been a huge increase in the number of clubs and bars offering shows involving at least partial nudity—with the pressure group Object identifying some 300 in Britain today, compared to a handful in the late 1990s. The Licensing Act has also been criticized by police forces and residents for allegedly turning some town centres into 'no-go areas' for older residents, particularly on Friday and Saturday nights. In its 2008 submission to a government review of the impact of the 2003 Act, the Local Government Association described it as 'a mistake', and its chairman, Sir Simon Milton, told an interviewer from *The Daily Telegraph* it had 'failed miserably'. The policy has also been openly condemned by everyone from the Archbishop of Canterbury, Rowan Williams, to former Labour Health Secretary Frank Dobson. A Freedom of Information Act 2000 request by *The Daily Telegraph* to all forty-three police forces in England and Wales, made just ahead of the publication of the Home Office's official review in February 2008, appeared to support their reservations, by uncovering official statistics confirming twelve forces had seen a 46 per cent rise in the number of antisocial incidents with which they dealt since the Act was enforced—with sixteen reporting an increase of 5 per cent in alcohol-related assaults, harassment, and criminal damage. Nationwide, serious violent offences in the early hours of the morning had risen by a quarter.

In the end, buoyed by reports from a number of individual police forces that pointed towards no significant increase in criminal offences—and, in some cases, suggested crime rates had fallen—the government's review recommended retaining the 'new' licensing regime when it was finally published in March 2008. Ministers did, however, introduce a new 'two-strikes rule' designed to deter off-licences from selling alcohol to underage drinkers.

As for the 'twenty-four-hour' aspect of the legislation, despite the initial expectation that all-night drinking would become a feature of most town centres, statistics obtained from 86 per cent of licensing authorities in November 2007 found that fewer than 500 English and Welsh pubs and clubs had ever been granted twenty-four-hour licences. Most 'late licences' have tended to cover only an additional hour or two of business, and only then at weekends in many cases. Of the 5,100 venues operating twenty-four-hour licences between April 2006 and March 2007, 3,300 were hotels, 910 supermarkets, and 460 pubs and clubs. Nonetheless, concerns about the links between late night drinking and unruly behaviour remain—prompting the Coalition government to announce a 'complete review' of the policy in May 2010. At time of writing, however, this had yet to materialize.

On a related note, councils have long had powers under statute to curb public drinking. In the early 1990s Plymouth and Bristol City Councils were among the first to invoke by-laws forbidding public consumption of alcohol in specified locations within their areas of jurisdiction, and similar measures have since been widely implemented. Additional powers were introduced under the Criminal Justice and Police Act 2001, enabling councils to pass alcohol-free zone orders—or, to use their official title, 'alcohol consumption in designated public places orders'—again related to specified locations. Once a zone is in place, police officers may require individuals spotted drinking there to stop immediately and, where necessary, confiscate their alcohol. In the last resort, those failing to comply may be prosecuted and, if convicted, fined up to £500. Some authorities have gone still further: within weeks of his election as London Mayor, Mr Johnson banned all drinking from London Underground and other public transport throughout the capital.

Shortly after, then Communities Secretary Hazel Blears launched a nationwide crackdown on problem drinking and related antisocial behaviour, in the guise of alcohol disorder zones (ADZs). Ministers gave individual local authorities the power to designate specific areas as needing extra policing to curb drink-related crime and disorder. The cost of the additional patrols would be met by pubs, bars, and other licensees themselves, in the form of a £100-a-head fee. While ADZs have been scrapped by the Coalition, it has taken with one hand and given with the other, by increasing the fines paid by off-licences and other outlets that sell alcohol to children, and giving licensing authorities new powers to set 'late-night levies' of up to £4,440 a year for pubs and clubs whose decisions to stay open into the night result in more costly policing arrangements. Meanwhile, 'early morning restriction orders' (EMROs) introduced by Labour to limit sales of alcohol between 3 a.m. and 6 a.m. have been toughened up to allow councils to impose them from midnight.

Such measures notwithstanding, unlike smoking (banned in all workplaces and enclosed public spaces, including bars and pubs, from 1 July 2007), Labour's attitude towards licensing was arguably more liberal than the Coalition's—which, at time of writing, was still murmuring about the possibility of revisiting the licensing laws more fully at a later date. The liberalism of the Blair government also extended for a time towards another popular British pastime—gambling—which he and then Culture Secretary Tessa Jowell planned to popularize still further by giving the go-ahead to at least one 'super-casino' in a major city and a network of smaller ones in other towns. The government's stated aim was to use the casinos as engines to attract industry, jobs, and private sector investment into deprived areas of the competing cities.

In January 2007 Manchester became the surprise choice of location for the super-casino project—beating off competition from, among others, Blackpool and London's former Millennium Dome. But within a short time of entering Downing Street, Mr Brown lived up to his puritanical image by scrapping the plans.

▌ Leisure and cultural services

Providing for citizens' quality of life arguably means more than managing public transport, clearing up refuse, and maintaining a social environment relatively free of crime and disorder. Among the 'softer services' traditionally offered by local authorities are those falling beneath the broad umbrellas of leisure and/or cultural services. These terms—increasingly fused together by some councils—cover everything from the maintenance of local swimming pools and sports centres to the provision of theatres, museums, and galleries, and the financing of festivals, like the Edinburgh International Festival or England's largest equivalent, the Brighton Festival.

Swimming pools, leisure centres, parks, and playgrounds

Under the Local Government (Miscellaneous Provisions) Act 1972 councils were given discretion—and ability to raise finance through local taxation—to provide 'such recreational facilities as they think fit'. These included:

- sports centres;
- pitches for team games and athletic events;
- swimming pools;
- tennis courts;
- stadiums, and premises for athletic and other sporting clubs;
- golf courses and bowling greens;
- riding schools;
- campsites;
- facilities for gliding, boating, and waterskiing;
- staff (including instructors) for any of the above.

As in most other areas of local service provision, compulsory competitive tendering was introduced under Mrs Thatcher to force councils to compete with private contractors for franchises to run leisure centres. Wearing another 'hat', however, they still have responsibility for ensuring *standards* of service meet statutory requirements, not least in terms of health and safety and disabled access.

Libraries, museums, galleries, and the performing arts

Under the Public Libraries Act 1850, emerging councils were empowered to *provide* libraries, but not actually to stock them with books. This changed under the Public Libraries 1919 Act, which allowed them to 'spend more than a rating limit of one penny in the pound on books'. Today there is no statutory limit and councils are obliged to offer 'a comprehensive and efficient library service' covering everything from books, newspapers, and periodicals, to records, CDs, and DVDs. Public libraries have also been required to offer free Internet access to the public since 2002.

There were fears that libraries might become the latest of a long line of 'added value' local services to fall prey to the Coalition's public spending squeeze when the Department for Culture, Media, and Sport announced plans to shake up local library services in August 2010.

With recent figures showing that only 29 per cent of British people now regularly visited their libraries, and that many local branches were home to dwindling, outdated stocks of books, Culture Minister Ed Vaizey launched a Future Libraries Programme to both generate cost savings and attract more users by reorganizing services in ways better suited to the pressures and routines of modern living. Among the ideas he floated was relocating libraries to premises other than conventional ones, such as shops and pubs. He revealed he had received fifty-one submissions for support from the programme, representing 100-plus councils. Ten—involving thirty-six councils—were being pursued in the initial phase, in counties ranging from Northumberland and Durham in the north-east to Cornwall and Devon in the south-west.

Libraries remain a sensitive topic, with 600-plus libraries having shut across England due to budget cuts by time of writing, including three in Liverpool, four in Warwickshire, and others in Wigan, Portland, and the London Borough of Barnet. While 'Big Society-style' social enterprises had been set up in Leicester and elsewhere, anger about the accelerating pace of library closures had led to the formation of a campaign group calling itself 'Speak Up for Libraries', whose leading lights include the authors Kate Mosse (founder of the Orange Prize for Fiction), Philip Ardagh, and bestselling children's writer Alan Gibbons. In November 2012, meanwhile, the Culture Media and Sport Committee of MPs warned that a number of councils were in danger of defaulting on their statutory duty to maintain a comprehensive service.

Although their statutory requirements to do so are less stringent, councils are 'allowed' to provide museums and galleries, and require neighbouring authorities to contribute towards their upkeep. Museum 'activities' beyond collecting, maintaining, and displaying objects—for example, public events like readings or classes—were until recently coordinated through area museum councils. This role was taken on by new 'hubs' (larger museums) set up by the Museums, Libraries, and Archives Council (MLA) and now assumed by Arts Council England (ACE) following the MLA's recent abolition. The Local Government Act 1972 also gave councils powers to establish theatres, concert halls, and other entertainment venues, maintain bands or orchestras, and foster arts and crafts.

Use of the broad-brush term 'cultural services' to encapsulate these many and varied 'quality of life' provisions has been increasingly criticized—not least by those directly employed by the organizations concerned. Whenever ministers offer councils a less-than-generous financial settlement—as at the present time—'non-essential' services like libraries, museums, and theatres are usually the first to suffer, as authorities move to protect 'core' areas like education and social services. The museums sector has increasingly suffered, as long-serving curators have retired without being replaced, while councils have sought to make economies by introducing job-shares and substituting specialist curators with generalist managers.

Hard-pressed councils have often also been 'forced' to withdraw funding from theatres and other venues. In 1990 Derby Playhouse faced closure after its annual £130,000 revenue grant from Derbyshire County Council was withdrawn overnight, following the authority's decision to scrap its entire arts budget. Although thrown a lifeline by ACE, the playhouse again narrowly avoided permanent closure in 2007, after Derby City Council withdrew a £40,000 grant, criticizing the theatre's poor management and what it described as 'unsustainable' losses.

In addition to their overarching role in promoting cultural venues and events for local benefit, councils play a part in encouraging tourism and monitoring its effects on their local economies. Towards the end of Labour's tenure, DCMS began formulating a new nationwide 'Tourism Prospectus' intended to define the future role of councils in promoting tourism alongside regional tourist boards, RDAs, and the national quango Visit Britain (formed by merging the British Tourist Authority and English Tourism Council in April 2003).

☰ Topical feature idea

Figure 19.1 is an edited item from the minutes of a meeting of Cambridgeshire County Council's Enterprise, Growth, and Community Infrastructure Overview and Scrutiny Committee, centring on concerns about the waste output of a proposed new PFI-funded biological treatment plant. With an hour until your deadline, your news editor on the *Cambridgeshire Evening News* has told you to develop this into a 'dispute' between the council, the company involved, and other interested parties. What principal angle(s) would you pursue, who would you contact, and what would you ask them?

Figure 19.1 Minutes of a Cambridgeshire County Council Enterprise, Growth, and Community Infrastructure Overview and Scrutiny Committee on 30 March 2012

WASTE PFI (WIC) CONTRACT

The Committee considered a report on an outline of the Private Finance Initiative (PFI) Contract and the implications of the delay in the commissioning of the Mechanical Biological Treatment (MBT) plant.

Councillor Shuter thanked Amey Cespa for kindly hosting the meeting and arranging a tour for Members prior to the meeting. He stressed the very positive view the County Council took, in regarding waste as an asset. The Council was three years through a 28 year contract with Amey Cespa. Whilst the infrastructure was in place, the MBT plant had not yet been fully commissioned, but Amey Cespa were working very hard to ensure that this was completed as soon as possible. It was noted that the plant was very flexible, and would help Cambridgeshire continue as one of the top recycling authorities in the country.

Members:

- commented favourably on the plant and were keen to see it fully commissioned;
- observed that costs were index linked to RPI, with no opportunity for the County Council to gain from any efficiency savings that Amey Cespa makes i.e. a 'pain/gain' arrangement.

Members were advised that one of the main benefits would be a reduction in fines relating to the Landfill Allowance Trading Scheme (LATS), and the annual Landfill Tax escalator of £8 per tonne annually, and more widely, benefit the environment.

Members asked a number of questions about the Compost Like Output (CLO):

- Expressed concern that markets had still not been found for the CLO, and asked the Cabinet Member how confident he was this could be found. The Cabinet Member

responded that this was all anticipated in the Integrated Planning process, and plans had been made on the basis of best assumptions in a changing world market.

- Asked if the intention was to export the CLO. It was confirmed that the objective was to get the best market for CLO— currently prices were very depressed, and there was a significant amount of CLO being exported from the UK. Amey Cespa advised that preference was given to local markets wherever possible.
- Asked if it would be more effective to burn the CLO, i.e. as Energy from Waste (EfW)? The Cabinet Member advised that EfW and Bioenergy options were being considered, and options and opportunities would be reviewed once the plant was fully commissioned. He advised that the RECAP Board had been visiting other authorities to look at the facilities and partnership arrangements they have. Sarah Clover advised that ultimately, the overall objective was minimising what goes into landfill, and that the flexibility of the plant meant that more could be recycled.
- Asked about the volumes of waste in and outputs out of the plant. It was agreed that this information would be circulated separately, as would the Amey Cespa Options report.
- Observed that PFI contracts were often 'sold on'. The Cabinet Member advised that the County Council was working very well with Amey Cespa on the PFI project and there was no intention of terminating the PFI contract. Sarah Clover advised that Amey Cespa was part of a larger group with considerable experience in the waste industry, including 48 waste treatment plants in Spain. In response to a question on Amey Cespa's construction partner BAM

Nutall, she advised that BAM Nutall had delivered on time and on budget, but the contract had been revised so that Amey Cespa could deal with issues in its own way. Observing that the plant was not unique, and that there were similar plants in other parts of Europe, Members asked why the commissioning was taking so long—had similar problems not been experienced with other plants? The specific issues that had led to the problems with the commissioning of the plant were outlined.

The Committee discussed the Council's ability to meet landfill targets, observing that the problem with collection of sufficient suitable recycling materials. The Cabinet Member advised that the RECAP Board, a partnership between both Waste Collection and Disposal Authorities in Cambridgeshire, was working very positively to increase the volume of recyclables and reduce the amount of residual waste going to landfill. It was noted that it was this residual waste which was dealt with at the MBT plant.

Noted the issues around the biodegradability of the materials, and how this would help the Council's targets.

A Member commented that she had been reassured by both the visit and the responses by the Cabinet Member and officers. She observed that the current high recycling rates (54 per cent) would be difficult to increase further, and there were some tough challenges ahead. She asked what the tipping point was: currently, due to the delay in commissioning, the County Council had benefited from a £1.5M windfall gain, but at what point does that relationship reverse, and should the Council be making provision in the Integrated Plan to recognise this risk? It was confirmed that risk/contingency had been built into the Integrated Planning Process. The role of managing risk was undertaken by the County Council through the PFI Board, the RECAP Board (working with the Districts), and regular meetings with Amey Cespa. The critical point was that if the amount going to landfill was reduced, the Landfill Tax liability was reduced. The County Council was working with the Districts through the RECAP Board to get a better quality of input.

Members suggested that incineration could be considered, particularly for CLO, and asked if a LGSS model was being considered for the RECAP partnership? In relation to the latter, the Cabinet Member advised ultimately a LGSS model was an objective, but currently the Districts were at different stages of development. However, it was clear from the RECAP visits to other authorities around the country that authorities in Cambridgeshire were ahead of the game.

✳ Current issues

- **Increased enforcement powers for Environment Agency and Natural England:** the statutory bodies charged with protecting the natural environment from unsympathetic development and pollution were awarded enhanced powers in 2010, including the ability to impose spot fines on businesses breaching environmental protection legislation.

- **Carrot rather than stick approach to recycling:** Labour proposals to introduce 'pay-as-you-throw' policies to encourage households and businesses to recycle more have been abandoned by the Coalition. Instead, Communities Secretary Eric Pickles aims to emphasize the incentives—taking his cue from Conservative-run Windsor and Maidenhead Council, which rewards households who increase their recycling with vouchers for use in local shops.

- **Cuts to local transport projects:** an early casualty of the Coalition's cuts was a tranche of local and regional transport projects that had been approved (and, in some cases, part-funded) by Labour. These have so far included plans to improve the Midland Metro tram system, linking South Yorkshire to Bristol and Tyne and Wear, and the Mersey Gateway Bridge Scheme, which was to have included a toll bridge between Widnes and Runcorn.

? Review questions

1. Which are the main highways authorities and how are their responsibilities divided up?

2. What are the main weapons available to local authorities and central government to tackle traffic congestion? Give some recent policy examples.

3. Explain the distinction between 'waste collection' and 'waste disposal'. What policies are being used to promote greener waste management in Britain?

4. What are the main duties of environmental health officers? How are their responsibilities in relation to food distinct from those of trading standards officers?

5. Outline the range of leisure and cultural services provided by local authorities.

→ Further reading

Docherty, I. and Shaw, J. (2003) *A New Deal for Transport: The UK's Struggle with the Sustainable Transport Agenda*, London: Wiley-Blackwell. **Critical overview of Blair government's sustainable transport policy, evaluating impacts against professed aspirations, by experts on transport and highways**.

Gumpert, B. and Kirk, J. (2001) *Trading Standards: Law and Practice*, Bristol: Jordans. **Comprehensive overview of statutory trading standards regulations, and how they work in theory and practice. Aimed at professionals, companies, and public**.

Lane, K. (2006) *National Bus Company: The Road to Privatisation*, Shepperton: Ian Allen. **Affectionate account of last years of National Bus Company monopoly, and revolution in public passenger transport ushered in by Thatcher government's privatization and deregulation reforms**.

Lang, C., Reeve, J., and Woolard, V. (eds) (2006) *The Responsive Museum: Working with Audiences in the Twenty-First Century*, Aldershot: Ashgate. **Thoughtful examination of present-day challenges facing public museums in light of diminishing support from state and local government, and increasing competition from other attractions and leisure pursuits**.

Morgan, S. (2005) *Waste, Recycling, and Reuse*, London: Evans Brothers. **Practical evaluation of West's mounting waste management problem, with suggested solutions, focusing on 'three Rs'—reducing, reusing, and recycling**.

Waters, I. and Duffield, B. (1994) *Entertainment, Arts, and Cultural Services*, London: Financial Times/Prentice Hall. **Informative look at changes in provision and funding of arts, entertainment, and other aspects of cultural services during 1990s, emphasizing the tensions between different parts of sector.**

 ## Online Resource Centre

www.oxfordtextbooks.co.uk/orc/Morrison3e/
Visit the Online Resource Centre that accompanies this book for web links and regular updates.

20

Freedom of information

The bulk of this book has been concerned with explaining *how* Britain is governed—both politically and through the nuts and bolts of public administration. We began by examining the UK constitution and the place within it of core institutions: Parliament, government, and monarchy. We went on to explore the concept of devolution, the place of individual spending departments, executive agencies, and quangos, and the role local authorities play in delivering day-to-day services to citizens.

This final chapter focuses not on who wields power, what that power amounts to, and how it is exercised, but on the means by which journalists (and taxpayers) can find out more about the decisions taken on their behalf and hold those responsible to account. Where can citizens go to obtain information about the precise composition and remit of the (often unelected) bodies that hold sway over their lives? What rights, if any, do they have to question or challenge them, and how can they exercise those rights?

▌ The origins of the Freedom of Information Act 2000—what is 'FoI'?

The concept of 'freedom of information' (FoI) rests on the notion that, in a democracy, citizens should be entitled to know as much as possible about the actions and decisions of the politicians elected to represent them and the officials appointed to implement their policies. More important still, to many, is the principle that participating citizens should be able to find out how public money—largely derived from the taxes they pay—is spent on their behalf.

Freedom of information was a long time coming in Britain. At least seventy other states had enshrined their citizens' rights to access details about how their money was being spent by the 'powers that be' long before the Freedom of Information Act 2000 (in Scotland, the Freedom of Information (Scotland) Act 2002) received royal assent. It was not until Tony Blair's election in 1997 that a British government committed to implementing such reforms. Even then it was several years into New Labour's first term before the party put its manifesto pledge into action—and in watered-down form at that. And not until 1 January 2005, towards the end of its second, did the full force of the new law come into effect, under the then Department of Constitutional Affairs (now Ministry of Justice).

The FoI concept has long been cherished in the USA, which has a nationwide Freedom of Information Act based on the principle of democratic accountability and numerous state-specific laws governing access to public documentation and the records of tax-levying entities. These Acts are collectively known as 'sunshine laws'. Elsewhere in Europe, where FoI legislation is commonplace, Acts are generally known as 'open records'. The European Union (EU) as a whole, meanwhile, is governed by Regulation 1049/2001, passed by the European Parliament (EP) and Council of Ministers on 30 May 2001. This sets out a detailed system of rules regarding public access to the main EU institutions.

Lest blinkered constitutional historians try to convince us Britain is the seat of democracy, it is worth noting that the earliest known 'open record' was passed in Sweden back in the late eighteenth century. And while some might scoff at the idea of openness and accountability operating under dictatorships it is intriguing to note that since 1 January 2008 even China has had an FoI law in place (at least notionally): the Regulations of the People's Republic of China on Open Government Information.

Given the huge number of FoI laws in force globally, perhaps unsurprisingly there is little conformity in their exact wording or provisions. Most share general traits, however—notably the principle that the 'burden of proof' falls on institutions from which information is being sought, rather than individuals seeking it. In other words, people making requests are not normally required to explain why they are asking for the information, whereas organizations questioned must give valid reasons for failing to supply the details requested. So what constitutes 'valid' in Britain?

Information the Act covers—and exempts

The UK's FoI legislation applies to more than 100,000 'public authorities', ranging from individual schools and hospitals to councils, quangos, and entire government departments. If a legitimate request is made under either Act the authority asked must first tell the questioner whether it holds the relevant information and, assuming it does, supply it *within twenty working days*.

The authority may, however, *refuse* to confirm or deny the existence of information—and/or to provide it—if any of the following conditions apply:

- the information is 'exempt';
- the request is 'vexatious' or similar to a previous request;
- the cost of compliance exceeds an 'appropriate limit'.

The term 'exemption' might invite the idea that any authority possessing information has free rein to refuse to disclose it, but according to the Acts even exempt material should sometimes be made available.

There are two broad classes of exemption: 'absolute' and 'qualified'. While the former may not be disclosed under any circumstances, the latter may be if the 'public interest' in disclosing it outweighs that in keeping it secret. For example, a public authority involved in security policy might legitimately refuse to disclose exempt information that could compromise public safety by jeopardizing counter-terrorism operations, but it would be hard pressed to do so if the information it was withholding were likely to *improve* safety—by, for example, revealing the expected time and location of an impending attack.

In addition to absolute and qualified exemptions, several entire categories of information are exempt. Authorities may also refuse requests they consider 'likely to prejudice' law enforcement or the UK's interests abroad. The three categories of exemption are listed in Table 20.1.

Even when none of the above exemptions applies, journalists should proceed with caution before reproducing certain kinds of 'information' wholesale in the media. Under the Re-use of Public Information Regulations, introduced in July 2005, some details disclosed by public authorities under FoI remain subject to their legal copyright. This means that, while the requester is entitled to answers, he/she does not necessarily have an 'automatic right' to reuse the information, other than for the purposes for which it was originally produced by the authority concerned. Although theoretically these regulations could be used by disingenuous authorities to delay or prevent media disclosure of perfectly 'free' information, in practice they tend to be invoked to protect the intellectual property rights of third parties whose work is included in the disclosed material: for example, freelance photographers, architects, or designers.

These, then, are the exempt categories of information, but what of the Acts' definitions of 'public authority'? Are any organizations or individuals that might be considered to fall under this umbrella exempted from FoI requests per se?

In short, yes.

The Queen and Royal Household

The Royal Family's website defines the status of the Queen and Royal Household thus:

> ❝The Royal Household is not a public authority within the meaning of the FOI Acts, and is therefore exempt from their provisions.❞

Table 20.1 Exemptions under the Freedom of Information Act 2000

Absolute	Qualified	Categories
Information supplied by, or relating to, bodies dealing with security matters	Intended for future publication	Information relating to investigations and proceedings conducted by public authorities
Court records and information related to impending prosecution	Related to national security (other than information supplied by/relating to named security organizations)	Court records
Information that would infringe parliamentary privilege	Which might limit defence of British Isles, or 'capability, effectiveness, or security' of Armed Forces	Formulation of government policy
Personal information *either*: 1. relating to person making request, which could be obtained under Data Protection Act 1998; 2. about another individual, if it would breach data protection principles	Potentially prejudicial to international relations between UK and another state, international organization, or court, or UK's interests abroad	
Information held by Commons or Lords that may be prejudicial to effective conduct of public affairs	Information that might prejudice relations between administrations within UK	
Information provided in confidence	Information likely to prejudice UK's financial and/or economic interests	
Prohibitions on disclosure where disclosure is prohibited by enactment or would constitute contempt of court	Information relating to investigations and proceedings conducted by public authorities	
	Information likely to prejudice law enforcement—defined as prevention or detection of crime, prosecution of offenders, assessment of taxes, etc.	
	Information relating to public authority with audit functions in relation to another public body (e.g. Audit Commission)	
	Information relating to formulation of government policy, communications between ministers, or operations of ministerial office	

(continued)

Table 20.1 (*continued*)

Absolute	Qualified	Categories
	Information held by public authorities other than Commons or Lords that may be prejudicial to effective conduct of public affairs	
	Information relating to communications between Queen, ministers, and/or other public bodies, including those relating to honours system	
	Information likely to endanger health and/or safety of individuals	
	Environmental information authority is obliged to make public under s. 74 of the Act	
	Personal information believed by institution not to breach data protection principles, but in relation to which individual who is subject of request serves notice that disclosure would cause 'unwarranted substantial damage or distress'	
	Subject to legal professional privilege	
	'Trade secrets' or information liable to prejudice individual's/authority's commercial interests	

It goes on to cite the 'fundamental constitutional principle' that communications between the reigning sovereign and ministers or other public bodies remain confidential—not least to ensure royals do not compromise their 'political neutrality'. As the site stresses, however, the fact the Royal Household is not bound by the FoI Acts does *not* mean it is unwilling to make certain information available voluntarily.

To this end it is happy to 'account openly for all its use of public money'. It does this by posting online every July a consolidated report, including a full annual account and breakdown of the Civil List and grants-in-aid (now the sovereign grant). In addition, the Prince of Wales voluntarily publishes details of his income from the Duchy of Cornwall estate—both before and after tax—on his own website.

→
see also
central
government,
pp. 22–4

What the sites fail to emphasize is the fact that no information about the Royal Household's funding was made public until 2001, when it was persuaded to agree to greater openness as part of its negotiation with HM Treasury over a new ten-year funding settlement. Perhaps even more remarkable is the amount of detail about its dealings the Royal Family still will *not* disclose. For example, nowhere will British taxpayers find details of the size of the Privy Purse (see p. 25)—that mysterious treasure trove, derived from the Duchy of Lancaster estate and reserved for the personal expenditure of the reigning monarch. Nor will they be able to access details about other aspects of the royals' personal finances, such as incomes derived by several members of the family from service in the Armed Forces, the Duchess of York's royalties for her series of *Budgie the Little Helicopter* children's books and numerous television talk show appearances, or the dividends and profits derived from family members' investments. Soon after the 2010 election, the Coalition pledged to give the National Audit Office greater access to the Queen's accounts, but this has yet to yield any major revelations.

The list of specific FoI exemptions for the Queen and the Royal Household are detailed in Table 20.2. The special treatment the Queen and her immediate family enjoy in relation to FoI requests became the subject of a public dispute in January 2012 between the Scottish Government and Scotland's then newly installed information commissioner, Rosemary Agnew. In an interview with *Scotland on Sunday* she criticized Alex Salmond's proposal to turn the 'qualified' exemption covering royal communications north of the border into an 'absolute' one—bringing the rules into line with those applicable elsewhere in Britain.

Despite this array of exemptions, which place the Royal Family in a significantly more privileged position than any other, recent annual disclosures of their public accounts have shed light on the huge lengths to which members appear to go to defend FoI applications. According to the Royal Household's 2006/7 accounts, it spent £180,000 of taxpayers' money in that one year shielding itself from FoI requests. Buckingham Palace explained at the time the sum was spent 'reminding' government departments of the exemption to prevent them releasing details of communications with the household.

In addition, it is normally possible for resourceful journalists to find ways of circumventing the royals' exemption. In June 2008 an FoI request to the Ministry of Defence unearthed the cost of Prince William's controversial flight in an RAF Chinook helicopter to an exclusive stag party on the Isle of Wight. The trip—one of five 'familiarization exercises' undertaken by the prince, which saw him stop off en route to pick up his brother, Prince Harry, in London—set taxpayers back £8,716. Embarrassing disclosures teased out of communications with the Royal Household only covered by qualified exemption have included the revelation that in 2004 the Queen asked ministers

Table 20.2 Specific FoI exemptions relating to the Royal Household

Exemption	Details
Financial and other personal matters	Information relating to personal affairs of sovereign and Royal Family members—including private finances and activities in personal capacity—exempt under s. 40 of FoI Act and s. 38 of Scottish FoI Act (Data Protection Act provisions).
Royal communications	'Absolute' exemption for letters, emails, and other correspondences sent by/on behalf of or to Queen, heir to throne, or second in line of succession introduced under Constitutional Reform and Governance Act 2010 in most of UK, with same exemption expected to be introduced in Scotland under forthcoming Freedom of Information (Amendment) Bill. 'Qualified' exemptions apply to communications with other Royal Household/Family members under s. 37 of FoI Act 2000. Latter may only be disclosed if 'balance of public interest' test deems it necessary to release information. All exemptions apply for whichever is longer of twenty years or five years after death of family member concerned.
Correspondences with family members now deceased	Personal information on recently deceased family members relating to communications with Queen, other members of Royal Family, or Royal Household. If contained in records less than thirty years old this may be exempt under s. 37 of UK FoI Act (s. 41 of Scottish FoI Act).
Other information relating to deceased royals	Information relating to recently deceased family members, disclosure of which would damage 'right to family life' of deceased's relatives, may be exempt under s. 44 of UK FoI Act and s. 26 of Scottish FoI Act and Art. 8—'Private Life and Family'—of Human Rights Act 1998.

for grants worth £60 million to improve the energy efficiency of Buckingham Palace—from a pot of money specifically targeted at low-income households. Among hundreds of other letters obtained by *The Independent* newspaper in September 2010 was one blowing the lid on a row between the Queen and ministers over who should profit from the sale of land around Kensington Palace.

Utilities, train operating companies, and other passenger transport operators

Controversially, the privatized utilities—water, electricity, gas, telecommunications, and rail operating companies—were excluded from automatic coverage by the FoI Acts when they entered their final draft stages. After being included in the remit of the government's 1997 White Paper, *Your Right to Know*, hopes were high that they would be subject to scrutiny when the Acts were passed. But after intensive lobbying by the companies concerned—many of which argued that being subject to FoI could jeopardize commercially sensitive operations—they were eventually omitted.

The decision to exclude companies involved in supplying British taxpayers with such vital 'natural monopolies' as energy and water was enough to infuriate many, but more baffling still was the fact that even Network Rail—the not-for-dividend company set up by ministers to take over maintenance of the railway infrastructure after the collapse of private firm Railtrack in 2001—was exempted. In a test ruling in January 2007 the Information Commissioner—the individual who hears FoI appeals (see pp. 598–600)—clarified that Network Rail was a 'private company' and therefore not a 'public authority' under the Act's terms. His ruling came in response to an appeal against the company's refusal to answer a request made in May 2005, under the Data Protection Act 1998, regarding information about a flood beside a railway line.

Although utility companies themselves are not subject to FoI, the regulators set up to monitor them—including the Office of Gas and Electricity Markets (Ofgem) and Office of Communications (Ofcom) (see p. 226)—*are*. The fact it is possible for press and public to access significant amounts of information from the utilities *indirectly* in this way has been used as an argument by the Confederation of British Industry (CBI) and other business lobbyists for retaining the 'light-touch' approach to the utilities which currently remains—though this is unlikely to last much longer (see p. 225).

Academies

Until recently one of the most contentious categories of organization exempt from FoI was academies—the new generation of 'independent' secondary schools operating within the state sector (see pp. 444–51). Their exemption—granted because of the involvement of private sponsors in setting them up and/or running their ancillary services—was widely viewed as a double standard, given that it enabled them to avoid having to reveal performance data that all other state schools were expected to publish. Some even suggested the exemption was a convenient way of masking academies' initially sluggish academic performance (when introduced in 2002 they were trumpeted as a way of turning round 'failing' comprehensives by pumping in private capital). Up to January 2011, when the law was amended to bring them within the ambit of the Act by Coalition Education Secretary Michael Gove, Labour's academies were allowed to publicize their exam results in a different way to other schools—omitting details of the subjects in which GCSE A*–C grades had been obtained, thereby making it hard for parents to take informed decisions about whether they were performing better or worse than others.

Some critics of this long-standing exemption also pointed to a clear contradiction between the government's public insistence that, despite being largely privately financed, they remained in the public sector—as opposed to representing the start of a creeping privatization of the state schooling system. In addition to bringing the first wave of academies under the ambit of FoI, in September 2010 Mr Gove extended the Act's remit to cover all those set up under the Coalition.

The Security Service, MI6, and other intelligence agencies

Just as most security-related material is exempt from the provisions of the FoI Acts, there is a blanket exemption for any information relating to the work of the Security Service (MI5), MI6, and other British intelligence agencies. Similar exemptions apply to Special Forces, such as the Special Air Service (SAS) and Special Boat Squadron (SBS).

How to make an FoI request—and how not to

Around 120,000 FoI requests are made each year in Britain—six out of ten by members of the public, one-fifth by businesses, and only around one in ten by journalists. That said, the exhaustive nature of some journalistic enquiries has taken its toll on authorities' time and resources. The overall cost of complying with media-related FoI requests was estimated at £35.5m in 2005 alone.

But how does one make a request? Although the exact procedure varies from one public authority to another, it entails writing to the organization either by email or post, detailing the specific question(s) to which an answer(s) is requested. If there is any ambiguity in the wording of a request the authority is encouraged to enter into dialogue with the requester to clarify the question(s) and supply the information as quickly as possible—provided it is not exempt. Authorities are also expected, where relevant or necessary, to supply additional explanatory material if it is likely to elucidate complex or confusing information and avoid the necessity for prolonged correspondence with the requester. As in other states, the requester must give his/her name and contact details when filing the request, but he/she is not expected to divulge 'reasons' for doing so. In principle, FoI requests are free and it is highly unusual for organizations to charge for answering them.

In addition to the aforementioned exemptions, authorities may refuse to respond to requests for other reasons. If a single request to a government department or body is likely to cost more than £600 in terms of the time and staffing needed to locate the information (£450 in the case of other public authorities), it may be refused. Alternatively, the authority may send the requester a notice that they will be charged a fee up to the cost of gathering and supplying the information. If the requester pays, the material requested must then be provided. There is also provision in law for authorities to decline to respond to 'vexatious' requests. The definition of this term was clarified by the Information Commissioner's Office (ICO) in a guidance note issued in July 2007. It ruled requests 'vexatious' if they imposed a 'significant burden' on the authority in terms of expense or distraction *and* one or more of the following statements applied—that they:

- clearly do not have any serious purpose or value;
- are designed to cause disruption or annoyance;
- have the effect of harassing the public authority;

- can otherwise fairly be characterized as obsessive or manifestly unreasonable.

Examples of 'vexatious' cases have included that of an individual refused information by Birmingham City Council after making more than seventy previous requests. In another case, West Midlands Transport Executive estimated it had spent 175 hours responding to one person's enquiries. Transport for London (TfL), meanwhile, reported it had received so many letters from a single enquirer it had had to devise a new internal management strategy to cope with them. But perhaps the most burdensome FoI addict to date was the individual who sent no fewer than 347 requests to police forces, 412 to the Ministry of Defence, and twenty-two to the Cabinet Office.

Just as authorities may reject vexatious requests, they may also refuse to answer 'repeated' ones—those identical to others to which they have previously responded in full (or refused to respond), particularly if they originate from the same individual or organization.

The Environmental Information Regulations 2004

The FoI Act was not the only new legislation designed to promote greater government openness to take effect in 2005. Under EU law the Environmental Information Regulations (EIR) 2004—in Scotland the Environmental Information (Scotland) Regulations 2004—came in at the same time, giving the British public access to information about the state of their natural environment, particularly in relation to potential hazards like pollution.

Unlike the FoI Acts, EIR requests—also generally made by post or email and subject to a twenty-day maximum response time—do not need to be made in writing, and may be lodged verbally. They also cover various private sector organizations currently outside the remit of general FoI legislation. For example, EIR requests may be made to privatized utilities, such as water and electricity companies, responsible for activities with a direct impact on the environment.

Environmental information covered by the Regulations may relate to:

- the state of the 'elements of the environment'—air, water, soil, land, fauna (including human beings);
- emissions and discharges, noise, energy, radiation, waste, and other such substances;
- measures and activities such as policies, plans, and agreements affecting, or likely to affect, the state of the environment;
- reports, cost–benefit, and economic analyses;
- the state of human health and safety, and contamination of the food chain;
- cultural sites and built structures—to the extent that they may be affected by the state of the elements of the environment.

As with the FoI Acts, there are certain 'absolute' and 'qualified' exemptions to the EIR's provisions, as outlined in Table 20.3.

Unlike FoI requests, enquiries made under the EIR tend to incur charges to requesters, provided these are set at a 'reasonable' level and authorities publish a schedule of all their charges. They may not, however, refuse requests on grounds of cost alone.

FoI versus data protection

The Data Protection Act 1984 (as amended by the Data Protection Act 1998) relates to the notion of protecting individuals' privacy, as its name suggests. On the face of it, this may appear to conflict with the more 'free-for-all' aspects of information disclosure ushered in by the FoI Acts. In practice, however, the two Acts largely complement and build on one another—a fact assured by ministers' decision to give the task of policing both of them to the Information Commissioner in 2005 (see pp. 598–600).

The 1998 Act applies to 'personal data'. This is defined as 'any data which can be used to identify a living person'—including names, addresses, telephone, fax, and mobile phone numbers, email addresses, and birthdays. It applies, however, only to data that is (or is intended to be) held on computer or in another 'relevant filing system'. The Act's scope is fairly broad in this latter context: an individual's paper diary may be considered a 'relevant filing system' if used for commercial purposes. The Act is underpinned by seven 'key principles' relating to the handling of personal data by public authorities, private sector companies, and other organizations as outlined in Table 20.4.

Table 20.3 Exemptions under the Environmental Information Regulations 2004

Absolute	Qualified
Information not held by authority (if so, it has 'duty' to refer request to relevant body)	Release would breach confidentiality of legal proceedings
Request 'manifestly unreasonable'	Might prejudice international relations between Britain and other states or international bodies, public security, or national defence
Request is 'too general' (although the authority should still fulfil duty to advise and assist)	Might jeopardize course of justice and right of citizens to fair trial
Requests for unfinished documents or data (in which case, estimated time for completion must be given)	Commercially confidential information
Requests for internal communications	Certain information related to intellectual property rights
	Related to personal and/or voluntary data
	Related to work of environmental protection

Table 20.4 Conditions relating to use of personal data under the Data Protection Act 1998

Condition	Details
Focus	Data may only be used for specific purposes for which collected.
Privacy	Must not be disclosed to other parties without consent of individual to whom it relates, unless there is legislation or other overriding legitimate reason to share information (e.g. prevention or detection of crime). It is offence for other parties to obtain this data without authorization.
Accessibility	Individuals have right of access to information held about them, subject to certain exceptions (e.g. information held for prevention or detection of crime).
Time-sensitivity	Data may be kept no longer than necessary.
Protection	Data may not be transmitted outside European Economic Area (EEA) unless individual to whom it relates consents or adequate protection in place (e.g. by use of prescribed form of contract). Entities holding personal information required to have adequate security in place—for example technical measures (such as computer firewalls) and organizational ones (e.g. staff training).
Regulation	Almost all entities that process personal information must register with Information Commissioner.

The Act gives anyone whose personal data is processed the right to:

- view any data held by an organization, for a small fee (known as 'subject access');
- request incorrect information be corrected—if the organization ignores his/her plea a court may order the data to be corrected or destroyed, and compensation may be paid;
- require data not be used in a way that causes 'damage or distress';
- require that his/her data is not used for direct marketing.

So how do the two Acts—governing 'data protection' on the one hand and 'freedom of information' on the other—coalesce in practice?

The first point to be made is that many enquiries individuals might think of making under the FoI Acts in relation to information about themselves will be exempt. However, this is only because the correct procedure for accessing such information actually falls under the 1998 Act. That said, if an individual seeks to make a request relating to themselves that will also disclose information about a third party, the correct law to use is indeed likely to be the FoI Act. Confusingly, though, the authority asked to supply this information must consider 'data protection principles' applicable under FoI before deciding whether to release the details.

Because many FoI requests tend to concern what might be termed 'corporate' information—procedural, statistical, and/or constitutional matters—rather than personal data, in practice the number of serious conflicts between the FoI and Data Protection Acts is relatively limited. There have, however, been notable altercations between the media and councils—particularly in relation to the salaries and perks of local authority chief executives and other senior officers. Councils have often tried to hide behind data protection legislation when asked for such details under FoI, arguing that, because officers are not elected representatives, such details constitute information of a personal nature, which should therefore be treated as confidential. The Commissioner has sought to clarify the legal position surrounding this, by distinguishing between information relating to the private lives of public officials (which should be exempt) and that concerning the discharge of their public duties. Sections 34 and 35 of the 1998 Act exempt individuals from data protection if the data requested consists of information the authority handling the request is obliged to make public by law or if a court order or other 'rule of law' has required its disclosure. Either of these can override personal data protections otherwise guaranteed by s. 40 of the FoI Act.

A landmark ruling by the Commissioner in June 2011 raised the prospect of a more 'free-for-all' approach to disclosing information about the salaries of public servants. Defying a Cabinet Office attempt to protect the identities of twenty-four senior civil servants earning more than £150,000 each, he ordered their names be made public—raising the prospect that a strongly resisted request by Communities Secretary Eric Pickles for councils to publish the names and salaries of all officers earning £58,200-plus (see p. 393) might return to haunt them. While the Cabinet Office had tried to avoid releasing the details of certain figures, ministers had already taken significant steps towards 'throwing open the books' in relation to mandarins earning more than the prime minister (£150,000 plus) a year prior to the Commissioner's ruling. In June 2011 the first wave of 'naming and shaming' took place, with disclosure on the http://www.direct.gov. uk web portal that the eleven 'top earners' in the public sector the previous year included John Fingleton, chief executive of the Office of Fair Trading, who took home between £275,000 and £279,999, NHS head David Nicholson, who earned £255,000–£259,999, and Joe Harley, IT director-general and chief information officer at the Department of Work and Pensions (DWP), who pocketed £245,000–£249,999. A month later it was the turn of quango bosses, with news that David Higgins, chief executive of the Olympic Delivery Authority, enjoyed a taxpayer-funded salary nearly twice that of David Cameron's (at £390,000–£394,999).

FoI appeals and the Information Commissioner

Anyone refused information under the FoI Acts has a right to appeal, initially through the authority's own internal review procedures but ultimately to the Information Commissioner's Office (ICO). In addition to its central London headquarters, the ICO has three offices based in the capitals of the devolved regions: Edinburgh, Cardiff, and Belfast.

It is the job of the **Information Commissioner** to ensure the twenty-three exemptions are not abused by authorities seeking to keep secret information they regard as embarrassing but which is not legally exempt. In Scotland complaints are made to the Scottish Information Commissioner. By way of underlining the importance of disclosure, citizens have a further right to appeal over and above even the Commissioners, via the Information Tribunal.

To aid public authorities in complying with the FoI Acts the ICO has published 'Ten Top Tips' for them to follow. These are listed in the table entitled 'The Information Commissioner's Office's "Ten Top Tips" for handling requests', to be found on the Online Resource Centre.

Complaints may be made to the ICO if an authority fails to:

- provide information requested;
- respond to a request within twenty working days (or explain why longer is needed);
- give proper advice and help;
- give information in the form requested;
- properly explain any reasons for refusing the request;
- correctly apply an exemption under the Act.

Complainants must provide the following material:

- covering letter, giving details of complaint;
- details of initial request;
- copy of authority's initial response ('refusal notice');
- copy of complaint they made to authority's internal review or complaints procedure;
- copy of authority's response;
- any other information they think relevant;
- their contact details.

Stories in which the Commissioner has played a prominent role in recent times have, ironically, had more to do with data protection than FoI. In June 2008 he confirmed he would serve formal enforcement notices—the toughest sanction available to him—against both HM Revenue and Customs (HMRC) and the Ministry of Defence over 'deplorable failures' leading to 'serious data breaches'. He was referring to two major data protection fiascos that embarrassed Mr Brown's government. In November 2007 HMRC confessed to losing two unencrypted discs containing personal details of 25 million Child Benefit recipients—every British family with a child under 16. The information—including names, addresses, birthdates, National Insurance (NI) numbers, and bank details—had been en route from HMRC's offices at Waterview Park, Sunderland, to the National Audit Office in London.

Table 20.5 Priority types of information covered by the FoI 'public interest test'

Category	Definition
Matters of public debate	Covers issues in relation to which public debate has been generated and debate cannot properly take place without information disclosure; issue affects wide range of individuals and/or companies; government has put its views on record; and issue may affect legislative process.
Public participation in political debate	Covers situations in which local interest groups need sufficient information to represent those interests, and requests relate to facts behind major policy decision—particularly one of 'unprecedented importance'.
Accountability for public funds	Matters relating to government accountability for sale of public assets, or legal aid spending, need for openness relating to tender processes and prices relating to public spending and services, misappropriation of public funds, accountability of elected officials whose propriety has been called into question, and need for public bodies to obtain value for money in spending receipts from taxpayers.
Public safety	Information relating to air safety, nuclear plant security, and public health, contingency plans in an emergency, and potential damage to the environment.

The second breach, revealed in January 2008, concerned the theft of an MoD laptop containing confidential details of 600,000 service personnel. In reporting the crime in a Commons statement, then Defence Secretary Des Browne revealed that two further thefts of departmental laptops had also occurred since 2005.

There is a welter of guidance on the ICO's website about the rights of public and media to access information under the Acts it administers. One of the most useful for journalists is the 'guidance notice' explaining how public authorities should weigh the 'public interest' of a request against any potential qualified exemptions (see Table 20.5).

▶ Freedom of information and the headlines—some case studies

Perhaps unsurprisingly, reporters working on everything from local weekly free sheets to national dailies have embraced FoI as a source of potential stories—not least because they enable a modicum of what might loosely be termed 'investigative journalism' to be carried out within the increasingly re-strictive parameters of modern newsrooms. Widespread cutbacks—from the offices of regional publishers to those of major national newspapers—have seen the size of many papers' reporting staffs dwindle in recent years. Papers are facing growing competition from the Internet and other forms of new media, and as a result new recruits are expected to 'multitask' as everything from video journalists and photographers to designers, subeditors, and bloggers. At the same time, the ever-tighter economies imposed on newsrooms mean that what conventional reporting is still being done is increasingly being carried out over the telephone and/or email, rather than in the face-to-face, hands-on fashion of days gone by.

The FoI Acts, therefore, offer means by which journalists with suitably forensic minds can target questions at relevant authorities and hold them to account 'on the cheap'. Whereas once they might have had to invest significant amounts of time (and money) in rooting out information organizations were keen to keep out of the public domain, much of this can now be obtained (at least theoretically) by sending a simple email. FoI legislation has also spawned several 'amateur' journalism websites almost entirely dedicated to using it as an investigative tool (notably http://helpmeinvestigate.com, http://www.whatdotheyknow.com, and http://www.opendemocracy.net).

The FoI bonanza did not begin in earnest until January 2005. Within days of the 2000 Act coming into force, the *Observer* ran a story listing a 'who's who' of celebrities and businesspeople who had been wined and dined by then Prime Minister Mr Blair at his country retreat, Chequers, since 2001. The luminaries—whose names it had obtained under the new FoI rules—included entertainer Des O'Connor, former Spice Girl Geri Halliwell, television presenter Esther Rantzen, Lord Lloyd Webber, Olympic champion rower Sir Steve Redgrave, and Tesco chief executive Sir Terry Leahy.

That August BBC2's *Newsnight* used an FoI request to expose the fact that Harold Macmillan's British government sold Israel sufficient quantities of uranium 235 and heavy water to enable it to develop its nuclear weapons programme. In a statement to the International Atomic Energy Agency (IAEA), then Foreign Office Minister Kim Howells denied Britain had been a party to any such sale, but in March 2006 *Newsnight* used a further FoI request to expose sales of plutonium to Israel during Harold Wilson's first term.

Perhaps even more shocking was the disclosure, in December 2005, of a hushed-up report by a Scotland Yard detective, Inspector Tom Hayward, into a brutal torture camp operated by British forces in post-war Germany. *The Guardian* used an FoI request to obtain a copy of the document, which detailed the outcome of interrogations of 372 men and forty-four women at the Bad Nenndorf camp, near Hanover. Among the grisly details included was an account of how two men suspected of being Communists were starved to death, another beaten to a pulp, and numerous others suffered serious injuries or lost toes to frostbite. Four months later the paper published images of emaciated prisoners after winning an appeal against the MoD's refusal to release photographs of the victims contained in the report.

But FoI requests do not always produce such sensational outcomes. In most cases they 'unearth' humdrum information—much of it unexciting and lacking in any obvious news value. Indeed, there is a feeling in some quarters—not least in the offices of the less well-staffed public authorities—that journalists have come to rely on the Acts too heavily. Before the concept of 'freedom of information' passed into British law, reporters were forced to rely on those time-worn qualities—guile, ingenuity, and perseverance—to tease out material organizations wanted to keep under their belts. If they received tip-offs that councillors were fiddling their expenses or public officials taking overseas flights using taxpayers' money, they would often have to confront the relevant authority's press office head on, citing phrases like 'public interest' and 'public domain' to remind them of their obligation to confirm or deny such activities, and where necessary supply details. Reluctant though authorities invariably were to expose themselves to criticism by admitting such abuses, more often than not they grudgingly put their hands up. Today, able to hide behind the cloak of having to 'dig out the information' or 'go through all the files', the same authorities can cheerfully take far longer to make disclosures—using the cover of the statutory twenty-day time limit to craft polished excuses and put off answering questions until any newsworthiness derived from them has dwindled or passed.

Seasoned FoI users—particularly those experienced enough to know the difference between stories requiring the Act and those that can be stood up using more conventional tactics—cite the counterargument that, given the relative ease and effectiveness of the legislation, too few journalists are taking advantage of it. Used in a targeted way it is certainly true that FoI provides an excellent source of off-diary stories (gold dust for news editors).

▌ The future of freedom of information— and moves to extend (or restrict) it

Labour made a big noise about its commitment to FoI during its first term, but by its third it appeared to be regretting laying itself open to quite so much scrutiny. Ministers' discomfort with some of the outcomes of FoI began emerging in May 2007, when Conservative backbencher David Maclean introduced a private member's Bill (PMB) into the House of Commons—the Freedom of Information (Amendment) Bill—which proposed exempting MPs from the 2000 Act (ostensibly to protect details contained in their personal correspondences, including the addresses of private individuals). It also proposed incorporating the cost of the time officials spend 'thinking' about whether (and how) to disclose information within the £600 limit above which requests become chargeable.

The issue came to a head that June after the Bill was provisionally approved by the Commons and passed to the Lords, where it appeared ministers were seeking a sympathetic peer to 'sponsor' it. When no one came forward, and the Bill was roundly condemned by both the Commons Constitutional Affairs Select Committee and Lords Constitution Committee, it finally fell—but not before Leader of the House Jack Straw had issued new guidelines urging public authorities to ensure MPs' personal details were not compromised by releasing correspondences between them and their constituents.

It is not only public authorities that occasionally gripe about the FoI Acts. In May 2007 the Commissioner used his address to the annual Freedom of Information Conference to urge people to act with 'restraint' when making requests. He cited an enquiry about how much the Foreign Office spent on Ferrero Rocher chocolates and another asking about the number of eligible bachelors in the Hampshire Police Force as examples of frivolous, time-wasting queries. Similarly, years after these events, Mr Blair confessed in an interview that introducing FoI was one of his biggest regrets about his premiership.

Beyond measures to *restrict*—or otherwise qualify—the Act's application, its scope is expected to be extended in coming months, through the inclusion of as yet unspecified new 'transparency' guarantees in a mooted 'Freedom' or 'Great Repeal' Bill. Such a measure would supersede an earlier Ministry of Justice (MoJ) consultation paper that mooted rolling out FoI to cover not only bona fide public authorities, but also private companies providing services on behalf of the public sector and those carrying out 'public' functions (including utility companies and independently run care homes with residents funded by social services departments), or private sector providers involved in treating NHS patients or running prisons. The MoJ has also mooted bringing other quangos and organizations within the scope of the FoI, ranging from university admissions service UCAS to the Association of Chief Police Officers. However, it has also been criticized for proposing new blocks to transparency—including the introduction of a small fee (perhaps £10) to deter nuisance requests.

▌ Other sources of information—accessing historic records

For decades there has been a rule (still present under the FoI Acts) preventing British governments having to make public Cabinet papers and other official documents until thirty years after they were written. However, in February 2010 Mr Straw announced this would be changed to twenty. The reform—which fell short of a fifteen-year limit for secrecy proposed by an inquiry headed by *Daily Mail* editor Paul Dacre—is due to be phased in gradually over ten years from 2013, allowing 2 million additional documents to be transferred to the *National Archives* (formerly the Public Records Office) at Kew, west London, at a rate of two years' worth of records per year. There will be some exceptions, though: as under FoI, communications with reigning monarchs and their heirs will be absolutely exempt from disclosure, while documents concerning British government policy and activities in Northern Ireland during 'the Troubles' would remain secret for a full thirty years, as before.

Though by definition they will relate to events that took place up to two decades earlier, records released under the new 'twenty-year rule' are likely to provide a magnet for journalists—if documents made public under the old rules are anything to go by. Previous disclosures have revealed everything from detailed preparations made by Margaret Thatcher's administration in 1981 for the possibility of nuclear war with the Soviet Union, to a private admission by her predecessor, James Callaghan, that his fatal decision to delay an election he might have won in autumn 1978 was inspired by his 'malicious' delight at the thought of confounding the Tories' expectations.

☰ Topical feature idea

Figure 20.1 is an edited story from *The Guardian* based on an FoI request to the Home Office focusing on the plight of supposed 'child' asylum seekers illegally held in detention by British authorities. Imagine you work for a local newspaper covering one of the towns where they were detained. How would you develop this story to paint a fuller picture of the scale of the issues identified, and who would you approach for interview to further 'humanize' the story? How would you track them down?

Figure 20.1 Article from *The Guardian*, 17 February 2012

£2m paid out over child asylum-seekers illegally detained as adults

Diane Taylor

The Guardian

17 February 2012

Web link: http://www.guardian.co.uk/uk/2012/feb/17/home-office-payout-child-asylum-seekers

Legal case involved 40 youngsters who were locked up in adult units under Home Office policy deemed to be unlawful.

The Home Office has paid compensation of more than £1m, plus £1m costs, in a case involving 40 child asylum seekers who were wrongly detained as adults, the Guardian can reveal.

It is thought to be the first case of its kind and the largest immigration detention payout for a single case.

Government officials accepted that the policy was unlawful and changed it as a result of this case. However, data passed to the

Guardian shows that children are still being detained.

The case that resulted in the £2m payout involved girls and boys, including 25 aged 14 to 16, from countries including Afghanistan, Iran, Sri Lanka, Nigeria, Eritrea, Uganda, Somalia and China.

The youngest was a 14-year-old girl from Sri Lanka. Some were survivors of torture in their home countries and some of the girls were survivors of rape and other forms of sexual violence.

Some of the children were locked up for more than a month. One boy was moved around the country and held in seven different adult centres including Dover, Campsfield and Harmondsworth during his 74-day detention. 'I cried myself to sleep every night,' he said. 'Nobody explained what was going on and I never knew what was going to happen to me when I woke up the next morning.'

A 16-year-old Eritrean girl who was detained said: 'I couldn't believe it. I had fled Eritrea to escape prison and thought I'd arrived in a safe country, but now I was being locked up again.'

Some of the 40 had been assessed by social services and declared to be children. They showed officials letters from social services stating that they were looked-after children, but the Home Office still detained them.

Mark Scott, of Bhatt Murphy solicitors, who acted for the 40 children, said: 'These children arrived in the UK as children, without the support of their families. They had committed no crime, yet were detained by the immigration service in conditions the Home Office admitted were unsuitable for them.

'One of the most shocking aspects of the case was that, despite the widespread concerns about what was going on, the Home Office did nothing to change the situation until they were forced to do so by children bringing litigation.'

When the 40 children were detained as adults there was no shortage of guidance about 'age-disputed' children available to the Home Office. The UN Refugee Agency, the Royal College of Paediatricians and the UN committee on the rights of the child all issued guidance on age assessment of asylum seeker children, emphasising that the best interests of the children should be prioritised. In March 2002, HM Inspectorate of Prisons expressed concern about Home Office handling of age-disputed asylum seekers.

Many of the children were placed in Oakington detention centre in Cambridgeshire, which was closed in November 2010 following the expansion of other detention centres.

Refugee Council data shows that 55% of 275 age-disputed cases sent to Oakington between November 2003 and January 2006 were found to be children when assessed by social services.

✳ Current issues

- **Widening the scope of the FoI Acts:** the Coalition agreement specified that the 'scope' of the FoI Acts would be widened to 'provide greater transparency' but failed to go further. Since then all academies have been brought within the ambit of the Act, but it has yet to be extended to privatized utilities.

- **Extension of Information Commissioner's powers to police data protection:** both Coalition parties proposed in their 2010 election manifestos to extend the powers of the Information Commissioner to audit public authorities accused of violating data protection principles to the private sector. Several external organizations, including the European Union Agency for Fundamental Rights, have previously criticized Britain for not doing enough to ensure that individuals' data is properly protected.

- **Relaxation of 'thirty-year rule':** the Coalition is in the process of making good on Labour's pledge to make public hundreds of thousands of government documents earlier than they would previously have been released under the long-standing 'thirty-year rule'. The release of material that is twenty years old is due to be rolled out gradually over ten years from 2013.

? Review questions

1. What are the main stated aims of the Freedom of Information Act 2000 and Freedom of Information (Scotland) Act 2002?

2. Outline the main types of exemption from the FoI Acts, introduced initially and subsequently, and give examples of how these exemptions apply in practice.

3. How and to whom does an individual make a formal complaint about a refusal by a public authority to disclose information under the FoI Acts?

4. How do the FoI Acts relate to the Data Protection Act 1998? Do they complement or contradict each other?

5. Give some examples of news stories to have been unearthed by FoI requests.

→ Further reading

Brooke, H. (2006) *Your Right to Know: A Citizen's Guide to the Freedom of Information Act*, 2nd edn, London: Pluto Press. **Step-by-step guide to making effective FoI requests by journalist who exposed MPs' expenses scandal. Includes introduction by Ian Hislop, editor of *Private Eye*, on his magazine's prolific use of FoI Acts.**

Carey, P. (2009) *Data Protection: A Practical Guide to UK and EU Law*, 3rd edn, Oxford: Oxford University Press. **Handy jargon-busting guide, now in its third edition, offering succinct explanations of UK's data protection laws and related EU rules—including Directive on Privacy and Electronic Communication, which came into force in December 2003 and governs potential for electronic privacy infringement arising from abuse of digital media.**

Macdonald, J., Crail, R., and Jones, C. (eds) (forthcoming) *The Law of Freedom of Information*, 2nd edn, Oxford: Oxford University Press. **Second edition of acclaimed legal handbook, offering forensic breakdown of law and how it applies in practice to UK public authorities.**

Wadham, J., Griffiths, J., and Harris, K. (2007) *Blackstone's Guide to the Freedom of Information Act 2000*, 3rd edn, Oxford: Oxford University Press. **Revised third edition of popular, user-friendly FoI guide, which contains clear pointers to making worthwhile requests, what not to bother requesting under the Acts, and full explanation of various exemptions.**

◉ Online Resource Centre

www.oxfordtextbooks.co.uk/orc/Morrison3e/
Visit the Online Resource Centre that accompanies this book for web links and regular updates.

Glossary

A

academy Labour's successor to Conservatives' **city technology colleges (CTCs)**, these semi-independent state secondary schools (many funded by private capital) are allowed to specialize and deviate from **National Curriculum**. Initially targeted at 'failing' comprehensives, academy status now available to all state schools, including primaries. Up to 10 per cent of pupils may be selected on basis of aptitude in academy's specialism(s).

adoption process by which registered 'children in need' taken into permanent care of family other than their biological one. Adopters become their legal parents, and recent reforms have extended adoption rights to gay and unmarried heterosexual couples, as well as married people. (cf. **fostering**)

Advisory, Conciliation, and Arbitration Service (ACAS) quango charged with mediating between employers and employees in industrial disputes. It is often asked to intervene by one of two parties to prevent industrial action, such as strikes, being taken in first place, but can be called in later to bring opposing sides back to negotiating table in pursuit of peaceful settlement.

agenda outline of timetable for meeting of subcommittee, committee, full council, **cabinet**/executive, or other body.

alternative vote (AV) electoral system used in Australia and proposed by Coalition as potential replacement for first-past-the-post (FPTP) procedure used to elect British MPs. Like FPTP, AV returns only one member per **constituency**, but rather than casting single vote electors place candidates in order of preference. If no candidate wins half or more of votes cast on first count, lowest-placed contender is struck off ballot paper and his/her second-preference votes distributed among remainder. Process repeated until someone finally achieves simple majority. A form of AV is used in Labour leadership elections.

antisocial behaviour order (ASBO) form of punishment issued by police and local authorities for 'antisocial behaviour' that falls short of criminal offence (e.g. shouting and swearing in street). This can be used to impose restrictions on individuals' movements or actions, with breaches leading to prosecution. ASBOs in process of being replaced by **criminal behaviour orders (CBOs)** and **civil crime prevention injunctions (CCPIs)**.

area of outstanding natural beauty (AONB) geographical area designated for special legal protection from development and commercial exploitation because of its natural beauty and/or rare or unique flora and fauna.

assembly member (AM) elected representative in **National Assembly for Wales**. There are sixty AMs—forty representing constituencies, the other four for each of five larger regions.

B

backbencher term referring to majority of members of Parliament in House of Commons, who represent **constituencies** but have no additional job title/responsibilities in government or Opposition, and therefore sit on 'backbenches' (seats behind front row on either side of House).

background paper document or file produced by local government officer for consideration as support for policy proposal to be considered at subcommittee, committee, **cabinet/executive**, or full council meeting.

balance of payments difference in value between imports to and exports from UK in given financial year, including *all* types of payment. This encompasses both 'visible' items (such as cars and refrigerators) and 'invisible' ones (such as legal and financial services), as well as value of financial transfers and debt payments to foreigners. If value of imports exceeds that of exports Britain is in 'balance of payments deficit'; if reverse is true it is in 'balance of payments surplus'. (cf. **balance of trade**)

balance of trade difference in value between imports to and exports from UK in given year, excluding financial transfers and debt repayments to foreigners. If Britain is importing consumer goods and services worth more than those it is exporting, it is in 'balance of trade deficit'; if reverse is true it is in 'balance of trade surplus'.

Bank of England Britain's central bank, based at Threadneedle Street in City of London. Has its own governor and was given independence from government by then Chancellor Gordon Brown within days of Tony Blair's 1997 election victory.

basic allowance standard fee (usually modest) paid to all councillors out of their local authorities' revenue budgets. It can vary from area to area.

Big Society Capital new state-sponsored but independent bank set up by Coalition to invest in projects launched by charities, community groups, and voluntary organizations aimed at addressing 'major social issues' in their areas.

billing authority local authority that sends out **Council Tax** bills to households, collects money, and keeps register of who has/has not paid. This is responsibility of **district councils** or **borough councils** and unitary authorities. (cf. **precepting authority**)

borough council type of local authority with same powers as **district council**, but which has right to call itself 'borough' because of historical connection to Crown.

Boundary Commission for England national **quango** responsible for periodically reviewing sizes and boundaries of English parliamentary **constituencies** to ensure they cover approximately same number of voters.

brownfield site area of land (usually in built-up area) previously used for development, which may still have extant buildings on it. (cf. **greenfield site**)

Budget annual statement of accounts of 'UK plc', beginning with Budget Statement by Chancellor of Exchequer, in which he sets out his tax and spending plans for coming year. This is followed by Finance Act enshrining changes in law.

building permission/building regulations additional consent required by private individuals or developers on top of **planning permission** in relation to work on extant buildings, normally relating to internal structural alterations. To attain *building permission* developers must meet series of *building regulations* relating to health and safety, energy efficiency, etc.

by-law form of **delegated legislation** that may be invoked by local authority to combat specific problem. Many councils have invoked by-laws allowing them to ban drinking of alcohol in streets to improve public order. (cf. **statutory instrument**)

C

Cabinet committee of senior government ministers, which meets at least once a week in Downing Street. (cf. **cabinet**)

cabinet form of executive arrangement introduced under Local Government Act 2000, which mimics Westminster **Cabinet** system. Most members of local cabinets drawn from party with greatest number of seats on council, with each handed specific 'portfolios' or briefs (e.g. housing).

Cabinet committees subsets of **Cabinet**, usually made up of groups of three or more senior ministers whose departmental responsibilities are related. Three types exist: standing (permanent); ad hoc (temporary); ministerial (permanent, but made up not of ministers but senior civil servants from related spending departments).

capital expenditure share of local authority's annual budget spent on building and repairing infrastructure, such as roads, schools, care homes, and libraries. (cf. **revenue expenditure**)

capping process by which central government (particularly under Conservative Party) has sometimes stopped local authorities raising **Council Tax** above certain level. It has also occasionally been used to cap spending in particular areas.

care order umbrella term for type of court order, for which local authority must apply in order to remove a child from his/her parents and into protective care. This can be temporary arrangement (**fostering**) or permanent one (**adoption**).

Care Quality Commission (CQC) regulator established in April 2009 through amalgamation of Healthcare Commission and Commission for Social Care Inspection. It handles complaints about National Health Service treatment and conducts regular inspections of social care services in England and Wales, including residential homes and day care facilities.

Chairman of the Conservative Party title held by official (often an MP) whose responsibility is to mastermind public image of party as a whole and coordinate its national fund-raising operation and membership recruitment.

chief constable most senior officer in local police force, responsible for hiring and firing junior officers and ensuring resources are spread effectively across area the force covers. He/she is held accountable by his/her local **police and crime commissioner**.

chief executive (also known as head of the paid service) most senior officer working for local authority. The chief executive will frequently take role of 'acting **returning officer**' for his/her area at local, general, and European elections.

child protection plan formerly known as 'child protection register', this is list of all recognized 'children in need' in each local authority area, which is shared between various public, private, and voluntary organizations involved in protecting them.

Children's Commissioner for England government regulator appointed under 'Every Child Matters' agenda to ensure all professionals and organizations involved in protecting recognized children in need are discharging their duties effectively.

children's trust all-in-one body, formed in 2008, comprising multidisciplinary teams of professionals involved in care of recognized children in need, including social workers, paediatricians, and child psychologists.

city council honorary title bestowed on certain **district councils**, **borough councils**, unitary authorities, and metropolitan borough councils granted Royal Charter status.

city technology college (CTC) type of semi-independent state secondary school, introduced by John Major's Tory government to specialize in maths, sciences, and information technology (IT), often with hands-on involvement from private sector. (cf. **academy**)

civil crime prevention injunction (CCPI) 'fast-track' **ASBOs** introduced by Coalition for lower-level antisocial behaviour. These can be imposed more quickly (within days or hours of

'offence' being committed) and require lower standard of proof than ASBOs.

clinical commissioning groups (CCGs) new consortia of GPs and other health professionals set up to commission NHS services from trusts and other private and third sector providers, in place of Labour's *primary care trusts* (PCTs).

coalition government form of Westminster government comprising ministers drawn from two or more parties, formed in event that no single party wins a working majority at **general election**. Britain's long-standing first-past-the-post electoral system tends to return majority governments, because of 'winner takes all' outcomes it produces in each **constituency**, but May 2010 poll resulted in Liberal Democrat–Conservative coalition—Britain's first since wartime 'National Government' ended in 1945.

code of conduct system of rules governing behaviour of councillors and officers that, since Local Government Act 2000, has had to be formally adopted by each council. It must set out details of unacceptable conduct and any penalties incurred.

collective responsibility principle that all members of parliamentary party's front bench (especially the government's) should either 'sing from same hymn sheet' publicly, whatever their personal views on some party policies, or be prepared to resign. Late Labour **Leader of the House** Robin Cook resigned in 2003 in protest at UK's impending invasion of Iraq. (cf. **individual ministerial responsibility**)

Commission for Local Administration (also known as the Local Government

Ombudsmen) there are three such independent officials, each covering different region, who investigate complaints from public, businesses, and other organizations about alleged incompetence by local government officials.

Commission of the European Union (also known as the European Commission) European Union's Civil Service, spread over twenty-seven departments known as 'Directorates-General'. Unlike British Civil Service, it *initiates* policy as well as implementing it on behalf of elected politicians. Each Directorate-General headed by commissioner.

committee stage third stage of Bill's passage through Parliament, this gives committee of **backbenchers** chance to scrutinize it line by line and suggest amendments. Type of committee that examines Bills known as **public Bill committee** (formerly 'standing committee') and normally sits in room outside main Commons chamber. Emergency legislation, however, and committee stages of international treaties due to be incorporated into British law are usually heard on floor of Commons itself—so-called 'Committee of Whole House'. (cf. **report stage**)

community care umbrella term for social care provided to elderly and adults with mental health issues in their homes or those of friends or relatives. Examples of help available under community care include 'meals on wheels'.

community school term used for LEA-controlled state secondary schools under 'New Labour'. Some community schools known as 'community colleges' because they provide adult education and evening classes on top of primary role as day schools.

Competition and Markets Authority (CMA) new super-regulator to be formed in April 2014 from merger of the Competition Commission—which vets prospective company mergers and acquisitions—and Office of Fair Trading (OFT), which polices the free and fair day-to-day operation of competitive markets.

comprehensive school colloquial term referring to all types of LEA-run maintained secondary school other than **grammar schools**.

Comprehensive Spending Review (CSR) method used by Treasury to encourage individual spending departments to plan strategically for future by announcing how much money it intends to allocate them on three-yearly basis, rather than annually through **Budget**. Three spending reviews—in 1998, 2007, and 2010—have been dubbed 'comprehensive' because of their more detailed nature.

compulsory purchase order (CPO) enforceable statutory order used by local authorities to force homeowners and businesses to sell up and move out of their properties, so they can be demolished to make way for new development.

concessionary fare schemes types of discount bus fare scheme, often operated by individual councils and passenger transport authorities, to allow qualifying individuals—such as children, pensioners, or students—to travel at reduced rates. Labour launched nationwide concessionary fare scheme in April 2008, allowing all pensioners to travel free on local buses anywhere in UK.

conservation area district of city, town, or village that is characterized by buildings of particular historical and/ or architectural vintage, and offered statutory protection from unsympathetic alteration (particularly to exterior appearance).

Conservative Campaign Headquarters (Conservative Central Office) national headquarters of Conservative Party and building it occupies at Victoria Street, Westminster.

constituency geographical area represented by MP. There are 650 constituencies in present Commons (due to be reduced to 600 in 2015) and all members (including ministers) must stand for re-election when **general election** called.

Consumer Council for Water consumer watchdog focusing on water industry.

consumer price index (CPI) government's preferred measure of **inflation**, this charts movement in value of notional 'basket' of goods regularly bought by typical British household. Unlike **retail price index (RPI)**, does not include mortgage payments and its readings therefore tend to be lower.

contributory benefits umbrella term for more generous social security benefits to which British people are entitled (subject to meeting other criteria) if they have made sufficient **National Insurance** contributions during previous periods in employment. For example, ESA is a contributory benefit related to illness and disability. (cf. **non-contributory benefits**)

council constitution each local authority has been obliged to adopt its own constitution since Local Government Act 2000, outlining its chosen form of executive decision-making arrangements and other procedural matters.

Council of Europe alliance of forty-seven European member states formed in 1949, prior to European Union. It aims to promote common legal and ethical standards in all member states, and its most celebrated achievement is European Convention on Human Rights (ECHR).

Council of Ministers of the European Union (also known as the Council of the European Union) European Union's supreme decision-making body. Composed of senior ministers from each member state—its precise composition varies according to issue being debated. If health policy is on **agenda** each state will send its most senior health minister. Council chaired by leading politician from country holding EU presidency, which rotates on six-monthly basis.

Council Tax form of local taxation currently paid by UK residents. It is charged to households and is predominantly property-based (under banding system from A–H, related to capital values of homes), but with elements of 'head tax'. It was introduced in 1993 to replace unpopular Community Charge (or 'Poll Tax').

councillors politicians elected at four-year intervals to represent local authority wards/electoral or county divisions. Councillors determine policies to be implemented by **officers**.

county council 'upper-tier' local authority in parts of England and Wales that retain a two-tier, rather than unitary, structure. Counties are responsible for service areas including children's and adult social services, schools, highways, and waste disposal.

county road major arterial road—normally an A-road linking one town or city to another—whole length of which falls within boundaries of single county. (cf. **trunk road**)

criminal behaviour order (CBO) one of two orders introduced to replace **antisocial behaviour orders (ASBOs)** by Coalition, these empower police and local authorities to impose 'bans' on antisocial conduct, if necessary forcing miscreants to attend programmes designed to improve their behaviour.

D

debt charge money local authorities must set aside each year in revenue budgets to repay interest on outstanding loans taken out for capital projects.

declaration of interest admission made by councillor on being elected or at beginning of business in full council, committee, subcommittee, or **cabinet** that he/she has outside vested interest in issue due to be discussed/voted on. He/she will be expected to leave meeting for duration of said item.

Dedicated Schools Grant (DSG) ring-fenced grant from central government paid to local authorities on proviso it is spent only on school staffing and maintenance.

delegated legislation (also known as secondary legislation) 'lower-tier law', derived from parent Act, which may be implemented by ministers without need to pass further Bills. There are three main types: **statutory instruments**, **by-laws**, and **Orders in Council**.

devolution constitutional concept of delegating degree of power from central parliament to regional and/or local assemblies. In UK, Scotland, Wales, and Northern Ireland all granted devolution in 1998—with the Scottish gaining most power, including right to vary Income Tax by up to 3p in pound. Devolution is distinct from independence, which is handover of full sovereignty.

direct taxes umbrella term for taxes, such as Income Tax and Corporation Tax, taken directly from individual or company, normally at progressive rate determined by their income levels in given financial year. (cf. **indirect taxes**)

directly elected mayor most senior and powerful local politician in towns and cities that have voted in local **referendum** to adopt one of two new forms of executive arrangement retained from Local Government Act 2000. They run their administrations with aid of **cabinet**. Ken Livingstone, the inaugural mayor of London, was Britain's first elected mayor.

dissolution procedure by which Parliament is formally 'dissolved' following resignation of government and before **general election**.

district council lower-tier local authority in two-tier area, responsible for services including housing, development control, environmental health, and **Council Tax** collection.

E

early intervention grant new specific local authority revenue grant introduced by the Coalition, at the behest of the Liberal Democrats, to fund initiatives designed to improve life chances of children from disadvantaged backgrounds. Though unfenced, it is meant to fund a variety of schemes, including the continuation of **Sure Start**.

elected hereditary peerage peerages passed from one generation to next. Until 1999 every hereditary peer was entitled by birthright to sit in House of Lords, but all except ninety-two (ninety of whom have since been elected to remain by colleagues) had this privilege removed in House of Lords Act 1999. Abolition of remaining hereditary peers is proposed in Coalition's House of Lords Reform Bill 2012. (cf. **life peerage**)

election deposit £500 deposit paid by each candidate who stands in **general election**. The payment is lost if they fail to poll votes from more than 5 per cent of registered electorate in **constituency**. It was introduced in 1929 as deterrent to 'frivolous candidates', but has been criticized recently for being too affordable.

Electoral Commission quango responsible for ensuring correct procedures followed in parliamentary, local, and European elections, and enforcing rules on party finance. Its responsibilities include keeping campaign spending by election candidates within agreed statutory limits, and it may refer cases to the Crown Prosecution Service if it feels electoral law has been broken.

electoral division term used for **constituencies** represented by county councillors and some unitary authority councillors. Each has between one and three councillors, depending on size of its population.

electoral register official list of all electors registered to vote in local, general, and European elections in given local authority area. It is compiled by electoral registration

officer employed by **district/borough council** or unitary authority.

emergency planning officer officer employed by county council or unitary authority to oversee strategic planning for civil emergencies, such as floods.

emergency protection order (also known as an interim care order) type of **care order** allowing local authority to take child into care immediately because of perceived threat to his/her well-being. Initially applies for eight days but may be renewed for further week.

Employment and Support Allowance (ESA) introduced by Labour to replace *Incapacity Benefit* (IB) for individuals judged too sick or disabled to work. From October 2013 ESA will be gradually absorbed into Coalition's new **Universal Credit**.

English Heritage national **quango** responsible for managing heritage monuments and properties, such as Stonehenge, on government's behalf. English Heritage administers **listed buildings** programme.

enlargement term referring to expansion of European Union. It has been enlarged twice in the past decade, with a number of former Soviet countries joining for first time: ten new states joined in 2004 and a further two—Bulgaria and Romania—in 2007.

Environment Agency **executive agency** of Department of Environment, Food, and Rural Affairs (Defra) responsible for regulating quality and safety of water in rivers and streams, and strategic planning for flood protection.

environmental health officer officer employed by **district council**, **borough council**, or unitary authority to investigate complaints about environmental health hazards, such as vermin infestation, rotting waste, and noise pollution, and inspect hygiene of business premises serving food.

Equality and Human Rights Commission (EHRC) **quango** formed through amalgamation of Commission for Racial Equality (CRE) and Equal Opportunities Commission (EOC), to ensure equal treatment of employees in workplace, regardless of gender, race, or age.

euro (€) single European currency, introduced in all European Union member states bar UK, Denmark, and Sweden on 1 January 2002. Since 2008 'eurozone' (seventeen countries using the euro) has been locked in crisis over sovereign debts of Greece and several other member states.

European Central Bank (ECB) based in Frankfurt, central bank of European Union, which issues **euro**.

European Commission See Commission of the European Union

European Council newly recognised as one of five governing institutions of the EU following ratification of the Treaty of Lisbon, this is a periodic gathering of heads of state/most senior politicians in member states, headed by a permanent president. Charged with charting the future strategic direction of the EU, it is not to be confused with either the **Council of Ministers** or the **Council of Europe**.

European Court of Human Rights (ECtHR) based in Strasbourg, ultimate court of appeal for citizens of states that have signed up to European Convention on Human Rights (ECHR)

and passed it into their own domestic law. Britain belatedly ratified convention by passing Human Rights Act 1998. Court was established by **Council of Europe** and has no link to EU.

European Court of Justice (ECJ) European Union's main legal body, this ensures EU law is correctly implemented in member states. Each state contributes one judge—twenty-seven in all—although only thirteen ever sit in session together. Only major cases go to full ECJ, with others heard by General Court. Warring parties have their cases presented to judges by one of eleven advocates-general.

European Parliament (EP) based primarily in Brussels, but moving to Strasbourg for one week every month, EP is elected every five years. Members of European Parliament (MEPs) sit in political groupings, rather than along national lines. For example, British Labour Party sits with Socialist Group.

executive agency subset of large government spending department, staffed by civil servants, charged with delivering particular area or areas of its policy. Examples include **Health and Safety Executive** within Department of Health, and **Highways Agency** in Department for Transport.

F

faith schools umbrella term for schools run by particular religious communities, including non-Christian groups. There are at least 7,000 faith schools in England, Wales, and Northern Ireland, many of which receive state funding.

federalism flip side of **subsidiarity**, this is idea promoted by Eurosceptics that further extension of EU powers will lead to individual member states surrendering autonomy for their internal affairs to centralized institutions, turning Union into 'United States of Europe' or 'European superstate'.

Financial Conduct Authority (FCA) part of new, tougher, tripartite regulatory system in process of being set up by Coalition to avert future banking collapses. Following passage of Financial Services Bill 2012 this will police overall conduct of every financial company authorized to provide services to public.

Financial Policy Committee (FPC) modelled on existing **MPC**, in March 2012 this committee of **Bank of England** assumed responsibility from **FSA** for identifying risks to stability of Britain's economy and taking pre-emptive action to combat them.

Financial Services Authority (FSA) part of tripartite 'light-touch' regulatory regime introduced by then Chancellor Gordon Brown to oversee finance sector in 1997, FSA was heavily criticized for failing to anticipate 2008–9 banking collapse. It is in process of being wound down and replaced by three new bodies: **FCA**, **PRA**, and **FPC**.

first reading formal introduction of proposed Bill to Commons. The reading usually consists solely of full title of Bill being read out by minister. (cf. **second reading**; **third reading**)

Fiscal Compact commonly used name for Treaty on Stability, Coordination, and Governance in the Economic and Monetary Union—agreed by all EU countries apart from Britain and Czech Republic in December 2011. It requires signatory states to maintain balanced budgets or budget surpluses or face fines from **ECB**.

forward plan list of upcoming **key decisions** due to be taken by local authority that must be made public at least a month in advance.

fostering the practice of placing vulnerable children in care with another family, often for short period of time, while more permanent situation sought. (cf. **adoption**)

foundation school like Conservative Party's grant-maintained (GM) school, this is self-governing state secondary school, permitted to spend its budgets as it pleases, within certain conditions set by central government. Money allocated to it via its local education authority (LEA), but it may hire and fire its own staff and set its own admissions and disciplinary policies distinct from those of local LEA-run schools.

foundation trust form of NHS hospital, ambulance service, or mental health trust permitted full autonomy over its own financial and contractual affairs, regulated by **Monitor**. Under Coalition all trusts are making the transition to 'foundation status'.

free schools key plank of Conservative education policy and its 'Big Society' vision of government, these are new generation of publicly funded secondary schools that parents, teachers, and other members of their community are setting up and running for themselves. Based on model devised in Sweden.

FT100 Share Index (FOOTSIE) *Financial Times* Stock Exchange 100 Share

Index (to use its full title) is most famous of number of 'indices', or lists, of major companies listed on London Stock Exchange. It lists hundred highest-valued companies at any time in order of share value.

further education (FE) umbrella term for post-compulsory education and training provided by tertiary colleges and school sixth forms. It can encompass resits of A levels and other qualifications aimed at those of school age, but primarily focuses on vocational courses and diplomas.

G

general block grant generic term for revenue grants paid by central government to local authorities that may be used for any service area, according to local needs and priorities, this is enjoying resurgence under Coalition. Often used as synonym for **revenue support grant (RSG)**.

general committee umbrella term for the three types of temporary parliamentary committee formed to scrutinize prospective legislation: the **public Bill committee, private Bill committee,** and **grand committee.**

general election name denoting elections for House of Commons. From May 2015 general elections due to be held at fixed five-year intervals following reform introduced by Coalition. Electoral system used to elect UK MPs is first past the post.

globalization term describing gradual convergence of national economies into bigger international whole. Used increasingly in relation to idea of free trade, free movement of labour between countries, and expansion of Internet.

grammar (selective) school type of maintained secondary school, phased out in much of UK, which admits only pupils who have passed academic test known as '11-plus'. Those who fail are admitted to standard **comprehensive schools.**

grand committee one of three types of **general committee** in Parliament, these are convened to debate the impact of prospective legislation on specific UK regions or to scrutinize Bills in the Lords on occasions when they are not debated on the floor of the House.

Greater London Authority (GLA) London's overarching 'council', which came into being in 2000 at same time as capital gained its first **directly elected mayor.** Individual London boroughs retain own councils to run local services at ground level, but GLA is responsible for taking strategic decisions for whole capital.

Green Investment Bank new Edinburgh-based institution, set up by Coalition from autumn 2012, backed by £3bn capitalization fund, to address private sector market failings by financing environmentally sustainable infrastructure projects.

Green Paper consultation document on tentative government policy proposal that may, in time, evolve into **White Paper,** and from there into proposed Bill. All government Bills (other than emergency legislation) will go through at least one Green Paper stage, although if public and/or interest groups react strongly against proposal, it is unlikely to go much further.

greenbelt term used for designated zones around towns and cities that have deliberately been kept free of development to prevent urban sprawl and protect wildlife.

greenfield site area of land on which there has been little or no prior development. (cf. **brownfield site**)

gross domestic product (GDP) total profit from all goods and services generated in Britain in given financial year, irrespective of which state benefits from them. (cf. **gross national product (GNP)**)

gross national product (GNP) total profit from all goods and services generated by British-based companies in given financial year, irrespective of where they are physically produced. For example, Far Eastern call centres owned by UK companies like BT or Virgin would still count towards state's GNP. (cf. **gross domestic product (GDP)**)

growth increase in value of **GDP** from one month/quarter/year to another, usually characterized by rises in bank lending and consumer spending and falling unemployment.

G8 (Group of 8) loose organization/forum devoted to promoting economic free trade and **globalization**, made up of world's eight leading industrial nations—currently USA, Britain, Japan, France, Germany, Italy, Canada, and Russia.

G20 (Group of 20) loose organization/ forum comprising world's twenty leading industrial powers.

H

Hansard official record of all parliamentary business in both Houses. Protected by legal privilege and now available to read online, it is nonetheless not an entirely verbatim record of proceedings (except for words used by serving **prime minister**).

head of the paid service See chief executive

Health and Safety Executive (HSE) **executive agency** of Department of Health, charged with setting and enforcing health and safety legislation in the workplace across UK. It recently merged with Health and Safety Commission (HSC), which had previously drawn up health and safety rules.

Health and well-being boards new local bodies to be formed by all 152 English local authorities, bringing together all commissioners of health and social care in each area, along with local representatives of **Healthwatch**, to promote integrated approaches to improving health. Boards to include local councillors.

health service scrutiny committee statutory body set up by county council or unitary authority comprises fifteen members, including chairperson, local councillors, and representatives from relevant voluntary sector organizations.

Healthwatch new national 'consumer-led' regulator of health services in England, with local branches based on the *local involvement networks* (LINks) set-up inherited from Labour.

High Representative for Foreign Affairs and Security Policy influential new permanent **European Commission** post created under 2007 Treaty of Lisbon. First holder of post, due to be backed from 2010 by diplomatic corps known as European External Action Service, was Britain's former EU trade commissioner Baroness Ashton of Upholland.

higher education (HE) level of education provided by universities for those who have acquired the right qualifications at post-compulsory/ tertiary level (e.g. A levels). HE begins with undergraduate degrees (BAs, BScs, etc.) and progresses to postgraduate degrees (Masters and doctorates) and beyond.

Higher Education Funding Council for England (HEFCE) quango that channels public money for teaching and research into universities.

Highways Agency executive agency of Department for Transport responsible for building and maintaining Britain's major roads.

honours list generic term used for two annual lists of individuals chosen to be honoured with ceremonial titles by Queen in recognition of their worldly achievements. Lists compiled by ministers and shadow ministers, and honours awarded in Queen's Birthday Honours List and New Year Honours List.

House of Lords Appointments Commission quango that vets potential candidates for **life peerages** after they have been nominated by political party leader. It may have an enhanced role as and when last hereditary peers are finally removed from Lords.

housing association not-for-profit organization formerly overseen by Housing Corporation quango. Housing associations are principal providers of social housing in Britain today, often working with, or on behalf of, local authorities.

hung parliament outcome of **general election** that leaves no single party with overall majority and largest one facing prospect of either ruling as minority administration or forging coalition with one or more others. The May 2010 election produced Britain's first hung parliament since 1974.

hybrid structure type of local government structure that exists in some English and Welsh counties, in which **two-tier structure** remains in certain areas while others have adopted newer **unitary structure**. East Sussex is example of hybrid county: Lewes covered by both district and county councils, while neighbouring Brighton and Hove has **city council**, which is unitary.

I

Income Support basic level of benefit paid to range of people who satisfy certain needs-based criteria but have paid insufficient prior **National Insurance** contributions to qualify for **contributory benefits**. Available to certain people between ages of 16 and 60 who are not in full-time work, such as carers or single parents. As with all other benefits paid to low earners and unemployed, it is due to be subsumed in single payment, the **Universal Credit** (UC), between October 2013 and 2017.

Independent Parliamentary Standards Authority (IPSA) new regulator created in 2009 to police MPs' and peers' allowance claims and pay their salaries. This quango, which began work in earnest only after the 2010 election, was introduced as replacement for in-house Fees Office following long-running scandal over parliamentary expenses, which led to several resignations and successful prosecutions.

Independent Police Complaints Commission (IPCC) national quango responsible for investigating complaints against **chief constables** and/or their forces. Commission automatically launches investigations whenever civilians killed by police officers.

independent remuneration panel body comprising at least three non-councillors, set up in each local authority area under Local Government Act 2000 to adjudicate independently on any application by council to increase its member allowances.

indirect taxes often referred to as 'hidden' or 'stealth' taxes, these are embedded in cost of items bought by individuals or companies. Value added tax (VAT) and excise duties on tobacco and alcohol are examples of indirect taxes. Because they are charged at flat rates on relevant items they are seen as regressive—that is, they do not take account of individuals' or companies' ability to pay. (cf. **direct taxes**)

individual ministerial responsibility principle that **secretary of state** should 'fall on his/her sword' and resign if major failing is exposed in his/her department. In practice, ministers often have to be pushed by **prime minister** (as happened in case of then Chancellor Norman Lamont after 'Black Wednesday' in 1992). (cf. **collective responsibility**)

inflation rises in prices of goods and services from one month to next. This is calculated using either **consumer price index (CPI)** or **retail price index (RPI)**, which monitor fluctuations in values of notional 'baskets' of goods containing items regularly bought by typical British households.

Information Commissioner statutory official appointed to police implementation of Freedom of Information (FoI) Act 2000, adjudicating on complaints from individuals and organizations of lack of transparency by public authorities in response to legitimate FoI requests.

interest rates instrument of monetary policy used to promote saving and investment and reduce consumer spending. Since 1980s, raising interest rates has been preferred method of controlling **inflation**. **Bank of England**'s **Monetary Policy Committee (MPC)** meets monthly to decide whether to raise or lower interest rates.

interim care order See emergency protection order

J

Jobcentre Plus replaced Benefits Agency in 2002 as main body responsible for administering benefits of all kinds, from **Jobseeker's Allowance (JSA)** and **Income Support** to sickness and disability-related benefits.

Jobseeker's Allowance (JSA) benefit paid to people over 16 who are registered unemployed and 'actively seeking work'. There are two types of allowance: contributions-based (related to prior **National Insurance** payments) and income-based. Due to be replaced by **Universal Credit** between October 2013 and 2017.

K

key decision policy decision affecting two or more **wards** or **electoral divisions** in local authority area and likely to involve 'significant expenditure' if approved. They are judged to be so significant that they must be presented for final say to full council and cannot be taken solely in **cabinet** unless delegated to individual portfolio-holder.

L

leader of the council most senior and powerful local politician in authorities that have either adopted second new executive arrangement retained from LGA 2000 or retained their pre-existing one. Like **prime minister**, they are normally leader of party with greatest number of seats on council.

Leader of the House government minister responsible for organizing weekly Commons timetable and proposing changes to its working hours and order of business.

life peerage honorary peerages conferred on individuals for life in one of two annual **honours lists**. As their name suggests, these titles die with recipients and cannot be passed on to their children. (cf. **elected hereditary peerage**)

listed building individual building or small group of buildings (e.g. a Georgian crescent) offered statutory protection against alteration or demolition because of link to specific historical personalities, events, or architectural movements. There are three levels of listing: grades I, II*, and II.

local enterprise partnership (LEP) alliances of local councils, businesses, and voluntary organizations introduced by Coalition to boost commercial investment in local areas. A more local-level replacement for the recently abolished regional development agencies (RDAs).

local government association regional coalitions of local authorities that lobby Parliament and central government. There is also the national Local Government Association (LGA).

Local Government Boundary Commission for England (LGBCE) national **quango** tasked with periodically reviewing boundaries between **wards** and **electoral divisions** to ensure each represented by correct number of councillors relative to its population size.

Local Government Ombudsman See Commission for Local Administration.

Local Housing Allowance the formula used to determine how much Housing Benefit (HB) the unemployed and low earners may claim to help with rental costs. Ultimately paid by **Jobcentre Plus**, it is administered by **district councils** or **borough councils** and unitary authority housing offices. Since April 2008 HB payments have been calculated relative to average rental prices in each postcode area (the LHA formula), rather than based on assessments of the value of specific homes rented by claimants.

local safeguarding children's board (LSCB) committees set up by every county council and unitary authority under Children Act 2004 to coordinate efforts of all organizations involved in looking after recognized children in need.

Local Services Support Grant (LSSG) replacement for Labour's *area-based grant*. Local authorities have received this non-formula, unfenced payment to spend as they see fit (within certain parameters) since 31 March 2011.

Lord Speaker recently introduced post designed to mimic that of Commons **Speaker**. This title is given to peer elected by his/her colleagues in the Lords to chair debate in chamber.

Lords Spiritual collective term for twenty-six most senior Church of England bishops, led by Archbishop of Canterbury, who remain entitled to sit in Lords.

M

mayor ceremonial title traditionally rotated between councillors on local authorities on year-by-year basis. Recipient spends twelve months chairing full council meetings on non-partisan basis and attending civic events.

member of the European Parliament (MEP) elected representative who sits in **European Parliament**, of which there are 754, elected every five years. Each state contributes number of members reflecting its population size.

member of the Legislative Assembly (MLA) elected representatives to Northern Ireland Assembly. There are currently 108, chosen in four-yearly elections using **single transferable vote (STV)** system of **proportional representation (PR)**.

member of Parliament (MP) elected representatives to House of Commons. As of May 2010 election there were 650 MPs, each representing average of 65,000 constituents—but number of seats due to be cut to 600 from 2015, with constituency sizes equalized.

member of the Scottish Parliament (MSP) elected representatives in Scottish Parliament. There are 129 MSPs at any one time, elected every four years using additional member system (AMS)—a form of **proportional representation**.

minister of state umbrella term for all ministers in government departments, including junior ministers.

ministerial code document outlining ten key 'principles' of conduct for ministers, including avoiding real or apparent conflicts of interest, and stipulating that **prime minister** should refer any alleged breach by a minister to *Independent Adviser on Ministerial Interests*.

minutes written record of proceedings of meeting of subcommittee, committee, full council, **cabinet/ executive**, or other body.

Monetary Policy Committee (MPC) committee of **Bank of England** that meets once a month to decide whether to raise or lower **interest rates**, on basis of previous month's **inflation** figures.

Monitor (Independent Regulator of NHS Foundation Trusts) quango responsible for promoting cooperation and regulating competition between **foundation trusts**.

monitoring officer senior local authority officer responsible for monitoring councillors' and officers' compliance with their council's **code of conduct**, and recording and reporting to members any cases of suspected maladministration.

N

National Assembly for Wales full title of Wales's devolved assembly, based in a purpose-built chamber in Cardiff Bay.

National Curriculum compulsory content that must be taught in maintained (state) schools in Britain in certain core subjects, such as English language and maths.

National Curriculum assessments (Sats) academic tests taken by state school pupils at three key stages in their **National Curriculum** learning. Key stages 1, 2, and 3 take place at the ages of 7, 11, and 14, respectively.

National Executive Committee of the Labour Party (NEC) often referred to as 'Labour's ruling NEC', a senior policy committee composed of representatives of all main branches of Labour Party, including MPs,

constituency party members, and trade unionists. Major changes to party's constitution must be approved by this committee.

National Institute for Health and Clinical Excellence (NICE) **quango** set up to vet medication before it is made available on National Health Service and carry out its own research into potential cures and treatments. Headed by *chief medical officer*.

National Insurance (NI) system of contributory payments deducted from employees' wages and topped up by employers to finance entitlement to future benefits should they be needed. System originally set up in 1911 to protect workers from poverty should they become unable to work through sickness or injury.

national minimum wage (NMW) minimum hourly rate to be paid to all employees in UK, introduced by Labour in 1998. There are lower NMWs for 16- to 18-year-olds and 18- to 20-year-olds.

national non-domestic rates (NNDR) (also known as uniform business rates (UBR)) local taxation paid by companies, the bills of which are calculated according to **rateable values** of business premises and national multiplier set each year by government (e.g. 50p in pound). Money collected locally but then funnelled through Treasury and redistributed around country according to need.

National Offender Management Service (NOMS) **executive agency** of Ministry of Justice responsible for recruiting and employing UK's 48,000 prison staff and overall policy regarding day-to-day running of its 135 jails. Prisons Service is now part of NOMS and is responsible only for publicly funded jails.

national park one of fourteen geographical areas of Britain designated for highest degree of protection from development or commercial exploitation possible under UK law.

Natural England **quango** responsible for conserving, protecting, and managing natural environment in England for current and future generations.

neighbourhood plan new form of local development plan to be devised by community itself. Local authority must adopt this in place of its own proposals if it is approved in local referendum—provided 51 per cent or more of residents who turn out to vote approve of it.

Network Rail not-for-dividend company set up by government in 2001 to take over repairs and maintenance of UK overland rail network (tracks, signals, and stations) from Railtrack—the private monopoly initially given those responsibilities following privatization of British Rail in early 1990s.

NHS Commissioning Board (NHS CB) new national **quango** charged with commissioning primary care and specialist health services at regional and nationwide levels.

NHS trust umbrella term referring to hospitals, ambulance services, and mental health services provided on NHS. Term 'trust' coined in early 1990s and relates to new levels of autonomy given to these bodies to run their own affairs. Each has its own board, like a company, and is designated a service 'provider'— rather than 'commissioner', like *primary care trusts* (PCTs).

1922 Committee often referred to as 'the influential 1922 Committee', this is made up of all backbench

Conservative MPs at any one time. 'Mood' of the Committee is crucial test of likely lifespan of its leadership, and it was widely credited with delivering knockout blow to Margaret Thatcher's premiership after she was challenged by Michael Heseltine in 1990.

non-contributory benefits umbrella term for lower-level social security benefits to which British people are entitled (subject to meeting other criteria) irrespective of their previous **National Insurance** contributions. **Income Support** is example of purely 'needs-based', non-contributory benefit paid to people in lieu of higher-level entitlement. (cf. **contributory benefits**)

North Atlantic Treaty Organization (NATO) military alliance made up of twenty-six predominantly Western powers, NATO was formed with signing of North Atlantic Treaty in Washington DC in 1949. Initially designed to act as bulwark during Cold War against expansion of Soviet Union and Warsaw Pact.

Northern Ireland Assembly based at Stormont, this is devolved chamber for Northern Ireland counties. Since March 2007, when power restored by British government to devolved institutions, has been elected every four years.

O

Office for Budget Responsibility (OBR) **quango** set up by Coalition to produce independent economic forecasts and comment on likely impact on jobs and inflation of government's budgetary decisions. For its first three months it was overseen by Sir Alan Budd, former economic adviser to Margaret Thatcher and founder member of

Bank of England's **Monetary Policy Committee (MPC)**.

Office of Communications (Ofcom) **quango** dubbed 'super-regulator' because of its all-embracing responsibilities for overseeing telecommunications, broadcast media industries (radio, television, and the Internet), and now postal services. Ofcom may fine broadcasters, including British Broadcasting Corporation (BBC), for breaking rules governing taste and decency, and it monitors their public service content (such as current affairs and news output).

Office for Fair Access (OFFA) regulator charged with ensuring **higher education (HE)** institutions that charge tuition fees above 'standard level' produce 'access agreements' detailing practical steps for attracting students from disadvantaged backgrounds.

Office of Gas and Electricity Markets (Ofgem) regulatory **quango** that oversees Britain's privatized energy market to ensure there is free and fair competition between suppliers, and bills are kept within acceptable bounds. Headed by Director General of Gas and Electricity Markets.

Office of the Schools Adjudicator (OSA) **quango** charged with ruling on disputes about local authority plans to change school admissions arrangements and resolve disputes over school reorganization by councils.

Office for Standards in Education, Children's Services, and Skills (Ofsted) central government inspectorate, headed by Chief Inspector of Schools, which visits maintained schools, preschools, education providers, and **further education** colleges on rolling basis to monitor standards of teaching and administration, and awards grades from '1' to '4'.

Office of the Qualifications and Examinations Regulator (Ofqual) independent national regulator established in 2008 to monitor standard of qualifications, exams, and tests in England. Ofqual headed by ruling committee.

Office of Water Regulation (OFWAT) See Water Services Regulatory Authority

officers civil servants employed by local authorities to implement policies agreed by elected **councillors**.

Order in Council one of three types of **secondary/delegated legislation**, this is legal instrument enacted by monarch on advice of **Privy Council**.

outline planning permission first stage of obtaining consent to develop a site, during which permission granted 'in principle', subject to submission of more detailed plan. (cf. **planning permission**)

overnight residency requirements Coalition's replacement for night-time curfews of up to sixteen hours Labour used to restrict movements of terrorist suspects in community. The new system will limit duration of overnight curfews to ten hours.

overview and scrutiny committee overarching 'super-committee' adopted by some local authorities under Local Government Act 2000, which scrutinizes workings of council departments and decisions taken by **cabinet** and senior officers. There will normally be several scrutiny subcommittees—or panels—focusing on specific policy areas.

P

parish meeting lowest form of local authority, this de facto parish council convenes once a year in small villages to discuss provision of local services and make representations to statutory authorities on behalf of local people.

Parliamentary Commissioner for Administration (also known as **Parliamentary and Health Service Ombudsman**) also responsible for overseeing administration in NHS, Commissioner hears complaints from public and organizations about alleged maladministration by Parliament, rather than corruption.

Parliamentary Commissioner for Standards a post created on recommendation of Nolan Inquiry, which was prompted by series of 'sleaze' scandals involving Conservative MPs in early 1990s, including 'cash for questions' affair, when Neil Hamilton accused of taking payments from Harrods owner Mohamed Al Fayed to ask parliamentary questions on his behalf. Commissioner polices rigorous system of disclosure of outside interests introduced after these scandals.

Parliamentary Labour Party (PLP) Labour's equivalent of **1922 Committee** in Conservative Party, this is collective term for all Labour **backbenchers**.

Parliamentary and Health Service Ombudsman See Parliamentary Commissioner for Administration

parliamentary private secretary (PPS) very junior government post often offered to upcoming MP judged to have ministerial potential. PPSs are 'link' between senior ministers and ordinary **backbenchers** in their party and are often used to float potential policy ideas to 'test the water' among their parliamentary colleagues.

parliamentary privilege constitutional convention allowing MPs and peers to speak freely within their respective chambers, even criticizing named individuals without fear of being prosecuted for defamation. Even under parliamentary privilege certain terms banned in reference to fellow MPs or peers, including the word 'liar'.

parliamentary sovereignty constitutional principle derived from 1689 Bill of Rights that elevated Parliament to position of supremacy over sovereign in governing England and Wales (and, in due course, whole UK).

parliamentary under-secretary lowest form of government minister: a junior minister below level of **minister of state** and **secretary of state**.

parole procedure by which prisoners released early from sentences for 'good behaviour'. Those convicted of more minor offences usually granted automatic early release after serving half length of their sentences, but serious offenders, including rapists and serial murderers, usually serve at least twenty years.

Passenger Focus (also known as Rail Passengers' Council) consumer watchdog representing interests of overland rail commuters and passengers.

permanent secretary most senior civil servant in government department. He/she offers day-to-day advice to **secretary of state** and other ministers, and therefore occupies **politically restricted post**.

planning obligations, planning contribution, or planning gain offer by developer of added value for local authority in exchange for being granted **planning permission** for major project. For example, developer may offer to finance new playground for children

in deprived **ward** as form of 'sweetener' to help its bid to build new supermarket.

planning inquiry public inquiry held into contentious development proposal to which there is strong opposition. It will be chaired by independent inspector appointed by Secretary of State for Communities and Local Government, and those immediately affected by proposal will be allowed to speak at it.

planning permission consent given to individual, company, or other organization to build new premises or extend/adapt existing ones. (cf. **outline planning permission**)

police and crime commissioners elected officials who replaced police authorities on 15 November 2012. As with their precursors, they are responsible for overseeing and holding to account their local police forces, with powers to hire and fire chief constables.

police community support officers (PCSOs) semi-trained officers employed as auxiliary police, with powers to arrest and issue some minor punishments, such as fixed-penalty fines for antisocial behaviour.

policy and resources committee traditionally most powerful local authority committee, because it is in charge of council's overall budget, this committee must be consulted on major decisions (e.g. to build new road) because it will have to approve funding.

political sovereignty constitutional concept of institution or individual holding political supremacy (or 'sovereignty') over nation's citizens. In Britain political sovereignty originally rested with reigning monarch ('sovereign') but passed to Parliament after 1689 Bill of Rights.

politically restricted post contractual position held by senior public officials (civil servants and local government officers) barred from canvassing openly for political party at elections, or standing for office, due to their close day-to-day working relationships with politicians.

postal vote means of casting votes in elections by post, rather than in person. British government is committed to extending rights to vote by post across UK, following several recent pilots, but this has provoked criticism from some quarters because of perceived risk of fraud in multi-occupancy households.

precepting authority all local authorities that receive some revenue funding through **Council Tax** are precepting authorities. Term 'precept' refers to 'invoice' that such authorities present to **billing authority**, outlining sum they wish to raise through Council Tax in coming financial year.

prescribed function role and responsibility formally delegated by council to its committees, subcommittees, **cabinet/executive**, and individual cabinet members. These will normally be spelt out in council's constitution.

President of the European Council recently created permanent post at helm of European Council—a powerful body comprising most senior politicians from each EU member state. Introduced under 2007 Treaty of Lisbon, its inaugural holder, ex-Belgian Prime Minister Herman van Rompuy, was re-elected for further two-and-a-half-year term in March 2012.

Press Complaints Commission (PCC) independent, self-regulatory industry body responsible for handling complaints from public about newspapers and magazines. It has seventeen members, including editors and representatives of the public relations (PR) and marketing industries, and enforces code of practice to which all print journalists must adhere. This prohibits practices such as major intrusions into personal privacy.

primary schools maintained schools that deliver primary teaching to pupils in core subjects such as English, maths, and science between ages of 4 (reception class) and 11.

prime minister (PM) commonly used title of senior minister who chairs Cabinet, officially the *First Lord of the Treasury*. PM or 'premier' is constitutionally seen as 'first among equals', in that he/she is elected constituency MP like any other but with more power than all others.

private Bill type of primary legislation introduced by government minister(s) for purpose of conferring specific powers or duties on a particular organization or regional entity. Act permitting Formula One racing in Birmingham stemmed from private Bill.

private Bill committee temporary Commons committee convened to scrutinize a prospective **private Bill**. One of the three types of **general committee**.

private finance initiative (PFI) main way in which major capital projects are now funded, this is an arrangement between public authority (e.g. council or government department) and private company, under which latter foots most of initial bill and former pays it back (with interest) over period of years. (cf. **public–private partnership (PPP)**)

private member's Bill (PMB) Bill proposed by individual **backbencher**, normally on issue dear to his/her heart, and/or one that concerns his/her constituents. While they may cast media's spotlight onto an issue, most PMBs never allotted sufficient parliamentary time to pass into law—but there have been exceptions, including 1967 Abortion Bill, introduced by future Liberal leader David Steel.

Privy Council ancient committee of state, originally formed as group of close confidantes for reigning monarch to counteract power of Great Council or *Magnum Concilium*, composed of peers of realm. Today all serving and past **Cabinet** ministers and leaders of Opposition appointed members for life and advise monarch on matters such as use of Privy Purse (monarch's personal pot of money, derived from Duchy of Lancaster estate) and issuing of **Orders in Council**.

proportional representation (PR) umbrella term for alternative electoral systems to 'first-past-the-post' (FPTP) process used in British **general elections**. Most Western countries use PR, including Ireland, which uses single transferable vote (STV). Liberal Democrats have been campaigning for STV to be adopted in Britain, arguing it is fairer than UK system, because number of seats won by party tends to bear stronger relationship to votes cast for them than does FPTP.

prorogation term denoting procedure by which Parliament is temporarily suspended (or 'prorogued') at end of parliamentary session.

Prudential Regulatory Authority (PRA) created as subsidiary of **Bank of England** in 2013 to prevent banks, building societies, or other financial companies taking imprudent risks with their investors' money. Part of new tripartite regulatory regime for finance sector.

public Bill primary legislation introduced by government minister(s) to change law of land. Public Bills usually begin with **Green Paper** then **White Paper**, before going through series of readings, committee stage, House of Lords stage, and finally **royal assent** by Queen.

public Bill committee temporary parliamentary committee convened to scrutinize and debate Bill or another prospective Act of Parliament. Formerly known as 'standing committees' because, being only temporary, their members were notionally not in post for long enough to warrant permanent seats at committee table. One of three types of **general committee**.

Public Health England new national quango charged with promoting public health initiatives across England, backed by £4bn fighting fund to finance locally run projects.

public health grant (PHG) new ring-fenced revenue grant introduced by Coalition from April 2013 to help councils take over funding of initiatives aimed at improving well-being of their communities—for example, by encouraging people to quit smoking.

public limited company (plc) type of larger registered company in UK that issues shares to general public to buy by 'floating' itself on London Stock Exchange. It has legal obligation to maximize profits for its shareholders and pay them *dividends*. Most household-name companies in Britain are plcs (e.g. BP).

public–private partnership (PPP) financial arrangement used to fund major capital projects, such as roads and prisons, whereby government department or other public authority will share cost of initial outlay with private company or companies. Bulk of upfront investment usually made by private sector, and public sector will pay it off (with interest) over period of years. PPP is 'New Labour's' successor to Conservatives' **private finance initiative (PFI)**.

public sector net cash requirement (PSNCR) formerly 'public sector borrowing requirement' (PSBR), this is sum of money British government will need to borrow through commercial loans or from public in given financial year to meet its public spending commitments—that is, difference between total taxation the Exchequer expects to raise in year and actual outgoings.

Public Works Loan Board (PWLB) body that can lend money to local authorities for major capital projects at lower rate than those offered by banking sector. PWLB is part of UK Debt Management Office, a Treasury **executive agency**.

pupil premium additional funding allocated annually by Coalition to schools with high numbers of pupils from disadvantaged backgrounds and/or on free school meals. The aim is to use one-to-one tuition and other strategies to intercept potential education inequalities.

Q

qualified majority voting (QMV) system of voting in **Council of Ministers of the European Union** that enables certain issues to be decided by majority vote in favour or against, rather than unanimously. Under QMV each member state is allocated certain number of votes in proportion to its population, meaning some have substantially more say in matters than others and that decisions are taken on 'qualified' majority basis. The UK, for example, has twenty-nine votes, while Malta has just three.

quango (quasi-autonomous non-government organization) non-departmental body set up by government department and partly funded by taxpayers, to regulate, monitor, or otherwise oversee particular area of policy delivery. UK quangos have own executive boards, like companies, and include Arts Council England and **Equality and Human Rights Commission (EHRC)**.

quantitative easing (QE) practice by which central banks (in Britain, **Bank of England**) purchase bonds or equities from retail banks to increase prices of those assets and reduce interest rates payable on them. Aim is to 'free up' finance for businesses and individuals in wider economy by encouraging banks to lend more and at lower rates.

Queen's Speech annual address given by Queen at State Opening of Parliament in October or November. Speech is actually list of legislation to be proposed by government during coming parliamentary session (year), and is written not by monarch herself but by sitting **prime minister** and **Cabinet**.

Question Time sessions of parliamentary business during which **backbenchers** and/or peers on all sides have opportunity of questioning individual departmental ministers on conduct of their ministerial business. Major spending departments each have a question time session at least once a fortnight, while most famous is 'Prime Minister's Questions', held every Wednesday lunchtime.

R

rateable value sum of money a business premises would be able to earn on rental market. Both **national non-domestic rates (NNDR)** and rates—the property-based domestic tax that preceded the Community Charge—are (or were) based on rateable values.

recession economic term used to describe rapid economic slowdown or negative growth. Technically, it refers to period of two successive quarters during which economy has 'shrunk'—that is, consumers have stopped spending, sales of goods and services dwindled, and manufacturers reduced production.

refer back term used for when local authority cabinet/executive and/or full council meeting asks committee or subcommittee to rethink its recommendations. Also used in the context of recommendations by **general committees** of the House of Commons.

referendum public vote on single issue. In Britain referendums are rare, but national referendum was held in 1975 on question of whether country should remain in European Community, and people of Scotland, Wales, and Northern Ireland were consulted in referendums about whether they wanted devolved government. Most recent national referendum, held in May 2011, rejected Lib Dem proposals to introduce **alternative vote (AV)** in place of 'first-past-the-post' electoral system for **general elections**.

register of members' interests (register of members' financial interests) a register of outside 'interests' (directorships, share holdings, etc.) of members of Parliament and peers introduced to improve transparency in 1974. Local authorities have been required to keep similar registers for their councillors since the passage of the Local Government Act 2000.

relative needs formula (RNF) calculation used by central government to decide how much to allocate each local authority in *formula grants* for given financial year. It is based on assessment of precise demographic factors in each area, including not only size of local population but its *nature* (e.g. number of pensioners).

relative resource amount (RRA) calculation used by central government to estimate how much money each local authority is able to raise itself for revenue spending in given financial year. RRA is subtracted from the **RNF** to calculate level of formula grants.

report stage stage immediately after **committee stage**, when **public Bill committee's** chairperson 'reports back' to Commons with its recommendations.

resolved items matters concluded at end of committee, full council, or **cabinet/executive** meeting. Vote will normally be taken to make final decision.

retail price index (RPI) measure of **inflation** (changes in prices of goods and services) preferred by most economists to **consumer price index (CPI)**, this charts movement in value of notional 'basket' of goods regularly bought by typical British households. Because it includes mortgage payments, it is usually higher than CPI.

returning officer official responsible for overseeing local and **general election** procedures on day of poll, ordering recounts where necessary, and announcing result. Officially, this post is held by chairperson or **mayor** of neighbouring or coterminous local authority, but senior council officer will usually perform duties in practice—often **chief executive** or electoral registration officer.

revenue expenditure share of local authority's annual budget spent on day-to-day running costs of schools, libraries, offices, and other local services. (cf. **capital expenditure**)

revenue support grant (RSG) one of three types of formula grant allocated to local authorities by central government for their revenue spending, this was traditionally biggest single chunk of money they received. It is calculated on basis of formula relating to demographic make-up of local area and may be used by councils in any area of revenue spending. Also known as **general block grant**, the proportion of funding channelled through RSG is increasing under Coalition.

ring-fenced grant one of two types of **specific grant** for local authority revenue spending (cf. **unfenced grants**), which must be used for purpose stipulated by central government. All but two ring-fenced grants have been scrapped by Coalition: **Dedicated Schools Grant (DSG)** and new **public health grant**.

royal assent 'rubber stamp' given to Bill by reigning sovereign to make it an Act. In practice, royal assent is formality today and no monarch has refused to give it since Queen Anne attempted to do so in 1707.

royal prerogative constitutional term used to refer to (now largely notional) idea that power in UK derives from authority of reigning sovereign. In practice, today most prerogative powers (e.g. ability to declare war and appoint ministers) rests with elected **prime minister** of day.

rule of law constitutional principle, derived from 1215's Magna Carta, stipulating that no one is 'above the law of the land', including (in theory) sovereign.

S

Schengen Agreement collective term for two European Union treaties—signed in 1985 and 1990 respectively—which formally abolished systematic border controls between member states.

Scottish Government (Scottish Executive) title used by devolved administration in Scotland.

Scottish Parliament Scotland's devolved assembly, based in purpose-built parliamentary building at Holyrood, at foot of Royal Mile in Edinburgh.

second reading first stage at which main principles of a Bill formally read out to House and debated. Normally takes place within few weeks of **first reading** and may lead to early vote on some aspects of Bill. (cf. **third reading**)

secondary legislation See delegated legislation

secretary of state umbrella term for most senior government minister in spending department (e.g. Secretary of State for Health).

select committee permanent parliamentary committee charged with scrutinizing day-to-day workings of government department and other public authorities related to responsibilities of that department. For example, Culture, Media, and Sport Select Committee examines work of the Department for Culture, Media, and Sport, as well as that of BBC.

separation of powers principle stipulating that three main seats of constitutional authority in UK—executive, legislature, and judiciary—should be kept separate to avoid concentrating power in too few hands. In practice there are overlaps, with **prime minister** and **Cabinet** (executive) also sitting in Parliament (legislature).

single transferable vote (STV) form of **proportional representation (PR)** used in general elections in Republic of Ireland, and long favoured by Lib Dems for Westminster polls. Candidates ranked in order of preference and all those who achieve 'quota' of votes up to predetermined number elected to multimember constituencies. If not enough candidates achieve quota, lowest ranked candidate is struck off ballot papers and their second choices redistributed among remaining contenders until enough reach required level.

site of special scientific interest (SSSI) area judged to have special or unique natural features. There are two types:

biological SSSIs (those with rare or unusual flora and/or fauna) and *geological SSSIs* (those of particular physiographic interest).

sovereign grant new all-in-one method of financing Royal Household from taxpayers' money, covering both day-to-day living costs previously funded through *Civil List* and upkeep of occupied palaces and royal transport traditionally paid as *grants-in-aid*.

Speaker member of Parliament elected by his/her peers, traditionally on motion moved by Father of the House (member with longest unbroken service to chamber) following **general election**, to serve as chairperson of debates and maintain discipline in Commons.

special responsibility allowance top-up fee added to **basic allowance** for councillor in recognition of additional responsibilities, such as sitting on, or chairing, local authority committee. Allowance can vary according to level of responsibility.

special school state school dedicated to teaching children with learning difficulties and/or mental or physical disabilities.

specialist school generic term for all state schools permitted to specialize in one or more subjects over and above teaching **National Curriculum**. **Academies** are, by nature, specialist schools—but, in practice, most **community schools** also have subject specialisms, enabling them to draw down extra funds to improve facilities.

specific grant one of two different categories of non-formula grant given to local authorities each year to help with revenue spending (cf. **area-based grants**). Specific grants can either be **ring-fenced grants** or **unfenced grants**.

spin doctor layperson's term for type of special adviser usually employed by senior figure in political party to put positive 'spin' on their policies to public and media. Alastair Campbell, former Downing Street director of communications, became one of Britain's most infamous spin doctors during Tony Blair's ten years in power.

standards committee committee set up by each local authority under Local Government Act 2000 to monitor councillors' and officers' compliance with council's **register of members' interests** and **code of conduct**. Committee must have at least one lay member.

standing order system of rules adopted by individual local authorities to govern day-to-day conduct of business in full council, and its committees, subcommittees, and/or **cabinet**.

statutory instrument the most common form of secondary legislation, this refers to the rules and guidelines issued by departmental ministers in order to implement the changes introduced in a new Bill on the ground.

subsidiarity loose constitutional principle underpinning European Union, which holds that member states retain primary sovereignty over their internal affairs, with EU acting as 'subsidiary' institution and last port of call if individual self-determination falters.

supplementary estimate when local authority is calculating level of revenue funding that it will need in next financial year, it will ask each department to estimate its projected spending. Occasionally, departments underestimate their needs and, at later date, ask for additional sum—the supplementary estimate.

Supreme Court of the United Kingdom Britain's final court of appeal for civil cases, and highest for criminal matters in England, Wales, and Northern Ireland, this was established in October 2009 in effort to emulate constitutional **separation of powers** in USA. It replaced Appellate Committee of the House of Lords—previously UK's ultimate court—which had been seat of 'Law Lords' for centuries. There are twelve Justices of the Supreme Court, all currently former Law Lords.

Sure Start government programme launched in 1999 to improve access for low-income families to early-years teaching and other support services.

T

tactical voting type of strategic voting by electors voting in 'first-past-the-post' (FPTP) elections, which sees them vote for candidate other than their 'sincere preference' in knowledge that to do so would be 'wasted vote'. Tactical voters instead opt for their 'least worst option'—choosing a 'bearable' third party to stop candidate they most oppose winning.

Tax-Increment Financing (TIF) form of capital finance for councils allowing them to borrow money for infrastructural/other capital investment against likely future income generated through business rates from companies likely to be attracted by that investment.

ten-minute rule one of three ways in which **private member's Bills (PMBs)** may be introduced into Parliament, and the one that most often grabs headlines. MP must have their idea for a Bill proposed and seconded by colleagues and obtain another eight members' signatures, and they will then be given ten minutes to introduce their proposals to Commons. MP who opposes Bill will then have same amount of time to make speech outlining his/her objections.

terrorism prevention and investigation measure (TPim) Coalition's replacement for the *control orders* used by Labour to restrict movements of those suspected (but not yet convicted) of terrorism plots. Unlike control orders they will lapse after two years.

third reading final stage of Bill's passage through Commons. It is at third reading that MPs are confronted with final version of Bill's wording, so it is an occasion for any major disagreements to be fought out in formal vote. (cf. **first reading**; **second reading**)

trading standards officer officer employed by county council or unitary authority to ensure local businesses adhere to regulations regarding issues such as product labelling and weights and measures.

Traffic Commissioner one of seven regional commissioners employed to license public transport routes and operators and long-distance haulage companies.

Transport for London (TfL) **quango** responsible for strategic planning and day-to-day running of London's transport network, including London Underground, Docklands Light Railway, city bus services, and river ferries.

trunk road major arterial road—A-road or motorway—linking towns and cities and sometimes crossing boundaries between counties. (cf. **county road**)

trust schools new form of **foundation school** introduced under Education and Inspections Act 2006. These are primary and secondary schools supported by charitable trusts that employ their staff, manage assets, and set admissions policies.

two-tier structure type of local government structure established under 1974 reorganization of local authorities, in which there are two levels of council operating in same area: **district councils** and/or **borough councils** responsible for services such as waste collection, housing, and environmental health; and overarching county council providing countywide services, such as education and highways (roads).

U

unfenced grant one of two types of **specific grant** for local authority revenue spending (cf. **ring-fenced grant**), it may be spent in whatever way council sees fit, subject to certain conditions. Coalition prefers unfenced to ring-fenced grants and has unfenced its new **early intervention grant**.

uniform business rates (UBR) See national non-domestic rates (NNDR)

UNISON main local government trade union, it counts among its members many departmental officers, social workers, and health professionals.

unitary structure type of local government structure that has replaced **two-tier structure** in many areas, in which single—unitary—local authority is responsible for all local services, from waste collection to education and social care.

United Nations (UN) global peacemaking body formed in 1945, as successor to defunct League of Nations established after First World War. The UN is headquartered in New York. Its main constitutional bodies include UN General Assembly and UN Security Council (which debates international conflict).

Universal Credit (UC) new 'all-in-one' welfare payment for low-paid and unemployed, due to supplant all other benefits between October 2013 and 2017 as part of Coalition's efforts to reduce social security bill and reduce complexity in system.

University technical colleges new vocational colleges introduced by Coalition to train 14- to 19-year-olds in hi-tech skills needed to 'rebalance' British economy towards technology.

V

virement process allowing councils limited discretion to transfer money from one spending area to another during given financial year, if former in surplus and latter in deficit. Councils' ability to use virement has been severely curtailed, due to roll-out of **ring-fenced grants**.

voluntary school type of school in state sector, land and buildings of which are owned by charity or local church. Voluntary aided schools receive some local authority funding but retain significant autonomy (for example employing their own staff and setting their own admissions policies), while voluntary controlled schools are run directly by LEAs.

W

ward the **constituency** represented by **district council, borough council,** and some unitary authority councillors. Each has between one and three councillors, depending on population size.

Water Services Regulatory Authority (also known as Office of Water Regulation (OFWAT)) one of three statutory regulators of privatized water industry, OFWAT monitors transparency of individual water companies' accounts and share policies.

Welsh Assembly Government (Welsh Executive) title adopted by elected devolved administration in Wales.

whip MPs and peers with job of 'whipping into line' their parliamentary colleagues, by making sure they attend important debates and votes and 'toe the line' by supporting their party.

White Paper crystallized version of **Green Paper**, containing more concrete proposals. If proposed government Bill has got this far it will normally proceed further into formal draft Bill and may well subsequently become an Act.

Work Capability Assessment (WCA) periodic medical test, introduced by Labour and continued by Coalition, to determine whether individuals claiming **ESA** are fit for work.

Bibliography

A

Atkinson, H. and Wilks-Heeg, S. (2000) *Local Government from Thatcher to Blair*, Cambridge: Polity Press.

B

Ball, S. J. and Junemann, C. (2012) *Networks, New Governance, and Education*, Cambridge: Polity Press.

Barron, J., Crawley, G., and Wood, T. (1991) *Councillors in Crisis: The Public and Private Worlds of Local Councillors (Public Policy and Politics)*, London: Palgrave Macmillan.

Betty, S. (2011) *The PFI; 'Teething Problems or Fundamentally Flawed?': A critical analysis of the UK's Private Finance Initiative*, Bury St Edmunds: Lambert Academic Publishing.

Blackman, T., Brody, S., and Convery, J. (eds) (2001) *Social Care and Social Exclusion: A Comparative Study of Older People's Care in Europe*, London: Palgrave Macmillan.

Blais, A. (ed.) (2008) *To Keep or to Change First Past the Post? The Politics of Electoral Reform*, New York: Oxford University Press USA.

Bomberg, E. and Stubb, A. (eds) (2012) *The European Union: How Does it Work?* Oxford: Oxford University Press.

Boynton, J. (1986) *Job at the Top: Chief Executive in Local Government*, London: Financial Times/Prentice Hall.

Braune, J. (2011) *Comparing Electoral Systems: First-Past-the-Post versus Proportional Representation*, Kindle edition: Amazon Digital Services.

Brooke, H. (2006) *Your Right to Know: A Citizen's Guide to the Freedom of Information Act*, 2nd edn, London: Pluto Press.

Brown, C. and Ainley, K. (2005) *Understanding International Relations*, London: Palgrave Macmillan.

Bryan, H. (1996) *Planning Applications and Appeals*, Oxford: Architectural Press.

Budge, I., Crewe, I., McKay, D., and Newton, K. (2007) *The New British Politics*, 4th edn, London: Longman.

Burnham, J. and Pyper, R. (2008) *Britain's Modernised Civil Service*, London: Palgrave Macmillan.

C

Campbell, A. (2012) *The Burden of Power: Countdown to Iraq*, London: Hutchinson.

Cannon, J. and Griffiths, R. (1998) *The Oxford Illustrated History of the British Monarchy*, Oxford: Oxford Paperbacks.

Carey, P. (2009) *Data Protection: A Practical Guide to UK and EU Law*, 3rd edn, Oxford: Oxford University Press.

Cooper, K. and Macfarland, C. (2012) *Clubbing Together: The Hidden*

Wealth of Communities, London: ResPublica.

Crewe, I. (ed.) (1998) *Why Labour Won the General Election of 1997*, London: Frank Cass.

Crook, D., Power, S., and Whitty, G. (2000) *The Grammar School Question: A Review of Research on Comprehensive and Selective Education*, London: Institute of Education.

Crossman, R. (1979) *The Crossman Diaries: Selections from the Diaries of a Cabinet Minister, 1964–1970*, London: Book Club Associates.

Cullingworth, J. B. and Nadin, V. (pending) *Town and Country Planning in the UK*, 15th edn, London: Routledge.

D

Daniels, P. and Ritchie, E. (1996) *EU: Britain and the European Union*, London: Palgrave Macmillan.

Denver, D. (2006) *Elections and Voters in Britain*, 2nd edn, London: Palgrave Macmillan.

Docherty, I. and Shaw, J. (2003) *A New Deal for Transport: The UK's Struggle with the Sustainable Transport Agenda*, London: Wiley-Blackwell.

E

Edwards, P. (2003) *Industrial Relations: Theory and Practice in Britain*, 2nd edn, London: Wiley-Blackwell.

Evans, G. and Newnham, R. (1998) *The Penguin Dictionary of International Relations*, London: Penguin.

F

Fischel, W. A. (2005) *The Homevoter Hypothesis: How Home Values Influence Local Government Taxation, School Finance, and Land-Use Policies*, Cambridge, MA: Harvard University Press.

G

Gallagher, M. and Mitchell, P. (2008) *The Politics of Electoral Systems*, Oxford: Oxford University Press.

Golding, P. and Middleton. S. (1982) *Images of Welfare*, Oxford: Mark Robertson.

Grimsey, D. and Lewis, M. (2007) *Public Private Partnerships: The Worldwide Revolution in Infrastructure Provision and Project Finance*, London: Edward Elgar.

Gumpert, B. and Kirk, J. (2001) *Trading Standards: Law and Practice*, Bristol: Jordans.

H

Hall, P. (2002) *Urban and Regional Planning*, 4th edn, London: Routledge.

Ham, C. (2004) *Health Policy in Britain: The Politics and Organisation of The National Health Service*, 5th edn, London: Palgrave Macmillan.

Hansen, R. S. (2001) *Citizenship and Immigration in Post-war Britain: The Institutional Origins of a Multicultural Nation*, Oxford: Oxford University Press.

Hardman, R. (2007) *Monarchy: The Royal Family at Work*, London: Ebury Press.

Harrison, K. and Boyd, T. (2006) *The Changing Constitution*, Edinburgh: Edinburgh University Press.

Hazell, R. and Rawlings, R. (2007) *Devolution, Law Making and the Constitution*, Exeter: Imprint Academic.

Hennessey, P. (2001) *The Prime Minister: The Job and its Holders Since 1945*, London: Penguin.

Hodge, M., Leach, S., and Stoker, G. (1997) *Local Government Policy: More than the Flower Show—Elected Mayors and Democracy*, London: Fabian Society.

Hollis, G., Davies, H., Plokker, K., and Sutherland, M. (1994) *Local Government Finance: An International Comparative Study*, London: LGC Communications.

I

Ishkanian, A. and Szreter, S. (2012) *The Big Society Debate: A New Agenda for Social Welfare?*, Cheltenham: Edward Elgar Publishing.

J

Jackson, R. and Sorensen, G. (2012) *An Introduction to International Relations: Theories and Approaches*, Oxford: Oxford University Press.

Johnston, R. and Pattie, C. (2006) *Putting Voters in Their Place: Geography and Elections in Great Britain*, Oxford: Oxford University Press.

Jones, A. (2007) *Britain and the European Union*, Edinburgh: Edinburgh University Press.

Jones, B. (2004) *Dictionary of British Politics*, Manchester: Manchester University Press.

Jones, B., Kavanagh, D., Moran, M., and Norton, P. (2006) *Politics UK*, 6th edn, London: Longman.

Jones, C. and Murie, A. (2006) *The Right to Buy: Analysis and Evaluation of a Housing Policy*, London: Wiley-Blackwell.

Jones, N. (2002) *The Control Freaks: How New Labour Gets its Own Way*, London: Politico's Publishing.

K

Klein, R. (2010) *The New Politics of the NHS: From Creation to Reinvention*, 6th edn, Abingdon: Radcliffe Publishing.

Knowles, R. (1993) *Law and Practice of Local Authority Meetings*, 2nd edn, London: ICSA Publishing.

L

Lane, K. (2006) *National Bus Company: The Road to Privatisation*, Shepperton: Ian Allen.

Lang, C., Reeve, J., and Woolard, V. (eds) (2006) *The Responsive Museum: Working with Audiences in the Twenty-First Century*, Aldershot: Ashgate.

Leach, R., Coxall, B., and Robins, L. (2006) *British Politics*, London: Palgrave Macmillan.

Leff, J. (1997) *Care in the Community: Illusion or Practice?* London: Wiley-Blackwell.

Leys, C. and Player, S. (2011) *The Plot Against the NHS*, Perth: Merlin Press.

Lowe, R. (2004) *Welfare State in Britain Since 1945*, 3rd edn, London: Palgrave Macmillan.

Lund, B. (2006) *Understanding Housing Policy*, Cambridge: Policy Press.

M

Macdonald, J., Crail, R., and Jones, C. (eds) (2009) *The Law of Freedom of Information*, 2nd edn, Oxford: Oxford University Press.

Malpass, P. (2005) *Housing and the Welfare State: The Development of Housing Policy in Britain*, London: Palgrave Macmillan.

Mansell, W. (2007) *Education by Numbers: The Tyranny of Testing*, London: Politico's Publishing.

Marr, A. (2008) *A History of Modern Britain*, London: Pan Books.

McCormick, J. (2008) *Understanding the European Union: A Concise Introduction*, London: Palgrave Macmillan.

Michie, R. C. (2001) *The London Stock Exchange: A History*, Oxford: Oxford University Press.

Midwinter, A. F. and Monaghan, C. (1993) *From Rates to the Poll Tax: Local Government Finance in the Thatcher Era*, Edinburgh: Edinburgh University Press.

Monbiot, G. (2001) *Captive State: The Corporate Takeover of Britain*, London: Pan Books.

Moran, M. (2006) *Politics and Governance in the UK*, London: Palgrave Macmillan.

Morgan, S. (2005) *Waste, Recycling, and Reuse*, London: Evans Brothers.

Mullin, C. (2010) *View from the Foothills*, London: Profile Books.

Mullins, D., Pawson, H., and Gilmour, T. (2010) *After Council Housing: Britain's New Social Landlords*, London: Palgrave Macmillan.

N

Norman, J. (2010) *The Big Society: The Anatomy of the New Politics*, Buckingham: University of Buckingham Press.

Norton, P. (2005) *Parliament in British Politics*, London: Palgrave Macmillan.

P

Phillips, R. and Furlong, J. (2001) *Education, Reform and the State: Twenty-Five Years of Politics, Policy, and Practice*, London: Routledge Falmer.

Philpot, T. (2007) *Adoption: Changing Families, Changing Times*, London: Routledge.

Pollock, A. M. (2006) *NHS plc: The Privatisation of Our Health Care*, London: Verso Books.

Pratchett, L. (2000) *Renewing Local Democracy? The Modernisation Agenda in British Local Government*, London: Frank Cass.

R

Reiner, R. (2000) *The Politics of the Police*, 3rd edn, Oxford: Oxford University Press.

Rogers, R. and Walters, R. (2006) *How Parliament Works*, 6th edn, London: Longman.

Roy, D. (2005) *Liberals: A History of the Liberal and Liberal Democratic Parties*, London: Hambledon Continuum.

S

Sanders, A. (2006) *Criminal Justice*, London: LexisNexis UK.

Seldon, A. and Snowdon, P. (2004) *The Conservative Party*, Stroud: The History Press.

Smart, G. and Holdaway, E. (2000) *Landscapes at Risk? The Future for Areas of Outstanding Natural Beauty in England and Wales*, London: Spon Press.

Stallion, M. and Wall, D. S. (2000) *The British Police: Police Forces and Chief Officers 1829–2000*, London: M. R. Stallion.

Stanley, J. and Goddard, C. (2002) *In the Firing Line: Violence and Power in Child Protection Work*, London: Wiley-Blackwell.

Stevens, A. (2006) *Politico's Guide to Local Government*, 2nd edn, London: Politico's Publishing.

Stewart, J. (2003) *Modernising British Local Government: An Assessment of Labour's Reform Programme*, London: Palgrave Macmillan.

Swann, D. (1988) *The Retreat of the State: Deregulation and Privatisation in the UK and US*, London: Prentice-Hall.

T

Thorpe, A. (2001) *A History of the British Labour Party*, 2nd edn, London: Palgrave Macmillan.

W

Wadham, J., Griffiths, J., and Harris, K. (2007) *Blackstone's Guide to the Freedom of Information Act 2000*, 3rd edn, Oxford: Oxford University Press.

Waters, I. and Duffield, B. (1994) *Entertainment, Arts, and Cultural Services*, London: Financial Times/ Prentice Hall.

Wilson, D. and Game, C. (2006) *Local Government in the United Kingdom*, 4th edn, London: Palgrave Macmillan.

Wilson, D., Ashton, J., and Sharpe, D. (2001) *What Everyone in Britain Should Know about the Police*, 2nd edn, London: Blackstone Press.

Wrigley, C. (2002) *British Trade Unions Since 1933*, Cambridge: Cambridge University Press.

Y

Young, J. and Kent, J. (2003) *International Relations Since 1945: A Global History*, Oxford: Oxford University Press.

Index